TALKS ON THE PATH OF OCCULTISM

TALKS ON THE PATH OF OCCULTISM

The Voice of the Silence

BY
ANNIE BESANT

GYAN

ISBN: 978-81-212-1912-9 Set (HB)
ISBN: 978-81-212-1936-5 Vol.1 (HB)
First Published, 1930
Published, 2018
Published by

Gyan Publishing House
5, Ansari Road
Daryaganj, New Delhi-110002
Phone: 011-47034999, 9811692060
www.gyanbooks.com
E-mail: books@gyanbooks.com

Printed at: G. Print Process, Delhi.

FOREWORD

THIS book is merely a record of talks by Mr. C. W. Leadbeater—now Bishop Leadbeater—and myself on three famous books—books small in size but great in contents. We both hope that they will prove useful to aspirants, and even to those above that stage, since the talkers were older than the listeners, and had more experience in the life of discipleship.

The talks were not given at one place only; we chatted to our friends at different times and places, chiefly at Adyar, London and Sydney. A vast quantity of notes were taken by the listeners. All that were available of these were collected and arranged. They were then condensed, and repetitions were eliminated.

Unhappily there were found to be very few notes on *The Voice of the Silence*, Fragment I, so we have utilized notes made at a class held by our good colleague, Mr. Ernest Wood, in Sydney, and incorporated these into Bishop Leadbeater's talks in that section. No notes of my own talks on this book were available; though I have spoken much upon it, those talks are not recoverable.

None of these talks have been published before, except some of Bishop Leadbeater's addresses to selected students on *At the Feet of the Master*. A book entitled *Talks on "At the Feet of the Master"* was published a few years ago, containing imperfect reports of some of these talks of his. That book will not be reprinted; the essential material in it finds its place here, carefully condensed and edited.

May this book help some of our younger brothers to understand more of these priceless teachings. The more they are studied *and lived*, the more will be found in them.

ANNIE BESANT

CONTENTS

PART 1

INTRODUCTORY

CHAPTER 1

THE OCCULT PATH AND THE INTERESTS OF THE WORLD

C.W.L.—*At the Feet of the Master* is one of three books—the other two being *The Voice of the Silence* and *Light on the Path*—especially intended to help people to set their feet upon the Path. It is most valuable for us, at the moment, because of its extreme simplicity, and because it bears especially the stamp and approval of the World-Teacher, who is so soon to come. It consists of teaching given by his Master to the young disciple J. Krishnamurti (called Alcyone in the series of his past lives recently published)[1] in the year 1909, when he was a boy of thirteen. His knowledge of English was not then perfect, and since the instruction was given in that tongue, both the teaching and the language had to be made especially clear. The Master Kūthūmi, with His marvellous power of adaptability, therefore put all that was necessary for the attaiment of the First Initiation into that wonderfully simple style which is one of the great recommendations of this little book.

The Light on the Path appeared in 1885, and *The Voice of the Silence* in 1889. Each of these books of

[1] *The Lives of Alcyone*, T. P. H., Adyar, 1924.

ethics has its own characteristics. Both the older ones are more poetical than *At the Feet of the Master,* although in it also there are some very beautiful expressions; it could not be otherwise, since it comes from the Master Kūthūmi. *Light on the Path,* we were told by Swami T. Subba Row, has several depths of meaning, one behind another, the most profound relating to the Initiation at the Mahāchohan level, a stage beyond where even our Masters now stand. *The Voice of the Silence* carries us as far as the Arhat Initiation. *At the Feet of the Master* applies especially to the First Initiation, so we will comment upon it first.

We have all heard often about the qualifications for the Path, but we shall continue to hear of them until we have succeeded in putting into practice everything that is written in such books as this. There is no difficulty in knowing exactly what ought to be done, and there is no obstacle in our path which is not of our own making, yet comparatively few people succeed in following these directions, because they have personalities which often get in the way. What is written in these books must be definitely applied by each person to himself. The teacher can explain and illustrate what ought to be done in various ways, but every one must tread the Path for himself. It is like training for a race or taking up physical culture: there may be a trainer who can give careful directions, but the candidate must exercise his own muscles; *nobody else can by any possibility do that for him.*

Millions of people around us are supposed to be living according to the precepts of their respective religions, but very few actually do so. Even those who live good and holy lives do not usually strictly follow all the precepts laid down for them. In some cases the teachings of exoteric religions are unessential or inappropriate, but in occultism no unnecessary precept is given; an exact adherence to all of them is required. This does not mean that we must have all of these qualifications in absolute perfection before we can be received by a Master—that would be the attainment of Adeptship; but they must be possessed to a reasonable extent, and they must be real, not merely polite fictions. When a professor of chemistry tells us that if we compound certain chemicals in a specified way we shall obtain certain results, we know that those results will follow, and that if the proportions are altered we shall not get what we expect, but something else. In religious matters people seem to think that a sort of vague approximation to the instructions given is quite sufficient, but in occultism that will not do at all; it must be taken as a science; and although we have heard so often about these qualifications, it is to be hoped that by going through them carefully and endeavouring to understand and follow with scientific precision exactly what is required, many who have not yet succeeded may be able to set their feet upon the Path.

These inner things are not far away and uncertain. Up to a few years ago they seemed more remote, because so few whom we knew had come into direct touch with the Masters, and a student might have thought to himself: "Yes, two or three men specially gifted, or in some way specially fortunate, have succeeded, but it does not seem to be for ordinary people." But now that a number have come into direct touch with Them, one may reasonably say to himself: "If these others have reached this, why not I?" The cause for non-success *must* be in ourselves, not in anything outside. It is certainly not the fault of the Masters, who are always there when the pupil is ready. In some there is one defect that bars; in others it may be only a general lack of development; but if there were not some deficiency we should all have succeeded. It is worth while to make a definite effort to find out what is the matter—what is lacking—and to remedy the defect.

There is a real inner world which surpasses in importance all this outer world, which is so incessant in its pressure upon us. Everywhere there are people who think themselves so busy and so wise in following their respective lines, and yet the truth is that all of them are working in the unreal and the outer, and few have realized that there is an inner and spiritual world which is of enormously more importance in every way than that which is external.

On the Path we have to play our parts in the world, but we do so only because of the true life inside. An actor plays on a stage because he has another life to live —a life which is consecutive and coherent. He may take various parts at different times, just as we come back in other incarnations and wear other kinds of bodies; but all the time the actor has his real life as a man and as an artist as well, and because there is that real life he wants to play his part well in the temporary life of the stage. Similarly, we wish to do well in our temporary physical life here, because of the great reality behind, of which it is but a very small part. If that is clear we shall see what is the relative importance of this outer life; that its only value to us is that we shall play our part well, whatever that part may be; what kind of part it is, and what happens to us in this mimic existence —these things matter little. It may be an actor's business to go through all sorts of pretended sorrows and difficulties; but these do not trouble him in the least. He may have, for example, to be killed every night in a duel; what does the feigned death matter to him? The only thing that concerns him is that he should acquit himself well.

It should not be hard to realize that the world about us is a mimic world, and that it really does not matter what experiences may come to us. All the things that happen to people from the outside are the result of their karma. The causes were set going long ago in other lives, and cannot now be altered. Therefore it is useless to worry about the things that happen. They come as the result of the past, and should be borne philosophically. Many people bear them foolishly and allow them to cause a vast amount of pain, suffering and worry. The right attitude is always to try to learn the lesson that they bring, and then to put them out of the mind as far as possible—like the bee and the flower, as our Indian brothers say. The way in which these things are borne moulds our character for the future, which is the only *important thing. One should use karma to develop* courage, endurance and various other good qualities, and then dismiss it from the mind.

This outlook is hard to reach because we are surrounded by thousands of people who are all taking the play as serious—as the only real life. What they say and do to us hinders to some extent, but a far greater obstacle in our way (though we never think of it) is the immense and incessant pressure of public opinion. That is simply stupendous, for there are many thousands who are ignorant to each one who knows the truth. They are thinking: "We must make haste to gain possessions and riches; what other people think of us is everything in life."

A great deal of thought is also poured out by those who want to gain positions and honours, to obtain invitations to certain dinners and balls, to get a duke or an earl on their visiting list, and so on. In religious matters too, there is a vast sea of delusion beating around us, for there are few who are liberal and millions who are not. Social delusions also abound, as for instance the prudery of England, where it is considered improper ever to speak of the sex side of things, so that for want of some small fragments of simple knowledge the young grow up in peril and sometimes fall into unexpected disaster, for there is a river of vice always running, into which it is easy for the ignorant to fall. People look upon the manners of the classical times of Greece and Rome as in many ways indecent, but from memory of those times I am bound to say that they were far less impure in thought than Europe is to-day.

We who understand more of the inner side of things have to stand against these really tremendous odds, and say to ourselves: "No, this is not so, all this is unreal, and we pray to be led from the unreal to the real." The real is the underlying life, the life which persists, the life which, as the Scripture puts it, is "hid with Christ in God". To live in that realization all the time and to regard the outer as not of essential importance is not easy, but that is exactly what has to be done. One of our Masters has said: "He who wishes to follow us must come out of your world into ours." This does not mean that one must give up one's daily life and live as a hermit—it implies that even more than before we perform heartily all the duties that are ours in this strange play of life—but it does mean that the aspirant must abandon his ordinary attitude and adopt that of the Masters.

Those who succeed in these efforts will some day find themselves accepted pupils of one or other of the Masters. When the man's thought becomes part of that of his Teacher the pupil can test his own thought by that of the Master, which is never affected by the crowd, and can see exactly what He thinks on any subject. Then he will soon get into the way of that and will understand His point of view; though at first he will be constantly meeting with unexpected shocks. Things that seemed of vast importance before do not now matter at all, and other things which he had passed by as comparatively unimportant, stand out as of great significance, because in some way, great or small, they affect our usefulness, and whatever affects our usefulness is important, because there we touch upon the real thing.

The pressure that comes upon the mind from all around in the mental and astral planes is not from on high at all. The ears must be closed to that, and open only to the sound from above, to the voice and thought of the Master. It is little wonder that in older days in India and other countries, whenever men set themselves to live the spiritual life, the first thing they did was to get out of ordinary life and go away and camp in a cave or jungle by themselves. They gained the advantage of escape from this pressure of ignorant opinion, and were freer then to follow their own way. Many of the Christian Saints also retired from the active world and became hermits and monks or associated themselves with people who were thinking on the same lines.

This advantage of retirement is still further increased for those who have the privilege of being in the aura of the Master or of one of His more advanced pupils. The vibrations of that aura are constantly acting upon the bodies of the pupil, tuning them up, shaking out unsuitable grades of matter and feeding them with what is required. The pupil should be always trying to develop some virtue—let us say love, for example. If left to himself he does so intermittently, for he constantly forgets about it; but the aura of his superior holds him to the higher standard of thought and feeling that he wants to establish permanently in himself. The effect is not unlike that aimed at in the treatment of the malformed limb of a child, when it is put into splints until it grows into proper shape. While in the aura of the Master the pupil feels that he could not think a wrong thought, even if he wanted to, which then seems to him impossible. In that position, we look smilingly down at our thoughts of yesterday, and say: "I never can have that feeling again; it has vanished like a dream." But to-morrow, when we are away from the Master, we may find ourselves struggling hard to maintain the higher attitude, which we thought so easy when in His presence.

At the present time those who are reaching towards the Path must try to achieve the same condition while they remain in active life, because it is intended that they shall help the world, not by meditation and thought alone—as no doubt the hermit and the monk did—but by mingling in its various activities. It is a very beautiful idea and a great privilege, but it is hard, very hard, to do.

The result of that difficulty has been that few have really achieved. Most have been content to take the Theosophical teaching much as the average Christian takes his religion: regarding it as very nice to talk about on Sunday, but not at all the thing to carry out every day and all day long. The earnest student of the inner life cannot be thus unreal; he must be consistent and practical, and must apply his ideals constantly to everyday life. To attain this constancy is difficult. It is not that people are unwilling to make some great effort for the Theosophical idea. If they could help a Master, could do some piece of work directly for Him, they would do it, though it cost them life itself. Remember what S. Augustine said: "Many there are who will die for Christ, but few there are who will live for Him." To become a martyr sounds magnificent, heroic; it is a great deed. But the martyr who does it has the feeling that he is making a mighty effort, and the consciousness of that bears him up and supports him through pain and suffering. He is keyed up for the moment to this great act of heroism. What has to be done now is much harder than that. It is not possible to keep oneself always strung to that pitch of heroism, amid the little daily troubles that are perpetually coming up. It is very difficult to keep the same equanimity of mind when dealing day after day with the same wearisome people, who will not do the things one thinks they should do. Living for Christ in all the small things—that is hard to do; and it is just because these things seem comparatively small that there is so much difficulty in following the Path.

Let us take these three books, let us follow their instructions, and see how far it is possible to apply them. Others have done it, and have succeeded in reaching the Path; why should not we? Success means the conquest of the self; it means that we take ourselves in hand and face the facts and, where there are weeds, pull them up. It does not matter how deeply they are rooted, or how much suffering it entails; up with them! Hard work, indeed; but those who have already entered on some of the higher stages tell us that it is very well worth while, infinitely worth while, to make any effort, great or small, whether it be once for all or many times.

CHAPTER 2

INITIATION AND THE APPROACH THERETO

C.W.L.—The name of this book was chosen by our President, out of thirty or forty which were suggested, and she is also responsible for the dedication

To Those Who Knock

the symbolism of which is obvious: "Knock and it shall be opened unto you; seek and ye shall find." In her preface Dr. Besant says:

> The privilege is given to me, as an elder, to pen a word of introduction to this little book, the first written by a younger Brother; young in body verily, but not in Soul.

Here is a point of great importance. In ordinary life, thinking only of this world and this one incarnation, we judge a person's age by the physical body; but in occult progress we consider the age of the ego, of the soul within. One must beware of judging by externals only, though almost everyone in the world does it. The soul grows steadily, and when it is highly developed it often begins to exhibit signs of its advancement in intelligence, emotion and occult power, even while the physical body is still young. Alcyone certainly showed this to be so in his case by the extreme rapidity of his progress. He responded to the teaching so fully that he was able to attain in a few months what would usually take many years, because for most it would mean a fundamental change in character.

Cases of this kind will be increasingly numerous in these days, because of the near approach of the World-Teacher. His principal disciples must be people in the prime of life and strength, most of them probably not much older than Himself in the physical body, and since He is to come soon those who are to be in that position then must be young now. It is exceedingly probable that some of those who are children now among us may in the future be prominent in the work, for it is likely that many of those who are destined for such good fortune will be born where they can have the teaching that will fit them for it, that is, in Theosophical families.

We should, therefore, watch for such possibilities, and see that any children that come in our way are told about the advent of the World-Teacher, so that they may know the possibility which is open to them. It must be left to them to grasp the opportunity, but at least it should be given. It would be very sad if any parent should hear from his son or daughter the reproach: "If you had told me about these things when I was young, I might have taken the opportunity, but you let me grow up without knowing anything about them; you let me grow into the worldly life, and therefore, when the opportunity offered, I did not take it." We must give the opportunity, but when we have done that, our duty is over, because it is not for us to try to force anyone into any line, or even to map out a future and expect these other and possibly greater souls to adhere to it.

The teachings contained in it were given to him by his Master in preparing him for Initiation.

The word Initiation has often been used in a very general way; but here it has a definite technical significance. Madame Blavatsky herself in the earlier days employed it somewhat loosely, but as our terminology has become more settled, the meaning of the word ought to be confined to the great Initiations, the five steps on the Path Proper, to use the old term. In the older writings we spoke of the Probationary Path, the Path Proper, and the Official Period as three stages in the advanced development of man. The Probationary Path means the period of probation for Initiation, the Path Proper is the Path of Holiness which begins with the first of the great Initiations (that in which a man "enters upon the stream") and ends with the attainment of Adeptship. Forty years ago we used to talk about "initiation into the Theosophical Society," and the word is used in connection with Masonic and other ceremonies; we must take care not to confuse those ideas with the great Initiations of the occult Path.

The period of probation for Initiation was in the early days spoken of as being divided into stages, which correspond to the four qualifications which are given in this book: discrimination, desirelessness, good conduct and love.

It is not correct to call these stages, or to speak of initiations between them. These qualifications are not at all necessarily taken up in the order given. They are written down in that order in the old Oriental books, but we are probably engaged in acquiring all of them simultaneously. We do what we can with all of them, and to some of us one qualification may be much easier than the others.

Discrimination has its position as the first qualification, because it enables a man to decide to enter upon the Path at all. The Buddhist name for it is *manodvāra-vajjana,* "the opening of the doors of the mind," which means that the man's mind is open for the first time to see that the spiritual things are the only real things, and that the ordinary worldly life is a waste of time. The Hindus name it *viveka,* which means discrimination. The Christian calls this realization 'conversion,' which is also a very expressive word, because conversion means turning and coming together with ; it is derived from the supine of *verto,* to turn, and *con,* together with.

It means that the man having previously gone his own way, having thought nothing about the Divine Will, has now realized the direction in which that Divine Will wishes the evolutionary current to flow, and has turned himself into line with it. With many Christian sects it has degenerated to mean a sort of spasmodic, hysterical condition, but even that contains the idea of turning about and going along with the Divine Will. It is very much what was expressed by the apostle when he said, "Set your affection on things above, and not on things of the earth."

As there are steps on the Path, so there are other definite steps which mark the degrees of the pupil's personal relationship to the Master who prepares him for the Initiations. Initiations are given by the Great White Brotherhood, in the name of the One Initiator who is its Head—and by His order alone. But the pupil's relationship with his Master is his own affair. One may be, first, a probationer, or, secondly, an accepted pupil; or, thirdly, what is called a son of the Master; these are private relationships and must not be confused with the Initiations which are given by the Great Hierarchy itself.

The First Initiation is that step which makes a man a member of the Great White Brotherhood. Before that he is not really on the Path at all, but is training himself in preparation for it. It is not conferred arbitrarily, but in recognition of his attainment of a certain stage of evolution—what used to be called the union of the higher and lower self, the joining of the ego and the personality. A man who wishes to put himself forward as a candidate for the First Great Initiation must acquire the qualifications described in this book, and make his personality an expression of the ego; there must be no lower personality left to thrust itself forward, and to have desires of its own in opposition to those of the reincarnating self.

The change that then takes place is shown in the illustrations given in *Man Visible and Invisible.* The astral body of the savage is full of colours which indicate all sorts of lower passions, and is irregular in outline, because the man has no control over it; and the causal and mental bodies show no relation to one another. The causal is apparently blank; the mental has a little development, but it has not much connection with the astral body. In the astral body of the savage there are all sorts of emotions and passions that have nothing to do with the mind. He does not think about them; he does not know how to think; they are simply there, and they run away with him.

In the advanced man, however, all those vehicles are closely linked. The causal body is full instead of being empty; all the different colours expressive of the higher virtues are developed in it, and it is already beginning to pour itself out in various directions for the helping of others. The mental body contains the same colours, somewhat denser, but still the finest of their kind, and they represent the causal body on the lower level. The astral body is in turn a mirror of the mental—there are the same colours, only just a little darker and denser, because a plane lower.

The self in the savage expresses itself in all kinds of different emotions and passions of which the ego could not possibly approve, but in the developed man there are no emotions but such as he chooses to have. Instead of being swayed by his emotions and carried off his feet, he simply selects them. He says: "Love is a good thing, I will allow myself to feel love; devotion is a good thing, I will allow myself to feel devotion; sympathy—that is beautiful, I will allow myself to feel sympathy." And he does this with his eyes open, intentionally. The emotions are thus under the dominion of the mind, and that mind is an expression of the causal body, so we are coming very near to the condition of complete unity of the higher and lower self.

It should not be imagined that there are two entities in man. There never is any lower self as a separate being, but the ego puts down a tiny fragment of himself into the personality in order to experience the vibrations of the lower planes. The personality then becomes much more vividly alive than the ego, because it is at a stage where it can respond to those vibrations; consequently it forgets that it belongs to the ego, and sets up in the business of life on its own account, and tries to go as it would rather than as the ego would. In the course of many incarnations, however, the ego grows strong, and then the man can recognize that the personality is nothing but an expression of himself, the reincarnating ego, and that whenever it tries to be master instead of servant it is going wrong and needs to be controlled. It is our business so to order the personality that it shall express the ego, and nothing else. That is what Mr. Sinnett called giving allegiance to the higher self. In *The Voice of the Silence* we are told that the disciple should slay the lunar form. This refers to the astral body. It does not mean that you should commit an astral murder; it means that your astral body should have no existence but as an expression of the higher, that instead of having its own passions and emotions it shall reflect only what the ego chooses.

This condition must be attained before one can be presented for the First Initiation. The man must have control of his physical, astral and mental bodies. All these must be servants of the ego. To gain that mastery would mean a very great deal of work for the ordinary person, and many people would say: "I cannot do that; it is no use talking about it." It is altogether too high an ideal to set before them all at once, but it ought not to be so serious a demand to make upon those who have been meditating and thinking on these matters for many years. Truly it is not easy to tread down one by one all sort of passions and desires, to curb the astral and mental bodies; these things are hard, but they are splendidly well worth doing, and the result attained thereby is quite out of all proportion to even the great efforts required. The thought of making ourselves capable of greater usefulness to the World-Teacher is an additional incentive and encouragement in this arduous undertaking. Those who take these Initiations do not do it for themselves, in order to escape from the sorrow and the suffering of the world, but that they may be of use in the mighty plan.

There are certain definite changes which outweigh all others in a man's existence. The first of these is when he individualizes and enters the human kingdom—when he comes forth from the animal stage and begins his career as an ego. His attainment of Adeptship at the Fifth Initiation is another; it marks his departure from the human kingdom, because then he enters a superhuman state. That is the goal which is set before all humanity; it is the point which we are to endeavour to attain in this chain of worlds. At the end of this period the man who has done what God has willed for mankind, who has carried out to the utmost the divine design for himself, will thus pass out of the human kingdom; and many of us may do it long before the end.

In between these two comes another point of quite as great importance, the definite "entry on the stream" at the first great Initiation. The words used in admitting the candidate to the Brotherhood include this statement: "You are now safe for ever; you have entered upon the stream; may you soon reach the further shore." The Christian calls him the man who is 'saved' or 'safe.' That means that he is quite sure to go on in this present stream of evolution, that he is certain not to drop out at the day of judgment in the next round, like a child in school who is too backward to go on with the rest of his class.

The Initiate has to pass the Second, Third and Fourth Initiations before he reaches Adeptship, which is the Fifth, but when he gains that stage he unites the monad and the ego just as before he had united the ego and the personality. When the man has achieved the union of the higher and the lower self, his personality no longer exists except as an expression of the ego; he has now to begin that process over again, as it were, and make that ego an expression of the monad. Whether beyond that there lies another stage of the same kind we do not know, but it is at least certain that when we attain Adeptship we shall find opening before us a still more glorious vista of progress.

People often ask what will be the end of this evolution which we see outstretched before us. I personally do not know whether there is any end or not. A great philosopher once said, "It is equally inconceivable that there should be an end or that there should be no end; yet one of those two must be true." Some speak of absorption into the Supreme; but of that we know nothing. We know that our consciousness continues to widen; that before it lies grade after grade above and beyond our own. We know that it is possible to touch the buddhic level, and thus attain an enormous expansion of consciousness, so that besides being oneself one is also other and greater people.

In this we do not feel that we have lost individuality at all, but that we have so widened it that we are able to feel through others as well as through ourselves. All who can do this in meditation should continue the practice, and expand until more and more is included in the consciousness—not only those far above, but those below as well, although those above come first because they are so much stronger, so much more tremendous in their power. Such expansion takes place gradually and one wins one's way through subplane after subplane of buddhic consciousness, until presently he learns to develop a buddhic vehicle—a body which he can use at that stupendous height where all the spheres seem as one, and he can traverse space without actually passing through it in our sense of the word at all.

Now, since that is in the experience of a number of us, we are justified in assuming that the further extensions of that consciousness will be somewhat of the same kind. We have attained that unity without losing our sense of individuality in the very least, without feeling ourselves merged in a shining sea, as the poet puts it, but feeling instead that the shining sea has been poured into the drop.

Paradoxical as it may sound, that is the sensation; the consciousness of the drop widens into the consciousness of the sea. That being so, so far as we know it, we are surely justified in assuming that there will not be any sudden change in the method. We cannot conceive of being merged into something else and losing that consciousness which we have taken so long to develop. I believe it will widen so that we may become one with God, but only in the sense in which Christ put it when He said: "Ye are gods; ye are all the children of the Most High."

We can look far back in evolution and can also see far forward. We can be sure of a future extending over millions of years of useful activity, on splendid levels whose glory and power and love and development are inconceivable down here; but what lies beyond that we do not know. If we consider the matter from a common-sense point of view, we can hardly expect to know. If the final end of it were something that we could now understand, it would be a very poor kind of ending, altogether out of proportion to all the stages which lead up to it.

Our intellect is a narrow thing—how limited no man realizes until he comes into touch with its higher developments, when he begins to see that the intellect about which we have boasted so much is in reality a poor affair, a beginning only, a seed of a future tree. In comparison to that of the future, men have now only a child intellect, though it is that of a hopeful child, for it has done much already, and shows promise of more. But compared with the intellect of the Great Ones it is still that of a very little child. Therefore it cannot yet reach great heights and depths, and we cannot expect to understand either the beginning or the end. I, at least, am more than willing to admit quite frankly that I do not know what goal the Supreme has in His mind; I do not know anything about the Supreme, except that He is.

The metaphysician and the philosopher speculate on these things, and gain from the effort considerable development of the mind and the causal body. Those who love such imaginations do no harm in indulging in them, but I think they should clearly understand that they are imaginations. The philosopher should not develop his theories into a system and expect us to accept it, for he is quite likely to be leaving out of account some of the most important factors. For myself, I do not speculate. I feel that the splendour and glory that unquestionably lie ahead of us are far more than sufficient to satisfy all our aspirations. "Eye hath not seen, nor ear heard, neither hath it entered into the heart of man to conceive the things which God hath prepared for them that love Him." That is true now, as it was two thousand years ago.

CHAPTER 3

HOW THE BOOK CAME TO BE WRITTEN

C.W.L.—Dr. Besant's Preface (which is dated December, 1910) then goes on to explain how Alcyone wrote the book.

> And were written down by him from memory—slowly and laboriously, for his English last year was far less fluent than it is now. The greater part is a reproduction of the Master's own words ; that which is not such a verbal reproduction is the Master's thought clothed in His pupil's words. Two omitted sentences were supplied by the Master. In two other cases an omitted word has been added. Beyond this, it is entirely Alcyone's own, his first gift to the world.

The following is my own account of what happened, as given in *The Masters and the Path* :

> The story of how this little book came to be written is comparatively simple. Every night I had to take this boy in his astral body to the house of the Master, that instruction might be given him. The Master devoted perhaps fifteen minutes each night to talking to him, but at the end of each talk He always gathered up the main points of what He had said into a single sentence, or a few sentences, thus making an easy little summary which was repeated to the boy, so that he learnt it by heart. He remembered that summary in the morning and wrote it down.

The book consists of these sentences, of the epitome of the Master's teaching, made by Himself, and in His words. The boy wrote them down somewhat laboriously, because his English was not then very good. He knew all these things by heart and did not trouble particularly about the notes that he had made. A little later he went up to Benares with our President. While there he wrote to me, I being down at Adyar, and asked me to collect and send to him all the notes that he had made of what the Master had said. I arranged his notes as well as I could, and typed them all out.

Then it seemed to me that as these were mainly the Master's words I had better make sure that there was no mistake in recording them. Therefore I took the type-written copy which I had made to the Master Kūthūmi and asked Him to be so kind as to read it over. He read it, altered a word or two here and there, added some connecting and explanatory notes and a few other sentences which I remembered having heard Him speak to Mr. Krishnamurti. Then He said "Yes, that seems correct; that will do"; but He added, "Let us show it to the Lord Maitreya." And so we went together, He taking the manuscript, and it was shown to the World-Teacher Himself, who read it and approved. It was He who said: "You should make a nice little book of this to introduce Alcyone to the world." We had not meant to introduce him to the world; we had not considered it desirable that a mass of thought should be concentrated on a boy of thirteen, who still had his education before him. But in the occult world we do what we are told, and so this book was put into the printer's hands as soon as possible.

All the inconveniences which we expected from premature publicity came about; but still the Lord Maitreya was right and we were wrong; for the good that has been done by that book far outweighs the trouble it brought to us. Numbers of people, literally thousands, have written to say how their whole lives have been changed by it, how everything has become different to them because they have read it. It has been translated into twenty-seven languages. There have been some forty editions of it, or more, and over a hundred thousand copies have been printed. Even now an edtition of a million copies is being prepared in America. A wonderful work has been done by it. Above all, it bears that special imprimatur of the coming World-Teacher, and that is the thing that makes it most valuable—the fact that it shows us, to a certain extent, what His teaching is to be.[1]

[1] *Op. cit.*, pp. 76-78. Second Edition, 1927.

CHAPTER 4

THE PRELIMINARY PRAYER

C.W.L.—Dr. Besant concludes with a good wish for all of us:

> May it help others as the spoken teaching helped him—such is the hope with which he gives it. But the teaching can only be fruitful if it is *lived*, as he has lived it since it fell from his Master's lips. If the example be followed as well as the precept, then for the reader, as for the writer, shall the great Portal swing open, and his feet be set on the Path.

In reviewing this book, Dr. Besant said: "Very rarely are such words as these given to men; teaching so direct, so philosophical, and so beautifully put." Therefore assuredly every word of it is worth our most careful consideration.

At the beginning of the book, before we enter even upon the Foreword of Alcyone, is set the old prayer, translated from the Sanskrit:

> **From the unreal lead me to the Real.**
> **From darkness lead me to Light.**
> **From death lead me to Immortality.**

The use of the word 'real' in this case may sometimes prove a little misleading. When we say 'real' and 'unreal,' the idea conveyed to our minds is that one thing has a definite existence and the other has not. The unreal is to us purely imaginary. But that is not quite what the Hindu understands by this sentence. Perhaps we should come a little nearer to his meaning if we said, "From the impermanent lead me to the permanent."

The statement that the lower planes, physical, astral and mental, are unreal, often leads to serious misunderstanding. They are not unreal at their own level, and while they last. Physical objects seem perfectly real while we are on the physical plane, but when the body falls asleep and we use our astral consciousness instead of the physical, those objects are no longer visible to us because we have passed into a higher plane. Therefore people sometimes say they are unreal. But there is just as much reason to say that the astral plane is unreal because we do not see its objects when on the physical plane. Both physical and astral objects are there all the time; they remain visible to those whose consciousness is on the respective planes.

So far as we know all manifestation is impermanent; only the Unmanifested is absolutely and always the same. All manifestation, even that of the highest planes, will one day pass again into the changeless, so the difference between what we commonly call the impermanent and those higher planes is only a matter of time, which in comparison to eternity can be as nothing. The physical plane, then, is just as real as the nirvānic, and just as truly an expression of the Deity, and so we must not form the idea that one of these things is real and the other mere dream or phantasmagoria.

Another very commonly held theory is that matter is evil; but that is not so at all. Matter is an expression of the Divine just as much as spirit; both are one in Him—two sides of Him. Matter often operates to hinder us in our progress, but only when it is so used as to delay us on our way; as well might a man who happens to cut himself with a knife say that knives are evil things. Considering the flexibility of the Sanskrit words we might equally translate the first line as "From the false lead me to the true". 'True,' 'permanent' 'real'—these words seem all of them to be included in the meaning; so what we are asking is rather that from the outer, where the illusion is greater, we may be led to the inner, which is nearer to the absolute truth.

The second petition is, "From darkness lead me to Light,"—that is, of course, from the darkness of ignorance to the light of knowledge. The prayer is addressed to the Master; we ask Him to enlighten us by His wisdom. There is also a secondary meaning attached to that in India, for in these words one is also supposed to be asking Him to lead one to the knowledge of the higher planes, and there comes in a rather beautiful thought which will be found in some of those old books, that the light of the lower plane is the darkness of the plane above it That is wonderfully true. What is thought of here as light is dim and murky, compared to the light of the astral world, and that in turn is poor in comparison with that of the mental. It is very difficult to put these distinctions into words, because each time you rise one plane in your consciousness you get the impression of something quite stupendously greater than you have ever known before—greater power, greater light, greater bliss.

When a man makes a definite advance in consciousness, he thinks: "Now for the first time I know what life really means, what bliss is, and how splendid all these things are." So each plane is quite out of all proportion superior to the one below it, so that, for instance, to return even from the astral, the very next plane, into the physical is like coming out of the sunlight into a dark dungeon. When a man can function consciously on the mental he finds an expansion in many directions absolutely beyond that which he knows on the astral. When he can touch the buddhic consciousness, for the first time he feels a very little of how God sees things. One is then coming into touch with Divinity, and beginning to know how He who is in all, feels through all. It is said that "In Him we live and move and have our being," and that "Of Him and through Him and to Him are all things";[1] and all that is not merely a beautiful and poetic expression, but represents an actual fact. There is a glorious unity—not brotherhood alone, but actual unity—and when the lowest fringe of that can be touched one begins for the first time very dimly to understand how God feels when He looks on His

[1] Rom., XI, 36.

universe and says: "It is good." And so from the darkness of the lower planes we ask to be led to the light of the higher consciousness—and it *is* light as compared with darknesss. No phraseology could be more apt; no expression could give more exactly what one feels.

Then we say: "From death lead me to Immortality." That does not mean what at first sight the ordinary religious person would take it to mean, because the Theosophist's attitude towards death should be very different from that of the man who has not studied these things—quite the reverse, in fact. Death is not a horror, not a king of terrors, but rather an angel bearing a golden key to open the door into a higher and fuller life. Of course we always regret those who pass away; but the regret is for "the touch of the vanished hand and the sound of the voice that is still". And when we ask to be led from death to immortality we do not at all mean what a Christian would have in mind: that he should live for all eternity in his present personality in some form or other. We have, however, a very definite wish to escape from death, and its inseparable companion, birth. What lies before men is the round which the Buddhist calls the *sansāra*, the wheel of life. The prayer here is: from this cycle of birth and death, lead us to immortality—to the life which lies above birth and death, which no longer needs to dip into the lower planes, because its human evolution is finished and it has gained all that matter had to teach it.

Although people never seem to see it that idea is prominent in the Christian scriptures also. Modern

Christianity suffers from certain obsessions—I do not think we can call them by any other name—and one of them is the terrible idea of an eternal hell. That belief has cast a cloud of misunderstanding over a number of other doctrines, too. The whole theory of salvation has come to mean salvation from this non-existent, eternal hell, whereas it does not mean that at all, and all the passages which are supposed to refer to that, which seem so incomprehensible, become clear and luminous when it is understood that it really is the birth of the Christ in the heart that saves the man.

The Christ often spoke to the people of the broad road which led to death or destruction, and the many who followed it. His disciples came to Him once and asked: "Lord, are there few that be saved?" Then He said: "Strait is the gate and narrow is the way which leadeth unto life, and few there be that find it." Men have actually taken those very beautiful and perfectly true words, and interpreted them to mean that the majority of mankind will be cast into eternal hell, that very few indeed will succeed in attaining heaven; but it is absolutely ridiculous to attribute that idea to the Christ. What He meant was perfectly clear. The disciples were asking how many people enter the path of Initiation, and He said, "Few," which is as true in our day as it was then. When He said: "Broad is the road that leadeth to death, and many there be that follow it," He referred to the road that leads to the cycle of death and birth. Of course, it is true that that road is broad and easy; there is no trouble at all about following that line of development, and those who so do will attain the goal easily enough, somewhere about the end of the seventh round.

But strait is the gate and narrow is the way that leads to Initiation, to the kingdom of heaven. When Christ speaks of the kingdom of heaven He never means the heaven-world, the state after death, devachan, but always the body of the saved, the company of the elect, that is to say, the Great Brotherhood. When He refers to the conditions of life between death and rebirth, we find a very different set of words. Remember the passage written by S. John: "And lo, a great multitude, which no man could number, of all nations and kindreds and peoples and tongues, stood before the Throne and before the Lamb, clothed with white robes, and palms in their hands." When they spoke of that condition they told of a vast multitude which no man could number, not of a few who found their way with difficulty.

CHAPTER 5

THE SPIRIT OF THE PUPIL

C.W.L.—We come now to the Foreword of Alcyone himself:

> **These are not my words; they are the words of the Master Who taught me. Without Him I could have done nothing; but through His help I have set my feet upon the Path.**

He plainly attributes all his progress to the influence and the help of his Master. We have much of the help that he then received, because we have the words of this book, which are the Master's words; but the enormous help of His presence and personal guidance is also ready and waiting for every one of us, too. That must sink into our minds as a reality; we may be confident of it as an absolutely certain fact. As Alcyone was helped, so will all be aided who choose to make themselves ready for it.

> **You also desire to enter the same Path, so the words which He spoke to me will help you also, if you will obey them. It is not enough to say that they are true and beautiful; a man who**

wishes to succeed must do exactly what is said. To look at food and say that it is good will not satisfy a starving man; he must put forth his hand and eat. So to hear the Master's words is not enough; you must do what He says, attending to every word, taking every hint.

It is not enough to *say*: "I will do all that is written in the book"; its teaching must be made to permeate every part of one's life. One must be on the watch for opportunities. There is a little bit of poetry at the end of the book which expresses this very well:

Waiting the word of the Master,
Watching the Hidden Light;
Listening to catch His orders
In the very midst of the fight;
Seeing His slightest signal
Across the heads of the throng;
Hearing His faintest whisper
Above earth's loudest song.

In the midst of all the noise, the whirl and excitement of the fight of life, one must listen all the while if one aspires to become a pupil of the Master. One must be eagerly looking out for opportunities to put into practice any of the teachings. This is not, after all, really difficult, because it is largely a matter of habit. *Ce n'est que le premier pas qui coute.*[1] When one has taken that, and has set up the habit, it is just as easy to be watching keenly all the time for this, as it is for the

[1] It is only the first step that costs.

business man who is looking for opportunities to make money. It is right that the man should keep up such constant watchfulness, for while he is doing business it is his duty to do it well. But if he can be eager about the temporary things, surely we might well be equally earnest about these things of the higher life.

It is very important that those who wish to reach the feet of the Master should understand His attitude. It is the same as that which is induced by Theosophical study. But the attitude is really what the study aims at, for Theosophy is a life to be lived, not merely a system to be learned. We must try, therefore, to bring our views into harmony with His, yet without forcing them at all. It would not be the wisest thing for any of us to adopt a point of view merely because it is the Master's, without understanding how He arrived at it. We should be quite safe in adopting it because He knows so much more than we do, but He would not wish it. Our intellect must be convinced, not merely our feelings influenced, by His thought.

The great requirement is to have it certain in one's mind that these things are the more real and permanent and important. The average Christian certainly says that the unseen things are more important, that that which is seen is temporary; but he does not act at all as though he believed it. Why? Because he is not certain of it. He is quite sure on the physical plane that money would be a good thing, and that the more he can get of it the better it will be for him; but he is not equally convinced that the spiritual things are real.

They belong to the group of subjects which he labels 'religion,' and there is not, somehow, the certainty and the practicality and the matter-of-factness about those things to him that there is in the affairs of ordinary life. We who are trying to make progress along these lines must introduce just precisely that matter-of-factness, that absolute and definite certainty, into these realms of the unseen. Mr. Sinnett said in his first Theosophical book: "These things must be as real to you as Charing Cross"; that is true; they must be as familiar as the things we see every day.

They may become so for us through reasoning about them, or through intuition, or best of all through direct experience. When we have completely convinced ourselves intellectually that a thing must be so, it grows into a fact for us. That is probably one of the advantages which the older students have over the newer ones. However enthusiastic the new ones may be, the older ones have had time to live into this thing and to make it, bit by bit, grain by grain, so to speak, part of themselves. Knowledge grows from more to more, as the poet puts it. There are some who as soon as they hear of the higher facts, spring at once into the state of absolute certainty about them, by a happy intuition, which is really their good karma from past lives. But for most of us, whose karma has not been quite so good as that, the steady growth tells very much. Of course, a person *may* be a member of the Society for thirty years and know no more at the end of the time than at the beginning. That is sad, because it is a waste of opportunity. But for those who have constantly thought about Theosophy and lived it, there is a feeling of certainty which has gradually grown. The experiences of life and thought on these things have accumulated for us proof after proof, until we see that they must be so.

In many cases the Theosophical ideas have appeared intricate and difficult at first, but later on simple and easy. They have become part of yourself. A child copies out a page of writing, and is very proud of it if there are no mistakes, but later on he will do the same thing without thinking of it—it has become a power. So long as we are making efforts to understand we have not yet realized the value of Theosophical truths; later on they will be a power in our lives.

Easier and more rapid is the path of the man who gets some personal experience. Few of us are entirely without that, and even one little bit of direct knowledge of that sort shows us—not, perhaps, that all the rest is true, but —that the rest is eminently probable. We have seen for ourselves that a part of what we have learnt is so; we recognize that the rest is probably so, since the entire philosophy is coherent; and this probability is so strong that it becomes for us practically a certainty.

If a hint is not taken, if a word is missed, it is lost for ever; for He does not speak twice.

A.B.—Many people fail to understand that those who hear these things again and again are worse off, not better off, than the people in the outer world who have not heard this message, if they do not try to carry them out. I do not say, it will be noticed, if they do not carry them out, but if they do not *try* to carry them out. It is the strenuous endeavour that is necessary, and it is this that is too often forgotten amongst us. It is true that the Master does not speak twice; He makes a suggestion; if it is not used, He lets it go; He does not repeat what He has said. Only His disciples, meeting the conditions of the world, repeat again and again the things that they have to say, until they produce an impression. If you were accepted disciples, your Master would not tell you to do a thing if it were not possible. If you did not take a piece of advice which He offered, He would not give it you any more. This is not because He is unkind, but because He cannot afford to waste any time; He has far too much to do. All this teaching was given to Alcyone, because he worked hard all the time. It is only those who are strenuously in earnest who can thus come into touch with the Master. I know that it is just this strenuous, unremitting effort which many of you find so difficult, but it is that which is needed, and without it you cannot enter upon the Path.

C.W.L.—We who follow the Master, and try to do some of His work in the outer world, have to speak twice constantly; we have to say over and over again the various things which are committed to us, because people are heedless and inattentive; but when one comes into touch with the Master Himself, he is not expected to be heedless any more; then a single hint should be sufficient, and certainly if it is not taken it will not be repeated, not because the Master is a proud Teacher, but because the pupil is not ready.

The method used by the Masters in training Their pupils should be understood. It is very rarely indeed that They issue any direct order. When I myself was taken on probation many years ago, almost my first question was, "What can I do?" The Master said in reply: "That is for you to discover." Then He explained: "I know quite well that if I tell you to do anything, of course you will do it at once. But in that case you will have only the karma of prompt and instant obedience; I shall have the karma of the deed. I want *you* to have it; I want you, for yourself, to do good things and to make good karma. It must be you who originate the idea, not I." The Great Ones very rarely give direct commands; but often from something that a Master says, or even from the glance of His eye, one forms the opinion as to whether He approves or disapproves of a certain thing; and those who stand round Him, more especially in the case of the Master Kūthūmi, learn very readily to note these things; they are always on the watch for any sort of hint.

The Master Morya was a King in the earlier part of his present incarnation, and He speaks with the command of a King. He more often gives direct orders, and if He disapproves of something, He generally says so clearly. The Master Kūthūmi has hardly ever expressed disapproval. His pupils have learnt to interpret His look, for He rarely says any word of blame. So it comes that they watch very carefully for anything whatever in the nature of a hint. When it is given they endeavour to take it, because they know that if it is missed that particular hint will not be given again. Nothing could possibly follow in the nature of blame or loss from not taking it, except to the pupil, who would be less likely to receive a hint on another occasion.

In *The Masters and the Path* it has been explained that the different Masters train their pupils in different ways, according to the rays to which they belong and the lines of work which they are destined to pursue. On the line of the Manu and Master Morya are people of the *kshattriya* kind—men of the governing type, judges, lawyers, soldiers, statesmen. On the line of the Bodhisattva and the Master Kūthūmi are those of the Brāhmana type—teachers, preachers, reformers. In addition to these there are five other great rays, with their special characteristics. A Chohan, who has passed at least the Sixth Initiation, stands at the head of each type, while under Him there are several Masters. Thus, on the second ray, for example, a pupil need not necessarily belong to the Master Kūthūmi; he might be attached to the Master Djwāl Kūl.

CHAPTER 6

THE FOUR INTRODUCTORY PATHS

C.W.L.—They tell us in the Eastern books that there are four main roads by which men may be brought to the beginning of the Probationary Path. They say that the most frequent method of such turning is through the companionship of those already on the Path. That makes them see its glory and beauty, and the necessity for following it. The influence of an advanced disciple is not limited to the words he speaks; it is the vibration of the life radiating from such a person that is so powerful. This fact is fully recognized in India, where there are many teachers of different sorts standing at different levels, of varying degrees of power, who are there called *gurus*. Each has his own set of followers, and teaches them his own ideas upon philosophy, and sometimes gives them *mantras* to recite, forms of meditation, and yoga practices to do. But it is not by any means mainly through these things that he helps them. The more important thing is that they shall be with him. If he is a peripatetic, wandering from place to place, they go about with him, just as the disciples of Jesus travelled with Him through Palestine. If he lives in one place, these disciples gather round him, sit at his feet and listen to any words of wisdom which he may drop, but the benefit they gain is not so much from what he teaches as from the influence of his presence.

This process is entirely scientific. The higher vehicles of the guru are keyed up to a higher rate of vibration than those of his pupils, who have come more recently than he out of the worldly life, where the vibrations are at a lower level. They are not entirely withdrawn from the selfish side of things, as he is. They must take themselves in hand, realize their faults and resolve to get rid of them and develop certain virtues, in brief, change their own characters, and that is usually a slow and tedious business. They can be quite immensely assisted in that process by being in constant contact with the *guru*, who has developed these virtues and extinguished those vices in himself. The pressure of the higher vibration is constant, whether they wake or sleep, and they are absorbing it and being attuned to it all the time. The principle of this is well known in physics: if you put close to each other two timepieces which are not moving regularly together in harmony, the stronger one will gradually bring the weaker into agreement with itself, or stop it altogether.

The second way of entering the Probationary Path is the hearing or reading of teaching upon the subject. A man who is interested in the matter gets hold of some teaching along these higher lines; it commends itself to his intuition, and immediately he seeks to satisfy his desire to find out more about it. This was my own experience. I came across *The Occult World*, and at once made up my mind: "If that be so—and it is so evidently—if there be these Greater People, and if They are willing to accept service from us, and to give us in return something of Their priceless knowledge—then I am going to be one of those who serve Them. I am going to pick up whatever crumbs I can, and the only thing worth doing from now on is to set to work to get into that position somehow." Of course there are many thousands who hear and read the teaching, and yet do not receive any impulse from it. That is a question of the man's experience in other lives. Only if he has already come into contact with the truth, and has convinced himself of its beauty and reality in a previous life, does he instantly feel it to be true when it comes before him in this life.

It seems to many of us amazing that everyone who gets hold of a Theosophical book is not converted. Theosophy is a wonderful teaching, and it solves a great many problems, and yet you know quite well when you try to lend Theosophical books to friends, half of them return them, and say "Yes, no doubt it is very interesting," but they have not really understood it at all. One's present understanding is the good karma of having studied it before; the more one has known of a thing before, the more he will see in it now. That is our experience with any good book that we may have read, say, twenty years ago. Read it again now, and see how very much more you will find in it than you did then. You are able to see in it that which you bring the power to see.

The third mode by which men are sometimes brought to the beginning of the Probationary Path is by what is called in the Indian books, 'enlightened reflection'. That means that by sheer hard thinking a man may come to see that there must be a plan of evolution, that there must be Those who know all about it—the evolved and perfected Men—and that there must be a Path by which They may be reached. The man who by such thinking comes to that decision then sets out to look for the Path; but those who traval by this road are probably few.

In some ways the most remarkable is the fourth way —the practice of virtue. That is an idea which would quite commend itself to the average Christian, because he often believes that all that is necessary is to be good. But the Theosophist recollects that in the early days of Christianity the purification, or saintship, which they now set before themselves as their goal, was considered to be only the first step. S. Clement says of it quite boldly that purity is merely a negative virtue, valuable chiefly as a condition of insight. Having achieved that, you are then fit to learn, to prepare for illumination, which was the second stage, and after that to pass into the third stage, called perfection. You will remember how S. Paul speaks of that. He says: "We speak wisdom among them that are perfect," but not to others.

This virtue leads to the beginning of the Path because, though the man who leads a good life through many incarnations may not thereby develop intellect, he will presently acquire sufficient intuition to carry him into the presence of the people who do know, to bring him in fact to the feet of some one who is a servant of the Master. It is admitted, however, that that method takes thousands of years and many lives. The man who practises virtue and does not develop his mind will reach the Path eventually, but it is a slow process. It would save him much time if he followed S. Peter's advice and aimed at knowledge as well.

CHAPTER 7

THE FOUR QUALIFICATIONS

Four Qualifications there are for this pathway :

> **Discrimination.**
> **Desirelessness.**
> **Good Conduct.**
> **Love.**

C.W.L.—These qualifications have been stated over and over again in the various religions, but this translation differs slightly from any that have been given previously. In the case of the first, discrimination, there has been little variation. I have already explained the words used for this by the Hindus and Buddhists, how they mean the same thing as conversion among the Christians, and how the pupil must unite the ego and the personality. On the Path proper the process has to be repeated between the Monad and the ego. The ego is a fragment of the Monad put down as far as the higher part of the mental plane; it also comes down for the collection of experience, to learn to receive and respond to vibrations such as cannot be sensed by the Monad at his own level. So the ego in turn has to learn that he is a part of the Monad, that he exists only for that Monad, and when that in turn is fully realized, the man is ready to take the Fifth Initiation and so become an Adept.

Those are the actual definitions of readiness for the two Initiations; for the First, that the higher and the lower self shall have been unified, that there shall be nothing but the ego working in this personality; and for the Fifth Initiation that there shall be nothing in the ego that is not approved or inspired by the Monad. Whenever the Monad touches our lives down here he comes in as a god from above. In all cases of Initiation he flashes down, and for a moment becomes one with the ego, just as they will be permanently one when adeptship is gained. At certain other times also the Monad comes down, as in the case mentioned in *The Lives of Alcyone*, when Alcyone took a pledge to the Lord Buddha.

By one or other of the foregoing means the man is led to discrimination—this knowledge of what is worth following and what is not worth following. Then he finds he has to develop the second qualification, to which the Master here gives the name of desirelessness. Dr. Besant previously translated it dispassion or indifference. This is the Hindu *vairāgya*, which means indifference to the result of one's actions. The Lord Buddha's statement of that is just a little different. For this second stage He uses the Pāli word *parikamma*. Karma or *kamma* always means doing or acting, and *parikamma* means preparation for action; so He calls that second stage preparation for action, the grade in which the emphasis is laid on learning to do right for right's sake, not for the sake of anything the man may gain from it in any way for himself. This must not be misunderstood. Many people say that indifference to the fruit of action means that one must perform duty without taking into account the effect on anyone else. As this book tells us later on, "that which is right you must do, that which is wrong you must not do," whatever the consequences may be; but it does not mean that people should go on doing just what they like without thinking how their action will affect others. In fact, it is that very effect which determines whether the action is right or wrong. The pupil of the Master does not think of the effect upon himself, but he does most emphatically think of that on others.

The third qualification, which is called Good Conduct, includes the six rules which the Hindus name *shatsampatti*. In the Pāli form, as given by the Lord Buddha, that qualification is called *upachāro*, which means 'attention' rather than 'conduct,'—one is to pay attention to conduct in the ways prescribed by those six jewels, as they are called. We shall come to the Master Kūthūmi's rendering of them presently, as we go through this book. By the Buddha they were given as *samo*, 'quietude,' that is, control of mind; then *dāmo*, 'subjugation,' that is, control of the body; then *uparati*, *titikkhā*, *samādhāna*, and *saddhā*, literally 'cessation, endurance, intentness, and faith'. I took the trouble to have all these words looked up in the principal dictionaries, and got these translations from the High Priest Hikkaduwe Sumangala Thero, who was then Head of the Southern Buddhist Church. The words also represent the current belief of that Church.

These are a little different from the translations which are given in this book. What is here called 'cessation' is translated 'tolerance,' because the cessation meant is from bigotry and superstition, the putting aside altogether of any idea that your way is better than anybody else's way, and the idea that any rite or ceremony is necessary. Endurance is simply cheerfulness in another form. Intentness is one-pointedness and balance, bringing all one's life to the focus of one's aim, and therefore also steadiness; and faith is confidence in one's Master and oneself. The qualifications are the same exactly in both cases, but the Lord Buddha spoke of them specially from the point of view of the necessity for wisdom, and the Lord Maitreya and the Master Kūthūmi are emphasizing more the necessity for love. In teaching Alcyone the Master also aimed more at giving the practical meaning than literally translating the old words.

The last qualification is called Love. It is in Sanskrit *mumukshatva*, which means "the intense desire for liberation from the round of births and deaths and for union with the Supreme". The Lord Buddha in His scheme called that *anuloma*, which means 'direct order' or succession. His meaning is that when the man has developed the other qualifications, he must desire to escape from the lower limitations and to become one with the Supreme in order that he may help.

Alcyone then goes on to say:

> What the Master has said to me on each of these I shall try to tell you.

And then begins the book proper.

PART II

DISCRIMINATION

CHAPTER 1

TRUE AND FALSE AIMS

C.W.L.—We now come to Section I of the book itself

> The first of these Qualifications is Discrimination ; and this is usually taken as the discrimination between the real and the unreal which leads men to enter the Path. It is this, but it is also much more ; and it is to be practised, not only at the beginning of the Path, but at every step of it every day until the end.

Those last few words show precisely the difficulties which stand in the way of most of those who see the glory and the beauty of the Path, and intend to enter upon it and come to the feet of the Master. They are all good, earnest, painstaking people, but the personality is wayward, and they have to face the great pressure of public opinion, as I have already explained. In addition there is also the fact that humanity is now but a little past the middle of the fourth round, and they are trying to do in it that which will be very easy to do at the end of the seventh round. Those who go on to that time will have, in their physical, astral and mental vehicles, matter far more fully developed than we have now, with all its spirillæ in activity instead of only about half, and all the forces surrounding them will be helpful and not hindering as they are now.

The Masters are on our side and Their forces help us. The force of evolution, slow as it is, also is on our side, and the future is with us: but the present is a very hard time to do anything of this sort. In the middle of the fifth round all the people whose influence is now bearing hard against us in an opposite direction will have been shunted out, and there will be none left but those who are going our way. In the seventh round things will therefore be wonderfully easy. One may then live in the outer world with all the advantages that can now be found only in a monastery under the direction of a spiritually developed man. Some might think: "Why then should we not wait for the seventh round?" Many among us have been drifting along comfortably and happily enough during the last twenty or thirty thousand years, and those who have not a keen desire from within to progress or to help the world may go on for another million years in just the same old line, and no doubt it will be very much easier in the end; but those who go through the dfficulties now will have the enormous privilege of helping forward evolution, and they will wear the crown of the helper. Remember the old Christian hymn which tells how a man went to heaven and, *looking round, found himself* somehow *different* from all the rest, and wondered what was the matter.

At last he met the Christ, and asked Him why this was so, and the Christ said in reply:

I know thou hast believed in Me
And life through Me is thine,
But where are all those glorious stars
Which in thy crown should shine?
Thou seest yonder joyous throng
With gems on every brow,
For every soul they led to Me
They wear a jewel now.

In the Christian Scripture it is said that they that are wise shall shine as the brightness of the firmament, as the light of the clear sky; but they that turn many to righteousness shall be as the stars for ever and ever—great glowing suns, sending out light and warmth and strength to thousands of other lives. That is the difference between doing the work now, and waiting to drift in with the current in the seventh round.

> You enter the Path because you have learnt that on it alone can be found those things which are worth gaining. Men, who do not know, work to gain wealth and power, but these are at most for one life only, and therefore unreal. There are greater things than these—things which are real and lasting; when you have once seen these, you desire those others no more.

A.B.—The question of the real and the unreal is a deeply metaphysical one, but we are not really concerned with that here, because the Master was teaching Alcyone as quite a young boy, and further the teaching was given on the astral plane. In such cases the Master is speaking to the lower mind as well as to the ego, and on this occasion he gave His teaching in a form suitable for the lower mind of a boy which had by no means reached its full development. However old the ego may be, the three bodies were young, so the teaching was expressed very simply, that on returning to his body the pupil might understand it in his waking mind.

The unreal is here taken to be everything which is not divine, everything that is passing in the phenomenal world, everything belonging to the personal self, including even the higher things for which men work for the sake of a material goal. Following the Master's thought, we may say that everything is unreal except that which is part of the will of God. Those who discriminate know the real things, so they work as agents of God, doing His will, He being the real doer. There is no suggestion that they should neglect material activity. Men should do their work better, not worse, because they are the agents of God, executing His actions in the outer world. "Yoga is skill in action," says the *Gītā*, and yoga is union with the Divine. Action must be skilful in the case of the man who has this union, for it is not he who does the work, but God in him. When Arjuna was asking Shrī Krishna about fighting, the Lord replied that He Himself had already killed the enemy, and He added: "Therefore fight, O Arjuna."

When the higher things have been seen, said the Master, the others are desired no more. That idea is familiar to students of the *Gītā*, in which it is said: "The objects of sense, but not the taste for them, turn away from the abstemious dweller in the body; and even taste turneth away from him after the Supreme is seen." When a man has seen the One, the very desire for the things of the senses dies out in him.

C.W.L.—It is a fact that when the greater things have once been seen one no longer has a taste for the lower things, but it must be absolutely that fact that induces one to refrain from following the latter. Very often people confound cause and effect, and think that to pretend not to care for the lower things—which, though quite good in their way, are yet so called in contradistinction to higher and spiritual things—at once puts a man on a high level. Of course it does not. It is another form of the very common delusion with regard to asceticism. A great many people follow what they call asceticism as an end in itself, and wrongly think that to avoid all the ordinary pleasures of life, to make oneself uncomfortable in various ways, is highly meritorious. That is a relic of the puritan idea which at one time dominated England and a good deal of Europe. It was distinctly of the essence of that puritanism that to be good you must be as uncomfortable as possible. Whenever a man was in any sort of way happy, he was surely infringing some of the divine laws, as he was not in the least meant to be happy down here; his body was a vile thing which had to be repressed in all sorts of ways, and if at any time it delighted in anything he was doing, he might be certain that that thing was wrong. That is all nonsense, but it does come from a perversion of the truth, and the truth is that those things which most people in the world enjoy and regard as great pleasures cease to be thought of as such by the man who, rising to a higher level, has altogether higher pleasures in view, which far more than take their place.

People in the world take great pleasure in all sorts of things which do not interest those who aspire higher—in horse-racing, for example, and drinking and gambling, and also in various forms of amusements such as dancing and card-playing, which are not necessarily harmful, but are rather like children's toys. As a little child grows up he abandons his toys. At the age of three or four he likes to play with bricks and dolls; when he gets a little older he takes to toy soldiers, kites, tops and marbles; when he gets again a little bit older he no longer cares for any of these things, but plays cricket or football, or some game of that sort which requires a great deal of out-door exertion. All these are stages through which the child passes, and each is quite proper in its turn. As he grows still older he abandons those things he had previously enjoyed, not because he thinks he ought to do so, but simply because they have ceased to interest him; he has found something which is more appropriate to his stage of development. But you can see at once that a little child of three would not become a big boy by choosing to ignore all the things of early childhood, and wanting to play cricket or football.

The highly advanced man does not care for a great many things which ordinary people think necessary, and the man of the world would probably find the life of the disciple intolerably wearisome, if he tried to live as many of us do, with no real interest outside Theosophy and the deeper problems of life. The average worldling would say that such people are always doing the one thing, and that they do not seem to know or care for anything else—which is quite true, because that includes all the rest. But he would not become an advanced man by pretending not to care for his own things, while all the time in his heart he really desired them.

> In all the world there are only two kinds of people—those who know, and those who do not know; and this knowledge is the thing which matters. What religion a man holds, to what race he belongs—these things are not important.

A.B.—The Master draws here a very luminous distinction. He divides men into two classes—those who know and those who do not know. That is the great division from the occult standpoint, and each should ask himself to which class he belongs. Both classes include many varieties of people, for outer distinctions and differences are things that do not matter. Those who do not know, work for what exists for one life only; but he who has once clearly seen the real things, is filled with the sole desire to work for the Logos, to fall in with His mighty plan and help in however small a way to carry it out. We can test our own knowledge to see whether it bears on that work or not. The mere brain knowledge which enables one to talk very intelligently, perhaps, and to teach others, is all unreal; the real knowledge is only that which is worked into one's life. There are very many people who make it their custom to sit quietly for a little time every night before going to bed, and review their day's work. That is a very useful thing, but if you do it, ask yourself not merely what you have done, what you have felt, and what you have thought, but what has been your attitude. If you have been submerged in the things you have done, the time has been largely lost : but if you had done the same things as part of the divine work—as acts of sacrifice—they would have helped and not hindered you.

The really important thing is this knowledge—the knowledge of God's plan for men. For God has a plan, and that plan is evolution. When once a man has seen that and really knows it, he cannot help working for it and making himself one with it, because it is so glorious, so beautiful.

C.W.L.—The spirit which makes men join political and temperance associations of various sorts which they think will help the world, is called forth in its very highest aspect the moment a man sees the real plan of the Logos for His system. He sees that it will be carried out one day, and that the time when that desirable consummation will be reached depends upon the number of people who are ready to work for it. If the whole world could be induced, in a few weeks or years, to see and to co-operate with it, everything that the Logos desires for His people would be very rapidly achieved. It is just because men are not yet sufficiently developed to see it, that we fall short so sadly, and so many sorrows and wrongs and wickednesses remain in the face of the sun.

Many students of Theosophy know something of the Plan. I do not say they have seen it yet, but they have been in contact with those who have, and know, therefore, what it is, and in what direction one must move if he would associate himself with it. But when the time of absolutely seeing it comes, it will be found that all that is said here of the enthusiasm is true. In the world, people often take up good causes and reforms with enthusiasm and vigour, but unless they know something of the larger plan of evolution, and see where their own work fits into it, mistakes may easily be made. They attach themselves to certain causes because they are impressed with their urgency and utility. Such is, for example, the cause of temperance, which they espouse because they have seen the tremendous evil caused by the drinking habit, and have realized in how very many ways the world would be quite infinitely better if that evil could be removed. They try to remove it, not by inducing men to give up the foolishness and wickedness of drink, but by prohibiting its sale, and so forcing the people into sobriety—a plan which by no means weeds out the desire, but only renders it impossible to gratify it. I am not for a moment speaking against the prohibition scheme; there is very much to be said in its favour. If we think it wise to place a restriction on the sale of arsenic or prussic acid, why should not the same be done in the case of a poison which is responsible for far more harm than both of them together? I am only pointing out that this remedy does not strike at the root of the evil; it tries to reform people by compulsion, not by persuasion.

Just in the same way people who have realized the awful suffering of the submerged tenth seek in all directions for a remedy for this great and crying shame; but unfortunately some think they have found it in extreme radicalism or even in anarchism. One cannot blame people for prosecuting unselfishly a line which they think will bring relief to their fellows. It is their heads which are at fault in such cases as this, not their hearts, which drive them to great personal loss and sacrifice in order, as they hope, to relieve the trouble of their fellow-men. They have to realize that there is a plan for human evolution, and to give themselves to its study, that their actions may become wise as well as unselfish. It is discrimination that is lacking; they see only one side of the difficulty, and so they plunge themselves into something which will lead to worse trouble than that which they are trying to assuage.

So, because he knows, he is on God's side, standing for good and resisting evil, working for evolution and not for selfishness.

C.W.L.—That is the touchstone by which we may recognize the people who know—it is not in the least by their religion or their race, but by the one and only fact that they stand for good and against evil. Wherever we find a man who is loyal to the highest that he knows, is standing for what seems to him to be good and resisting what seems to him to be evil, we must see in him a brother working on God's side, even though some of the work he does is hardly such as we could approve, or think of as being pleasing to God. There are numbers of people who are utterly good and loyal to their convictions and yet have most crushing limitations. These earnest, devoted persons actually sacrifice their energy, their whole time, and everything they have, to bring other souls to Christ, as they would put it; yet they have the most limited and bigoted conceptions. They show in some cases a feeling of bitter opposition, practically amounting to hatred, for those whose belief is a little different in certain ways from their own.

One of the most striking features of the work of the great Hierarchy is that in every such case its members extract the good and put aside the evil. They take up the force which that devotion and earnestness generates, and use every ounce of it, putting aside all the evil which, on this plane at any rate, so largely prevents the good from showing itself. There are many Christian communities where the bigotry so overshadows the loving-kindness that all the outward impression one gets is of its bitterness. The Brothers of the Hierarchy deplore the bigotry and see the evil done by it even more than others can, but nevertheless They draw out from it all the force of loving-kindness and devotion and good intention, utilize it, and give credit to those who pour it out; and every one of those people will get all the benefit that follows from his goodness, although at the same time for his anger and his bigotry there will also be exactly the due results according to kārmic law.

Wherefore it behoves us to be charitable in dealing with these other people and to try in all cases to fix our thoughts on the good things, to "pounce upon the pearls," as the Master said, instead of everlastingly flying at the flaws, as so many people do.

> If he is on God's side he is one of us, and it does not matter in the least whether he calls himself a Hindu, or a Buddhist, a Christian or a Muhammadan, whether he is an Indian or an Englishman, a Chinaman or a Russian.

A.B.—This is a thing that aspirants to the Path should never forget, for unless it is lived, you are still very far from the Portal. There no one will ask what your race is, or your creed, but only what you have added to your character in the way of qualities. All of us pass through different races in turn. We find ourselves now in a particular sub-race of a particular root race because we need to acquire the good qualities in which it specializes, and which it can therefore give to us, whatever they may be; yet at the same time many people are busy developing the weaknesses of that particular sub-race as well. It would probably be quite right to say: "No other race would be so suitable for me just now, to remove my defects and fill in my character," but it is not intended that we should take up, say, English methods and glorify them to the exclusion of all others, and feel that none can be as good as those. Each race has its part to play in the harmony; each contributes its share to the mighty whole. In whatever race you happen to be, the part of the harmony which is played by that race offers for the moment the easiest and most natural work for you. But you will pass through that and learn to play some other part later. If people understood this, they would be less prone to foolish pride of race, and criticism of other races.

When I hear some one complaining of some one else with the implication that the fault of the other exists because he is an Englishman or an Indian, it shows me at once that the speaker is still deluded by the unreal. The same thing occurs when a person excuses his own shortcomings by saying that they are those of his sub-race. You must try to acquire the best qualities of your race and sub-race, not its deficiencies. The Indian, for example, should try to acquire spirituality, harmlessness, tolerance, and capacity for action with non-attachment—for these are the qualities that the first family of the Aryan race was meant to show out.

Yet sometimes we find that non-attachment is accompanied by carelessness and slipshod work, rising from the wrong idea that because one should be indifferent to the fruits of action the action is unimportant. But what is really wanted is perfection of action with indifference to the fruits of action. With the Englishman, it is often quite the reverse. He is generally competent and careful in action; but is apt to get excited about the fruits of it, because he often lacks the quality of indifference.

It is the business of each to try to acquire what he lacks; the Indian should try to practise action, the Englishman indifference, without loss of the qualities which are already theirs. If this were done differences of race would work for the enrichment of all races, for each could learn from the other what he himself lacked.

C.W.L.—To be patriotic, to admire your own race, to feel that you owe something to it, and to be ready to serve it, are all good things. But take great care lest you show your admiration by depreciating the others. Our permanent relation is to humanity as a whole. We are citizens of the world, not of any one race. Yet patriotism is good, just as family love is good. In both cases, however, we must not let ourselves carry our virtue to such extremes as to put evil in the place of good. Truly family affection is a splendid thing, but that of the robber barons of the Middle Ages, which led them to murder other people for the sake of enriching their own families, was certainly a virtue carried to an excess, and become a vice. In exactly the same way patriotism is good, but if it leads to aggression against other races, it becomes bad. But if you can do something for your race, without injuring others; if you can show yourself to be a worthy member of it, so that it shall be the better for your passing through it, you may then have some cause for satisfaction. It is precisely the same with religion. We have all been through many of the great religions. Each one emphasizes certain virtues, but all are necessary for the progress of mankind.

Those who are on His side know why they are here and what they should do, and they are trying to do it; all the others do not yet know what they should do, and so they often act foolishly.

C.W.L.—Here is a touch of the teaching of the Lord Gautama Buddha that all evil comes from ignorance. The fact that those who do not know often act foolishly makes it true that the wicked man is always to be pitied, not to be disliked or hated. What impresses itself most upon people generally is that he is acting in selfishness—for his own interests, as he thinks—and they are a little apt to forget his ignorance of the facts. To take an instance—there have been certain great millionaries who won their way to temporary prosperity by throwing out of business a number of smaller people and beggaring them. They are regarded with execration by those people whose livelihood they have taken away, and everyone says how utterly selfish and brutal these people are.

Yes, but when they are so it is because they are ignorant. Such a man is doing exactly what he set out to do: to crush out those other people because he thinks he can do all that business better. Perhaps he can turn out better results, and make a fortune for himself at the same time, but he would never have set out to do it had he known that he was doing far more harm to himself than to any of the other people, that he was making for his own future a karma that would be quite infinitely worse than that of those men whom he crushed. Instead of execrating that man for his selfishness the wiser part would be to pity him for his ignorance.

> **And try to invent ways for themselves which they think will be pleasant for themselves, not understanding that all are one, and that therefore only what the One wills can ever be really pleasant for any one.**

C.W.L.—It is a great motto of utilitarianism to pursue the greatest good of the greatest number. It is a great improvement upon the previous idea that the good of only a few should be considered, and that the others were a negligible quantity. But the minority cannot be ignored; indeed every one must be taken into account, because all are one. This cannot be understood until the consciousness of the buddhic plane has been developed to some extent, and even then only by slow degrees can one learn how utterly all are one. We think of it as a sort of religious duty to believe it to be so, or as a sort of pious aspiration that some day all will become one. We say: "We have all come forth from the same great Father, and therefore we are all brothers, and we are all one." We do not, however, understand the reality and the depth of that until we experience it in buddhic consciousness.

Some suggestion of it may be given, nevertheless, if we say that all consciousnesses are one, that all the world is one, that all the love in it is the one Divine Love, that all the beauty in it is the one Divine Beauty, and all the holiness of the world is the one Holiness of God.

Christ expressed that when a man came to Him and called Him "good Master", He said: "Why callest thou Me good? There is none good but One and that is God." The goodness of each man is the goodness of God showing itself forth in him, and all the beauty and glory of the world, as we see it, in the earth and sea and sky, is nothing but part of the one Divine Beauty; and as we rise to different subplanes, from level to level, more and more we see that beauty opening itself out before us, until we learn to see all beauty through each beautitul thing. It is all one.

When that is learned, the glory of the Divine will be seen in and through everything, and all its other glories through each of those, so that when a beautiful landscape opens before us, it will not be merely the scene which we shall admire, but all that it suggests—the infinite whole of which it is only a tiny part. Then life will become wonderfully happy for us, and full of love. Through that happiness we shall experience something of the Eternal Bliss, and through that love we shall realize the Eternal Love. It is only in that way that great advancement can come, only when we realize that we ourselves are nothing but a point in the whole; then our consciousness is in a condition to merge into His, so that through us He may see all this beauty, and we, as in Him, may see it and realize it too.

They are following the unreal instead of the real. Until they learn to distinguish between these two,

they have not ranged themselves on God's side, and so this discrimination is the first step.

But even when the choice is made, you must still remember that of the real and the unreal there are many varieties; and discrimination must still be made between the right and the wrong, the important and the unimportant, the useful and the useless, the true and the false, the selfish and the unselfish.

C.W.L.—Those are all subdivisions of the great distinction between the real and the unreal, and their enumeration shows us how discrimination must ramify down into the smallest affairs of life, if we are to tread this Path. Little points are constantly arising which we have to decide this way or that way, so always we have to bear the idea of discrimination in mind, and keep constantly watchful. To stop and think all the time is wearisome. Many good people get tired when they try it; the perpetual strain of it is too great for them. That is very natural, but those who give in fail to achieve; therefore however wearisome it may be, we must continue the life of recollectedness.

Between right and wrong it should not be difficult to choose,. for those who wish to follow the Master have already decided to take the right at all costs.

A.B.—If anyone hesitates between right and wrong he does not really wish to follow the Master. Those who decide to do so must make up their minds to take the right at all costs on all occasions, small and great, no matter what the consequences may be. In the *Yoga Sutras* it is said of the five great qualities called *yama*, which include harmlessness, truth, honesty, and other virtues, which are prescribed at the very beginning of the Path, that "these are called the great vows, being universal," which means that they are to be kept under *all* circumstances, that no gain for himself or others could justify the disciple in breaking one of them. The man who has attained this position will never tell, or act, an untruth, however great may be the apparent advantage of so doing. This will be so not only in money matters but in everything; he will never take any more credit than belongs to him, for example. You must ask yourself whether you always choose the truth *instinctively*, for until this is so you are far from the first Portal. On this subject the Master does not think it worth while to say any more; it is so clear, so palpable.

C.W.L.—This idea refers not only to the question of conduct, but also to the fact that there are right and wrong ways to go about any piece of work that has to be done. He who is not strict in following this rule does not really desire success deep down inside. People sometimes say: "How I wish I were clairvoyant; how I wish I could see astrally, how must I begin? What is the first step?" The first step is to purify all the vehicles; you must be careful that the physical body takes no food but the most suitable. Many would like astral sight, but when it comes to the point they prefer what they call a good dinner. They feel that they must have that, because they are used to it, and for the time they forget all about their desire for astral sight. The feeling, however, is simply due to habit, and when we know about this peculiarity of the body we can proceed with confidence in the wearisome task of wearing down the old bad or unsuitable habits, and setting up new ones. It is encouraging that the principle of habit can be made a powerful ally in our work, although it is a hindrance in the beginning; for when once we have established good habits, they will go on automatically, and we can forget them, and give our attention to other things.

In conduct there is no question as to choosing between right and wrong. Anyone who is likely to be interested in this book, or who wants to reach the Master's feet, will not hesitate in choosing the right, when he sees it. Let us hope that none of us would try to cheat a fellow-creature—I hope we have got past that —or be guilty of the slightest untruthfulness, even to do apparent good. We should probably not be obtaining a living in any objectionable way, such as by the slaughter of animals, nor be of the number of those who wear articles of dress or adornment which can only be obtained by the killing of animals,—sometimes by the slaughter of, say, the mother-bird under peculiarly revolting circumstances. All people who continue to wear such things do not really desire to follow the Master; they prefer to follow the fashion.

CHAPTER 2

THE LIFE OF THE BODIES

But the body and the man are two, and the man's will is not always what the body wishes. When your body wishes something, stop and think whether *you* really wish it.

A.B.—Here the Master gives His pupil the decided order that when his body wishes something, he must stop and consider whether he himself really wishes it. Many people will find that stopping and thinking every day and all day long very difficult and irksome ; but the fact must be faced that it is an important part of the preparation. It is very difficult, I know, and therefore many aspirants get tired of making the effort.

Those who give up because they are tired do not achieve, that is all. The effort to do this must be great and prolonged—it all means such a regulated life, in which there shall be no hasty action, no hasty speech, not even hasty thinking, but all the pupil's activities, physical, emotional and mental, must be entirely under control.

C.W.L.—If one wants really to do his best in this matter of progress it is worth his while to make a careful study of his different vehicles and see exactly what they are. Here it is said quite clearly that the physical body wishes for things that the man does not wish for, and that is equally true of the astral and mental bodies. If the constitution of these vehicles is understood, one can see that what they are likely to want would be undesirable for the man. We are speaking of them almost as though they were separate persons, and in a way they are. Each of these bodies is built of living matter, and the life in them joins itself together, and acquires a kind of corporate consciousness.

In the astral body that forms what we sometimes call the desire-elemental, who is practically an entity composed of the joint life of all the astral cells that make up that body. Each cell by itself is a small, only partly-conscious life, struggling on its upward way—or, rather, its downward way, because evolution for it is to pass down into the mineral kingdom. When these lives find themselves all joined together in an astral body, they do to a certain extent practically club together and act as though they were a unit, and you get the effect of an astral body that has strong instincts of its own, so strong, in fact, that you could almost say that it has a will of its own. The way for it to evolve is to get stronger and coarser vibrations, connected with all those feelings and emotions which we do not want to develop, such as envy, jealousy and selfishness: that is why its interests are so often opposed to ours. The far more delicate, more rapid and really more powerful vibrations of love, sympathy and devotion, all belong to a higher part of the astral body, consequently they are of the type that the body itself does not want, though we do.

People of unregulated life, who want to be free, as they often call it, to say and do what they wish, are really slaves to their astral bodies. We must not blame the astral body for this, nor regard it, as the mediæval Christians did, as a tempting demon. It does not know anything about us or our existence; and it is not tempting us at all, but is simply trying to find expression for itself, to evolve, in its own way, just as all other creatures are doing.

People have sometimes asked the question, "Ought not we to give this elemental a chance for its evolution; ought we not to let it have its coarse vibrations?" No, that is mistaken philanthropy, and could not be done thoroughly, anyhow. The kindest thing one can do with the coarser matter—which is in our astral bodies because in some previous lives we have allowed the lower emotions to play strongly through us—is to shake it out, and let it fasten itself upon some savage, or a dog or a cow, where its vibrations can act with no harm to anybody.

The desire-elemental is in its way quite cunning. We cannot quite put ourselves in its place and realize consciousness at so very low a stage, but evidently it feels that it is surrounded by something finer than itself—the mental matter—and appears to find out by experiment that if it can get that to vibrate along with its matter, it obtains a much more intense vibration, and more of it, than it otherwise could. If it can make the man think that he wants what it wants, it is much more likely to get it, so it tries to stir up that finer matter. If it can thus induce an impure thought, for example, it will presently get the impure emotions that it likes, or if it can arouse a jealous thought there will presently be a feeling of jealousy rankling, which is what it wants; not, however, because it is evil, for to it it is nothing but a very strong coarse vibration such as it enjoys. In this way the elemental often proves more than a match for the human being, though it is very low in the scale of evolution. It is rather humiliating, when you think of it, to realize that you are being overcome and used as a tool by something that is not yet even a mineral. We have to face it and purify the astral body against its will by changing any bad habits that may be ours from the past, and putting in their places good emotions for the future.

There is a mental elemental and a physical elemental as well. The latter is engaged in the building up of tissue and looking after the body generally. If one gets a scratch, a cut or a wound, it is the physical elemental that at once hurries the white corpuscles to the spot, to try to build together new cells. There is a great deal that is very interesting about the work of this elemental in the physical body; some of its activities are eminently useful to us, but at the same time it is liable to have impulses which are not for our good.

For *you* are God, and you will only what God wills; but you must dig deep down into yourself to find the God within you, and listen to His voice, which is *your* voice.

C.W.L.—The idea of our unity with the One Self is difficult to realize. I will tell you how it was first brought definitely home to me, though it was not by a method that I can recommend to others. I was at the time trying to concentrate the whole of my power in the atomic part of the mental plane, in order to discover how far one could utilize what we call the short cuts which run between the atomic subplanes of the different planes. In rising through the planes one can travel up the physical plane from subplane to subplane to the atomic, from that to the lowest astral, and on by degrees to the astral atomic, and then to the lowest mental, and so on. Or one can take a short cut from the atomic physical to the atomic astral, and from that to the atomic mental.

I had heard, among higher pupils, of another kind of short cut, at right angles, as it were, to that. They said that if one's consciousness were focused in one of our atomic subplanes one could get a line of communication open to the corresponding cosmic plane. Therefore, by focusing oneself entirely in the atomic mental, there would be a possibility of coming into touch with the mental division of an entirely new set of planes, (that is to say, the cosmic mental plane) altogether above all the planes that we know.

I had not, of course, any hope of reaching such a plane as that, but there was a possibility of communication. I tried, and found that I was able to see—I cannot describe it, I am afraid—the corresponding subplane in the cosmic mental, two whole sets of planes above where we are. I could not actually reach it in any sort of way—I do not think even an Adept could do that—but I could see it. It was as though I were at the bottom of a well and were looking up at a star—but I could see that higher consciousness. The one thing that was then borne in upon me, with an intensity which I cannot describe, was the fact that if before I had supposed that I had a will, that I had an intellect, that I had emotions, they were not mine, they were His; it was His will, His feeling, not mine at all. I have never forgotten the experience, as it impressed that fact upon me with a certainty that I cannot describe.

That certainty that the Divine is within us can be gained also through the buddhic consciousness, as I have already explained. As soon as we achieve that, we find the sea of consciousness opening round us, and we know that we are part of it, and yet at the same time many others are in it and share it along with us; and presently, in addition to that feeling, we come to realize that this is all one consciousness, penetrating us and all others—that we are God. That realization gives one a sense of the utmost safety and confidence, the most tremendous impulse and stimulus of which one could possibly think. Yet I can quite imagine that at first it might alarm some people, because they might feel that they were losing themselves. They are not, of course; but remember what Christ said, "He that loseth his life for My sake shall find it." Christ represents the buddhic principle, and is saying: "He who for My sake—for the Christ development within him—will put aside the causal body in which he has been living for so long, will find himself, will find the far grander and higher life." It needs some courage to do it, and it is a startling experience the first time that one is wholly in the buddhic vehicle and finds that his causal body, upon which he has been depending for thousands of years, has vanished. When any one has one or other of the experiences I have described, he will know with absolute certainty that the Self is one. The idea cannot be conveyed, but it will be known when the thing is experienced, and nothing will ever again shake that certainty.

> Do not mistake your bodies for yourself—neither the physical body, nor the astral, nor the mental. Each one of them will pretend to be the Self, in order to gain what it wants. But you must know them all, and know yourself as their master.

C.W.L.—The Master speaks of these bodies quite definitely as though they were separate persons, referring, of course, to the elementals which we have already considered. Their empire is absolutely unchecked for most people in the world, who not only make no effort to throw off their dominion, but do not even know that there is any yoke to throw off. They do not separate themselves from their bodies. The disastrous teaching about man *having* a soul is responsible for much harm in this direction. If people could only realize that man *is* a soul and *has* bodies, at once they would begin to disentangle things a little. So long as a man has the idea that the soul is something vague floating above him, there is very little hope of doing good. When we find the elementals rising in us, we should say: "This emotion is a vibration in my astral body, and I will vibrate as *I* choose. I am the centre for the time being of this set of bodies, and I will use them as *I* want."

> When there is work that must be done, the physical body wants to rest, to go out walking, to eat and drink; and the man who does not know says to himself: "*I* want to do these things, and I must do them." But the man who knows says: "This that wants is *not* I, and it must wait awhile."

C.W.L.—You will notice that very strongly in the case of children. If a child wants to do a thing, it is heaven and earth to him; he must do it then and there in a moment, and if he cannot he thinks the universe is falling round him. Savages also are like that—creatures of impulse, which is so strong that just to do some trifling thing they will sometimes kill a man. The civilized man would say: "I will wait and consider what will happen." The child dashes off and plays, and far too often we who are older blame and scold him, not understanding the child nature. He says, "I did not remember." That is absolutely true, but we doubt it because we know that *we* should remember. We have forgotten our own childhood and that of the race. We ought to say, "I know you have an impulse, but really you must not do that just now. It will upset the arrangements of a great many other people. You shall do it some other time." That is the way education progresses. It is the same with the savage, who in course of time learns that certain impulses must not be followed. It takes him several births to do so, and he generally gets killed in the process, but gradually he becomes a little less savage and more civilized. But the advanced man is dealing with the body as a separate entity, as a thing he can manage.

> Often when there is an opportunity to help some one, the body feels: "How much trouble it will be for me; let some one else do it." But the man replies to his body: "You shall not hinder me in doing good work."

C.W.L.—Dr. Besant remarked with regard to this that there are very many cases where there is obviously a good piece of work to be done, but most people look at it and say: "Yes, that is a thing that must be done. Some one will do it some day; why should *I* bother about it?" but the person who is really in earnest says: "There is a piece of work that ought to be done; why should not *I* do it?" and he will plunge in and do it at once.

> The body is your animal—the horse upon which you ride. Therefore you must treat it well, and take good care of it; you must not overwork it, you must feed it properly on pure food and drink only, and keep it strictly clean always, even from the minutest speck of dirt.

C.W.L.—The idea that the body is an animal is really very useful; it sounds so obvious, and yet the more closely the simile is followed, the nearer we shall be to doing what is required. Suppose you keep a horse—I am taking it for granted that you are a reasonable and kindly person, and that while you want your work done, at the same time you want your horse to be as happy and comfortable as possible, and in good health. First of all, then, you want to make friends with him, to get to know the creature, and get him to know you and to feel that you are kindly disposed towards him. Then you find out what kind of food suits him best, and how much of it he needs, and give to him. You take care that he shall have enough, but you do not give him the things that will be bad for him. At the same time you work him, because that is the object of having a horse; yet you do not overwork him in any way. You find out what he can do, and set him to do it. You have taught him to trust you so that he will obey you, and when you suggest anything he will follow what you want, knowing that all will be well with him, and then he will trust you even when he is frightened. So you get the most work out of him with the least possible trouble. A bad trainer will sometimes terrorize a horse; but never after that will he get really good work out of him. You do not want that; you want to have a friendly arrangement with the creatures.

The body is exactly like that horse. We ought to find out the best way to deal with it. It is a great mistake to apply severe Hatha Yoga methods. We must be kind to it, and get out of it as much as we comfortably can, but never overwork it, for one may do harm in an hour that it will take years to repair. There is great strain and stress in modern life. Men constantly say in business: "I really must do a little more"; but very often that little overstrains the mechanism, and that which is overstrained does not return to its normal condition. It is very easy to do this harm, because the body is such a very delicate piece of machinery—a *living* piece of machinery. It is wonderfully recuperative, and in many cases what we know as "a good body" will stand a great deal of ill-usage. But the fact that it survives the ill-usage, and that the man lives through it, does not by any means prove that no harm has been done. On the contrary, very often a slight overstrain leaves a permanent mark. Therefore I would caution any who are attempting anything in the way of occult development to be very careful, and to realize fully that, as our President has said, what we have not time to do is not our work.

Then comes the question of nourishment. The theory that anybody can live on anything is not one that commends itself to the practical man. People differ enormously in their dispositions and capacities. It is an old proverb that what is one man's meat is another man's poison, and that is true in this matter of food values. I know there is a tendency to think that people who pay much attention to food are worrying themselves unnecessarily about purely physical things. Certainly I would say do not overdo it, but take the middle path and be wise. Each one owes it to his body to find out what it can take and what amount of that suits it best. Within reason we should give the body what it wants and likes, but never things which are bad for it, like alcohol or meat. Never try to force anything, but always aim at what is wanted with understanding of what you are dealing with, and thus gain the co-operation of such intelligence as the creature may have.

People very often have trouble in changing to vegetarianism from a meat diet. In England when people begin to be vegetarians they often misunderstand the whole matter; they have been living principally on meat, with cabbage and potato. Their idea of being vegetarians is to give up the meat and try to live on cabbage and potato. Now potato is practically all starch and cabbage is mostly water. A man cannot live on starch and water: other elements are needed—foods that will form flesh, bone and blood—and there are many different kinds of them, so assuredly one can with a little trouble find what kinds suit his body best, and then live principally on those. If any one has trouble with digestion he is probably taking the wrong things; he should try others, for there is always a way out, unless he is hopelessly diseased. When little children keep caterpillars in order to see them turn into butterflies they take a good deal of trouble to find what kind of a leaf the caterpillar will eat—they know that only one kind of leaf will suit it. Surely we might take as much trouble over the animal which is to serve us for so many years, and feed it properly on pure food and drink only.

Very great care must be taken about cleanliness. There are various reasons for it—not only for health, nor simply because it is the refined thing to do, but also because the Master particularly uses those who are in close relation with Him as channels for the outpouring of His force. That is generally confined to His pupils, who are in close touch with Him, but any person who is seriously trying to live by the principles laid down in such books as this, is under His eye, and therefore it is not impossible that such an one might be needed, and might be used as a channel for force. It might well happen that in any given place there was no pupil quite suitable for some kind of outpouring; but there might be some other person who, though not so far advanced, was suitable for that particular purpose. In such a case the Master would want to use him.

Many varieties of force are poured out by the Master for different purposes; sometimes one person is suitable as a channel and sometimes another. Watching the case of two pupils side by side, one sees that one is used always for one type of force and the other for another type. This outpouring is physical as well as astral, mental, and buddhic, and on the physical plane it issues mainly through the hands and feet. If, then, the physical body of the person selected failed him for a moment in this most important matter of cleanliness, the Master could not utilize it, because the man would not be a suitable channel. It would be like pouring pure water through a dirty pipe—it would be fouled on the way. Therefore those who are in close relation with the Master are exceedingly careful about perfect bodily cleanliness. Let us take care, then, that we shall be fit in this respect if we should be needed.

Another point about which we need to be careful if we wish to be of use is to avoid distortion, especially of the feet. Not long ago I stayed for a few weeks in a community where it is the custom to walk barefooted, and I was horrified to see the twisted and crippled appearance of the feet of many of the students, and to observe how seriously this deformity interfered with their usefulness as channels for the Master's force. The natural course for that force under ordinary conditions is to fill the whole body of the pupil and rush out through the extremities; but in cases where unhygienic foot-gear had produced permanent malformation the Adept could utilize only the upper half of the body; and as that imposed upon Him the additional trouble of constructing each time a sort of temporary dam or barrier in the neighbourhood of the diaphragm of the pupil, it inevitably followed that others who were free from this disfigurement were employed far more frequently.

For without a perfectly clean and healthy body you cannot do the arduous work of preparation, you cannot bear its ceaseless strain.

C.W.L.—Under present circumstances preparation for the Path is truly arduous, and if it is hurried it is a ceaseless strain, which we cannot bear unless all our bodies, including the physical, are in good order. Therefore perfect health is a necessity for rapid progress, and wherever it fails there is a delay at once. Those who are in charge of the progress of any pupil always watch most carefully to see that there is no overstrain, and they will not put the least extra work upon one under their care until they see that he is perfectly able to bear it with a suitable margin.

But it must always be you who control that body, not it that controls you. The astral body has *its* desires—dozens of them; it wants you to be angry, to say sharp words, to feel jealous, to be greedy for money, to envy other people their possessions, to yield yourself to depression. All these things it wants, and many more, not because it wishes to harm you, but because it likes violent vibrations, and likes to change them constantly. But *you* want none of these things, and therefore you must discriminate between *your* wants and your body's.

A.B.—I suppose that most thinking people clearly realize that they are not their physical bodies, but the examples that the Master gives here show how continually they identify themselves with their astral bodies. You may sometimes find yourself saying, "I am angry, or irritable." Even those who do not like to think of themselves as the lower emotions often still confuse them with the higher. Probably they will not say, "I am jealous," when they become conscious of the feeling of jealousy within them; for though men may identify themselves with their feelings they try to veil the lower ones, and in this case they deceive themselves into believing that their feeling is not jealousy, but love; "I am hurt because so-and-so, whom I love, loves some one else better than me."

Love is such a far-reaching, all-embracing virtue, that men like to shelter under it, and they manage to attribute to it all sorts of things with which it has nothing whatever to do. It is far better for us to examine our feelings honestly, and not to play with these serious matters and deceive ourselves with pretty words. In the case under consideration, you are not hurt because you love your friend, but because you desire to appropriate that friend to yourself. Whenever there is this feeling of being hurt it springs from selfishness, which is the opposite pole to love. You—the real Self—cannot feel jealous, but your astral body can; nor can you be angry or irritable; these are all moods of the astral body.

The Master also mentions further examples—greed, envy and depression. Aspirants for the Path are not so likely to yield to the first two of these as to the third. Often people are less careful about depression than about their other feelings because they are under the delusion that it affects only themselves. They think: "If I feel sad or low, after all it is only my business, and it concerns no one else." But that is not true; it does injure other people. The mechanism of this process is well known to all students of occultism. The vibrations of depression spread around, and affect the astral bodies and even the mental bodies of other people. This is a far more evil thing than is generally realized, because many of the people whom your thought may touch may be of a less-developed type, and may also be in circumstances in which they are exposed to conditions that tend to crime.

Those who are familiar with the history and statistics of crime know that a large number of crimes, especially such as murder and suicide, are committed after a period of deep depression. The prisoner in the dock often says: "An overwhelming feeling of despair came over me; I felt I could not help myself." There are many people in the lower stages of evolution who may be affected in this way; and some may suffer imprisonment and death, who yet were not really responsible, or only partly so for the crime committed by their hands. We are living in a world where few people understand these inner laws and very imperfect justice is rendered in our courts for want of simple knowledge of the rudiments of psychology.

Perhaps I feel this all the more keenly because I used to be subject myself to moods of great elation, and then of equally great depression when the pendulum swung back. Many people have the same temperament; one day the world seems full of happiness, the sunshine is bright, nature is beautiful, all things are joyful and fair. Then follows the inevitable reaction; a feeling of great sadness comes over you, and the whole world seems darkened. If you look at the matter quietly, you will realize that the outer causes to which you may attribute your changes of mood are not sufficient to account for such large results. Still, this temperament has some advantages. I certainly could not speak so effectively if

I had not brought it into the world with me; it is part of the orator's temperament to know these extremes of feeling. But, like every other temperament, it has its drawbacks as well as its uses. One must not yield to these violent alternations of feeling.

I doubt whether one can get rid of this defect by merely saying to oneself: "I ought not to feel depressed"; but even the worst cases can be overcome if one remembers that one ought not to yield to it because of its deplorably bad effect on other people. Do not therefore simply try to drive it away, but replace it with a strong thought of courage and cheerfulness, to which should be added the warmth of your unselfish feeling.

The astral body does not wish to do any harm, as the Master points out. It acts as it does simply because it is made up of elemental essence which is on the downward arc, and is evolving by violent and constantly changing vibrations. This constant desire of the astral body for violent changes is a thing that should help the student to realize that it is not himself, but something that brings about moods for no apparent cause, and not approved by the reason, because they are independent activities of the astral body. One must realize this, and not allow oneself to be the playground of all these changing moods. Study your own astral nature, and find out what are the undesirable things that it particularly desires. Then quietly determine that you will not allow it to have them. That done, do not think any more about them; do not brood over them. Pick out the opposite moods, and practise them all day long. If your astral body wants to be impatient, set your mind on patience; think patience in your morning meditation, and practise it throughout the whole of the day. If your astral body wants you to feel jealous, simply observe the fact, and then do not think any more about jealousy, but think of unselfishness and practise it hard, and then there will be no room for jealousy. Your mind cannot be filled with two opposing things at the same time.

Remember that all difficulties constitute opportunities for the would-be occultist. It is no credit for the disciple to show out love when all around are kind, or gentleness when all are considerate. The most ordinary person does that. Those who wish to be disciples must show out right emotion when the wrong is being shown to them; otherwise they are just like all the rest. This should be remembered in difficulty and temptation; the aspirant should spring forward to meet them as opportunities for the payment of debts. To a disciple, every trying person and circumstance he meets is not a temptation, but an opportunity. It is when he is returning good emotions for evil ones that the disciple resembles his Master; it is then that he is showing forth the Master's qualities.

Think, then, in your morning meditations, of the qualities that you want; if you are irritable, for example, think of patience. Then, when you meet an irritable or tiresome person during the day, you will at first respond to him with irritability through force of habit, but a moment after you have made the mistake you will think of patience. The next time you will think of patience while you are making the mistake; a little more practice, and you will think of it the moment before, and then you will feel the irritability, but will not show it; at last you will not even feel irritable. The first of those stages shows that your meditation is beginning to bear fruit.

I know many people who have set themselves to do this and have kept it up for a few days or weeks and then said: "I will not meditate along these lines any more: I am getting no results. My meditation is doing me no good. I am not making progress." It is exactly the same as if a person started on a three days' journey to some place, and after an hour or two sat down, saying: "It is no use my walking; I do not seem to be getting there." Everybody can see how silly such conduct would be down here in the physical world; the other is not a bit less foolish. Meditation *must* produce results, just as walking must carry you over the ground. It is as certain as that. Scientific rules act at all times, and every force you set going must produce results. If you do not at once gain what you are aiming at, it is because there is still more to be overcome, and the force is going into that, to neutralize it and then to conquer it completely. Do not think of the question of results. Just direct the thought to the quality of patience, or whatever it is that you are going to develop, and the results will take care of themselves.

C.W.L.—It is not, after all, very difficult with a little practice to realize that we are not this physical body, that it is only an overcoat, but the astral body—our emotions and desires—presents more difficulty, because it seems often to be a very intimate part of ourselves. One finds people in every-day life everywhere who feel themselves to be their emotions and desires; some are so full of them that if you could imagine these taken away there would seem to be nothing left—the whole person is desire and emotion. It would be very difficult for such an one to separate himself from his astral body, and yet that is what has to be done. The fact that the astral body is constantly changing its moods ought to help people to realize that it is not the Self, the 'I'. As soul one is not changing; one wishes always the same thing—advancement to be able to help others to walk alone the Path intended by our Masters. Surely, therefore, it is clear that this emotional body is not the Self.

The astral elemental gains a certain continuity because the permanent atoms attract round them just the kind of matter we possessed in our previous life. It is therefore difficult to turn round suddenly and check this creature. It can be done, however, and the best way is to discover by careful examination along what lines of undesirable activity one's astral body wants to run. Each person has his own difficulties. One perhaps is nervous and irritable or prone to jealousy, or is greedy for money. When he finds out, he must quietly set himself to check that particular thing. Suppose it is irritability, which is very common under the horrible conditions and the noise of modern life. The person should make up his mind that he will not be irritable. It is a good thing to take it as a subject for meditation; yet in that one should not set to work to combat the vice, but rather to meditate upon the opposite quality of patience. Never think of the evil thing and of fighting against it, because that stirs it up the more.

The same method must be applied also when you are trying to help others by your thought. If you are helping some one who has this fault, instead of dwelling upon his irritability and what a pity it is, and thereby intensifying it, you should think: "I should like him to be calm and patient." Then all the strength of your thought goes in the direction of making him so.

At first, when we meet an irritating person we shall probably be irritable, because we are in the habit of it; and afterwards we shall remember, "I did not mean to do that." It is something even to remember afterwards like that. Perhaps the next time, or the twentieth time, we shall remember at the moment, instead of just afterwards. In the third stage, we shall remember just before we say the irritable thing; the feeling of irritability is there, but we shall not show it. The next step is that we shall not feel the irritability at all, and then it is conquered and we shall have no more trouble with it in this life or other lives to come.

It is also necessary for the mastery of the astral nature that we should have no personal feelings at all that can be hurt or offended. The better feelings, such as sympathy and love, we may and must have to the uttermost. But it must be impossible for us to have our feelings hurt, to be offended. He whose feelings can be hurt is thinking about himself, and that we have no right to do if we have given ourselves to the Master. It may be that there are some people so thick-headed that they cannot see an insult—that is not desirable ; but when you do see it, be wise enough to take no notice of it, which is always the better way. If people say nasty things about you, never mind; people have been saying nasty things about other people ever since the world began, and until we are all well on the way to Adeptship they will continue to do so. And after all it does not matter what another person says. It is a passing vibration of the air, and it is no more than that unless we allow it to be so. If a person says something about you which is unpleasant, if you do not hear it, it does not hurt you in the least. If you do happen to hear it and get into a fume of anger and horror and despair and all the rest of it, that is not the doing of the original sinner ; you are hurting yourself. Take it quite philosophically. Say, "Poor creature, that is all she knows about it!" Be quite gentle and kindly about it. What other people say is of very little importance, because they never know. Remember "the heart knoweth its own bitterness". In each case a man has his own reasons for what he says and does and thinks ; from the outside you never know the whole of his reasons because you are looking at them superficially, and usually quite wrongly. Until you reach the buddhic plane therefore, give him the benefit of the doubt, or more wisely still do not attempt to attribute motives to anyone. If you feel that a person's action is wrong the kindest thing is to say : "I should not do that ; to me it seems to be wrong ; but I assume that that person has his reasons, though I do not know what they may be."

When a person is rude, it is often because something has gone wrong, and the result is that he feels all out of tune—and you happen to be the next person who speaks to him. He is not really angry with *you*. Something else has upset him; perhaps he had not a good dinner. We have to learn to make allowances for other people and say: "Poor fellow, I suppose he cannot always feel as perfectly amiable and agreeable as I always am!" Probably that person will be rather sorry afterwards that he spoke a little rudely, or else he will not even realize that anything out of the common has been said. Any feeling of being offended or hurt must spring from a thought of self. If we were not thinking of ourselves we could not feel hurt or offended. This thought of self is precisely what we must weed out and cast away. Wherever there is a case of jealousy, there is also this thought of self. If the person were thinking only how much he loved the other, it could not matter to him how much that other loved some one else. The delusion of the separate self is at the back of nearly all our troubles.

The selfish man is now an anachronism—still carrying on what was useful and necessary for him twenty years ago, but it is not useful and necessary for him now, and he is simply behind the time. Our business is to be up-to-date. We are living for and thinking of the future that the great World-Teacher will make for us; and because of that we must brush away all these antiquated ideas.

When you examine yourself to find the faults that you intend to overcome, beware of being upset by delusions about remorse and repentance. Remember the story of Lot's wife, and do not look back—that is a very profitless occupation. You may say quite calmly when you have made some bad mistake: "That was a foolish thing to do; I will never do it again." Talleyrand is reported to have said: "Any man may make a mistake—we all make mistakes—but the man who makes the same mistake twice is a fool." A Master once remarked: "The only repentance which is worth anything is the resolve not to do it again." Remember; "The man who never made a mistake never made anything at all." You do not worry about what you did in past lives; why then worry about yesterday? Both are equally past. Remorse is a waste of time and energy—worse than that, for it is a form of selfishness.

It is easy to be loving and kindly to those who are so to us, but if we have made any real progress we shall pour out love even when we meet with the lack of it. The Christ said: "If ye love them which love you, what reward have ye? do not even the publicans the same?"[1] His command was to love your enemies and pray for them which despitefully use you.[2] That is the time when a disciple of the Master can show his true value; when he can do what the Master would do; when, although people speak ill of him, and ill-treat him, he still thinks of them kindly and lovingly, and makes excuses and allowances for their foolishness. That is what we have to do. It is not enough to return love and kindliness; we

[1] S. Matthew, v, 46.

[2] S. Luke, vi, 27-29.

must be able to pour it out upon people who as yet scarcely know what it means. It was said of the Christ that when He was reviled, He reviled not again; when He suffered, He threatened not; but committed Himself to Him that judgeth righteously.[1] We are all wronged and misjudged and misunderstood sometimes. No one need worry about it, for karma will see that all is put right. "Vengeance is mine; I will repay, saith the Lord."[2] Leave it to Him. Justice will always be done, and all that is wrong will some day come right, and those who now misunderstand will some day realize their error, and be sorry that they misunderstood. No injustice will be done: the total will come out as it should.

The Logos Himself is setting the example of Love all the time. Many people speak ill of Him; many misunderstand and flout Him. He makes no answer, but the steady outpouring of the divine love goes on for ever, and in so far as we wish to be an expression of the divine that must characterize us also.

Your mental body wishes to think itself proudly separate, to think much of itself and little of others.

C.W.L.—Here again we must differentiate between what the mental body desires and what we ourselves desire, and realize that we are not the mind. We are in the habit of saying, "I think so-and-so," but about nine times out of ten the fact is not "I think," but the mind thinks. Many of us have been trying to control and

[1] I Peter, II, 23.
[2] Romans, XII, 19.

train our thoughts, yet if we review them we shall see how few are worthy to be attributed to us—to the Self—and how many belong merely to the lower mind.

The lower mind flies from one thing to another, flits over the surface of a variety of subjects, but usually deals fully with none. It is not its desire as a rule to deal exhaustively with anything, but simply to pass from subject to subject in order to get constant change of vibrations. We shall probably find, if we look back, that we have, during even a short space of time, thought a great number of quite insignificant things. When you are walking along the street, for instance, you will find that though *you* are not specially thinking, there is something that is doing so all the time; that is the mental body. If you do not hold it in control, it will pass in review a vast number of things, useless to you, though not necessarily bad, unless they are self-centred or selfish. It has the habit of association of ideas, also, by which it will sometimes twist one's most beautiful thought and carry it away to something quite different and trivial. We must control and change all that. I know it is hard every moment to keep check upon what the mind is doing, but it ought to be done, because the mind is a mighty power, by far the strongest thing we have about us. If the will can be directed through the mental body there are few things one cannot do by its means. This enormous power can be ours, be we rich or poor, young or old—a valuable instrument in our service of the Master, if we will practise constant vigilance until new habits of mind are formed. Many things can be done with thought, which cannot otherwise be accomplished. Affectionate thought that is sent out to some one whom we know to be in need of assistance may be of far greater help than the gift of a sum of money—it may produce a life-long effect. The results of this may not even show on the physical plane, but it is none the less real work for the Master.

The background of the mind should be a thought of the Master, to which it will turn whenever the Self is not really thinking about something that requires attention. This thought should be as precise as possible. There are many people whose thought of the Master is a kind of vague beatitude, a sort of semi-ecstasy, a species of religious coma in which they are not really actively thinking of anything. Instead of vaguely bathing ourselves in a thought which has no precision about it, we should let our devotion to the Master take a definite form, such as "What can I do to serve Him, in what direction can I employ my thought-power ?"

You will find again and again in this book the strongest insistence upon the fact that there is really only one thought, only one will, only one work for us. The one thought is the thought of service to the Master, the one will is to do that work, the one work is the devotion to Him, and for His sake to the world. Though there is the most complex variety in the work that will come in our way to do, it is all for Him and for the world. There is only one thought in the Master's mind—that of service; and if we wish to be one with Him that must be our only thought, too. It implies that we shall make ourselves fit for service, and in that way it includes some progress for us, not because we want to be great, but because we desire to be good instruments.

Many people are developing their mental bodies. Great scientific men do it for the pure pursuit of knowledge. Sometimes there may be a side thought in the man's brain that if he makes a great discovery he will become famous, but I do not think that is true of most scientific men. There is usually a wish in the background to make the knowledge useful, but first of all there is in the scientific mind an intense desire to know. It is a noble line, and in it there are many noble souls, doing great service to mankind.

We too must endeavour to cultivate our mental bodies, to make them keen, active, useful. Why? Why does a carpenter sharpen his plane? Not in order that he may have a sharper plane than some other carpenter, but in order that it may cut the wood well, and that his work may be well done. It is precisely for that reason that our mental bodies must be trained. But we must all the time have in view the thought: "I am making an instrument for the Master's work." One who keeps this ideal will be free from spiritual pride, and so will avoid many of the pitfalls into which mere intellectual development does undoubtedly lead people.

Even when you have turned it away from worldly things, it still tries to calculate for self, to make you think of your own progress, instead of thinking of the Master's work and of helping others.

A.B.—The thing which has perhaps struck me most in this teaching of the Master is that it invariably centres round and returns to the idea of one thought, one will, one work. It seems to radiate that unity so strongly, that you feel that the Master can have only the one thought, that he has blended Himself so perfectly with the One that He could not think of anything else, that He could not forget it, whatever might be occupying His attention. That is the ideal for the disciple. He must think always of the Master's work and of helping others; that one idea must dominate all else. If it is otherwise, then it is your mind which is thinking, not you. But if you have that idea, you have everything else. Suppose you think of a virtue in meditation; why do you want it—to be admired, or to bring yourself nearer to initiation? Or do you want it in order to be a better instrument for the Master's work? That is the test by which you may know whether it is your mind or you which is thinking.

It is a good plan to put the test to yourself in a definite way. Suppose the case—and I do not think it an inconceivable one, though as a general rule the more developed a man is the more useful he is also—of a piece of the Master's work which called for qualities far inferior to others which you had developed. Would you be willing to take it and to work away at that, instead of going on using your higher talents and improving yourself on those lines? Would you be willing to be less, in order to be more useful? You would if you always kept in mind the one motive of being useful for the

Master's work. In that work there will be plenty of opportunity for the cultivation of our mental bodies, that they may be keen, active, useful. If we improve ourselves for this purpose we shall be in no danger of falling into the heresy of separateness. In the lower world we must continually keep our eyes open to turn to account the opportunities which other people have left aside because they thought them unimportant. A disciple always looks for the things left undone by others, that he may supply what is lacking. Such an attitude means that the mind is coming under control.

C.W.L.—The Master's work must dominate all else in our minds. If we find any other thought than that, any other reason coming forward for doing anything, then that which is putting forward a reason is the mind, not the ego—an important distinction to make. The mind is indeed proud and separate, and when it has quite given up all the earthly kinds of pride, its next stage will be to try to make us proud of our progress, of our position in relation to the great Masters, or something of that kind. When we have trodden that down, and are rid of any pride in these things, it will try to make us proud of not being proud. Do not blame the subtle mental elemental; it has no idea of you, but it is simply trying to get the varieties and kinds of vibrations which it needs for its own evolution.

When you meditate, it will try to make you think of the many different things which *it* wants instead of the one thing which *you* want. You are

not this mind, but it is yours to use; so here again discrimination is necessary. You must watch unceasingly, or you will fail.

C.W.L.—They say in India that the mind is the rāja or king of senses, and that of all parts of our nature it is the most difficult to control. In that respect we in the West are perhaps even worse off than the Indian, because we have been especially developing this lower mind, and have prided ourselves on the rapidity with which it can change from one subject to another.

However, by patient effort you may bring to bear upon this elemental the mighty power of the force of habit; you may get it into a groove, and induce it to understand that you, the ego, intend to preserve your dominant idea all the time, but that in connection with that idea there are infinite ramifications, for there is nothing that cannot be brought into the service of the Master. Then presently this curious unmanageable elemental will come to understand that, on the whole, it gets more by working with you, whom it does not understand, than by working against you; and afterwards it will work pleasantly and harmoniously along with you.

CHAPTER 3

RIGHT AND WRONG

Between right and wrong Occultism knows no compromise. At whatever apparent cost, that which is right you must do, that which is wrong you must not do, no matter what the ignorant may think or say. You must study deeply the hidden laws of Nature, and when you know them arrange your life according to them, using always reason and common sense.

A.B.—If you look honestly at it you will find that ordinary life is a series of compromises. Men are constantly doing a little less than what they know to be right in order to meet that deadliest of questions: "What will people say?" Knowing quite well in a given case what is best to do, they shift it a little, tamper with it, fall short of it, in order to make the way smoother for themselves. This fear of the opinions of others is partly due to a weakness which is amiable at its root—the desire to please. This desire is very common in India, but if you want to tread the occult path properly, you must never let yourselves be led by it into compromises, where principles or matters of importance are concerned, such as in the big religious and social questions. Take, for example, the case of child marriage. There are many cases in which these marriages are consummated too early. I have spoken again and again on the public platform about the cruelty of making a girl a mother before she is full-grown, and of the injury that such a practice does to the vitality of the race. Many a man knows that it is wrong, and openly says so; he asks why other people marry their children too young, and yet he still does it himself, because of what people would say if he did not. Out of such material as this you cannot make the occultists.

Putting aside for a moment the great questions on which the future of a nation largely depends, let us turn to the small matters of every-day life. Here also there must be no compromise. You must make up your mind as to what is right, and then keep firmly to it. I know that you cannot carry out your highest ideals immediately, any more than you can get from the bottom of a mountain to the top by taking one step. But if you mean to scale your mountain, every step must be taken with a view to reaching the summit, every step must bring you nearer to it. Never lower your ideal; that is fatal. As the Upanishad says: "One thing is the right, the pleasant another; right unto pleasant the wise man preferreth."

Try in little things to do what your conscience thinks right. You are not responsible for what another person's conscience thinks, nor for whether he follows his own conscience; but your are responsible for following your own, at whatever apparent cost. It is only *apparent* cost, mind you; you cannot lose by doing what you believe to be right. Of course, care must be taken not to identify your whims, prejudices and fancies with the right; as to that the Master gives a warning here, when he says: "Study deeply the hidden laws of nature." First find out what is right, and then live according to your knowledge.

The Master adds the important suggestion in the last few words of this passage: "Using always reason and common sense." Always consider the feelings of other people, but never let them interfere between you and what you know to be right. If you have to choose between hurting people's feelings and compromising with your own conscience, then choose the former. An occultist will always discriminate, in dealing with people, between the real person and the prejudices of his various bodies. He will never hurt a person, but he will hurt his prejudices rather than do wrong. Still, he will not hurt even his prejudices unnecessarily; but if he must do so, he will at the same time know that really the person is being helped, not hurt, and that he himself is being used as an instrument for breaking down a limitation which is cramping the man inside. Even in that case, his action will be gently and considerately carried out. Many people find this difficult. It is much harder to do a thing with quiet reason; a rush of emotion makes it easier. The emotion, be it good or bad, supplies an impulse which carries a man through without further effort on his part. If you would be an occultist you must not act through impulse, as ordinary men do; you must develop reason, power of discrimination, and in this effort you will begin unconsciously to unfold the buddhi.

C.W.L.—People usually have their prejudices—plenty of them; and they identify these with the right. Having been brought up along some particular line, it has never occurred to them to question it, so they are liable to think that the man who does not fall in with their particular method is wrong, especially when it is followed by the majority. Popular prejudices are usually very unreasonable, and therefore we cannot allow them to influence us in matters of right and wrong. I do not say that there are not often some grounds of reason to be found behind a popular prejudice, if we dig down deep to it—not probably the reason that people are alleging at all, but some other reason. But usually that fragment of truth is distorted and misapplied on account of the mass of error in which it is swathed.

The occultist never allows himself to be forced to do a wrong thing for fear of hurting other people's prejudices, but he will never offend those prejudices unnecessarily. Reason and common sense must rule in all things. There is something, let us say, that you want to do because you know it is a good thing, and important. Very well, but do not charge at it like a bull at a gate. He possibly gets through, but at the cost of considerable damage to himself and the gate. One should always show sweet reasonableness in all that is done. If we let ourselves become stirred up and angry about a thing there is a wave of emotion that carries us through; but to do the thing gently and quietly, without any feeling against those who oppose, is much more difficult; yet that is quite obviously the right way to do it.

One must not act on impulse, as most people do. They cannot bear this and that; they do not understand, and do not want to take the trouble to understand; they just drive ahead and take it for granted that they are in the right; but we have to consider others—to take into account their feelings, and to think, too, of the possibility that they may be in the right, and we in the wrong, in a particular case.

> You must discriminate between the important and the unimportant. Firm as a rock where right and wrong are concerned, yield always to others in things which do not matter. For you must be always gentle and kindly, reasonable and accommodating, leaving to others the same full liberty which you need for yourself.

A.B.—This is a very tender and beautiful passage, and it balances the previous one, which, taken by itself, might sound rather hard. Now, as the things for which people generally care most are those which do not matter the occultist can afford to let them have their own way, in many cases. What is important to him is a certain thing that has to be done; he points his will to the one thing in the middle that really matters, and with regard to the rest he lets people do exactly as they like. As he yields to them in those things, they realize what a delightful person he is to work with; and they gradually follow him quite happily on the important point, hardly conscious that they are following at all. In the world this quality is called tact. In occultism it is called discrimination.

It is this quality that the fanatic overlooks, and therefore he does not succeed, while the occultist always succeeds. This fanatic never knows the difference between the important and the unimportant, so he will not yield even in things which do not matter; therefore he rubs people's fur up all the wrong way, and then they will not follow him, however much he may be in the right, and however important his main object may be. If, instead of that, you smooth their fur down, they purr and come along after you. This is based upon a universal fact in nature. In both men and animals it is an instinct to pull in opposition to anyone who is trying to pull them. I saw a little instance of this fact the other day. A man was trying to pull a calf along, and, of course, the calf had planted its four feet firmly into the ground, stuck its tail out, and was pulling against the man for all it was worth. If that man had been sensible he would have stopped pulling, and then the animal would have stopped pulling against him, and with a little patting and coaxing he could have got it to follow him willingly.

There was a valuable lesson in that. If people will not do what you want, look for the fault in yourself; you will generally find that it is something in your way of acting that sets them against you. I follow this plan myself. When there is friction and trouble connected with my work in any place, I sit down and think it over, and try to find out what I am doing that produces these difficulties, and to discover some other way of doing the work. This is far better than trying to make people follow your way. You can force them to a certain extent, no doubt, but that is wrong in principle, and also in practice it only creates opposition and trouble. It shows a great lack of the qualities of leadership—a faculty which the Masters will want in us in the future. The Masters will want you to know how to lead, so that you may help people on, instead of hammering them along.

C.W.L.—Some seven hundred years from now many of us will have the opportunity of working in the development of the Sixth Root-Race, and in the meantime we shall have much to do with preparing the world for the coming of the World-Teacher. Some of us will be alive when He comes, and we shall work under Him; therefore we shall have to develop the qualities of leadership. The first necessity of a leader is tact.

Because the occultist never gives up in any work of importance, he always succeeds in the end, though he may meet with a check, and be thrown back for the time. The French Revolution was an instance of this sort. Those who stood at the back of the movement towards liberty in France were unable to control the mad passions of the people, so that terrible carnage and crime ensued, and the Star set in blood for the time. Never think for a moment that They approved of the madness, of the devilish lust for slaughter, of the unspeakable filth and cruelty, of the treachery and terrorism, of all the indescribable loathsomeness of that awful time. The power passed into the hands of a rabble, maddened by abominable tyranny and oppression, who showed themselves far lower than the beasts of the field. Never imagine that their incredible atrocities were countenanced by Those who were working towards civilization. But later on They managed to gain Their end in some other way, and at the present day that country and many others have all the freedom for which those people were struggling. That is so with all other great reforms that They introduce, and all the other work that They take up—They succeed in the long run, though not always just at first.

We shall have to do just precisely that—never accept defeat, always go on with the work—but to do it well we must acquire the art of helping skilfully. A great many good people want to drive everybody. But that is not the way—we must show others the delight and joy and glory of man's future and the Masters' work, and then they will come along with us of their own accord. If you cannot get on with certain people, look for the defect in yourself. Do not bother about their faults, although no doubt they have plenty, but see what it is in you that prevents you from getting on with them. You will probably find something if you look closely enough.

Try to see what is worth doing: and remember that you must not judge by the size of the thing. A small thing which is directly useful in the Master's

work is far better worth doing than a large thing which the world would call good. You must distinguish not only the useful from the useless, but the more useful from the less useful.

A.B.—As I have already said, the things which are worth doing from the standpoint of the real are those about which people usually care nothing at all. They are interested in unimportant things. The disciple is required therefore to practise this kind of discrimination, and must not waste his time in all the useless occupations which fill the days of worldly people.

Then comes a subtler point; you must not judge the value of a thing by its size. The acts of a statesman which are looming large in the eyes of the world may possibly be quite unimportant from the Master's standpoint—mere dust on the wheel. Some small thing done by an unnoticed person may be infinitely more important if it is exactly in line with the Master's work.

Then comes a still more subtle distinction—that between the more and the less useful. You cannot do everything, so you must do what in your own judgment will serve the Master best. Everything which helps the world is useful for the Master's work, but as your time and energy are limited you must take the more useful, whenever the choice is open to you. The Master gives a typical illustration of this in the next two sentences, when He speaks of feeding the souls of men in preference to their bodies. By helping the soul you are striking at the root of all the evils in the world, for without exception they grow out of ignorance and selfishness.

> To feed the poor is a good and noble and useful work; yet to feed their souls is nobler and more useful than to feed their bodies. Any rich man can feed the body, but only those who know can feed the soul.

C.W.L.—It has sometimes been brought as a reproach against the Theosophical Society that it does not engage itself in active philanthropic work such as the distribution of food and clothing to the poor. Some of our Lodges have done a good deal in that way, but it is not their principal work. Any man who is rich and kindly disposed could do that, but there is much work which only those who know can do. It may perhaps seem to some that we are rather conceited to arrogate to ourselves the title of "those who know". But we are not really praising ourselves in doing that. We can quite clearly see that there are plenty of good people who have nothing whatever to do with Theosophy who are intellectually far in advance of many of us; but it has been our karma to study these subjects, and because of that we know more about them than all those excellent people who have not studied them. There are many among those people of greater intellect, spirituality or devotion, who will go rapidly ahead when they acquire this knowledge that we have of the way in which our forces ought to be directed. They will pass us on the way, perhaps, but we on our part shall welcome them and rejoice to see it, for there is no jealousy on this path and every one on it hails the advance of a brother.

Meantime this Theosophical knowledge is the great talent which is put into our hands for use. If we did nothing for others with it, but simply hugged it to ourselves and enjoyed all that it brings us in the way of freedom from worry and trouble, comprehension of difficult problems, and so on, we should be exactly like the man in the Bible who buried his talent. But if we do our best to spread the light that comes to us and to help in every possible way, then at least we are putting our talent out to interest. 'One who knows' can feed the souls of the poor and the rich alike with his knowledge. This is in no way less practical than the other work, even from a material point of view. What is the cause of all the poverty and suffering in the world? Ignorance and selfishness. If we attack the ignorance and the selfishness by trying to put before men knowledge of the laws of life, and to show them why they must necessarily be unselfish, we are doing more even from the most material point of view to bring about the welfare and happiness of people on the physical plane than we should do by merely distributing food. Not for a moment would one say that that is not good and necessary, that it should not be done. The need of the moment must be met; but it is a greater service to remove the cause of all the trouble. We are doing what the purely physical plane helper could not do.

Wherever there has been any wisdom, any knowledge at all on these lines, those who know have been set free from the other work in order that they may teach. You may read, for example, in the Acts of the Apostles, how, in the early Christian Church, they had community of goods, and when there was some trouble about the distribution of the food supply, the Apostles were requested to settle the dispute—to deal with it themselves, in fact. They said: "It is not reasonable that we should leave the word of God to serve tables," and told the other people to elect from among themselves those who would do that work, and abide by their decision, but not to expect them, whose business it was to expound the word, to devote themselves to the purely physical side of things. It was not that those things were to be neglected, but that the proper people to attend to them were those who could do that but could not do the other work.

A.B.—We in the Society have knowledge which those outside have not, and therefore the spreading of Theosophy is the one thing we ought to do. Those in the Society who are not yet ready for that work—for lecturing or writing or teaching in some other way—should do other kinds of work while they are preparing themselves. I established the Order of Service for those who cannot teach, so that everyone who joins the Society may find something to do. The one thing that a person in the Society should *not* do is to be idle. All members should be active in the Master's work.

C.W.L.—It is hard to realize how many people are reasonably near the position where they might make rapid progress if only they could be awakened to it. I have myself, I suppose, seen it most among the young, because my work generally lies there. I see boys and girls by the score in almost any country who could make good progress along Theosophical lines, if the matter could only be put before them. But it is not, and they plunge off into the work-a-day world, and become very good people of the ordinary type. They will go on in that way for twenty or thirty incarnations, or more, though they are capable of taking up Theosophy and would be interested in it, if it were properly put before them. Surely that state of affairs throws a serious responsibility upon those who possess this knowledge. It is therefore our business to be capable and ready to put Theosophy forward whenever there is a suitable opportunity. There are plenty of people who might just as well enter upon Theosophical development now, as in twenty lives' time. It is, of course, a question of their karma, but it is our karma to give them the opportunity, to put the matter before them—whether they take it or not is their affair. Until we have done our best we do not know whether it is their karma to be helped or not.

> If you know, it is your duty to help others to know. However wise you may be already, on this Path you have much to learn ; so much that here also there must be discrimination, and you must think carefully what is worth learning. All knowledge is useful, and one day you will have all knowledge ; but while you have only part, take

care that it is the most useful part. God is Wisdom as well as Love; and the more wisdom you have, the more you can manifest of Him. Study then, but study first that which will most help you to help others.

C.W.L.—The Master here advises study, but He tells his pupil to choose so far as he can what will help him to help others. I take it that that means that one should try to understand Theosophy thoroughly and first of all, but should in addition acquire the knowledge and education of the time that make a cultured man. I know that there are many in the Theosophical Society who find themselves, for various reasons, uneducated, but yet are very earnest and devoted, who say: "Why should we bother ourselves about the details of education? We want to get at the reality of the thing, and to present the truths somehow." Yes, but the uneducated man is likely to present them in a form that will probably at once estrange and repel the educated and cultured. I have heard people say that an intuitional man who hears the thing badly put will rise above the form to the truth that lies behind; but unfortunately most men are not intuitional and we have no right, on account of our own laziness, to put an additional obstacle in the way of anyone who might otherwise be induced to take an interest in the subject. It is distinctly and emphatically our duty to make our presentation as nearly perfect as we can.

Work patiently at your studies, not that men may think you wise, not even that you may have

the happiness of being wise, but because only the wise man can be wisely helpful. However much you wish to help, if you are ignorant you may do more harm than good.

A.B.—Here is advice especially important for our younger members. I often come across young men at college who are touched by the new spirit; they are very eager to help, and often want to put aside their studies. "What is the use of these studies to us?" they ask. The advice I always give in such a case is: "Continue your studies and become an educated man. Although there may be many things among those you learn which have not much importance, the training of the intelligence is all-important. That is where the use of your studies lies; they render your mind logical and accurate. If you do not go through this mental discipline, afterwards you will be badly hampered in your work."

It is not enough to be able to recognize Theosophic truths; if you want to help others to know, you must have that intellectual training which enables you to present them properly. If a person is uneducated, one sees it at once in the way he presents a subject. There is no part of my own training which I am more glad to have gone through than the scientific part. First of all it has helped me to put things in a rational, logical way, which gains a hearing from intellectual and cultured people; and secondly, it supplies me with many illustrations, which appeal to the mind because they are drawn from subjects which can be definitely proved.

Those among us who are older can be of much use to the younger with whom they have opportunities of dealing if they will, without damping their enthusiasm, explain in a kind and sensible way the importance of their making themselves what the world calls educated. When one has the higher things, one is apt to be a little impatient with these lower studies. Therefore the Master says to His young disciple, who had still much of his intellectual training to go through: "Work patiently at your studies."

C.W.L.—History emphatically supports this counsel. Many good people, with the best intentions, have blundered in the most terrible manner, and have injured their cause, whatever it may have been, far more than any outside attack could have done. Theosophical work has frequently suffered from faulty or negligent presentation. We do not wish that Theosophy should be spoken ill of because of our personal defects or disabilities. If you are set to do work for the Society and do not do it satisfactorily, then go to work and learn to do it satisfactorily. If you are asked to read something and cannot do it, learn how to do it properly. If you cannot lecture—presently, when you know enough and take the trouble to prepare, you will learn to do that. But, at any rate, be doing something and try to do it well. It is our duty as Theosophists to master the correct grammar and the correct expression which will enable us to put these things acceptably before the people that we wish to reach. Any truth, however glorious, may be eclipsed, if clumsily and wrongly put. It is our duty to do our best in this matter. We must be educated if we are to present these truths properly.

CHAPTER 4

BE TRUE ALL THROUGH

You must distinguish between truth and falsehood; you must learn to be true all through, in thought and word and deed.

A.B.—One might wonder, if one were not following the Master's thought as well as His words, why this point comes where it does. Discrimination between truth and falsehood—surely this should have come first! The Master places it later because it is a very difficult thing. You must be true all through, He says, and it is not easy to make onself so in thought and word and deed. You will notice that thought comes first; this is the regular occult order, which puts thought first, then speech and action. The Lord Buddha also gave them in this order, as right thought, right speech and right action.

In thought first; and that is not easy, for there are in the world many untrue thoughts, many foolish superstitions, and no one who is enslaved by them can make progress.

C.W.L.—We think in Theosophy that we are absolutely free from superstition; I am not quite sure that

that is always true. There is a possibility, it seems to me, of a Theosophical superstition. The man who believes a thing because "it is written in the Bible" is no doubt superstitious to that extent, because he has no good basis for that belief. Still, it is only one step forward from that superstition to say, "Thus saith Madame Blavatsky" or "It is written in *The Secret Doctrine*". It *is* a step, because there is a great deal more evidence that Madame Blavatsky knew what she was talking about, than that, let us say S. Paul did, or any of the older writers; but the thing is no more our own because Madame Blavatsky said it, than because it is attributed to S. James or S. Peter. We must understand a thing and make it part of ourselves, grow into it and let it grow into us. So long as we are only reading things parrot-wise those things are superstitions. The very belief in the truth may be a superstition, if it has no better basis for us than that it is written here or there. When it becomes part of our mental system, we can say, "It is part of me and it is mine; I know why I believe it, and therefore my belief is an intelligent belief and not merely superstition." I am afraid there is a great deal of unintelligent belief even in the truth, in many cases.

A.B.—It is so difficult for a person to free himself from superstition, from taking the unessential for the essential (for this is the essence of superstition) that he is not expected wholly to do so until after the First Initiation. This shows that it is a deep and subtle thing, which works into the very nature of the man. No one who is enslaved by it, says the Master, can make progress. That is a sweeping statement, but we must observe the word enslaved. He does not say that no one who is in any degree superstitious can make progress, but that no one who is a slave to superstition can do so. Superstition is a great thing for holding people back. How many religious people one knows who are good, pious, philanthropic, who lead beautiful and earnest lives, but are superstitious! They think that their ceremonies, their formulæ, their ways of doing things, matter. But they do not matter a bit.

Let us take as an example the perfomance of a particular function, that intended to help the dead. The Roman Catholic celebrates the Mass for the dead; the Hindu performs the Shrāddha ceremonies for the same purpose. Both ceremonies are inspired by the same wish to help those who have passed over, and both effect their purpose, though they are widely different in form. Yet a Hindu or a Catholic in clinging to these *forms* would be superstitious. The goodwill and the earnestness that they put into it, the love that they pour out towards the departed—these are the real things, and they produce the result. The good wish matters very much, but the specific character of the outer form does not, for the garment of their wish is local and unimportant. That outward form depends on where you happen to be born, for you are born into a religion as into a race and country. Of all the superstitious belief in rites and ceremonies, in the efficacy of mere outward forms, you must rid yourselves. For a long time this belief was very important, a good thing, because it is the only thing which can get people out of sloth, carelessness and indifference. These outward things are crutches; they are necessary for those who cannot yet walk alone, but when once you can walk without them you must cast them aside.

> Therefore you must not hold a thought just because many other people hold it, nor because it has been believed for centuries, nor because it is written in some book which men think sacred; you must think of the matter for yourself, and judge for yourself whether it is reasonable.

C.W.L.—Those are the words of the Master Kūthūmi. They were also, twenty-five hundred years ago, the words of the Lord Gautama Buddha, when men came to Him asking: "There are so many teachers and so many doctrines put before us, and they all seem good; how are we to know which is the best: how can we decide among them?" His reply to that question is given as follows in the Kālāma Sutta of the *Anguttara Nikāya*:

> Our Lord Buddha has said that we must not believe in a thing said merely because it is said; nor in traditions because they have been handed down from antiquity; nor rumours, as such; nor writings by sages, because sages wrote them; nor fancies that we may suspect to have been inspired in us by a deva [that is, in presumed spiritual inspiration]; nor from inferences drawn from some haphazard assumption we may have made; nor because of what seems an analogical necessity; nor on the mere authority of our teachers or masters. But we are to believe when the writing, doctrine, or saying is corroborated by our own reason and consciousness. "For this," says He in concluding, "I taught you—not to believe merely because you have heard, but when you believed of your own consciousness, then to act accordingly and abundantly." [1]

[1] See *A Buddhist Catechism*, by H. S. Olcott, question 131.

One of the exercises set by the Masters for Their pupils is to find out how much they really know and how much they only believe. It is a good practice to observe how much of our mental furniture we can definitely claim as belonging to ourselves, how much is ours because we have thoroughly understood and assented to it, and how much we have accepted from others almost without having thought about it. In every case people are born into religions as they are into countries. It is the same with a great number of customs. For example, when you go out to dinner you must wear a certain dress. It is the custom, and one does not want to go against custom in a matter which is of no importance, in which there is no question of right or wrong.

A.B.—It is a very useful exercise to examine the contents of the mind from time to time, and observe, first, how many things you believe simply because many other people believe them; second, how many things you believe only because they are old beliefs; third, how many things you believe because they are written in some sacred book. And when you have swept out these three classes of belief, notice how much remains, and these will show you what real basis you have for your beliefs. That is one advantage of going through the Freethought experience, as I did. No one who has not been through it can quite understand, I think, what it means to have to give up one's religious beliefs if they have been really sincerely held; what the final crash is like, when the foundations that you have been standing upon give way. It very nearly killed me; I was physically prostrate for weeks. But when once you have done it thoroughly like that, you need not do it over again. So, when I came into touch with Theosophy, although I felt sure of it with a perfect inward conviction, I tested it all with my mind as I received it.

> Remember that though a thousand men agree upon a subject, if they know nothing about that subject their opinion is of no value.

C.W.L.—That is a matter which is very hard for the modern world to realize. People seem to think nowadays that, if you only pile up enough ignorance you will somehow get knowledge out of it. But you do not. The ignorant must have those who know to direct them.

A.B.—In one way, the multitude of books that we have at the present day is a disadvantage. It induces reading without thinking, which produces superficiality and fickleness of thought. That is why I always advise people to read a little and then reproduce what they have read, not by memory, but out of the clear grasp of the subject that they have obtained. Only what you have thought out is really yours, and only by thinking over and understanding what you read and hear, can you make it your own. Otherwise, the more you read the more superstitious you become. You go on adding more beliefs to those that you already have, none of which has any sure foundation.

I once employed a man who kept accounts very badly. Whenever he got his accounts into a muddle, he began a new account book, and hoped in that way to get them straight again. In the same way, people nowadays always want something new because they have not gained any real satisfaction out of their superficial acquaintance with what they already have. Those among our members who quote Bishop Leadbeater's books and mine all over the place are also superstitious. However true the statements they quote may be, they are not true *to them*; for if they had grasped them they would not need to fall back upon us as authorities. If they quote what we say at all, they should only quote our words as opinions, and not try to force them on anyone. There is only one authority in the world, and that is wisdom.

He who would walk upon the Path must learn to think for himself, for superstition is one of the greatest evils in the world, one of the fetters from which you must utterly free yourself.

C.W.L.—That superstition is a very big and subtle thing is evident from the fact that it is the third of the fetters which men must cast off on the Path after the First Initiation. The Pāli name for it is *sīlabbataparāmāsa*, "belief in the efficacy of rites or ceremonies of any kind".

Your thought about others must be true; you must not think of them what you do not know.

C.W.L.—If we think of other people what we only suppose about them, the thought is probably the merest speculation. We really know remarkably little even about those who are very near to us, still less about casual acquaintances; and yet there is constantly much profitless babble about the doings and sayings and supposed thoughts of other people, and most of it, fortunately, is hopelessly untrue.

A.B.—Opinions about other people are mostly untrue. We can only think truly of another when we really know him, when we can see his thought and understand it. That knowledge is impracticable to most people, yet they have very definite opinions about others; they constantly judge them and think unkindly of them.

A little further on the Master says: "Never attribute motives to another." That is an enormously important piece of advice which, if carried out in the world, would do away with at least half the trouble that exists. If a person does a thing which you do not understand, leave it at that; do not invent possible motives. A person does something, for what reason you cannot know; but you hunt round for a possible motive, generally an unworthy one, and fasten it on to the act; then you blame him for what you have thought and done yourself. By thus attributing motives men add to any evil force that may possibly exist in the mind of the person criticized, or they supply it if it is not already there, Christ said: "Resist not evil"; this is a case where that applies; it is not our business to search in people's minds for evil to battle against; leave the thing alone and it will die.

Do not suppose that they are always thinking of you.

C.W.L.—This happens perpetually: whatever some other person says or does is taken as referring to ourselves. Because we are always thinking of ourselves we imagine that other people must be thinking of us also; but if we are always thinking of ourselves, it seems more sensible to assume that other people are probably thinking about *themselves*, not that they are thinking about us. They make themselves the centre of their own circle, round which all their thoughts and emotions revolve, and they think of everything as it affects them. They are running round themselves in a circle all the time, and because they are running round themselves they think everyone else must be running round them, too. But they are not. Each man is in his own circle—an equally vicious one, no doubt. Probably nine-tenths of the cases in which people take offence at what others do and say, are rooted in this idea.

If a man does something which you think will harm you, or says something which you think applies to you, do not think at once: "He meant to injure me." Most probably he never thought of you at all, for each soul has its own troubles and its thoughts turn chiefly around itself. If a man speak angrily to you, do not think: "He hates me, he wishes to wound me." Probably some one or something else has made him angry, and because he happens to meet you he turns his anger upon you. He is acting foolishly, for all

anger is foolish, but you must not therefore think untruly of him.

C.W.L.—That is plain commonsense, but how very few people ever practise it! When I was a priest in the Church of England I once preached a sermon about some ordinary trial or temptation which I thought might come in the way of the farmers and labourers who were my congregation. I explained how a man might get into trouble along a certain line. After the service a farmer came into the vestry in a towering rage, and asked me what I meant by preaching a sermon directed at him. Of course, poor man, he gave himself hopelessly away. I had never before supposed that he was guilty of this particular thing, but evidently it was a sore point, and my remarks had gone home to him. I have no doubt that to this day that man really thinks I singled him out, and preached about him.

In this crowded life which we are all living, it is inevitable that there should be a certain amount of friction, which need not be taken seriously, or regarded as of great importance. As we walk along the streets of any great city thousands of people, each full of his own business, are pushing ahead and not thinking in the least of others. Inevitably it happens that people jostle each other, but it never occurs to anyone to take it seriously as an insult; that would be ridiculous. The same thing is bound to happen mentally and emotionally. Where there are great crowds there is inevitably a certain amount of mental and emotional jostling. We ought to take that in exactly the same spirit, realizing that the man who happens to tread on our mental corns did not mean to do so in the very least but that he was following his own line of business and not thinking of us. We must not take all such little frictions as serious things, any more than we do the daily jostling in the street.

At the same time, while we hold that attitude with regard to the absorption of other people in their business, it is our duty to see that we in turn are not so absorbed in ours as to forget the little courtesies that make life go so much more smoothly.

The Theosophist ought to be distinguished from the rest of the world by his courtesy, and by his calm and unchanging cheerfulness. Be gentle, be patient; there is always time to be friendly and gentle, however much one may be hurried. One should decline to be swept off one's feet by the waves of irritability which come from overstrained nerves, which are so common in these crowded times.

A.B.—The suggestion that the Master makes here is very wise. Do not suppose that everybody is thinking about you, because you are thinking about yourself. The other people are also thinking about themselves and not of you; they are concerned with their own affairs just as you are with yours. It would add greatly to the happiness of nations if people would only take up this idea and put it into practice. When some one jolts up against you in the bustle and hurry of life do not think that he means to injure you, or that he has any personal intention at all. Unless you are sure that a person meant to harm you, it is much better to think the reverse.

Suppose a man speaks angrily to you. If you would remember then not to attribute wrong motives to him, and not to get angry also, you would make very rapid progress in self-control. Generally people remember this afterwards. If a man is self-controlled he will not *show* irritation, but if he is *perfectly* self-controlled he will not even feel it. Even if the other man is at fault, it is, after all but a weakness of his, and he who would be an occultist must remember to be charitable to the weaknesses of others. One must also remember that the angry speech, or the hasty and irritable answer, very often means that the person who makes it is under a great tension arising from some trouble or anxiety, and is not quite strong enough to bear the strain and show no signs of it; his nerves are highly strung; that is why he acts as he does.

It is true, of course, that he acts foolishly, as the Master says. But we must make allowances. Most of the little difficulties that people have arise in this way. A heavy strain on a person will cause him to take offence at almost anything. Think how many troubles there are in the world—troubles of all kinds constantly pressing on people and worrying at them. We do not know the troubles of all those around us, of course, because no sensible person goes about proclaiming his difficulties. Ordinary dignity forbids that. But if we would remember that they exist, and make allowance for them, we should obtain that perfect peace which the Master is aiming at in this teaching.

> When you become a pupil of the Master, you may always try the truth of your thought by laying it beside His. For the pupil is one with his Master, and he needs only to put back his thought into the Master's thought to see at once whether it agrees. If it does not, it is wrong, and he changes it instantly, for the Master's thought is perfect, because He knows all.

A.B.—An accepted pupil can always test his thought by laying it beside that of the Master. If he feels a jar he knows that the thought is wrong. To use a physical analogy, it is like a false note in music. The pupil does not need to call the Master's attention; he simply puts his thought beside the Master's, and if it does not ring true, he casts it out at once, and sets to work immediately to bring his thought into harmony with that of the Master. He does not argue about it, nor try to make out that his thought may be right after all, because if it is faulty, its error at once becomes apparent. Those who are not accepted pupils cannot quite do this, and that presents a difficulty to many aspirants. As the consciousness of the pupil is one with that of the Master, the latter will not accept anyone against whose thought He would afterwards find it necessary to build a wall.

C.W.L.—It is said that the pupil is one with his Master. That is true in a sense which only the Master knows perfectly. The pupil knows it too, but less perfectly. Those who have not yet entered into that relation cannot understand the intensity of that unity. The pupil becomes an outlying section of his Master's thought, belonging to Him in a way not at all unlike that in which the personality belongs to the ego. The ego puts down a small piece of itself—that is not quite correct, but it is more accurate than the idea of reflection would be—into the conditions of the lower planes, where even the best of physical, astral and mental bodies can give only a very imperfect expression of him. That ought to be a comfort to us when we feel depressed at our own various weaknesses down here. One may say to oneself; "At any rate the ego knows better than that; therefore I need not despair. It is only needful for me to bring more of myself down into this lower manifestation to make it a purer expression of what I really am up above, and then my defects will become less."

In the same sort of way the pupil not merely represents the Master; he is the Master in a very real sense, but the Master under tremendous limitations—the limitations not only of the lower planes, but also of the personality of the pupil, which is by no means perfectly transcended. If the disciple's ego had gained perfect control of its lower vehicles, so that they were nothing but reflections or expressions of the higher, he would be able to express the Master far more perfectly than he does now, but even then there would be a limitation of what must be called the *size* of him, because the pupil is a smaller ego than the Master whom he follows, and therefore can be only an incomplete representative of

Him. Still, whatever thoughts the pupil has, those are in the Master's mental and astral bodies also. Partly for that reason all pupils have to pass through a period of probation, during which the living image of the probationary pupil is constantly before the eye of the Master. The Master wants to know exactly what are the thoughts and feelings of His prospective pupil, because otherwise He might find constantly obtruded into His own astral and mental bodies thoughts and emotions which were out of harmony with the work He is doing all the time. It is only after He has seen for some considerable time that such thoughts and emotions as would not harmonize are very rare in the pupil, that He accepts him, and makes him a part of Himself.

Even then the Master still retains the power to interpose a veil between His consciousness and that of His pupil. It is the latter's earnest desire not to be shut off, but still we are fallible people down here on the physical plane, and it may often happen that some thought or feeling comes to us which should not. The Master does not want that, so He shuts it quietly away from Him. There is, it is true, a later period at which the Master renounces even the power to do that—when He accepts the pupil as His 'son,' but that comes only when He is quite sure that there will be nothing that needs to be excluded.

On account of this intimate association with his Teacher's consciousness the pupil is able to lay His thought by the side of the Master's thought. It is not necessary to call the Master's attention at all; he is not seeking His opinion on the question in hand. He is simply going back along the line of that oneness to discover what is the idea in the Master's mind with regard to this particular question. "How," you may ask, "would the pupil do it?" There are various ways, according to the extent to which he has realized the unity. He would make a vivid image of His Master; he would raise himself into it with all his force, and then would think his thought and see whether there was the slightest jar or disharmony, and if there were he would, of course, alter his own thought at once.

There is here a great difference between the occult and the worldly point of view. In the world if there is a difference of opinion between yourself and another man, you at once proceed to argue in favour of your opinion, or try to justify it. In occultism we never argue; we know that the man who stands on the higher level knows better, and we simply accept his view. It would never occur to us for one moment to set up our own opinion against that of the Master, because we know (it is not a matter of opinion; but of actual knowledge) that He has access to all kinds and sources of information that we have not; therefore He knows what He is talking about. His opinion is based on far greater knowledge than our own. Afterwards we may try to find the reasons which gave rise to it—that is quite another matter—but in the meantime we do not oppose it, and we should never think of doing so. When the pupil lays his thought beside the Master's he does not argue. When you have an instrument out of tune you do not argue that perhaps that is a better pitch; you tune it up.

In the occult world we never criticize, we take it for granted that every man who is working for the Hierarchy is doing his utmost; and if he is doing his best, then to his own Master he stands or falls—not to us. Of course it may sometimes be possible, if we see failure in some direction, to make a little suggestion in the most delicate way we can: "If so-and-so were done, do you not think that things might perhaps be a little better?" The way in which people recklessly criticize others of whose troubles and difficulties they know nothing whatever is entirely foreign to occultists or those who aspire to become such. We simply do not go that way at all; we should consider it wrong.

Those who are really in earnest about getting on the Path would do well to follow the custom of the Masters' pupils in this matter. We should not plunge into criticism of people who are doing their work; most people are doing the best they can from their point of view. We may possibly have a much higher point of view, but at any rate they can work only according to their own light, not according to ours. When an official is appointed, for example, to do something in our Society, we should give him his chance; if he does not do the work satisfactorily, then we may in due course give the work to some one else, but in the meantime we should not hamper the man. He should be given a chance to show what he is made of, to try the ideas which are in his mind. It is a bad thing to be always interfering.

It would be a very much worse thing to be always in a critical frame of mind—constantly looking for holes, always trying to find weak spots. That is not the way in occultism. We often hear people say, "I cannot help criticizing; that is my nature." If that is your nature it is a very bad nature, and you had better try to transcend it. When you say a thing is natural, human, you mean it is what the average man would do; but if a man has really taken himself in hand he is trying to be a little more than the average. We are here to change our natures. There need be no pride in this; the aspirant is seeking to raise himself above the average in order that he may be able to advance that average—which he could not do if he were on the same level or below. Anyone who wills to do so can give up the bad habit of criticism.

Sometimes one would like to say to people, "Do get out of the way of your higher self and give him a chance to do what he can. You are letting the lower personality stand in the way of what the higher would and could do quite easily." No one should ever say, "I cannot." If you take that line, you have already prejudged the case, and foredoomed yourself to failure. Set up rather the thought-form, "I can do this thing, and I will do it"—then it is already half done. People often fail in their efforts; that is very natural. While they continually try, however, force is being accumulated, and this will presently bring success. We must not think when a failure comes that everything is lost; for the force which has been gained, though it may not be enough to bring immediate success, is all the same a substantial gain, and if we go on putting more and more to it the time will come when success will crown our efforts.

There is a vast gulf between these two attitudes: to sit down and despair, and to get up and do something. It has been said that the world is divided into two parts: the people who go and do something, and the people who sit still and say: "Why was it not done some other way?" We ought to be among the former, and not mind in the least what is said by the other kind of people who never move a hand to do it themselves.

> Those who are not yet accepted by Him cannot do quite this; but they may greatly help themselves by stopping often to think: "What would the Master think about this? What would the Master say or do under these circumstances?" For you must never do or say or think what you cannot imagine the Master as doing or saying or thinking. You must be true in speech too—accurate and without exaggeration.

C.W.L.—If we could keep that always in mind, never to think or say or do anything that the Master would not think or say or do, there would not be much need of correction in our lives. We might make some errors, perhaps, as to what we thought He might think or say or do, but on the whole ours would be a life wonderfully pure and near to Him. No doubt many people may feel: "If I had to stop and think that, I should never say anything." The world would probably not be greatly the poorer if they did not, for most of what is said is not particularly useful. If a man each time before he speaks really seriously sets himself to think: "Would the Master say what I am going to say?" he will speak a great deal less. The process of referring to the thought of the Master may be slow at first; but presently it becomes a habit, and then it takes place like a flash.

Thought moves with the rapidity of light, probably even faster, and if, as the physicists tell us, light travels about 1,86,000 miles per second, your thought of England, for example, which is 12,500 miles away, would be there like a flash of light. The speed of thought is one of the questions of occult physics amidst which we are only stumbling as yet. We are trying all the time to learn new facts about occult science, and are making experiments blunderingly, much as did the old alchemists, out of whose effort emerged the beginnings of chemistry, which has slowly evolved into a great science comprising many thousands of facts. I believe that out of the stumbling experiments which are now being made by only a few people, there will arise, as the years roll on, a development of occult science generally which will be of great importance to the world.

Usually our thoughts do not move as fast as they might, because we have not practised using them apart from speech and action to any great extent. It is one of the fruits of meditation that it trains us to use thought apart from these other things. From success in that one obtains really wonderful results. Dr. Besant has made a study of this. I have heard her say that when she is giving a lecture in public, while she is speaking one sentence, the next comes before her thought in three or four different forms, and she deliberately selects that one which she thinks will be most effective, while she is speaking the previous sentence. Very few people could do that. It is a matter of using thought altogether apart from action, and with a rapidity which would be hard to calculate—but it shows what may be done. It is quite worth while to try to practise using thought as thought. The pupil, following out the excellent practice of thinking before he speaks or acts, will find it not only fruitful in bringing his life into harmony with that of his Master, but also a useful training in swift thought.

Never attribute motives to another; only his Master knows his thoughts, and he may be acting from reasons which have never entered your mind.

C.W.L.—Every man is an enigma even to those who are nearest and dearest to him, and if sometimes, long afterwards, you do get at his reasons for having done something, they are usually surprising—something which would never have occurred to you has been the controlling influence in his mind. I have seen that many times more, perhaps, in India than anywhere else, because the Indian mind differs greatly from ours in many ways, and most of our Hindu brothers are moved to action by ideas that never would have occurred to an Englishman. Their mind is infinitely more subtle, and its activities are based upon a set of traditions foreign to our ways of thought. If, therefore, even in our own race it is never advisable to supply a motive to anyone for what he or she says or does, it is far less safe in a foreign country, where you are dealing with another civilization altogether. Hopeless misunderstandings occur because we supply motives, and we must not do it. It is not our business to know why a certain thing was done. We need not trouble about it.

> **If you hear a story against any one, do not repeat it; it may not be true, and even if it is, it is kinder to say nothing.**

A.B.—If, having heard this, you go and tell a story against some one, you are disobeying the Master's direct command, because it has been passed on to you, and so is directed to you personally. It is easy enough to hold your tongue; it may be difficult to control your thought, but surely you can control your body! The story that you tell may not matter much, but if it is untrue and you repeat it, you are telling a lie, and that matters very much for those who are striving to prepare themselves for Initiation. It sounds hard to call it lying, perhaps, but it is a fact, and we have to face facts.

It is obvious that we cannot spend our lives in enquiring into the truth of such stories, so the only safe course is never to repeat them at all. Quite apart from the question of injuring ourselves and our own prospects, and even supposing you know such a story to be true, it is kinder to say nothing. Why should you wish to harm any person? Why should you wish to repeat anything which shows another in an unfavourable light?

Of course, if we happen to find out that a man is a rogue or a swindler and is bent upon doing injury to unsuspecting persons, it is our duty to expose him, or at least to warn those who are in danger from him; but that is a matter altogether different from those which form the pabulum of common gossip. This is, however, a duty which should be exercised only with the greatest care and forethought, and certainly without the slightest ill-feeling or indignation.

Think well before speaking, lest you should fall into inaccuracy.

C.W.L.—This has been preached for many years and yet even our own people go on making inaccurate statements. People sometimes talk in a most exaggerated way. If a thing is a hundred yards away they say it is "miles off". If a day comes that is hotter than usual, they say it is "boiling". Our command of English is poor if we are not able to find words to express different gradations of thought without plunging into these wild, meaningless superfluities. It is a lack of education as well as of accuracy, and I do not think we ought to be careless about this matter. Not without significance the Christ is reputed to have said that for every idle word that men shall speak they shall give account in the day of judgment.

Be true in action; never pretend to be other than you are, for all pretence is a hindrance to the pure light of truth, which should shine through you as sunlight shines through clear glass.

A.B.—Truth in action is a very difficult thing to carry out. It means never to do a thing before people in order to impress them with a high opinion of you, and never to do when you are alone anything of which you would be ashamed in the company of others; but to be perfectly honest always. Let people see you just as you are, and do not pretend to be anything else. Most of us have a kind of ideal of what we should like other people to think us to be; consequently there are all sorts of small things which we do when we are alone, but would not do if others were present, because they are not quite the things that we feel they would expect of us.

Whenever you are inclined not to do a thing because somebody is there, check the feeling: if it is right, never mind other people's opinion about it; if it is not, never do it at all. I know the feeling well, for I used to have it. I used to feel that I must behave before people as they would expect an author and lecturer and all the rest of it to behave. In the past, I sometimes found that this feeling came up about some quite harmless thing. To give an example; on board ship, where I never feel well, I was at one time in the habit of playing patience—a most harmless recreation, I consider. It came into my mind one day to wonder what the passengers would think when seeing me play it on a

Sunday, knowing I was a teacher of occultism—whether it would shock them. Then I thought: "It does not matter whether people see me or not. If wrong it ought to be dropped; if right, their opinions do not alter the fact." Madame Blavatsky was remarkable in this way. She always did what she wanted, and cared not in the least what people thought about it. If people thought her behaviour was not what they considered that of an occultist should be, what on earth did it matter? They knew nothing whatever about it, anyway.

An occultist does not go about with a grave and solemn face, taking care to do things in a very dignified manner, though that is the notion which many people have of him. The popular views are entirely false on the subject. An occultist is supremely natural. I think one reason why it is important, at the present time, to lead a perfectly true and frank life, is that it may serve in a small degree to prepare the way for the great Teacher who is coming; it may make His path a little bit smoother. For the Great Ones are not always what the people expect them to be. They do not run in moulds prepared for them, but They come to reform the world, generally to alter radically the popular outlook; and while They are very considerate of people's feelings, They are not always so of their prejudices. We, by living frankly and openly, may help to prepare the people's minds, so that when the Lord Maitreya comes they will already have loosened some of their prejudices, and there will be a chance of their being less offended than might otherwise have been the case. Let us, then, lead a perfectly open life, always provided that we do not fall below our ideal. We must not make the mistake of thinking that it does not matter how we act before people; but we must be equally careful and honest in private and in public.

C.W.L.—It is quite true that we should never pretend, that there is a falsity about any kind of pretension, but take care that in the effort to avoid it you do not run into the opposite extreme. Sometimes people say, "I want to show myself just as I am naturally," and then they proceed to show the worst and coarsest and most vulgar part of themselves. They are not showing themselves naturally, but a very low and poor and degraded copy of what they should be. That in man which is highest and best and noblest is nearest to the real self; therefore, to be natural we should be at our best.

Sanctimoniousness is a form of untruth. If you find a person giving himself out as an occultist, and at the same time talking very largely about his own loftiness and tolerance, hinting at his great powers, and trying to win the admiration of credulous people, like the hypocrites of old who "love to pray standing in the synagogues and in the corners of the streets, that they may be seen of men" and the scribes and Pharisees who "for a pretence make long prayer,"[1] you may know that he is not a real occultist. The genuine occultist is never sanctimonious, though he is determined to live far above the standard of what is usually called the "natural" man.

[1] S. Matthew, vi, 5, and xxiii, 14.

People often fail to recognize a Master because they have a rigid idea of what a Master must be, and the real, living Master may not be like that at all. He does not adapt Himself to our prejudices and ideas; He is that which He is on His own plane, and if we are hidebound by our own prejudices we may not know Him when He appears. Some have already made up their minds as to what the World-Teacher will do and say, and how He will carry Himself. Do not risk shutting yourself off from Him by preconceptions. We know that He will teach the doctrine of love, but the manner and detail of it will be settled entirely by Him. Let us recognize Him to the full, and be ready to follow wheresoever He will lead.

CHAPTER 5

UNSELFISHNESS AND THE DIVINE LIFE

You must discriminate between the selfish and the unselfish. For selfishness has many forms, and when you think you have finally killed it in one of them, it arises in another as strongly as ever. But by degrees you will become so full of thought for the helping of others that there will be no room, no time, for any thought about yourself.

A.B.—The Master here describes what is I believe the only way to become perfectly unselfish. It is possible to get rid of one particular form of selfishness, certainly, if we turn our efforts to its eradication, but, as the Master says, it comes up in another form. Working in this way, you may spend a long time in killing one form of selfishness, and then find yourself like Hercules when he was killing the hydra—as soon as he had cut off one head, another grew. But the way that is recommended here goes straight to the root of the matter.

One of the valuable results of devotion lies here—I am inclined to think, the greatest of all: the thought of another person, who is the object of devotion, occupies the whole mind, and the man becomes unselfish without any special effort. That is the proper way of growth, to "grow as the flower grows, unconsciously, opening its heart to the sun". Efforts are all signs of weakness; if you can find clever ways of getting round yourself, as it were, it is a great advantage. You circumvent your thoughts and turn your force into a good channel, and the undesirable quality gets starved out. This is the best way of getting over one's faults; for thinking of them, even regretfully, strengthens them.

Be full of thought for others, and then, as the Master says, there will be no room, no time, for thinking about yourself. Then, too, you will be happy. I have found that this is true in my own case. If ever I found myself inclined to grieve, to feel the least regret about anything which affected me personally (I do not think that I am ever inclined to do so now, but at one time I was) I filled my mind at once with the thought of helping and of working for others. Grieving over things which affect oneself is selfish, and it only serves to make one unhappy. Yet it is what many people do. They sit down and say: "Oh, how sad it is. How hard it is. This thing is very hard on me. That person does not care for me, does not look after me, does not love me"—and so on indefinitely.

All that is selfishness. The remedy, both for your own grief and the selfishness, is to go at once and do something for someone else. Go and work. Your mind cannot be filled with two things at once, and the moment you cease to think of yourself you begin to be happy.

When you can say: "I do not want anything from anybody around; I love them and need nothing in return"—then you will be happy. What people generally call love is a little love underneath with a great coating of selfishness over it. The moment that there is pain through love, it means that selfishness is also there.

That is a hard lesson for the warm-hearted and the affectionate to learn, I know, but it has to be learned; and when learned it brings happiness and peace. I speak to you from my own experience. Learn to love all, without asking anything in return, and when you do that you will find plenty of people to love you; but so long as you keep on grabbing, their natural instinct is to draw back. A hard lesson it is, but once learned it brings a peace that nothing can shake, not even when a person you love dearly is for the time being disagreeable. What does it matter? You know he will come round again some day, and in the meantime you go on pouring out your love on him just the same. If you suffer, just make up your mind not to trouble about it. Say to yourself: "I do not mind how much my lower nature suffers." What are we—our lower selves at any rate—that we should care if we suffer, or that we should claim to be loved? By taking up this attitude towards your suffering you will overcome it.

C.W.L.—To think about a fault is to strengthen it. That is the mistake often made in the Christian system, where men are urged to repent of their faults and to feel remorse for them. The more sorry one feels and the more he turns his fault over in his mind the stronger it grows. But if one goes ahead and does some work for someone else, the thought-form is not intensified; it dies a natural death, drops away, and is forgotten. Morbid introspection often magnifies small failings into great sins. It reminds one of little children who constantly pull up their plants by the roots, to see how they are growing. Thus, a person eagerly takes up some good and noble work, then begins to doubt himself, and says: "I am not sure that my motive was pure; I must have done it because I was inwardly proud," or, if he relieves suffering, he thinks: "It was not really unselfish; I could not bear to see the suffering, and so I relieved it." In the Church of England they say: "Lord, have mercy upon us miserable sinners." We may be sinners, but we need not aggravate the offence by being miserable about it, and so making others miserable too. Never brood over the past, but set to work to do better in the future. It is useless to wish that you had not done so-and-so; much better to say: "I did that; it is a pity; never mind, this is the present condition of affairs, and I must see what I can do to make the best of it." I do not say that it may not be possible at some exalted level to alter the past, but it certainly is not practical for us to take that into consideration.

In the Lord Buddha's Noble Eightfold Path, the last step but one was Right Remembrance. He said to His people: "You must be very careful what you allow yourselves to remember. If you say you cannot help remembering everything, then you have no control over your memory, over the mind which is a part of yourself. It is as though you went along the street gathering up all the rubbish which came in your way; you are sweeping into your memory all kinds of useless and undesirable things. You should remember the right things and be particularly careful to forget the others." Then He enumerates elaborately and definitely the things that people should forget, and among these He mentions all unkind words spoken to them, all fancied slights and injuries. Those are among the things which one should permanently and absolutely forget, whereas, among the things one should remember are all the kind words that ever have been spoken to one, all the kindly deeds, and all the good qualities one has ever seen in one's neighbours.

We must learn to love all whom we contact. I do not say all alike; that is not expected. The Lord Buddha Himself had His favourite disciple, Ananda, whom He loved more than the others, and the Christ had His beloved disciple S. John, who leaned upon His breast at the Last Supper. We are not expected to love people all alike, to feel towards everyone the same love that is felt for father or mother, wife or child, but to hold the attitude of active goodwill or love towards all, and of hate to none. We are to hold this attitude also without asking any return for it; the moment one begins to make demands he sets up a claim; he is introducing the factor of desire again, and once more thinking of himself, not of those he loves. To pour out love and not expect any return is the only thing that deserves to be called love. Without that unselfishness people get entangled with jealousies, envyings and many other desires, and their love, instead of showing the pure glorious rose-colour, is seen as a sort of brownish-crimson, a poor-looking thing, and unpleasant also in form, because instead of outraying like sunlight, it is hooked and grasping, and makes a closed curve, often affecting no one but the sender.

The worlds are moved by the divine unselfish love that pours out in great open curves, and never returns and does not mean to return. It is poured out in other dimensions and other planes, to do the work of God in God's own way. This is the lesson to be learned—it is hard because it means the destruction of the lower nature, but it is the path to peace.

> You must discriminate in yet another way. Learn to distinguish the God in everyone and everything, no matter how evil he or it may appear on the surface. You can help your brother through that which you have in common with him, and that is the Divine Life; learn how to arouse that in him, learn how to appeal to that in him; so shall you save your brother from wrong.

A.B.—This is the final lesson in discriminating between the real and the unreal. However evil a thing is from the outside, God is there, for it could not exist at all if God were not at its heart. This truth is told again and again in the Hindu scriptures. "I am the gambling of the cheat," says the Lord in the *Bhagavad-Gītā*. That statement sometimes shocks people dreadfully; but it is true, because the cheat has something to learn in that way which he is refusing to learn in a better way. If a person cannot learn quietly by precept, he must learn from experience of natural laws. What we call the laws of nature are the most material expression of the Divine Mind.

The laws of nature stand there like rocks; if a man goes and bruises himself against them the pain that results teaches him to avoid a similar mistake in the future. When a person will not learn by precept or example (and there are plenty of both of these in the world) he must do so through the pain that comes from breaking the law. He must be carried on at all hazards towards unity, for the divine will is for evolution, and his own innermost will is one with the divine. I think that is the meaning which underlies also the words of the Hebrew singer: "If I ascend up into heaven, Thou art there." So far it is plain; we all know God is in heaven, but then: "If I make my bed in hell, behold, Thou art there also."[1]

See therefore the divine in everything around you; the rest does not concern you. In that way, and in that way only, you can help your brother, for the one thing you have in common is the divine life; all the rest is different, but in that you are at one, and you can use that as a lever for helping him in all ways. When you want to help a man to overcome a fault, remember that

[1] Psalm, cxxxix, 8.

he is just as anxious as you can be to get rid of the wrong thing in him; it injures him, and if you can only reach the real man inside, you will find that he wants to be rid of it. This is the right way to help; the inside way never hurts or offends anybody.

C.W.L.—All that exists on this plane, as much as on any other, is a manifestation of the divine Life: and therefore all of it—the good and the evil alike—must be an expression of God. Nothing can exist of which God Himself is not the heart and root. That fact is emphasized in all the scriptures. We have it in the Christian Scriptures: "I form the light, and create darkness; I make peace, and create evil; I the Lord do all these things."[1] People cannot understand how all that men commonly call evil can somehow be also divine, yet we must face the fact. There are black magicians and evil people of all sorts and kinds, but the life in those people is the Divine Life, because there is no other life.

If a man introduces evil into his life by his own stupidity, by his wrong-headedness, out of it good will nevertheless come; it is the only way to evolve that particular man. The cheat will cheat; he has it in his mind to do that. He is under the Divine Law still, and although he is doing wrong, out of it good for him will come, because he will learn by doing that, and by failure, to step into the right path. It is, as it were, the last resort, but it is a resort, and therefore we must acknowledge it to be within the Divine Plan.

[1] Isaiah, 45, 7.

There is a sense in which everything absolutely *is* God. Still it is not exactly in that sense that these words are written; it is the divine spirit in every one which makes him man. If you can see through the personality which is so warped, which has gone so far wrong, and get at the divine life in the man, you can appeal to that. We must remember that the "evil" man, as a soul, wishes to make progress just as much as we do. He wishes to get rid of the evil which is haunting and obsessing and troubling his personality, and therefore if we can get back to that soul through all this outer crust of hardness and evil, he will rush forward to help us in our endeavour to assist the personality.

I have been a priest and lay-helper most of my life, and have worked in some of the very worst parts of England. I have seen many men whom one would think hopeless criminals; but I have never seen one who had not some spark of good in him somewhere. It might be his love for a child, or his love for a dog, that seemed to be the only human touch in what was otherwise a brute, and a dangerous brute; but there is the One Life stirring in him somewhere, and if one can get into touch with him at that point there is just a chance that he may be helped upward through an appeal to that one thing.

A.B.—The Master's last words on the subject are: "So shall you save your brother from wrong." Here He makes the strongest appeal; it is to that which is the very object and end of life to the disciple, for his one aim is to become a saviour of the world. Far stronger is it than any appeal to the disciple for his own personal advantage could possibly be. The Master lives only to help the world; and the more we can bring service into our lives the more we shall reflect in them the beauty of His.

PART III

DESIRELESSNESS

CHAPTER 1

THE REMOVAL OF DESIRE

A.B.—We come now to the second qualification, which in the Sanskrit is *vairāgya*, for which, speaking in English, the Master uses the word desirelessness. That is a very accurate translation. In the past I have used the word dispassion, but henceforth I shall translate the term as the Master does.

> There are many for whom the Qualification of Desirelessness is a difficult one, for they feel that they *are* their desires—that if their distinctive desires, their likings and dislikings, are taken away from them, there will be no self left.

A.B.—Practically all those who sincerely desire to tread the Path feel the truth of the first sentence, in which the Master says that the qualification of desirelessness is a difficult one. The difficulty arises because people identify themselves with their desires. So long as a desire which is not gratified makes you unhappy, so long are you identifying yourself with your desires. It is well to recognize this, admit it to yourself; for it is quite easy to think that you have separated yourself from your desires, when in reality you have not done so. Very many people like to think that they have conquered the desire-nature, when their whole life, their every act, shows that it is not so. It is far better to recognize the fact, if you have not yet done so, and then you are prepared to adopt the remedy.

The first step that should be taken is to dwell on the idea; "I am not my desires." Here you can call to your aid what I have already explained with regard to moods; your desires, like your moods, are changing, and anything that changes is not the Self, who is not subject to fluctuations. For instance, I have known people who think one day: "How delightful it is to be at Adyar; how beautiful to think of all the great things that are going to happen"; and the next day they feel depressed, discouraged. Now, neither of these changing moods, neither the enthusiasm nor the depression, is yourself; both are merely passing vibrations of the astral body, roused by some contact from the outside.

It is for this reason that people are advised to meditate every day; for you cannot meditate properly until your desires are quiescent. If you meditate regularly and faithfully, you will little by little realize a Self behind your desires, and as you go on meditating, and also during the day practise the attitude required, you begin to realize that Self all the time. Then you will no longer identify yourself with your desires, and constantly feel: "*I* want: *I* wish; *I* desire"; but will think: "It is not I; it is the lower self."

This is the first great lesson which the Master gives about the second qualification. You are not required to have desirelessness perfectly before Initiation, but what the Master does expect is that you should have it to a great extent, and what He expects is law. All the swinging between the two poles of depression and elation must go before you can reach Initiation.

C.W.L.—Large numbers of people make no effort to distinguish between their desires and themselves, but say: "I am as God has made me. If I have a bad temper, or a weak will; He gave it to me. If I am not strong enough to resist temptation, that is how I was made." They do not understand that they have made themselves by their past lives, but they are in the habit of taking their character as a sort of inalienable something which is given to them, as one may be born blind or with a lame leg. They do not realize that it is their business to change a nature which is undesirable in its character. They do not know that they can, and furthermore, often they do not particularly see why they should.

There is usually no adequate reason held up to the average man why he should take all the very great trouble necessary to change his character. Some may say that unless he does so he will not go to heaven, but many reply that the conventional heaven would bore them inexpressibly, and they are hoping for something different. It is obvious, in fact, that though teaching concerning the heaven-life has been widely spread, it has had little practical influence on most people's character probably because it is so lacking in verisimilitude. The only theory that I have ever heard that seems to me adequate as an inducement to effort is that of Theosophy. It shows what is worth doing, and shows us that there is every opportunity and sufficient time for complete success. If a man understands God's plan, and seeks to co-operate with Him, he has the strongest possible motive to throw himself into the work of evolution, and to fit himself for it. He sees then that it is possible to make the most fundamental changes in his character and disposition, and that success is absolutely assured.

The never-changing desire of the ego is for progress, for the unfoldment of the higher self, and the bringing of the lower vehicles into tune as its instruments. Whenever we find other desires which are not part of that, and do not agree with it, we know that those are not from the soul, and so we do not say, "I desire this" but, "My desire-elemental is moving again; he wants so-and-so; but I, the ego, wish to progress; I wish to co-operate in the divine plan. These changing moods and desires are not mine." As long as an ungratified desire can cause unhappiness a man may know that he is still identifying himself with the desires of the elemental.

> But these are only they who have not seen the Master; in the light of His holy Presence all desire dies, but the desire to be like Him. Yet before you have the happiness of meeting Him face to face, you may attain desirelessness if you will.

A.B.—This recalls once more the verse in the *Bhagavad-Gītā*: "The objects of sense, but not the relish for them, turn away from an abstemious dweller in the body; and even relish turneth away from him after the Supreme is seen." All desire dies when a glimpse of the one desirable object has been obtained. Hence to realize the presence of the Master will rid you not of desires only, but of desire itself. Desire is a root that sends forth many shoots; you may lop off the shoots, but while the root remains it will send forth new ones. But union with the Master will finally rid you of the root of all desires.

Even before that, however, the Master says you may attain desirelessness if you will. Those three words "if you will" are specially important. They show us where the difficulty lies. It is not the ability, it is nearly always the will to do a thing, which is lacking. If you could put into your work on the path the same amount of will that you put into your worldly work, your progress would be rapid indeed.

C.W.L.—We have here one of the specially beautiful sentences in this very beautiful book. It is true that when you see the Master and realize what He is, all lower desires are simply not there any more; your whole being is filled with something higher.

Many people speak of their wish to attain desirelessness, and are yet all the time hugging the objects of desire and would be unhappy without them. They do not in reality wish for this desirelessness; they only think they do; on the surface they do, but deeper down in the personality they do not. It is well to question ourselves on this matter, to search deeply and see whether we have really got rid of all these lower desires. A Theosophist often thinks that he has, and thinks that it is merely an elementary matter; but a great many of these elementary things go very deep. Superficially one gets rid of them, but they crop up again in different forms, and it is hard to be sure that one has really disposed of them. Fortunately, it is not expected of us that we shall be utterly free from them at this stage. Initiation may be attained with the roots of some of these things still within us, but after that one must weed them out entirely. Still, it is better to root them out utterly even now, so that our progress may be smoother and more rapid. It is practicable, for the Master never suggests to us anything that we cannot do, though He does set before us many things which will tax our endurance or moral strength, because that has to be done if we want to get on rapidly.

> **Discrimination has already shown you that the things which most men desire, such as wealth and power, are not worth having; when this is really felt, not merely said, all desire for them ceases.**

A.B.—Desires for wealth and power clothe themselves in a variety of ways, not only in connection with money and social or political influence. Wealth is the thing which most people want above all others; but it is not in itself a good thing to have, for it only fosters desires, and does not give happiness, as may be seen by looking at rich people, who are by no means a happy class of beings. It is the same with power, social or political; it is all dross and tinsel, not gold. The *Gītā* says that the wise man is content with whatsoever cometh—which means that he will cheerfully make use of what is available, and not waste his time and energy in craving for something different.

Few people attain high social or political positions, but the temptation of power is often present without that. Power includes all wish to control other people, to interfere with them and tell them what to do, instead of minding one's own business. Though there may not be much desire for social or political power, there still is frequently an unhealthy desire to make others do what we think they ought to do. That must go if we mean to make progress. Those who mean business will soon find out, as many of us have done, that we have quite enough to do to manage our own lower selves, without trying to interfere with anybody else. The Self in others is the same as the Self in us, and the way in which it chooses to manifest in them is their business, not ours. Therefore all tendencies to interference must be weeded out.

You have no right to interfere except when it is your duty, and that is only when you have a certain limited control over a person who is placed under you by nature, as in the case of your own children, or by karma, as in the case of servants or workmen. Your control of a child should be protective control, exercised when and as long as there is weakness which needs protection;

and it must gradually disappear as the ego inside becomes able to take possession of his own vehicles. With your equals—I use the word in a wide sense—you clearly have no right of interference.

C.W.L.—People often want to interfere with others only because they think they can manage affairs better than those others can; but after all they do not *know* that. The divine power is working through each man; we had better let it do so in its own way. Remember how the Christ reminded the Jews that their Scriptures told them, "Ye are Gods", and that they were all children of the Most High. It may be that the other man is not doing his work in the very best way, or possibly that he is making some mistakes, but so long as he is honestly and earnestly doing his best it is well. Let him have his innings, even if he is not so good a batsman as you are. Sometimes one may very tactfully, very respectfully and delicately, offer advice, but there are many cases where even that would be an impertinence; one should never under any circumstances attempt to force an opinion on any one. Our first care should be that our own affairs are well managed, for each man is responsible to himself.[1]

[1] S. John, 10, 34, and Psalm, 82, 6.

CHAPTER 2

THE ONE GOOD DESIRE

Thus far all is simple; it needs only that you should understand. But there are some who forsake the pursuit of earthly aims only in order to gain heaven, or to attain personal liberation from rebirth; into this error you must not fall.

C.W.L.—The desire for personal liberation from rebirth is found chiefly in India, because most of the people there believe in reincarnation. To the average Christian, heaven is also a release from earth. These instructions were given to an Indian boy; therefore first of all and most of all they refer to Indian conditions, though the ideas can be applied to our Western world as well. We Theosophists are not particularly likely to make violent efforts in order to gain the happiness of the heaven-world, in which men spend hundreds and even thousands of years between incarnations. Many of us would prefer to avoid it altogether and return quickly to work upon earth, and that is possible to those who really desire it. That does need a certain amount of strength, however, as we must then carry the same mental and astral bodies over into the new physical body.

It is not that the astral body and the mental body are capable of fatigue, like the physical brain. There is, however, another consideration: the astral and mental bodies that we have in this life are the expression of ourselves as we were at the end of the last incarnation. As we go on through life we modify them considerably, but that cannot be done beyond a certain point. There is a limit to which, for example, a motor-car is susceptible to repair or improvement, and very often it is better to buy a new car than to try to bring the old one up to date. It is somewhat the same with the astral and mental bodies. A radical change in them would take a great deal of time, and might perhaps be only partially accomplished after all. If a man's capacities in this life have greatly increased, it might be better for his progress that he should get a new astral and mental body in which to express himself, instead of trying to patch up and alter the old one. Therefore quick reincarnation is not always quite a practicable thing. Yet we may take it, as things are now—with the special need of workers on account of the coming of the World Teacher—that any person who has worked well in this life and is earnestly desirous of taking an immediate incarnation in order to continue in service, may be able to achieve his desires.

There is an ordinary course of life after death for all men, and for those who pass through it there is no need to make any special arrangement; but if a man wishes to depart from that he has to make what amounts to an application, or it has to be made for him. It has to be submitted to a higher authority, who can give permission if He thinks it desirable; but He would quite certainly refuse it if He did not think it to be in the best interests of the person. I think those who have anxiety on this subject may set their minds at rest, however, for those who have worked well now will certainly have further opportunities of continuing that work. A man who wishes rapid reincarnation must make himself indispensable, so that he will be known as one who would be useful if he did come back at once. That also, incidentally, is the best way to bring the mental and astral bodies into the required condition.

> If you have forgotten self altogether, you cannot be thinking when that self should be set free, or what kind of heaven it shall have. Remember that *all* selfish desire binds, however high may be its object, and until you have got rid of it you are not wholly free to devote yourself to the work of the Master.

A.B.—We must remember that the astral and mental planes are material, though they are made up of subtler matter than the physical. They also are objective, and full of objects of desire. The desire for heaven, which is in the lower mental plane, is therefore just as much a desire of the lower self as is the desire for earth—only it is further off and more impalpable. The advantage of the former desire over the latter is that it gives a check to the desire-nature, because it cannot be gratified at once; so it helps the man to get rid of desire in general, and at the same time it causes him to select more refined pleasures, and to dwell upon those in his thought rather than the coarser ones. There are many men to whom it would obviously be useless to say, "Kill out desire". If you want to help a man who is addicted to the pleasures of eating and drinking and sex, you may put before him the desire for heaven, in order to help him to starve out the lower desires. Therefore it is that all religions make so much of the teaching of heaven and hell. Even the Lord Buddha spoke of these when he was addressing the ordinary people.

Those who wish to tread the Path must give up not only desire for heaven, but also that for personal liberation from the round of births and deaths, that is, for *moksha*. The reason is quite simple, and the Master gives it here. If you have forgotten yourself altogether, you cannot be thinking of those things which affect yourself. You must be free from desire for those things, if you mean to devote yourself to the work of the Master.

There are many people who wish to serve, in one way or in another, but the disciple must wish to serve the Master in the way He wills, and where He requires the service. Such unconditional service is not possible while the heart is bound up in anything. As one of the Upanishads says: "Until the bonds of the heart are broken, man cannot attain immortality." That sounds a hard thing to say, if we think of the bonds of the heart as including the qualities of love, to which we attach the greatest value. It does not say, however, that the heart must be broken, but that the bonds must be broken, so that the heart's love may be boundless. Do not misunderstand me, and think that I have said that to love is not desirable. It is not the love which binds, but the elements of selfishness which are too often mixed with it. The love of the Self in one man for the Self in another is in its very nature everlasting; we could not change that even if we would, but when love for the Self is mixed with love for the form, it begins to bind, and thus even love itself may become a bondage.

There is no way to reach the condition that makes you free for the Master's work but by constant effort to break every bond that restricts you. If you find in your love anything which can cause you pain, there is selfishness in it, which must be eliminated. Get rid of it, and your love will remain, stronger, nobler, purer; and such love can never interfere with the Master's work. Suppose you have a wish to go to a certain place because there is a particular person there with whom you like to be; well, give up the idea of going. That is just one instance of the way in which you may deliberately break the bonds that tie you by selfishness to special persons and things. Break off such ties.

I say this only for those who are in dead earnest—not for those who wish to go gently and quietly along the road of progress. There is no blame attached to this latter course, mind; each is free to go forward slowly or swiftly as he chooses. But I am speaking now for those who mean business, for those who are wholly in earnest. The Master is always looking out for this earnestness, and does not find too much of it. Once more I am speaking from my own experience, for I have had difficulty in this way. Then I began to train myself, and when I found that I had a great wish to be with some one, I would try to keep away from that person. If you have tact and strength, you can often untie yourself inside, so to say, without showing others that you are doing it. You remain just as loving as before, and your outward manner shows no alteration, but you are loosening the personal bond inside your own heart. It is by thus clearly seeing what ought to be done and then deliberately doing it that some of us have made more progress than most people. You will find such an effort easier if you keep in mind the fact that you cannot devote yourself entirely to the work of the Master until nothing remains that can bind you.

C.W.L.—This passage shows us that desire for heaven belongs to the personality. It is not, however, by any means a bad thing at an earlier stage of development than that of the disciple. It has its place in the evolutionary scheme. The primitive man is full of thoughts about eating and drinking, and similar pleasures. It would be quite useless to talk to him about desirelessness, as he must first pass through a stage of higher and more refined desire. The utmost we can say to him is: "Try to refine your desires; there are other and grander things than these of which you are thinking, and you cannot rise to those in the future unless you are prepared to check the outrush of your feeling." Men can rise only step by step, and only the strongest can climb the great heights of the Path rapidly. Yet those who read the words of this book, and wish to do as Alcyone has done, must resolve at once to get rid of all selfish desire, because it binds. As I have said, even love itself is a bond of the heart if there is in it a grain of selfishness, but when it is utterly free from any thought of selfishness it is a power of the heart. Until the bonds are broken, until the selfishness is weeded out, even love itself may be a hindrance as well as a help.

There has been much misunderstanding in India and elsewhere on this subject, on account of the confusion of love (which is unselfish) with desire (which is selfish). Some philosophers try to harden themselves so as to be indifferent to what happens, to escape suffering by avoiding love. But that is the wrong way; it produces men half-developed, intellectual but unemotional. We must have the power to express even great surges of feeling, but they must be reflections of the higher emotions of the Self, strictly under control, not astral waves sweeping us along at the will of the desire-elemental. To control emotion by killing it is something like that other idea of trying to avoid bad karma by doing nothing at all. The Master's way for us is that we should become increasingly useful to humanity through our actions, emotions and thoughts, and the more we can do in all three ways the better it will be for all concerned.

When all desires for self are gone, there may still be a desire to see the result of your work. If you help anybody you want to see how much you have

helped him; perhaps even you want him to see it too, and to be grateful. But this is still desire, and also want of trust.

A.B.—This is what the *Bhagavad-Gītā* calls not working for fruit. The result is the fruit. If you are really working you have no time to notice results, no time to stop and look at a piece of work which is finished. As soon as one thing is done there is something else at hand to be done. You are wasting time if you are looking at the results; if you are thinking of what you have already done, how are you to carry on the next piece of work? And when it comes to personal help, which is the pleasantest of all to give, because there is personal love at the back of it, do not look to see if the person whom you have helped appreciates what you have done. That is like running after one to whom you have made a present, in order to see if he is grateful, and to claim thanks. One who acts like that has not given; he has sold. It is barter; so much help for so much gratitude. You must not barter here! Remember how the Christ drove from the temple those who were selling, although they were selling things for sacrifice, saying to them: "Make not my Father's house an house of merchandise."[1]

C.W.L.—No one is busier than the occultist. The moment he finishes one thing he goes on with another, and he does not stand gazing to see what has resulted from what he did before. Suppose you were acting as a

[1] S. John, 2, 16.

nurse or a helper on the battle-field; you would have to do the best you could for one case, and instantly turn to another; you could not stop to watch for half-an-hour to see exactly what was going to be the final effect; you could not even stop to see whether the man was likely to recover or not. It is just the same with the Master's work; we have not time to stop and think about the ultimate results, and above all we have no time to think about ourselves in connection with those results. It is but human to desire that our efforts should meet with success, and to be elated when it comes, but we must rise above such human frailties, because the goal at which we aim is superhuman. If a thing is well done, we may rejoice in the fact, but we must feel just as glad if the success is another's as if it were our own.

It speaks here of sometimes wanting the man you have helped to see it too, and be grateful. If one has any feeling of that sort he is not giving at all, but selling. The only giving which is recognized in occultism is giving as God gives, pouring out love as the sun pours out life.

> When you pour out your strength to help, there must be a result, whether you can see it or not; if you know the Law you know this must be so.

A.B.—In the book *Of the Imitation of Christ* it is asked: "Who will serve God for naught?" The disciple must work for the sake of the work, not for seeing the result, and even without the happiness and satisfaction of thinking, "*I* am serving". He must give himself to the world because he loves it. There *must* be a result, of course, because we live in a world of law; that is why we need not make it our concern. Very often the nature of our work is such as not to bring about immediate results on the physical plane, but to bring something nearer to accomplishment; some one else will put the finishing touches to the work, but without those who have toiled and seen no results the thing could not possibly have been done.

You cannot do important work without trusting the law, because all great work is slow work. Consider, for example, the work of a Manu: thousands upon thousands of years go by before anything you would call a result is seen. Even in building a big house the same rule holds good, for deep foundations are necessary. Our work is largely the laying of foundations, which are not seen; later some one will come along and put a row of bricks above the surface; those will at once be seen. Are the foundations useless, then?

Results are inevitable. Therefore work in a quiet, scientific way, and you will never be disappointed. All disappointment is due to a desire for fruit. You may go on working strenuously for a long time without seeing any consequences, and one day the result will flash into sight. A chemist making a saturated solution goes on dropping a salt into the water, and for some time the liquid remains to all appearance unaffected; then the last grain is added, and the whole suddenly turns solid. So it is with our work; suddenly it will be manifest complete. We are preparing for the coming of the

Great Teacher. We must put all our force into this work, quietly, confidently, patiently; sacrificing ourselves wholly to the work. When the Lord Maitreya comes, He will take up all that we have done, and the result of it will then be manifest to the world.

C.W.L.—It often takes the work of a number of people, following one another, to achieve some great result. When there is a great reform to be introduced in the world, it usually happens that one man, or one group of men, will see the need and begin to talk and write about it. He or they will be ridiculed, and it will seem that their work is without result, but they will convert a few people to their cause, and these will carry it on, until at last society accepts the reform. What was done by the later men would have been impossible without the apparently resultless work of the pioneers.

Very often it may be the nature of our work to bring something near to its accomplishment. Somebody else will step in and put the final touch to the work; his efforts will then be recognized, and he will be considered as having done the whole thing. Never mind; we must care nothing whatever about getting the credit, but be happy to be allowed to do the work. One must not think: "That is rather hard on me." Our karma will take care of what we have done, and it does not matter what the world does or says about it at the present time. One who works scientifically, understandingly, without a thought of the result, except that somehow, somewhere, all good work must do good, will never know disappointment.

When the Lord comes He will take up all our work, carry it on and complete it; and so it will appear that it is all His work. In a sense it all is His, as we have been inspired by Him; yet a great deal of it will have been made possible by the unseen, or apparently profitless work done by a number of humble people beforehand. That we should have a chance of being among those people is assuredly the very greatest privilege we could desire.

In all cases, when one knows the laws of nature one can use them. This is as true of all the work that we are constantly doing on the inner planes, as of that in which we are engaged on the physical plane. Every thought of ours makes a form on the astral or mental plane, and this goes to the person or thing of which we are thinking, and hovers around or discharges itself, for good or ill according to its nature and quality. It is no more trouble to make a helpful thought-form than a harmful one. It all depends upon the attitude of the mind. One may think: "My attitude of mind matters only to me, and only just now." But it matters to others as well, and also it will matter to you the next day, the next month, or even the next year, because it generates thoughts which react upon you. Every thought intensifies itself, by calling up repetitions of itself. It rests with us to make forms which will be beneficial in every way; for though they be invisible to ordinary sight, they infallibly do their work.

So you must do right for the sake of the right, not in the hope of reward; you must work for the

sake of the work, not in the hope of seeing the result; you must give yourself to the service of the world because you love it, and cannot help giving yourself to it.

C.W.L.—Love is indeed the greatest of all motives. All through the teaching of this book, and of some later ones which have been moulded to a large extent upon it, it will be observed how strong and constantly repeated is this need of love as the motive in life, as the explanation of everything, and as the remedy for all ills. It is because that will be the key-note of the teaching of the World Teacher Himself when He comes, that it is already so strongly foreshadowed in that of those who are trying in their small way to prepare for Him.

Another thing the student will note is that all through this book the Master takes it for granted that we are all utterly in earnest, and that the work is the one thing for us. That is certainly the very best way of bringing us into that frame of mind, if there are still some lingering fragments of other ideas hanging about us. The fact that in His mind there is clearly no thought of anything but service, is the greatest incentive for us to make ourselves what He desires.

We often get in our own way; we have to stand aside and give the Self in us a chance to work, for as long as we have some reservations, as long as there is something which we are not prepared to give up for the sake of the Master's service, we are standing in our own way. It is a rare thing to find one who has no reservations whatever, who will give himself utterly to the service of the Master, who will stop at nothing, but give all. It is rare, but the man who has that quality will go far and very fast.

CHAPTER 3

PSYCHIC POWERS

Have no desire for psychic powers; they will come when the Master knows that it is best for you to have them.

A.B.—The term "psychic powers" properly includes all the manifestations of the powers of consciousness through organized matter, in the physical body, or the astral, or the mental. All powers of the intellect are therefore psychic powers. The distinction which has grown up between the ordinary powers of the mind shown through the brain, and the various kinds of clairvoyance and similar powers, is an unfortunate one. One hears many people speaking against the acquisition of psychic powers, while they themselves are using them all the time through the physical body. They denounce astral vision while they are using physical sight. It is illogical to denounce astral sight, unless you are prepared to take up the logical position of some of the Indian yogis, who regard the use of both physical and superphysical senses equally as a hindrance. These men are quite rational; they do not value any of the senses, because they consider that these only bring them into closer touch with the worlds of illusion from which they wish to escape. I do not agree with those people. I think that it is better to be healthy and to have the use of one's faculties on all planes; but unless their thorough-going attitude is adopted a good deal of the talk against psychic powers is foolish.

What is true is that in the early exercise of one's astral senses there is always a possibility of being misled. But one's physical senses also may deceive one. Certain sight-illusions, for example, are due to bad digestion and liver disorders, though I would not include in this category many things which the average doctor does, which are in reality instances of etheric or astral sight. The commonest illustration of the way in which our senses deceive us is that of the rising of the sun; you know that the sun does not rise, but you see it doing so.

The senses have always to be corrected by the reason, which is higher than all sense perceptions. Your astral vision constantly deceives you, when you begin to exercise it. That is why anyone who is being trained by a Master is put through a definite and thorough course of practice. He is asked what he sees, and his replies at first are mostly wrong; then his mistakes are pointed out to him, and explanations are given.

Suppose that a person who is not being trained by a Master awakens that sight. This frequently happens, for in the normal course of evolution the astral senses are unfolding, so that many people are beginning to possess them. Such a person is in the same position on the astral plane that a baby is in here. You know how a baby will stretch out its hand to grasp a lighted candle which is at the other end of a room. The baby's mistakes get corrected naturally by his elders; he will find out that certain objects that attract him are at a distance, by being carried to them. So our astral baby—as we may call the person newly functioning with his astral senses—makes many mistakes, which would not matter in the least if he were in the midst of his elders. Neither would they matter so much if only people would have common sense. But unfortunately the person who receives an astral communication, or sees an astral vision, too often thinks himself distinguished from all the rest of the world by being vouchsafed a special revelation. They are thus not in a position to learn from their elders in this sort of knowledge, as a baby is willing to be taught by grown-up people, and so a good deal of trouble arises.

C.W.L.—Those who become pupils of the Masters are put through a long course of training with regard to this matter of higher sight and higher impressions generally. I suppose that to many that training would be very wearisome. An elder pupil will take the younger and pass before him a number of different objects and ask him what he sees. The young pupil is generally quite wrong at first, because he has got the thing out of focus. He does not know the difference between the astral body of a dead man and of a living man, nor that between the man himself and a thought-form made by some friend. In these and many other ways the untrained observer is liable to deception. Patiently the teacher will show him these things again and again, and show him how to recognize them, pointing out the minute differences.

No one should think that because this training is necessary the astral senses are especially unreliable. All senses are unreliable until they are trained, and even then when they are not used along with the rational intelligence. Every morning in fine weather, if we are up in time, we may see the sun rise; we know perfectly well that it does not rise and yet we see it doing so. Sometimes illogical people say with regard to things a little outside the range of most people's experience that they will not believe in what they cannot see, but if they see they will believe. Some go further and say that they will be convinced if they can touch the thing. A simple test will show the fallacy of this. Take three bowls and put into them water at different temperatures; very hot, icy cold, and of temperate degree. Put one hand into the hot and the other into the cold water; let them remain there for a few minutes, then move them both into the temperate water. The hand that has been in the hot water will tell you that this bowl of water is very cold, and the other hand will tell you that it is very hot. This demonstrates that the senses are not always to be implicitly relied upon. Their testimony must be checked by the use of reason, and this has to be done just as much with the astral and mental senses as with the physical.

If a man wishes for psychic powers he must work at their development and it is often a matter of years before the man is perfectly certain of his accuracy in all cases. It is difficult to realize the extent of the area over which this clairvoyant vision extends. Take one example only: in the astral plane there are two thousand four hundred and one different varieties of what is called elemental essence, and if one wishes to be reliable and to do his work well and quickly, he must learn to distinguish one from another, and know when they are to be used. The work can be done without any of this knowledge, but wastefully—on the principle of emptying a bucket of water over a man to wash his little finger.

We are told, however, that waste of energy is precisely one of the things we must avoid. Energy is capital, and we are bound to make the most of it. We are responsible for any waste of it, just as we should be if we let it lie idle and did nothing with it.

It would be of no use for a pupil of the Master to say: "I know already." That is not the spirit in which we approach these things. We are always eager and anxious to acquire further information, but always that we may serve the better, in order that we may be more useful. That is the idea, and most assuredly there is no knowledge which comes amiss in the work we have to do. Everything he knows enables the occultist to illustrate points, and often to understand points which otherwise might not be clear to him. They say at the end of this evolution we shall attain all knowledge; we shall get rid of ignorance. All our work is tending in that direction, and we shall certainly need to be most wonderfully well informed to do the higher work well when our turn comes. Meantime, it is wisdom to use to the full the powers one has, and to have no desire for psychic powers until the Master sees fit that we should develop them.

> To force them too soon often brings in its train much trouble ; often their possessor is misled by deceitful nature-spirits, or becomes conceited and thinks he cannot make a mistake ; and in any case the time and strength that it takes to gain them might be spent in work for others.

C.W.L.—The deceitful nature-spirits, of which there are many different kinds, are a very real feature in the case. Most of them are rather small creatures, and they think it is very amusing if they can make a great big man do what they say, when they order him about. They do that very often merely by pretending to be Julius Cæsar, Napoleon Bonaparte or any great and well-known personage whose name happens to occur to them, and it is great fun for them to see big people who belong to a higher stage of evolution than their own doing what they suggest. It is perhaps a little hard on the people, but they should have brought their reason and common sense to bear on their visions.

If you hear an astral voice sometimes, do not immediately jump to the conclusion that it is that of the Master or of a great Archangel. Dead people often manage to communicate and offer advice, and nature-spirits play their little tricks frequently, so it is more likely in most cases to be one of these. So, take the voice quite calmly; it is an interesting phenomenon, not necessarily because of what you may get out of it, but because anything a little out of the ordinary is in itself interesting, and there is generally something to be learned in connection with it. But do not start by denying that there is a communication—that again is an unwise thing to do. One may think of a thing as improbable, but it is not safe to say it is impossible. Listen respectfully to the revelation, but, unless you have good reason to do so, do not let it affect your conduct in any way. Action should be the consequence of one's decision, following upon one's own reasoned thought, not of something said by somebody else, one does not know who.

A great number of people have revelations which they think are going to remodel the world. Though they are usually quite good, there is generally nothing very striking about them, and they are apt to be somewhat indefinite in outline, and vague in their teaching. As far as they go they are generally an improvement upon the very limited and cramped orthodox theories. They are nearly always along Theosophical or New Thought lines —Theosophy and water, the water predominating. They are usually given out with perfectly good intentions, by some dead man, who has now realized certain broad facts of life which he wishes to impress upon those whom he has left behind. He thinks that if these higher ideas were accepted the world would be a much better place, and he tries to impress them upon the people on the general theory of Dives in the parable, that if some one came to the people from the dead they would repent, forgetting, of course, the sage answer of Abraham: "If they hear not Moses and the Prophets, neither will they be persuaded though one rose from the dead."[1]

Such a man forgets that he himself paid no attention whatever to spirit messages when alive. If such come our way—they are sure to, more or less, if we are what is called psychic—we should receive them quite respectfully, but at the same time without undue excitement. Many of those who receive the message think that they are going to revolutionize the planet, but that is not easily done. When they are brought to our notice, we apply to them, if necessary, certain means of testing the truth and validity of such communications. Most people have not those means immediately at their disposal, but if they will just apply plain common sense to their superphysical experiences they will get along very well in regard to most of them. There are two attitudes which are adopted by most people; either they receive them blindly or else they scoff and say it is ridiculous. Both these extremes are silly. Everyone who has studied these things knows that they do come, but for the most part only from people who can tell us nothing new and accurate. A dead man, if he is wise enough to do it, may learn certain things which as a living man he could not get to know, but nearly all the dead neglect this opportunity, and go on contentedly with the limitations and prejudices they had on earth.

[1] S. Luke, 16, 31.

Experiences of the super-physical are now on the increase, because the time of the coming of the World-Teacher is drawing near, and that fact is widely known on all the planes. In the physical world there is a strong expectation of His coming, quite outside the Theosophical ranks. There are many people who feel the nearness of His approach, and consequently are more likely than before to be the recipients of such communications. They invite them by their attitude of expectancy. Therefore it is quite certain that there will be a great deal of information and misinformation spread abroad with regard to the coming of the Lord. He Himself said a long time ago that there would be many false Christs who would come. The average Christian probably thinks of the false Christs as anti-Christs, deliberately deceiving the people. But most of them will be entirely well-meaning people, who have really persuaded themselves that they are overshadowed by the Christ, and the very fact that they are well-meaning will render them more dangerous, because people will feel their earnestness, and be carried away by that.

The Theosophical attitude about false Christs may be expressed somewhat thus: it is a pity that people should be misled into thinking that some one who is very ordinary is the World-Teacher. Nevertheless, if the teachings are good and the people follow them heartily and nobly, their lives will be improved. The fact that they have wrong impressions on certain points will not prevent them from receiving the karma of their good lives. It would be better that they should see the truth clearly, but we must not make the mistake of thinking that people who are in error with regard to a certain important truth are necessarily wrong in every other respect—because they are not.

I hope, however, that we who are students of Theosophy shall be free from this particular error, because we are expecting the coming with a clearness and a definiteness which most of the sects have not. As the time draws nearer more than ever shall we have to use our own common sense, never denying the possibility of anything, but exercising judgment and reason always. We may adopt the attitude of Gamaliel: "If this counsel or this work be of men, it will come to nought; but if it be of God, ye cannot overthrow it; lest haply ye be found even to fight against God."[1] Let us take whatever comes of good, from any source whatever.

The Masters influence many people, and care nothing about whether the instruments that They use know Them or not; therefore we must be prepared to find that quite outside Theosophical organizations other forces are working towards the same great goal. And while we follow our line and serve our own Society firmly, strongly, faithfully, loyally, keeping to that because it is obviously the way for us, yet we should be careful not to condemn or to speak against any other forms of manifestation outside it, which may be tending in the same general direction, and we must not expect such manifestations to be all pure or perfect. In all sorts of ways

[1] Acts, 5, 38-39.

spiritual power will be outpoured from now on to the time of the coming. The Hierarchy itself is pouring upon the world floods of influence which may perhaps touch but little the man who is entirely wrapt up in worldly matters, but which mean a great deal to those who are sensitive; to those who are ready to profit by it, it will mean the making of a new heaven and a new earth.

That there will be unusual happenings is certain. *The Light of Asia*, which is a very faithful transcript of the Buddhist books, referring to the life of the Lord Buddha, relates again and again how various non-human entities knew of His coming and rejoiced in it, and how devas and nature-spirits everywhere felt His wonderful magnetic influence and gathered round when anything specially great was going to happen—at the time of His birth, when He was about to attain Buddhahood, and at the time of His first sermon. There is much truth in that idea. Whenever any great manifestation of the higher power is taking place, the other and more sensitive evolutions feel it much more than humanity does. Because men have given themselves largely to the development of the lower mind, and for a long time have neglected the hidden side of things and been so entirely wrapped up in themselves, they are generally at present less sensitive than some of the lower creatures. I have known cats and dogs that were more sensitive to higher influences than human beings—not that they could get so much from them, but they were aware of them when human beings were not.

When the Lord comes He will no doubt take up the experiments made by those who have prepared for Him and carry them through to a successful conclusion, so probably He will leave the world in all sorts of ways different from the condition in which He will have found it. He will not only preach His religion, but it may well be that all sorts of other reforms as well may be introduced as a consequence of His teaching. One cannot say definitely, of course, because there will probably be opposition this time, as there was before.

I do not think we can assume that He will carry the world before Him. Probably many teachers will have to come before His pure doctrine wins the allegiance of the world in general. When He came two thousand years ago men barely heard of Him. We must expect the life of the Teacher and those around Him to be anything but easy. The world at large is always ready to take up and circulate evil reports, so we may as well be prepared for a vast amount of petty annoyance and discomfort, if nothing worse. All sorts of vested interests will obviously find the changes which He may propose unpalatable to them. The vested interests murdered Him last time after only three years of teaching. How it will be this time we cannot know, but we hope that at least a nucleus of people will exist in every country, who may be able to make it profitable for Him to stay and work with us longer than three years. The Order of the Star in the East has definitely set itself the work of preparing for Him, with a full knowledge of what it means and what lines His teaching is likely to follow.

There may well be also other individuals and organizations inspired to work in the same way, often without any means of obtaining such knowledge as we are privileged to have. We hope that our service will make possible what was not possible before. We hope, but we cannot say. We can only do our best.

Those who are destined by karma to work with the great Lord of Love are now of necessity coming into incarnation. We often hear, therefore, of the birth of extraordinary children. They must come now, in order to be in the prime of life when the Lord arrives. It is likely that they will differ in certain ways from other children, so do not be surprised when you hear of young people who remember previous births, or have other superphysical experiences of their own; all these things are quite natural and to be expected, because of the special time in which we live. Dr. Besant once gave directions as to how people should treat such cases as came within their ken. She said: "Do not be excited with regard to any such things, and do not recount alleged identifications of such children too readily, for very few people know who they were in previous births. Remember that all such children are unusually sensitive, therefore you must be very kind and very gentle in your dealings with them. There must never be a harsh word or gesture of any sort; you must never startle or alarm them, for they feel much more acutely than other children. You must guard them from crowds or from the neighbourhood of undesirable people. You should let them know but few people, and should surround them with harmonious magnetism, which should not be changed too often. You should not send them to school, but you should surround them with a specially loving home atmosphere."

A.B.—Here the Master adds a further reason why one should not desire to obtain psychic powers: the time and strength that it takes to gain them might be spent in work for others. Notice how constantly the advice that the Master gives has for its aim service and the getting rid of selfishness in every form. Instead of using time and strength to acquire psychic power for yourself, give them to the service of those around you. If the Master sees that you are thus using every power you already have in the service of others, so that more can be entrusted to you because it is certain that you will also use those unselfishly, then He will step in. If you can honestly say that you are using every faculty *you have, be sure you are on the threshold of having fresh powers entrusted to you. But there are very few* who can say *it*, and *if you* are not one *of those* you had better set to work to attain this condition.

This is the meaning of the parable of the talents—the name is equally applicable whether you take the word talent in its modern meaning or in its original one of a certain measure or weight of money. A man went away on a journey, entrusting some money to his servants; one had five talents given to him, another two, another one. On the employer's return, he asked how the talents had been used. Those who had five and two talents respectively had traded with them, and were able to return them with interest. But the servant with one talent only had hidden it away, and now he brought it and handed it back. Then the lord took it away from him; while the other servants who had been faithful in small things he made rulers over many things. And he said: "Unto everyone that hath shall be given, and he shall have abundance: but from him that hath not shall be taken away even that which he hath."[1] It seems paradoxical, but the occult meaning of the words is clear. He who uses his powers to the full shall be entrusted with more; he who does not use his powers, and who therefore from the occult standpoint does not possess them, shall lose even the possibility of using them; they will atrophy.

No one should complain that he is not receiving from the Masters all the help to which he thinks himself entitled. There is only one way in which to satisfy your wish to come into touch with the great Teachers, and that is to be useful to your fellow-men. That is the only claim which the Masters recognize; they look not at the capacity of a person, but at his usefulness. I came into touch with the Master in this life when I did not know of His existence, and so was obviously not thinking of reaching Him. It is true that I had been His disciple for many lives, but it was not that which caused Him to reveal Himself to me; He did so because I was straining every nerve to help the people about me—the poor, the miserable, the down-trodden—because it was worth while for Him to pour His strength into me, when it was passed on to thousands.

[1] S. Matthew, 25, 29.

So, instead of crying out to the Master in your meditation, asking Him to reveal Himself to you, see what good work there is that ought to be done in your town or village, and go and do it. It does not matter to the Master whether or not His instrument knows that He is using it. There are many great helpers scattered throughout the world who are assisted and inspired by the Master. Many outside the Theosophical Society are so inspired.

> They will come in the course of development—they *must* come; and if the Master sees that it would be useful for you to have them sooner, He will tell you how to unfold them safely. Until then, you are better without them.

C.W.L.—People often say: "I hear of these wonderful powers which make their possessors so much more useful. I want to be useful. I should like to have them too." There is nothing wrong in that, only one had better follow the advice which is given here, and wait until they come naturally, or until the Master Himself tells one how to open them. Is He likely to do that? Yes; when you are ready. My own experience tells me that. I had none of these powers, and was not thinking about them, because we thought in the early days of our movement that they could be developed only by those who were born with a certain amount of psychic faculty to begin with, and I had none. One day, however, the Master Himself, when visiting Adyar, gave me a hint in that direction. He advised me to try a certain sort of meditation, and said: "I think you will get good results from it." I tried it and got the results. The same thing will be said to everyone who works for the Master, when the right time comes. We may take that as quite certain. In what form He will signify His wish cannot be foretold, but He will do it in some way.

The best way to make oneself fit for such an effort is unquestionably to use for service to the fullest possible extent all the powers one has. Any person who is doing that without thought of self is likely to receive some new powers.

It is the old parable of the talents again. You remember those who made good use of their talents were able to go on, and were given charge of far greater work. It was said to them, "Thou hast been faithful over a few things, I will make thee ruler over many things: enter thou into the joy of thy lord."[1] Very few people stop to think what that means—the joy of the Logos, the joy of the Masters. It is not vague pleasure or bliss, or entry into heaven. The making of the worlds is joy to Him; it is the play of Bacchus in the Greek Mysteries, and of Shri Krishna among the Hindus. The Logos has chosen to throw Himself into this mighty work of evolution; that is the joy of our Lord, the joy of carrying out this splendid plan of pouring out His love through the universe; and if we are to enter into the joy of the Lord we must take part in that work and the bliss which it brings. If we are not using all the powers that we have, the Master will not help us to obtain others.

[1] S. Matthew, 25, 21, 23.

He will wait until He sees that we are making full use of what we already have. People do not always understand that. They want to become invisible helpers; we tell them always, "You must be visible helpers first. If your whole life is full of helpfulness on the physical plane where you are fully conscious, then quite certainly you will be useful also in the other planes."

CHAPTER 4

SMALL DESIRES

You must guard, too, against certain small desires which are common in daily life. Never wish to shine, or to appear clever.

C.W.L.—Most people rather like to appear clever, to appear to the best advantage. But no man who has met the Master face to face could ever think about shining himself. When he has seen that glory he realizes in a moment that any light he can show is as a farthing rushlight compared to the sun. Therefore the idea does not occur to him, or if it was there before it is now dissolved. The man who thinks that his tiny light is going to make a vast impression in the world is the one who has not yet seen the higher lights, and therefore has not the means to compare.

Yet in every possible way we must make the best of every quality that we have, in the Master's service. What light we have is not to be hidden under a bushel. It is not only the mighty beacon of the World-Teacher that is needed; let the lower lights be borne along the shore. The great light shines out so brightly that it dazzles some; others never lift their eyes, and hardly know of its existence. The lesser lights, which are nearer to their own comprehension, may appeal to these. There may be many whom we can help who as yet are not at all ready to be helped by greater people. So each has his own place; but never desire to shine for the sake of shining, that would be foolish.

> **Have no desire to speak. It is well to speak little; better still to say nothing, unless you are quite sure that what you wish to say is true, kind and helpful. Before speaking think carefully whether what you are going to say has those three qualities; if it has not, do not say it.**

A.B.—People who want constantly to talk have not enough to say to be able always to talk sensibly, and so they say things which are not worth hearing, and thus add to the tremendous stream of gossip which there is in the world. Thus they do incalculable harm, if they allow the tongue to be their master, instead of themselves mastering the tongue. Then comes a teaching which I have often heard from the Master: think before you speak whether what you are going to say is true, kind and helpful, and if it has not those three qualities do not say it. This will make you slow in conversation, so that gradually you will find that you talk less, and that will be a good thing.

Talkative people fritter away their energies, which ought to be employed in useful action. The person who talks a great deal is generally a poor worker. You may think, perhaps, that these remarks about speaking might very well be applied to myself, as I am constantly lecturing. But I do not speak much outside my work. I have lost the capacity for small talk, so that people often find fault with me for my silence. In the West I have often to force myself to talk, because silence is frequently mistaken for moroseness or pride, or a disinclination to make oneself agreeable. Naturally, then, my facility of speech is not great unless I have something definite and useful to say. Speak, by all means, when you have good cause to speak, when you have something to say that is worth saying, when it is done out of kindness to others. It is not such speech, but useless talking, that must be stopped. Every useless word is another brick built into the wall which separates you from the Master, and that is a serious consideration for those who want to reach Him.

He who speaks much cannot be truthful. I do not mean that he is consciously and wilfully untruthful, but he cannot always be accurate, and inaccuracy is untruth. There is scarcely anything worse than to have around you an atmosphere of untruthfulness, such as is always created by inaccurate speech. I often receive letters, for example, which are a mass of verbiage, with perhaps a little kernel of fact in the middle of it all. In all the ordinary affairs of life we learn to discount exaggeration; so also, when I receive a letter containing a complaint against somebody else—and there are many such —I judge how much ground there is for it largely by my knowledge of the writer's character and also by sensing the mood in which he was when he wrote it.

The Manu said that he who had mastered the tongue had mastered all; and a Christian teacher said: "The tongue is a little member, and boasteth great things. Behold how great a matter a little fire kindleth! And the tongue is a fire, a world of iniquity: so is the tongue among our members, that it defileth the whole body."[1] To master the tongue is to master the lower nature. The small troubles which people have are mostly the result of their idle words; the reaction from them. Little headaches, indispositions, depressions and so forth arise in this way. If people who have these would learn silence, they would soon improve their physical health, partly because they would no longer lose all the nerve-energy which now trickles away in talk, and partly because they would not have constantly to pay the little kārmic debts which result from their idle words. It will be remembered that Pythagoras imposed two years' silence on his pupils; that fact should weigh with us, because he was the Master whom we now know as Kūthūmi, the teacher of Alcyone and also of Bishop Leadbeater.

In India there are many yogis who are called *munis*; they have taken a vow of silence, as their name implies. The value of that has always been recognized in this country. I know one man who has carried out this vow for ten years, and it has given him great peace and dignity; because of it he is leading a far more spiritual life than he could have done without it. Of course, most of us cannot take such a vow when we are living

[1] James, 3, 5-6.

in the world and have all kinds of work to do in it; but we can and should follow the spirit of it, keeping silent whenever it is possible to do so without giving offence.

The need of constantly watching and judging is also valuable as a training in greater self-recollectedness. You must say something, but you have to determine not to say more than will fulfil the occult rule as to kindness and usefulness. It is a good practice to make a resolution on this point for one day at a time; determine in the morning that you will speak no idle word during the day —that will be one day to the good, at least. Our Jain brethren make use of similar exercises in order to learn watchfulness and self-recollectedness; they determine in the morning that during that day they will not do a certain thing—which may be quite unimportant in itself —and they do not do it, and the habit of watchfulness thus engendered does away with carelessness. The Lord Buddha also spoke very strongly on the subject of carelessness, the lack of thoughtfulness which leads men into so many blunders.

C.W.L.—People who are all the time chattering cannot always be speaking sensibly or profitably; furthermore, they cannot be truthful. If people are always talking loosely, quite certainly some of the things they say will not be true, though not intentionally false. They make all sorts of inaccurate statements, and afterwards say: "I did not mean to be inaccurate, so it does not matter." It is not what you mean, but what you do that produces results. If you do a foolish thing, the fact that your intention was good does not alter its character, nor relieve you from the karma of it. The good intention, if definite, will be beneficial to you, but the foolish thing will bring you bad physical karma. A man will say something, and later correct himself: "I see I was wrong; it is not quite like that." He has told a falsehood: he did not mean it, but he has made an assertion which is not true. To say that he did not mean it is like the plea of a man who happens to shoot some one by accident: "I did not know the gun was loaded." He ought to have presumed that it was loaded until he knew it was not.

It would be a good thing if we set ourselves just for one day to make quite sure that we spoke nothing that was not true, kind, and helpful. It would be rather a silent day, but perhaps the world would not lose much, and it would be very good for us. Of course, it would be impossible to carry on a rapid and animated conversation because we should have to stop and think. These rules are based upon the laws of the higher life. If a man wants to make more rapid progress, he must try to keep these higher rules. He must change himself to suit them, even when they seem to bring him into conflict with ordinary life and its methods. That may appear hard, perhaps; but if, after carefully thinking it over, he feels that the demands of the higher life are too hard for him, let him wait a life or two before trying to make real progress. We cannot do the two things: have an easy life without any effect and exertion, and have the rapid progress; but we can do either one, and there is no blame attached to the man who feels that as yet he is not equal to the strain.

It is well to get used even now to thinking carefully before speaking; for when you reach Initiation you must watch every word, lest you should tell what must not be told.

C.W.L.—That might possibly be misleading if one did not understand the facts with regard to Initiation. If anyone thought of divulging the real secrets of Initiation, before he uttered the words he would have forgotten that there was anything to betray. Therefore the real secrets are perfectly safe; they have never leaked out, and they can never do so. Still, there is great danger for the Initiate who may become careless. He may put himself in a very awkward position indeed. I myself am possessed of certain information of various kinds, as to which I cannot see that any particular harm would be done if it were published in the daily newspapers; but I was told not to repeat it so I do not; I do not know why. A promise is a promise, and must be kept as a sacred thing. If there are any who do not feel that way about it, they had better give up at once all thought of occult progress.

Much common talk is unnecessary and foolish; when it is gossip, it is wicked.

C.W.L.—Often what we must call unnecessary talk is nevertheless spoken with intent to help to pass the time pleasantly for some one. It is, perhaps, the unfortunate custom of our period to spend a great deal of time in talking which really might be employed much more profitably in thinking. There must be times when we say things which are not absolutely necessary, just in order to please other people who would misunderstand us if we were persistently silent. Yet outside that there is a great deal of unnecessary talking which does not fall under that head at all, done apparently just for the sake of saying something. That is a mistake. Real friends can be silent and yet enjoy one another's company, and realize a close community of thought; but if people are in a condition where they are afraid of gaps in the conversation and must keep on talking, then unfortunately there will be a great deal said which would be much better not said. Garrulous people are not the wisest, and are not, as a rule, notable for thought.

So be accustomed to listen rather than to talk ; do not offer opinions unless directly asked for them.

C.W.L.—Some people cannot hear a statement made which they think to be wrong or incomplete without instantly contradicting it and creating disharmony and argument. We must realize that it is not our business to correct opinions, or to try to put right everybody who is wrong. It is our business to go about helping people as much as we can in a quiet sort of way, and if our opinion is asked on the subject to state it very calmly and temperately, and not in a spirit of opposition. We need not assume that our opinion is of great interest to anybody else; sometimes it is not, and then it is wrong to thrust it upon people. A man may be quite sure that the fact is so-and-so, and we may know very well that it is not so, but it is better to let him talk; it probably pleases him and does not do us any harm. He may choose to believe that the earth is flat or that the sun goes round it—it is his own affair. If one were in the position of a schoolmaster and were appointed to teach certain boys, then one would gently and quietly correct them, because that would be one's duty; but no one is appointed as a schoolmaster to the general public.

Of course, if we heard some one's character being taken away it would be our duty to say, "Excuse me, you are not quite right; that is not true" and as far as possible put the thing right before people. That would be a case of a helpless person being attacked—then it is one's duty to defend him.

> One statement of the Qualifcations gives them thus: To know, to dare, to will, and to be silent; and the last of the four is the hardest of them all.

C.W.L.—The Rosicrucians held that he who would make occult progress must resolve to know, dare, will and be silent. We must know the truths of nature, and dare to use them. To use the great powers that become ours on this Path we must have a strong will that can control them, and control ourselves too. Then, when these things are done, we must know enough to be silent about them.

CHAPTER 5

MIND YOUR OWN BUSINESS

Another common desire which you must sternly repress is the wish to meddle in other men's business. What another man does or says or believes is no affair of yours, and you must learn to let him absolutely alone. He has full right to free thought and speech and action, so long as he does not interfere with any one else. You yourself claim the freedom to do what you think proper; you must allow the same freedom to him, and when he exercises it you have no right to talk about him.

C.W.L.—One should not interfere with other people's beliefs and actions, as long as their actions are not obviously to the common harm in any way. If a man comports himself so as to be a nuisance to his neighbours, it may sometimes be our duty to suggest something; but even in such cases it is often best to go away and let things quietly right themselves.

We of the Anglo-Saxon race boast much of freedom, but we are not in the least free really, for we are hidebound by custom to an almost inconceivable extent. We cannot dress as we like, or go about as we choose.

A man might prefer the ancient Greek—it is probably one of the most beautiful costumes in the world—but if he put it on and walked down the street he would probably have a crowd of people round him, and might be arrested for blocking the traffic. In any land of liberty he would be quite free to dress and act as he liked, so long as he did not make himself a nuisance to others. But there is no real freedom at all; we cannot depart from the line which other people take, or at least only very slightly, otherwise a great deal of trouble and disturbance is caused. It is a pity, because real freedom would be so very much better for all concerned, especially for those who want to interfere with others.

A.B.—I suppose that most of us who are earnest and enthusiastic are so sure of the value of what we have learned, so convinced, and rightly so, of its supreme importance, that we want other people to feel the same; and sometimes we should almost like to force them to see as we do. That is a fault of almost every enthusiastic nature. But a man can only receive gladly what he already knows inside, though he does not yet know it in the brain and therefore cannot yet articulate it to himself. Until that preliminary stage has been reached he is not in a position to accept a truth presented to him from the outside, and to try and force it upon him does far more harm than good.

In the same way conscience cannot be created from the outside; it is only the fruit of past experiences. Therefore the acceptance of all teaching and advice implies that the outer presentation has stirred knowledge *already possessed by the man inside, and it has then flashed down into the brain. All that the teacher can do* along these lines, therefore, is to bring to a man's physical-plane knowledge that which he already knows on other planes. One of the great Teachers has pointed out that many people are taught much Theosophical knowledge while out of their bodies during sleep. The real man then learns, and the knowledge that is thus acquired can then be regiven to him by a physical-plane teacher, whose words help the man to bring it down into his brain. That is all that the physical-plane teacher can do.

We have all to learn by repeated disappointments that we cannot help a man along the way which he is not yet ready to tread. Thus we become much quieter—ready to help when help can be useful, also ready to stand aside and wait when our help would be no help at all, that is, when the person could not profit by what we could tell him. This attitude often gives the ignorant the idea that we are indifferent, whereas the truth is that the person who is more advanced knows exactly where he can help and where he cannot.

For those who cannot see exactly where help can be given the policy ought to be tentative. Suggest a thought; if it is met with indifference or is repelled, you see that you cannot help the person whom you are addressing along that particular line. Then you must wait or try some other way, as the case may be. That is much better than forcing upon him all that you know; do not drown or choke the person mentally by pouring all your knowledge out upon him or trying to ram it into him. People are often very willing to claim freedom for themselves but extraordinarily reluctant to give it to others. That is a serious fault, for other people have fully as much right to their views and to the expression of them as we have.

Sometimes the fault is the other way. Do not run into the other extreme of thinking that you must accept other people's opinions. You have the fullest right to disagree. You may say quite frankly, " No, I do not agree with that," or you may keep silent ; but what you must not do is to attack another for holding his own opinion. When you hear a person making some statement, use your own common sense first of all ; always exercise your reason on every statement you hear. Leave other people free, but do not enslave yourself.

> If you think he is doing wrong, and you can contrive an opportunity of privately and very politely telling him why you think so, it is possible that you may convince him ; but there are many cases in which even that would be an improper interference. On no account must you go and gossip to some third person about the matter, for that is an extremely wicked action.

A.B.—You may sometimes be able to help a person whom you know to be morally doing wrong, but here great circumspection is required, since it is so easy to do more harm than good in such cases. Help so given must certainly be offered only in the private and utterly friendly way which the Master indicates. If the person is self-opinionated we can but leave him to learn by experience, which fortunately is a great teacher.

If a person has got hold of some mistaken idea, and he comes and expresses it to you, it is not necessary to say that it is wrong, unless you are sure that he has more confidence in your judgment than in his own, or at least is willing to consider seriously what you say; in many cases, he is bound to find out the error for himself, and then it is better to let him do so. People often come to me and make some great announcement of what is going to happen, according to their belief; generally I listen quietly and politely and do not express an opinion. When the prophecy fails of its fulfilment, the person who made it sees that he made a mistake, but one leaves him to draw the conclusion for himself. It is inevitable that such things should happen when many people are coming into touch with occultism. Sometimes they become confused, because many of their former standards of judgment are swept away, and they wonder how many of their criteria are going to fall to pieces among all the earthquakes that are taking place. The only thing to do under these circumstances is not to hurry, but to keep calm and cool and steady; gradually things will become clear, that which is false and mistaken will pass, and the real things will remain.

If you see a case of cruelty to a child or an animal, it is your duty to interfere.

A.B.—In the case of cruelty to a child or an animal interference is a duty, because strength is taking advantage of weakness, which it ought always to protect, because weakness cannot protect itself. Whenever, therefore, a child or an animal is being ill-treated, the duty of one who is stronger is to step in between and not allow an infringement of its rights, nor permit the liberty of another to be taken away. So whenever you see a case of cruelty to a child you should interfere, and try to make your interference effective.

If you see any one breaking the law of the country, you should inform the authorities.

C.W.L.—A great deal has been said about that passage, and various people have taken exception to it. This is curious because, as a matter of fact, if you conceal a crime you become an accessory to that crime, before the fact or after the fact as the case may be, and you are so regarded by the law. People say, "But are we to spy upon others to see whether they are breaking the law?" Certainly not; you are not constituted a detective to go and find people breaking the law.

Law gives cohesion to a country; it establishes order for the good of all; therefore it is the duty of every citizen to uphold it. Still, one must use common sense. No one is expected to obey obsolete laws, though they remain on the statute book. Nor need anyone go out of his way to report minor delinquencies. Let us take, for example, the question of trespassing on another man's property; if you see a man taking a short cut across another man's park, I do not think you are thereby bound to go and report the matter. If you are asked about it, then, of course, you must say so. Or take the law against smuggling things through the customs. I should say a good citizen would obey that law, and not think of endeavouring to smuggle in goods of any sort. At the same time it seems to me that if some fellow-traveller is trying to smuggle some cigars or something like that through, it is not exactly my business to inform the authorities, because that is not a matter of the breaking of a law which injures anyone else.

I would not myself break it, because I think that when a law is made it should be obeyed, and if it is a bad law we should endeavour to use constitutional means to change it. We have in some cases laws which it would be difficult to obey. In some places there is a law of compulsory vaccination. Personally I should object to being vaccinated, and should refuse to submit to it except by major force. I should be prepared if necessary to go to prison rather than have that done, because it is an evil thing. These are all matters on which each person must pass his own judgment.

In India it is especially laid down what crimes must be reported if seen—they are, of course, all the serious crimes. If one were to see a murder or a robbery it would be one's duty to report it, but with regard to a host of minor things, one does not legally, in India, make oneself an accessory by not reporting them.

A.B.—It is the duty of every citizen, whenever he sees the law being broken to put a stop to the wrong,

This is one of the elementary duties of citizenship. Yet the other day an objection was raised to this teaching. A student came to me and said that here was a thing in the book which he could not accept; it seemed to him to suggest a general prying about, a spying into other people's affairs. Of course, it intends nothing of the kind; but when you see the law broken you must interfere, because the law is what gives cohesion to a country, establishing and preserving order, and binding its people together. It is the duty of every citizen therefore to uphold it; no one has the right to conceal a crime which he knows is going to be committed, and if he does so he becomes a partaker in it. This is so generally recognized that a person who knows of the crime and fails to report it is held legally to be an accessory to it and is punishable by law. I could only suppose that my objector had not considered what he was saying, for a country whose citizens do not recognize this simple duty and act accordingly goes down, because of the lack of public spirit.

If you are placed in charge of another person in order to teach him, it may become your duty gently to tell him of his faults.

C.W.L.—That is obvious. A child, a pupil, or a servant is placed in our charge because we are older and wiser. If we do not tell him of any faults which he commits he is losing the advantage of our wisdom and experience; therefore we should be so far failing in our duty towards him, neglecting to do that which we are placed there to do.

Except in such cases, mind your own business, and learn the virtue of silence.

A.B.—Think how different society would be if this were practised! Instead of being constantly on guard against his neighbours, a man could live his own life freely and openly, for people would leave one another alone to act as each might think best, and mutual tolerance and goodwill would replace interference and criticism. Our fifth race, which dominates the world to-day, is aggressive, combative and critical, but we have to try to live the life of the future, that of the sixth root-race, which is to be reached by tolerance and active goodwill. This will lead on to the general idea of brotherhood, on which the sixth race will be established.

C.W.L.—It does not seem difficult to mind one's own business, but very few people do it. What is meant here is that a general attitude of tolerance and goodwill should replace what is so painfully common at present—the spirit of interference and criticism. If a person does something quite unusual I am afraid many people fly to the conclusion that he has some nefarious reason for so doing. It does not at all follow; he may have his own private reason, and anyhow, unless he is doing something clearly wrong or interfering with others, we should let him go his way and do what he will.

Like some of the other common present-day faults, this springs largely from an excess of our fifth race and fifth sub-race qualities. Our race is developing the critical faculties of the lower mind, and that carried to excess makes us liable to be aggressive, combative and argumentative. Those who aim at occult progress are supposed, however, to develop the next quality—buddhi, the unifying quality, that which gives synthesis rather than analysis, and tries to see the points of contact rather than those of difference. The development of that will be the business of the sixth root-race, and also, in a subsidiary way, of the sixth sub-race, which is now dawning in America, Australia and some other places.

In the Theosophical Society we uphold the idea of brotherhood, and this is a way of practising it—find something not to blame but to praise. Something to praise as well as something to blame can be found in everybody and in everything, if you look for it; and there is every reason why we should concentrate our attention on the good qualities, not on the blameworthy things. We might try thus to bring down the side of the balance a little. We can afford to leave the fault-finding to the rest of the world, who are certain to continue to attend to the business of blaming, and will do it with more gusto than we possibly could. It is a valuable exercise to pick out the good things, because until we begin to look for them we do not really understand how many good things there are in everybody. When we do this, we shall begin to find all kinds of beautiful qualities in people whom we have been regarding very unfairly. It is easy to form an opinion of people whom we do not know well, based on only one or two things: we saw them looking angry, and therefore think of them as irritable people; or we saw them one day looking discontended, and so put them down as usually that sort of people. Probably we have simply stumbled upon them just at an awkward moment, and their life in general may not be at all coloured as we conceive it to be.

If we must err now and then, let it be on the good side; give a person credit for a little bit more than his due—that will not hurt him or us. A Master once said, "In everyone there is good, and in everyone there is evil." Beware of thinking of a person as bad; for you may expect him to act badly, and then, when he does not do so, you may be disappointed, because it shows that you were wrong in your judgment. It is much better to think too well of hundreds of people than to think too badly of even one. Let us live the buddhic life at least to the extent that we look for the things which are good and not for the things which are evil, not only in the interests of truth and justice, but because we know that our thoughts are powerful, that to think of another as bad tends to make him so, but to see the good in him diminishes the evil and helps that good to grow.

One of the chief things we have to learn is not to let the lower mind run away with us and make us attribute unworthy motives to other people. Our experience of human nature has shown us that it is a fallible thing, that people are not always swayed by unselfish considerations; therefore the natural tendency is to look for something selfish in the way of a motive, rather than for something high. But we must not allow ourselves to be dragged down to that level of suspicion and unkindness; not only for our own sakes, but for the welfare of others it is necessary that we should look first for the highest motive, and, even when we do not see it, should give the person credit for meaning well. When we think of a bad motive we are intensifying it by our thought, for the mind is very receptive. If a man has slipped back a little, and we give him the credit of meaning well, he will soon become ashamed of the lower motive and will replace it by the higher. Besides, in attributing the best possible motives to all our friends we are sure to be right in nine cases out of ten. Of course, the outer world in its cynical way will say to the man who does this. "You are a simple fellow." It is better to be the simple fellow who does good in this way than the clever one who cannot think well of anybody.

Practically no one is intentionally wicked. One should therefore avoid the common mistake of thinking that those who do what we should call wrong, do so through wicked motives. We must guard against doing injustice by supposing, for instance, that those who eat meat think anything about it, and are doing what they know to be wrong. They are not usually acting against their better feelings; they are following the custom without thinking about it. Such people are quite good; indeed, good people burnt one another in the middle ages, with no more thought. But one of the Masters said: "Our object is not to make good people, but to make mighty spiritual powers for good."

PART IV

GOOD CONDUCT

CHAPTER 1

CONTROL OF MIND

The six points of Conduct which are specially required are given by the Master as :

1. Self-control as to the Mind.
2. Self-control in Action.
3. Tolerance.
4. Cheerfulness.
5. One-pointedness.
6. Confidence.

[I know some of these are often translated differently, as are the names of the Qualifications ; but in all cases I am using the names which the Master Himself employed when explaining them to me.]

A.B.—As Alcyone says, the Master's translation of some of these qualifications is a little different from that to which we have been accustomed. The first three are not unlike the translations that I have been using for a great many years, but the last three are somewhat dissimilar, though of course the essential meanings are unaltered. The third of these points of good conduct

I have always translated "tolerance", as the Master does here, but that rendering is not acceptable, I know, to a good many people. The Sanskrit word is *uparati*, which means literally "cessation". We take the cessation as referring to qualities like criticism and discontent, and the positive side of this virtue is therefore tolerance.

The fourth, *titikshā*, I have always called endurance; of course, the idea of cheerfulness is the same, for a person who has endurance will necessarily be cheerful. Here the Master, who is—if I may venture to use the word—particularly sunny, gives the translation that emphasizes this aspect of the quality, and it is well that all should meditate upon it. Then comes one-pointedness; that is the Sanskrit *samādhāna* which I have given as balance—and again the idea is the same, for the one-pointed person is balanced, and vice versa. Lastly comes *shraddhā*, which I have always called faith. Here it is confidence; but once more the meaning is unchanged because I have always defined faith as utter belief in the God within and in the Master. It is well to note the differences as well as the likenesses, because these help us to grasp the meaning better.

1. *Self-control as to the Mind.*—The Qualification of Desirelessness shows that the astral body must be controlled; this shows the same thing as to the mental body. It means control of temper, so that you may feel no anger or impatience; of the mind itself, so that the thought may always be

calm and unruffled; and (through the mind) of the nerves, so that they may be as little irritable as possible.

C.W.L.—Control of temper is precisely one of the things which are difficult for us, because we are trying the new experiment of raising ourselves in evolution (which means much refining all our vehicles and making them more and more sensitive) while remaining in the midst of the life of the world. Our victory is so much the greater because of these difficulties, the overcoming of which shows that we have progressed further in strength of will than has the monk or the hermit.

Sometimes people succeed in weeding out the angry feeling, and yet find it difficult to control the outer vehicles entirely; there may still be a movement of impatience when really the feeling which used to be behind it has absolutely gone. It is not so bad as having the feeling and not showing it, but we must get rid even of that, because it misleads other people. If you look clairvoyantly at the astral body of the average man in the street, you will see that the whole thing is a swirling mass, and instead of having definite striations, and colours clearly marked and circulating as they should be, it has on the surface fifty or sixty little vortices or whirl-pools in violent agitation, each of which, because of the rapidity of its motion, makes a hard knot resembling a wart. If you examine these vortices you will find that they all arose in the little outbursts of temper, or small worries, or feelings of offence, jealousy, envy and perhaps even hatred, which the man has had some time within the last forty-eight hours. Larger vortices, lasting much longer, are made when the man renews a number of times the same kind of thought about the same person.

While a man is in that state it is quite impossible for him to think with the clearness and definiteness that might otherwise be his; if he wants to think or write on any subject, his views are bound to be coloured and distorted by these vortices, even though he has forgotten the feelings which caused them. Men forget their feelings of annoyance, and do not realize that the effect is still there; most of them keep up their stock of vortices at much the same level.

Prejudice shows itself in this way very clearly to astral and mental clairvoyance. The matter of the mental body ought to be in rapid circulation; not all over it, but in certain zones or areas. Broadly speaking, it tends to arrange itself according to its density, so that the coarser matter, while circulating to some extent all over the body, tends to gravitate towards the lower part of the ovoid, so that people who have a preponderance of selfish thought and feeling look like eggs standing on their larger ends, while those who are notably unselfish or occultly developed resemble eggs standing on their smaller ends. There are four zones or slices in the mental body, just as there are departments in the brain which deal with particular types of thought.

Imagine a man who is very illiberal in his religious thought. The mental matter, instead of flowing freely in that particular department, piles up until it actually projects and becomes a heap, and begins to fester and decay. As his thought on religious subjects must pass through this division of the mental body, it can never be true, because its vibrations are overcome by what is literally the mental disease that has fastened upon it. His view is bound to be prejudiced, until he sets to work and cures himself by deliberate control and purification of the mind. Only then may he learn to think truly—that is, to see things as does the Deity, who knows absolutely the whole of His system exactly as it is.

Prejudices are not necessarily against persons or things; quite often they are in favour. Even so, they are a form of untruth, and they show the same corruption in the aura. One of the commonest cases is that of the mother who cannot believe that there ever before was such a baby as hers since the world began. Another example is that of the artist who is incapable of seeing good in any other school of art than his own.

All those things, from the point of view of psychic force, are like open sores, through which the will-power of the man is leaking away all the time. That being the condition of the average man, when you get a person who is by nature a worrier, you have naturally a still worse case—a person who is all one sore, and has no force left, for all is spent. If we want to conserve our energies and do good work with them, as must be the case if we are to be occultists, the first thing to do is to check all these sources of waste. Suppose we want to put out a fire; we must have a jet of water. It must be pumped at high pressure, and there must be absolutely no leak in the water cylinders and pipes. That means for us calmness and control of mind.

The average man seems to have little or no will-power; when trouble comes he simply lies down under it and groans and complains, instead of directing his will to deal definitely with it. There are two reasons for this weakness. The degree of power that comes down into any man varies according to his realization of the true Self—the extent to which the One Self, the Deity, is unfolded within him. In essential nature we are all of equal strength, but men differ in the extent to which they have unfolded the divine strength in themselves. The ordinary man has not developed much of that, and even what he has he is wasting.

Many among us would like to realize more fully the presence of the Master, and to bring various other good influences from the higher planes down into the physical brain. Such influences must come down through these different vehicles—must be reflected from one to another. Look at the reflection of a group of trees on the surface of a lake or river. If it is quite calm we get a perfect picture, in which every leaf is clearly seen; but the least ripple distorts the picture altogether. If there is a storm, it is completely destroyed. That is exactly true with regard to the astral and mental bodies. They must be kept calm and held still if through them any true or valuable influences are to come from above. People constantly ask, "Why don't we remember all that we do in our sleep?" That is one of the reasons—because their vehicles are not quiet enough. Now and again they may become calm enough to bring something through, but even then the impression is usually somewhat distorted, because the medium is not perfectly clear. It is like looking at something through cheap bottle-glass instead of good plate-glass; it altogether alters the proportions of things.

When we have become calm we can work in the midst of disturbance and trouble, but of course it is always a strain to hold the bodies calm under these conditions. It is so great a strain that some people cannot do it at all; but they must gradually acquire strength.

The occultist learns through self-control to work on two planes at once, that is, to be partly out of his body at the same time that he is working on the physical plane; so that while he is writing or speaking he may be doing other things with his astral body. I have heard it said, for example, that when I have been lecturing various people in the audience have seen astral entities standing on the platform and coming up and speaking to me. That is correctly seen so far; it is often the case that they come up in that way, desiring answers to questions or wanting something done, while the lecture still goes on. That is only a small and passing example, but often there are much more serious pieces of work to be done, in which the occultist uses his consciousness in that complicated way.

This double concentration is performed to some extent quite frequently in ordinary life also. Many ladies can knit and go on talking, because the knitting is a mechanical action to them. I had much to do once with one of the great banks in London, and I have seen there men, who were used to it, rapidly and steadily adding up long columns of figures, and at the same time singing a song for the entertainment of their fellows. I must admit that would be impossible to me, but I have seen it done over and over again.

A.B.—In the section on desirelessness the Master has dealt with the control of the astral body and its numerous forms of desire, and in the section on discrimination He spoke much about truth, which involves the purification of the mental body. Now He deals further with control of the mind, and also of the emotions; an emotion is a combination of thought and desire. Emotions are desires which are penetrated by the thought-element. In other words, emotion is desire mingled with thought. When the Master speaks here of control of temper, He is speaking of emotion, because impatience and similar feelings proceed partly from the desire-body and partly from the mental body. The would-be occultist must certainly not let himself be carried away by temper, for until the control of that is gained, so that his emotions cannot be upset, he will not be able to see definitely or clearly. The vibrations of emotion will arouse corresponding excitement in purely mental matter, and all the man's thoughts will be disturbed and distorted, so that he will not be able to see things correctly.

The Master then says that the thought itself must be calm and unruffled; this is necessary because only in such conditions can influences be thrown down into the lower mind from the higher. I think it is in *The Occult World* that Mr. Sinnett quoted a letter from the same Teacher in which He told him that if he wanted to write usefully he must keep the mind calm, and then thoughts from the higher mind would reflect themselves in it, as mountains in a calm lake.

It is a good plan, if you want to write a letter on a serious subject—about Theosophy, for instance—or to produce an article, to sit quiet for some minutes, steadying yourself before you begin to work. This is not a waste of time, for when you begin writing you will then find that your thought will flow quietly and without effort, and you will not have to pause in the middle and consider how you are to go on. This will be so because the higher mind is being reflected in the mirror of the lower. This practice is especially important for those who cannot yet shut off the outer things at will.

One may make use of outer disturbances to practise concentration. As a child I was made to learn my lessons in a room where other children were being taught different things, so gradually I acquired the power to work at a task of my own while all sorts of other activities were going on around me. In consequence I have now the power to work undisturbed by what may be happening near by, though I must admit that I find it difficult to perform calculations under those circumstances. I have always felt grateful to my teacher, Miss Marryat, for this. The power comes with practice, and is then useful in a variety of ways. I found, for example, that I could also use it when partly out of my body, as when I was writing one of the lives of Alcyone.

In the Indian household this faculty is developed as a matter of course, because there it is customary for people to do different things in the same room, and there are generally children running about and numerous other small happenings. In the village school, and in the home too, a number of children are taught a variety of things at the same time, all reading aloud, each his own special subject, while their teacher follows it all, and corrects their mistakes as they are made. I do not think it is an ideal method of teaching any particular subject, but the children are learning how to concentrate, and that will be very useful to them afterwards.

If you can get that power of concentration so much the better; hence, if you have to live amid noise, do not complain of it but profit by it. That is the way in which the student of occultism works. I mention this especially, because it is by such means that occultists are made. To learn to work under difficult conditions means progress. That is one of the reasons why some of us have made progress, and others not so much. I personally have always tried to take everything as it came, instead of complaining. By this means one seizes every opportunity.

This last is difficult, because when you try to prepare yourself for the Path, you cannot help making your body more sensitive, so that its nerves are easily disturbed by a sound or a shock,

and feel any pressure acutely; but you must do your best.

A.B.—The Master says that it is difficult to control the nerves. That is so because the physical body is that over which thought has the least power. You can affect your astral and mental bodies comparatively easily, because they are made of finer matter, more affected by thought; but the heavier physical matter is much less responsive and therefore harder to control. Yet it must be mastered in time.

The pupil must be sensitive, and yet have the body and nerves completely under control. The greater the sensitiveness becomes, the more difficult is the task; there are many noises which pass unheeded by an ordinary person which are torture to one who is sensitive. There are certain diseases which produce excessive sensibility of the nerves; in such a case the bark of a dog may throw a person into convulsions. That example is sufficient to show how acutely sensitive the nerves may become.

The nerves of an occult student are not diseased—if they were, he would not be under training—but he is like a tense string, vibrating to the least touch. His nerves thus become so sensitive that he has to use great force of will in order to prevent irritability. The strain on the body under these circumstances may become so great that in some cases, like Madame Blavatsky's, it may sometimes be wiser to let go, to allow the body to go on as it likes at times, lest it should go to pieces altogether. It was necessary that she should keep her body for the work that she had to do, so she could not allow the strain on it to reach the breaking point. This, however, was an exceptional case; the aspirant who wants to follow the Master's teaching must do as He says here, and try as hard as he can to gain control over his nerves. He may fail again and again—that does not matter. The Master's last words on the subject are: "You must do your best." That is all that He asks, so do not let failures discourage you, but go on doing your best.

Sometimes a similar disturbed condition is set up from within, because of an exaggeration of scrupulousness and conscientiousness, into which the most earnest students are liable to fall. There are two tendencies among aspirants; one is to be careless, the other to torment oneself. In the second case conscience may reach a point when its condition is like that of the overstrained nerve. Thus it often happens to the best class of students to make too much fuss over little failures. Do not sit down and brood over such things till they have grown to the dimensions of a serious crime. Make your path between these two extremes. You cannot be too scrupulous before the event, but you may easily make yourself too unhappy afterwards. Do not brood over your faults and failures. Only look at them to see the reason why you failed, and then try again. So doing, you will starve out the tendencies which led you into them; whereas thinking about them only gives them new strength.

C.W.L.—The physical body is that over which the will has the least power. People say, "Oh yes, you can learn to do a thing with your physical body, you may even control your feelings but it is a much harder thing to control your thoughts." I know it is a popular idea that of all things that is the most difficult. In one way it is; because the mental matter is finer and more active, there is much more to control in the way of motion and of initiative. On the other hand, the mental body is much nearer to the ego within, and therefore more under his control: he has greater forces with which to grasp the mental matter and deal with it, than he has down here in the physical plane; and also the physical matter is less responsive. People think it easier, because they are in the habit of controlling the physical body, but not the mental body.

It is often said that you can control pain on the physical plane, but cannot ignore mental suffering. Really, exactly the contrary is true. The mental or emotional suffering ceases to exist if one grasps it and just puts it away from oneself, but actual severe physical pain is most difficult to ignore, though it can be very largely diminished by removing from it the mental element. The Christian Scientist does that by declaring that there is no pain; he leaves only the physical side of it, and that is comparatively small.

We should learn to control the mind so that the mental part of physical suffering is eliminated, because as pupils of the Masters we have to make ourselves exceedingly sensitive. Then it becomes painful to sit near a man who drinks alcohol, smokes tobacco and eats meat. It is positive torture to go about in a city, along a business street, with its tremendous roar of all sorts of hideous noises. It goes all through the physical body and makes it shiver, but if one thinks about it, that makes it much worse; whereas if no notice is taken at least one feels it less. The pupil who is trying to reach the higher planes, has to learn to eliminate the mental part of it, and not import into it any thought that makes it stronger.

Those who are practising meditation will find that they are more sensitive than the people who do not meditate, and because of that the strain on the physical body is sometimes enormous. One frequently hears it said that Madame Blavatsky used sometimes to have outbursts of temper. There was a very good reason for that, certainly, as she had a very unfortunate physical body; there was probably never an hour when she had not some acute physical suffering. The body was old, broken down and worn out, but it was the only body available for the particular work she had to do, and she had to keep it; she could not throw it away, as many of us might do. The opportunity was once offered to her to do that, but she said: "No, I will hold it till I have finished *The Secret Doctrine*"—the work in which she was engaged. That meant that the physical body was in a condition of terrible strain, and sometimes for relief she let it do what it liked. Of course, many people did not understand, but we around her came to know that these things did not mean much. We had many curious instances of that. For example, she would be in a wild tirade, apparently quite angry about some trifling thing, but while the newer people who did not know shrank away from her in fear, we discovered that if in the middle of that excitement some one suddenly asked her a philosophical question, the whole thing dropped away, was cut off as you might cut a thread with a pair of scissors; immediately the rage disappeared and she proceeded to answer the question. A person in an ordinary rage could not have done that. Many people misunderstood her and turned away, but I know quite well that she had sometimes to let go or her body would have gone to pieces.

> The calm mind means also courage, so that you may face without fear the trials and difficulties of the Path.

A.B.—Courage is a quality upon which immense stress is laid in the Hindu Scriptures. It has its root in a recognition of the unity of the Self. "What fear, what delusion is there for one who has seen the Self?" it is asked; and the phrase is used: "the fearless Brahman." In *In the Outer Court* I recommended students to meditate upon the ideal character, using the list of qualities given by Shrī Krishna at the beginning of the sixteenth chapter of the *Gītā*. The first quality that He mentions there is *abhayam*, fearlessness or courage.

Courage grows out of the realization that you are the divine Self within, and not your outer vehicles, which are the only part of you that can be hurt. All differences of power between people arise from the degrees of strength which the Self within has unfolded. Essentially we are all equally strong, but there are stages of evolution. When you realize that you are yourself divine, you know that your weakness or power depends upon the amount of unfolded strength of the Self within you; so your refuge, when you feel fear, is to call out the power from within.

This realization of yourself as the Self is one of the things that ought to come to you through your meditation. Those who do morning meditation should include in it an effort to realize the Self; some of the strength they gain through that effort should then remain with them throughout the day. That will help to give them the courage that is needed for progress upon the Path. On it there are many difficulties which call for fortitude and endurance, if they are to be met and overcome, and these qualities are forms of courage. There is a novelty in things on the Path which also calls for courage. I know of no way of acquiring this quality except by realizing the Self.

C.W.L.—Much stress is laid upon the necessity of courage in all systems of occult training. If a man enters upon the Path he will have to face misrepresentation, calumny and misunderstanding. That has always been the lot of those who try to raise themselves above their fellows. Moral strength is necessary to meet that, and to enable a man to maintain his position and do what he thinks right, whatever those around him may think or say or do. Such strength is required to carry out the teaching as given in this book—and plenty of fortitude and determination as well.

Actual physical courage is needed, too. There are many dangers and difficulties on the Path not by any means symbolical, or on higher planes only; tests of bravery and endurance do come to us in the course of our progress, and we must be prepared for them. A man who is faint-hearted will not make progress on this Path, where is required, not merely goodness, but strength of character that cannot be shaken by the unaccustomed or the alarming.

I knew an occult society in England which tried for many weeks with various invocations to raise certain kinds of spooks, and at last they did raise something; but nobody stayed long enough to see what it was. Similarly, people try to obtain results on higher planes, but as soon as they get them they are afraid. The first time a man goes out of his body in waking consciousness, he may feel a little alarmed and may have a passing wonder whether he will get back again or not. He must realize that it does not much matter whether he does or not. He is used to certain limitations, and when those suddenly drop away, he is quite likely to feel that there is no certain base left to stand upon. We shall find as we go further on, that courage—plain, straightforward bravery—is a thing which is very much needed. All sorts of forces have to be encountered; it is not child's play.

When we realize and remember that we are one with the Divine, we fear nothing; but sometimes when sudden danger arises, men forget that and shrink back. The Self within is utterly unaffected, utterly uninjured, by any of the passing things, so if we can realize that we are that Self and not the outer vehicles, we shall have no fear. If ever fear of any sort is felt, the thing to do is to call up more power from within, not to appeal for help from some one from without. The common Christian teaching on that subject has been very unfortunate. They tell people always to take refuge in prayer, which literally means asking, and should not be applied to the highest form of aspiration, as it so often is. The word prayer comes from the Latin *precari*, which means to ask—nothing but that. If we hold that God is all-good, we should follow the advice of the Lord Buddha: "Do not complain and cry and pray, but open your eyes and see. The light is all about you, if you will only take the bandages from your eyes and look. And it is so wonderful, so beautiful, so far beyond anything man could think of or pray for, and it is for ever and ever."

I know that many people have the habit of calling upon the Master for help when they find themselves in difficulties. We may be sure that the Master's thought is always near, and assuredly He can be reached; but why should we trouble Him for something that we ought to be able to do ourselves? It is true that we may call upon Him if we wish; but surely if we can call upon the God within, and bring out more of that, we shall thus draw nearer to the Master than we could by calling feebly on Him for help. One does not question a man's right to do that; but knowing how the Master is always occupied in work for the world, surely we should not wish to call upon Him while there was any possible resource left to us whereby we could, by any means, do the thing for ourselves. To fail in doing it is to fail in faith; it is a want of confidence not in ourselves only, but in the divine power.

The practice of meditation also ought to prepare one to meet emergencies, so as not to be upset by them. Those who have grasped the inner laws should remain calm and composed whatever may come, realizing that to do so is a necessary condition of real progress, and that the shock and upsetting which result from an hysterical outburst will leave their scars on the sensitive vehicles of a pupil for a long time afterwards.

> **It means also steadiness, so that you may make light of the troubles which come into every one's life, and avoid the incessant worry over little things in which many people spend most of their time.**

A.B.—Steadiness is the next requirement mentioned by the Master; it is the quality that is necessary so that the pupil may not be blown about by every wind that comes. Such a dependence upon outside things gives rise to endless worry because the man is then not in control of his own affairs, and so cannot decide upon a definite line of work. It is worry that wears people out, not work. Worry is the going over and over again of a certain painful sequence of thought. It is difficult for a timorous person to prevent himself from falling into this habit in one or other of its different forms.

In some cases there is a tendency of the mind to dramatize, and then to live in its self-created drama. It is a thing I used to do to some extent myself. I am mentioning this and similar personal experiences because I think they will make what I have to tell you more living and useful than merely abstract thought would be. Most aspirants have probably done some such mental dramatization, for we are all made up in much the same way. I used to imagine that some friend of mine must have been hurt by some word or action of mine; I then imagined my next meeting with that person—the first words, the whole ensuing conversation. When we actually did meet the whole thing failed to work out as I had anticipated, because the first remark of my friend was always something quite different from what I had imagined. Sometimes people conjure up in this way an unpleasant scene, and imagine how they will act in the trying conditions they have invented; and at last they arrive at a painful condition of mind upon which they expend much feeling and emotion. Nothing of all this has as yet taken place, and probably none of it ever will: it has all been a pure waste of force.

All this sort of thing is merely unnecessary trouble, and it weakens the mental and emotional nature. The only way to get rid of this habit is to make yourself stand outside the scene, and observe whether the first thought in the series is a thing over which you have any control or not. If you have, then control it; if you have not, it is of no use to think about it till it comes, and this, after all, it may never do. It is useless to let your mind brood over possible happenings in the future. It is equally useless to let it run over and over the things which have happened; you cannot alter past events, so it is palpably useless to worry about them.

Many good people make their lives a burden by brooding over the past, thinking; "Perhaps if I had, or had not, done so and so, this trouble would never have happened." Suppose that is true, the thing is done, and no thinking will change the past. People lie awake at night and worry all day over unalterable past things or possible future eventualities. This action of the mind is like the racing of an engine or of the heart when normal resistance is lacking, which injures both heart and engine much more than work does. Recognize the futility and the positive harmfulness of such mental racing, and you will stop it, and learn to put out your strength effectively instead. It is pure silliness; it comes down to that. It is a thing which nearly everybody does, but ought not to do, and the would-be disciple simply must not do it.

C.W.L.—Of all mental difficulties, worry is the worst to deal with. It is an absolute bar to anything like proper progress. It is impossible in that condition to bring oneself into the state of mind for meditation. Some people worry about the past, others about the future, and by the time they have dropped one worry they have picked up another to take its place, and so they are never in a state of calm, and cannot hope to meditate with any prospect of success.

The best cure for it is to replace the trouble by a thought of the Master, but it takes unusual strength to do that. Suddenly to try to impose calmness on an astral body or a mental body in that condition is like trying to press down with a board the waves of the sea during a storm. Often the best thing to do is to get up and do something physical—weed the garden or go for a bicycle ride. There can be no permanent calm until the vehicles move rhythmically together; then all these other practices may be undertaken with some reasonable chance of success.

Often people worry over their own defects. Everyone finds himself falling into faults and failings now and then; it would be better not to do so, but that is hardly to be expected yet, for if we had no faults and failings we should all be Adepts. It is, of course, wrong to be careless about these things and think they do not matter, but it is also equally wrong to worry unnecessarily about them. In worry the mind races madly round and round, to no purpose. If you have been on board a steamer in rough weather you may remember that now and then the screw rises out of the water and races madly in the air. It is just a matter of mechanics that that does far more harm to the machinery than a great amount of regular work. That is exactly like worry.

Periodically troubles arise in our Society. I have seen a good many of them in my time. I remember very well the excitement over the Coulomb affair in

1884, and how many Theosophists were greatly disturbed and worried over that, and their faith in Theosophy was in some cases quite destroyed, because they supposed that Madame Blavatsky had been playing tricks upon them. That really, had nothing to do with the case. Our faith in Theosophy does not rest upon the statements of Madame Blavatsky or anyone else, but upon the fact that it is a perfect and satisfactory system which has been given to us, and that remains true even if it had been the case that Madame Blavatsky had deceived them—which was not so, of course. If people rest their belief on personal grounds, it can easily be shaken, but if our belief is based upon principles which we understand, it would remain unshaken even if a trusted leader did suddenly fail us.

> **The Master teaches that it does not matter in the least what happens to a man from the outside: sorrows, troubles, sicknesses, losses—all these must be as nothing to him, and must not be allowed to affect the calmness of his mind, They are the result of past actions, and when they come you must bear them cheerfully, remembering that all evil is transitory, and that your duty is to remain always joyous and serene. They belong to your previous lives, not to this ; you cannot alter them, so it is useless to trouble about them.**

A.B.—Here the Master gives a reason for not worrying which, I fear, many people will not appreciate. He says that it does not in the least matter what happens to a man from the outside. The things which come to us in this way are quite beyond our control, because we ourselves made them in the past; they are our karma.

This does not mean, however, that there is nothing that we can now do in the matter. On the contrary, we can do much; we can meet them in the right way, and thus enormously modify their effect upon us. To do this is like changing a direct blow, which has force enough to knock one down, into a glancing blow, which is comparatively unimportant. It all depends upon changing the angle at which you meet to blow. If you meet every affliction that comes to you with the feeling: "This is only the payment of a debt; it is well to clear it off," then the sorrow will weigh upon you but lightly. A man who knows how to meet life will be calm and happy in the midst of difficulties, while one who does not know may be crushed by troubles that are half imagination.

How much of the trouble and pain that you feel is really caused by the mind, you can test for yourself when you are suffering physically; if you will then stand outside it all, as it were, you will find that the suffering will diminish very much. This fact can be realized in another way, by considering the state of the animals. An animal that has broken its leg will eat quite comfortably, dragging its wounded leg behind it. Now, that is a thing which a man could not do, yet a horse will do it, and the horse, so physiologists tell us, has an even more delicate nervous system than man has, so that its nerves are more sensitive to pain than his. Do not misunderstand me, and think that I say that animals do not suffer, or that their sufferings do not matter. Quite the reverse. But man intensifies his own suffering and prolongs it, because of the way in which he dwells upon it in his mind.

If you learn to check the effects of pain on your astral body, you will know how to diminish the pain itself very greatly. Those who call themselves Christian Scientists thus reduce pain very much, because they take away the mental element that usually mingles with it and increases it. I have had also some experience of the same thing, when I have had to lecture while suffering acutely physically; the result has been that during the time of lecturing I did not feel the pain. Why? Simply because my mind was entirely engrossed by my lecture. If you could completely withdraw your mind from paying attention to the physical body, as you would do perforce were you lecturing, any physical hurt which you might have been feeling would disappear to a large extent. If you have complete control over your mind you can do that, and so leave the outside things to affect only the outside body. People often do it under sufficient stimulus. Sometimes the soldier on the battlefield does not feel his wound until the excitement of fighting is over; and certainly some of the religious martyrs did not feel the flames around them, on account of the ecstasy that they felt in suffering for their Lord. Similarly, if a child meets with an accident, its mother will forget all about any pain that she herself may be suffering, as she rushes forward to rescue and help her child.

It is possible to learn this sort of control without the stimulus, and then you can largely neutralize the effect of any pain upon your astral and mental bodies. I do not say that it is easy to do this, but that it can be done. Personally, I do not think it is worth while to use a great deal of force, or make a very special effort, to obtain so little result as the stopping of a mere physical pain. Instead of turning your mind to the service of the body, as most people do, it is better to turn it away and occupy it with something profitable. If you take up the right attitude to life you will see that these outside things do not matter, and you will leave them alone to have their effect only on the outside of yourself. They have to be gone through, and their only value lies in the strength which you gain through them. By looking at them in this way you will gain great peace of mind.

All evil is transitory. You will realize that this is so if you look at the larger cycle of your life, and realize your past, not in detail, for details do not matter, but in its general sweep and trend. If one realizes how often before one has been through these things that grieve and trouble one—friends taken away by death, sicknesses, losses, troubles of all sorts—they sink into something approaching their true relative insignificance. It is important to make this effort, because the present is so insistent that it blocks out with its petty anxieties the deeper knowledge. The realization of your own long past will make you stronger, and then when some misfortune occurs you will think, "Why trouble? It will pass!"

I feel sure that I could not lead my present life at all if I did not refuse to bother, and to react to circumstances. Troubles of all sorts come pouring in daily, and if I reacted to them I should be dead in a week. In the past I have come through many movements of the kind with which I am now connected, and have found that they are always accompanied by turmoil. It is better not to anticipate trouble, but to attend to it when it comes, and afterwards to put it aside and forget all about it.

Your duty, says the Master, is to remain always joyous and serene. A warning was once given against casting dross into the crucible of discipleship. The evil and danger of doing so is carried to an extreme point at a place such as Adyar, where any dross—any form of trouble, suspicion, anxiety, doubt, and the like—acquires much more force than that of the person who sent it out. If sometimes you cannot at once rid yourself of depression, vexation, or any other undesirable feeling that you may have, then at least keep it to yourself. Do not let it pour out and infect the atmosphere, and make things harder for others. After training yourself in this way you will look back with surprise at your former condition, and wonder how such trifles could ever have troubled you as they did.

C.W.L.—The man who knows remains calm and happy even in the midst of what would be very serious trouble to other people. The man who does not know is very often crushed by the trouble, because of his own attitude with regard to it. There is a vast deal of imagination at the back of our sufferings. The real amount of payment exacted by karma is often small; but by taking it wrongly people frequently double their necessary suffering or even multiply it by ten; it is not fair to charge that to ancient karma, for it is the karma of the present foolish action—what Mr. Sinnett called "ready-money karma."

The amount of the debt to be paid cannot be altered —the karma which comes calls for a certain amount of suffering on our part; but as it can be increased, so it can be decreased. By an effort of our own we can apply new force, and change what would be the effect of a direct blow into one that glances off, as our President has expressed it, so that it will be much less felt. Every such putting forth of strength is the introduction of a new force into the case; therefore there is in it no sort of injustice, or interference with karma. That force which otherwise would have been spent in some other way is now spent in modifying the blow.

All evil is necessarily transitory. There was a Persian king who took as his motto: "Even this will pass away." It is a good motto, because it applies equally to pleasure or to suffering, and to good or evil fortune, whichever may be dominant at the time. The only things that do not pass are the real progress and the bliss which come from within—those remain for ever. Whatever is our suffering now, it will pass; we have had suffering before in other lives and have passed through it. If this can be realized it will help very much. Things that troubled us early in life seem quite unimportant now. We say: "Dear me, those things were not of any importance; I wonder why I worried so much about them?" The wise man learns from looking back. He says: "Here are these other things which are worrying me now, surely they are just as unimportant." Of course they are, but it takes a wise man to make that deduction.

Think rather of what you are doing now, which will make the events of your next life, for that you *can* alter.

C.W.L.—Your next life will depend very largely upon the karma you make in this. More than that—the World-Teacher will come soon; things are moving fast now; the force which is being outpoured is tremendous, and because all that plays round us to some extent, we who are trying to prepare for His coming may modify not only our next life but the remaining part of this.

The karma of the pupil engaged in this work is more intense than that of most other people. There are probably many things which the man of the world does constantly and may do without much harm resulting in any way; but if these things were done by those who are nearing the Path, they would be very decidedly harmful. In the case of a disciple, whatever happens to him happens to the Master, because He has made him part of Himself. "No man liveth to himself, and no man dieth to himself"; this is true of everyone, but those who are drawn to the feet of the great Masters must be doubly careful. Especially anything whatever which puts difficulties in the way of a fellow-student in occult matters is a thing which makes serious karma.

> Never allow yourself to feel sad or depressed. Depression is wrong, because it infects others and makes their lives harder, which you have no right to do. Therefore if ever it comes to you, throw it off at once.

C.W.L.—Anybody who suffers from serious depression will probably shake his head and say: "That is very good advice, if one could only take it." But, as I said before, a thought of its effect upon others will give a man strength to throw it off when nothing else would. Depression is wrong, because it affects one's fellow-students and other people, and makes their way harder. Nothing can affect us that does not come from ourselves—from our own past lives, through our own karma. One may learn from that to be very careful that no one else shall be hurt by us. If some one has said or done something not quite creditable, we should think; "I will not pass this on; I will not do or say anything myself which will make the day harder for some one else." We can also determine not to be the instrument whereby the bad karma of others works itself out. If one hurts or offends some one, it is true that one is only the instrument of that other's karma; but it is a very ungenerous rôle to play. We should be the instruments of the good karma, in helping people and bringing them blessing and comfort; the evil karma must work itself out through other channels, not through us.

> In yet another way you must control your thought; you must not let it wander. Whatever you are doing, fix your thought upon it, that it may be perfectly done.

C.W.L.—It ought to be a simple matter to fix our thought upon whatever we are doing, so that it may be perfectly done. If we are writing a letter, for example, we can concentrate on that and see that it is what the letter of an occultist should be. An ordinary man writes his letters in a rather careless or slipshod way; he says what he has to say without making any special effort to see that it is well done. It appears to be quite a new idea to some people that ordinary little matters like that ought to be well done. I receive a number of letters, and I must say that many of them are not such as I should think of sending out myself. Frequently they are faulty in expression, and often so badly written that they waste a good deal of my time.

This sort of carelessness matters very much for those who are occultists or endeavouring to become such. The letter of an occultist should be carefully expressed, and well written or typed, as the case may be. It should be a nice thing to look at; a pleasure to the person who receives it. Whatever we do, it is emphatically our duty to do it decently well. I do not mean to say that one can always spare the time to write everything like copper-plate, or to make of every letter a finished work of art; that cannot be done in these days. But even outside of occultism, as a matter of common politeness to a correspondent, one should write clearly and legibly. If you write hurriedly and badly to save a few moments of your own time, remember that it is done at the sacrifice of, perhaps, four times the amount of the other person's time. We have no right to do that sort of thing.

Every letter that we send out should be a messenger; we should make it a message of the Master. It may be about business or any ordinary subject, but it should be charged with good feeling. This can be done in a moment: as we are writing the letter we should have in mind strong kindly feeling; that will affect the letter without any further action on our part, but when we are signing it we should take a moment to send into it a current of good feeling of some sort. If one is writing to a friend, one should pour affection into the letter, so that when he opens it there shall rush out at him the feeling of brotherly affection. If the letter be to a brother Theosophist, put into it a thought of higher things and of the Master, so that it will recall to him the higher thought which Theosophists always desire to cherish. If we are writing to some person whom we know to be in want of a particular quality, we should pour that quality into the letter, taking the opportunity to give what is needed. So let us see that each letter is well written, and also that it has a soul.

The same service may be rendered when we meet others directly. Some of us come into contact with many people during the day; we have to speak to them, and sometimes to shake hands with them. We can take advantage of that direct physical contact to pour in a rush of vitality or nerve force or affection or higher thought, or whatever may seem most suitable. One should never shake hands with anybody without leaving something of that nature behind—it is an opportunity. Our business, if we aspire to become pupils of the Master, is to watch for such opportunities to serve. A man who is not in some way or other being useful to his fellow-men is not on the road to being accepted. I suppose it is doing no injustice to the average man to say that his idea in making a new acquaintance is very largely: "What shall I get out of this man in some way or other?" It may not be in money; it may be in amusement, or social benefits; but at any rate he thinks about getting something. Our attitude must be exactly the reverse: "Here is a new opportunity for me, what can I give?" If I am introduced to a stranger I look him over and throw out something or other in the shape of a good thought; it will stick there and penetrate when its time comes. The pupils of the Master do that as they are walking about the streets or riding on the trams and ferries. They watch for cases where they see a good thought is needed, and they give it—a hundred times perhaps in the course of a single morning's or afternoon's journey.

When a greeting is given to anyone it should be a reality, not merely a form of words. The greetings into which the name of God comes, and which invoke His blessing, such as are customary among the Muhammadans, for example, are sometimes only formal, but sometimes they are hearty good wishes, and the thought of God is really there. We say, "Good-bye." Few people know that this is a contraction of "God be with you," but we should know it and mean it. These seem small things, but it is the small things in everyday life that make the difference. They show character and they shape character, and if we do all these small everyday things carefully and well, we shall soon develop in ourselves a character which will be careful and self-controlled and accurate about all sorts of things, great as well as small. One cannot have a character that is careful in great things and careless in small things. It is inevitable in that case that we shall sometimes forget and be careless at the wrong time, but we must learn to be careful altogether. Again, many small things taken together mount up to a big thing, and with a little practice one may learn to give not a small, but a very large amount of help to a person by the touch of a hand or the writing of a letter.

The Master says: "Whatever you are doing, fix your mind upon it." This applies even to the things we do in order to rest our minds, such as the reading of novels or magazines. The best kind of rest, apart from deliberate relaxation and sleep, is generally some other form of exercise, so even when people are reading something for the sake of amusement or rest, the mind should be their servant, not they its slave. If you are reading a story, fix your mind upon it and try to understand it, to see what the author meant by it. Often people read so vaguely that by the time they reach the end of the story they have forgotten the beginning; they are so utterly vague that they could not give you a sketch of the plot, nor say what it is meant to teach. But if we want to train our minds when we are reading for pleasure or recreation we ought to do it well. Similarly, when we are resting. There are actually millions of people in the world who do not know how to lie down and rest themselves properly. They have not learned that ten minutes of relaxation is worth two hours of lying down in a tense and strained condition. Quiet control of the mind is necessary even for success in resting. Such control forms a habit like everything else, and those who practise it presently find that they cannot do things in the old slipshod way; if they rest, they must rest properly.

Do not let your mind be idle, but keep good thoughts always in the background of it, ready to come forward the moment it is free.

A.B.—That ought to be a very easy thing for the ordinary Hindu to do, because he has been taught from childhood to repeat good sentences in unoccupied moments. Even the quite uneducated people in India do so. You may often hear some man who has finished his work suddenly begin to repeat, "Rām, Rām, Rām, Sītārām, Sītārām, Sītārām," over and over again—just the sacred name and nothing else. Some people may think that that is a senseless thing to do; but it is not, for it has a very real effect upon the person who is reciting; it steadies his unoccupied mind on a soothing and elevating thought. That is infinitely better than allowing the mind to roam as it will, occupying itself most likely with the affairs of its owner's neighbours, and so leading to gossip and all the untold harm that that does. Of course, if you can control your mind without any outward repetition, it is all the better; but many people do neither the one nor the other.

It is a good plan, which you will find recommended in many religions, to choose in the morning some phrase which you then learn by heart. It will come up of itself in the mind during the day, and will drive away other less worthy thoughts at times when the mind is unoccupied. You can select a phrase or sentence from any good book, and the repetition of it a few times in the morning (perhaps while you are dressing) with your thoughts fixed upon it, will make it come up of its own accord during the day. One can see how easy such automatic repetition becomes to the mind when one remembers how a chance piece of music, a catching tune, will impress itself upon the mind, will take possession of it and be repeated by it over and over again. For many years I have kept the thought of the Masters in the background of my mind, and now it is always there, so that the moment my mind is released from a piece of work it reverts naturally to Them.

C.W.L.—Thoughts of the Master should be always present in the background of our mind, so that they come forward when it is not occupied by other work. If one is reading or writing a letter or doing some physical work, one is not necessarily thinking actively about the Master; but the resolution is made at the beginning: "I will do this well for the sake of the Master." Having done that, one is thinking of the work, not of Him, but as soon as the work is finished, the thought of the Master returns into the foreground of the mind. Such a thought not only ensures that the mind shall be well occupied, but it also causes our thinking on other subjects to be clearer and stronger than it otherwise would be.

Sometimes people practise the repetition of the names of God, in order to form such a background for the mind. In India you often find people muttering to themselves as they stand waiting for a train or walk along the road, and sometimes you hear them saying a sacred name over and over again. One of the special criticisms which missionaries have always made against the "heathen" is that they are "given to vain repetitions". The Muhammadan goes about reciting texts; he always has the name of Allah upon his lips. It may be that sometimes he does not think much of Him, but often it does mean something to him. It is true that a man may say things of that sort merely as a matter of habit, and give no thought to it: a Christian may repeat his prayers, and his thoughts may be wandering somewhere else all the time. Even a priest may go through his hours of prayer without necessarily concentrating much thought on them, because he knows the whole thing by heart; he may utter his "Ave Marias" and "Paternosters" without ever thinking of Our Lady or our Father in heaven. In any religion it is possible to be a formalist, to retain the outer shell, having lost most of its inner spirit; but that is not done more in Hinduism and in Buddhism than it is in Christianity—I should be inclined to say not nearly so much. It is a fact that the repetition of names like "Rāma, Rāma, Rāma," does help to keep the thought of the Deity in the minds of people, and when it does that assuredly it is good. If we can think equally readily and fruitfully of the Master without needing the repetition of His name, that is a still better thing; but it is infinitely better to do the physical repetition than not to have the thought.

There is a certain rate of vibration in the mental body which is appropriate to these devotional feelings; in time that rate becomes a habit, so that devotion easily arises and is built into the character. This habit also serves to keep out evil thoughts. If the mind is vacant, any passing thought can enter and influence it, and such a thought is more likely to be bad, or at any rate useless, than useful. It comes from the vast quantities of thought floating round us, representing the average level of the country, but we are aiming at something higher. We want to be in a position to lift our average brother, and we cannot do that until we first attain a higher level ourselves.

Use your thought-power every day for good purposes; be a force in the direction of evolution.

C.W.L.—We have been educated on a namby-pamby sort of theory that the one thing necessary is to be good; but it is not enough to be pious and to abstain from doing evil things; we must go ahead and *do* something with our goodness and piety. Why are we on earth at all? Why should we encumber the ground, unless we can do something? To sit down and be good (though it is better than sitting down and being bad, of course!) is simply a negative state. We are here to be channels for the divine Force. We, the Monad, came forth from God long ago as a glowing spark of the divine Fire. Truly, as *The Secret Doctrine* says: "The spark burns low"—very low, in many cases—but we must rekindle it with the fervour of our enthusiasm and faith and love, and make that spark into a living flame that will warm other people.

> Think each day of some one whom you know to be in sorrow, or suffering, or in need of help, and pour out loving thought upon him.

C.W.L.—Thought-force is just as real and definite a thing as money, or as the water we pour out of a jug into a glass. If we send a definite stream of it to anybody, we may be absolutely certain that it will get there, though we may not see it. Most of us know somebody in sorrow and suffering, who could be greatly helped by the stream of thought that we may send. Even if it should happen at any time that we know of no one in particular who is in such need, we can send out our thought in a more general way, and it will find some one among the many who are in trouble.

If one knows of a person who is in touch (as is Dr. Besant, for example) with a great many people who are in need and sorrow, one may send thoughts of devotion and strength to her, so that she will have a little more to pour out. It is the same with the Masters. When anyone pours out a thought of devotion to Them, it calls down upon him the answering thought of the Master, which is in the nature of a blessing. But besides that, a little more is added to the Master's store of force, and He uses that for the good of others.

A.B.—I must say that until I read this it had not occurred to me to make such a definite and regular practice of this mental helping of others. It is certainly a very good thing. Decide in the morning upon some person whom you will help during the day in your odd moments—there are always plenty of people needing help, unfortunately. Then, whenever during the course of the day your mind is free, instead of letting it be used as a kind of hotel for the most casual visitors, engage it in sending the person thoughts of strength, comfort, happiness, or whatever it is that he most needs. This practice is a stage beyond that of the repetition of a good sentence.

In one way or another you should close your mind against undesirable thoughts, until it is so strong that these helps are not needed. The thought of the Master should always be in mind; it is one that always goes out in help, and it does not prevent any of the higher activities of the mind. It does not exclude other ways of helping, but throws greater force into them. After a time it will fill the whole of your mental horizon, and then all that you do will be better and more strongly done because of it.

Hold back your mind from pride, for pride comes only from ignorance.

C.W.L.—There is a great deal of subtle pride amongst students of occultism. They cannot help realizing that they know a little more of the real facts of life than do people who have not studied these things. It would be foolish not to recognize the fact, but they must take care lest they have a feeling of despising the ordinary man who does not know these things as yet. In this particular respect students of occultism are ahead of the ordinary man, but there may well be other matters in which the ordinary man is far ahead of them. The man who knows, literature, science, or art thoroughly, for example, has spent very much more time and trouble in learning that than many of us have in studying Theosophy, and surely he deserves credit for the work he has done, and the amount of selfless labour that he has put into it. It is not the mark of a wise man to despise the work of another, but to realize that all alike are progressing.

Many people have what is called a good conceit of themselves; they like to think of themselves as always right, as very good persons, and so on. But the points on which they admire themselves are generally not at all what the ego would acknowledge. In the ego, so far as any quality is developed, it is pure. If, for example, affection is there, it is utterly untainted with jealousy, envy, or selfishness. It is a mirror of the divine love in so far as he can reproduce it at his level. Sometimes we pride ourselves on progressing fairly well. That is very like a little child of four years priding himself on the fact that he is getting on very well. So he may be—for that age—but it will be different with the man of twenty-one. Our powers of intellect, devotion, affection, sympathy—exist in us but in a small degree, as compared with what they will be. Instead, therefore, of stopping to pat ourselves on the back, we must press on and try to gain more of such qualities.

In this work, meditation is a great help. If a man really sets himself to develop affection, meditates upon it and works to try to feel it, he will be surprised at the strength of the quality evoked in himself in a short time.

Pride, the Master says, comes always from ignorance. The more a man knows the less likely he is to be proud, because the more he is able to see that he does not know. Most especially is this true if it be his good fortune to come into touch with one of our great Masters. Such a man will never feel proud again, not even proud of that fact, because whenever he thinks he can do anything, or that he possesses any quality, it cannot but come into his mind: "But I have seen that quality in the Master, and what is mine beside His?"

The virtues in Them are so magnificently developed that to know one of Them is an absolute and instantaneous cure for anything like pride. Yet discouragement never comes from the Master. In ordinary life you think you can do a little bit of something, but when you come into the presence of an expert in that line, you see at once how little you can do compared with the great man, and you feel rather crushed and hopeless. But that is not the feeling one gets in the presence of the Master. You realize your own incompetence and insignificance acutely, but at the same time in His presence you realize your own potentiality. Instead of feeling that there is an abysmal gulf which can never be passed, one feels, "I can do this; I am going to set myself to imitate that"; that is the stimulus which any touch with the Master always gives. In His presence one feels very much what the Apostle says: "I can do all things through Christ which strengtheneth me."[1] Because of this strength of the Master, a person thinks at the time: "I shall never again be depressed; I can never again feel sorry; I can never again fall into the silly mistake of irritability which I committed yesterday. I look back and see that some things worried me. How ridiculous; why should anything ever worry me?" It may be that, later on, having passed out of the direct rays of that divine influence, we do fall back, forgetting that it can reach us just as well when the rays are not visible and direct, that we may live always in the Master's aura if we choose to do so.

The man who does not know thinks that he is great, that he has done this or that great thing; the wise man knows that only God is great, that all good work is done by God alone.

[1] Philippians, 4, 13.

A.B.—Here we have a great lesson of the *Gītā.* It is the one will that works through us all. All work is done by the whole, not by the parts; and the most that any of us can do is to make ourselves good organs for the one divine activity to work through. It is as foolish for us to boast as it would be for one of the fingers of our hands to do so. Make yourselves healthy organs of the divine will; then you will find that the one Actor is using you, because you are convenient for use.

We have come back to the point where we began. We saw that realization of the Self destroys all fear; we now see that it destroys all pride. That is the one great basic truth. It is good to see how these multifarious things all lead us back to the one truth—the one Life seated equally in all beings.

C.W.L.—God is in everyone, and whatever goodness or greatness there is in any man is the God in him shining through. All that we do He does through us. This may appear strange. You may say that it seems to destroy the feeling of individuality, but that is only because our physical brains cannot grasp the real relationship. Not without reason the mediæval Christians used to say: "To God be the glory." For one of us to be proud of anything that he has done is just as though, when one is playing a piece on the piano, one of his fingers should say: "How well I struck that note! It was I who made that tune so beautiful!" After all, all the other fingers did their part, and they all acted, not with separate volition, but as instruments of the brain behind. We are all fingers of His Hand, manifestations of His power. I know quite well that it is practically impossible for us fully to realize that; but the more we develop the higher consciousness the more acutely we feel it, and sometimes in meditation, in moments of high exaltation, we get a momentary grasp of that unity.

CHAPTER 2

SELF-CONTROL IN ACTION

Self-control in Action.—If your thought is what it should be, you will have little trouble with your action.

A.B.—This sentence emphasizes the fact, with which every occult student is familiar, that thought is more important than action. This is exactly the reverse of the ordinary point of view; but it is true, because thought always precedes action. There can be what is called spontaneous action; but that only means that to find the preceding thought you must go further back, perhaps even to a former life.

When sufficient thought-force has been accumulated in the mind in any given direction, and then an occasion presents itself for the expression of that particular kind of thought, it inevitably overflows into action. Every thought along a given line acts as a little added impulse, until at last the stored-up force of the impulses carries you over into action along that line. The Hindu quite rightly looks upon action, or karma, as made up of the three parts—thought, desire and act. It is true; so you may have in any life an act which is unpremeditated so far as the immediate past is concerned, an act committed on the spur of the moment. Those are cases in which the thinking having been completed, the act—that is the last part of the whole action—must follow, as being the net impulse along that line. Thus it may happen that on any line of thinking you may exhaust your power of selection, and then, even when you have exerted to the full your power of control, on the first occasion that presents itself your thought will manifest in action. It may lie latent for a long time, if opportunity for expression be lacking, but as soon as ever the circumstances permit the action will be done.

Hence the great importance of understanding the working of thought. Guard your thought and lead it along good lines, for you cannot tell when the moment will be reached and your next thought will be embodied in action. This is one reason for the stress laid on the importance of thought by all the great Teachers of the world, and here in this book the student is reminded of it again. It may be well to remember at this point that manas, the mind, is itself activity. You have in the Monad the three aspects of will, wisdom and activity, and these embody themselves in ātmā, buddhi and manas. Here you have the recognition that thought embodies itself in action.

C.W.L.—It is a truism to say that thought precedes action. There are occasions on which we act, as we say, without thinking, but even so it is the result of previous thought—we have a habit of thought on certain subjects or along a certain line, and we act instinctively in agreement with that. A man does a thing, and then explains: "I could not help doing it; I did not think." But the fact is that he is carrying out thought belonging, perhaps, to previous incarnations. Although a man has not usually the same mental body now as in his last incarnation, he has the same mental unit, which is the nucleus of that body and is to a great extent a kind of epitome of it, and that carries from life to life the impressions of the type of thought to which the man has been accustomed.

It has often been pointed out that a man can take over from life to life, in his causal body, only his good qualities. That is quite true. The causal body is constructed from the matter of the higher subplanes of the mental plane—the first, second and third—and matter of those levels cannot vibrate in response to any of the lower or less desirable qualities. Therefore a man can actually build into himself only good, which is very fortunate for us, because otherwise we should all have built in a great deal that is not good, which would retard our evolution instead of helping it. But he carries over with him the permanent atoms belonging to the different planes—mental, astral and physical—and so the vibrations which belong to them come up as inherent qualities in his new vehicles.

In this way one brings over the possibilities of qualities, rather than actual qualities. Madame Blavatsky used to call these, among other things, "privations of matter," that is, forces which would operate when the matter was there for them to work in, but were suspended until it gathered round the ego again. So when a man acts "without thinking" he does so according to the momentum of those old thoughts. That is one of the reasons why we should so carefully guard our thoughts; we never know when they will overflow into action. The man who yields himself to some evil thought, thinking that he will never allow himself to act upon it, may some time find it translated into action almost before he is aware of it.

Great use can be made of this knowledge for the helping of children. When the ego takes up his new vehicles, parents and friends can do very much to help him by encouraging the good qualities as they show themselves, and giving the bad ones no opportunities to manifest. We give the greatest help to the child when we get the good qualities into action, and make them into a habit before those which are bad can assert themselves. The latter will sooner or later manifest, probably because the outer world will stir them up, but if there is already a strong momentum in favour of the good qualities, those which are evil will find it very difficult to make any impression. The whole will of the ego is then acting through his vehicles against their impacts, and in such a case they will probably be entirely weeded out in the course of that life-period, so that in the following incarnation the ego will come in without any trace of them at all.

Yet remember that, to be useful to mankind, thought must result in action. There must be no laziness, but constant activity in good work.

A.B.—Here is a very important reminder—thought to be useful must result in action. That is a point on which many of us are defective; we have in our minds thoughts which do not result in action, and all such are sources of weakness. The Master Morya once said that a good thought not acted upon acts like a cancer in the mind. That is a graphic simile, which should help us to realize that such a thought is not merely negative, but positively harmful. We should not enfeeble our moral fibre by good resolutions not carried out, which act as an obstacle and make it more difficult to carry out the same thought into action when it arises again. Do not delay, therefore. Do not put things off; do not leave them undone. Many of us stultify our growth by good resolutions not put into practice. An English proverb says that the way to hell is paved with good intentions.

A good intention not carried out becomes a force for ill, as it acts like a drug which dulls the brain. Be careful to regulate your thinking, and when from the higher Self comes an impulse of service go and carry it out; do not leave it for to-morrow. This putting off is a reason why so many good people in the world are marking time. It is quite a common thing to meet a really good person after a lapse of about ten years, and find him just the same as he was when you knew him before. Thus people remain for years, having the same difficulties and temptations, the same weaknesses and strength. That ought never to be true of a member of the Theosophical Society, for all of us ought to know something of the way in which these laws work.

That it is sometimes true is very much due, I think, to the failure to understand that good impulses not carried out make barriers. If you put into effect those which you receive, more and more will come. No favourable outer circumstances or additions of outer knowledge can make up for the want of inner effort and resolution, and for failure to carry out into action what you already know. Your thought ought always to result in action. Make that a rule. I do not mean that you will always be able to carry out your thought at once, because circumstances may not permit it: but presently opportunities will come. In such cases put your thought by, not losing it. It will then be like fruit that is ripening. If you do that, the unembodied thought will not harm you, and as soon as the time is ripe you will carry it out.

> But it must be your *own* duty that you do—not another man's, unless with his permission and by way of helping him. Leave every man to do his own work in his own way; be always ready to offer help where it is needed, but *never* interfere. For many people the most difficult thing in the world to learn is to mind their own business; but that is exactly what you must do.

A.B.—A warning is now given which is needed by those who have a very active—a rājasic—nature. We have to consider now the other side of the razor-path; laziness must be shunned on the one hand, but interference must be avoided on the other. Very active people are prone to want, as the saying is, a finger in every pie. But other people's pies are their own pies, and you ought not to put your fingers into them. You may remember how often in the *Bhagavad-Gītā*, which is a gospel of activity—for its constant burden is, "act! act!"—the warning is given against wrong activity. The duty of another, it says, is full of danger.

The reason is clear. If you, with your own line of thought-activity behind you, mix yourself in the action of another person, who similarly has his own line of thought-activity behind him—which is a different one from yours—you are sure to spoil what he is doing. His action is the logical outcome of his thought-activity; it is not, and could not be the right and proper outcome of yours. The energetic type of person must learn that he only creates confusion by mixing himself in another person's action. I used to want to set other people right, according to what was my view of what was right for them, which was my own right, of course; but I learned in the course of discipleship that that was not the way to work.

Even if another person's way is not the best way from the abstract standpoint, it may yet be the best for him. It has the force of both his faults and his virtues behind it, and it marks the line of evolution proper for him. Suppose that a man holds his pen in some particular way that is not the best one, when he is writing: if you interfere and induce him to hold it in a different way, you will make him write worse, not better. He will lose all the advantage of his long practice in the old method, and it will cost him a great deal of time and trouble to make that good. Of course, if he himself wants to change his way of writing because he is convinced that another way is better, and he asks your help in this, the case is different; he has a right to do as he pleases, and he will then have the force of his own will behind his action.

It is clear that a strong person can easily dominate another for a time. History affords many examples of great men who dominated all around them while they lived, but whose work fell to pieces when they died. They forgot that they were mortal and should therefore have provided for the gap that their death would leave; the unfortunate karma of their error, their self-centredness, lay in that result of things tumbling to pieces as soon as they were gone. That shows at once that those men did not understand the conditions of successful activity. They did not realize that a worker and leader should gather fit people together and trust them, and leave them independent in their own part of the work, independent along their own lines—that one should not try to look after every detail oneself; moreover, it cannot be done.

The world is made up of a great variety with an underlying unity. The lower types in the world obey law, because, unknowing of the fact themselves, they are compelled to do so. But man is left comparatively free—free within a great circle of laws outside which he cannot get, but inside which he may do as he pleases. In doing his work in his own way lies his development.

The divine plan is such that more and more liberty is bestowed on man as he progresses and can be trusted to use it wisely; so that bit by bit, step by step, we come to perfect freedom. The animal, at the lower end of the scale, obeys perfectly, unconsciously; the Master at the upper end of it obeys perfectly, consciously; and we all stand somewhere between those two.

We must remember too, that interference extends to the mind, and non-interference has also to do with the previous qualification, that of self-control as to the mind. Interference by thought is very potent. Take for example such a case as the following. One of us has a particular difficulty which he is trying to overcome; perhaps it arises from some weakness in his character, perhaps it is an undesirable way of thinking or acting, along which from force of old habit he is inclined to go. Whatever it is, he is doing his best to overcome it. Then some one comes along and suspects him of that particular line of weakness or difficulty—suspects, and goes on his way, never thinking that he has done any particular harm.

That second person does not realize that he has given a little push to his brother, which may just determine the latter's action and send it along the wrong line. The two forces of habit and effort were perhaps trembling in the balance, and the suspicious thought turned the scale. That is why suspicion is so wrong. It is always wrong. If unfortunately it is true, it only gives the man suspected an additional push in the wrong direction; if it be untrue, it may make it a little easier for him to go wrong in that particular way at some other time. In any case it is sending out an evil thought against him; so it is wrong either way. We ought always to think well of people, even if our thought of them is better than their practice; thus we throw out to them a thought which will work only for their good.

It is also important to remember these facts, because a mass of evil thought is sooner or later directed by the dark forces against every person who is advancing rapidly on the Path. Because you are having a mass of evil thrown against yourself, tending to push you into wrong actions, you should realize the harmful way in which suspicion works, and should be extra careful of your own thoughts and actions. You should think of what is happening to yourself merely with a dry recognition of the facts, without any feeling of anger or resentment, and whenever you come across a great outburst of hatred, remember that you ought, to use the Biblical phrase, to gird up the loins of your mind, and simply bring to bear upon the situation an added force of a contrary nature to neutralize the evil one. Do that, and the mass of evil thought directed against you will not harm you; on the contrary, you will draw advantage from it, as it will help you to see what are your weak points; it will bring them into the light when otherwise they might have remained hidden from you. Also your very resolution in the face of attack will strengthen you, and lead you onwards to the time when all these things will beat against you with small effect.

Therefore you should do your own work perfectly, and leave the work of other people alone unless they ask you for help. Do your own work to the utmost of your ability, and leave other people's work alone to the extent of your ability..

C.W.L.—A good deal of interference with others is due to religious misconceptions. Orthodox Christianity makes it its business to interfere with everybody. It starts out to save other peoples' souls, instead of recognizing that each man's business is to let his soul save him. Most assuredly no one has a right to interfere between the lower and the higher self of another under any circumstances whatever. The torturers of the Inquisition thought it right to do any frightful thing with a man's body in order to save his soul, by making the body say this or that. It was never even suggested, so far as I can understand, that you could make him *believe* it, but if you could make his body *say* that it believed a certain thing, that statement, even if false, somehow or other saved the soul. If those people *really* believed that (I wonder whether *anybody* ever *did* really believe so monstrous a lie!) they could actually justify all the horrible things they did; for whatever the horrors to which you subjected the unfortunate body for a few hours or days, they would be as nothing compared with the frightful pain lasting for all eternity from which you were saving his soul. The torture of your neighbour under those circumstances becomes quite a laudable action. It is difficult for us to believe that anyone could take up this position, yet it appears to have been held by great numbers of people—even after allowing for those who were using the power of the Church for political purposes.

> Because you try to take up higher work, you must not forget your ordinary duties, for until they are done you are not free for other service. You should undertake no new worldly duties; but those which you have already taken upon you, you must perfectly fulfil—all clear and reasonable duties which you yourself recognize, that is—not imaginary duties which others try to impose upon you. If you are to be His, you must do ordinary work better than others, not worse; because you must do that also for His sake.

A.B.—We sometimes find that when a person comes into occultism he begins to do his ordinary work worse, not better than before. That is altogether wrong. His great outburst of enthusiasm for his new studies and his effort to reach the higher things have their danger as well as their advantage; and the danger is precisely that the worldly duty appears unimportant. There is truth in the idea, and it is in the truth that the danger lies; all errors are dangerous only on account of the truth that lies at the base of them. It is the little bit of truth in an error that gives it its strength, not the great wrapping of falsehood that overlies the scrap of truth.

The perfect carrying out of the duties that have to be done in the world is what shows that the force coming down from the higher planes is being turned in the right direction. "Yoga is skill in action."[1] If a man is disciplined on the higher planes his lower plane activities will be good; but if he is undisciplined they will not be good. Even this last, however, is very much better than not to care about the higher things at all. The unwise activities of a man in this plight may work much temporary harm, but not permanent harm, because the motive power behind them is good.

The disciple must try to carry out physical plane duties better than other people. Very often, when he acts unwisely, a Master may have to step in in order to balance up his unwise activities. That is one reason why a Master puts a chela on probation, and the long time that the probation often lasts is sometimes due to this. Generally people need a fairly long time to balance up their enthusiasm and activity with wise moderation and forethought.

The first test of discipleship is usefulness to others. The aspirant should never think that his esoteric work is more important than his exoteric work. If, being a Theosophist, he neglects his Lodge and his work for the Society for the sake of his own progress in esoteric matters, he is blundering. If he neglects outside work for the sake of study, to take another example, he is doing quite wrong. Study is good, but it should subserve usefulness; you should study in order to be more useful, not cease to be useful for the sake of studying. And whenever a conflict arises between outer duties and such studies, the outer ought to take precedence.

[1] *Bhagavad-Gītā*, II, 50.

In all such matters as these, we must never forget that the path of occultism is narrow as the edge of a razor. It would be quite possible to give almost every moment of one's waking time to small services for others, but in such case many of them could not be well chosen, and most of them would not be well done. Just as one must spend time in sleeping and eating, in order to have strength to work the rest of the time, so must one spend time in meditation and study, and in considering what work should be done and how it should be done. This aspect of the matter was dealt with by the Master in the section on discrimination. Every portion of His teaching directs the pupil back into the middle path ; if he follows any piece of advice to excess, he will only fall over again. It has been said that the track of the best ship is not a straight line, but is made up of thousands of tracks, now to one side, now to the other. The life of the disciple is similar to that ; the captain on the bridge is the Master, who points out the stars by which he can guide himself, and assists him to keep as close as possible to the direct line. One meets so many people who fasten on to one good idea, and then let it ride them to death.

The master tells his pupil that he should undertake no new worldly duties. The man who has pledged himself to the Master's work should know the importance of being always ready to serve Him in any way and anywhere that He needs him. I can give you a striking example of this out of my own experience. When I was young my children were taken away from me against my will. I fought against the separation by every means that the law allowed, but lost my case; the law broke the tie, took away from me the duty of protection which a mother has to her children. My daughter came back to me as soon as she was free to do so; for ten years I had not seen or written to her, but my influence held and she came straight back to me. I was then living with Madame Blavatsky, and she warned me: "Take care that you do not re-knit the ties which karma broke for you." If I had taken up my old life again then, after I had taken my pledge to the Master, I should have done wrong. It did not mean, of course, that I was to neglect the girl—she came and lived with us, and stayed with us till she married, but she had to come second, not first.

You are responsible for the duties which you have to fulfil, not anybody else; you are responsible to your Master and not to anybody else. If people try to force upon you what they imagine to be your duty, and you see that it is not so, you must simply disagree with them —good-temperedly, but firmly. *You* must decide. You may do so rightly or wrongly, and if wrongly you will suffer, but the decision must be yours. That responsibility of an individual to himself and to his Master must not be interfered with by anyone. To your own Master you are responsible, and you must do your ordinary work better than other people do, for His sake.

C.W.L.—This principle that the occultist should do ordinary work well was understood in the old religions. In the story of the youth of Prince Siddhārtha, who afterwards became the Lord Buddha, for example, it is related that he devoted himself very much to study and meditation, but when it became necessary that he should win his bride by skill in various manly sports, he showed that when he wished he could excel in those as well as the higher things. In the *Bhagavad-Gītā* it is said that yoga is skill in action; it is doing the right thing carefully, tactfully and courteously. Disciples of the Masters have therefore to learn balance in their lives, to know when the lower may safely be put aside and when it should not be put aside.

A man who has pledged himself and his time and strength to the Master's service ought not to undertake anything new which is not actually His work. He must not let people force upon him duties which he does not recognize as his. I can quite imagine, for example, that people might sometimes expect members of the Theosophical Society to attend various social functions. A member might say, "I am willing to give up a reasonable amount of time for the sake of friendliness," but he is quite justified in reserving most of his time for any work that he has taken up for the Society.

This instruction concerning duties had special reference to Alcyone's life at Adyar, while the Master was teaching him. In one special case, for example, he was being pressed to devote a whole day to some ceremony in connection with a distant relation. The matter was submitted to his Master, and He said: "Yes, for the sake of the rest of the family who might be shocked or troubled, you may go down for an hour at such and such a time, but be very careful that, during that time, you repeat nothing whatever which you do not understand, that you in no case repeat things blindly after the priest, and that you do not allow anything to be done for you that you can do for yourself—that is, in the way of ceremonies and blessings."

CHAPTER 3

TOLERANCE

3. *Tolerance.*—You must feel perfect tolerance for all, and a hearty interest in the beliefs of those of another religion, just as much as in your own. For their religion is a path to the highest, just as yours is. And to help all, you must understand all.

A.B.—I suppose tolerance is one of the virtues most talked about at the present day, but one of the least practised. It is one of the most difficult virtues to acquire, for where a belief is strongly held and highly valued people not unnaturally tend to try to push it on others. Out of that aggressiveness all religious persecutions and wars, both public and private, have grown; but even that aggressiveness is better than indifference, which is so often confused with tolerance. Indifference is not tolerance, and should never be mistaken for it.

Nowadays there is very little State persecution, but there is still much social and family persecution. Some State persecution of religion does still exist in certain countries, where the free-thought party has the upper hand. Free-thinkers were so much persecuted that the temptation to retaliate has been too strong, though of course they are acting in direct violation of their own principles. I hope it is only the reaction of the persecution that the religious party meted out to them, and that it will soon cease.

There still exists in the world much of the spirit out of which all persecution grows, and sometimes the State finds it necessary to impose forbearance, as in India, for fear of disturbances and troubles arising. The sufferance that we find existing between members of different creeds in countries where various religions are more or less evenly balanced is largely due to mutual fear. Thus what tolerance there is springs generally from some motive that is more or less unworthy.

The occult student must aim at the kindly feeling which grows out of the recognition that the Self in each finds his own road. This is the only right attitude, and nothing less than recognition of it will make tolerance a widespread virtue. We must recognize that each man has his own way of searching for the highest, and must be left absolutely free to follow it. This implies not only that you will not try to draw a person into your own religion, but that you will not try to force arguments and opinions upon him, will not try to shake his beliefs which he finds helpful. Such perfect forbearance is the object at which you have to aim. It is far as the poles are apart from what men of the world often think to be tolerance—semi-contemptuous feeling that religious things do not very much matter, but are useful merely as a kind of police force to keep people in order. But a man's religion must be sacred to you, because it is sacred to him. The White Lodge will not allow anyone to come into its Brotherhood who has not developed this attitude to a considerable extent.

C.W.L.—There is perhaps in the present day more tolerance than there has been since the time of the great Roman Empire, and it is very much like that which then existed. We hear curious things of the way in which the Romans are supposed to have treated the early Christians. Careful research shows that the greatest of the persecutions about which so much has been said never happened at all; but it is true that the Christians frequently got themselves into trouble. I do not mean to say that the conditions were not in some ways barbarous; but the early Christians seem to have been an anarchical set of people, and when they came into collision with the authorities it was not on account of their religion, but because of the things they said and did. The Romans did not welcome the kind of brotherhood that the early Christians preached. It was far too much like: "*Sois mon frère ou je te tuerai.*"[1] In some cases they would not perform small ceremonies which were considered matters of loyalty; they would not throw a pinch of incense on the altar or pour out a drop of wine to the Emperor—actions more or less equivalent to taking off one's hat in London when the King passes. The Roman Empire was the most tolerant in the world about other religions. They did not care in the very least what god anybody worshipped, because they did

[1] "Be my brother or I will kill you."

not believe there were any gods. They had a huge pantheon, where they set up temples to all the gods, and when they realized that the Christ was being worshipped they promptly set up a statue to Him. Their tolerance really amounted to indifference.

Many of those ancient Romans are incarnated in the English race. There are many people now who are tolerant to all forms of belief, just because they themselves do not believe in anything. They look on religion as a pleasant fable to amuse the ladies, but of course for a man it is not a serious matter. That is not the kind of tolerance at which we are aiming. Ours must come from a recognition that the beliefs of others are also ways to the highest. When one goes into a temple or church of some form of religion which is not one's own, one who is really tolerant conforms to the customs of the place, not simply because it is the custom, but because he respects those people who are different from himself, and that religion which is different from his own. There are people who go into a church and then refuse to bow to the altar and even make a point of turning their backs upon it. I have known people who tried to go into a mosque without taking off their shoes. One has no business in the church or the temple of another faith if one is not prepared to behave so as not to hurt the feelings of the worshippers. If you think it is wrong to genuflect before the altar of a Catholic church you can always stay outside, and if you feel it would be wicked to take your shoes off you need not go inside the mosque.

All men are manifestations of the One Self, so the form another's aspiration takes is to be respected. Often childish manifestations appear, but no good man would make fun of them, or try to turn people against them, for the less developed intellect cannot be expected to take the view that appeals to one much more advanced. Tolerance will always direct us to say, with the old Romans, "Since I am a man, nothing human is foreign to me," and try to understand the other man's point of view; even as an exercise for oneself that method would soon show us at how many different angles the rays of truth may be reflected by the human mind. The world would be monotonous if all things were done in one way only. It would be like a prison, where everything is done at the same time each day, and in the same way.

There are certain broad divisions, such as you find, for example, in the minds of the Catholic and the Protestant. Each of them approaches Christianity from his own point of view, and many on both sides are quite incapable of understanding the other. The Catholic takes the view that a great deal of ceremony should appear in his ritual, that it should be made in every way as beautiful as it can be, in order that it may glorify the God whom he worships, and that it may appeal to the people. He feels keenly that the ritual and the ceremony and all these beautiful surroundings are of the greatest help to him in his devotions. The Protestant, on the other hand, thinks all that to be very wicked and dreadful, because it distracts the mind from the inner meaning. The Protestant's mind is, perhaps, such that if he had to attend to all these ceremonies he would not at the same time be able to keep before him the inner things. What appeals so strongly to the Catholic type of man would be to him rather a nuisance, a disturbance —something which interferes with his inner devotion.

There are many people who feel their devotion and aspiration to be vague and uncertain when only subjective methods of worship are employed. To them the outer form gives great comfort and help; why should they not have it? Those who find the ceremony, the statue, the picture, the physical-plane manifestation, an intense satisfaction and inspiration, belong definitely to one of the seven great rays of life, one of the seven great lines of human endeavour that lead to the throne of God. Those who wish for none of these things, who find them rather troublesome and distracting, are also following their own different line; let them enjoy it; why should we trouble them?

As each one of us has his own language, in which he was born, so he has what might be called his religious language—a way in which his thoughts and feelings and aspirations most readily express themselves. It would be in the highest degree foolish to despise a Frenchman because his language is different from our own, and equally so to despise anyone because his religion is different from ours. A Frenchman says *maison* instead of "house": it means exactly the same thing; it would be absurd to argue that one is a better word than the other. One recalls the celebrated Mr. Lillyvick, a character in *Nicolas Nickelby*, who, after hearing that *l'eau* meant "water" in French, decided that it was a poor language. There is also a story about an old woman in the time of the Napoleonic wars who prayed to God that the English might be successful, and when some one reminded her that probably people on the other side were praying for the success of the French, she replied, "What does that matter; how can God understand them when they speak such nonsense?"

There can be no possible reason why each man should not follow the way which he finds to be best for himself, in the path to God which seems to him the most direct. All that is needed for peace and harmony is that both should recognize that fact. Each should say, "I prefer my path, but I am perfectly willing that every other man should have the same privilege, that he also should take the path which seems best to him." That does not seem much to ask, yet few will concede it. Each feels that what is best for him must be best for others. The larger mind sees that there are many paths, that they all lead equally to the summit of the mountain, and that each man should be left to take that which can most inspire him.

I confess that there is one disposition I personally find it hard to understand—the very gushing type of religious devotion, which applies to the Deity all sorts of endearing terms collected out of love-poetry and novels. It gives me a shock, and an impression of irreverence, though I know perfectly well that it is sincere and well-meant. Probably those who like it think me cold and expressionless, because my disposition is to take a common-sense view of everything and try to reason about it and understand it.

The devotional books written for the higher type of people in every religion are remarkably similar. If one compares, for example, those familiar to the Roman Catholic with those used by the followers of Shrī Rāmanujāchārya, one finds the closest resemblance. The life, too, of a good Christian is the same as that of a good Hindu, or Buddhist, or Muhammadan, or indeed a good man of any religion. The same virtues are practised by all; the same objects are striven for; the same evils are shunned.

> But in order to gain this perfect tolerance. you must yourself first be free from bigotry and superstition.

A.B.—The bigot is the man who considers only his own opinions, and not those of anyone else. I was once told by a very good lady—but also a very bigoted one, of the straitest sect of the evangelicals—that I ought never to read a book which was not written exactly from my own religious standpoint. That is the position of the bigot—never read another view lest it may shake your own. It is the very opposite of that of the seeker after truth, the man who wants to lead the higher life. He tries to read all round a subject, in order to see at how many different angles the rays of truth have struck the human mind and been refracted by it. If you would reach the truth you must study all these different views and opinions, and then assimilate what little, or great, truth they may contain.

It is well also to study people's superstitions; for, as the great phrase in the Upanishad says: "Truth alone conquers, not falsehood." Superstitions derive their strength from the little bit of truth which they contain. You should find that fragment of truth. The bigot, of course, will see only the falsehood in them, but you ought to know something of all religions; not studying them in the spirit of the missionary, but sympathetically. And the same plan should also be followed in political and social questions.

You must also destroy superstition, which is characterized later in this book as one of the three great sins which do most harm in the world, because it is a sin against love. Religion and superstition have been so muddled together in the world that it is necessary to separate them in our minds by careful definition. My favourite definition of superstition—though it does not cover the whole ground—is the taking of the unessential for the essential, the mistaking of a side issue for one of importance. In religious controversies people fight over some unessential matter, and each side as a rule represents a different misunderstanding of the truth.

Another definition of superstition—which also does not cover the whole ground—is that it is a belief which has no rational foundation. Thus, many truths are superstitions to the people who hold them, because they have no good and sound reason for doing so. The Lord Buddha said that the only right ground for believing a thing is that it commends itself to your reason and common sense, so that you may be said to know it yourself. If we apply that test, the greater part of most people's religion comes under the heading of superstition. For them that does not really matter, but for those who are trying to reach the Path all that cannot justify itself to the intuition and reason should be put aside for a time. As that higher sense in you which knows truth at sight gradually unfolds, you will be able to take in more and more of the truth. Then there will grow up in you a deep inner conviction, and when a truth is presented to you, you will know it is true. This sense corresponds to eyesight on the physical plane. It is the faculty of buddhi, pure reason. We should all try our beliefs by this test, for we inherit a great many of them which are only superstitions to us. As we do so, and to the degree that this attitude of mind becomes habitual to us, shall we get rid of superstition and develop tolerance.

C.W.L.—Superstition has often a very strong hold indeed on the minds of men, so that sometimes it has been said that it is impossible to have religion without it. It is true that there is much confusion in religious thought, and much of it is unreasonable, but whenever there is a belief that has a very wide hold, there is probably a fragment of truth somewhere behind it. Generally speaking, superstitions are not mere inventions, but distortions or exaggerations of facts. Our President once cited a celebrated Indian instance of superstition. There was once a holy man who had a pet cat which was so fond of him that when he wanted to perform his religious ceremonies he found it necessary to keep it quiet by tethering it to the leg of his bed. People seeing this thought the tying up of the cat was a necessary part of the ceremony, and in course of time the rest of the ceremony fell away, and the only part that remained of the devotion was the tradition that a cat should be tethered to the leg of a bed.

The scribes and Pharisees, whom Christ denounced as hypocrites, and likened unto whitened sepulchres, showed a similar form of superstition. They paid tithes, He said, of mint and anise and cummin; because they were ordered to pay a tithe of all they had, they took into account most punctiliously the little things corresponding to our pepper and salt; but they entirely forgot the weightier matters of the law—justice, mercy and faith.

The superstition of Sunday is a serious trouble in some parts of Great Britain, especially in Scotland, where the day is made unutterably tedious. The idea was to minimize the amount of ordinary work that must be done on that day, and make it a day that could be devoted to spiritual things. However, the divine service aspect has dropped very much into the background, and there is more drunkenness and general looseness in other ways on Sunday than on other days—certainly an instance of taking the non-essential for the essential. Because there is one day at least on which people are supposed to be religious, men often seem to have the feeling that on other days it does not matter seriously if one fails to observe religious precepts and ideals. I have noticed that the people who do not keep Sunday—

Hindus, Buddhists and others—have religion permeating their lives in a way that is not found among Christians. I do not say that they are all good people, any more than the Christians are, but religion means more to them than it does to the average Christian, who often thinks that if he attends service one day a week he has discharged all his religious obligations.

Superstition has also been defined by our President as the holding of any belief without a reasonable foundation. It is quite rational to believe in the rotation of the earth, in the existence of foreign countries which we have not seen, in the reality of atoms and electrons which are beyond physical sight altogether, because we have good reason to believe all these things. But many popular beliefs are not in this class. The ordinary belief of the Christian in eternal fire and everlasting punishment is nothing but a peculiarly pernicious superstition. There is no rational basis whatever for it, yet if you told that to the average Christian he would say that you were an atheist and that you were making a mock of his religion. The first man who taught it may or may not have believed it, but millions of people have done so since, thereby most assuredly yielding themselves to superstition.

The only thing which from the Christian point of view ought to be of importance in connection with it is what the Christ Himself said on the subject. There are, I think, eight passages in which He is supposed to mention this eternal punishment: and every one of those can be quite plainly shown to have nothing to do with the popular idea which is attributed to them. There is a very valuable book on this subject called *Salvator Mundi*, written by a Christian clergyman, the Rev. Samuel Cox; he very carefully goes into the original Greek of what the Christ is alleged to have said, and shows at once and conclusively that there is no scriptural basis for the belief in everlasting punishment. There certainly is no rational basis, for if God is a loving Father it is absolutely impossible.

One would have expected modern Christians to have outgrown that horrible superstition, which works enormous evil in this world, but millions of them have not done so, and it is still being taught. I saw not long ago a Roman Catholic catechism for children, and in that the old ideas of hell as a place of everlasting torment were set forth in the same old foolish way. We might be still living in the most brutal part of the Middle Ages as far as the teaching given to little children is concerned. It is a very sad thing. There are many Christian sects which have risen above that, but the oldest and largest of them still clings to its mediæval teachings. There are individual priests who explain the whole thing away very much as we might do, but the printed word which they teach to little children is an utterly horrible and blasphemous thing, because it starts them in life with an altogether wrong idea of God, filling their lives and minds with fear and cruelty, to the serious detriment of their character and evolution.

The teaching of the Lord Buddha about belief and reason, which I have already quoted, was very fine. At the council called after His death to determine which of the many reports current should be accepted as His sayings, the very first rule they laid down was: "That which is contrary to reason and common sense is not the teaching of the Buddha." They ruled out everything that did not satisfy them from that point of view, saying: "This is obviously not common sense; He could not have said it." They may perhaps have cast aside one or two good things which they did not understand, but they saved their religion from a vast amount of superstition. The Founders of the great religions, with the exception of Muhammad, did not give Their teachings to the world in written form. It is said, however, that the Lord Buddha wrote a book, which is kept by the Adepts, not published to the world. Usually, three or four generations have elapsed before the teachings have taken written form, and then those writings have been compounded from many sources. For example, in the Book of Isaiah, scholars have found eight different layers of tradition—three Isaiahs, one after another, then a committee, and so on. There is deterioration in the religion when people write down not what they know but that they have been told, and then quarrel about minutiæ.

There is also another source of confusion in the fact that when a new religion is launched it spreads like a wave of conquest over the existing ones, but does not obliterate them. A wise general, conquering a new country, tries to adapt his rules to the people, so as to minimize trouble; so have the religions become adapted to the various communities who adopted them. Thus the Chinese and Japanese still reverence their ancestors, and follow the ancient way, the Shinto, but they have added thereto the Buddhist ethics; while in Ceylon, they hold a materialistic form of the religion, and will tell you that nothing of a man passes on from life to life but his karma, yet they speak of their previous lives and their hope to reach nirvāna in a future life. The Christians also adopted the festivals of the nations among which the religion spread, but conveniently found names of Christian saints by which to call those days.

Traces of the old traditions are thus found everywhere —devil-dancing in Ceylon, the Kālī cult in India, and so on—and these are sometimes taken for the real thing, and thus form a prolific source of superstition.

One may sometimes know a thing to be true without being able to reason it out—that is the other side of the question. The ego knows, and has good reason for his knowledge; but sometimes he cannot impress his reasons on the physical brain, though the fact comes through that he knows. So, when a new truth is presented to us, we know at once whether we can accept it or not. That is not superstition, but an intense inner conviction. I do not think anybody will ever be found with that intense inner conviction about hell. They believe that they will be burnt for ever because they have been so taught. This sounds, perhaps, a little like abandoning reason in favour of intuition, but then it must be remembered that that very buddhi which we translate "intuition" is known in India as "pure reason". It is the reason of the ego, which is of a higher type than that which we have in lower planes.

The Master goes on to give instances with regard to this question of superstition :

> You must learn that no ceremonies are necessary ; else you will think yourself somehow better than those who do not perform them. Yet you must not condemn others who still cling to ceremonies. Let them do as they will ; only they must not interfere with you who know the truth—they must not try to force upon you that which you have outgrown. Make allowance for everything ; be kindly towards everything.

C.W.L.—The Master spoke so strongly about ceremonies perhaps because the life of the youth of the high Brāhmana caste to which Alcyone belonged begins to be very full of them at about the age which he had then reached. There is a tendency at that time for a boy to consider himself very important on account of them, for he is quite the centre of a great deal of attention which surrounds the *upanayana* or initiation of a boy into his full caste privileges. The life of an orthodox Brāhmana is full of ceremonial ; there are gestures to be made and texts to be recited at the time of rising, bathing, eating and almost every other action. Some people round Alcyone were probably trying to make him do these very fully, because they feared that modern education and the European friends he had made might possibly divert him from the old cult of his people ; so the Master guarded His pupil by saying that they were not absolutely necessary and that when doing them or when giving them up he must take care not to fall into the error and folly of thinking himself superior on that account.

Christian ceremonials differ from those of the Hindus and Buddhists in being generally done by a number of people together. Worship is nearly always individual among the latter, but in Christendom it is mainly collective. Though all these ceremonials are not necessary (except for the people whose temperament is so strongly in favour of them that they cannot really be happy without them), they are nevertheless a form of science, dealing with natural forces of the inner planes in perfectly definite ways.

There are many ways in which spiritual force can be poured out upon the world. That which we find in the ceremony of the Mass, the Holy Communion or the Holy Eucharist, is one instituted by the Founder of Christianity Himself, for the distribution through His Church of what is commonly called the divine grace—certain spiritual forces of the higher planes, which are, of course, not supernatural, but superphysical. He arranged it so that the priest, whatever his nature might be, doing the ceremony would be a channel for the distribution of this force. It would be all the better that the priest should be a really good man, full of thoughts of devotion and service, but it has been arranged that the ceremonial shall be effective in any case, for the benefit of the people. The general Christian scheme is that there shall be Churches dotted over the land, so that the outpouring may radiate out and reach everybody. This ceremony does enormous good to millions of people, but to say that it is necessary for salvation would be superstition.

Various forces are tapped by different ceremonies. They all, no matter how spiritual, work under the laws of nature, and if, therefore, the benefit of them is to be felt in the physical world there must be a physical mechanism through which they can work. It is the same in the case of electricity; the force exists all about us all the time and is always in activity, but if you want it to perform a particular work in a particular way in a particular place you must provide certain physical machinery through which it can operate.

A.B.—The Master says that no ceremonies are necessary, and all the religions recognize this truth. In India, the man who is highest and most respected of all is the sannyāsī, who performs no ceremonies at all. He breaks and throws away the sacred thread, which was his most important possession, put upon him when as a boy he was initiated into his caste, and worn throughout life as his most sacred symbol, until he became a sannyāsī.

Ceremonies are only necessary so long as a man has not reached realization and true knowledge, so long as they help to give him right emotions, quiet thoughts and noble aspirations. The great majority of people are still undeveloped and need all the help that can be given them in any way. Therefore no wise man will condemn ceremonies, though they are not necessary for him. The *Bhagavad Gītā* is the gospel of the sannyāsī, yet it is there written: "Let no wise man unsettle the minds of the ignorant, attached to action, but acting in harmony with Me, let him render all action attractive."[1] The child who is learning to walk catches hold of any thing that is firm enough to help him to sustain himself on his feet—chairs, table-legs and walls. So ceremonies are supports, intended for the man who is not strong enough to support himself. As a man develops, his ceremonies become more refined, more beautiful and symbolical, and at last he arrives at a stage when they are no longer of any use to him and he lets them go. There are two kinds of people who do not perform ceremonies—those who are above them, and those who are beneath them.

The responsibility of choosing the point when he shall abandon ceremonies rests entirely with the man concerned; each must decide for himself. None can take the responsibility of saying when a man should become a yogī. So also with ceremonies; none must criticize when a man decides to give them up, or chooses to retain them. Sometimes a man may still feel bound to attend them after he feels that he no longer needs them himself, on account of his position in the community. He alone is responsible for his choice, so we must not condemn those who perform ceremonies, nor those who do not perform them.

Ceremonies may be dangerous as well as helpful. In ancient Hinduism there was a strict rule forbidding the utterance of certain formulæ in a crowd; it was not made in order to withhold any benefit from the people, as nowadays is sometimes ignorantly supposed, but to avoid the harm that certain vibrations might do to some

[1] *Op. cit.*, III, 26.

people. It was on this account that Manu laid down the law that only Brāhmanas who were learned and of good life should be invited to the *shrāddha* ceremonies. A person who has some power but does not understand when he should use it and when he should withhold it might possibly, if he assisted at certain ceremonies, put strength into the formulæ which might injure the people present; for that reason one who has begun to gain such power might do well to keep away. I found, for example, when I attended some *shrāddha* ceremonies at Gayā, that had I added my force to them, I might have injured the priests, for some of the mantras which they were reciting were exceedingly powerful. They, however, did not bring out the power, since they were ignorant and not very clean-living men. Madame Blavatsky advised students of occultism not to go into a crowd unless they were in perfect sympathy with it, not merely because of any effect it might have on their own auras, but because their force might do more harm than good. In such cases, a man with knowledge might find it better sometimes not to take part in certain ceremonies, while another who did not understand how to say the formula in such a way as to bring out the power which is really in it might attend with perfect safety to the people around him, no matter what kind of people they might be.

Now that your eyes are opened, some of your old beliefs, your old ceremonies, may seem to you absurd; perhaps, indeed, they really are so. Yet

though you can no longer take part in them, respect them for the sake of those good souls to whom they are still important. They have their place, they have their use; they are like those double lines which guided you as a child to write straight and evenly, until you learnt to write far better and more freely without them. There was a time when you needed them; but now that time is past.

A.B.—Inevitably, as we grow older and wiser, some things in which we used to believe take on an aspect of non-reality and even absurdity; yet we can look at them kindly and sympathetically, as we can look on a child nursing a bundle of rags which she makes believe to be a doll. From one point of view the child's action is somewhat grotesque, but it is doing her a real service, for it develops the mother instinct in the little girl—she does not see the rags; she sees a child; and as she fondles and comforts her imaginary child she practises maternal tenderness and protection, and care of the weak and helpless. So, when we smile at that little child, our smile is a very tender and gentle one. It is the same with our old beliefs and ceremonies; they had their place; they had their use.

If one finds a savage tribe performing ceremonies which to us seem quite absurd, or when we see, as we frequently do in India, a rag tied to a village tree as an offering, we should not despise the poor outer expression of the savage's or villager's devotion—we ought to look at the feeling underlying it. Their humble offerings may mean as much to them as the costliest one could mean to us; the same spirit is underneath.

All outer offerings are unnecessary; the only acceptable one is the offering of the heart, and where that accompanies the gift the poorest gift becomes acceptable. Therefore it says in the *Gītā* that even a leaf, a flower, a fruit or a little water, if offered with devotion, is acceptable to the Supreme.[1] It would be a hard and unbrotherly act to discourage these things—to tear away the rag from the tree, for instance, as has sometimes been done—it would show a complete lack of the feeling of unity.

C.W.L.—Always be gentle and kindly towards childhood—that of the children, and the general childhood of the human race at its present stage as well. Our President has spoken of a little child nursing a bundle of rags and pretending that it is a doll. That is a superstition, of course, but at the same time it does not occur to anyone indignantly to scold the child for it. On the physical plane it is a bundle of rags, but in the child's imagination it is perhaps almost a living thing, with all sorts of qualities. One cannot disturb the idea in the child's mind without injuring the development of good feelings that are being aroused.

She has also mentioned the practice of the common people of India, who sometimes tie a piece of rag on a tree as an offering to the deity. The average Christian missionary would come along and be very angry about

[1] *Op. cit.*, IX, 26.

it, thereby showing his own ignorance, because the offering is made in all good faith. The comparatively primitive and childlike soul meant it well, and the thing should be taken like the child's rag doll, for what it means. They pour out a little water as a libation, or they offer a flower—a very small offering truly, but why should it be despised? The Christ Himself said that those who gave even a cup of cold water in His Name and for His sake should by no means lose their reward. It must be remembered, too, that probably no people, not even the most primitive, think of the statue or the form as a reality, but all have some sense of the Deity behind it.

> A great Teacher once wrote: "When I was a child, I spake as a child, I understood as a child, I thought as a child; but when I became a man I put away childish things." Yet he who has forgotten his childhood and lost sympathy with the children is not the man who can teach them or help them. So look kindly, gently, tolerantly upon all; but upon all alike, Buddhist or Hindu, Jain or Jew, Christian or Muhammadan.

A.B.—You have there an exact description of the occultist; he is the man who has not forgotten his childhood. He has grown to manhood, but he remembers what he has passed through, and so he can help all. In order to train ourselves in this power of sympathy for all and help towards all, it is a good practice to translate your religious thoughts into the language of some particular exoteric religion, to put your thought into its formulæ. We all have one particular language of our own, in which we express things to ourselves, until we reach the stage when we have a common language in which we can speak to anybody. The student will do well to study some language or form other than his own. Those who have been brought up as Christians might practise speaking and thinking in terms of Hinduism; then they would learn to see things from the Hindu standpoint, and would be quite astonished to see how different they looked from what they had imagined them to be. Hindus might similarly learn to speak and think in terms used in Christianity.

Shrī Rāmakrishna Paramahamsa, the guru of Swāmī Vivekānanda, trained himself in that way. He took several religions in turn, and for the time being followed their methods and practices. He took up Christianity: prayed in the Christian way, thought in Christian terms, and even dressed in Christian dress; and thus he went through one religion after another, learning to identify himself with each. He used every outside help that he could contrive in order to help himself in this effort. When he was trying to realize the mother side of nature, that which is represented by the Virgin Mary in the West, by the Shaktis in Hinduism, he dressed himself as a woman and thought of himself as a woman. Certainly the result of these practices in his case was very beautiful, for all outer religious differences ceased entirely to affect him.

How different is this line from that which most people pursue! Yet it is only by learning to identify oneself with all around that one can fit oneself for discipleship. Shri Rāmakrishna was fundamentally a bhakta, a devotee, and he learned through emotion in this way.

The aspirant should try for a time, then, to think of himself as a Hindu, or a Buddhist, or a woman—something which he is not. How few men ever try to think or feel as a woman does, to see things as she sees them! I suppose, too, that not many women really try to see things from a man's standpoint; but it is more marked in men—a man always wants to feel himself "he". Even among Theosophists it seems to me that the fact of our brotherhood being without distinction of sex is sometimes overlooked.

Learn also to understand how things would appear to you if coming to you through some particular atmosphere to which you are not accustomed. You have to cure yourself of the habit of looking at things exclusively from your own standpoint—that is contrary to occultism. Do this, and in the world you will be blamed; your impartiality and sympathy will be called indifference. That does not in the least matter. I have been accused of being "too Hindu" in the West, and of being "too Christian" in the East; because in the West I speak in Western terms and the people in India do not like it, and in the East I speak in Eastern terms and the people in the West do not like it. My answer to such complaints always is that I speak to the people in the language which they understand.

Such complaints and such blame rise from looking at things from the lower pole instead of from the higher. To learn to speak many religious languages is one of the lessons necessary for the man who is to carry the message to many lands. This is no new truth, and the blame which follows such action is also not new. The great reproach made against S. Paul was that he was all things to all men. He wrote: "For though I be free from all men, yet have I made myself servant unto all, that I might gain the more. And unto the Jews I became as a Jew, that I might gain the Jews; to them that are under the law, as under the law, that I might gain them that are under the law; to them that are without law, as without law, (being not without law to God, but under the law to Christ,) that I might gain them that are without law. To the weak I became as weak, that I might gain the weak; I am made all things to all men, that I might by all means save some."[1] From being one of the straitest, he became one of the most liberal of men; he belonged to one of the strictest sects of the Jews, yet became the apostle of the Gentiles—a remarkable transformation.

The occultist belongs to no religion or to all religions, according to the way you like to put it—to none exclusively, to all inclusively. Nothing less than that is tolerance. The reason why it is good to keep out of controversies is that for the time one may become intolerant; it is difficult to be quite impartial, if one is to be effective, when controverting a one-sided presentment.

[1] I Corinthians, 9, 19-22.

Always put the truth from the standpoint of unity, not from that of difference; then only will you be able to help all, and all alike. Then only will you be able to see the good in each and all, overlooking and looking through that which is defective.

C.W.L.—The Theosophist aims at brotherhood without distinction of race, creed, caste, sex or colour. That brotherhood can best be lived when we are able to enter into the feelings and thoughts of those of other races and creeds, and of the other sex. A man forgets the fact that he has had many births in feminine form; a woman also forgets that she has had many incarnations in masculine bodies. Though not easy to do, it is an exceedingly good exercise for the man to try to put himself in thought in the woman's place and to understand her way of looking on life; and so also for a woman to try to see how a man envisages things. The two points of view are surprisingly different in various ways. One who can identify his consciousness with that of the opposite sex has already taken a step towards a brotherhood which transcends the idea of sex. Having tried to understand the point of view of his sisters or mother or wife, a man may then extend this practice to people of other religions and races than his own. It is a most helpful exercise, because when anyone can really understand and thoroughly sympathize with another person's point of view, he has widened his own outlook by just that much.

Concerning tolerance there is a good story in the Talmud, about Abraham, when once a traveller came to him, and he was about to give him food and drink, as is the custom of the desert. Abraham called upon his visitor to praise God before eating, but when he refused and said he did not know anything about God, Abraham rose in anger and turned him out of his tent, and would not give him anything at all. Then the Lord came along, as apparently He used to do in those days, and said: "Why did you send him away?" Abraham replied, with great indignation, "Lord, He refused to recognize Thy Name; he is an infidel of the worst type." "Yes," God said, "but I have borne with Him for sixty years; surely you might bear with him for one hour."

Some of us who are Theosophists still have an outward religion to which we cling, yet I think we ought to be able to say that we belong to no religion exclusively, but to all of them inclusively. I myself, for example, am a Christian Bishop, but I am also a Buddhist, because I took the vows and obligations by which I accepted the Lord Buddha as my guide. In that, I was not asked to renounce any other religion. Buddhism is perhaps the widest of all religions in that respect—they do not ask you what you believe, but whether you will follow the teaching of the Lord Buddha and live so far as you can the life He commends. A Christian, Muhammadan or follower of any other religion might say, "The teaching is good teaching, I will undertake to follow it", and thereby become a Buddhist, without leaving his previous religion. Theosophy is the truth which lies behind all these religions. We study comparative religion, not merely to see that the Theosophical truths do appear in all religions, but also that we may understand the different presentations of truth and be able to help along all these lines.

Our President shows us the value of this. She speaks as a Hindu to the Hindus; she quotes from their Scriptures in support of what she says, using some of their own Sanskrit terms—and that appeals to them just as the sonorous Latin appeals to a Roman Catholic. When she speaks to the Buddhists she says exactly the same things, but quotes the sayings of the Lord Budhha, and uses the terminology of Buddhism. In the Western world you will hear her speak to Christians in their own terms, not in the least changing her own belief or religion, but simply speaking their language. She is, of course, learned in all those religions. When we know the truth behind all religions, even though we cannot begin to compare with her in knowledge and skill of utterance, many of us can by a little study of a primer of any particular religion, understand it well and become able to present the truth in its terms, and to explain the meaning of much that is obscure to others. I have heard Colonel Olcott do it again and again. He was not a man of the student or scholar-type, but he was an exceedingly good practical lecturer. He would speak effectively to audiences of Hindus, Parsis and Buddhists, and learned men of all those faiths agreed in saying that he had given them new light on their respective religions. That shows how Theosophy is the master key to all the religions. At the great conventions of our Society at Adyar the same fact appears in another way, for people of many different religions and races, gather together, and no one who attends can fail to be deeply impressed with not merely the tolerance, but the active affectionate brotherhood that is shown there.

CHAPTER 4

CHEERFULNESS

4. *Cheerfulness.*—You must bear your karma cheerfully, whatever it may be, taking it as an honour that suffering comes to you, because it shows that the Lords of Karma think you worth helping.

A.B.—This is the qualification which, as I have already explained, was formerly frequently translated endurance. Endurance may be a somewhat negative virtue; but what you have to do is not so much to endure things which you cannot help as to take them cheerfully and brightly, facing all trouble with a smile. The word cheerfulnees gives you the whole idea of what is required by the great Teachers with regard to this particular endowment. Many people can endure, but they do so sadly; you must take all your trials and troubles brightly. On that point a great deal of stress is laid in some of the Hindu books; things are to be taken gladly.

That karma is very much quickened for people who come forward and offer themselves as candidates for the Path is a fact that been much emphasized; this is done first in order to warn people beforehand of what they have to expect, and secondly, in order to cheer them up and when the experience comes to them practically, instead of only theoretically—for that makes a great difference.

Karma, being a law of nature, can be avoided for a while or else can be brought immediately into effect, that is to say, you can put yourself into conditions where it will affect you or into others where you will be sheltered from it for the time being. It is necessary to repeat very often that the laws of nature are not enactments; they do not command us to do anything. To take a common illustration: electrical forces are always in activity about us, but if we want them to produce certain effects at a given place and time, we require a special apparatus in order to bring them into manifestation. Similarly, karma is a law of nature, and the apparatus which may start its forces working in the life of an individual may be his appearance on the stage of physical life through the process we call birth. Some changes in an individual's life may very much intensify and quicken the working of the law of karma upon him. When, for example, you offer yourself as a candidate for rapid progress, Those who administer the laws of karma may, by your consent, which you have given, modify the apparatus, so to speak, and let the force which is there show itself more strongly, exhaust itself upon you in a shorter time. Your will is the real cause of the alteration in the apparatus.

If the expressed desire to grow more rapidly, and therefore to get rid quickly of his evil karma, is a real wish on the man's part, so that his soul is set in that direction, then his wish reaches the Lords of Karma, and They put in motion the karma he has made in the past and let it descend upon him. The karma was there; it is not that the man is creating anything new, but he begins to clear off what he has stored up.

If you realize what is taking place, you will not be surprised at anything that may happen to you. Consider the lives of Alcyone, and see how many terrible things occurred in them. In one life his child was murdered; in another he was executed for a crime he had not committed, and so on. You scarcely realize these things when you read them like a story; but you would think them very dreadful if any of them were to happen to you in this life. All those misfortunes and sorrows were so much clearing off of bad karma.

When troubles fall quickly on you it shows that the Lords of Karma have taken notice of your prayer, and that is a very good sign. If things were to go on very smoothly it would mean that They had not yet taken notice. So in this matter again the occult view reverses the judgment of the world: the things which the world calls evil are, from the occult standpoint good.

When to the pain and loss which fall upon you there is added the censure and ungenerous criticism of those around you, then you have the best karma of all. Some misfortunes at once awaken sympathy in others, and all the sympathy poured out on the man who is suffering helps him a great deal. But other misfortunes may excite blame; you may have done your best but acute suffering has fallen upon you, and in addition the world turns against you and blames you. When this happens one is clearing off a great amount of past karma; that additional disagreeable factor enables one to work it off quickly and thoroughly.

It is easy to see that these things are true theoretically, as you hear or read them; but what you have to do is to remember them at the right moment. What people generally do is to admit them till the time comes for their practical realization, and then promptly to forget them. Try to get these facts so thoroughly into your mind that you cannot forget them, so that the thought of them shall strengthen you when suffering and enable you to help others when they are suffering. It may help a little towards the clear understanding that is needed if you look around you and see how constantly troubles come to very good people, who have done, as so often one hears it said, nothing to deserve them—that is, nothing in their present lives, which are noble and useful ones. Our tendency is to compare ourselves with those who are more fortunate than we are; it is well sometimes to do so with those who are less fortunate, that we may feel gratitude for all the good that we have received. We are liable to forget how much there is for which we should feel grateful, because we think always of whatever pain and loss fall to our share; but we ought not to do this.

C.W.L.—No one who really understands and believes in the law of karma can fail to be cheerful. It should be made quite clear that karma is a law, like gravitation, and it is always acting. People sometimes think of it and speak of it as though it came into operation occasionally when they do something. This is not true; we are under its operation every moment. A man provides conditions in which the law of karma can act upon him when he does or thinks or speaks some definite thing. The law of karma for each of us at this moment has an account with us, the sum total of our good and our bad deeds. Because we have all come up through savage states when we did all sorts of uncontrolled things, there is likely to be a certain amount of evil karma waiting for all of us, unless we have spent many lives working it out. When we find suffering coming upon us, we should assume that we are working out, perhaps, the last part of that karma. If we read the stories of some of the greatest of the saints we shall find that they passed through an immense amount of suffering. All the people who have tried to help the world have suffered terribly. It is part of the training for Initiation, but it is absolute justice always, for not even for the purposes of training can any injustice take place.

The Lords of Karma are simply the Administrators of that Law. In some ways perhaps the word Lords is a little indefinite, because it rather suggests that They direct and rule karma. You cannot direct or rule gravitation; but you can make arrangements to use it at certain points and in certain ways. So with the law of karma; those who are working in connection with it are its administrators. One function of the Lords of Karma is to select a certain part of a man's store of karma and give it to him to work out in his forthcoming incarnation.

They cannot take more of good or more of evil than there is in the man's karma, but They do select from that what They think he can work through. Still, the man's will is free, and if the selected karma is worked through sooner than They had expected, if one may put it that way, They may give some more. "Whom the Lord loveth He chasteneth"—that is the meaning of that extraordinary statement. People also make much trouble from themselves which is not within their karma from the past, by taking things hardly instead of philosophically, and also by downright folly—but the Lords of Karma are not responsible for this.

However hard it is, be thankful that it is no worse.

C.W.L.—The tendency of almost everyone who suffers is to say how hard it is and to think of other times when things were better. We may take it the other way and say, "Things might have been much worse than this," and also, "I am very glad to be working off all this karma; I might have had much more to work out; at least let me make the best of it."

Remember that you are of but little use to the Master until your evil karma is worked out, and you are free.

A.B.—From the Master's standpoint it is a very good thing for a man to get rid of a piece of bad Karma which is hanging over him in the background, for we have to remember that the Master is hampered by the bad karma of those who wish to serve Him; it prevents His using them as freely as He otherwise could do. Madame Blavatsky, who always spoke very openly about herself, being truthful through and through, said of the Coulomb trouble: "I have not deserved it now, but for my past." It was a vital thing for her to get rid of this karma, and so the scandalous and shameful way she was treated throughout that affair was the greatest blessing for her; she recognized this when she looked at the matter philosophically, but at times she was disturbed by it on the surface.

All aspirants ought to be helped by that thought, helped to look away from themselves to Him and to think: "These troubles that I am going through make me more useful to Him."

If you have asked that your karma shall be quickened it is unreasonable to complain when your request is granted. Keep the inspiring idea always in your thoughts: "I shall be of more use to the Master the freer I become." A gift, once given, must not be taken back. This idea is very common in some of the old Indian books, recurring over and over again in the stories told in them; a gift once given, or a word once spoken, cannot be taken back. If a gift that you have once given should be put back into your hands by circumstances you must give it again; it is not yours, and to keep it would be theft. So, when there is this gift of yourself—the highest and noblest gift of all—you must never take it back. People continually give themselves verbally to the Master, but keep a finger on the gift in order to be able to pull it back if the Master goes too far—that is really what it comes to. They draw back, if the Master takes them at their word, as sometimes He might do, in order to let them see that they had been deceiving themselves, and had promised more than they were prepared to fulfil.

C.W.L.—If all one's bad karma were exhausted one would have the whole of one's time and strength free for the Master's work. It has been explained that the Master is hampered by our bad karma, and therefore in getting rid of it quickly we are making ourselves more fit to serve Him. Madame Blavatsky took that view very strongly with regard to the attacks made upon her by Madame Coulomb and others in Madras about the year 1884. While she was indignant that the attacks should be made, and sad at the ingratitude which they showed, and also disturbed lest they should reflect upon her Society and injure it, yet she said: "At least there is this to remember, that all these troubles make me more fit to serve Him."

We can apply that idea to the Society's troubles as well as to our own. Think always of the service of the Master when the Society is getting rid of what is evil; it goes forward the moment it has passed through some particular trouble, for it has got rid of some bad karma and so become more useful, a better instrument for its true owners.

Having disposed of that portion of its karma the Society could move onward to greater things. Such karma shakes out the dead material, the people who have reached their "saturation-point for truth", as

Madame Blavatsky used to express it, and cannot go further. They may previously have been a great help, but they have become a hindrance to future progress. Yet the rest of us are often very sorry to lose those friends. In the last trouble, it seemed to me that I was somewhat of a storm-centre, and that there was very good excuse for many of the people who misunderstood, so I ventured to represent to the Mahāchohan that the test was very hard for them, and to ask for an act of grace for them. Naturally, He smiled kindly at my presumption, and said: "Will you be satisfied if the same people throw aside Mrs. Besant?" "Oh, yes," I said, "of course." I felt they would not do *that*, but a few months later they did turn against her, and the Mahāchohan said, with the same gentle smile: "You see; for this life their sun has set. But there are other lives, and the sun will rise again to-morrow."

No one is indispensable, though it does sometimes happen in India that a Lodge grows up round some influential member, and fades away again when he removes to some other town. When Madame Blavatsky went, many of us, accustomed to daily inspiration from her, felt that all would be dark. Another great individuality arose in the person of our present President. Yet I am sure that she would be the first to say that we need not be anxious for the Society when her turn comes to leave us. The instruments change their bodies—"in the sight of the unwise they seem to die." But the Masters who stand behind do not die, and while They are there some one will always be found to continue Their work.

By offering yourself to Him, you have asked that your karma may be hurried, and so now in one or two lives you work through what otherwise might have been spread over a hundred. But in order to make the best out of it you must bear it cheerfully, gladly.

A.B.—According to the way in which an old debt is paid, a new cause is started. That should never be forgotten. If you make the best of what looks like bad karma you set in motion new forces for good, whereas if you take bad karma unwillingly and pay your debts grudgingly, the reverse happens. Remember how the Christ said in the sermon on the Mount: "Agree with thine adversary quickly, whiles thou art in the way with him."[1] That is good counsel to follow in the adverse circumstances that come to you. Your troubles and losses appear to you to come as adversaries; meet them bravely, agree with them quickly, and then they will be done with. We should rid ourselves of our bad karma very much more rapidly if we did not sow new while reaping the old.

C.W.L.—People sometimes talk of giving themselves to the Master, and are then afraid that the Master will ask too much. That is the spirit of Ananias and Sapphira. That unfortunate couple had assuredly the most perfect right to retain part of their goods for themselves if they wished to do so, but they made a mistake when they pretended that they were giving everything. To say,

[1] S. Matthew, 5, 25.

"I can give this; I can do this much for Him, but I cannot give myself unreservedly", marks a stage through which we pass. But when one offers himself to the Master it ought to be in the same whole-hearted spirit that he would give any other gift. It should be offered without reservation as to how it should be used, and one should not want to take any of it back. No one need fear that He will want too much. If we offer ourselves to the Master we must not be surprised and hurt if suffering comes suddenly upon us. That shows that the offering has been partially accepted. Many things that the world calls evil and suffering may therefore be taken as signs of swift progress. Instead of sympathizing with us people often blame us, but generally that is the best karma of all. To be misunderstood, so that our good shall be evil spoken of, as Ruysbroek put it, seems to come always when people are drawing near to their final goal. It has happened to every great occult or mystical teacher all through history. To bear it all cheerfully in itself makes good karma and develops in us various valuable qualities—patience, perseverance, endurance, long-suffering, determination. So, out of evil long past, we may bring good.

> Yet another point. You must give up all feeling of possession. Karma may take from you the things which you like best—even the people whom you love most. Even then you must be cheerful—ready to part with anything and everything.

A.B.—We come now to a thing that is enormously more difficult than the preceding. The bearing of past karma is far easier than this. You must eliminate of all feeling of ownership—first of all for things, and then for persons. The latter is a more subtle task; have you given up all sense of possession with regard to the people you love best? Even when people think they have done so, circumstances arise to test them, and often show that they have not. Can you let a life go out of your own, which is more to you than your own life? You may call this the last and most difficult test of your real devotion to the Master. It is a point on which all aspirants should try to test themselves, before the test comes upon them by circumstances, because they can lessen the blow by practising beforehand. Do not try to kill out the love you feel towards anyone—that is the way of the dark powers. You might practise by loving a person all the time, but withdrawing yourself for a time from that person's society, by doing some work which has to be done away from the person who makes life happy for you, or in some such way as that. If you can do that cheerfully and gladly, you are well on the way to answer the call when it comes—the call to leave all and follow the Master.

Remember how much stress is laid upon that in the accounts that have come down to us of what took place when the Lord Maitreya was in Palestine. Not everyone who was called rose to the height of his opportunity, but some did so. Those who forsook all and followed Him became teachers after He went away; the others never heard of Him again. Remember the case of the rich young man who went away sorrowing, although it was only riches he was asked to abandon. People think that they would have obeyed the call at once, had they been in that young man's place, yet I am not sure that there are many people who would leave great possessions to follow a vagrant preacher—for that was how the Christ appeared, as a wandering teacher surrounded by some half-educated people. Yet this is the test of discipleship, to forsake everything—the things you most like and the people you love best—and follow the Master.

C.W.L.—We must realize that nothing is ours in the personal sense, that whatever we have is given to us in trust for the work of evolution. If one has money or is in a position of influence, that is because it gives the opportunity of doing more for the work. Nothing is our own, in the sense that we may make a separate use of it; one is always in the position of the trusted manager or employee who is using the firm's money, but is in every respect just as careful with every penny of it as he would be if it were his own. That ought to be the attitude of every rich man, and every man in a position of power.

The attitude of living as a representative of humanity is very wonderfully and beautifully expressed by the Masters. They regard Themselves merely as stewards of all the mighty powers which They possess. That is why the Master makes no karma, either good or ill, to bind Him to the human condition. Those who are the greatest actors and performers make no karma that binds Them, because They do all impersonally, utterly without personal desire. They do it all as a soldier fights in battle, with no thought of the particular enemy whom he happens to kill, but with the feeling that he is working for a cause, as part of a mighty machine. So They work as part of the Great Brotherhood, as part of the Hierarchy, part of humanity, and all the good they do comes back to humanity and helps to uplift it.

First we must have no feeling of possession about things, and then about people, which is harder still ; they may be taken from us by death, as it is called, and also perhaps for service to humanity. Of many thousands that was true during the Great War ; the wife gave her husband, the mother her son, to go forth and fight for the right. Surely it is not for us ever to hesitate to do as well in the Master's service as so many thousands of others have done in the service of their nations. It is difficult to let a life go out of ours which is more to us than our own life, and yet many have had to do that—some under very sad circumstances, others in conditions which made the sacrifice holy and beautiful.

It is the way of those who follow the darker magic to kill out love and so escape all this suffering. But those who would be of the Great White Brotherhood must make their love ever stronger, yet kill out the selfishness that so often mars it. Remember how a sword pierced the heart of our Lady Herself, the Blessed Virgin Mary. She might have escaped that sword if she had chosen to tear out from her heart all remembrance of her Son and forget Him altogether. In many cases it is as Christ said of Himself, "Think not that I am come to send peace on earth: I came not to send peace, but a sword."[1] He meant that His new teaching would be taken up here and there by one in a family, and that the others would object and so cause division, or that one might have to leave his old home and friends for the sake of some special work that he could do. Similarly there have been cases where one member of a family has seen the Theosophical truth and the rest have not, and that has led to suffering and division. Often, in modern days, one will leave the family to go to the other side of the earth in order to make money, and no one objects to that; but if one should propose to do it for the good of humanity there is immediate protest—so unevolved is the spirit of our time.

Remember the difficulties that King Suddhodana created when Prince Siddhārtha wished to devote himself to the religious life. He spent vast sums of money and a great part of his life in endeavouring to keep his son back from the high destiny that opened before him—endeavouring to make him, instead of the greatest religious teacher the world had ever known, the greatest king in India—an alternative future that the astrologers had foretold for him. The king knew that to become a religious teacher would mean poverty and self-abnegation for his son, and he did not realize that it would be in reality a higher position than that of any king. It is not the great king whose name goes down longest and

[1] S. Matthew, 10, 34.

furthest in history, but the great religious teacher. King Suddhodana wished enormous power and fame without parallel for his son, and it came, but not in the way for which he had hoped and planned. The power of Lord Buddha is greater than that of any earthly monarch, and his renown has spread all over the world.

The Christ said to the people: "Forsake all and follow Me." When our Christian friends read this in the Gospel they feel that they would have done it at once. That is not so certain. Let us try to put ourselves into the place of the people of that time. Remember the young man with great possessions and great riches who came to Him; those possessions probably brought their duties which he felt he had to fulfil, and therefore he could not forsake them. All the public opinion of the time, all the respectability, and all the orthodox powers were arrayed against the Christ; He was only a poor wandering Teacher who had nowhere to lay His head. Would we have followed Him in the face of all that? Is it so certain that we would have forsaken everything to follow Him whom all the elders and the high priests and the orthodox people stigmatized as a fanatic? Would we not have felt a doubt as to whether, after all, we might not be throwing away the substance and grasping at the shadow? It is not so certain. In the present day, perhaps, it looks like that still, and yet those of us who have thrown away other things for the sake of following Them have never for one moment regretted it.

Often the Master needs to pour out His strength upon others through His servant; He cannot do that if the servant yields to depression. So cheerfulness must be the rule.

C.W.L.—Constantly all through this book the same reason is brought forward for everything that is to be done, that it is for the sake of the service of the Master. We might expect many other reasons to be given against depression—that it is bad for the person and it has an unpleasant effect upon others; but the one point which is emphasized here is that the Master cannot use us as a channel for His force if we yield to it.

A.B.—Here the reason why cheerfulness must be the rule is given, for again that inspiring idea is presented, that the Master needs your help, that you can be of use to Him! His force is all joyous because it is part of the force of the Logos; it cannot therefore pour out through a pipe that is choked with depression.

It may sound strange to say that the Master is unable to do this or that, yet the fact is so. Now and again one will hear the Master say of something: "I could not succeed in doing it." Their power is limited when They work down here, by the conditions that exist on the physical plane. Often They cannot reach a person on the physical plane except through an intermediary; therefore They need the help which perhaps you can give Them. Without that help, things have to remain undone, and later on, in consequence, obstacles have to be removed which need never have been there.

CHAPTER 5

ONE-POINTEDNESS

5. ***One-pointedness.*****—The one thing that you must set before you is to do the Master's work. Whatever else may come in your way to do, that at least you must never forget.**

C.W.L.—In ordinary life one-pointedness is necessary for real success. The one-pointed man always wins in the end, because all his powers are working together, while other people have a variety of aims, and are constantly changing them. The man who sets himself to make money, for example, and uses all his thought and will for that purpose, and watches and plans for it all the time, is almost sure to gain his object. If one determines all the time to serve the Master with constantly increasing power, and is willing to put aside *all* other things for that, his progress will be swift indeed.

Yet nothing else *can* come in your way, for all helpful, unselfish work is the Master's work, and you must do it for His sake. And you must give all your attention to each piece as you do it, so that it may be your very best.

C.W.L.—A good deal of a pupil's work consists in preparing himself for more responsible work for the Master in the future. Some of it is not directly useful in the Master's present plans, but may be compared to much of the work of a boy at school, who in learning, for example, Latin, is not doing any particular good, but is or ought to be developing powers of mind and qualities of character which will be useful in later life. The duties of common life often combine something of both these things, for they provide a splendid training and education for those who do them well, and also offer many occasions for helping other people to progress in character and ideals, which is most emphatically the Master's work. All the varied activities of daily life will come within our one-pointed endeavour to serve the Master, when we learn to do them all in His name and for Him. The Master's work for us is not something peculiar and apart from our fellows. To raise a good family who will serve Him in turn, to make money to use in His service, to win power in order to help Him, with it, are all part of it; yet in doing these things we must be ever on guard against self-deception, that we are not cloaking with the holiness of the Master's name what is, underneath, a selfish desire to wield power or handle money.

That same Teacher also wrote: "Whatsoever ye do, do it *heartily*, as to the Lord, and not unto men." Think how you would do a piece of work if you knew that the Master was coming at once

to look at it ; just in that way you must do all your work. Those who know most will most know all that that verse means. And there is another like it, much older : "Whatsoever thy hand findeth to do, do it with thy might."

C.W.L.—The whole world exists within the consciousness of the Lord of the World, the One Initiator, and therefore everything that we do is being done in His Presence. From that is derived the old Christian idea of the omniscience and omnipresence of God, of whom it is said, "In Him we live and move and have our being." It is not a poetic fancy, but a scientific fact, that we live within the aura of the great Spiritual King of the world. Of course, a consciousness that can grasp all the world simultaneously is to us inconceivably incomprehensible, yet one day we shall reach His stupendous level.

The old conception of God used to make His omnipresence a terrible thought ; God was supposed to be one who was always watching to find fault, looking eagerly for any breach of His rules that He might come down in wrath upon the hapless offender. Many a child has suffered terribly because of that thought that God sees everything that he does ; he feels it in a way unfair that there can be no privacy. This is especially so because a frightened child cannot tell how his mentor will take anything that he does. But if instead one realizes the mighty divine Love, then one begins to see that His omnipresence is our safety and our greatest blessing.

A.B.—The test that the Master gives here should be applied to all our work. Suppose you are writing a letter; if you knew that the Master would come and read it over, it would be very carefully written, both as to its contents and its form. Whatever your work is, it is His work, if it is the best you can do; whether it is something that the Master wants done for some immediate purpose, or something that prepares you for future work. Everything is for Him, if we are His; it cannot be for anybody else. Make this your normal and continual attitude of mind, and you make the atmosphere in which one-pointedness can grow.

If we had that real one-pointedness, how splendidly everything would go. That thought of doing all because of His service is one which I keep in my own mind, just as younger disciples can do, though I have more force of habit to help me than they have as yet. "Why should I answer this letter?" I sometimes ask myself; and the answer to my own question at once comes up in my mind: "It has come in my way to do, and so it is Master's work."

You will continue to hold this thought foremost in your minds all through the time that you are disciples; all have to make the habit, and when it is made they must go on strengthening it. That will help us to do with all our might whatever work we have. We must do it with our might because so it becomes part of the divine work, and because of the training of character that it gives. Make your work quite true, allowing nothing second-rate to pass.

One-pointedness means, too, that nothing shall ever turn you, even for a moment, from the Path upon which you have entered. No temptations, no worldly pleasures, no worldly affections even, must ever draw you aside. For you yourself must become one with the Path; it must be so much part of your nature that you follow it without needing to think of it, and cannot turn aside. You, the Monad, have decided it; to break away from it would be to break away from yourself.

C.W.L.—The statement that the individual must become one with the Path is made in other Scriptures besides this. The Christ said to His disciples, "I am the Way"[1]; Shrī Krishna made a very similar observation: "I am the way along which the traveller must walk." The same idea is put forward in *The Voice of the Silence*, where it said: "Thou canst not travel on the Path before thou hast become that Path itself." What is happening really is that one is becoming one's own true self. Patañjali, defining yoga, says that when a man has gained control of his mind he "resides in his own true state". The Monad is our true Self, the God in man, but he has put down a shadow of himself to form the ego, and that again has incarnated in a personality. Not until a man is considerably evolved can the ego manage the personality; before that, he looks down upon it without trying to do much in such a hopeless cause. Then comes the First Initiation, the

[1] S. John, 14, 6.

point when the personality has ceased to have a will of its own, and lives (except when it forgets) only to serve the higher. The ego is now active through it in the lower planes, and is beginning to realize the existence of the Monad, and to live according to its will. The Monad has determined the path for the ego's evolution; and he can choose no other, because he is becoming himself, gaining release from the bondage even of the spiritual planes. Constantly, while on the Path, the pupil will be swayed from side to side, but when he has achieved one-pointedness he will always swing back to the one right way.

A.B.—People often forget that they are the expression of the Monad. The real you is the Monad, and therefore whatever you do down here is done of your own true will, not through outer compulsion of another will. The Monad's will is your will; your desires are not your will at all, but you are drawn to outer things because one or other of your bodies wants to take a particular pleasure. It is not you who like the pleasure; it is the elemental material that wants to taste and experience it. Against this state of affairs you must oppose your true "I", which points undeviatingly to the highest. You must be like a strongly magnetized compass whose needle may indeed be drawn aside, but returns ever back. Until you are so strong that nothing can draw you aside, you must constantly practise bringing yourself back to the one will.

You are not matter; you must make matter your instrument. It is absurd that you should give way to the piece of material that you have picked up to fashion to your use. It is as though the hammer in the hand of the carpenter struck where *it* chose instead of where he chose, and crushed his finger instead of driving in the nail. It happens sometimes that a man crushes his own finger with his tool, but that is because he is a clumsy workman. Learn fidelity to your purpose, to your true will, and the time will come when you cannot turn aside from it.

One-pointedness can also be developed by concentration. Fix your attention on a small area at any given time; concentrate upon one thing at a time, so as to do it well. A quantity of water which is sufficient to make a strong current when penned into a channel, becomes a mere film when it is allowed to spread over a large surface. So is it with your energies. Take up one piece of work after another, and do each thing definitely and forcefully, instead of vaguely trying to do everything. If you follow this advice steadily you will soon begin to see some definite result, very small each week perhaps, but as the weeks pass the results accumulate and soon become very considerable in quantity of work done as well as in increase of power.

CHAPTER 6

CONFIDENCE

6. *Confidence.*—You must trust your master; you must trust yourself. If you have seen the Master, you will trust Him to the uttermost, through many lives and deaths. If you have not yet seen Him, you must still try to realize Him and trust Him, because if you do not, even He cannot help you.

C.W.L.—These are partly the words of Alcyone, who is speaking here of His Master; but the Master Himself spoke similarly of others greater than He, because just as we speak and think of the Masters so do They in turn speak and think of the Lord Buddha, of the Lord Maitreya, and others greater than Themselves.

It is practically impossible for us to realize a Master. We may try to do so; we may think of the highest ideals we know; but the Master embodies so many kinds of greatness that we cannot even imagine, that the highest ideal we can form of Him is still far too low. Such being the case, uttermost trust in His wisdom is but simple common sense.

Utter trust in the Master is largely a question of one's past. If we look at the lives of Alcyone we can see how that has been so in his case. He has been in close association with his Master through many past lives. From the same set of lives, I see, for example, that I myself have been in similar association with my Master, and so have others. I suppose I must take that as accounting for the fact that the moment I read of the Master I instantly felt the strongest possible attraction towards Him. When I had the privilege of seeing Him, it never for a moment occurred to me to distrust Him. In such cases it may be said that the ego knows, either by being aware of the Master's presence on the higher mental plane, or by memory of past lives in which the Master has been known. Sometimes the ego knows but cannot send that knowledge down into the personality, and sometimes it is transmitted imperfectly or incorrectly, or again, in other cases the ego simply does not know. The ego is never likely to be wrong; he is, apparently, not deceived about anything, but that he is ignorant of certain matters is quite clear, and indeed the very purpose of his incarnation is to remove that ignorance.

Those who have no proof of the existence of the Masters may well consider the reasonableness of the idea, the certainty that since man is evolving and many stages lie behind him, there must be other stages of evolution in front of him. We cannot regard ourselves as the crown of the ages. There is also much testimony to Their existence coming from those who have met and spoken with such Men.[1]

[1] This subject is dealt with at length in *The Masters and the Path*.

There are some who have actually seen the Masters and yet, incomprehensible though it may appear, have afterwards fallen away from full trust in Them. I remember very well, for example, a certain Mr. Brown of London; he has written a pamphlet describing his life, so there is no harm in referring to him. Many years ago he went to India, and there had the most unusual privilege of meeting in the physical body one of the two Masters who started the Theosophical Society. They come down very rarely from Their Tibetan home, but both of Them have been in India since I have been a member of the Society, in the earlier years of the movement. In *The Occult World* there is an account of the visit of the Master Kūthūmi to Amritsār, where the great Golden Temple of the Sikhs is. He said: "I saw our Sikhs drunk on the floor of their own temple, . . . I turn my face homeward to-morrow." More and more, I suppose, They find They can use Their energies to best advantage upon higher planes, and leave the work on the lower to those who are now gradually gathering round Them in the world. Young Mr. Brown had first seen the astral appearance of the Master Kūthūmi, and then he happened to be travelling in the far north of India as secretary to Colonel Olcott, when the Master came in His physical body to see the Colonel. Mr. Brown was sleeping in the same tent as the Colonel, but in a separate division of it. The Master spoke for some time with Colonel Olcott, and then came round into the other division of the tent. I do not understand why, but Mr. Brown wrapped his head up in the bed-sheet and was afraid to face the Master. Naturally, one would be highly conscious of one's faults, but to adopt the ostrich-like plan of putting one's head under the bedclothes does not seem to me to help much, because the bed-clothes, of course were also transparent to the higher sight. The Master, however, spoke to him patiently. "Take your head out of the bed-clothes," He said, "I want you to see if I am the same person you saw in your astral body." Eventually the Master gave up and left a little note for him, and only then Mr. Brown recovered his senses. He had there an opportunity for which many would give a very great deal. He had deserved it, of course, but he did not make the best use of it. And afterwards he doubted the existence of the Masters. There have been others also who have had the privilege of seeing Them, and yet have somehow fallen away.

Some people, owing to the experience of their past lives, have built up a sceptical nature; others are over-credulous. Neither of these extremes is good for a man's progress; both alike are unscientific. Each man has a general scheme of things in his mind. If new facts which are told him at once fit in with that, he is ready to accept them as probable without demanding exact proof. We say, "Yes, that seems very likely; that fits in very well; probably it is so." But if, on the other hand, the average person is told of something which does not in any way gear in with what he knew before, he altogether refuses to accept it. When one has had experience in the study of the inner side of things, one soon abandons the attitude which refuses to accept a statement because it does not gear in with what one already knows. One learns to suspend judgment, neither accepting nor declining to accept, but simply saying: " From what I have seen so far that does not seem to me very likely; but I do not deny it, I shall put it aside and wait for further light." It is futile to say that because a thing is not in one's experience therefore it cannot be. That is the tendency of ignorance.

Generally speaking, the less people know the more certain they are, down here on the physical plane. In ordinary science, those who dogmatize are the students. The great scientific men will usually say: " I have had experience of such-and-such things, but of course I cannot pretend to lay down the law." The Lord Chancellor once said: " I am as certain of that as the youngest barrister present." He is certain because he has not learnt that there are many possibilities, that you cannot lay down the law too definitely. Those who have been studying for years are much more thoughtful of the way in which they express themselves. There are vast numbers of realities before us all the time, which as yet we do not know. A generation ago many of what are commonplaces of our daily life now would have been derided by most people as utterly impossible. It is well to recognize that fact from the beginning and to be prepared for new discoveries, which may constantly be expected, as man evolves.

It is distinctly useful for us as students of these higher matters to try to get out of the attitude of being bound by our preconceptions. We must be sufficiently plastic to accept even revolutionary truths when they have good reason on their side. Failing that, we must simply put them aside and say we do not yet see, without condemning them or the people who hold them. Truth is many-sided, and to see it from all sides at once is not commonly given to any one man or set of men; consequently there may always be a modicum of truth in that which at present seems to us unreasonable.

One great trouble is that many people who know nothing whatever about a subject are persuaded that they know all about it; especially in matters of religion people who know little are nevertheless clamorously insistent that others should believe the particular delusion that happens to occupy their minds. Sometimes they say their conscience is thus directing them. Even if that be so in some cases, we cannot always depend upon the conscience, since the ego whose voice it is does not know everything. History records that people have burned and tortured others for conscience' sake. An ego who recommends such ideas is distinctly ignorant on very important points. One must, of course, give heed to one's conscience, when one is sure the voice is that, but always remember Bishop South's celebrated reply to a dissenter: "By all means follow thy conscience, but take heed that thy conscience is not the conscience of a fool."

While it is well to have confidence, one cannot make oneself believe, any more than one can make oneself love. But just as we can dwell upon a person's good points and so gradually acquire reason for loving him, so we can think over the reasons for belief, and perhaps gradually attain it thereby. Strictly, of course, one should not desire to believe anything in particular, but only whatever may be true; yet that truth may come to us only after considerable study of the matter, if we have no conviction arising from the past.

It is not the method of great spiritual teachers to make everything easy for us. I first came into touch with occultism through Madame Blavatsky. She gave occasional crumbs of knowledge to her people, but she constantly applied rigorous tests to them. It was a drastic method, but those who really meant business remained with her, while others very soon abandoned her. She cured us of conventionality, but there was much searching of hearts among her followers in the process. Many people said she did things which a great spiritual teacher ought not to do. My own feeling was always this: "Madame Blavatsky has this occult knowledge, and I am going to get that knowledge from her, if she will give it to me. Whatever else she does is her affair. I am not here to criticize her; to her own Master she stands or falls, and not to me. She may have her own reasons for what she does; I do not know anything about that. She has this knowledge, she speaks of these Masters. I intend to get this knowledge; I intend, if it is humanly possible, to reach the feet of those Masters." I gave up everything else to follow her lead, and I have never regretted the confidence I placed in Madame Blavatsky. If one is critical by nature it is his karma; he will learn much more slowly than the man who is prepared to accept things reasonably.

We have to remember that we cannot play with occultism. If we do, no benefit results from it and we are doing no good; if it is not the first interest in life it is of no value. We cannot give to it the second or the third or the seventeenth place in life as so many good people try to do. It must actually be the first thing in life and everything else must be subsidiary to it. Confidence in the Master does mean that we believe that He knows exactly what we ought to do, and that He says what He means; and so when, as in this book, He lays down certain definite rules we must do our very best to follow them. I know it seems difficult, and it is very hard to make people believe just that thing. They say: "Well, He means an approximation to that. He means something like it." But He means exactly what He says, and if we do not believe Him, and therefore we fail, we must blame ourselves. In occultism we have to pass from the insincerity of the world into the light of truth, out of our world into Theirs.

Unless there is perfect trust, there cannot be the perfect flow of love and power.

C.W.L.—If one is in a condition of doubt as to the existence of the Master, or doubt as to one's own power ever to reach Him or to make progress, then that very doubt sets all the vibrations going the wrong way, and the person having it will not be a channel which can be used. Therefore the pupil must have confidence in the Master and love for Him, and yet at the same time love for mankind which is quite impersonal. It is all the time the Master's one idea to do what has to be done with as little expenditure of spiritual force as possible, so that He may have the more to use in other work. If anyone is in any such condition as I have described he is not a good channel and so is useless to the Master. It would be indeed sad to fail Him just when He wanted our service—to have vibrations in our various vehicles that would repel His influence instead of transmitting it.

I remember a case of one who aspired very strongly to become a pupil of a certain Master. He had already served Him well in various ways, and his greatest desire was to see the Master. I was myself staying in that person's house when the Master came in His physical body to visit the city where he lived; but He did not come to the house. I met Him outside and spoke to Him for a long time, but He could not come to see the one who wished to be His pupil, because just at that time that person's astral body was very violently affected—it was all torn with ignoble passion along certain lines. Thus the opportunity of a lifetime was lost—perhaps the opportunity of many lifetimes. If that person could have known how near the Master was, I am sure that all his passion would have fallen away in a moment. Yet for the Master to use His power to drive that away in order to show Himself would have been a waste of His force.

It must not be thought that the Master resents want of trust or any attitude of that nature, or that He is hard when He does not spend his time in removing this or that state of passion from an aspirant. He will do only what will best serve the work, and He will not be swayed by sentimental reasons of any description. When there is real business to be done you must take the best man that offers, whether he be a friend or not, and to put him aside and take a less efficient one, because he was a friend, would be to fail in your duty. In the case of a great war, for example, you must take the best available man to lead your forces, to be at the head of this Ministry or that, or to carry on a particular department of the work. It is not a time for nepotism, to consider whether somebody's nephew could be found a certain post; you must have the man who can best do the work, because it is above all else important to everyone that the work should be well done.

The work of occultism is of that nature: it has to be done, and Those who direct it will employ the best man. Years of service to Them do not constitute any claim to office or to attention from the Master. It is the Master's duty to take the man who can do the work, whether he be one who has just come to Him or one who has been serving Him for many years.

Anyone who puts the work first cannot but rejoice at seeing another do it better than he himself could. Long ago Ruskin said of a certain piece of work: "Be it mine or yours or whose else it may, this also is well; it is well done." You should not hesitate to say that it is well done even though you did it yourself; you should not fail to recognize the better work of another, because it does not matter who did it. There are wonderful passages in Ruskin; he knew, so far as I am aware, nothing of occultism, nor did I when I knew him, yet there is very much in his writing which bears the true stamp of occultism.

You must trust yourself. You say you know yourself too well? If you feel so, you do *not* know yourself; you only know the weak outer husk, which has fallen often into the mire. But *you*—the real you—you are a spark of God's own fire, and God, who is Almighty, is in you, and because of that there is nothing that you cannot do if you will. Say to yourself: "What man has done, man can do. I am a man, yet also God in man; I can do this thing, and I will." For your will must be like tempered steel, if you would tread the Path.

A.B.—When the various instructions that we have been considering are placed before some people, and they are advised to cease their old foolishness or wrongdoing, they sometimes say: "I cannot help it; it is my nature." Many people try to shelter under that excuse. But you are not really in earnest if you say that, and you must be earnest; you cannot afford to play with things that are so serious. You can do anything you set yourself to do, though perhaps not at once.

Of course, if you say, "I cannot help it", you cannot; for you paralyze yourself by the thought. It is a fatal fault; it prevents all progress, and leaves you where you are for months and years. It is as though a man tied his legs with a rope, and then said, "I cannot walk." Certainly he cannot, as he has been at pains to tie himself up; let him undo the rope if he does not wish to sit where he is, and then he will be able to walk well enough. You *can* do things! Get rid of the false idea that you allow to incapacitate you. Make up your mind that you can, and that you will; then you will be astonished at the rapidity of your progress. If you will not do this, you are not in earnest, or at least you are not in earnest in the way in which the Master wants you to be; you are merely playing at being in earnest. I do not say that you are not trying, but it is trying in a way that does not count for much.

See what I mean by applying it to worldly things, to the business by means of which you feed wife and children. You know quite well that if a thing stood in your way there, you would at once make up your mind to remove it, and would exert yourself to the utmost to do so. You would not sit down and say, "I cannot help it." Use some of that seriousness here. You have much of it for all the things which are not serious. It seems as if the one thing which matters is that in which earnestness is the most lacking.

It is of no use applying to the Master for help, if you make no effort to help yourselves. It is as though you held a cup which you carefully covered over with your hand, and prayed for water; when the water is poured down to you it flows over the covering hand and round the cup, and you are none the better for it. So long as a man is trying to do a thing with all his available strength, he is doing it in the occult manner. The results of his efforts may not show themselves in the outer world at once, but he is all the time gathering up his force which at last will pour out in successful action.

The things that you have to do have been done and can be done, but as long as you think that you cannot do them, you cannot. But if you say to yourself: "These things have to be done, and I will do them", then you can do them. Do that, and your thought will be a guardian angel, ever near you, enabling you to accomplish. Otherwise you have near you—as the Christian would put it—a devil, created by yourself with your own thought. You need not create such devils; make instead an angel, a great thought-form—"I *can* and I *will*."

C.W.L.—It is quite true that there is nothing a man cannot do, but it is not said that he can do it at once. That is where people sometimes make a mistake. I know this very well, because I receive scores of letters from people who are in some serious difficulty, fallen perhaps under the influence of drink or drugs or of some kind of obsession, and they often say, "We have no will left, it is all gone; we cannot overcome our difficulty; what can we do?" Those who have not met with any such cases have no idea how terrible the hold of such a thing is on the man, how entirely his will is sapped away and how he feels that he can do nothing at all.

Such people sometimes contemplate suicide. That would be fatal. Even if a man is maimed for life, he should take what opportunity he has to repair the harm, should gird up his loins and valiantly continue the struggle. Suicide would mean a return to conditions similar to those from which escape is sought, with the added bad karma of the act. Let the sufferer realize that the will is there, however much it may be hidden. If he had to create the will for himself, he might very well despair, but let him remember that the will is there; it is the will of God which shows forth in every man. It has yet to be unfolded and developed, but that can be done gradually. Sometimes the devotion of a relative or friend, endowed with great love and patience, proves a veritable godsend in such a case as this.

What has that man done to be in such a condition? Probably for the whole of this incarnation, perhaps for one or two previous lives, he has been deliberately yielding himself to the desire-elemental, to the temptations of the lower nature—deliberately letting it seize upon him. At first he could have struggled against it, but, since he did not check it, he has an accumulated momentum of the evil force—so much of it that he cannot all at once stem it. But he can begin to do so. We may use the example of a man pushing a railway truck or carriage. At a country station where they have plenty of time you will sometimes see a railway porter shunting a carriage from one line to another. See how he goes to work; there is a huge object weighing tons; he pushes against it steadily, and at first he makes no impression. Presently the thing begins slowly to move. He continues pushing, and it moves faster and faster. Then he goes to work to stop it. Now he cannot stop it all at once; if he stood in the way and refused to move, it would run over him and crush him; so he sets himself to oppose it steadily, giving way yet pressing all the time, until gradually he brings it to a standstill. He had put into it a certain amount of force; he cannot take it out again, but can neutralize it by a similar amount of energy.

The man who has yielded himself to the desire-elemental is in a similar position. He has put great force into the thing, and he must meet and face it. One may say: "But there is so much of it." Yes, but it is a limited amount. If only he could look at the matter not sentimentally, but abstractly, as a problem in mathematics, he would not say, "I am a degraded worm, and the force is too great for me", but would go to work and oppose it. He can be absolutely certain that he put into it only a limited amount of force. But now he has unlimited force at his disposal. Just because we are sparks of the Divine Fire we have all the power of God behind us. Only a very little can come through us at a given time, but it is coming all the while.

All this must be looked at from the point of view of the ego; he can do these things and he will. One can never do instantly anything that is worth doing in the work of occult development; just as it is not enough to have music in one's soul, but the ear and hands must be trained so that one can become a suitable channel for the power of the music. The ego has to train his vehicles patiently in a similar way.

People sometimes say: "If I cannot overcome this bad habit now, let me wait till I get another body." Such a person forgets that his next body will have the character and qualities of the present one, if he does nothing to change them, and the hopeless conditions will continue in the next life. But if he makes a determined fight against them now, even though they dominate him to the very end of his life, he will begin with a very much better body next time. It is the same way at higher levels. A man may so injure his mental body by debauchery that in this life it never can come back to its pristine condition. Nevertheless, if he makes a determined attempt against the evil he will get a good mental body next time, instead of having one which reproduces his present defects. In this, as in other cases, the chief struggle is at the beginning; confidence grows and becomes strong a little later on.

Just as many people want to introduce sentiment into their relations with the Master, so some people also want to obtain exemption from the working of the laws of nature; they want to be suddenly taken out of all their sin and sorrow. The emotional type of Christian says: "You will be saved by the blood of Jesus here and now. You will be taken right out of your trouble and be as though it never had been." That is in some ways attractive, but it is not true. What is true is that when you turn round and go the right way along with the divine Will, you at once become free from all the troubles and difficulties ***within you*** which have arisen from fighting against that; but it does not follow that the outer consequences of what you have already done will be wiped out. You have made the change; you are a converted man and you are going in the right way now, but you have still to deal with the results of having gone the wrong way.

You may change your attitude in one moment; and of course you are forgiven—there is nothing standing against you spiritually; you are absolved. But even an orthodox priest will tell you at once: "I do not profess to put right all the results of the wrong you have done. If you have lived a life of debauchery, if you have undermined your constitution, I cannot put that right—these results will remain and it will be part of your penance to try to undo them. What I can put right is the guilt—to use the ecclesiastical term. You have set yourself at odds with God; I can put you straight again. There my absolution will do something for you; it is the power of the higher will and not the lower. It will take you when once you want to be taken; it will help to keep you in the right line; but the physical results cannot be undone. You yourself can change your attitude; the priest can put you right on the higher planes where you lack the power. I do not say that a person could not do this for himself, but he would do it with great effort, clumsily, unscientifically. That is the power that lies behind the absolution; but it cannot take from a man the results of his sin—the laws of nature do not work that way.

There is another consideration to be added to what has been said: Until a person has developed his will and taken hold of himself he cannot really offer himself to the Master. People say, "I give myself entirely to the Master," but is it not obvious that one has not the entire self to give when part of it is in possession of evil qualities of various sorts? For this reason also we must develop the will. The Master said that that will must be like tempered steel. I remember the occasion very well because Alcyone did not understand what was meant by tempered steel, and a little materialization was necessary, to show him. It must be not simply a will of iron, but of tempered steel, a will that cannot be turned aside. The will is there; the divine power is in us; we have but to unfold it and so become masters of ourselves, and then we may make the glorious offering of that will at the feet of the Master.

PART V

LOVE

CHAPTER 1

LIBERATION, NIRVĀNA AND MOKSHA

Of all the Qualifications, Love is the most important, for if it is strong enough in a man, it forces him to acquire all the rest, and all the rest without it would never be sufficient. Often it is translated as an intense desire for liberation from the round of births and deaths, and for union with God. But to put it in that way sounds selfish, and gives only part of the meaning.

C.W.L.—We have said that in this book there are several departures from the ordinary translation of these qualifications. Of all those departures this one is the most daring—the presentation of *mumukshatva* as Love. The word is composed from the root *much*, "to release or set free". In the desiderative stem the root is reduplicated, and other changes occur, to form *mumuksh*, "to desire release". *Mumuksha* is the noun form, meaning "desire for release", and *mumukshatwa* means "the state of desire for release". The termination *twa* has somewhat the meaning of our *ness*, as in "eagerness". From the same root comes also the word *moksha*, "deliverance", "release", or "liberation".

The question has often been asked whether *moksha* is the same as nirvāna. The words mean different things, but they may be taken as attributes of the same state of being—or rather state beyond what we know as being. Nirvāna comes from the root *va* with the prefix *nis*, "to blow" or "to blow out", so it is translated "the blowing out". Moksha is release from the cycle of births and deaths, and nirvāna is the blowing out of that part of man which binds him to that cycle—which means all that men can usually think of as man. Some Hindus think of *moksha* as a negative condition, and work to destroy all personal desires and human interests, so that neither things nor persons can attract them back to rebirth, and so they win freedom from the wheel of births and deaths for long periods of time, but the conception of most of them is of an indescribable state of happiness, beyond the illusion of separateness, called *kaivalya*, independence, absolute oneness. Some Buddhists think of nirvāna as a complete blotting out of man, but others think of it as the attainment of wisdom and bliss that blots out all previous conceptions of self and experience, because it is superinenarrable. So we see that even in the same religion men hold different views.

We Theosophists sometimes apply the term nirvāna to the state of consciousness on the ātmic or spiritual plane, but we also speak of nirvāna as the condition of those supermen, or Adepts, who have taken the Fifth Initiation, who choose among the seven paths open to them that which resembles the true Buddhist nirvāna—not the "blowing-out" of the Southern Church of

Buddhism, but the indescribable rest and bliss of the Northern Church.

It is the Arhat, he who has passed the Fourth Initiation, who can raise his consciousness to the nirvānic plane, and there experience the flood of life that I have tried to describe in *The Inner Life* and *The Masters and the Path.* That consciousness is so much wider than anything that we know down here that one hesitates to call it his consciousness at all. He has become one with a very much greater consciousness; he has lost the sense of being separate. All efforts fail to put these ideas into words because we have not words to express them.

It is very difficult to get the right shades of meaning in translating Sanskrit books, but he who has had a touch of the nirvānic consciousness will best know what the old writers, who had themselves experienced it, meant by nirvāna; the mere lexicographer cannot be expected to give exact meanings to words of that kind. Suppose that a man who knew nothing about the Christian religion tried to understand such a word as "grace". If he looked it up in the dictionary he would become entangled with words like "graceful" and "gracious" and get quite another meaning. That is so also with "dispensation", in ecclesiastical language; it is quite a different thing from what it is in ordinary life. Every religion has a number of terms which in process of time come to have their special religious meaning, and unless one has been brought up in that faith, approaching it from the inside, it is not easy to realize the exact shade of thought. In the beginning of the Theosophical movement none of us knew Sanskrit. Madame Blavatsky understood something of the religions of India, but she did not know Pāli or Sanskrit. Her method was to describe as well as she could what she herself saw, and then say to any Indian friend who might be present, "What do you call that in your system?" He often did not fully understand her meaning, but he gave her the nearest term he could. The next time she wanted a word she would ask another man, but she never paid any attention to the fact that the first man might be a Hindu and the second a Buddhist—or that the various Hindus might belong to different schools of philosophy.

In addition to this, Madame Blavatsky was not in the position of a teacher of science, who is expounding a theory which he is illustrating with suitable experiments, brought forward as proofs as he goes along. She was not working with a plan or skeleton, into which one would try to fit every new piece of knowledge. She would make several statements which did not agree as far as words were concerned, and if asked for explanations would say, "Never mind the contradictions. Go and think over the statements." Her ideas were wonderfully clear, and her knowledge definite.

Hers was the opposite method of working to that of our day, when words are first defined very carefully and given fixed meanings. Often, it is to be feared, the result of that is that science and philosophy become a kind of game, like chess, where the moves that a piece can make are strictly prescribed. With her, words were living things—thought-forms on the physical plane, as it were—used as a means to awaken in the hearer's mind the knowledge already existing in her own.

If we wish to understand all the complicated relationship between the ego and the personality, we must first of all have a clear idea in our mind of what these things respectively are. This matter has been dealt with at great length in Theosophical literature both in the earlier days of the Society's teaching and also quite recently. I have said something about it in *The Masters and the Path.* Putting it very briefly and crudely, let it be understood that we can think of man as existing in the three divisions which S. Paul used long ago—body, soul and spirit. The corresponding Theosophical terms would be the personality, the individuality and the Monad. The Monad is definitely divine—a spark of the eternal flame—to all intents and purposes a part of God Himself. It is of course true in the highest sense that everything is a part of God—that there is nothing which is not He; and that is true of matter as well as of spirit. Nevertheless there is a very special sense in which the Monad may be thought of as a fragment of the Deity coming down into manifestation. I know quite well that is unphilosophical, unscientific, inaccurate to speak of a fragment of that which is indivisible; but there are no words to express the conditions of higher planes, so that whatever we say must be utterly inadequate and therefore to some extent misleading. Some writers who have tried to express these relations have spoken of the Monad as a reflection of the Logos, the ego in turn as a reflection of the Monad, and the personality as representing the ego in a similar way. There is a sense in which that expression has its advantages, and yet it seems to me to give somewhat less of the true relation than this other suggestion—that the Monad may be considered as a fragment of the Deity, the ego a fragment of the Monad, and the personality in its turn a fragment of the ego.

As part of the eternal unfoldment it has pleased the Logos of our system to project from Himself a vast host of these Monads. If we may use the simile with all reverence, they are thrown forth from Him as sparks in order that after their passage through various material planes they may return to Him as great and glorious suns, each capable of giving life and light to a magnificent system, through which and by means of which millions of other Monads may in turn develop.

The stupendous height from which this divine manifestation which we call a Monad originally comes cannot be measured in terms of any planes of which we know anything; but the lowest point which the Monad appears able to reach in his outrush is that which for that very reason we call the Monadic plane. It will be remembered that according to our great President's nomenclature the highest of the seven planes about which we are taught is called the divine, the second (coming downwards) being the monadic, the third the spiritual, and the fourth the intuitional. A still further descent into matter is necessary that the purposes of the Logos may be achieved. The Monad as a whole appears to be incapable of further descent, but it can and does put forth what we must call a part or fragment of himself which is capable of descending to the upper part of the mental plane. On the way down this fragment so put forth manifests itself on the spiritual or nirvānic plane as the triple ātmā. Of that triple spirit the first manifestation remains on that plane, while the second descends to the intuitional plane and clothes itself in buddhic matter. The third aspect or manifestation descends one plane more and resides in the higher part of the mental plane, where we call it the higher manas. Thus the ego (which is the name given to this fragment put down by the Monad) consists of ātma, buddhi and manas, which we represent somewhat inadequately in English by the terms spiritual will, intuitional wisdom and active intelligence.

The ego in his turn puts down a minute fragment of himself through the lower mental and the astral planes and eventually manifests himself in a physical body. Each of these successive descents is a quite indescribable limitation, so that the man whom we meet down here on the physical plane is at the best a fragment of a fragment, and as an expression of the real man is so inadequate as to furnish us with nothing even remotely resembling a conception of what that man will be at the end of his evolution.

The egos with whom we have to do in daily life are at different stages of this incredibly prolonged evolution. In all cases the ego exists primarily on his own plane, which as we have said is the higher part of our mental plane. At that level quite apart from his manifestation as a personality, he may be already wide awake, conscious of his surroundings and living an active life; or on the other hand he may be somnolent, almost entirely unconscious of his surroundings and therefore capable of experiencing anything like an active life only through his personality on much lower levels. As man raises his consciousness through the various planes he finds the vibrations on each one far more rapid than on that next below it. When we speak of the ego as developed on his own plane we mean that he is able fully to respond to all the vibrations of that plane; if he is not so conscious then these very rapid vibrations pass over him without affecting him, and in order to attain consciousness he must put himself down lower and draw round himself a vehicle of the matter of a grosser plane to whose vibrations he can already respond. By much practice in that lower plane he will gradually grow to be able to respond to its higher vibrations and then very slowly and by degrees to the vibrations of the plane next above it; so that the consciousness has to work its way up level by level.

His consciousness therefore in the personality should be reaching upwards all the while towards the ego; and when the consciousness of the ego is by this means fully developed, he in his turn will begin to reach upwards towards the Monad. The whole course of the movement downwards into matter is called in India the *pravritti marga* or the path of outgoing. When the lowest point necessary has been reached the man enters upon the *nivritti marga* or the path of return. He returns from his day's work of harvesting, bearing his sheaves with him in the shape of the fully awakened consciousness which enables him to be far more useful on those higher levels than he could have been before his descent into matter. On this path there is always the temptation for that lower part of the ego to forget its connection with the higher, and to identify itself entirely with the lower manifestation which is so much more vivid to it, and in that way to cut itself off from the higher and as it were to set up in business in the lower world on its own account. Presumably the ego himself as part of the Monad is liable to a similar temptation on his very much higher plane; but we are for the moment dealing with the relations between the ego and his personality; and furthermore we are viewing it from the point of view of the personality looking up towards the ego and trying to become one with him.

The ego has associated himself with the personality because he has a hunger, or thirst, for vivid experience. He is undeveloped on his own plane, unable to respond to the high vibrations of that region; the slower vibrations of the lower planes mean more to him, so he comes back again and again for them. As he develops, the hunger abates little by little, and sometimes when he is advanced and has become sensitive to the delights and activities of his own plane, he goes to the other extreme of neglecting his personality—caught as it is in the grip of karma, sunk in conditions which are now full of sorrow or of boredom for him because he feels he has outgrown them.

This diminution of his thirst for the lower planes has taken place as he developed his personality. When he gained full consciousness on the astral plane the physical life began to appear dull by comparison; reaching the lower mental world he found the astral dark and dismal; and all three of the lower levels lost their attraction when he began to be able to enjoy the still more vivid and luminous life of the causal body. Many people have reached the point of evolution at which they can travel about and do useful work on the astral plane during sleep. All students of occultism have their astral bodies well developed and ready for use, though many of them have not yet acquired the habit of using them. The lowest part of the mental vehicle is also in order, and is ready to come into activity; regular meditation develops this and brings it under control. At this stage the man may be taught to use that body, and he can then leave his astral with the physical vehicle during sleep. When this has been accomplished, the process is repeated at the causal level, and the ego is then awake and active on his own plane.

All the lower vehicles are temporary vestures which we put on in order to learn how to use the forces of their planes, and when we have done that completely, and the ego is working perfectly in his causal body, which happens at the Fourth Initiation, there is no need to incarnate again at those levels. Having triumphed over them, a man can at any moment materialize a temporary astral and mental body, show himself on those planes and do what he wants to do. One who has reached this stage need no longer go through the wearisome round of birth and death, which is so unpleasant. Perhaps we do not always think of it as so unpleasant, because we do get a little enjoyment out of life; true, but if we could look at it from the standpoint of the ego we should realize what an unspeakable bore it is to the eternal spirit to be down here "cribb'd, cabin'd and confin'd" in a body that cannot do this and will not do that. While we are in it we make the best of it, but it is only a temporary vehicle put on for the purpose of learning, and when we have learned the lesson we are very glad to get rid of the whole thing.

The man who has had some experience of the causal levels sometimes feels very deeply the oppressive limitations of the three lower worlds. He misses all the glorious freedom and love and truth of the ego's own regions. He realizes the cause of his descent into this state of darkness, and may then say to himself: "I will rid myself of this desire, which is the primary cause bringing me down into incarnation, and I will balance my karma by acting without attachment." The man who can say this is already a developed man, who has thought a good deal about these things; he is a metaphysician and a philosopher. He says deliberately: "I will shut off this desire; I will balance the karma accurately, and then there will be nothing to bring me back." That can be done. When he succeeds—and there have been many in India, all though its history, who have succeeded in doing it—the man escapes from this round of births and deaths. He lives in the heaven-world, or perhaps he may reach the causal level; but he does not, as a rule, rise any higher than that. He has attained what he would call *moksha.*

The man who can do that must be a man who has raised himself above all lower passions and desires, otherwise the thing would be impossible, but all the same he has forgotten one side of evolution. He has understood the action of the law of karma perfectly, and therefore he has been able to release himself from it. But he has not learned perfectly the law of evolution and he has not freed himself from that. He is like a clever boy at school, who might get far ahead of his companions and take several examinations in advance, and then do nothing for three or four years while the others were coming up to his level. That is precisely what happens to the man who attains *moksha*; he has not attained the goal which is set for humanity, because the evolution of humanity ends in Adeptship.

Now, an Adept is not only a man, free from birth and death, but he is also a living power; he has become one with the Monad, who is, in turn, a spark of the Deity. But the method of the Deity is to put Himself down, to pour Himself out in utter self-sacrifice into this whole plan. Therefore the man who becomes one with the Deity must be also filled with this spirit of self-sacrifice. The Adept does more good works than the greatest philanthrophist could possibly do, and is doing them all the time on higher planes, but He does them on behalf of the humanity of which He is a part, Therefore the karma resulting from them comes to humanity and not to Him, so there is nothing to bind Him to rebirth; but the whole of humanity gets a little uplift. It is not a great uplift; that amount of karma spread all over the world is not a very large amount for anyone, but it does mean a steady uplift for all. Therefore, in a sense, everyone gets just a little more than he may appear exactly to deserve. There is no injustice in this, however, because like the rain that falls on the just and the unjust, it is the same for everyone.

Therefore, after the lapse of thousands or even millions of years the man who has attained *moksha* finds that the tide of evolution has risen to his level and laps round him once more, and he has to come back and be reborn, and proceed with his development. He who seeks *moksha* generally knows that his liberation is not for ever, but he thinks that he will be called back in a remote future, and the world will probably be better by the time he has to return. He says: "I can afford to risk that; I shall gain thousands of years of freedom and be all that time in the heaven-world enjoying myself."

Our ideal is perfect consciousness on the highest level we can reach. We do not propose to rest satisfied at any level whatever. But on the other hand, we decline to give up our consciousness and go into trance, as some people do for the purpose of reaching a level beyond the scope of their waking consciousness. People talk sometimes about "passing into *samādhi*", and some, who are fond of the rolling Sanskrit, talk of going into *samādhi* when they meditate. We were in much confusion as to the meaning of this word, until we realized that it was a relative term. *Samādhi* for anyone is the point which is just beyond that at which it is possible for him to retain his clear consciousness. If one is conscious on the astral and not on the mental, then for him *samādhi* would be the next level—the mental. It is to get just beyond the point where one can be conscious, to pass into a sort of trance from which one emerges with all sorts of glorified and beautiful feeling, but not generally with clear consciousness. People should not go into *samādhi* when they meditate; they should retain their consciousness, so that when they come back they can remember what they have seen. I know that many have passed into *samādhi* and have experienced a great feeling of happiness and beatitude. That, however, does not mean progress, because they lose hold and do not know clearly what they have been doing. There is always a certain danger in that—one does not know that he will be able to return.

Dr. Besant and I were once watching some tremendous outpourings of life from the higher planes, great waves that came pulsating forth from the Solar Deity. She said: "Let us throw ourselves into that wave, and see where it takes us." We should have plunged in had her Master not intervened, and told us not to do it. Afterwards Dr. Besant asked Him, "if we had thrown ourselves into that wave, where should we have found ourselves?" He said, "You might have washed up in a million years or so somewhere on Sirius or some other solar system." Manifestly it is not wise to throw ourselves into outpourings of that sort, when we do not know exactly what is happening. It is not a good plan to lose consciousness; it is much better to try to keep control of our vehicles and see a little bit where we are going—otherwise we may lose the physical body and end our temporary usefulness. Our method is to keep full consciousness on any plane that we can reach, and try to be of use on that plane. Our Masters never speak of mere passive contemplation. Our aim is not to sit down and enjoy ourselves anywhere, but to be active in the Master's work at all times.

This paraphrase that the Master has given of the fourth qualification, Love, is eminently characteristic of Him. He goes behind the word itself to the reason for it. He says: "What is your reason for wanting liberation? In order that you may be free to help better, you are trying to make yourself one with God. What is this God? God is Love. You must develop Love if you want to be one with Him. Therefore this qualification is in reality Love." Readers of *Man: Whence, How and Whither* will remember how it explains that different bodies of people came over from the other chains to this, and how certain of those groups of people were spoken of as boat-loads of servers. Practically all members of the Theosophical Society belong to one of those groups; so this idea of service is a very strong factor in our dispositions. We know how hard it is to get away from anything with which we are born.

Our nationality, for example, carries with it many little points of view, very difficult to avoid. That is the nationality of the personality; but this idea of service we may call the nationality of the ego, or perhaps of the Monad. He was born with that streak in him, and it has been cultivated ever since.

It is difficult for us to understand that there are other types which are just as good as this one under consideration. The solar Deity manifests Himself through three aspects: will, wisdom and love. That is the way they are given in this book. Men appoach Him along all these three lines. Each man's own way is the best for him, but he should remember that the other man's path is better for him and that, in the long run, they all merge. We must acquire the ability to look out simultaneously through all the aspects and know that in truth they are all one. We are told, in the Athanasian Creed, that we must hold this doctrine of the Trinity neither confounding the Persons nor dividing the Substance; we must learn that through all eternity there is only one God, although His manifestations are through Three Persons.

It was said in the beginning that if love is strong enough in a man it forces him to acquire all the other qualities. It makes people act, according to their power. Take one of the very best and most beautiful examples: mother love. Let us see how that operates among a savage race. The mother savage does not know much, but at least she is prepared to defend her child, and even if necessary to sacrifice her own life for him. The civilized mother among ourselves would do just the same thing in the same circumstances. Now and again you hear of a mother losing her life in saving her baby from a burning house, or more often as a result of attending to it when it has some infectious disease. In ordinary life among us that strong love makes the mother think. Her love for the child induces her to study hygiene, all about food and things of that sort. So love leads to both mental and physical activity.

A man must have this love, which is an intense desire for service, if he would reach the Master. S. John said: "We know that we have passed from death unto life because we love the brethren. He that loveth not his brother abideth in death,"[1] and: "He that loveth not knoweth not God."[2] All that is perfectly true. It is a very good thing to know the technical terms of Theosophy, and to understand its philosophy and science, and to be able to distinguish and employ the two thousand four hundred and one types of elemental essence is very useful for practical purposes—but love makes the true Theosophist.

I remember well, long ago, when Babu Mohini Mohun Chatterji, who was a disciple, came to London to instruct us, he told us for the first time about these qualifications, which were not expounded in Mr. Sinnett's books, or in *Isis Unveiled*, which were almost the only books we had. He told us quite plainly that without this fourth qualification, this intense desire for liberation

[1] I John, 3, 14.

[2] *Ibid.*, 4, 8.

(that is the way he put it), for union with God, the six points of good conduct "watered but the desert"; they would be really arid and all but valueless to us unless we had this intense desire to be one with God and to do as He does. We did not then realize that it meant service so fully as we do now, though the Masters had emphasized from the beginning Their love for "the teeming millions of humanity, the lowly and the despised". We were mainly occupied in trying to learn Theosophy. All was so new, so interesting, so exciting, that our time was mainly given to that—much more, perhaps, than it ought to have been, were it not that one must learn something before one can be of real service to others.

It is not so much desire as *will*, resolve, determination.

C.W.L.—Will is pre-eminently the quality of the first ray, on which the Master Morya stands. The Master Kūthūmi is on the second ray, that of wisdom and love; but here He spoke as a first ray man would do. I remember one occasion on which Alcyone mentioned his desire to attain a certain quality. The Master said: "Do not desire a thing; desire is feeble. Will, because you are God. If you want to acquire a quality, will to do so, and go and do it." That emphatically is the standpoint of the Hierarchy. It is very important indeed for us to understand the Master's attitude and way of looking at things, which have brought Him where He is now, and can do the same for us.

To produce its results, this resolve must fill your whole nature, so as to leave no room for any other feeling. It is indeed the will to be one with God, not in order that you may escape from weariness and suffering, but in order that because of your deep love for Him you may act with Him and as He does. Because He is Love, you, if you would become one with Him, must be filled with perfect unselfishness and love also.

C.W.L.—The pupil of the Master has only one desire and that is to serve. For this, he is willing to give up all personal pleasure and ambition, and remain but a small wheel in the great machine. The ordinary man has not yet begun to think very seriously of anything higher. He takes life very much as he finds it, and his desire is not to get out of this kind of life into something higher and nobler, but rather to succeed in it. If you suggested that he should give up all that we call the lower self, he would ask: "But what will be left of me if I do that?" It is true that there would in such a case not be very much left, as far as he could see, although the whole of the reality would, in truth, remain.

It is difficult to explain to such a man what we mean by "becoming merged into the Divine Life". I knew a very good and clever man, who was making a considerable study of Northern Buddhism. He came to me one day and said: "I can't make anything out of this; it does not seem to me worth following up. It is quite interesting as a study in archæology, but the only object they put before you seems to be to become one with the Buddha. I can't see that that would be of any value to Buddha, and it would certainly be the end of me." That is the point of view the average man takes of these things. Yet there is a real, glowing, burning meaning to it all; if one can get hold of that it will revolutionize his whole conception. This widening of the consciousness does not take away any freedom, nor destroy individuality in the least degree. It is not that I am absorbed in the universe, but the universe becomes I. People say, "That Self am I." That is a delusion as applied to the lower self, but when one realizes "I am God", then the sense that God is God is not an illusion at all, and the sense that what I thought was I is in reality an expression of Him is not an illusion. It is the idea that anything can exist outside That or can be separated from the one Self that is illusion.

In every-day life there are some things that will serve as an example of this inclusion of the smaller in the greater. You have a great mercantile house, and some young man joins it as a junior clerk. At first he regards the house as a task-master, and it is a great trouble to him to have to come at regular hours and do all his work. But after he has been there for some years and has been raised to a more responsible position, he begins to say, "We do this," and "We do that," and then he is beginning to identify his interest with that of the house. So he goes on, until he becomes a manager, and at last a partner. Then he speaks always for the house; and when he considers any of the business, it is "the firm" he has always in his mind. He is just as free and as capable of taking the initiative along any line as ever, yet he is now certain to use his will along the right lines. The firm has not coerced him into that attitude, but he has grown into it. That is only a small illustration, but it gives an idea of the way in which a man may identify himself with a greater power, yet his will may be as much his own as ever.

There will come a time when we shall have become the Path itself, when we shall never fail in any of the qualifications because they will have grown into us and become part of our very nature. We are close to the living God all the time, because He is in us and about us and with us always, yet it is for us to learn to realize that, to raise our consciousness step by step, employing all the means that come in our way, until we can really grasp that idea. We are to become one with God in His highest manifestations, in the internal manifestations, not in the merely material form. The very matter in our bodies, and around us also, is His outer garment—but it is not the garment, it is He with whom we wish to become one. When we become one with Him, He on His side recognizes that and uses us as living channels through which His force can be outpoured. We are channels for the divine force on these lower planes, but we are effective channels only when we have reached the point where we have no separate personality in opposition to Him. He works through such means always, and His ministers, the great occult Hierarchy, do likewise. No doubt They could work miracles by direct action on people, but it would unnecessarily use up a great amount of Their force, so They work through the means which They have arranged.

There is a large class of people who never try to understand the principles of life. They think that nature must bow to them, and they will not accept things in the way that is ordained. They are, in their way, like those investigators at spiritualistic séances, who want to prescribe the conditions under which manifestations should take place. It is a very absurd attitude of mind, because there is no line of investigation in the world in which you can prescribe what the laws of nature shall do. One has heard of savages to whom electrical phenomena were shown, who declared that they were due to trickery. The savage chief would say, "I see all this is connected by wires; you are doing it with those wires. Cut them away and then I shall believe you." The electrician smiles and says in reply: "You do not understand the law. The wires conduct the electricity; without them the force could not come through." Then the man says: "I have exposed your trickery." People do the same thing at spiritualistic séances. They will not take the way ordained, but want to strike out another way. There is a certain amount of individuality about the idea of compelling God to do things in one's own way which, I suppose, recommends itself to some types of minds, but it does not appeal to mine any more than the idea of telling God in prayer what to do. I always feel profoundly that He knows infinitely better than I do, and if by any utterly inexplicable chance He should change His intention on account of my asking Him, I know I should be infinitely worse off under that scheme than I should have been under His.

The idea that one should will to be one with God may not have occurred to many of us, but it is very familiar to our brothers in India. The Master uses that sort of phrase several times in this book when He speaks of God. In an earlier life He was a prominent Buddhist teacher named Nāgārjuna, and in that incarnation He made many great speeches and wrote much. In His books which have been preserved, He is very strongly opposed to any idea of personality in the Deity. He objects even to the use of that word or that name, and goes deeply into metaphysical questions connected with it. Indians, knowing all that philosophy of Nāgārjuna, have often said, " How curious it is that, in this little book, our Master, who has spoken so strongly against personality in the Deity, should now use that word God. The Lord Buddha also spoke very strongly against anything like personality in the Deity." The answer to that objection is this: In this book the Master is not going into the question of the Absolute; He is not speaking of *That*—the Supreme, the Eternal; He is speaking primarily to an Indian boy, about *Īshwara*—that is, the solar Logos, the solar Deity—and it is in that sense undoubtedly that our Master uses the word God here. As Nāgārjuna he was speaking to students many of whom knew the systems of Indian philosophy, and so he spoke strongly against any endeavour to degrade the conception of the Deity by making it personal in the way in which many of our Christian brothers now do.

Then He says that you must make yourself like Him. This brings up the question: what do we know of Him? We know that He manifests Himself through three Aspects. Some approach Him through one of these Aspects and some through another. Our way is the way of active love, because that is the way of our Masters. There are seven great rays of the divine life, and therefore seven types of men. One is the line of devotion, another that of will, another that of wisdom. Men seek God in various ways, but as our Masters are on the line of active love, all who wish to follow Them must use the powers of his own special type in active service for love of God and man. Take, for example, the case of devotion, of which there may be three types or kinds. One person casts himself down before the object of his adoration and just longs to become one with it. I suppose this type is found in our Western races only among some few monks and nuns, whose desire is simply to spend themselves in perpetual adoration of the Deity. That is a splendid thing, but for the moment, at any rate, the man is not thinking of others, but only of becoming one with the Deity. If you ask him about others he will say: "Let them do what I am doing." I knew a man in India whose one idea was just precisely that—to sit in adoration before the image of his Deity, and try to become one with Him. That is the goal he set before himself, and it is the future he will gain. He will spend the whole of his heaven-life, probably a very long one—thousands of years—in a sort of swoon of adoration. Such pure devotion means the development of his various vehicles, and certain advance for himself.

A second kind of devotion scarcely deserves the name —that lower devotion which demands a *quid pro quo* of the Deity, and says: "If you repay me so much in the way of riches and promotion and general assistance, I will give you so much devotion."

A third devotee will say: "I love that Great One, or that Teacher so much that because of that I must be doing something to help others to know Him and understand Him as I do. I must do good works in His name." This is a very noble and practical kind of devotion. Those of us who are on the devotional ray will not be purely devotional, but will have this variant of activity which will make us want to do something on account of our devotion. So also if any of us be on the line that wishes above all things to know, we shall also have the same characteristic in our nature. There are those who desire to become wise merely in order to know and understand. That is a very wonderful quality in a man, and there are many who make great progress in that way. But those among them who are servers will find in themselves the complex resultant: "I want knowledge, but I want it only that I can be really useful to others." Such a person would see very clearly the mistakes made by other people who, though they desire with all their hearts to serve, yet, because of foolishness, do more harm than good. "Let me have perfect knowledge, then I shall be able to serve really well," such a man would say.

We wish to become one with God, not merely that we may be one with Him, and may bask in all that glory and joy, but that we may act as He does, and as His great action was to pour Himself out in utmost self-sacrifice into matter, in order that we might come into being, therefore he who will be one with God must himself show forth the same spirit of utter forgetfulness of himself for the sake of the work which is to be done for the God who is all Love. That one sentence: " You, if you would become one with Him, must be filled with perfect unselfishness and love also," really epitomizes the whole Path. Will, wisdom, love—each one of these carried to perfection and employed in service brings in all the others, so it is really true that "love is the fulfilling of the law."[1]

[1] Romans, 13, 10.

CHAPTER 2

LOVE IN DAILY LIFE

In daily life this means two things; first, that you shall be careful to do no hurt to any living thing; second, that you shall always be watching for an opportunity to help.

C.W.L.—Those are two sides of the same thing—the passive that you shall do no hurt, and the active that you shall do good. People sometimes say that the Oriental religions are negative, that the idea of service which we import into them is in reality a Christian idea. That is not so. Though the modern Christian has relegated it to a back seat, it is true that in original Christianity service was expressed and emphasized very strongly. "But he that is greatest among you shall be your servant."[1] The same idea appears in the old religions also.

In Buddhism—which has always been spoken of as the most negative of religions—it certainly does give you directions as to the things you must avoid. But its five precepts are not more negative than the Jewish ten commandments. The Buddhist religion does not say "Thou

[1] S. Matthew, 23, 11.

shalt not", though it asks its people to promise to avoid certain things. The wording is: "I observe the precept to refrain from taking life, to refrain from taking that which does not belong to me, to refrain from saying that which is not true, to refrain from taking intoxicating drinks or stupefying drugs, to refrain from unlawful sexual intercourse." That is the form; it is not a command but a promise.

In the summary of the religion in one *sutta* or verse, given by the Buddha Himself, we see its positive aspect:

> "Cease to do evil;
> Learn to do well;
> Cleanse your own heart:
> That is the religion of the Buddha."

The same thing comes out clearly in the Noble Eightfold Path, in which you have: "Right views, right aims, right words, right behaviour, right mode of livelihood, right exertion, right mindfulness and right meditation." Most of this is very positive indeed.

In the *Bhagavad-Gītā*, which is practically the gospel for millions of Hindus, you find taught the most positive activity. There God is described as the great Actor, and it is said that he who will not follow His example, and work for the welfare of the world, lives in vain. Inaction, it says, may be really an action in a deadly sin. It warns people, as Madame Blavatsky used frequently to do, that sins of omission are as much to be feared as sins of commission. And as to the sannyāsī, the man who has renounced the material life, it says that he must constantly perform acts of charity, sacrifice and austerity. The great historical Scriptures of the Hindus are full of accounts of men who devoted themselves to the public weal, and teachers, many of them considered to be divine incarnations, who taught the service of our fellow-man.

Nowhere could public service be more emphasized than it has been in those religions, yet they have always had their contemplative sides, as had Christianity all through the middle ages. It is only in recent years that, in the intensity of our activity in the fifth sub-race of the fifth root race, we have become secretly inclined to despise the monk and the nun and to magnify the man of action, the great commander in war, the great ruler or statesman in peace. The whole idea of the contemplative orders is, however, a very beautiful one. The plan was that the active orders of the monk and the friar would preach to the people and perform acts of charity, while the contemplative orders would shut themselves up and devote themselves wholly to meditation and supplication. Translating it into other terms, that would mean the formulation of good and high thought, and the sending of it out with a definite view to the helping of people. It was their business to make a speciality of prayer and meditation and to do it for their brethren who, for various reasons, were unable to do it so well and so thoroughly for themselves. The theory in every religion was that they were a part of humanity supplying a need of humanity; they were not merely lazy monks retiring from active work. They were doing very much harder work, which the others could not do, in connection with higher planes, and doing it generally under circumstances of self-abnegation and asceticism which would appal the ordinary man.

That the life of the monk, however, when it was not so definitely ascetic, attracted many who wanted a comfortable, lazy existence, is also true. Such people escaped physical work, but did not substitute for it the work of the higher planes. Among the Buddhist monks there are some of this kind, who are looked down upon and called "rice monks"—men who are monks for the sake of the assured living, which, though it is not a very luxurious one, will never fail while anyone in the country has any food at all. The same was true, perhaps to a somewhat greater degree, of the monastic orders of the middle ages in Europe. There were people who joined them for the sake of power and influence and did not mind, in many cases, the lack of possessions. Though the individual monk had no possessions, the monastery as a body did acquire a very great deal, which was at the disposal of the individual to a large extent.

> **First, to do no hurt. Three sins there are which work more harm than all else in the world—gossip, cruelty, and superstition—because they are sins against love.**

C.W.L.—When one hears of sins which work more harm than all others one is apt to think of murder and robbery and such crimes, and perhaps is surprised to find such comparatively ordinary things as gossip, cruelty and superstition at the head of the list. The Master is taking into account the quantity of these sins, and their far-reaching effect. Murder and robbery are universally recognized as serious sins, and consequently respectable people avoid them, unless you dignify them by the name of war. But gossip is universal; and if one thinks of the harm it does in any individual case, of the great amount of mental suffering which it may cause, of the depreciation of ideals which it often brings about, then multiplies that by the millions of cases which are going on all the time, one will very soon see that it does vastly more harm than the other. It is a terrible thing to destroy a person's ideal, to cheapen it and lower it, and make him feel that after all it is not so good or high or noble as he had thought. Sometimes there is talk of the destruction of idols as a good thing. The destruction of a person's idol may be the most serious injury one can do him. If he idealizes something which to us is low and mean, we may, perhaps, be able to lead him to some higher ideal, but it is a most evil and wicked thing to take away his ideal without leaving him something higher and better to take its place. It is not for us to point out the flaws or to try to belittle anyone under any circumstances.

Many of us know, probably by personal experience, what a wonderful amount of good Dr. Besant has done. Tens of thousands have seen the light through her lectures and writings, but still the gossip that has been circulated about her has prevented thousands of others from listening to her and reading her books. They say: "I have heard so-and-so about Mrs. Besant. Why should I read a book by a person of that sort?" There have been many in that way turned aside from what would have meant their salvation in this particular incarnation. Thousands of people also write to her and ask her advice about all sorts of difficulties in which they find themselves involved. Many people have been prevented from applying for such advice by the evil and utterly false reports that have been circulated about her.

I think I know no one who has been more frequently and more fully attacked than our great President. Long before she became a Theosophist she was before the public as a teacher of free-thought. She was assailed and vilified first of all because she republished what is called the Knowlton pamphlet, dealing with sex problems which ought to be faced and studied, and not prudishly hidden. This pamphlet had been written long before she was born, but its publication had been discontinued on account of a threat of prosecution. Our President took the matter up partly because she believed that the question should be ventilated and that the poor should be put in possession of the information which the pamphlet gave, but still more, I think, as a matter of protest against the suppression of facts and in vindication of free speech and free publication in regard to everything that concerned the public health and public good generally. Her reissue of the pamphlet was fully intended as a challenge to what she considered a bad law; she announced beforehand to the police her intention of selling this work and invited them to come at a certain hour and officially buy a copy. They accepted the invitation, came and formally purchased the incriminating document and then proceeded to prosecute her, but the case ended in *nolle prosequi.* Then she wrote a more carefully worded pamphlet on the subject. Her reward for that—at any rate on the physical plane—was to have her personal character attacked in the most abominable manner. Later she withdrew the pamphlet, having come to the conclusion that it did not present the best way of dealing with this social difficulty; but I am sure she has never regretted that she did her best to deal with the facts as she then understood them. Such unselfishness and courage are rare in this world.

A great deal of gossip was also started by jealous people against Madame Blavatsky. Wild and mad accusations were brought against her; these appeared instantly and obviously ridiculous to all of us who knew her personally, yet many people have been deterred by them from a careful examination of Theosophical truths. She died in 1891, yet to this day it is quite a common experience, if you mention the Theosophical Society, to be met by the remark: "Oh, yes, that was founded by Madame Blavatsky, who was exposed as a charlatan. We do not want to spend our time and energy considering the teaching of a fraud. It is not likely to contain the truth." In this way many have missed the Theosophical knowledge that might have changed their lives.

From these instances alone we see that immeasurable harm may be done by spiteful and foolish gossip. This form of selfishness also very much hurts the feelings of the person at whom it is aimed. That the person can be hurt shows a weakness in his character, but that does not excuse the gossip, or relieve him from the evil karma which he has made. Our President is quite impervious to gossip about her, though if she is abused for more than the usual time along one particular line she does sometimes say: "This is getting very monotonous; I wish they would find something else to discuss." I also have been much abused, but it has never cost me a night's sleep. Thus karma falls back from us. But the harm done to others by the gossip brings its karma to those who started it and passed it on. It is more difficult not to care what is said about somebody else, and I confess I still find it hard not to be angry when some one speaks ill of our President, for example, or when unworthy thoughts, which to us who know Them are nothing less than blasphemous, are directed to the Masters.

Gossip is not real criticism. Unfortunately the very word criticism has come to mean picking holes. It is derived from the Greek *krinein*, to judge, and should mean a judicial attitude, but now it does not. Justice is one of the manifestations of God; therefore to judge a man's words or actions without their context is wrong and leads to evil. I suppose there is not a scripture in the world, no matter how holy and beautiful, which could not be made ridiculous by taking some words away from their context and putting them by themselves. We are always doing that with the thoughts of other people. We find a man to be irritable; he speaks sharply, perhaps roughly, and we at once assume that this indicates his character. But we do not know the reason for his irritability. Possibly he has been sitting up all night with a sick child; somebody else may have jarred him or annoyed him intensely in some way and we get the reflex action of that, although he is not really annoyed with us. If he were a great Adept he would not be annoyed, but we are not all great Adepts yet, and so these things happen.

I first learnt this as a small child, from an old coachman. I was near him one day when a man approached and spoke to him very roughly. The old coachman answered without seeming to pay any attention to the gruff tone of the other. After the man had gone, I said, "Why, John, what have you done to make that man so angry with you?" "Oh, nothing, sir; he's not angry with me," the old servant replied. "I haven't annoyed him; but probably his wife or somebody else has." And he explained to me that when once a man got thoroughly upset he was likely to vent his feelings on anyone who came in his way.

The grip of unkind judgment on a man's mind and the tenacity and virulence of its poison would be unbelievable, did we not have thrust upon us constant evidence of it. A man gets a wrong idea, and his whole outlook is coloured by it. We have seen that even in regard to this book. When I first heard this teaching about gossip given to Alcyone, long before the book was published, I was much impressed by its importance, so I repeated it on several occasions. When the book was issued some people immediately pounced upon the fact that these statements had been made months before it was published, and said that therefore part of it must have been my work.

I have mentioned that there were two periods in the development of Alcyone's memory of astral plane experiences; one during which he could not remember perfectly, when I would repeat to him the special precept given to him by the Master as applying to the next day; the other, in which he could bring through the memory. I found that in Bombay the story was being circulated that the whole book had been repeated to him by me in that way. But, as a matter of fact, the book was written in the second period, when he was able to remember what the Master had said to him, and he wrote it down by himself. When people get a little twist like that they distort everything. I have suffered from all sorts of injustice and misconception in consequence of such distortion of facts. I do not mind in the least, but it shows me very clearly how easy it is for people to misunderstand when they start with a wrong idea. I have seen the most ludicrous mistakes made, in which every event that occurred was made to bolster up some idea for which there was no foundation in fact, but which was simply imagination from beginning to end.

One of the experiments we have to make in the course of our occult training is to identify ourselves with the consciousness of certain animals. It is merely a question of practice; a pupil is set to do that in order that he may be able to learn later how to do the same thing with other and higher forms of consciousness. We consider ourselves far superior to any kind of animal, and rightly, since we belong to a higher kingdom. It should therefore be perfectly simple for us to understand the mind of that animal, yet from the experience I have had I imagine almost everybody who pays any attention to animals must be misrepresenting their ideas and motives all the time. When you really find out what an animal is thinking, you discover that it has reasons for what it does which never occurred to you. Since we are unable to understand the animal, whose lines of thought are few and simple, we are even less likely to understand our fellow-men. We are nearer to the human being, of course, but I doubt whether any human being ever understands another human being at all. Strange as it may sound, we are all isolated; each stands by himself. There is another way in which it is true that we are a mighty brotherhood, yet as far as our minds are concerned, each lives in a tower of his own. The circumference of his mind touches that of another man's only at a point, and even there only doubtfully and uncertainly.

Against these three the man who would fill his heart with the love of God must watch ceaselessly.

C.W.L.—One would think it fairly easy to avoid the three evils mentioned. It is not, because they are so painfully common and so much a matter of habit that few people realize their existence. They are our special difficulties because of the place where we stand in evolution. We have been developing the lower mind which looks first for points of difference. Because of that people notice first the points which they do not like in anything which comes before them; then comment and criticism almost invariably follow. The man who is devoting his energies to picking holes and finding differences is behind the times—a hopeless anachronism. We ought now to be studying synthesis and trying to find the divine and good in everything, because we should be beginning to develop buddhi. We are trying to live for to-morrow, not for yesterday; therefore we must not let ourselves be swept away by this tide of ignorant obscurantism; but we have constantly to remind ourselves not to give way, otherwise the stream will so surround and press upon us that we shall occasionally slip back.

CHAPTER 3

GOSSIP

See what gossip does. It begins with evil thought, and that in itself is a crime. For in everyone and in everything there is good; in everyone and in everything there is evil. Either of these we can strengthen by thinking of it, and in this way we can help or hinder evolution; we can do the will of the Logos or we can resist Him. If you think of the evil in another, you are doing at the same time three wicked things.

C.W.L.—The Master speaks of evil thought as a crime. When we remember how exceedingly careful and balanced is the speech of the Master always, we realize that that against which He speaks so strongly must be evil indeed.

An attempt to understand the motives of another man, to follow his line of reasoning, is very likely to be incorrect; therefore the least we can do is to give him the benefit of the doubt. Most people are on the whole quite respectable and well-meaning, therefore we should give them the credit of good intentions. If we are wrong, our slightly higher thought about the person will act upon him and actually do him good. When you hear something to the disadvantage of another, ask yourself whether you would repeat that piece of gossip and send it on to be magnified if it were about your own son or brother ? No, emphatically you would not. You would combat it in the first place, and in any case you would not circulate it. Why should you act differently with regard to somebody else's son or brother ?

> **(1) You are filling your neighbourhood with evil thought instead of with good thought, and so you are adding to the sorrow of the world.**

C.W.L.—The world is very much to us what we make it and as we take it. If a man is pessimistic, bent upon finding evil and darkness, looking for a chance to be offended or hurt, he can find it. There is evil in the world and much sorrow in these lower planes, as the Lord Buddha pointed out. We can magnify these things into serious difficulties, or we can approach the world optimistically, in a cheery spirit of determination to make the best of everything. In the latter case we shall find that there is a great deal that is bright, and shall also be making the world more cheerful for others by our outer life and our thought-power.

There are many people who have been practising regular meditation for many years. They must inevitably have learnt to think a little more definitely than those who have made no such attempt; their thoughts are therefore more powerful. If these people should think evil of others, it is very much worse in a great number of ways than if the ordinary person did it. First, because they know better, they are, as it is expressed in the Church, "sinning against light". Secondly, their thought produces definite and relatively permanent forms, which often have considerable influence in the astral and mental atmosphere. Use your power, therefore, to make the world brighter and happier. You have no idea how much that can be done, simply by putting away all sorrowful and selfish thought, and filling yourself with love that will radiate all around you.

> (2) If there is in that man the evil which you think, you are strengthening it and feeding it ; and so you are making your brother worse instead of better. But generally the evil is not there, and you have only fancied it ; and then your wicked thought tempts your brother to do wrong, for if he is not yet perfect you may make him that which you have thought him.

C.W.L.—The clairvoyant can see the thoughts of one person going to another and buzzing round him like a crowd of mosquitos. They cannot get in while the man is busy with some other matter, but when his thoughts for the moment slacken, when he is meditative or tired, or absent-minded for a moment, they take their opportunity. The thought-form then fastens on his aura like a burr, and by its vibrations gradually colours the part on which it has impinged, and from there its influence spreads. Thus it suggests the bad or good idea, and if there be something in him that is akin to it, as is usually the case, it sets that in motion.

A little impetus given to another might not matter so much sometimes, but in some cases it makes all the difference in the world. School boys running about often push one another; cases have been known in which a boy has quite unintentionally pushed another over the edge of a precipice. You never know when a man's thought may be on the verge of some wrong course of action, and one evil thought about him may just push him over. On the other hand, when a man is in that way balanced between the good and the evil, one strong, helpful, good thought may push him definitely on the good side and set him going on a career which may mean for him rapid development.

I have seen cases in which an evil thought about a man led to a course of evil action on his part the result of which would last for many lives; it was near the surface, but it had not materialized itself in action; there came an evil thought from some one else, which gave just the push which sent him over from thought into action, and committed him to a course of crime. Till you see that clairvoyantly you will scarcely be able to realize it; but see it once, and you will be careful forever, with a care born of horror. It gives you a new sense of responsibility, sometimes rather overwhelming. Remember how the poet Schiller wrote about clairvoyance, how he desired the welcome blindness of the senses again; "Take back your cruel gift; take back this dreadful gift," was what he said.

(3) You fill your own mind with evil thoughts instead of good; and so you hinder your own growth, and make yourself, for those who can see, an ugly and painful object instead of a beautiful and lovable one.

C.W.L.—Many people take much trouble about their physical personal appearance, and the grace and gentleness of their manners, not merely because they are anxious to appear at their best and to be thought well of, but also because it is recognized to be a duty to society in general. In ancient days it was understood to be every man's duty to make himself as perfect and as beautiful as possible in every way; in attire, appearance, speech and action, he was to learn the right, the graceful, the proper way to do everything. Not only one's personality but one's surroundings also were to be not merely useful but also beautiful. If a man built a house it was his duty to his neighbours to put up something that would be graceful and beautiful, though not necessarily costly; and his pottery, as well as his statues and pictures, was to be good. In these days many think only of building as cheaply as they can, regardless of the hideous effect produced. A man builds a great ugly house or factory, and everybody who is sensitive shrinks back from it at once, and all who look at it are the worse for doing so. The man who is responsible for the building actually makes bad karma. Some think such things do not matter, but they do. Our surroundings are of very great importance. True, the strong soul can conquer, but why should we not have things which would help us instead of those which hinder us? Everybody who builds a beautiful house deserves well of his fellow-citizens, because he has put up something the sight of which will benefit everyone who sees it. The touch of pleasure that you get when you see something beautiful is no light thing. I always feel that our gratitude is due to anybody who wears a beautiful colour, because of the effect that colour produces in this terribly grey civilization of ours.

All that is true of beauty physically is even more evident on other planes. The man who makes for himself a radiant and beautiful astral body, full of love and devotion, which he pours out on all around him, deserves the gratitude of his fellows. The audience on the astral plane is generally larger than that on the physical. If we allow ourselves to appear badly in the astral world, a far greater number of people are scandalized by our appearance or annoyed by it, than could possibly be the case on the physical plane. Not only do the inhabitants of the astral world see the beauty of it, but everyone, even those who do not see, feels it. These vibrations act upon them, and the people are helped thereby. The man who yields himself to ugly, selfish, evil thoughts is spreading unpleasantness about him, besides being a horribly disagreeable and unpleasant sight. In the physical plane people hide their loathsome diseases, but the astral leper carries his sores in full view.

Not content with having done all this harm to himself and to his victim, the gossip tries with all his might to make other men partners in his crime. Eagerly he tells his wicked tale to them, hoping that they will believe it; and then they join with him in pouring evil thought upon the poor sufferer. And this goes on day after day, and is done not by one man but by thousands. Do you begin to see how base, how terrible a sin this is? You must avoid it altogether. Never speak ill of any one; refuse to listen when any one else speaks ill of another, but gently say: "Perhaps this is not true, and even if it is, it is kinder not to speak of it."

C.W.L.—It requires a certain amount of courage to say this, but it should be done, in kindness to the gossip, as well as to the person who is being criticized. One may do it gently by using the first person plural: "Perhaps we had better not say any more about it." Then you have not appeared to assume superiority, which is both unoccult and irritating, and probably the man will agree with you, and let the matter drop.

CHAPTER 4

CRUELTY

Then as to cruelty. This is of two kinds, intentional and unintentional. Intentional cruelty is purposely to give pain to another living being; and that is the greatest of all sins—the work of a devil rather than a man. You would say that no man could do such a thing; but men have done it often, and are daily doing it now. The inquisitors did it; many religious people did it in the name of their religion.

C.W.L.—Cruelty is the work of a devil rather than a man; that is how it looks to a Master. Very often in daily life a man does or says something in order to cause pain to somebody else. He comes under that condemnation; he is doing a thing which is worthy of a devil rather than a man. It seems incredible, but people can be found who do it.

Horrible things have been done in the name of religion. Read the oldest literature we know, the Vedas, and we find evidence of them cropping out very strongly there. We find the Aryans pouring down into the plains of India and proceeding to put to the sword the people who were there. Nothing is too dreadful to be done to these people; they must be wiped off the face of the earth! Why? For one all-sufficient reason: because their rites are different! The Muhammadans swept over a large part of the world offering their Koran or the sword to the people they conquered. Christians have been no better. The same spirit led to the persecutions by the Inquisitors, the atrocious treatment of the South American Indians, and all the rest of such things. We think we are becoming more civilized now, yet even to-day religious feeling is very strong and bitter in some quarters. It is the fashion to say that even if the law permitted such persecutions as used to take place, our higher civilization would prevent us from ever resorting to the horrors of the past. I am not so sure of it. I know places in England where a person of unorthodox religious views is regarded as to be excluded from social functions, and to be suspected of all sorts of bad things. We do not put people on the rack, and wrench out their teeth, as our forefathers did. *Autres temps, autres moeurs!* I do not think I should like to see absolute power given into the hands of any of the dogmatic sects.

Vivisectors do it.

C.W.L.—There is no excuse for practising deliberate cruelty to animals. They are our younger brothers, and though not yet men, they will become so after a greater or lesser number of incarnations. The practice of animal experimentation involving cruelty is abhorrent, and can never really benefit mankind, because the law of karma cannot be changed, and as man sows so shall he also reap. I have heard Dr. Besant say that no lives ought to be saved by such methods as that. We know that the instinct of self-preservation is strongly implanted in every man and every animal, so that the body which has been acquired at the cost of considerable effort and trouble may give service to the life within as long as possible, and that therefore human life must be saved when it can rightly be done. But that end cannot justify all possible means. We rightly admire the men who face death rather than dishonour ; surely it is great dishonour to human beings to have their lives saved by anything obtained in such a diabolical manner as this. Our President said she would rather die than be saved in this way.

There is very varied opinion on this subject among members of the Theosophical Society, in which everyone is free to have his own beliefs, but the Master's opinion, as quoted above, is definite. Whatever may be our abhorrence of the cruelty of vivisection, however, we must make allowances for the fact that many doctors and others who support and practise it do so regretfully —not for the pleasure of cruelty (though the existence of such things in our midst does give an opportunity for that to some ghouls in human form), but because they think it the only way to save human bodies from suffering and death, and they sincerely believe that the end justifies the means in this case. However much, therefore, we may disagree with them, let us condemn the sin but not the sinner. There can be no question but that karma will bring great suffering to those who practise vivisection. Many who view them with indignation approaching hatred would change their feeling to pity did they realize this fact.

All vivisectionists are not cruel to the same degree. I know, for example a member of our own Society, who is one of the leading surgeons, who has performed vivisections of a certain kind. There are certain tubes in the human body which sometimes become severed. They are so fine that when one tries to join the severed ends again the inevitable scar always blocks the tube. It was for a time impossible to save people in this condition until it occurred to this doctor that if one made a larger incision it might be possible for the wound to heal and yet at the same time to keep the tube open. He did this by making an incision in the tube near the end of one piece and on the side of the other, and let them overlap and heal in that way. In order to see whether this would work, he tried it upon a number of dogs. He told me that he tried this experiment on about half a dozen stray dogs. They were thoroughly well fed and brought into perfect health before the operation, some anasthetic was then administered, and the dogs were nursed very carefully until they had recovered, and it was found that the operation had been successful. The result was that this which before had been thought impossible became a recognized possibility. The operation is now a common one all over the world, and is known by the name of the doctor who invented it. The principle was wrong, but there was practically no cruelty to the animals concerned, and they were much better off, instead of worse, for the time being. This experiment was thus quite different from what usually occurs, and I think it would be entirely inappropriate to attack this doctor in the way in which anti-vivisectionists constantly attack the mass of the vivisectors.

Some of the experiments that one reads about are atrociously cruel, such as that of seeing to what degree of temperature an animal can be baked before certain functions disappear, and dozens of other ghastly and obviously useless horrors. And there are thousands of others performed needlessly for the general instruction of students, and to try all kinds of effects, many of which are quite useless, because the human constitution differs from those of different animals in a variety of ways. For example, a goat, among its other miscellaneous food, will eat freely of henbane, with no apparent injury; but if a human being takes it he will pass on to the astral plane. Again, when an animal is in frightful pain and terror, that must change the fluids of its body and render any observations with regard to them of very uncertain value.

The proper substitute for all this cruelty is, of course, clairvoyance. It is very far better for the doctor if he can see into the interior economy of the living man while the body is whole, than it is to deduce certain things about it by cutting into the living body of an animal which differs from the man. Those who feel that they *must* do vivisection had better form a society in which they will agree to practise on one another; in that way they will have human subjects giving reactions likely to be useful when those of an animal are not, and they will avoid horrible cruelty to defenceless creatures, which in God's world they have no right to inflict. This is unnecessary, however, for a tenth part of the trouble, and study and research that is put into these experiments would produce an army of reliable clairvoyants; indeed, the attention that is given by the average student to his long training would generally be quite enough to develop his clairvoyance.

There is serious danger of another form of cruelty rising out of the great authority claimed by the orthodox medical fraternity. We do not want to become slaves to them, as our forefathers were slaves to the Church. Though they have done good in various ways, that gives no authority for the establishment of scientific "inquisitions" with power to penalize the heretic who does not wish to submit to their creed of the moment. True, it would be only the civil law that would punish, but that was also the case with the Church—those who would not believe and submit, it handed over to the civil authorities, with the hypocritical prayer that there should be no shedding of blood, which prevented those in power from cutting off their heads and made them burn their victims instead. There has been trouble with the enforcement of vaccination, and it is still compulsory in some countries; though it is an arguable question as to whether the remedy is not worse than the disease which it is professed to prevent. There are very frequent changes in medical opinion, yet each fad is frantically supported while it lasts. The interests of a community in power have often in history given rise to terrible oppression and widespread misery. Let us have no scientific "inquisitions".

There are some people who try to excuse any cruelty to animals on the old Jewish theory that they exist only for the sake of man. We know better than that. They exist for the Logos; they are stages of evolution permeated by His life. It is, however, justifiable for us to make use of animals, so long as we promote their evolution. They benefit by being in contact with man. It is true that we interfere with the wild horse when we capture him, but in other ways, especially mentally, he gains much development.

Some even extend the old Jewish idea to children. There are parents who think that children exist for them —to be used as servants, to be a source of pride, to provide for their old age, and so on. And that leads on to the inhuman notion that a child should be forced to become what we think he ought to be, regardless of the special interests and aptitudes that are his because of his past lives. This leads to superfine cruelty.

Many schoolmasters do it habitually. All these people try to excuse their brutality by saying that *it is the custom ; but a crime does not cease to be* a crime because many commit it.

C.W.L.—The beating of children is a widely spread custom, but that is no excuse for it. It is not, however, a universal custom; I am happy to say that there are a few countries which in that respect have attained civilization. I believe that Japan is one of them. I know from my own experience that Italy is another. I lived for some considerable time in one of the Italian cities, in a house which overlooked the grounds of a large school, and I watched with very great interest the relations between the masters and the boys. Because of their more excitable and freer natures they did not treat discipline as we do. The boys, would all be drawn up in line and at any moment one of them would suddenly leave the ranks and rush up to the master, seize upon his arm and say something to him in quite an impassioned way. The master would smile and pat his head, evidently granting his request or saying something about it. They were all on the most friendly terms. I noticed, too, that whenever those boys met their master in the street, they immediately sprang upon him and pulled him about, and were the very greatest of friends out of school hours also. That was a very good sign, because the man whom children love is always a good man at bottom—their instinct is infallible. In Italy anything like the cruelty that exists in most English schools could not happen, because the customs are different. To lay a hand upon a person is the one unforgivable sin in that country; it involves knives and duels and things of that sort. So the children are perfectly safe.

Punishment has long been a custom, but that does not prevent it from being both cruel and futile. First of all, it is not our business to administer chastisement.

The law of karma will attend to all that, and it cannot make mistakes, as we often do. Frightful legal injustice has been committed again and again; the severest penalties have been imposed upon quite innocent people. The criminal has done more wrong to himself than to anybody else, and vengeance may be left to the course of nature.

Apart from that, punishment is applied to inspire fear—in the offender for the future, and in the possible offender at large. The idea of beating a child is the same as that of punishing a criminal by law; these things have in them the elements of revenge. They seem to say: "You do such-and-such a thing, and I will make it very uncomfortable for you." Often a teacher gets angry, and his feelings are the cause of the punishments he applies—not any reasoned judgment as to what is best for the child. I know it is said that punishment by law is intended to prevent people from committing crimes. But it does not act in that way. A hundred years ago the punishments of the English law were very severe. For example, a person would be hanged for stealing anything to the value of one shilling and sixpence. I remember having seen it recorded at the entrance to Newgate prison—and in other places there is the same sort of thing—that such-and-such a person was hanged for stealing a pair of gloves, valued at two or three shillings. When such severe punishment was meted out, the proportion of crime was much greater than it is now. The amount of crime has little to do with the punishments meted out; it is chiefly a question of general education and civilization.

Punishment by the law or by the school generally has no relation to the crime committed. A man steals something; then he is shut up in a prison for a certain time. What is the relation between the two things? He might reasonably be made to do some work which should return the value of the article stolen, to the person from whom it was taken. The punishment should fit the crime in some way. Merely to shut a man up because he has stolen something is a kind of nightmare. So also among us a child does not learn a certain lesson and they beat him. What is the connection between the two things? There would be some reason in saying: "You have not learnt the lesson; you will be behind the others in your class, therefore you must stay and learn it when otherwise you would be playing." There is no sense in this kind of thing, and it is radically wrong. The idea of giving intentional pain is always wrong, and no amount of custom can make it right. All sorts of eminently undesirable and foolish things have been the custom—foot-binding in China, for example, and some of our own fashions at different times. We must not get the idea that because a thing is the custom, even if it has been so for hundreds of years, it must be a good or necessary thing, because very often it is not.

A community might reasonably say to some habitual criminals, as they did to such people in ancient Peru: "We are a civilized race. With great trouble we have arranged our State upon a certain scheme, and it is intended for people who will keep its laws. If you do not intend to keep these laws, go out and live with some one else." There, exile was the only punishment; and to be cast out among the barbarian tribes was the greatest disgrace, as well as a discomfort. Society has the right to restrain a dangerous person. When you get a Malay running amuk you must stop that man, even though it should be at the cost of having to take his life. But except in emergencies, when it is unavoidable, we have no right to kill; and no one ever has the right to torture—that is absolutely certain. Capital punishment, if it is revenge, means that we become as brutal as the criminal who has aroused what we euphemistically call our righteous indignation. If it has the purpose of saving us further trouble with that man it is wrong in principle, since the State has a duty to every citizen, not only to those who are normal, and also it should think of the real man, not merely of the body. To seek the easiest way out of our difficulty by killing the man is thus positively criminal; and it does no good because much evil passion is aroused, and the man will reincarnate in unpleasant kārmic relations with us in the future. The real criminal—who is rare, because most offenders are products of unfortunate environment—is really a pathological case. What he requires is not torment and brutalization, which accentuate his anti-social tendencies, but the right treatment and training that will bring him physically and emotionally within the ranks of normal citizenship. The State cares for the physically and mentally defective; it must deal in the same way with the criminal, who is generally either mentally or emotionally defective. This would be the attitude of love, the standpoint of the Master.

These ideals are real, and quite clear and practical. Both the criminal and the child must be helped by education, not driven by fear. The system of terrifying children produces exceedingly evil results. It introduces into their lives fear and pain and deceit, and is generally disastrous to character and good citizenship. It is another form of the old Church idea of hell; but the hell is to be here, and it can be escaped by one with sufficient cunning. People thought they could make others good by frightening them. It is odd how that idea still holds. One of our principal living novelists wrote to me some time ago and said that once at the seaside he met a young man and gave him some Theosophical ideas, in the course of which he explained to him that the hell theory was all nonsense. Later on this youth's mother, full of anger, paid the novelist a visit. She said: "That is the only way I have been able to keep this boy in order—by the fear of hell, by threatening him with it every day and all day long. Now that you have persuaded him that there is no hell, what am I going to do?" Perhaps if she had known a little better, and had explained things to him from the first there would have been no need to adopt this very unpleasant form of terrorism.

Liberty and love are great factors in the development of the human soul. There are many people who are quite willing to give liberty to others, if they will do exactly what they prescribe! But true liberty means the freedom to try in one's own way. In general there is far too much interference; too much direction from the outside diminishes the very life-activity that it seeks to protect or assist. This is seen in school life, where quantities of unnecessary rules are made, when individual freedom would give more opportunity for growth. That is one of the great differences between the English scheme of government and that of some of the other nations. England tries on the whole to leave its people as free as possible. Some countries try to avoid trouble and danger and to assist the people by all kinds of restraints. I remember an official of a foreign state saying to me once: "Well, sir, in a really well-managed country everything would be forbidden!" In travelling about the world I have been much struck by the different forms in which the regulations are expressed. In one country you will find a stern prohibition; in another, a request. Some obviously adopt the military plan, which is good only for very young souls; but others appeal to the good sense and goodwill in a man. I remember, for example, reading one sign, forbidding certain unpleasant practices, which ran: "Gentlemen will not, and others must not" do so-and-so. That was in America, which is one of the newer countries. I thought it was rather well put.

There are cases where you must assert compulsion in the interests of the community; but it is always better when possible to have the wills of the people with you than to drive them along. I am afraid that is only very slightly understood with regard to education.

Everything is prescribed; all the time it is: "Do this, do not do that." Even in teaching the child his interest is not usually engaged, but he is told: "This is a lesson and it must be learned."

In the newer methods, such as that of Mme. Montessori, the lesson is made interesting, so that the child mind opens like a flower. There is only one way in which you can really and usefully teach a child anything, and that is by making him love you to begin with. You exercise a certain amount of moral suasion afterwards, because you look injured and pained if he does wrong. That is quite legitimate, because you really do feel the pain. If you start ruling by love you call out the love of the pupil, and get something done. To teach children one must have a clever mind, a heart full of love, and patience as wide as the sea; one must understand the mistakes that children make, and be able to show them how to do things properly, but in their own way. If you start with force and brutality you call out nothing but hostility, and then you do not get anything worth while done.

It is the same in ordinary life. If one business man wants to deal profitably with another, he speaks pleasantly to him, and tries to convince him that the business he proposes will be to their mutual advantage. It would not occur to him to start out by trying to drive the other man; it would only antagonize him and make anything like friendly relations between them impossible. Boys and girls are human beings, too, and you can get more out of them if you have them on your side than if you set them against you to start with. These are matters of experience to those who try to teach. No teacher, however skilful, however learned, is worthy of that highly honourable name unless he can interest the children and get them to love him. It is an absolute prerequisite. That is the way in which the Masters teach: never by force, never by issuing commands, but by showing the right way and encouraging us to try to imitate Them.

> **Karma takes no account of custom; and the karma of cruelty is the most terrible of all. In India at least there can be no excuse for such customs, for the duty of harmlessness is well-known to all.**

C.W.L.—The man who takes up the profession of a school-master does so in order to earn his living, just as he might enter any other profession. The Lords of Karma do not, however, regard the matter from that point of view. They put a man into such a position with the idea of giving him a magnificent opportunity. If he should take it, and carry his work through carefully, tactfully, lovingly, it will lead him to another life in which he will probably be a religious teacher. From that the way is open to become a great saint, a great benefactor of mankind. The teaching profession lies straight in the road to some of the highest prizes of life, from the point of view of the Lords of Karma.

The teacher should realize that each child is an ego; and should give all the help possible to the development of its character. He naturally has a vast opportunity, because the children are in his care to learn, and he can make of them very much what he will. As to the strength of this influence, a well-known Jesuit once said: "Let me have a child up to the age of eleven, and after that he can go where he pleases." The teacher's influence upon the young operates quite as much by what he is and the way in which he acts, as by anything directly said to them. He who is what he ought to be radiates love in a strong and powerful influence. His position is also one of great responsibility, for if instead of rousing love and good qualities in his charges he awakens fear and deceit, he is hampering the progress of those egos, and thus doing serious positive harm.

Misuse of such an opportunity involves a terrible fall for the man. Cruelty in such cases produces very horrible results; on certain occasions we have found it to bring a sort of repayment in kind, but quite often it brings insanity as its result, and short of that, a great many conditions such as hysteria and neurasthenia. In many cases also it has resulted in a remarkable and cataclysmic descent in the social scale. A person who has been cruel in a reasonably good position finds himself thrown down among the drugs of the populace because of that cruelty. For example, I have seen cases of Brāhmanas reborn as pariahs, in consequence of cruelty to children. So it is evident that the Lords of Karma, demonstrating the great laws of the universe, take the same view of these things as the Master does.

. . . . .

An opportunity somewhat similar to that of the schoolmaster is given to a man who is the manager of a factory or the head of a large business of any kind. A man thinks of such a place as one to be desired because it gives him an opportunity of getting a good salary or of making a good deal of money and obtaining a certain amount of power. But the Lords of Karma would regard that, again, as an opportunity to help all those other men who came under his control. An employer often regards his men with a sort of scarcely veiled hostility; he thinks they want to get as much out of him as they can and to take advantage of him in various ways. On their part, the men usually think he wishes to grind them down, to get all he can out of them, paying them as little as possible in return. It is true, unfortunately, that in some cases both sides are right in thinking as they do. There are employers who have that attitude; and there are very many workmen who take that line towards their employers: but the man who understands will look at it not in the least from that point of view. That the position gives the man an opportunity of being a helpful influence in the life of a number of people is the only aspect of the matter which concerns the Lords of Karma. The Lords of Karma do not usually look at things from our point of view. Mankind generally, for example, regards death as a terrible thing and a heavy punishment: but it is often given as a kind of reward—as a release leading to better and more promising conditions.

The fate of the cruel must fall also upon all who go out intentionally to kill God's creatures, and call it 'sport'.

C.W.L.—As regards conditions in the country in England Punch's satire, "It is a fine day; let us go out and kill something" was not very far wrong. As a clergyman in a country parish in England I was in close relation with a typical set of the people who shoot and hunt and fish. They did all these things as their regular daily occupation, and that formed also the principal subject of their conversation. Yet, however hard one may find it to believe, these people were perfectly gentle and kindly towards their fellow-men; the men were good fathers and husbands, lenient judges and kind friends, but they did not see the wrong in this particular thing. One of those very men, who would kill deer and shoot as many pheasants as he could in the most reckless way, would nevertheless sit up all night with a dog that was sick, showing that he had a kind heart, and that even towards the animals he felt a certain brotherhood. The cruelty is all due to a kind of mental blindness. They do not lack intellect, but on this matter they have never thought, but have taken it for granted that all these creatures were created for their use, and for the enjoyment which they could derive from their skill in killing them. People eat meat with the same thoughtlessness. As a young man I did so, and it never dawned upon me that it was wrong until I found a book on the subject—that was long before the Theosophical Society was founded.

When we have once seen that such "sport" is a horrible thing, and that in following it we are taking part in the slaughter of God's creatures, we wonder why we never noticed it before. Thousands of people have not yet seen the evil. The glamour of custom is upon them, and they have never thought of the frightful harm that is being done. The same thing is true in connection with some articles of attire. There are certain kinds of feathers, for example, that can only be procured at terrible cost in animal life—not only the pain and death of the creature concerned, but generally of other young creatures depending upon it. People who wear these things are certainly criminally careless. They are not desperately cruel—not in the least: they are simply following the custom. Still, karma will operate. A man may be in a brown study and walk over a precipice; the fact that he did not know where he was going does not alter the result.

Such things as these you would not do, I know; and for the sake of the love of God, when opportunity offers, you will speak clearly against them.

C.W.L.—Here we must note the words "when opportunity offers". We do not want to thrust our ideas upon other people, so one speaks on such matters usually only when an opinion is asked, or when the subject comes forward in a natural way. To thrust forward one's own ideas, however excellent they may be, generally does more harm than good. The aggressive people who do this always arouse resentment. A man who accosts you in the street and wants to know whether you have found Jesus, or whether your soul is saved, does not impress you favourably, and most people are inclined to feel that since he is so tactless his religion cannot be of great practical value. If a suitable opportunity occurs one may lend a book or a pamphlet, or converse gently and quietly on the subject. But if you find yourself among a number of sportsmen, I should not advise you to start out by saying: "This is a very wicked thing" —although it is. If I were asked, I should say quietly: "I hold that all life is sacred, that these animals are really younger brothers of ours, and you have no more right to go out and kill them for pleasure than you would have to kill a man for your pleasure." They would be surprised, no doubt; perhaps they would sneer covertly at me; but they would not be so strongly set against the idea as they would if they were attacked.

We who are vegetarians often feel great disgust if we have to sit at the same table with people who are eating meat, yet it is frequently unavoidable when travelling. Still, it is not well to show our feelings; that is certainly not the way to convert other people, but if they ask about our views we can express our opinions temperately, forcefu y but quietly. If we do this it is quite probable, if the man begins to think about it, that he will come over to our point of view.

But there is a cruelty in speech as well as in act; and a man who says a word with the intention to wound another is guilty of this crime. That,

too, you would not do; but sometimes a careless word does as much harm as a malicious one. So you must be on your guard against unintentional cruelty.

C.W.L.—Some people pride themselves on speaking out just what they think, even if it hurts others, and they seem to regard this as a virtue. The Master, who never uses words carelessly, says it may be a crime, if the words are cruel. In debate or discussion we need not refrain from putting our side of the case, but we can put it carefully and courteously. The Apostle said: "Let every man be fully persuaded in his own mind."[1] That does not mean that he is to try to persuade other people, but that he himself should understand why he holds certain beliefs. When that is the case he will be able to state his views, when necessary, gently and temperately.

It is a curious fact that many people cannot differ in opinion from others without getting more or less angry, although they know that there are thousands upon thousands of questions in the world upon which there is so much to be said on several sides that one point of view is almost as defensible as another. A discussion between a Catholic and an Orange-man is exceedingly likely to end in blows, which, after all, do not constitute a form of argument which carries conviction with it. If a person differs from another's opinion it appears to be taken as a kind of slight; such a person is so sure that

[1] Romans, 14, 5.

his own idea is right that any other man who disagrees is wilfully of malice prepense declining to accept it ! We have therefore to be careful how we put our views before others.

There is a special temptation in regard to Theosophy, because we definitely base our belief on reason, and we only try to show people this; yet often the other man cannot see it. Reason, however perfect, however logical, does not necessarily impress the ordinary man at all; he does not live in his reason, but in his feelings, and if these are roused by what is said, no amount of reason will convince him, and the more we talk the angrier he will become.

It comes usually from thoughtlessness. A man is so filled with greed and avarice that he never even thinks of the suffering which he causes to others by paying too little, or by half-starving his wife and children. Another thinks only of his own lust, and cares little how many souls and bodies he ruins in satisfying it. Just to save himself a few minutes' trouble, a man does not pay his workmen on the proper day, thinking nothing of the difficulties he brings upon them. So much suffering is caused just by carelessness—by forgetting to think how an action will affect others. But Karma never forgets, and it takes no account of the fact that men forget. If you wish to enter the Path, you must think of the consequences of what you do, lest you should be guilty of thoughtless cruelty.

C.W.L.—By paying a little less than what a thing is worth one may be causing much suffering to the workman, and his wife and children. The reduction of a few pence from a day's wages may mean that the family has insufficient food. Business is business, I know, but it is better if necessary, to make less rather than fall into the sin of grinding down the poor. Employers are finding that it pays to give "good wages", as has been the experience of Mr. Henry Ford, who is said to be now the richest man in the world. As a priest, I used to go among the poor and see things from their standpoint, and often found people taking advantage of their helplessness. This was so also in India, where sometimes in the Pariah Schools children actually fainted from hunger, until we were in a position to give them food.

CHAPTER 5

SUPERSTITION

Superstition is another mighty evil, and has caused much terrible cruelty. The man who is a slave to it despises others who are wiser, tries to force them to do as he does.

C.W.L.—Superstition never takes into account the differences of temperament between people. It has some form of belief which it wishes to impress upon all alike, not realizing that you never can impress any belief, except, perhaps, some dry scientific fact, upon all people alike, because there are as many attitudes towards life as there are people. Even if you know a great number of people, you will rarely find two who are alike in the way in which circumstances affect them. You can predict certain general possibilities with regard to the great majority of men, but until you know them very well you cannot judge accurately how they will react to certain things. So superstition implies among other things a very great want of sympathy. The man who is subject to it does not understand that there are other ways than his own of looking at things.

Superstition is not only bad for the person himself, but when prominent it always leads to attempts to coerce other people. All through history, superstition in religion has led to frightful trouble. On its account the followers of Muhammad have at different times spread bloodshed and slaughter over vast tracts of Asia, Europe and Africa, offering "the Koran or the sword". The superstition which produced the Inquisition has been previously discussed. The massacres of St. Bartholomew and the Sicilian Vespers, when the Protestants and the Catholics respectively massacred each other were other terrible results of superstition. The last were partly political, but the former was a matter of "religion". The ill-feeling between the different sects of Christians was very largely responsible for the massacre, though no doubt political considerations also had their share in it, as they had also with Constantine when he became a Christian, thinking it a good card to play in the then state of affairs in the Byzantine Empire.

The Crusades were another mighty superstition. Because of a story which had little foundation in fact, as to the life and death of the teacher Jesus, twenty million men lost their lives in those Crusades, trying to get into Christian hands the country where His life story occurred. If they could have been brought to understand that it was the life story of every Initiate, and that that has been led in all countries of the world at one time or another, all that loss of life might have been avoided. Perhaps it was not all loss, however, because by going out to fight with the more enlightened Saracens the Christians brought back, some useful information into Europe, and that they were willing to die for an ideal counted to them for righteousness. There was something chivalrous and beautiful, no doubt, in the idea that the sacred places of a religion ought to belong to the people of that religion. Time has proved, however, that in this case it was fortunate that the Christians did not succeed. In that holy land the Muhammadan soldiers have had to keep peace between the rival Christian sects—the Latin and the Greek—because they always fight for precedence about the holy fire and at the sepulchre.

At the present day we have in India a similar problem, but no one dreams of trying to settle it by the method of the Crusades. The holy places of the Buddhists—the place where the Lord Buddha was born, the place where He attained His Buddhahood, the place where He died—are all in the hands of people of the Hindu faith, a religion which is as different from Buddhism as Christianity is different from Muhammadanism. The Buddhists earnestly desire to possess their holy places, but it has not occurred to the Buddhist nations to start upon a war of conquest. We may be very thankful for that, for the Buddhists number about five hundred million people. Their religion forbids them to do anything so irrational. Some Buddhists have tried to buy back the site, and they nearly succeeded in doing so. The Theosophical Society assisted them, but unfortunately a great part of the money was lost in a law suit, and the plan fell through.

There is no great religion except Buddhism which has never persecuted. It could not do so because of its inherent principles: it is bound to toleration by the very words of its Founder. Who is a Buddhist? He is a man who follows the teachings of the Lord Buddha; not a man who believes this or that, but a man who lives as the Lord Buddha said men should live. Ask a missionary what will become of the really good Buddhist, and he will usually answer, "If he does not believe in Christ, there is no hope for him", or at best he will leave him to the uncovenanted mercies of God, if he is a very good man. If you ask a Buddhist the same question about a good Christian, he will say, "He is quite a good Buddhist; he calls himself a Christian, but he is following the teachings of the Lord Buddha; all will be well with him." Such is the tolerance of Buddhism, as I have explained before. Of course, every religion really forbids intolerance and violence, but the level of ignorance and fanaticism in some of them has blinded their people to this simple fact.

The form of superstition called race hatred, in which one race instinctively dislikes another *en bloc*, is also foolish, because there is good and bad in every race. I remember that in remote villages in England the attitude of the peasantry towards a foreigner was always one of suspicion and ridicule. The fact that a man spoke a different language was something to laugh at, among those ignorant people. There are other peasantries who, in that particular respect, are less uncourteous than our common folk. I always feel that if a foreigner visits our country we are in the relation of host towards him, and it is our duty to make his path easy, and to give him as good an impression of our people and our country as we can.

In the Napoleonic era there was a superstition in England that all Frenchmen were practically devils, fighting against us with the full knowledge that they were on the wrong side and against the light. To-day you may get cases where a vast number of people are obsessed by one dominant idea, resulting in a kind of national monomania. Under the influence of such a temporary monomania dreadful atrocities occur, which the same people would never dream of committing at other times. In this case the individuals are responsible only to the extent to which they allow themselves to be swept off their feet in that way; the things that they do are done by the monomania more than by the individuals themselves. It is in much the same way that a man will sometimes lose his temper and say unpleasant things; it is the temper that speaks and not the man. He is to blame in that he allows the temper to get control of him, but we must take into consideration that in all probability he will afterwards very much regret what he has said.

Think of the awful slaughter produced by the superstition that animals should be sacrificed.

C.W.L.—Mention of animal and other sacrifices in connection with religion raises the whole question of the relation of God to man. There are only three fundamental views that we can take upon this subject: the first is that God started this scheme of things and left it to take care of itself afterwards, being quite indifferent as to what happened to it ; the second is that He retains what must be called a malevolent interest in it, desiring to enjoy blood or other sacrifices; the third is that He remains always the all-loving Father of His creation.

The first theory is practically modern materialism plus the idea of an original creator. The second represents God as a monster full of blood-lust. Many of the old scriptures misrepresent Him in this way. In one case in the Old Testament the Jews boast of sacrificing a hundred and twenty-two thousand bullocks at one time. Probably they were exaggerating, as was their habit in those early days. Jehovah demanded sacrifices, and did not in the least care how much suffering he caused so long as he could get what he wanted. He was always clamouring for sacrifices, which must be made to him, and to no other deity. The Jews of the present day would recoil in horror from such a thing, but evidently they did not do so in the days of David and Solomon. It follows that the Jehovah whom they then worshipped was not what we call God, to which conception they could not then rise, but one of the great elemental deities coming over from Atlantean days. The Jews had before then contacted the civilization of Egypt, but its great ideas had made little impression upon them; but later, during the Babylonian captivity, they learned of a supreme God. They at once identified Him, characteristically, with their own Jehovah, and their later prophets wrote magnificently of Him, but still with frequent outcroppings of the old ideas.

Blood-sacrifices belong only to early stages of human evolution. They involve the primitive magic of elemental worship, and are always connected with elementals which live on the fumes of blood. The elemental wants the sacrifices because he absorbs the aroma of the blood and obtains from it the power to materialize himself. Among some hill tribes the people say that if they do not perform such sacrifices troubles come upon them—their crops are spoiled and their houses catch fire; the hill gods of India are therefore also probably great elemental deities of Atlantis.

We may be sure that the Great Ones have never countenanced such sacrifices. In India, for example, the original revelation of the Vedas certainly did not contain them, but they came from the aboriginal traditions, which still exist to some extent. The Lord Buddha spoke against animal sacrifices, and induced King Bimbisara to issue an edict abolishing them in his realm.

Clearly no Deity whom we could wish to worship would want offerings of blood, though there are elementals and nature-spirits who do. We must, therefore, regard those portions of Scripture which deal with such offerings as belonging to a period in human evolution long outgrown. Some people do not like to say this openly, because they reverence the Scriptures, but it is nothing but superstition to regard one particular set of words as sacred and sacrosanct for all time. We ought to be eclectic about the Scriptures, as about everything else. We take up a book, and value and remember those passages in it which we find especially beautiful and helpful. In the same way, we should take from any scripture what is noble and beautiful and grand for all time, and we may with advantage drop all those parts which do not come up to our standards. Although blood-sacrifices are mentioned in the Psalms and other parts of the Bible, we must face the fact that God could never have wanted them; they invariably belong to the type of religion that considers the Deity as an evil being, who must be bought off.

It has been the great tragedy of Christianity that this idea became mingled with the pure teaching of the Christ about God the loving Father. True, animal sacrifices to the Deity have not disgraced Christianity, but the idea of God as a being who will do harm unless bought off is still taught by the great Christian organizations. They invented the amazing theory that God sacrificed his own Son instead of all the other people who would otherwise have been sent to hell. I suppose most people never stop to think what kind of a god it could be who would require or permit such a sacrifice. You can imagine what would be said of any earthly king who condemned quite casually a number of people to horrible tortures and then released them because his own son came forward and said, "If you must kill somebody, kill me. I have not done anything wrong; but nevertheless, kill me, and let these people go free." That theory is not Christianity.

Colonel Ingersoll was right when he said that an honest God is the noblest work of man. It is true that only a nation which was already highly developed could rise to the conception of a really grand and glorious Deity. It is true that our remote forefathers, who ran about in the woods and painted themselves blue, and the ancient war-like Jews, and others, had crude conceptions of the Deity, but there is absolutely no reason why we should carry them on at the present day.

The third theory, which we hold in Theosophy, is that God is beneficent, that He has brought the whole scheme into existence for a purpose which He is steadily pursuing all the time, and that therefore everything that happens is part of His work. He allows a certain amount of free-will to His creatures and they do things which are clearly not in harmony with His great plan; yet as their will is part of His plan, all is ultimately His work.

When we say that God allows man some independence or freedom, we must make it clear that we understand it to be limited, and growing. If a man uses well the freedom and power that he has, more will be given to him. The method seems to be like that by which a little child is taught to walk. The teacher allows him to try, and tumble, and try again; if he were always carried in some one else's arms, so as to avoid all possible tumbles, he would end as a cripple. But what the teacher does not do is to let the child learn to take his first steps alone on a marble floor, at the head of a staircase or in other dangerous places. Later, when he has grown up, he may walk on the edge of a precipice to admire the view, if he so chooses. In some such manner the Logos guards us while He trains us, so that we cannot wreck our lives or hurt ourselves beyond repair.

This third theory is steadily gaining ground. For a long time now, Christianity has been much better than its creeds, and very many Christians have held wider views than their Churches have officially authorized. The Church of England, for instance, formulates what it supposes to be its theory of things in a certain predication called "The Articles of Religion". The clergy have to assent to them, but if one of them should ask, "How am I to accept these Articles; they are evidently contradictory?" he is told that at the time they were written there were two irreconcilable parties, and something had to be said to please them both. They say: "The Bishop and the rest of us have all signed them, we have all taken them in this philosophic way, and since we have done so, I think you may do so, too." The young man will probably say. "Well, I suppose if you assure me that it does not mean anything, I may as well accept it." But the position is not quite dignified.

I have no objection to the Christian Creeds; there is a far deeper meaning underlying them than the Christian usually suspects.[1] But I do object to the Thirty-nine Articles and the Confession of Faith, because with some most beautiful ideas they contrive to intermingle others which are absolutely impossible. If in the Catechism they had only stopped at the end of the first question and answer: "What is the chief end of man? To

[1] See *The Christian Creed*, by C. W. Leadbeater.

glorify God and enjoy Him forever", that would have been magnificent.

Christianity has gone very much ahead of its authorized pronouncements and beliefs. I came across a passage the other day which shows that rather clearly. There is a book by the Dean of Ripon, in which he says: "The development of Christ in man is the object of Christianity." Then he goes on to explain what the Christ in man is: "It is the wisdom of the man of science; it is the eloquence of the lawyer; it is the fairness of the judge; it is the love of beauty in the artist; it is the love of man in the philanthropist," and so on. That kind of Christianity we will all accept. There is very much the same idea in the *Gītā*. "Of rulers," says Shri Krishna, "I am the sceptre; of those who seek victory I am statesmanship; and of secrets I am also silence; the knowledge of knowers am I." "Whatsoever is glorious, good, beautiful, and mighty, understand thou that to go forth from a fragment of My splendour."[1] The Christian Dean is very nearly in agreement with the writer of the *Bhagavad Gītā*, a scripture of immense antiquity, very much older than the *Mahābhārata*, of which it became a part. Much of the glorious teaching incorporated in the *Gītā* existed among the Atlanteans residing on the plains of India long before the Aryan invaders entered the country. I know that that is not the generally accepted idea, but it represents certain facts which we have seen.

[1] *Bhagavad Gītā*, x, 38, 41.

Assuredly we may trust God utterly, because He knows and we do not know. We know, in a general way, what is expected of us in the helping forward of His scheme of evolution, but we do not know the details. Yet we know that those details are in competent hands. What our karma will be we do not know, but the great Powers who are managing the matter know it all, and will decide wisely how much of it can usefully be brought down upon us now, and how much should be reserved for the future. If it were possible for the Great Ones to listen to us, and to change our destiny in accordance with what we think we should like at any time, it would assuredly be the worse for us. I do not say that our own aspirations in the matter are useless—very much the reverse, for if we have good aspirations, those are new factors introduced into the case, and they may well enable the Great Lords to modify the working out of our karma, perhaps to bring down more so that we may the sooner be rid of it, perhaps to alter its incidence and bring it down in some other way. But whatever is done, is done for the best for every one and not for a few only, and so we surely should not try to alter God's will; we should thankfully accept whatever comes to us, and should always make the best of it, not the worst. We should take our difficulties as something to be dominated, yet be always glad because we know that God is behind it all, and He is utterly beneficent.

And by the still more cruel superstition that man needs flesh for food.

C.W.L.—That *is* a superstition, because, there are many millions of people who exist in perfect health without it. There are probably some few people who, owing to bad heredity and their own karma, are really unable to make their bodies digest the purer form of food, but they are very, very few. I have myself known of a few instances, among many hundreds of Theosophists, of people who after really trying for a long time to adopt a vegetarian diet, found that they were unable to do it; but all the rest, after a certain amount of difficulty just at first, were able to maintain and often improve their health on vegetarian food.

It has been proved unquestionably that most people can be perfectly strong without saddling themselves with the crime of taking part in the slaughter of animals. It is but a small percentage of physical bodies that cannot be adapted to vegetarian food. It is an unfortunate condition for these persons, but if one has really tried intelligently to reform one's diet in this way, and finds it impossible, one must accept it as karma. In such a case it is not always wise or right to say, "I will force my body to do what I will, or let it go. I will live on pure food or not at all." It may be that one has duties towards others, which cannot be fulfilled if the body is weak, duties which demand rude health. I know, of course, that advice of this kind may very easily be used as an excuse by those who do not like the higher form of food or who shrink from the trouble of adapting the body to a new diet, but it must be given because there are some few unfortunates who must needs continue in their old ways.

Flesh food is undesirable because it is cruel to kill animals, and also because it brings undesirable particles into our bodies, which coarsen them, and excite animal desires in the elementals of those bodies. There are many other reasons also, which I marshalled together once in a lecture which may be found in my book *Some Glimpses of Occultism.* This is one of the few subjects in which practically all the arguments are on one side, for there is nothing to be said for meat-eating, except that people follow the practice because they like it. I think we can make it abundantly clear to any enquirer that it is entirely in his interests to abstain from flesh food. It is not only a question of principle, although surely that is enough for us, but a vegetarian diet means better health, and the avoidance of certain fearful diseases; and definite facts show that the vegetarian has relatively greater endurance.

People sometimes object to this idea and say that in any case we must destroy life in order to live, that those who are vegetarians also destroy life. That is true, to a very limited extent. I suppose we may be said to be destroying the vegetable life, but that is much more primitive, and has not the acute sentiency of the animal.

The fundamental objection to killing is that it interferes with the course of evolution. If you kill a man, you really do no harm to that individual, so far as his pleasure and happiness are concerned; he goes usually to a plane where he will be far happier than he ever was on the physical plane; and the mere destruction of the body is not necessarily cruel, because a man killed suddenly does not feel it. The wrong you have done is to cut him off from the opportunity of evolution which he would otherwise have had in that body. He will have a further opportunity in another body later on, but you are delaying him, and giving the Lords of Karma the trouble of finding another place for that man's evolution, and of carrying him on again through babyhood and childhood before he has the opportunity for development that the conditions of mature manhood provide. That is also why it is so much more serious to kill a man than an animal; the man has to develop an entirely new personality, but the animal goes back into his group-soul, from which incarnation is a comparatively easy matter. Still, in the case of the more evolved animal, which is a more complicated manifestation, it causes, if we may reverently put it so, a great deal of trouble to the evolutionary Powers. The killing, say, of a mosquito is an infinitely smaller matter, because it flows back into its group-soul and comes out again in a very short time. The trouble caused by the destruction even of hundreds of thousands of those insects is as nothing compared to the killing of one horse, or cow, or cat, or dog.

There is no conceivable case in which it could be the right thing to kill a man for any purpose of one's own, except in emergencies in self-defence or the defence of another. The yogi does not even defend himself; he leaves the whole matter in the hands of karma. Still, I believe that we are justified in defending our lives when they are attacked, and I am quite certain we are justified in defending a friend or a child, even at the cost of killing the aggressor. The same thing holds good with regard to all kinds of animals. If an animal attacks you, endangering your life or your safety, you have, I think, the right to kill it if necessary. The whole question is : which will cause the greater harm ? If, for example, you are troubled by mosquitos, which have left their own natural food to attack you and poison your blood, and perhaps spoil some important work, it might very well be the lesser evil to kill the mosquitos. If you can take refuge behind a mosquito net, or drive them away, so much the better. The mosquito is vegetarian by nature and by instinct. There are millions upon millions of them which have never tasted blood. Bring them into contact with human beings and give them that vitiated taste and you know how it turns out. It is exactly the same with a variety of other small pests. They are good in their proper place, but that is not in close contact with human beings. Not only do we ourselves suffer if we permit them to overrun us, but we also subject other human beings to infection from which they would have been free if it had not been for us.

Though, with our imperfect knowledge, it gives us no special justification to kill or exterminate any creature offensive to us, it is a fact that some forms are now intended to die away, either because they have run their course, or because they are experiments that have been improved upon and are therefore no longer needed. It is not irreverent to think of the great evolutionary Powers as experimenting to some extent. The Lord Maitreya, when He succeeded the Lord Buddha as World-Teacher, tried some new methods in religion, which might conceivably have failed. Madame Blavatsky used sometimes to speak guardedly of certain plants and animals as failures, whose life-form was being permitted to flow on and die out gradually, being used sometimes for the indwelling of creatures lower than those originally intended to occupy them and sometimes even for those undergoing involution. She spoke of certain loathsome forms of insect and reptile life as "by-products", and considered that the killing of these was by no means the same thing as the destruction of evolving forms of life.

The theory of the non-destruction of life is carried to extremes in certain places, as for example, where people decline to kill vermin, and allow themselves to be eaten by them. That does not commend itself to any civilized person. Again, a person who has a library of useful books will sometimes find them attacked by little silver-fish. It would be preferable to drive them away, but it is better, certainly, to destroy those insects than to allow good books, which might be of use to others besides oneself, to be rendered useless. There are many small forms of life which if we permit them, would render our lives practically impossible. For the yogi, who never destroys life, food is always provided, but the agriculturist who provides it has to protect his crops from grubs and worms. In Australia he has particularly to deal with rabbits, which having been imported into the country, have increased in such millions that if left free to do so they would destroy every vestige of cultivation.

It is not only for the sake of food for man that one must destroy some of the pests, but also as a matter of protection, for if one cultivates plants, or trees or vegetables, one has a certain responsibility to the life that takes up its dwelling in those forms. I think we should use common sense in all these matters all the way through. In any case, to kill any animal in self-defence is surely a different thing from killing highly evolved creatures, such as cows and sheep, to gratify a low form of taste, when it is absolutely unnecessary.

> Think of the treatment which superstition has meted out to the depressed classes in our beloved India, and see in that how this evil quality can breed heartless cruelty even among those who know the duty of brotherhood.

C.W.L.—The depressed classes in India, sometimes called the panchama, or fifth caste, really the outcaste, the pariah—are the descendants of the original inhabitants of India, whom the Aryans found there when they came over the Himālayas. The caste rules ordained by the Manu, which were good eugenic and magnetic rules at the time, forbade the settlers to intermarry or mix or eat with them. Beyond that, however, they have been treated with great cruelty. For instance, the pariah is not allowed to approach the caste well to draw water, because he will contaminate it for the caste people; consequently he has to depend upon such inferior wells as he can make or find, and this often causes serious hardships, especially as in some parts of the country the outcaste villages have been driven to unfavourable plots of land, and often forced to move. Until quite recently a pariah could hardly attain a good position in life, except by the undesirable expedient of becoming a Christian or a Muhammadan, a course which removes some of their most serious social disabilities.

This, and even worse than this, has been the treatment which superstition has meted out to these depressed classes, even among people who make a speciality of brotherhood. In this case they have forgotten what brotherhood means, because of their superstition. One hopes that in time they will come to form a respectable and clean community. Modern conditions, such as the mingling that takes place on trains and tramcars, tend to facilitate this process.

It is the duty of the better classes of the Indian people, and also a kārmic obligation upon them, to uplift these outcastes whom their ancestors conquered. Their very nobility, their innate Aryan quality should urge them to this necessary task. If a child is not clean we do not recoil from him, but we take him to be washed; so must we not shrink from the pariah, but provide him with conditions in which he can acquire health, cleanliness and knowledge. It is not necessarily a question of eating together, but it is assuredly our duty to be kindly and compassionate to our younger brothers.

It is true that birth in a given caste or community always offers a man certain definite opportunities, but it does not follow that he is making the best of them. To be born into the family of a good man of lower caste would offer better opportunities in some ways than to belong to the family of an unworthy Brāhmana. Often men strive for some goal, and when they attain it they fail to make good use of opportunities which it brings; hence a bad Brāhmana may be one who is taking his first incarnation as such, or who has neglected or misused his opportunities in a former birth. It is true only in rare cases that:

> Who toiled a slave may come anew a Prince
> For gentle worthiness and merit won;
> Who ruled a King may wander earth in rags
> For things done and undone.[1]

As a general rule those who are in the great mass of the working classes will only gradually raise themselves into the bourgeoisie, and then higher. Most of a man's karma is made with the class of people among whom he is, and he needs similar conditions for working it out in a future life. The way of evolution is also by gradual advance in culture and refinement, so a sudden transition into a distinctly higher or lower class is somewhat in the nature of a surgical operation, necessitated by very exceptional karma. Still, mankind is one family, and the duty of brotherhood applies to all without exception.

Many crimes have been committed in the name of the God of Love, moved by this nightmare of superstition.

[1] *The Light of Asia*, Book VIII.

C.W.L.—One other point about superstition is that the man who does the most harm because of it is the one who has the best intentions, who is standing loyally to the letter of his law. A really selfish bad man—there are such people, though perhaps not very many—is concerned mostly with gratifying his own desires. He does not want to interfere with others unless they obstruct his way; so, after all, he does not do so much harm in the world. The stupid person with good intentions is really a far more serious danger, because he always wants to interfere with others. Missionaries, for example, are often a case in point. I do not doubt that the missionaries sent out from Europe and America have done much good among Central African savages and people of that type, but in India, where any common labourer in the street usually knows more than the missionary about the philosophy of religion, about all the greater and higher ideas, the missionary is ridiculously out of place. His intentions are good enough, but he does a great deal of harm. Many wars have been caused by the irrational methods of missionaries; their State has to step in and save them when they are in danger of what they call martyrdom. It has come to be a regular thing: first the missionaries, then those selling brandy and gin, and after them a conquering army. Poor old ladies in England and America even go without the necessities of life in order to help these missions, and think they are doing it for Christ's sake! They have absolutely no conception that thousands of years before Christ India had a profound religion and philosophy, and that their money could be better employed in converting the heathen in England itself.

> **Be very careful, therefore, that no slightest trace of it remains in you.**

C.W.L.—The emphasis which is laid upon it clearly shows that there is a danger that we may be superstitious without knowing it, so it is well that we should carefully watch. There are always at least two sides to any question. No one sees the whole thing—not even the Theosophist. When we become consciously one with the Logos on His own high plane, then we shall see all round everything, and be able to say: "My view is right", but when that occurs our view will probably include all the others, because there is generally some germ of truth in all.

> **These three great crimes you must avoid, for they are fatal to all progress, because they sin against love.**

C.W.L.—That love should govern our lives and vivify all our other powers is the special teaching of the line to which the Master Kūthūmi belongs. It is difficult for many to understand exactly how the Masters, who contain within Themselves all the highest and the noblest qualities which we can imagine, can yet somehow have one quality more than another. The Master Morya, who represents to us the First Ray, has for His greatest characteristic will and power, yet it would be a mistake to suppose that He has any less of love or of wisdom than any of the other Masters. So also should we be quite wrong in supposing the Master Kūthūmi to have any less power than Masters of the First Ray. These are differences beyond mere human knowledge.

In the same way there are distinctions of level among the Great Ones; the Bodhisattva stands far higher than our Masters. To us They all appear so great that we cannot venture to make any distinction between them. They are all suns of blinding light, and to us there seems no difference between a great Angel and a Devarāja; yet one is a whole kingdom, a whole evolution above the other. It must be that the Solar Logos has greater power than all these that are parts of Him; although it seems as though no being could have more than They. The knowledge and the power of the Master are so much greater than ours that for us the whole thing is one blinding glory; but the distinction exists.

CHAPTER 6

SERVICE

But not only must you thus refrain from evil; you must be active in doing good. You must be so filled with the intense desire of service that you are ever on the watch to render it to all around you—not to man alone, but even to animals and plants. You must render it in small things every day, that the habit may be formed, so that you may not miss the rare opportunity when the great thing offers itself to be done.

C.W.L.—We may very often miss a chance of helping some one if we have not formed the habit of watchfulness; but if we have that habit we are not likely to pass many opportunities, because it will assert itself, even in the most unusual surroundings or in the greatest emergencies. That is the whole reason of the long, rather painful drill through which soldiers are put; not only that they may know exactly what to do when certain orders are given, but that they may have certain habits instinctively part of them. In battle in the old days, if not to-day, the soldier found himself in absolutely novel surroundings, that might well try his courage, however brave he might be, conditions such that a man might well be excused if he lost his head. But even in such an emergency habit would assert itself, and the man would obey orders and do what was required.

This remark about being active in doing good is not directed in any way against those whose activity is on other planes. Such a remark as that might easily be wrongly used against the contemplative orders of monks and nuns, or the Brāhmana caste in India. The theory in the old days was that the Brāhmana was the spiritual leader of the nation, and he was supposed to devote all his time to the performance of ceremonies and rites, and to study and teaching and giving advice, which would benefit all the community. The other people, whose lives were taken up in ordinary work, and in making money, supported him because he was doing this spiritual work for them. A similar idea in Catholic countries is behind those orders of monks and nuns whose time is taken up in praying for the dead. In the days when those arrangements were made it was recognized that the dead and the living were one community, and that this was a far higher service to the community than the growing of corn; therefore those people received their living in charity and were in nowise ashamed of it, and those who gave to them felt themselves highly honoured. The whole conception was entirely different from the modern one; there was no shame whatever attached to begging for a living; in fact, those who did it were the most spiritual of the people, bound by the vows of poverty, chastity and obedience. To condemn the people who lived in that way is to make exactly the same mistake as was made in the French Revolution, when they said that a philosopher or a writer was a man living an idle and useless life, and that he ought to be breaking stones upon the road.

> For if you yearn to be one with God, it is not for your own sake; it is that you may be a channel through which His love may flow to reach your fellow-men. He who is on the Path exists not for himself, but for others; he has forgotten himself, in order that he may serve them.

C.W.L.—The whole idea of this book is to get people into a certain attitude. What is aimed at is not nearly so much to know as to be; that is, to live the Theosophical life, to be filled with love for all and with an intense desire to help forward evolution, so that we forget ourselves in the service of others. If you ever saw a surgeon perform a big operation, you know how a man in the most intense activity and with the keenest use of brain and hand, can yet be absolutely absorbed in the work he is doing, with his whole life, as it were, in the ends of his fingers. In war, too, a man sometimes forgets himself utterly in the effort to save a wounded comrade or to perform some necessary but dangerous deed.

The Logos is omnipotent in His system; He pours out force at all levels in that system. We cannot but suppose that He could flood the whole system with that force at any level and to any extent that He chose. As a matter of fact He does not do that; the force poured out at each level seems to be a definite amount, and of a definite kind only, and so it remains that we, who are sparks of His fire can do certain things which the Great Flame of which we are a part does not do, except through us, who are parts of Him. We cannot say that He could not do it, but that He does not, apparently. It is within our power, with our intense devotion, setting our wills to work along with His will, to draw down more force from higher planes, to transmute it and send it out. That is work which would not be done, as far as we can see, unless we did it. It would seem that He counts on our co-operation. Yet that is also His, because there is no force that is not His.

I have several times used the simile of a channel or pipe to help in describing the fact that the force of the Master is distributed on lower planes by a pupil. One may use also the simile of the transformer of electricity; you have great quantities of electricity sent at high pressure, perhaps hundreds of miles from the generating station, to the transforming station in a city; there are there transformers which receive it at that high pressure, and convert it into huge volumes of current at lower pressure, suitable for lighting and other purposes. So a pupil in Sydney, for example, may receive the Master's force coming on higher planes from the Himālayas, and transform it into force of the lower planes, so that it may be distributed around him or directed to those for whom it is intended.

Every Initiate is thus a transformer of spiritual force; through him it can flow at a certain level, according to his stage or degree. The divine force is all round us, just as the sun is shining all the time. When the sunshine does not reach the earth it is the earth's doing, except during a solar eclipse, because it raises clouds which come between it and the sun; so also do men raise clouds of selfishness and ignorance between themselves and the Logos, who is raying out a great variety of His forces on every plane. The Initiate takes a definite step which enables him to be a better channel for these forces. It is not that the forces are themselves in the least affected—they are there all the time, but they pass us by when we are not ready to receive them.

Let us take the analogy of prāna on the physical plane. Every body draws in prāna, but sometimes when a man falls ill he is unable to specialize it for himself, and soon begins to feel a great lack of vitality. Although he is then unable to specialize prāna for himself, he can still use that which has been prepared by another; another man, abounding in vitality, may pour it upon him and give him the strength that he requires to enable him to recover his normal condition. Similarly, the Initiate takes up many of the higher forces and transforms them into a condition in which they become readily assimilable by others. As more and more of our mankind reach the stage at which they can do this work the evolution of men in general will increase in rapidity. Though it is true that there is a limit to the amount of sunlight that plants can bear, it is also true that it is impossible to pour upon any man too much of the spiritual light.

Do not, however, think of these channels as merely passive. They are living channels. The pupil is not sitting still and simply acting as a pipe. There are forces that do come through like that, and the pupil of the Master is often conscious of the nature of the force pouring through him and knows to whom it is going. But there is also a great amount of it which he can at any time employ as he will, which he can turn this way or that, as he sees it to be needed. His own adaptability and tact are thus called into play, and his life is very full indeed of positive activity of this kind. His is not, therefore, a life of blind obedience—on the contrary, he is busy when others are idly thinking about themselves.

Ordinary men cannot commonly be used in this way, because they are not sufficiently developed on the higher planes, and because even when the ego is somewhat advanced the thread of connection with the personality is very narrow. The Master can use the pupil because the channel is open; so also can the One Initiator use the Initiates for the force of the Hierarchy. In these cases the man is the higher self, and even when he is engaged in the duties of the physical plane there is the feeling always in the background of the mind: "I am I; a spark of the Divine; I can do nothing unworthy of That; *noblesse oblige*."

Because of the importance of the work, the relation between Master and pupil is never based on sentiment, though it is full of the deepest affection that the world can know. The Master does not accept a man as a pupil because some other member of his family is a pupil or because He has known him in previous lives. Both Master and pupil think only of what was called in Egypt "the hidden work", the building up again of the riven body of Osiris, the reuniting of the scattered fragments. They know of "the hidden light" in every man, "the jewel in the lotus", through which he can always be helped when the appeal is rightly made. This was the work of the Initiates in ancient Egypt, as it is of those of to-day. They use the power that made the worlds, the love of God, which is not personal. No one is bound to come forward into occultism, but if he does so he must adopt the motto and attitude of the Brotherhood, which is to live not for himself, but for others, not for personal advancement or satisfaction, but for the work.

> **He is as a pen in the hand of God, through which His thought may flow, and find for itself an expression down here, which without a pen it could not have.**

C.W.L.—It would seem that He must have calculated that at a certain stage of evolution He would have many such pens through which He could write, that God Himself, as a poet puts it, "needs you and me." Our help is part of the plan. That is a grand idea and very logical; we see at once that if we have been able to reach a level of knowledge, of love, of power which is a little higher than the standard about us, we have done it in order that we may be of use in distributing it to others.

> Yet at the same time he is also a living plume of fire, raying out upon the world the Divine Love which fills his heart.

C.W.L.—There is a story of two Alexandrian monks who wanted to keep themselves perfectly pure; one did it by making round himself a shell of protective thought, but the other was so full of the love of God that it rayed out from him all the time and kept him pure. There are always the two ways of the occultist, who progresses by work in the world, and the mystic, who retires into himself. In many cases the aim of the mystic is simply to become utterly one with God; yet it is not right to call him selfish, because even in the act of so becoming he must and does shed a tremendous influence on all around him. Our aim, that of the occultist, should be to raise ourselves step by step through all the different stages until at certain high levels of Initiation we can merge our consciousness in the Third Aspect of the Deity, then with the Second Aspect, and finally with the First. The mystic throws himself into the Divine Life here as he stands, but it is a lower manifestation of the Divine Life; then he has to work upwards in order to feel himself one at higher levels also.

> The wisdom which enables you to help, the will which directs the wisdom, the love which inspires

the will—these are your qualifications. Will, Wisdom and Love are the Three Aspects of the Logos ; and you, who wish to enrol yourselves to serve Him, must shew forth these aspects in the world.

C.W.L.—That is a beautiful ending, my brothers. As Alcyone achieved, may you attain.

INDEX

INDEX

Printed by C. Subbarayudu, at the Vasanta Press,
The Theosophical Society, Adyar, Madras

TALKS ON THE PATH OF OCCULTISM

TALKS ON THE PATH OF OCCULTISM

The Voice of the Silence

BY

ANNIE BESANT

GYAN

ISBN: 978-81-212-1912-9 Set (HB)
ISBN: 978-81-212-1938-9 Vol. 2 (HB)
First Published, 1930
Published, 2018
Published by

Gyan Publishing House
5, Ansari Road
Daryaganj, New Delhi-110002
Phone: 011-47034999, 9811692060
www.gyanbooks.com
E-mail: books@gyanbooks.com

Printed at: G. Print Process, Delhi.

FOREWORD

THIS book is merely a record of talks by Mr. C. W. Leadbeater—now Bishop Leadbeater—and myself on three famous books—books small in size but great in contents. We both hope that they will prove useful to aspirants, and even to those above that stage, since the talkers were older than the listeners, and had more experience in the life of discipleship.

The talks were not given at one place only; we chatted to our friends at different times and places, chiefly at Adyar, London and Sydney. A vast quantity of notes were taken by the listeners. All that were available of these were collected and arranged. They were then condensed, and repetitions were eliminated.

Unhappily there were found to be very few notes on *The Voice of the Silence*, Fragment I, so we have utilized notes made at a class held by our good colleague, Mr. Ernest Wood, in Sydney, and incorporated these into Bishop Leadbeater's talks in that section. No notes of my own talks on this book were available; though I have spoken much upon it, those talks are not recoverable.

None of these talks have been published before, except some of Bishop Leadbeater's addresses to selected students on *At the Feet of the Master.* A book entitled *Talks on "At the Feet of the Master"* was published a few years ago, containing imperfect reports of some of these talks of his. That book will not be reprinted; the essential material in it finds its place here, carefully condensed and edited.

May this book help some of our younger brothers to understand more of these priceless teachings. The more they are studied *and lived*, the more will be found in them.

ANNIE BESANT

CONTENTS

SECTION II

THE VOICE OF THE SILENCE

PART VI: FRAGMENT I: THE VOICE OF THE SILENCE

PART VII: FRAGMENT II. THE TWO PATHS

PART VI

FRAGMENT I

THE VOICE OF THE SILENCE

CHAPTER XXX

THE PREFACE

C.W.L.—Even from the superficial and wholly physical point of view, *The Voice of the Silence* is one of the most remarkable books in our Theosophical literature, whether we consider its contents, its style, or the manner of its production; and when we look a little deeper and call to our aid the power of clairvoyant investigation, our admiration is by no means diminished. Not that we should make the mistake of regarding it as a sacred scripture, every word of which must be accepted without question. It is by no means that, for, as we shall presently see, various minor errors and misunderstandings have crept into it; but anyone who on that account regards it as unreliable or carelessly put together will be making an even less excusable mistake in the opposite direction.

Madame Blavatsky was always very ready to admit, and even to emphasize, the fact that inaccuracies were to be found in all her works; and in the early days, when we came across some especially improbable statement of hers we not unnaturally laid it reverently aside as perhaps one of those inaccuracies. It was surprising in what a number of such cases further study showed us that Madame Blavatsky was after all correct, so that presently, taught by experience, we grew much more wary in this matter, and learnt to trust her extraordinarily wide and minute knowledge upon all sorts of out-of-the-way subjects Still there is no reason to suspect a hidden meaning in an obvious misprint, as some too credulous students have done; and we need not hesitate to admit that our great Founder's profound knowledge in occult matters did not prevent her from sometimes misspelling a Tibetan word, or even misusing an English one.

She gives us in her preface some information as to the origin of the book—information which at first seemed to involve some serious difficulties, but in the light of recent investigations becomes much more comprehensible. Much of what she wrote has been commonly understood in a wider sense than she intended it, and in that way it has been made to appear that she put forward extravagant claims; but when the facts of the case are stated it will be seen that there is no foundation for such a charge.

She says: "The following pages are derived from *The Book of the Golden Precepts*, one of the works put into the hands of mystic students in the East. The knowledge of them is obligatory in that school the teachings of which are accepted by many Theosophists. Therefore, as I know many of these Precepts by heart, the work of translating has been relatively an easy task for me." And, further on: "The work from which I here translate forms part of the same series as that from which the stanzas of *The Book of Dzyan* were taken, on which *The Secret Doctrine* is based." She also says: "*The Book of the Golden Precepts* . . . contains about ninety distinct little treatises."

In early days we read into this more than she meant, and we supposed that this work was put into the hands of *all* mystic students in the East, and that "the school in which the knowledge of them is obligatory" meant the school of the Great White Brotherhood itself. Hence when we met with advanced occultists who had never heard of *The Book of the Golden Precepts* we were much surprised and a little inclined to look askance at them and doubt gravely whether they could have come altogether along the right lines, but since then we have learnt many things, and among them somewhat more of perspective than we had at first.

In due course, too, we acquired further information about the Stanzas of Dzyan, and the more we learnt about them and their unique position the clearer it became to us that neither *The Voice of the Silence* nor any other book could possibly have in any real sense the same origin as they.

1. The original of *The Book of Dzyan* is in the hands of the august Head of the Occult Hierarchy, and has been seen by none. None knows how old it is, but it is rumoured that the earlier part of it (consisting of the first six stanzas), has an origin altogether anterior to this world, and even that it is not a history, but a series of directions—rather a formula for creation than an account of it. A copy of it is kept in the museum of the Brotherhood, and it is that copy (itself probably the oldest book produced on this planet) which Madame Blavatsky and several of her pupils have seen—which she describes so graphically in *The Secret Doctrine*. The book has, however, several peculiarities which she does not there mention. It appears to be very highly magnetized, for as soon as a man takes a page into his hand he sees passing before his eyes a vision of the events which it is intended to portray, while at the same time he seems to hear a sort of rhythmic description of them in his own language, so far as that language will convey the ideas involved. Its pages contain no words whatever—nothing but symbols.

When we came to know this fully, it was somewhat startling to find another book claiming the same origin as the sacred Stanzas, and our first impulse was to suppose that some strange mistake must have arisen. Indeed, it was this extraordinary discrepancy that first led to our investigating the question of the real authorship of *The Book of the Golden Precepts*; and when this was done, the explanation proved to be exceedingly simple.

We read in the various biographies of Madame Blavatsky that she once spent a period of some three years in Tibet, and also that on another occasion she made an unsuccessful attempt to penetrate into that forbidden land. On one or other of these visits she seems to have stayed for some considerable time at a certain monastery in the Himālayas, the head of which at that time was a pupil of the Master Morya. The place seems to me to be in Nepal rather than in Tibet, but it is difficult to be sure of this. There she studied with great assiduity, and also gained considerable psychic development; and it is at this period of her history that she learnt by heart the various treatises of which she makes mention in the Preface. The learning of them is obligatory upon the students of that particular monastery, and the book from which they are taken is regarded there as of exceeding value and holiness.

This monastery is of great age. It was founded in the early centuries of the Christian era by the great preacher and reformer of Buddhism who is commonly known as Āryasanga. I think a claim is made that the building had already existed for two or three centuries before his time; but, however that may be, its history as far as we are concerned begins with his temporary occupancy of it. He was a man of great power and learning, already far advanced along the Path of Holiness; he had in a previous birth as Dharmajyoti been one of the immediate followers of the Lord Buddha, and after that, under the name of Kleinias, one of the leading disciples of our Master Kūthūmi in His birth as Pythagoras. After the death of Pythagoras, Kleinias founded a school for the study of his philosophy at Athens—an opportunity of which several of our present Theosophical members took advantage. Centuries later he took birth at Peshawar, which was then called Purushapura, under the name of Vasubandhu Kanushika. When he was admitted to the order of Monks he took the name of Asanga—"the man without hindrance"—and later in his life his admiring followers lengthened this to Āryasanga, by which he is chiefly known as author and preacher. He is said to have lived to a very great age—nearly a hundred and fifty years, if tradition speaks truly—and to have died at Rājagriha.

He was a voluminous writer: the principal work of his of which we hear is the *Yogāchārya Bhūmishāstra*. He was the founder of the Yogāchārya school of Buddhism, which seems to have begun with an attempt to fuse with Buddhism the great Yoga system of philosophy, or perhaps rather to adopt from the latter what could be used and interpreted Buddhistically. He travelled much and was a mighty force in the reform of Buddhism; in fact, his fame reached so high a level that his name is joined with those of Nāgārjuna and Āryadeva, and these men have been called the three suns of Buddhism, because of their activity in pouring forth its light and glory upon the world. The date of Āryasanga is given vaguely as a thousand years after the Lord Buddha; European scholars seem uncertain as to when he lived, but none assign him a later date than the seventh century after Christ. To us in the Theosophical Society he is known in this life as a specially kind, patient and helpful teacher, the Master Djwāl Kūl—one who has for us an unique position, in that when some of us had the honour of knowing Him about forty years ago, He had not yet taken the step which is the goal of human evolution—the Aseka initiation. So that among our Masters He is the only one whom we knew in this present incarnation before He became an Adept, when He was still the head pupil of the Master Kūthūmi. The fact that as Āryasanga He carried Buddhism into Tibet may be the reason why in this life He has chosen to take a Tibetan body; there may have been kārmic associations or links of which He wished to dispose before taking the final initiation as Adept.

In the course of one of His great missionary journeys in His life as Āryasanga He came to this Himālayan monastery and took up his abode there. He stayed there for nearly a year, teaching the monks, organizing the religion generally over a very large section of the country, and making this monastery a kind of headquarters for the reformed faith, and He left upon the place an impression and a tradition which last until the present time. Among other relics of Him is preserved a book, which is regarded with the greatest reverence; and this is the scripture to which Madame Blavatsky refers as *The Book of the Golden Precepts*. Āryasanga seems to have commenced it as a sort of commonplace book, or a book of extracts, in which he wrote down anything that he thought would be useful to his pupils, and he began with the *Stanzas of Dzyan*—not in symbol, as in the original, but in written words. Many other extracts he made—some from the works of Nāgārjuna, as Madame Blavatsky mentions. After his departure his pupils added to the book a number of reports (or perhaps rather abstracts) of his lectures or sermons to them, and these are the "little treatises" to which Madame Blavatsky refers.

It was Alcyone, in his last life, who prepared and added to *The Book of the Golden Precepts* the reports of the discourses of Āryasanga, three of which form our present subject of study. So we owe this priceless little volume to his care in reporting, just as in this life we owe to him our possession of the exquisite companion volume *At the Feet of the Master*. That life of Alcyone began in A.D. 624, and was spent in Northern India In it Alcyone entered the order of Buddhist monks at an early age and became deeply attached to Āryasanga, who took him with him to the monastery in Nepal, and left him there to help and direct the studies of the community which he had re-organized—a service that Alcyone performed with distinguished success for about two years.[1]

It is in this sense, and in this sense only, that *The Voice of the Silence* claims the same origin as the Stanzas of Dzyan—that the two are copied in the same book. We must not forget also that though we have undoubtedly much of Āryasanga's teaching in these treatises, it cannot but be coloured considerably by the prepossessions of those who reported it; and it is probable that at least in some passages they misunderstood him and failed to convey his real meaning. As we examine the work in detail we shall find verses here and there which express sentiments that Āryasanga could hardly have held, and show ignorance which for him would have been impossible.

It will be noticed that Madame Blavatsky speaks of translating the precepts—a remark which raises some interesting questions, since we know that she was unacquainted with any Oriental tongue except Arabic. The book is written in a script with which I am unfamiliar, nor do I know what language is used. The latter may be Sanskrit, Pāli, or some Prakrit dialect, or possibly Nepalese or Tibetan; but the script is not any of those now commonly employed to write those languages. It is at any rate reasonably certain that on the physical plane neither script nor language can have been known to Madame Blavatsky.

For one who can function freely in the mental body there are methods of getting at the meaning of a book, quite apart from the ordinary process of reading it. The simplest is to read from the mind of one who has studied it; but this is open to the objection that one gets not the real meaning of the work, but that student's conception of the meaning, which may be by no means the same thing. A second plan is to examine the aura of the book—a phrase which needs a little explanation for those not practically acquainted with the hidden side of things. An ancient manuscript stands in this respect in a somewhat different position from a modern book. If it is not the original work of the author himself, it has at any rate been copied word by word by some person of a certain education and understanding, who knew the subject of the book, and had his own opinions

[1] See *The Lives of Alcyone*.

about it. It must be remembered that copying, done usually with a stylus, is almost as slow and emphatic as engraving; so that the writer inevitably impresses his thought strongly on his handiwork.

Any manuscript, therefore, even a new one, has always some sort of thought-aura about it which conveys its general meaning, or rather, one man's idea of its meaning and his estimate of its value. Every time the book is read by any one an addition is made to that thought-aura, and if it be carefully studied the addition is naturally large and valuable. A book which has passed through many hands has an aura which is usually better balanced, rounded off and completed by the divergent views brought to it by its many readers; consequently the psychometrization of such a book generally yields a fairly full comprehension of its contents, though with a considerable fringe of opinions *not* expressed in the book, but held by its various readers.

With a printed book the case is much the same, except that there is no original copyist, so that at the beginning of its career it usually carries nothing but disjointed fragments of the thoughts of the binder and the bookseller. Also few readers at the present day seem to study so thoughtfully and thoroughly as did the men of old, and for that reason the thought-forms connected with a modern book are rarely so precise and clear-cut as those which surround the manuscripts of the past.

A third plan, requiring somewhat higher powers, is to go behind the book or manuscript altogether and get at the mind of the author. If the book is in some foreign language, its subject entirely unknown, and there is no aura round it to give any helpful suggestion, the only way is to follow back its history, to see from what it was copied (or set up in type, as the case may be) and so to trace out the line of its descent until one reaches its author. If the subject of the work is known, a less tedious method is to psychometrize that subject, get into the general current of thought about it, and so find the particular writer required, and see what he thinks. There is a sense in which all the ideas connected with a given subject may be said to be local—to be concentrated round a certain point in space, so that by mentally visiting that point one can come into touch with all the converging streams of thought about that subject, though of course these are linked by millions of lines with all sorts of other subjects.

Supposing her clairvoyant powers to have been at that time sufficient, Madame Blavatsky may have adopted any of these methods of getting at the meaning of the treatises from *The Book of the Golden Precepts*, though it would be a little misleading to describe any of them as translations without qualifying the statement. The only other possibilities are somewhat remote. There is at present no one in that Himālayan monastery who speaks any European language, but since it is probably at least forty years since Madame Blavatsky was there, there must have been many changes. It is recorded that Indian students have occasionally, though very rarely, come to drink from that fount of archaic learning, and if we may assume that the visit of some such student coincided with hers, it might also be that he happened to know both English and the language of the manuscript, or at least the language of other inmates of the monastery who could read the manuscript for themselves, and so could translate for her.

Strangely enough, there is also just a possibility that she may have been taught in her own native tongue. In European Russia, on the banks of the Volga, there is a fairly large settlement of Buddhist tribes, probably Tartar in their origin; and it appears that these people, though so far removed on the physical plane from Tibet, still regard it as their holy land and occasionally undertake pilgrimages to it. Such pilgrims sometimes remain for years as pupils in Tibetan or Nepalese monasteries, and as one of them might very well know Russian as well as his own Mongolian dialect, it is obvious that we have here another possible method by which Madame Blavatsky may have communicated with her hosts.

In any case it is obvious that we must not expect an exact verbal reproduction of what Āryasanga originally said to his disciples Even in the archaic book itself we have not his words, but his pupils' recollection of them, and of that recollection we have now before us either a translation of a translation, or the recording of a general mental impression of the meaning. It would of course be quite easy for one of our

Masters or for the author himself to make a direct and accurate translation into English; but as Madame Blavatsky distinctly claims the work of translation as her own, this evidently was not the plan adopted.

At the same time, the account which we have from an eye-witness of the speed with which it was written down does certainly seem to suggest the idea that some assistance was given to her, even though it may have been unconsciously to herself. Dr. Besant writes on this subject:

> She wrote it at Fontainebleau, and the greater part was done when I was with her, and I sat in the room while she was writing it. I know that she did not write it referring to any books, but she wrote it down steadily, hour after hour, exactly as though she were writing either from memory or from reading it where no book was. She produced in the evening that manuscript that I saw her write as I sat with her, and asked me and others to correct it for English, for she said that she had written it so quickly that it was sure to be bad. We did not alter in that more than a few words, and it remains as a specimen of marvellously beautiful literary work.

Another possibility is that she may have done the translation into English beforehand while at the monastery, and that at Fontainebleau she may really have been reading it at a distance, just as our President says she appeared to be. I have often seen her do that very thing on other occasions.

The six schools of Hindu philosophy to which she refers on the first page of the preface are the Nyāya, Vaisheshika, Sānkhya, Yoga, Mimānsā and Vedānta. She states that every Indian teacher has his own system of training, which he usually keeps very secret. It is natural that he should keep it secret, for he does not desire the responsibility of the results that would follow if it were tried (as, if known, it certainly would be), by all sorts of unsuitable, ill-regulated people. No real teacher in India will take charge of a pupil unless he can have him under his eye, so that when he prescribes for him a certain exercise he can watch its effect and check the man instantly if he sees that anything is going wrong That has been the immemorial custom in these occult matters, and unquestionably it is the only way in which real progress can be made with rapidity and safety. The first and most difficult task of the pupil is to reduce to order the chaos in himself—to eliminate the host of minor interests, and control the wandering thoughts, and this must be achieved by a steady pressure of the will exercised upon all his vehicles through a long period of years.

Our author tells us that if the systems of instruction differ on this side of the Himālayas in the esoteric schools, on the other side they are all the same. We must emphasize here the word esoteric, for we know that in the exoteric religion the corruptions and evil magical practices are worse on the northern side of the mountains than on the southern. We may perhaps even understand the expression "beyond the Himālayas" rather in a symbolical than in a strictly geographical sense, and many suppose that it is in the schools owing allegiance to our Masters that the teaching does not differ. This is very true in a certain sense—the most important of all senses; but capable of misleading the reader if not carefully explained. The sense in which all are the same is that all recognize the virtuous life as the only path leading to occult development, and the conquest of desire as the only way of getting rid of it. There are schools of occult knowledge which hold that the virtuous life imposes unnecessary limitations. They teach certain forms of psychic development, but they care nothing for the use which their pupils may afterwards make of the information given to them. There are others who hold that desire of all sorts should be indulged to the utmost, in order that through satiety indifference may be attained. But no school holding either of these doctrines is under the direction of the Great White Brotherhood; in every establishment even remotely connected with it, purity of life and nobleness of aim are indispensable prerequisites.

The next paragraph in the Preface happens to contain two of the trifling inaccuracies to which I have referred. Our author mentions "the great mystic work called *Paramārtha*, supposed to have been delivered to Nāgārjuna by the Nāgas". Nāgārjuna's great book was not called Paramārtha, but *Prajnā Pāramitā*—the wisdom which brings to the further shore; but it is very true that the subject treated in that book is the paramārtha satya, that consciousness of the sage which vanquishes illusion. Nāgārjuna, as already mentioned, was one of the three great Buddhist teachers of the earlier centuries of the Christian era; he is supposed to have died A.D. 180. He is now known to Theosophists under the name of the Master

Kūthūmi. Exoteric writers sometimes describe Āryasanga as his rival, but, knowing as we do their intimate relation in an earlier birth in Greece, and now again in this present life, we see at once that this cannot have been so. It is quite possible that, after their death, their pupils may have tried to set up the teaching of one against that of the other, as pupils in their undiscriminating zeal so often do; but that they themselves were in perfect accord is shown by the fact that Āryasanga treasured much of Nāgārjuna's work and copied it into his book of extracts for the use of his disciples.

It is not, however, certain that the *Prajnā Pāramitā* was the work of Nāgārjuna, for the legend seems to be to the effect that the book was delivered to him by the Nāgas or serpents. Madame Blavatsky interprets this as a name given to the ancient Initiates, and that may well be so, though there is another very interesting possibility. I have found that the name of Nāgas or serpents was given by the Āryans to one of the great tribes or clans of the Toltec sub-race of the Atlanteans, because they carried before them as a standard when going into battle a golden snake coiled round a staff. This may well have been some totem or tribal symbol, or perhaps merely the crest of a great family. This tribe or family must have taken a prominent part in the original Atlantean colonization of India and the lands which then existed to the south-east of it. We find the Nāgas mentioned as among the original inhabitants of Ceylon found when Vijaya and his companions landed there. So a possible interpretation of this legend might be that Nāgārjuna received this book from an earlier race—in other words, that it is an Atlantean scripture. And if, as has been suspected, certain of the Upanishads came from the same source, there would be little reason to wonder at the identity of teaching to which Madame Blavatsky refers on the same page.

The *Gnyāneshwari* (transliterated *Dhyāneshwari* in the first edition) is not a Sanskrit work, but was written in Mahrāthī in the thirteenth century of our era.

On the next page we find a reference to the Yogāchārya (or more accurately Yogāchāra) school of the Mahāyāna. I have already mentioned the attempt made by Āryasanga, but a few words should perhaps be said as to the vexed question of the Yānas. The Buddhist Church presents itself to us to-day in two great divisions, the Northern and the Southern. The former includes China, Japan, and Tibet; the latter reigns in Ceylon, Siam, Burma and Cambodia. It is usually stated that the Northern Church adopts the Mahāyāna and the Southern Church the Hīnayāna, but whether even this much may be safely said depends upon the shade of meaning which we attach to a much-disputed word. Yāna means *vehicle, and it is agreed that it is to be applied to the* Dhamma or Law as the vessel which conveys us across the sea of life to Nirvāna, but there are at least five theories as to the exact sense in which it is to be taken:

1. That it refers simply to the language in which the Law is written, the Greater Vehicle being by this hypothesis Sanskrit, and the Lesser Vehicle Pāli—a theory which seems to me untenable.

2. Hīna may apparently be taken as signifying mean or easy, as well as small. One interpretation therefore considers the Hīnayāna as the meaner or easier road to liberation—the irreducible minimum of knowledge and conduct required to attain it—while the Mahāyāna is the fuller and more philosophical doctrine which includes much additional knowledge about higher realms of nature. Needless to say, this interpretation comes from a Mahāyāna source.

3. That Buddhism, in its unfailing courtesy towards other religions, accepts them all as ways of liberation, though it regards the method taught by its Founder as offering the shortest and surest route. According to this view, Buddhism is the Mahāyāna, and the Hīnayāna includes Brāhmanism, Zoroastrianism, Jainism and any other religions which were existing at the time when the definition was formulated.

4. That the two doctrines are simply two stages of one doctrine—the Hīnayāna for the Shrāvakas or hearers, and the Mahāyāna for more advanced students.

5. That the word Yāna is to be understood not exactly in its primary sense of "vehicle", but rather in a secondary sense nearly equivalent to the English word "career". According to this interpretation the Mahāyāna puts before a man the "grand career" of becoming a Bodhisattva and devoting himself to the

welfare of the world, while the Hīnayāna shows him only the "smaller career" of so living as to attain Nirvāna for himself.

The Northern and Southern Buddhist Churches are related somewhat as are the Catholics and protestants among the Christians The Northern resembles the Catholic Church. It has added to the teachings of the Lord Buddha. For instance, it adopted much of the aboriginal worship which it found in the country—such ceremonies as those in honour of nature-spirits or deified forces of nature. When Christian missionaries went among the Northern Buddhists, they found ceremonies so similar to their own that they said it was plagiarism due to the work of the devil, and when it was conclusively proved that these ceremonies antedated the Christian era, they said it was "plagiarism by anticipation"!

In the Buddhist, as in all other scriptures, there are contradictory statements; so the Southern Church has founded itself on certain texts; anxious to avoid excrescences, it ignores the others, or calls them interpolations. This has made it narrower in its scope than the Northern Church. To take one example. The Lord Buddha preached constantly against the idea that was evidently prevalent in His time, of the continuation of the personality. That notion is common also among Christians—that our personalities survive to all eternity. But while He taught that nothing of all that which men generally identify themselves lasts for ever, he made most unequivocal statements about the successive lives of men. He gave examples of preceding lives; and when some King asked him what it was like to recover the memory of former lives, He said it was like remembering what one had done yesterday and on preceding days when visiting this village or that. Yet the Southern Church now teaches that only karma persists, not an ego; as though man in one life made a certain amount of karma, and then died, and nothing was left of him, but another person was born, and had to bear the karma which he did not make.

Still, while the Southern Buddhists teach that only the karma survives, they speak at the same time of the attainment of nirvāna; so that if you ask a monk why he wears the yellow robe, he will answer you: "To attain nirvāna," and if you say: "In this life?" he will reply at once: "Oh, no, it will need many lives." So also, after every sermon that a monk preaches he blesses his congregation with the words: "May you attain nirvāna"; and again, if you asked him whether they could attain it in this life, he would say, "No, they will need many lives." So a practical belief in the continued existence of an individual persists, in spite of the formal teaching to the contrary.

Madame Blavatsky devotes a couple of pages to the question of the various forms of writing adopted in the Himālayan monasteries. In Europe and America the Roman alphabet is so widely spread, so almost universally employed, that it is perhaps well, for the sake of our Western readers, to explain that in the East a very different condition of affairs prevails. Each of the numerous Oriental languages—Tamil, Telugu, Sinhalese, Malayalam, Hindi, Gujarati, Canarese, Bengali, Burmese, Napalese, Tibetan, Siamese, and many others—has its own alphabet and method of writing, and a writer in one of them, when quoting a foreign language, expresses that language in his own characters, just as an English writer, if he had to quote a German or Russian sentence would probably write it not in German or Russian type, but in Roman. So that in dealing with an oriental manuscript we have always two points to consider—the language and the script, and these two are by no means always the same.

If I take up a palm-leaf book in Ceylon, it is almost certain to be written in the beautiful Sinhalese script, but it does not at all follow that it is in the Sinhalese *language*. It is quite as likely to be in Pāli, Sanskrit or Elu. The same is true of any of the other scripts. So that when Madame Blavatsky says that the precepts are sometimes written in Tibetan, she may very likely mean only in Tibetan characters, and not necessarily in the Tibetan language. I have not seen any instances of the curious cryptographs which she describes, in which colours and animals are made to represent letters. She speaks in the same paragraph of the thirty simple letters of the Tibetan alphabet. These are universally recognized, but it is not clear what is meant by the reference a little later on to thirty-three simple letters, since if she takes them without the four vowels there are but thirty, while if the vowels are included we should of course have not thirty-three but thirty-four. As to the compound letters, their number may be variously stated; a grammar which is before me gives over a hundred, but probably Madame Blavatsky refers only to those in general use.

I remember an interesting illustration of her statement as to one of the Chinese modes of writing. When I was in Ceylon there came one day to visit us two Buddhist monks from the interior of China—men who could speak no language with which any of us were acquainted. But fortunately we had some young Japanese students staying with us, in pursuance of Colonel Olcott's splendid scheme that each Church, the Northern and the Southern, should send some of its neophytes to learn the ways and the teaching of the other. These young men could not understand a word of what these Chinese monks said, but they were able to exchange ideas with them by means of writing. The written symbols meant the same to them, though they called them by quite different names, just as a Frenchman and an Englishman would each perfectly understand a line of figures, although one would call them "un, deux, trois," and the other "one, two, three". The same is true of notes of music. So I had a very curious and interesting interview with these monks, at which every question which I put was first translated into Sinhalese by one of our members, so that the Japanese student might understand it; then the latter wrote it down with a paint-brush in the form of writing common to Chinese and Japanese; the Chinese monk read it and wrote his reply in the same characters, which the Japanese student then translated into Sinhalese, and our member into English. Under these circumstances conversation was slow and a little uncertain, but still it was an interesting experience.

CHAPTER XXXI

THE HIGHER AND THE LOWER POWERS

These instructions are for those ignorant of the dangers of the lower Iddhi.

C.W.L.—To this opening sentence of the first Fragment there is a note by Madame Blavatsky as follows:

The Pali word Iddhi is the equivalent of the Sanskrit Siddhis, or psychic faculties, the abnormal powers in man. There are two kinds of Siddhis—one group which embraces the lower, coarse, psychic and mental energies, while the other exacts the highest training of spiritual powers. Says Krishna in *Shrimad Bhagavat*:

"He who is engaged in the performance of Yoga, *who has subdued his senses and who has concentrated his* mind in me [Krishna], such Yogis all the Siddhis stand ready to serve."

There is a vast amount of misunderstanding on this subject of psychic powers, and *it will save the student a great deal of* trouble if he will try to get a reasonable conception of it to begin with. First, let him not attach a wrong interpretation to the word "abnormal". These powers are abnormal only in the sense that they are at present uncommon—not in the least in the sense that they are in any way unnatural. They are perfectly natural to every man—indeed they are latent in every man here and now; a few people have developed them from latency into activity, but the majority have as yet made no effort in that direction, and so the powers still remain dormant.

The simplest way to grasp the general idea is to remember that man is a soul, and that he manifests himself on various planes through bodies appropriate to those planes. If he wishes to act, to see or to hear in this physical world, he can do so only through a body made of physical matter. Similarly if he wishes to manifest in the astral world, he must have an astral vehicle, for the physical body is useless there and even invisible, just as the astral body is invisible to our physical sight. In the same way a man who wishes to live upon the mental plane must use his mental body.

To develop psychic faculty means to learn to use the senses of these different bodies. If a man can use only his physical senses, he can see and hear only the things of this physical world; if he learns to use the senses of his astral body, he can see and hear the things of the astral world as well. It is merely a matter of learning to respond to additional vibrations. If you will look at the table of vibrations in any book of physics, you will see that a large number of them evoke no response from us. A certain number appeal to our ears, and we hear them as waves of sound; another set impress themselves upon our eyes, and we call them rays of light. But in between these two sets, and above and below them both, are thousands of other sets of oscillations that make no impression at all upon our physical senses. It is possible for a man so to develop himself as to become sensitive to all these undulations of the ether, and of matter even finer than the ether; we call a man who has done that clairvoyant or clairaudient, because he can see and hear more than the undeveloped man can.

The advantages of such an unfolding of the inner sight are considerable. The man who possesses it finds himself free of another and far wider world; or to speak more accurately, he finds that the world in which he has always lived has extensions and possibilities of all kinds of which he has previously known nothing. His studies may already have informed him of the presence all round him of a vast and complicated non-physical life—of kingdoms of devas and nature-spirits, of the enormous army of his fellow-men who have laid aside their dense bodies in sleep or in death, of forces and influences of many sorts which can be evoked and used by those who understand them; but to see all these things for himself instead of merely believing in them, to be able to contact them at first-hand and experiment with them—all this makes life far fuller and more interesting. He who can thus follow on higher planes the results of his thought and action becomes thereby a more efficient and more useful person. The gain of such an unfoldment of consciousness is obvious; but what of the other side of the story? Madame Blavatsky writes of the dangers of this development, and of two kinds of it, a lower and a higher. Let us take this latter point first.

All information which reaches man from without comes to him by means of vibrations. Vibrations of the air convey sounds to the ears, while those of light bring sights to his eyes. If he sees things and creatures of the astral and mental worlds, it *can only be through the impingement of vibrations of astral* and mental matter upon the bodies respectively capable of responding to them. For man can see the astral world only through the senses of his astral body, and the mental world through those of his mental body.

In each of these worlds, as in this, there are coarser and finer types of matter, and, roughly speaking, the radiations of the finer types are desirable, while those of the coarser kinds are distinctly undesirable. A man has both kinds of matter in his astral body, and he is therefore capable of responding to both the higher and the lower vibrations; and it is for him to choose to which of them he will turn his attention. If he *resolutely shuts out all the lower influences, and accepts only* the higher, he may be greatly helped by them even at astral and mental levels. But Madame Blavatsky will have none of these—not even as temporary aids; she groups them all together as "lower, coarse, psychic and mental energies" and urges us to sweep onward to far higher planes which are beyond the illusions of the personality. She evidently regards the dangers of ordinary psychic development as outweighing its advantages; but as a certain amount of this development is sure to come, in the course of the evolution of the disciple, she warns us of some points as to which extreme care is necessary.

In our own experience during the forty years that have elapsed since Madame Blavatsky wrote this, we have seen something of these dangers in cases of various students. Pride is the first of them, and it bulks very largely. The possession of a faculty which, though it is the heritage of the whole human race, is as yet manifested only very occasionally, often causes the ignorant clairvoyant to feel himself (or still more frequently herself) exalted above his fellows, chosen by the Almighty for some mission of world-wide importance, dowered with a discernment that can never err, selected under angelic guidance to be the founder of a new dispensation, and so on. It should be remembered that there are always plenty of sportive and mischievous entities on the other side of the veil who are ready and even anxious to foster all such delusions, to reflect and embody all such thoughts, and to fill whatever *rôle* of archangel or spirit-guide may happen to be suggested to them. Unfortunately it is so fatally easy to persuade the average man that he really is a very fine fellow at bottom, and quite worthy to be the recipient of a special revelation, even though his friends have through blindness or prejudice somehow failed hitherto to appreciate him.

Another danger, perhaps the greatest of all, because it is the mother of all others, is ignorance. If the clairvoyant knows anything of the history of his subject, if he at all understands the conditions of those other planes into which his vision is penetrating, he cannot of course suppose himself the only person who was ever so highly favoured, nor can he feel with self-complacent certainty that it is impossible for him to mistake. But when he is, as so many are, in the densest ignorance as to history, conditions and everything else, he is liable in the first place to make all kinds of mistakes as to what he sees, and secondly to be the easy prey of all sorts of designing and deceptive entities from the astral plane. He has no criterion by which to judge what he sees, or thinks he sees, no test to apply to his visions or communications, and so he has no sense of relative proportion or the fitness of things, and he magnifies a copy-book maxim into a fragment of divine wisdom, a platitude of the most ordinary type into an angelic message. Then again, for want of common knowledge on scientific subjects he will often utterly misunderstand what his faculties enable him to perceive, and he will in consequence gravely promulgate the grossest absurdities.

The third danger is that of impurity. The man who is pure in thought and life, pure in intention and free from the taint of selfishness, is by that very fact guarded from the influence of undesirable entities from other planes. There is in him nothing upon which they can play; he is no fit medium for them. On the other hand all good influences naturally surround such a man, and hasten to use him as a channel through which they may act, and thus a still further barrier is erected about him against all which is mean and low and evil. The man of impure life or motive, on the contrary, inevitably attracts to himself all that is worst in the invisible world which so closely surrounds us; he responds readily to it, while it will be hardly possible for the forces of good to make any impression upon him.

But a clairvoyant who will bear in mind all these dangers, and strive to avoid them, who will take the trouble to study the history and the rationale of clairvoyance, who will see to it that his heart is humble and his motives are pure—such a man may assuredly learn very much from these powers of which he finds himself in possession, and may make them of the greatest use to him in the work which he has to do.

The Siddhis are enumerated at considerable length in the third chapter of the *Yoga Sûtras* of Patanjali. He speaks of them as being attained in five ways—by birth, by drugs, by mantras, by tapas, and by samâdhi.

We have come to birth in a particular kind of body as the result of our actions in previous incarnations, and if we find ourselves by nature in the possession of psychic powers we may take it for granted that we have worked for them in some way in previous lives. Many clairvoyants of the present day, in whom the faculty has been easily awakened, but perhaps reaches no great heights of spirituality, have been in such positions as those of the vestal virgins of Greece and Rome, the minor yogis of India, or even the medicine-men of various half-savage tribes or the "wise women" of the middle ages; there has always been a very wide range in these matters.

What will happen to such people, how their spiritual lives will be shaped, depends largely upon those with whom it is their karma to come into contact. If that karma is good enough to lead them to Theosophy, they will have the opportunity of learning something about these dawning faculties, and of being trained in its Esoteric School in the preliminary qualities of character and purity of physical and magnetic life that are prescribed by all true occultists, so that a little later on they may develop their psychic powers in safety, and become of great service to mankind.

If on the other hand they come into touch with the spiritualistic school of thought, they are quite likely to find themselves following a line which frequently results in passive mediumship, the very opposite of what we are trying to attain.

There are those who turn to pseudo-occultism for the attainment of magical powers in order to gratify personal ambition. That path is full of the most serious dangers. Sometimes such people sit in a passive condition and invite unknown entities of the astral world to work upon their auras and organisms and to adapt them to their purposes; sometimes they practise various forms of hatha yoga, consisting mainly of peculiar kinds of breathing, which have unfortunately been widely taught in the Western world during the last thirty years or so. As a result of such proceedings mental and bodily disorders of a serious character often arise, while at best the contact which is gained with the inner worlds seldom extends beyond the lower astral levels, from which nothing can come that is uplifting to mankind.

As to the second method—the use of drugs—there is a note by Vyâsa, in his commentary upon the *Yoga Sutras*, to the effect that these are used "in the houses of the asuras" for the purpose of awakening the siddhis The asuras are the opposite of the suras, and the word may roughly be translated as "the ungodly"; the suras are the beings on God's side, those who work for His plan of upward-evolving life.

Patanjali does not recommend this method; he is merely enumerating the ways in which the siddhis can be acquired. A study of the *Sutras* shows very clearly that he favours only the last of his list of five methods—that by means of samâdhi or contemplation.

We can understand to some extent the action of drugs on the body, when they are used as a means of awakening psychic powers, if we remember that in the fourth root race clairvoyance through the sympathetic nervous system was quite common. Then the astral sheath, not yet properly organized into a body or vehicle of consciousness, responded in a general way to the impressions made upon it by the objects of the astral plane. Those impressions were then reflected in the sympathetic centres in the physical body, so that consciousness in that body received astral and physical impressions together, and often scarcely distinguished between them. Indeed, in the earlier days of that race, and in the Lemurian race, the activity of the sympathetic system was far greater than that of the cerebro-spinal system, so that the astral experiences were more prominent than the physical. But since then the cerebro-spinal system has become the dominant mechanism of consciousness in the physical body, and man in consequence has paid more and more attention to the physical-plane experiences, as they have grown stronger and more insistent. Therefore the sympathetic system as a purveyor of impressions has gradually lapsed, its business now being to carry on in an involuntary manner many bodily functions to which the man need not attend, because his life is mental, emotional and spiritual rather than physical.

The objection to the use of drugs, therefore, is not only that they upset the healthy working of the body and bring the sympathetic system once more into a prominence which it ought not to have, but even from the point of view of the psychic powers attained they merely re-awaken that system and bring again into the physical consciousness indiscriminate impressions from the astral world. These come generally from the lower part of the plane, in which are aggregated all the astral matter and all the elemental essence concerned with exciting the lower passions and impulses. Sometimes they come from slightly higher regions of sensuous delight, such as are described in the visions of the Count of Monte Christo in Dumas' famous novel, or in De Quincy's *Confessions of an Opium Eater;* but these are scarcely better than the others.

All that is entirely contrary to the plan of evolution laid down for humanity. We are all intended to unfold clairvoyance and other cognate powers, but not in that way. First there should be a development of the astral and mental bodies, so that they may be definite vehicles of consciousness on their own planes; then may come the awakening of the chakras in the etheric double by means of which the valuable knowledge gained through those higher bodies may be brought down to the physical plane consciousness. But all this should be down only when and as the Master advises; remember, in *At the feet of the Master* the Teacher said: "Have no desire for psychic powers."

The third method mentioned is by the use of mantras. The term mantra is applied to certain words of power which are used in meditation or in ceremonial rites, and are often repeated over and over again. These are to be found in Christian rituals as well as in the East, as has been explained in *The Science of the Sacraments*. In many religions sounds are thus used, and are associated with pictures, symbols, signs and gestures, and sometimes dances.

The term *tapas*, used to describe the fourth method, is often associated with ideas of extreme austerity and even self-torture, such as the method of holding the arm extended until it withers, or lying on a bed of spikes. These practices certainly develop the will, but there are other and better ways of doing that. These hatha yoga schemes have the great demerit of making the physical body useless for that service of humanity which is above all other things important for the Master's work. The will may be just as effectively developed in dealing with the difficulties of life that come to us by nature and through karma; there is no necessity to *make* trouble.

In the *Gitā* Shrī Krishna speaks strongly against this superstition. He says, "The men who perform severe austerities, which are not prescribed by the Scriptures, wedded to vanity and egoism, impelled by the force of their desires and passions, unintelligent, tormenting the aggregated elements forming the body, and Me also, seated in the inner body—know these as *asuric* in their resolves."[1] Such antics cannot be the real tapas. The word means literally "heat", and perhaps the nearest English equivalent to that when it is applied to human conduct is "effort". The real meaning of the teaching with regard to it seems to be: "Do for the body what you know to be good for it, disregarding mere comfort. Do not let laziness, selfishness, or indifference stand in the way of your doing what you can to make your personality healthy and efficient in the work that it ought to be doing in the world."[2] Shrī Krishna says in the *Gitā*: "Reverence to the Gods, the elders, the teachers and the wise, purity, straightforwardness,

[1] *Op. cit.*, xvii, 5-6.

[2] See *Raja Yoga*, by Ernest Wood, p 18.

continence and harmlessness are the *tapas* of the body; speech truthful, pleasant and beneficial, and study of the sacred words are the *tapas* of speech; cheerfulness, balance, silence, self-control, and being true to oneself are the *tapas* of mind."[1] These descriptions, given by one whom most of the Hindus regard as the greatest incarnation of Deity, certainly do not indicate any of the dreadful developments of which we sometimes see such sad examples.

It is the fifth means, that of samâdhi, that the *Book of the Golden Precepts* advocates, and, as in the *Yoga Sûtras* and other standard works of the kind, this is preceded by dhāranā and dhyāna, which are commonly translated as concentration and meditation, while samâdhi is interpreted as contemplation. These one-word translations from the Sanskrit are, however, often rather unsatisfactory; the Sanskrit words, coming down to us through the ages, have acquired a marvellous complexity, have added to themselves many fine shades of meaning which are not to be found in any modern English expression. The only way really to understand them is to study the terms in their context in the ancient books.

The siddhis may be divided into two classes, not only as higher and lower, but also as faculties and powers. The world acts upon us through the senses, through our faculties of sight, hearing and the rest; but we also act upon the world. This duality applies also with regard to super-physical accomplishments. We receive impressions through the newly unfolded powers of our astral and mental vehicles; but we can also act through them. It is usual in Hindu books to speak of eight siddhis: (1) *animā*, the power to put oneself in the position of an atom, to become so small as to be able to deal with that tiny thing; (2) *mahimā*, the power to be as if of monstrous size, so as to deal with huge things at no disadvantage; (3) *laghimā*, the power to become as light as cotton borne on the wind; (4) *garimā*, the power to become as dense and heavy as anything can be; (5) *prāpti*, the power of reaching out, even as far as the moon; (6) *prākāmya*, the will power with which to realize all wishes and desires; (7) *Ishatwa*, the power to control and create; and (8) *vashitwa*, the power of command over all objects. These are called "the great

[1] *Op. cit.*, XVII, 14-16.

powers", but others are mentioned, such as steadiness and effulgence in the body, control of the senses and appetites, beauty and gracefulness, and so on.

We students of these later days approach all these problems from a point of view so totally different from that of the Hindu writers of thousands of years ago, that it is sometimes difficult for us to understand them. We are the product of our age, and the quasi-scientific training through which we all pass makes it a mental necessity for us to try to classify our knowledge. Each man endeavours to build for himself some kind of scheme of things, however crude it may be, and when any new fact is presented to him he tries to find a niche in his scheme for it. If it fits in comfortably he accepts the fact; if he cannot make it fit in, he is quite likely to reject it, even though it may come to him with the weightiest evidence. Though some people seem capable of holding, quite happily, beliefs which are mutually contradictory, there are others who cannot do this, and it is often a painful process for them to reconstruct their thought-edifice to admit a new fact—so painful that they not infrequently avoid it by conveniently forgetting or denying the fact. Our ancient Indian brethren seem to me to have catalogued their observations and left them there—to have made no special attempt to relate them to one another or to classify them by the planes on which they occurred or the kind of faculty which they required.

We have no difficulty in recognizing the first and second powers on this list of siddhis; they are instances of the alteration of the focus of the consciousness; we sometimes call them powers of magnification and reduction. They mean the adaptation of the consciousness to the objects with which it has to deal—a feat which presents no difficulty to the trained occultist, though it is not easy on the physical plane to explain exactly how it is done. The third and fourth mention the possibility of becoming light or heavy at will; this is achieved by the comprehension and use of the repulsive force which is the opposite of gravity. I am not so sure about the fifth; it *may* refer merely to the power of travelling in the astral body, since the limit of astral migration is indicated by the mention of the moon; but I rather suspect that it means the power of producing a definite result at a distance by an effort of will. The sixth and eighth are only developments of will-power, though very remarkable developments; the seventh is the same, with the addition of the special knowledge required for the dematerialization and rematerialization of objects. In this list there seems to be no direct reference to clairvoyance at all, either in space or in time.

It is to be noted that *The Voice of the Silence* does not say that the lower *iddhis*, those belonging to the astral and mental bodies, are to be neglected altogether; it merely points out that there are serious dangers connected with them. We shall have to deal with them a little further on, for he who would climb the ladder must step on every rung.

> He who would hear the voice of Nada, the "Soundless sound," and comprehend it, he has to learn the nature of Dharana.

To this there are two footnotes, as follows:

> The "Soundless Voice," or the "Voice of the Silence." Literally perhaps this would read "Voice in the *Spiritual Sound*", as Nada is the equivalent word in Sanskrit for the Senzar term.

> Dharana is the intense and perfect concentration of the mind upon some one interior object, accompanied by complete abstraction from everything pertaining to the external universe, or the world of the senses.

The word that is here translated concentration comes from the root *dhri*, to hold. The word dhārana, with a short final vowel, means *holding or supporting in general*, but here we have a special feminine substantive, with the long terminal vowel, as a technical term signifying concentration or holding of the mind.

It is described in some places as a kind of pondering or dwelling upon a given thought or object, and it is said in the Hindu books that meditation and contemplation will not be successful unless this is practised first. It is obvious that while the mind is responding to the appeals of the physical, astral and lower mental planes, it is not likely to hear the message that the ego is trying to transmit to the personality from his own higher planes.

Concentration is requisite, that attention may be given to the chosen object, not to the restless activity of the lower vehicles. It is usual to begin the practice of concentration with simple things. On a certain occasion some people came to Madame Blavatsky, and asked her upon what they should meditate; she threw a matchbox down on the table, and said: "Meditate on that!" It startled them somewhat, because they had expected her to tell them to meditate upon Parabrahman or the Absolute. It is very important that this concentration should be done without strain to the body. Dr. Besant has told us that, when Madame Blavatsky first instructed her to try it, she began with great intensity; but her teacher interrupted her, saying: "My dear, you do not meditate with your blood-vessels!"

What is required is to hold the mind quiet, so that one looks at the object of thought with perfect calmness, just as one would look at one's watch to see the time, except that one keeps on looking for the length of time prescribed or decided upon for the period of concentration. People often complain of headaches and other pains as a result of meditation; there should never be any such result; if they will take care to keep the physical body calm and free from tension of any kind, even in the eyes, they will probably find their concentration much easier and more successful, and free from physical trouble and danger. Various books have been written on this subject, and some of them offer exceedingly dangerous suggestions Anyone wishing further information on this should read Professor Wood's book, *Concentration—a Practical Course*, of which Dr. Besant wrote: "There is nothing in it which, when practised, can do the striver after concentration the least physical, mental or moral harm"

In her footnote, H. P. B. associates dhāranā with the higher mental plane, for she says the mind must be fixed upon an interior object and abstracted from the world of the senses; that is, from the physical, astral and lower mental worlds. That is a *prescription for the candidate who is already on the Path,* and is aiming at the samâdhi of the nirvânic or âtmic plane. But the three terms concentration, meditation and contemplation are also used in a general way. To fix one's thought on a verse of scripture—that is concentration. To look at it in every possible light and try to penetrate its meaning, to reach a new and deep thought or receive some intuitional light upon it—that is meditation. To fix one's attention steadily for a time on the light ,received—that is contemplation. Contemplation has been defined as *concentration at the top end of your* line of thought or meditation. It is usual for the Oriental student to begin his practice on some simple external object, and from that to carry his thought inward or upward to higher things.

CHAPTER XXXII

THE SLAYER OF THE REAL

Having become indifferent to objects of perception, the pupil must seek out the Raja of the senses, the Thought-Producer, he who awakes illusion.

The Mind is the great Slayer of the Real.
Let the Disciple slay the slayer.

This refers to what has to be done during the practice of concentration. In the Hindu books on the subject it is explained that prior to the actual concentration the student who sits for the practice must withdraw his attention from the objects of sensation; he must learn to take no notice of any sights or sounds that may come within his range; he must not be attracted by anyone or anything that comes within his view, or affects his sense of touch. He will then be ready to observe what thoughts and feelings rise in the mind itself, and to deal with them.

As I have already explained, in most persons the mental and astral bodies are in a constant state of activity, full of vortices, which must be removed before real progress can be made. It is these that create the mass of illusions which beset the average man, and render it exceedingly difficult for him to get a true view of anything at all. It is an axiom of Shrī Shankarāchārya's teaching that just as the physical eye can see things well when it is steady, but not when it is roaming about, so the mind can understand things clearly when it is still. But if it is full of vortices they are sure to distort the vision and so create illusion.

The mind is called the rājā or king of the senses. Sometimes it is spoken of as one of them, as in the *Gītā*:

> A portion of Mine own Self transformed in the world of life into an immortal Spirit, draweth round itself the senses, of which the mind is the sixth, veiled in matter.[1]

That the mind does act as a kind of sense is obvious, since it corrects the evidence of the five senses and also indicates the presence of objects beyond their reach; for example, when a shadow falls across your threshold, you may infer that somebody is there.

What *is* the mind, that has to be dealt with so severely by the aspirant? Patanjali speaks of it when he defines yoga practice as *chitta-vritti-nirodha*, which means restraint (*nirodha*) of the whirlpools (*vritti*) of the mind (*chitta*). Among the Vedāntins, or in Shrī Shankarāchārya's school, the term *antahkarana* is not used as we generally employ it, but indicates the mind in its fullest sense. It means with them literally the entire internal organ or instrument between the innermost Self and the outer world, and is always described as of four parts: the "I-maker" (ahamkāra); insight, intuition or pure reason (buddhi); thought (manas) and discrimination of objects (chitta). It is these last two that the Western man usually calls his mind, with its powers of abstract and concrete thought; when he thinks of the other processes he imagines them to be something above the mind.

The Theosophist ought to recognize in these four Vedantic divisions his own familiar ātmā, buddhi, manas and the lower mind. Madame Blavatsky called the last kāma-manas, because it is the part of manas that works with desire and is therefore interested in material objects. Kāma is to be taken not only as relating to low desires and passions, but also to any sort of desire or interest in the external world for its own sake. The whole of the triple higher self is from this point of view nothing but the *antahkarana* (or internal agency) between the monad and the lower self. It has become a tetrad, because manas is dual in incarnation.

The three parts of the higher self are considered as three aspects of a great consciousness or mind; they are all modes of

[1] *Op. cit.*, v, 7.

cognition. Ātmā is not the Self, but is this consciousness knowing the Self; buddhi is this consciousness knowing the life in the forms by its own direct perception; manas is the same consciousness looking out upon the world of objects, and kâma-manas is a portion of the last immersed in that world and affected by it. The true self is the Monad, whose life is something greater than consciousness, which is the life of this complete mind, the Higher Self. Therefore Patanjali and Shankara are quite in agreement; it is the chitta, the kâma-manas, the lower mind, which is the slayer of the real, and has to be slain.

Much that is now called the astral body by Theosophists must be included in the Indian idea of kāma-manas or chitta. Madame Blavatsky also speaks of four divisions of the mind. First there is manas-taijasī, the resplendent or illuminated manas, which is really buddhi, or at least that state of man when his manas has become merged in buddhi, having no separate will of its own. Then there is manas proper, the higher manas, the abstract thinking mind. Then there is the antahkarana, a term used by Madame Blavatsky merely to indicate the link or channel or bridge between higher manas and kâma-manas during incarnation. Finally there is kāma-manas, which is on this theory the personality.

Sometimes she calls manas the deva-ego, or the divine as distinguished from the personal self Higher manas is divine because it has positive thought, which is *kriyāshakti*, the power of doing things. Really all our work is done by thought-power; the sculptor's hand does not do the work, but thought-power directing that hand does it. The higher manas is divine because it is a positive thinker, using the quality of its own life, which shines from within it; that is what is meant by the word divine, from *div*, to shine. But the lower mind is only a reflector; like all other material things, it has no light of its own; it is something through which the light comes, or through which the sound comes—merely *persona*, a mask.

The antahkarana is usually considered in the Theosophical works as the link between the higher self or the divine ego, and the lower self or personal ego. The *chitta* in that lower self puts it at the mercy of things, so that our life down here may be compared to the experience of a man struggling to swim in a maelstrom. But this will be followed sooner or later after death by a period in the heaven-world. The man has been whirled about; he has seen many things; he has not dwelt upon them, however, with a calm, steady mind, but with kāma-manas; *therefore he has not understood their significance for the soul.* But in the heaven-world the ego can widen out the antahkarana, because all is now calm; no new experiences are to be gathered. *The old ones can be quietly turned over and dwelt upon,* and their essence taken up, as it were, into the deva ego, as being of interest to him. So, very often, the *ego* really begins his personal life-cycle with the entry into the heaven-world, and pays a minimum of attention to the personality during its period of collecting materials.

In that case the aspect of mind that is antahkarana (in Madame Blavatsky's classification) functions but little before the period of the heaven-life. But if a man is to become expert on the astral and mental planes during the life of the physical body, he must bring the positive powers of the higher self down through that channel, by the practice of dhāranā or concentration, *and so make himself entire master of his personality.* In other words he must clear out the astral and mental whirlpools. A man who is genius on some line may find it easy to apply tremendous concentration to his particular kind of work, but when he relaxes from that, his ordinary life may quite possibly be still full of these whirlpools. That is not what we want; we are aiming at nothing less than the complete destruction of the whirlpools, so as to comb out the lower mind and make it the *calm and obedient servant of the higher self at all times.*

These whirlpools may and do constantly crystallize into permanent prejudices, and make actual congestions of matter closely resembling warts upon the mental body. Then if the man tries to look out through that particular part of that body he cannot *see clearly; everything is distorted, for at that point* the mental matter is no longer living and flowing, but stagnant and rotten. The way to cure it is to acquire more knowledge, to get the matter into motion again, and then one by one the prejudices will be washed away and dissolved.

It is in this way that *the mind is the great slayer of the* real, for through it we do not see any object as it really is. We see only the images which we are able to make of it, and everything is necessarily coloured for us by these thought-forms of our own creation. Notice how two persons with preconceived ideas, seeing the same set of circumstances, and agreeing as to the actual happenings, will yet make two totally different stories from them. Exactly this sort of thing is going on all the time with every ordinary man, and we do not realize how absurdly we distort things. The disciple *must* conquer this; he must "slay the slayer". He must not of course destroy his mind, for he cannot get along without it, but he must dominate it; it is *his*, but it is not *he*, though it tries to make him think so. The best way to overcome its wandering is to use the will; its efforts are just like those of the astral body, which is always trying to persuade you that its desires are yours; you must deal with them both in a precisely similar manner.

Even when the whirlpools that fill the mind with prejudice and error are gone, much illusion still remains. The translation of the Sanskrit word *avidyā* as ignorance is perhaps not very fortunate, though it is universally accepted. So often in Sanskrit there are delicate shades of meaning which it is difficult to convey in English. In this case perhaps what is intended is not so much ignorance as unwisdom. A man may have vast stores of knowledge, and yet be unwise, for knowledge is concerned with objects and their relations in space and time, whereas wisdom is concerned with the soul or consciousness embodied in those things. The wise politician understands the people's minds; the wise mother understands her children's minds. However much one may know about material things, if one has only the matter-sight and not the life-sight, one has in reality only unwisdom or avidyā. "It is at the expense of wisdom that intellect generally lives," said Madame Blavatsky. Then, out of that unwisdom or ignorance spring four other great obstacles to spiritual progress, making five altogether, which are called the *kleshas*.

If avidyā be the first obstacle the second is *asmitā*, the notion that "I am this", or what a Master once called "self-personality". The personality is developed through life into quite a definite thing, with decided physical, astral and mental form, occupation and habits; and there is no objection to that if it be a good specimen. But if the indwelling life can be persuaded to think that he *is* that personality, he will begin to serve its interests, instead of using it merely as a tool for his spiritual purposes.

In consequence of this second error men seek inordinate wealth and power and fame. When a man looks over his country houses and his town houses, his yachts and cars, his farms and factories, he swells with pride, thinking himself great because he is called the owner of these things; or he hears his name on everybody's lips, and feels that thousands of people are thinking of him with praise (or even with condemnation, for notoriety is often pleasing to men who cannot attain fame) and he thinks himself a very great person indeed. That is "self-personality", one of the greatest superstitions in the world, and a great source of trouble for one and all. The spiritual man, on the other hand, counts himself fortunate if he can be the master of his own hand and brain, and he wishes to hold the images of thousands of others in his own mind that he may help them, rather than to rejoice in the thought that his image is multiplied and magnified in *their* minds. Hence self-personality is the greatest obstacle to the use of the personality by the higher self, and so to spiritual progress.

The third and fourth obstacles may be taken together. They are *rāga* and *dwesha*, liking and disliking, or attraction and repulsion. These too spring from this same self-personality. That it should show its likes is inappropriate; it is as though a motor-car should have a voice of its own, and should raise it in great discontent when its master drives over a broken road, or in a purr of delight when he goes over a good road. The road may be a bad one for the car, but from the point of view of the driver it is a good thing that there is a road at all, because he wants to get somewhere, which would be a difficult matter without a road. It is nice to have our armchairs and fires and electric light and steam heat, but he who would make progress has to go over new country, sometimes materially, and always in thought and feeling. People like the things that consort with their settled conveniences and habits; anything that disturbs those is "bad"; anything that fits in with them and enhances them is "good". Such an outlook upon life does not harmonize with spiritual progress; we do not refuse comfort when it comes, but we must learn to be indifferent to it, and to take things as they come; this emphasis upon liking and disliking must go, and the calm judgment of the higher self as to what is good and what is bad must take its place.

The fifth obstacle is *abhinivesha*, the outcome of the last, the state of being fixed, settled in, attached to a form or mode of life, or to the personality. From this arises fear of old age and of death—events which can never exist for the man himself, but must come in due course to the personality. A veritable death in life may arise out of this fifth trouble; people waste their youth in preparation for comfort and safety in age, and then waste their age in seeking for their lost youth, or are afraid to use their bodies, lest they should wear out. They are like a man who buys a beautiful motor-car, and sits in his garage, enjoying his new possession, but unable to bring himself to run it out on the road, lest it should be spoiled. Our business is to do what the higher self wants, and to be utterly willing to die in his service if need be.

All the whirlpools arise from these five obstacles. Concentration and meditation are the means to dispel them completely. When the kāma-manas no longer gravitates downwards, the manas can turn upwards, to become *manas-taijasī*.

Another Sanskrit word connected with this self-personality is *māna*, sometimes translated pride, but perhaps better rendered by conceit. This root appears in the word *nirmānakāya*, which means a being who is beyond this illusion—*nirmāna* Madame Blavatsky said that there were three kinds or modes of incarnation; first, that of the *avatāras*, those who descend from higher spheres, having reached them in a cycle of evolution prior to ours; secondly, those of an ordinary kind, when a person passes through the astral and mental worlds and then takes up a new body; and thirdly, that of *nirmānakāyas*, who incarnate again without interlude, sometimes perhaps after only a few days. In *The Secret Doctrine* she cites the Cardinal de Cusa as an instance of this, he having been born again quickly as Copernicus; and she says that such rapid rebirth is not an uncommon thing. She speaks of such people as adepts, not using the word quite as we employ it now, but meaning that they are adept or expert on the astral and lower mental planes; she says that they sometimes act as spirits at séances, and that they are particularly opposed by the Brothers of the Shadow, presumably because of the progress that they are making for themselves and also for mankind in general.

She explains that there are two kinds of *nirmānakāyas* those who have renounced the heaven-world, as above explained.

and those who at a later and higher stage renounce what she calls *absolute nirvāna, in order to remain to help the progress* of the world. Modern Theosophical literature confines the term to this latter class, but here we are concerned with the lower class. The man who has slain the slayer has largely destroyed the five obstacles, and has become the servant of the higher self, with nothing in him but what is favourable to its purposes. He has his *antahkarana* widened out so that during his bodily life he is in full touch with the higher self, and all the time that self is taking what it needs; the bee can visit the flower when he will, for there is no storm raging; and when the physical body is dead, the subtle part of the personality can be used again in the next incarnation, because it is not full of whirlpools which represent fixed desires and rigid opinions, and selfish habits of feeling and thought.

CHAPTER XXXIII

THE REAL AND THE UNREAL

For when to himself his form appears unreal, as do on waking all the forms he sees in dreams; when he has ceased to hear the many, he may discern the One—the inner sound which kills the outer.

C.W.L.—The simile of dreaming and waking is frequently used in Oriental philosophy. It has its use, but we must take care that it does not lead us into a misapprehension. When we wake from an ordinary dream we realize that our senses have been deceived, that what we thought at the time to be a real experience was in truth nothing of the kind. But this is not exactly what happens when we wake to a perception of spiritual reality. We awaken to a higher and broader life; we perceive for the first time the crushing yet entirely unsuspected limitations under which we have hitherto been living But that does not mean that our life before that time was nothing but a useless deception. The awakening to higher things causes our previous state of mind to appear irrational, but, after all, it was only relatively so. We were acting then according to our lights, upon such information as we had; now we have so much more that all our lines of thought and action are completely changed.

Even the Vedantist does not deny that this physical plane dream of ours has its value for the production of enlightenment. A man may dream that a snake is threatening him, and be much alarmed thereby; at last in his dream the snake strikes him, and with that shock he wakes, and is much relieved to find that the whole experience was an illusion. Yet it was the blow of the illusory snake that awoke him to a more real life. Similarly, in the *Gītā*, Shrī Krishna tells his pupil that wisdom is better than worldly goods, because, he says, "All actions in their entirety culminate in wisdom."[1] That great Teacher did not deprecate a life of activity, but encouraged it to the utmost; yet he said *that one should not be attached to the activities and the things* with which they deal, but should seek only the wisdom that can be obtained from them. *It is in the wisdom that man has his* own true being, as he is a part of the Logos. If he listens to the voice of wisdom he will become increasingly the master of himself and his life; the inner sound will thus put a stop to the outer clamour which directs the feverish activities of ordinary men.

It is very true that a man should cease to give his attention to the many things which surround and play upon him, and should turn it inwards to the one witness of all these things; but he is not entirely free to do this until he has fully performed his dharma in the outer world. Any man at any time, whatever his duties may be, may set his affection upon things above, and not upon things of the earth. But he may not be at liberty to devote his whole life to higher work until he has satisfied the demands of the karma which he has made in past lives, or in the earlier part of his present life. He may certainly *feel* vairāgya, but while any physical duties still remain to him, he must retain sufficient interest in them to do them as perfectly as they can be done.

If his desire for liberation is strong enough, and unless his karma places some insuperable obstacle in his way, he will probably find that the path to freedom will soon open before him. I myself had an experience of that kind; I received a message from my Master offering me certain opportunities which I most thankfully accepted. But if that gracious offer had been made a little earlier, I should have been unable to accept it, because I should not have been free; there lay upon me a clear duty which I could not possibly have neglected.

Vairāgya has two parts; there is the *apara* or lower vairāgya, and the *para* or higher vairāgya.

There are three stages in the abandonment of attachment to external things. First, the man becomes tired of the things

[1] *Op. cit.*, IV, 33.

which used to give him pleasure, yet he is sorry that he is tired of them; he desires still to enjoy them, but he cannot. Then, because of that satiety, he seeks elsewhere for satisfaction. Finally, when he has caught a clear glimpse of the higher things his spiritual desires awaken, and they prove so attractive to him that he thinks of the others no more. Or else, having learnt of the existence of the higher things and decided to follow them, he in the second stage either sets himself to observe the defects of the lower things, so as to create a sort of artificial disgust for them, or he fixes his will in rigid determination to reject their attractiveness and starve out desire for them. Finally, as in the former case, perhaps only after many fluctuations, the man sees the higher; he hears the inner sound which kills the outer. Then he has the higher vairāgya.

In the middle stage of struggle, it often happens that the man conceives a positive repugnance for the things of his erstwhile pleasure; that is usually a sign that he has only recently escaped from bondage to them and he still fears their attractiveness; he feels that he is liable to be tainted by their proximity, so he shudders and avoids them, or he attacks and tries to destroy them with unreasoning vehemence. All these different aspects of the second stage are forms of the lower vairāgya.

> Then only, not till then, shall he forsake the region of Asat, the false, to come unto the realm of Sat, the true.

Let us be careful here not to misunderstand. Many have supposed that this passage implies that the lower planes are mere illusion, but that is by no means what is intended. I have already written on the real and the unreal and have explained that each plane is real to the consciousness which functions upon it.[1] What is true is that until a man is able to hear the inner voice and to look upon life from the standpoint of the higher planes he has no real grasp of the truth which lies behind all this complexity of manifestation that surrounds us.

> Before the Soul can see, the harmony within must be attained, and fleshly eyes be rendered blind to all illusion.

[1] *Ante*, pp. 9, 23.

> Before the Soul can hear, the image (man) has to become as deaf to roarings as to whispers, to cries of bellowing elephants as to the silvery buzzing of the golden fire-fly.
>
> Before the Soul can comprehend and may remember, she must unto the Silent Speaker be united, just as the form to which the clay is modelled is first united with the potter's mind.

The harmony within is that between the ego and his vehicles, and also, of course, between those vehicles themselves. In the average man there is a perpetual strain going on between the astral body and the mental body, between the desires and the mind; and neither of these bodies is in the least in tune with the ego, or prepared to act as his vehicle. The personality must be purified, and the channel between it and the ego must be opened and widened. Until this is done the personality sees everything and everybody from its own very limited point of view. The ego cannot see what is really going on; he perceives only the distorted picture in the personality, which is like a camera with a defective lens that distorts the light rays, and a faulty plate or film which makes the result all blurred, indistinct and unequal.

That is why in most people the ego cannot derive any satisfaction from the personality until it is in the heaven-world. The ego knows the true from the false, he recognizes the true when he sees it, and rejects the false; but generally when he casts an eye downwards into the personality he finds so crazy a confusion of inconsequent thought-forms that he can distinguish nothing definite; he turns away in despair, and decides to wait for the quietude of the heaven-world before attempting to pick the fragments of truth out of this unseemly chaos. Under those more peaceful conditions, as the emotions and thoughts of the recent physical life come up one by one and envisage themselves in the vivid light of that world, they are examined with clear vision, the dross is thrown away and the treasure is kept. The disciple must try to bring about this condition while still in the physical body, by purifying the personality and harmonizing it with the soul.

The possibilities of personal error are almost infinite. Suppose that a worm, a bird, a monkey, and a traveller simultaneously look at a tree. The first will think of it as food, the second as a house, the third as a gymnasium, the fourth as a kind of umbrella; the pictures will all be different from one another, and different again from the tree's conception of himself.

While seeing has reference to looking outward, hearing refers to what comes from within. The man must become quiet if he is to hear the still small voice. Dhāranā or concentration will produce this quietness. If the soul is to hear the inner voice with certainty and accuracy, the outer man must be unshaken by all external things—by the clamour of the big breakers of life that dash against him, as well as by the delicate murmur of the softer ripples. He must learn to be very still, to have no desires and aversions.

Intuition can scarcely ever be invoked except when the man is utterly willing to receive its behests as the best and most acceptable guide, without intruding his personal desires It would be of little use to ask from the intuition any solution of a problem of conduct, if at the same time the man wished that the answer should be this or that. Except on rare occasions when it is unusually strong, it is only when personal desires and aversions have ceased to exist, when the voice of the outer world can no longer command him, that a man can hear the inner voice which should be his unfailing guide

Before the soul can fully comprehend the drift of all the tuition which comes to him from without, and the intuition that comes from within, another harmonizing process must take place, in which the manas gradually becomes attuned to the will, which gives *direction* to his life.

There are three stages in the development of consciousness. On the probationary path the man's highest consciousness works upon the higher mental plane; after the First Initiation and until the Fourth, it is climbing steadily through the buddhic plane; at the end of that stage it enters on the ātmic or spiritual plane. He has then become united with the will, the directing agent, controller of his destiny. While in the middle stage he might have said: "Thy Will, not mine, be done," but now he says: "Thy Will and mine are one." Just as the design of the pot that is to be made is first in the potter's mind, and just as the model for a race of men is in the Manu's mind, He having received it from above, so is the goal of achievement for every one of us already marked out by the Monad, and then brought down into the evolving life of the conscious man by the spiritual principle within him.

There is thus a reason for the use of the word soul in these three verses. It is the soul that treads the path of progress, not the personality. On the first half of the path it unites itself more and more completely with the buddhi, forming the spiritual soul, manas-taijasī. But all the work is done under the direction of the ātmā, the voice of the silence.

CHAPTER XXXIV

THE WARNING VOICE

For then the Soul will hear, and will remember.
And then to the inner ear will speak

THE VOICE OF THE SILENCE,

and say:

If they Soul smiles while bathing in the sunlight of thy life; if thy Soul sings within her chrysalis of flesh and matter; if thy Soul weeps inside her castle of illusion; if thy Soul struggles to break the silver thread that binds her to the Master; know, O disciple, thy Soul is of the earth.

C.W.L.—In occult books we have frequent reference to the voice of the silence, and we often find that what is said in one place does not agree with what appears in others. In the early days of the Society we used to puzzle over its exact significance, trying to make it always mean the same thing. Only after much study did we discover that the term is general. The voice of the silence for anyone is that which comes from the part of him which is higher than his consciousness can reach, and naturally that changes as his evolution progresses. For those now working with the personality the voice of the ego is the voice of the silence, but when one has dominated the personality entirely and has made it one with the ego so that the *ego may work perfectly through it*, it is the voice of the ātmā—the triple spirit on the nirvānic plane. When this is reached there will still be a voice of the silence—that of the Monad on the plane above. When the man identifies the ego and the Monad and attains Adeptship, he will still find a voice of the silence coming down to him from above, but then it will be the voice, perhaps, of one of the Ministers of the Deity, one of the Planetary Logoi, as They are called. Perhaps for Him in turn it will be the voice of the Solar Logos Himself; and if even for Him there is such a thing as that, it must be the voice of a higher Logos. But who can say?

"The sunlight of thy life" refers to those periods in our personal existence when fortune smiles upon us, and everything seems bright and fair. The ego who basks in that pleasure, and mistakes it for the true happiness of the higher self, has not yet the higher vairāgya which kills the outer sounds. In *The Ancient Wisdom* our President has explained how the man who feels that nothing on earth can satisfy him, not even those things that give the greatest delight to ordinary mortals, may through a strong but calm effort of the will rise to and unite himself with the higher consciousness and find himself free of the body; but that is only for those who obey the first condition, who cannot be satisfied with anything less than that union.

The three bodies, physical, astral and mental, which with their habits constitute the personality, are in truth a chrysalis, in which a butterfly is gradually being formed. In our present caterpillar state the soul must be in the body and the world; yet it must not be *of* them; it must not accept that life as its own, but must realize that it is independent of its vehicles. Here again we must be careful not to misunderstand. It is indeed well, it is even necessary that the soul should rejoice on its upward path, that it should smile, that it should sing within its chrysalis; there is no harm in that—there is even much good in it. What it must *not* do is to sing *because* of the chrysalis, or of anything that happens to that outer shell. It would be wrong, terribly wrong, that the soul should weep within its castle of illusion, because depression and sadness are always wrong. But that, true as it is, is not what is meant here. What Āryasanga is trying to tell us in his graceful poetical language is that the soul must neither rejoice nor sorrow because of anything whatever that is connected with the chrysalis or the castle, or any outer form; it must be indifferent to that form, unaffected by what happens to it. If it is *not* indifferent, it is still of the earth, still entangled with this lower world, and so not yet ready for perfect freedom.

All around us eternal change is taking place; but the soul must press forward on its way resistless, undeterred by change, for to be influenced by these outer things shows weakness. Remember how Shakespeare writes in his *Sonnets*:

When I have seen by Time's fell hand defaced
The rich proud cost of outworn buried age
When sometime lofty towers I see down-razed,
And brass eternal slave to mortal rage;
When I have seen the hungry ocean gain
Advantage on the kingdom of the shore,
And the firm soil win of the watery main,
Increasing store with loss and loss with store;
When I have seen such interchange of state,
Or state itself confounded to decay;
Ruin hath taught me thus to ruminate,
That Time will come and take my love away.
This thought is as a death, which cannot choose
But weep to have that which it fears to lose.

Since brass, nor stone, nor earth, nor boundless sea,
But sad mortality o'er-sways their power,
How with this rage shall beauty hold a plea,
Whose action is no stronger than a flower?
O, how shall summer's honey breath hold out
Against the wreckful siege of battering days,
When rocks impregnable are not so stout,
Nor gates of steel so strong, but Time decays?[1]

But time is really the friend of the aspirant, for it is precisely the finer, the higher, the inner things which are least subject to its ravages. This truth the occultist learns as a matter of certain experience and knowledge, so the changes in outside things at last come to trouble him not at all.

Silver is the thread—as befits an emblem of purity—that binds the soul to the higher self; every traffic that the soul has with impurity of body, emotions or thought is a struggle

[1] *Sonnets*, XLIV, XLV.

to break that silver thread, a temptation to ignore the still, small voice.

Madame Blavatsky adds the following footnotes:

> The "great Master" is the term used by chelas to indicate the Higher Self. It is the equivalent of Avalokiteshvara, and the same as Adi-buddha with the Buddhist occultists, Atma with the Brahmanas, and Christos with the ancient Gnostics.
>
> Soul is used here for the human Ego or Manas, that which is referred to in our occult septenary division as the human Soul in contradistinction to the spiritual and animal Souls.

Madame Blavatsky here employs the word Master in an unusual sense, saying that it is so used by the chelas or pupils. In later Theosophical literature this title has been reserved for that limited number of members of the Great White Brotherhood who accept pupils from among those who are still living in the world. That number is small; it would seem that one Adept on each of the rays is appointed to attend to that work, and all those who are coming along His particular ray of evolution pass through His hands. No one below the rank of Adept is permitted to assume full responsibility for a pupil, though those who have held the position of pupil for a number of years are often employed as deputies, and receive the privilege of helping and advising promising young aspirants. These older pupils are gradually being trained for their future work when they in turn shall become Adepts, and they are learning to take more and more of the routine work off the hands of their Masters, so that the latter may be set free for higher labours which only They can undertake. The preliminary selection of candidates for chelaship is now left to a large extent in the hands of these older pupils, and the candidates are temporarily linked with such pupils rather than directly with the great Adepts. But the pupils and the Master are so wonderfully one that perhaps this is almost "a distinction without a difference".

The terms which Madame Blavatsky uses in these footnotes will be better understood if we study a little the various trinities in the universe and in man. It is in the experience of everybody that there is a duality of the knower and the known, of the one who sees and the things that are seen, of the subject and the object. This is the old division of the world of experience into two parts, spirit and matter, using those words in a general or common sense. Spirit or consciousness and matter are a pair of opposites—the spirit is an active principle, the matter a passive one; the spirit has a centre but no circumference, the matter has a circumference but no centre; the spirit is self-moving, the matter is moved from outside. In these two we have also the division of reality into the divine and the material; the free and the bound; that which shines with its own light and that which has only reflected light.

When one looks closer still, one sees that those two are playing, as it were, on the stage in one's presence, that they are not No. 1 and No. 2 principles, as many people think, but they are No. 2 and No. 3; for the one that now witnesses their interplay is No. 1. No. 2 is the *God who is seen*, but No. 1 is the God who is the real Self, who is the cause of all the interplay between No. 2 and No. 3.

In Christian terminology, Christ is the God who is seen. "No man hath seen God at any time."[1] Yet said Christ: "I and my Father are One."[2]

That brings us to the term Avalokiteshvara. This word is a compound of *avalokita* (seen), and Ishvara (God, the Ruler). It thus means the Higher Self in the duality of spirit and matter in the universe. "There are three that bear record in heaven," said S. John, "the Father, the Word and the Holy Ghost."[3] The Word, the Logos, Avalokiteshvara, is the Second. He is the Christos, the God that is seen This is the universal spirit, or purusha, as distinguished from the matter, or prakriti. Man is consciousness looking at matter, and this God is glorified or universal Man, the supreme subject. Analyze yourself, and you will find the reflection of this—the inner God in yourself. Still,

[1] I John, 4, 12.

[2] St. John, 10, 30.

[3] I John, 5, 7.

that God that is seen only bears witness to the real God—in man to the Self, the "I" which embraces both the subject and the object.

This "I" is not a new subject, witnessing the old subject and object, put together and now made into one new compound object. It is "I"—that is all there is to say. Every thinking man can look at his own body, and in some cases his astral and mental bodies as well, and call it "it", that is, he can look upon it as an object. He can also have a conception of the consciousness or subject in his neighbour, and infer that it is of the same nature as that consciousness (containing will, feeling and thought) which he finds in himself. *But on this point he now makes a great mistake*, by giving two different names to one thing—he calls the same thing "you" when he sees it in his neighbour, but "I" when he looks at it in himself! Let him look upon the consciousness or subject within himself (all of it) as he does upon that in others, and call it "you", regarding it as just one of the great sea of "yous" that make up the Logos, as drops of water make up the ocean, and he will be ready to transcend consciousness and reach the real "I", the Self or God that is not seen.[1] The consciousness, the "you", is a portion of Avalokiteshvara, the God that is seen, the Christ, the light that lighteth every man that cometh into the world, just as much as the bodies are parts of the ocean of cosmic matter; and both equally are not the Self. No one hath *seen* the supreme God at any time—not even the Son.

This trinity has been considered in various ways:

Avalokiteshvara has been described as follows by Swāmī T. Subba Rao: "Parabrahman by itself cannot be seen as it is. It is seen by the Logos with a veil thrown over it, and that veil is the mighty expanse of Cosmic Matter." And again: "Parabrahman, after having appeared on the one hand as the Ego, and on the other as Mūlaprakriti, acts as the one energy through the Logos" The danger of all such descriptions is immense; the use of the word "it" alone in this connection can undo everything. In *oneself* deliverance, the truth, must be sought—only I being I can solve this mystery, which is so easy, but that people will not see. There is also the strongest

[1] This argument is expounded in *The Seven Rays*, by Ernest Wood, Ch. xxi.

objection even to the word God as applied to Parabrahman—for to think of God is to think of the seen, that is, of Avalokiteshvara; and that God is, after all, a "you", or rather all "yous".

The conception of a subject or "you" involves a time limitation; that of an object or "it" involves a space limitation. But motion in both time and space is a mystery. Some ancients argued that nothing could really move, "because it cannot move in the space where it is, and it certainly cannot move in the space where it is not". But subjects can move in time, and objects can move in space, because all move in Parabrahman. Both time and space are secondary to motion, properly conceived.[1]

"And these three are one."[2] Mūlaprakriti, the root of manifestation, basic matter, external being, is not something other than Parabrahman, but is the same, as seen through the time limitations of consciousness. Parabrahman is beyond that time limitation, and therefore seems to be still, and from that arises the appearance of space, the characteristic of Mūlaprakriti—which is in reality a space containing everything which ever existed or will exist in all of the three periods of time—past, present and future. Then universal consciousness, the great Man, also called Daivīprakriti (the divine manifestation), as against Mūlaprakriti (the material manifestation), is Avalokiteshvara, the Īshvara or Ruler or God *who is seen*, in contradistinction to Parabrahman, the first member of the Trinity, who is not seen directly even by Him

Now, in the higher triad in the consciousness of man we have a reflection of this great Trinity. Therefore Madame Blavatsky says that the Higher Self, by which she means buddhi or the intuitional love, is the *equivalent* of Avalokiteshvara. Any confusion in thought of the universal reality with ātmā, buddhi and manas—the three modes of consciousness in man—would result in serious error, but there is an analogy between the two. The great Trinity is reflected in man in various ways, and appears in one form in those three aspects of his consciousness. So ātmā, buddhi and manas reflect in their smaller sphere the characteristics of the universal trinity. Ātmā is the consciousness of self, and also the will, which gives self-direction.

[1] See *The Seven Rays*, Ch viii.

[2] I John, 4, 12

Manas, at the other pole, is consciousness of the world, and its thought-power does all our work, even that which is effected through the hands. But buddhi, between the two, is the very essence of consciousness, of subjectivity. Thus the greater Trinity is reproduced in the consciousness of the ego.

Beyond this middle member, triple in character, is the Monad in man, representative in him of Parabrahman, the state of his true and absolute nirvāna, beyond consciousness. The ātmā is the state of his false and relative nirvāna of the nirvānic plane, his last illusion, that persists between the Fourth and Fifth Initiations. As the Monad lies above the trinity of consciousness, so the personal bodies lie outside or beneath it—they are known only in reflection in manas. On the first half of the Path (from the First to the Fourth Initiation) the man is busy shaking himself free from those personal limitations, from the illusion of "it". On the second half he is engaged in releasing himself from the illusion of "you".

There are still a few more points to consider in Madame Blavatsky's notes. Her reference to Ādi-Buddha and Ātmā requires some comment, though that to the Christos of the Gnostics will be abundantly clear from what has been said above. The "Ātmā of the Brāhmanas" is rather what the Buddhists thought that the Brāhmanas meant by the term (and what perhaps many of the Brāhmanas who missed the true point of their philosophy really did think); it is that spiritual soul in man which the *Buddha declared to be not utterly* permanent. Yes, even the Christ (the higher self) in man is at last mortal. Beautiful and wonderful, and far beyond *the vision of ordinary men as it lies, it must at last give up* its life, to be one with the Father. It is the "you" masquerading as the "I" in spiritual men—just as, far earlier in evolution, the absurd personality, the "it" pretended to be "I". But when he says that their belief in ātmā is wrong, the orthodox Buddhist has not understood the height of true Brāhmana thought, and especially the teaching on this point of Shrī Shankarāchārya, who was really one with the Buddha in His anātmā doctrine, because by ātmā He meant the Monad, the indescribable Parabrahmic aspect of man. The *Buddha saw that people called "you" the ātmā, the Self*, and tried to dislodge them from that error by saying that what they called "I" was perishable.

In the foot-note Madame Blavatsky says that Avalokiteshvara is the same as Ādi-Buddha. She amplifies her statement on the subject in *The Secret Doctrine*, as follows:

> In the esoteric, and even exoteric Buddhism of the North Ādi-Buddha, . . . the One Unknown, without beginning or end, identical with Parabrahman, emits a bright Ray from its Darkness. This is the Logos, the First, or Vajradhara, the Supreme Buddha, also called Dorjechang. As the Lord of all Mysteries he cannot manifest, but sends into the world of manifestation his Heart—the "Diamond Heart," Vajrasattva or Dorjesempa. This is the Second Logos of Creation.[1]

In this extract she clearly shows that the First and Second Logos are respectively Ādi-Buddha and Avalokiteshvara, for the latter is the same as Vajrasattva. Therefore when she speaks of them as one it can only be as the Christians speak of the Christ as one with the Father. I wrote as follows on this subject in *The Inner Life*, Section II:

> There has been much discussion as to the exact meaning of the terms Ādi-Buddha and Avalokiteshvara. I have made no special study of these things from the philosophical standpoint, but so far as I have been able to gather ideas from discussion of the matter with the living exponents of the religion, Ādi-Buddha seems to be the culmination of one of the great lines of superhuman development—what might be called the abstract principle of all the Buddhas. Avalokiteshvara is a term belonging to the Northern Church and seems to be the Buddhists' name for their conception of the Logos European scholars have translated it: "The Lord who looks down from on high' but this seems to have in it a somewhat inaccurate implication, for it is clearly always the manifested Logos; sometimes the Logos of a solar system and sometimes higher than that but always manifest. We must not forget that while the founders of the great religions see and know the things which They name. Their followers usually do not see, they have only the names, and they juggle with them as intellectual counters, and build up much which is incorrect and inconsistent[2]

We have already seen that by the term Higher Self Madame Blavatsky means the buddhi in man, the central member of the trinity of his immortal consciousness That is the wisdom in man But it is a reflection of the universal wisdom, without which there could be no human wisdom.

[1] *Op cit.*, Vol. I, p. 624.

[2] *Op. cit.*, Vol. I, p. 169.

CHAPTER XXXV

SELF AND ALL-SELF

When to the world's turmoil thy budding Soul lends ear; when to the roaring voice of the great illusion thy soul responds; when frightened at the sight of the hot tears of pain, when deafened by the cries of distress, thy Soul withdraws like the shy turtle within the carapace of selfhood, learn, O disciple, of her silent God thy Soul is an unworthy shrine.

When waxing stronger, thy Soul glides forth from her secure retreat; and breaking loose from the protecting shrine, extends her silver thread and rushes onward; when beholding her image on the waves of space she whispers, "This is I"—declare, O disciple, that thy Soul is caught in the webs of delusion.

C.W.L.—At the beginning of this passage, in the expression "budding Soul" we have a suggestion of the idea of evolution. For many centuries in Europe people did not think of evolution; they had the idea that the world and all the various creatures in it had been created quite suddenly, and they did not suppose that the more complex forms had evolved out of inferior ones, and would evolve further into something more perfect. Then came the idea, within about the last century and a half, that the material forms of living creatures were undergoing evolution, an unfoldment which has been believed by some to be due to an impulse of the indwelling life, and by others merely to the selective agency of natural environment.

But long ago there existed a theory of evolution of the Soul, which has all along been a central doctrine of the Hindu and Buddhist traditions, and has been spread extensively in the Western world by Theosophists during the last fifty years, along with the doctrine of reincarnation. This is put forward as the most logical and ethical theory of human destiny, once it has been established, on scientific or religious grounds, that the Soul of a man survives the death of his body. The soul incarnates many times for the sake of experience, and each one will thereby become at last not merely a genius in some field of human thought or work, but a perfect man, ready for full conscious divinity.

There are two great stages on the path of the soul's evolution—the first is called the pravritti mārga, the way of forth-going, and the second the nivritti mārga, the way of return. In the former the development of personality takes place, accompanied by the accumulation of much karma as the soul pursues its restless career of seeking the satisfaction of its multitudinous desires in the external world. In the latter the soul little by little turns its back upon the world, and with its face towards the divine, its source and goal, proceeds with the task of perfecting itself so as to finish up the human stage of its evolution.

It is this second stage, the nivritti mārga, that is divided up into the probationary path and the *Path of Initiation*, which have been fully described in *The Path of Discipleship*, *Initiation, the Perfecting of Man*; and *The Masters and the Path*. This mārga implies a course of voluntary evolution, in which the candidate is deliberately training himself in the higher qualities of character; the evolution of the lower creatures and of men on the pravritti mārga is involuntary, they seek and respond to experience, and learn without clear realization of what is happening to them.

In a foot-note to the word illusion, Madame Blavatsky calls it Mahā-Māyā, the great illusion, the objective universe. The meaning of the term *illusion*, as applied to the external world, has already been discussed. It is not the same idea as that referred to in the text as "webs of delusion," which has reference, as another foot-note says, to "Sakkāyaditthi, the delusion of personality".

When the Lord Buddha revealed to men the Noble Eightfold Path, the way to liberty, the practical means to bring sorrow to an end, he told them about the ten fetters which the candidate must cast off—one after another. The first of these was called Sakkāyaditthi, the delusion of personality. Let us see how this arises. A child is born subject to karma—the result of its deeds in previous lives. It has a certain kind of body, and various things happen to it. In course of time it hears what people say of it, and it finds out what it can and what it cannot do. It sees itself in these things as in a mirror—one of those distorting mirrors which are sometimes set up in exhibitions to amuse people with their grotesquely flattened or elongated images. It thus obtains ideas about itself—that it is clever, or stupid, beautiful or ugly, weak or strong. As its education proceeds it acquires social standing or position or character, assumes the habits of body and mind of doctor, lawyer, house-wife—whatever it may be—and thus acquires a settled *personality*. When it thinks itself to be that personality it has what has been called "self-personality"—exactly the same delusion that obsesses the unfortunate people in the lunatic asylums, who imagine themselves to be tea-pots, ear-drums, north poles, Queen Elizabeths and Napoleons.

A definite well-trained set of bodies and personality, with useful habits, is, of course, a good thing, just as is a good set of tools, or a good motor-car. We do not want to have weak or nondescript personalities But however good our personality may be we should not think it to be ourself, and we should be able to enjoy all our native will-power, love-power and thought-power while using it for our purposes, for our spiritual life in the material world. These personalities should not set themselves up as candidates for immortality, and try to intrench themselves against the ravages of use and time that beset all material things. A middle-aged gentleman once said to his son, who volunteered to relieve him of some work: "No, no, my boy. Always use up the old ones first!" The personalities must be willing to be used, to be adapted to the spiritual purposes of the moment, to be worn out—and must be content with the sole reward of a *long and glorious devachan*, that will follow the death of the outer body in the case of all those who have thus served the divine indwelling self, except, of course, the servants of the Masters who *renounce this reward* and take speedy rebirth in order to work for the world.

> This earth, disciple, is the hall of sorrow, wherein are set along the path of dire probations, traps to ensnare thy Ego by the delusion called "great heresy".

That *the physical plane is a place of sorrow* is a widespread Buddhist and Hindu thought. Uncongenial and often disfiguring or debilitating labour, oppression, disease, indignity and dread fall to the lot of the majority of mankind. Those whose fortune has set them in places of ease may say that they *find much pleasure in it; but Patanjali says: "To the* enlightened *all* is misery." There are many things that give no trouble to the relatively unevolved—such as the smell of alcohol, meat or onions, the noise of factory sirens or coarse music, gross manners, hideous clothes and buildings, and a thousand other things that afflict those who are more sensitive. In addition to these there is hunger to gain what we want, and fear to lose it when it is in hand, and *suffering for others all round us, if not for ourselves.* Surely men must be mad to hug such chains as these. Surely this world is indeed a hall of sorrow. Think how poor is its best in the sight of those who know the higher planes.

But it is so chiefly because man has made it so. Think of the vast sea of life that fills the mineral, the vegetable and the *animal kingdoms of nature, and how* all that *is throbbing with* pleasure. Even the dreadful picture of the poet, of "nature, red in tooth and claw with ravin" loses most of its lurid colour when we realize that the animals do not "think before and after" as men do, with painful longing and fear, and that while *their battles* are on, and the blood and wounds distress the human beholder, the excitement of the animal consciousness is at its greatest height and is often experiencing its greatest pleasure. Earth is a hall of sorrow only for man, who with his greed and anger, born of a strong imagination that feeds the *flames of hot desire,* has poisoned with innumerable horrors both his personal and his social life.

Yet it only needs the conquest of *selfishness* to remove every one of these horrors, and open to all mankind the joys of this world—the thrill and deep strong peace of beauty, of discovery, of creative work, of social and bodily well-being.

Madame Blavatsky's foot-note then speaks of:

> Attavada, the heresy of the belief in Soul, or rather in the separateness of Soul or Self from the one universal, infinite Self.

Atta is the Pali equivalent of the Sanskrit ātmā, and *vāda* means doctrine. The doctrine of ātmā, which we have already considered, is the great source of cleavage between the Hindus and Buddhists, but as a matter of fact the distinction is merely one of words, because when the Hindu says that the Self or ātmā in man is one with the universal Self, he does not mean by the word what people usually mean when they think or speak of themselves, but something altogether deeper, which only the advanced yogī can even imagine. There is a passage in the *Shrī Vakya Sudhā* which warns the aspirant that when he repeats the great religious formula "I am That," he must take care what he means by "I"; it explains that the separate individual should be understood as threefold, and that it is the union with Brahman only of the highest of these three that is proclaimed by "Thou art That" and such sayings. As already explained, the personality is not "I", and even the "you" in me is not "I", but the "I" is something indistinguishable from the universal Self in which the many and the One are one. The Lord Buddha's teaching denies the permanency of the "you" that men call "I".

It is an unfortunate thing that two such great religions as Hinduism and Buddhism should be separated mainly by so small a misunderstanding, and also that because of it the modern Theosophical movement has spread very slowly among the Buddhists. We have developed a large Theosophical literature, in which the words ātmā and Self figure extensively, and this has alienated a good many Buddhists who have not taken the trouble to clear away this obstacle of words which we have inadvertently put in their path.

This earth, O ignorant disciple, is but the dismal entrance leading to the twilight that precedes the valley of true light—that light which no wind can extinguish, that light which burns without a wick or fuel.

In this and some later verses we have poetical names for the planes of nature. As previously stated, it was common among Oriental occultists to bunch together the astral and lower mental planes, and Madame Blavatsky often followed that plan in her teaching. This combining of the two is indicated in this picture of a "twilight that precedes the valley of true light". That description of the valley of true light shows it to be the region of the Soul and the Higher Self, the planes where buddhi and higher manas have their habitat.

If we divide the planes by a line separating the lower from the higher mental, we find that there is a radical difference between those which lie below the line and those which are above. In the former, matter is dominant; it is the first thing that strikes the eye; and consciousness shines with difficulty through the forms. But in the higher planes life is the prominent thing, and forms are there only for its purposes. The difficulty in the lower planes is to give the life expression in the forms, but in the higher it is quite the reverse—to hold and give form to the flood of life. It is only above the dividing line that the light of consciousness is subject to no wind, and shines with its own power. The symbol of a spiritual fire is very fitting for consciousness at those levels, as distinguished from the lower planes, where the symbol of fire burning fuel is more appropriate.

Saith the great Law: "In order to become the knower of All-Self, thou hast first of Self to be the knower." To reach the knowledge of that Self, thou hast to give up self to non-self, being to non-being.

In a foot-note Madame Blavatsky distinguishes between the Ātmajnānī who is mentioned here, and the Tattvajnānī. In Hindu literature generally the distinction is slight and is usually ignored, but she says: "The Tattvajnānī is the knower or discriminator of the principles in nature and in man; and Ātmajnānī is the knower of Ātmā, or the universal One Self." Jnānī means a knower and tattva means the truth or the real nature of things.

It has always been a teaching of Theosophy that to make progress we must apply the old Greek formula "Know thyself". In consequence, a very large part of our modern Theosophical literature deals with the constitution, history and destiny of man. It is by the study of the various principles and bodies of man that we are able gradually to distinguish what he is, and to separate him in thought from the vehicles that he uses, until at last we arrive at the real Self. Then, through that real Self in us, we shall realize the universal Self; in fact, the two are one.

But to know the real Self in oneself, the lower self must be set aside, must become as naught. As we have already seen, the utter destruction of "self-personality" is the very first task of the Initiate on the Path proper, since sakkāyaditthi, the delusion of the personal self, is the first fetter which must be cast off.

> And then thou canst repose between the wings of the Great Bird. Aye, sweet is rest between the wings of that which is not born, nor dies, but is the Aum throughout eternal ages.

On the Great Bird, which occupies a prominent place in Oriental religious symbolism, Madame Blavatsky has the following foot-note:

> Kala Hamsa, the bird or swan. Says the Nadavindupanishat (Rig Veda) translated by the Kumbakonam Theosophical Society—"The syllable A is considered to be the bird Hamsa's right wing, U its left, M its tail, and the Ardhamatra [half metre] is said to be its head."

The word Aum, generally pronounced Om, is used at the commencement of every good work or thought, because it is a word of power, symbolizing divine creation Innumerable

Sanskrit books repeat the statement that hearing, touch, sight, taste and smell are correlated respectively with the orders of matter named *ākāsha* (ether or sky), *vāyu* (air), *tejas* or *agni* (fire), *apas* or *jala* (water), and *prithivī* (earth), which are our familiar five planes of human manifestation, the ātmic, buddhic, mental, astral and physical. These planes were created in this order, beginning with the ātmic, where sound was applied as the creative power. Of course, that could not be the same thing as our physical sound, which is a pulsation in the air or some other physical substance; it was of the nature of the voice of the silence, the will of ātmā. Yet even on our physical plane sound is a great builder of forms, as every student of elementary science knows, who has made Chladni's figures or performed similar experiments. There is a great deal of symbolism in the Hindu Scriptures connected with this idea that the world was created by sound.

The word Aum is said to have special value as a mantra because it is the most complete human word. It begins with the vowel A in the back of the mouth, continues with the vowel U sounded in the centre of the mouth, and closes with the consonant M, with which the lips are sealed. It thus runs through the whole gamut of human speech and so represents in man the entire creative word. Its three parts are also taken as symbolical of the manifestation of the Trinity, in a variety of ways, to explain which one might fill a book. Thus we have Parabrahman, Daivīprakriti and Mūlaprakriti; Shiva, Vishnu and Brahmā; will, wisdom and activity; ānanda, chit and sat, or happiness, consciousness and being; ātmā, buddhi and manas; tamas, rajas and sattva; and many another. Aum is thus a constant reminder of this triplicity running through all things; it is a key therefore to the solution of many mysteries, as well as a word of power. The head of the bird is then taken as the unmanifested origin of the triple word.

Kāla, a word which means "time", is one of the names of Vishnu or Avalokiteshvara. Kāla-hamsa therefore means the swan of time or in time, hamsa being a swan. This symbol of a bird contains the implication of time, since it is proceeding through space. It is a characteristic of consciousness that it progresses or evolves, and so exists in time. The consciousness of the Logos *is* time, it does not begin nor end in time, and is therefore without birth or death.

This bird is thus a symbol of the Second Logos, which is also the great Wisdom. There is a well-known Hindu fable which connects the hamsa or swan with this idea of wisdom also, for it relates of that bird that when a mixture of water and milk is placed before it, it can separate the milk from the water. So does wisdom operate even in human life, selecting from our mixed experience the essential nutriment of the soul. Wisdom remains in the spiritual soul of man when experiences have died away, since, as the *Bhagavad-Gītā* says: "All actions in their entirety culminate in wisdom."[1]

A man on the Path who has passed the Third Initiation is also called a Hamsa, or swan. He is busy getting rid of rāga and dwesha, the fourth and fifth fetters, which are liking and disliking, and is therefore especially practising wisdom. People in the world are full of likes and dislikes, and they therefore suffer greatly from their own opinions about things. Throwing these two fetters off, the Hamsa becomes like the sage described in the *Gītā* as one satisfied with wisdom and knowledge, to whom a lump of earth. a stone and gold are the same, who regards impartially friends and foes, the righteous and the unrighteous. It is not that this man does not value gold and friends; he does, but he values also clay and foes. The wise man can profit from every kind of experience; all are useful for the soul. Epictetus asserted this when he declared: "There is only one thing for which God has sent me into the world—to perfect my own character in virtue; and there is nothing in all the world that I cannot use for that purpose."

Again, Hamsa is also a form of the saying "Aham Sah" or "I am That," or, as it is frequently used, "So'ham," which consists of the same words reversed. So when the aspirant repeats this sentence he also remembers that the way to bestride the Hamsa or bird of life is to realize that he is the Self. It is said that the devout yogī utters this formula with every breath, of which there are said to be 21,600 in a day and night, for the air is considered to come in with the sound of "sah" and go out with that of "ha".

As long as the bird is flying, the creative word is sounding, time exists. Although this time has neither beginning nor ending it is nevertheless a measurable period—which is a great

[1] *Op. cit.*, IV, 33.

mystery. On this point Madame Blavatsky has the following note:

> Eternity with the Orientals has quite another signification than it has with us. It stands generally for the 100 years or age of Brahma, the duration of a Maha-Kalpa or a period of 311,040,000,000,000 years.

This part of the subject is concluded with the words:

> Bestride the Bird of Life, if thou would'st know.
> Give up thy Life, if thou would'st live.

To these are appended the following notes:

> Says the same *Nadavindu*, "A Yogi who bestrides the Hamsa [thus contemplates on Aum] is not affected by karmic influences or crores of sins."

> Give up the life of the physical personality if you would live in Spirit.

A crore is ten millions. It must not, however, be assumed that the yogī is permitted to perform these sins; if he did he would not be a yogī. This expression is only an Oriental way of indicating that he is utterly free from taint by the material world. The man who thinks and works without personal desire, with utter unselfishness, suffers no kārmic consequences. The fruit of all his efforts goes into the great reservoir of spiritual force for the helping of the world, as has already been explained.

CHAPTER XXXVI

THE THREE HALLS

Three halls, O weary pilgrim, lead to the end of toils. Three halls, O conqueror of Mara, will bring thee through three states into the fourth, and thence into the seven worlds, the worlds of rest eternal.

If thou would'st learn their names, then hearken, and remember.

The name of the first hall is Ignorance—Avidya.

It is the hall in which thou saw'st the light, in which thou livest and shalt die.

The name of hall the second is the Hall of Learning. In it thy Soul will find the blossoms of life, but ? under every flower a serpent coiled.

The name of the third hall is Wisdom, beyond which stretch the shoreless waters of Akshara, the indestructible fount of omniscience.

C.W.L.—The three halls may be interpreted in two ways: as objective planes, or as the subjective condition of man.

In the former case the hall of ignorance is the physical plane, and the hall of learning, described in a foot-note as "the hall of probationary learning" is what may perhaps be called the astro-mental plane (the astral and lower mental planes taken together). When I wrote *The Inner Life* sixteen years ago it seemed to me probable that by the term hall of learning Madame Blavatsky meant the astral plane, and by the hall of wisdom the lower mental plane, but having thought the matter over and discussed it many times since then, I now lean to the opinion that we shall more accurately represent her thought if we take the hall of learning to include not only the astral but also the lower mental, and if we raise the hall of wisdom so as to include within it the planes of higher manas and buddhi.

That Āryasanga was not thinking of the astral plane as the hall of learning and the lower mental world as the hall of wisdom is shown a little further on, when he speaks of the latter hall as one "wherein all shadows are unknown, and where the light of truth shines with unfading glory". The lower mental world does not answer to this description; far more glorious and delicate than the astral plane as it is, it is still a material world and the habitat of the personalities of men. Further, the teacher also says that that which is uncreate abides in the hall of wisdom, and it is the ego, not the personality, which is uncreate. And in the lower mental plane, as well as in the astral, there is a serpent coiled under every flower; for if passion and foolish desires infest the one, pride and prejudices inhabit the other. In the higher mental plane, though there may be much that the ego does not know what it does know it knows correctly; but the lower mental is a region of personality and error.

The extent to which the lower planes are worlds of illusion is also seen in the way in which our senses and powers work in them. To take sight as an instance—we see because our sight is obstructed. If one could see perfectly through the wall one could not see the wall. It is the same with walking; we have some freedom to move about, because the earth resists the free motion of our feet. In the higher planes one lives in the light.

The combination of the astral and mental planes is not uncommon in the Oriental schools of occult training. The Vedantins speak of one body (called the manomayakosha, the body made of mind),[1] where our Theosophical literature usually

[1] See *The Secret Doctrine*, Vol. I, p. 181.

distinguishes the two (the astral and the mental), and to that body when awakened and functioning they ascribe the experiences proper to both planes. The candidate for the path of yoga in the Rāja Yoga schools was always trained to work from the mental down to the astral. This very cautious procedure is also shown in the teaching of Patanjali; who makes his first two steps moral, and requires definite progress in these before the practices leading to the siddhis or yoga powers are taken. In *Rāja Yoga: The Occult Training of the Hindus*, Prof. Wood has called these first steps "The ten commandments", and has translated them as the five restraints: "Thou shalt not injure, lie, steal, be incontinent, be greedy", and the five observances: "Thou shalt be clean, content, self-controlled, studious and devoted." These methods were in full force long before the time of Āryasanga; Pandit N. Bhāshyāchārya and some other Sanskrit scholars maintain that Patanjali, who in turn was not the originator of the system, gave his famous *Sūtras* to the world as far back as in the ninth century B.C.

In *The Masters and the Path* I have explained that in the old Initiations it often happened that much time was taken in instructing the candidate in astral work, as the awakening of the pupil to work at that level was left to a relatively later stage than is customary among the modern Theosophists, who often have already done much astral work and have thus learnt the detail of the astral world long before Initiation.

If we think of the three halls subjectively, as stages of progress in human development, we have the following familiar divisions: (1) The man who lives ignorantly in the world, attracted and repelled by the things around him, impelled to action by his own uncontrolled passions and desires—this is the ignorant stage. (2) The man who is learning that nature has definite laws, and is realizing that by working with them he can gain much more power than he had in the days of his ignorance—this is the hall of learning (3) The man who has realized that there are spiritual laws, and is learning to obey them. He knows about reincarnation and karma, and the ethical and moral laws that govern the progress of his own soul and those of others. He is aware that outer things exist only for the purposes of the evolving soul, and lives according to this knowledge. He is in the hall of wisdom.

Madame Blavatsky describes the four stages of consciousness:

> The three states of consciousness, which are Jagrat, the waking; Svapna, the dreaming; and Sushupti, the deep sleeping state. These three Yogi conditions lead to the fourth—the Turiya, that beyond the dreamless state, the one above all, a state of high spiritual consciousness.

These states of consciousness are not fixed, but may be correlated to the sets of planes or objective halls above mentioned, in the case of the candidate who is being prepared for the arhat initiation. In this case the waking state may be the physical, the dreaming state the astro-mental, the sleeping state the higher mental and buddhic, and the turiya state the ātmic.

The rather curious terms waking, dreaming and sleeping seem to have been selected from a physical plane point of view to name the heights of consciousness reached by the candidate at different times. When the man was going about his business in the physical plane, with all his faculties awake to this world, he was in the first state. To understand the second state we have to remember that there are two kinds of dreams—the often nonsensical productions of the brain (physical and etheric), *and the true experiences of the man away from his physical* body, working and learning in the astro-mental regions. It is to these latter that this term dreaming applies. The candidate sleeping, or almost going to sleep in a day-dream, would afterwards remember some such experiences, and then ascribe them to the "consciousness of the dream state". Suppose, however, that the aspirant out of the body should at any time go into *what may be called a second sleep, and rise into the next set of* planes, to be conscious for a time at that higher level. Probably on waking physically he would remember nothing of what had been happening out of the body—his brain not being attuned to record the experiences coming from planes higher than his "dreaming state". So it would seem to him that he had had deep dreamless sleep, and usually his only feeling would be one of great satisfaction and well-being. The "sleeping state" is therefore consciousness in that still higher region.

Now, the fourth state is sometimes called *trance*, for the following reason. It has often been explained that an aspirant when out of the body can rise a stage higher than when in it. It is possible also in deep meditation for the disciple to rise in trance to the higher state and afterwards bring that experience down into the waking memory. Thus the Arhat can touch the buddhic level while in the physical body, and the ātmic or nirvānic plane when out of it, or in deep meditation or trance. The term akshara, which is here applied to this fourth region, means simply that which does not melt away; it is the undecaying.

The same set of terms may be used as a relative series for less advanced occult students. One may have his waking consciousness on the physical plane, his dreaming state on the astral plane, his deep sleep on the mental; another, who is able to use his astral faculties in his physical waking consciousness, will have his dream consciousness on the lower mental, and his sleep state on the higher mental, and so on. The turīya is a higher state reached in every case by a special effort of will and meditation, which is a means to ultimately raising the whole set of three states to a higher level than before. While the transition is in progress, before the new level is established, there will always be this fourth stage.

This is seen in meditation. The candidate will sit down and fix his waking consciousness on some object—suppose it is a cat. Then he will rise to the " dream state ", and try to realize the astral aspect of the animal. Next he will ascend to the " sleep stage ", and give his attention to the mental being of the creature. The fourth step would be samādhi—or contemplation—an attempt to realize its significance and reality for the ego, to go beyond the three forms of the cat into its subjective meaning. The fixing of the mind on the cat in the first case is concentration; the process of elevation of the consciousness is meditation; the final concentration in a higher field of vision, beyond what was reached before, is contemplation (or samādhi). The last effort may be like piercing a cloud or fog, out of which the new vision will gradually form itself, or from which it may come like a flash of lightning. In either case the practitioner must hold himself very still in order to retain the impression as long as possible—one thought of self, of the old personal relativity, can dismiss the whole thing, so that there remains not even a memory of what it was like.

The three halls, it is said, lead to the end of *toils*—*not* to the end of *work*, it must be observed. In these lower worlds we have a sense of work which is certainly quite different from that of higher levels. To us down here the word is almost synonymous with toil, and often with drudgery, but from a higher point of view work is really play. Drudgery is merely action; it does not create the man who does it. But the least bit of work done occultly, done heartily "as to God and not unto men", done better than ever before, is good for the evolution of him who does it. If, in writing a letter, for example, one is at pains to do it neatly, even beautifully, and to express oneself briefly, clearly and gracefully, one has developed hand, eye and brain, thought-power, love-power and will-power. True work, such as that of an artist, is full of creative influence and of joy. We find some toil even in these things, however, because of the obstructions of the lower planes. Yet even down here there is no clear dividing line between toil and play. If one goes out, for example, on a long ride, the earlier part of the journey will be full of delight for both man and horse, but insensibly that passes away as fatigue increases, until suddenly the man realizes that the ride which was play in the beginning has now become work, or rather drudgery. In other cases, there may be a task, not prolonged, but a little beyond our strength; then there is a sense of toil. But all work in reality is play when there is willingness and no fatigue or overstrain.

We have much to learn from the animals, and even from the plants, in this respect. "Grow as the flower grows," says *Light on the Path*, "opening your heart to the sun." Said the Christ: "Consider the lilies of the field, how they grow; they toil not, neither do they spin: and yet I say unto you, That even Solomon in all his glory was not arrayed like one of these."[1] It is deadly fear of the morrow that makes men's work a toil, that makes them sweat in bitterness. But the Law says: "Do the wise and right thing to-day, and leave the result to take care of itself." This is not a doctrine of idleness, but of work that is play instead of toil.

An illustration of this is also to be seen in the way in which different people take a long journey. One man will get into the train at Chicago, and remain in a fever of impatience for the three or four days' time which the train takes to go to San

[1] S. Matthew, 6, 7.

Francisco, his destination. He has fixed his mind on something that he wants to do there; in the meantime his journey is a toil and a misery. Another finds a thousand things of interest on the way—the scenery, the people, the train itself; for him the journey is a happy holiday. And in the end he has accomplished much more than the other man. The Hindu villager lives very near to nature, and certainly grows as the flower grows. A man will set out from his village to get the mail from the Post Office or to post some letters there, perhaps sixteen or twenty miles away. He does not tramp along stolidly and painfully, jarring his nerves with the graceless movements that spring from a discontented or impatient mind. The vision of his mail is not a mania that shuts out all other interests, and makes him curse the length of the track. No; there are insects, birds, flowers, trees, streams, clouds in the sky, fields, houses, people and animals, and lastly the blessed earth itself, to lie on which for awhile is to be on velvet in the divine arms. How little the white man knows of life, how much of toil!

The Hindus have long held that God plays. The Līlā or play of Shrī Krishna, as it is called, is the great work of evolution, which looks so toilsome to us that we shudder at the long ages of work that lie in front, and cry out for rest. Think of the 311,040,000 million years of our mahākalpa. What an illusion! When we come to the end of toils life will be all play, all happiness.

The end of toils, though not of work, comes with the entry of the candidate, on the fourth Path, into the nirvānic plane. He has finished the toil of casting off the first five fetters—self-personality, doubt, superstition, liking and disliking—all of which marked his bondage to material things, with which his life was one long struggle on an up-hill road. But now his remaining five fetters are internal; he has to conquer them, truly, but his weapon will be serenity, quietness, calmness—the use of the will, which is the quietest thing in the world. These fetters are: desire for life in form and formless life, pride, agitation and ignorance. Little profit is to be derived from examining these in detail in this place; it is enough to notice their internal character, and to say that to destroy them the man must quieten himself and his vehicles above the line that divides the personality from the ego.

At earlier stages, before the end of toils, the student will do well to organize his life wisely, so that his work for the Master may be as far as possibly play. It should be pure delight, unmixed happiness—such a condition would make for the swiftest progress. Toil is not meritorious, nor especially profitable, though sometimes it may be necessary. How often a student does meditation, feeling it an irksome thing, but regarding it as a duty to be done, though with travail and suffering. *Do it happily and rejoicing, as play, or at least look forward* to the time when you can do so. Some men sink luxuriously *into the arms of the present, and say, "We will enjoy ourselves* now, and let the future take care of itself." Others stand aloof in proud strength and say, "We refuse to respond to that which can distress us." But the disciple must bare his back to the strokes of time, rejoicing in the long future, in the game in which every move can be a dancing poem of delight.

On the subject of the seven worlds, Madame Blavatsky says:

> Some Oriental mystics locate seven planes of being, the seven spiritual Lokas or worlds within the body of Kala Hamsa, the swan out of time and space, convertible into the swan *in* time, when it becomes Brahma instead of Brahman.

All the manifestations of seven in nature, such as the seven principles in man, or the seven planes in the world, come from a sevenfold division arising from Parabrahman. Three of the seven principles are manifest in the universal consciousness, and three more in *mūlaprakriti. One remains at its* source and includes all the others, for the presence of many *does not mar* the unity of That which is truly One. So, at his lower level, the man who transcends his middle set of principles (ātma-buddhi-manas), and rises into the first (the Monad), though he escapes from the worlds or planes, finds them all present in that new state of real nirvāna, which is beyond the consciousness-state as much as that is beyond the mere matter-state. We speak thus of it, in the third person, only as a *concession to ignorance,* and must *point out that* what has been said should be translated into terms of "you" for consciousness and "I" for the true life of super-conscious nirvāna, if it is to be understood. These "worlds," however, are not entered by the Arhat, but by the full Adept.

There are several other ways in which the Arhat may be thought of as entering the seven worlds of rest eternal:

In one way those worlds are the sub-planes of the ātmic plane, through which the Arhat begins to climb. The characteristic of the man who dwells in them is a changeless serenity, for everything is seen as in the One Self, and where that is realized fear and anxiety can have no place. As the *Gītā* says: "For the sage enthroned in yoga, serenity is called the means."[1] It is not that there is any lack of activity in those regions—it is one vast wave of ever-moving life—but there are no obstructions to the will of the One. On the buddhic plane we have still duality in a sense, since there one sees others, though the same Self is seen dwelling in them as in ourselves. But buddhi has to be transcended, for love implies a duality.

The serenity that the Arhat increasingly acquires puts a new face on the common planes of our existence. He enjoys in them a liberty that others do not know; he has found that work is play. Having touched the vale of bliss, he has discovered that life not only there but on all planes is pure delight. He not only sees and loves the advancing life behind the perishing forms, but feels and rejoices in the Divine Will behind the changing life. The rest eternal that he enjoys is not idleness, but the utter internal peace of one who knows that all is well, that the Divine Will is present even in what may to others seem the obstructions to progress, as well as in the apparent progress itself. A philosopher once caught a glimpse of this idea when he said: "Be serene; for if you fail through no fault of your own, the failure is a success better than you knew, since the Divine Will is being done." The Arhat knows something of the peace that passes understanding, because he is beginning to dwell in the Eternal. This is, Madame Blavatsky says, "The region of the full spiritual consciousness, beyond which there is no longer danger for him who has reached it."

If thou would'st cross the first hall safely, let not thy mind mistake the fires of lust that burn therein for the sunlight of life.

[1] *Op. cit.*, vi, 3.

If thou would'st cross the second safely, stop not the fragrance of its stupefying blossoms to inhale. If freed thou would'st be from the karmic chains, seek not for thy Guru in those mayavic regions.

The wise ones tarry not in pleasure-grounds of senses.

The wise ones heed not the sweet-tongued voices of illusion.

Seek for him who is to give thee birth in the Hall of Wisdom, the hall which lies beyond, wherein all shadows are unknown, and where the light of truth shines with unfading glory.

The guru here spoken of is the Master, the Teacher Madame Blavatsky puts it:

The Initiate who leads the disciple, through the knowledge he imparts, to his spiritual, or second birth, is called the father, Guru or Master.

A statement of the lives and work of the Gurus or Masters has been given in *The Masters and the Path*. A glimpse of the marvel of Their exalted powers is seen in the account there given of a meditation of the Master Kūthūmi. As He sits in His garden or His room He seems to be meditating, but is, in fact, giving attention to some millions of people, dealing with each one as individually as an ordinary man could if he were to give his full attention to that one.

Every ego is being helped by one of the Masters, so the man who can vivify the link in himself between the lower self and the higher may receive that help in his personal life. The gurus who are to be met with on the physical plane are generally Initiates, advanced pupils of the full Adepts, as stated before.

That which is uncreate abides in thee, disciple, as it abides in that hall. If thou would'st reach it and blend the two, thou must divest thyself of thy dark garments of illusion. Stifle the voice of flesh, allow no image of the senses to get between its light and thine, that thus the twain may blend in one. And having learnt thine own Ajnana flee from the Hall of Learning. This hall is dangerous in its perfidious beauty, is needed but for thy probation. Beware Lanoo, lest dazzled by illusive radiance thy Soul should linger and be caught in its deceptive light.

This light shines from the jewel of the great ensnarer (Mara). The senses it bewitches, blinds the mind, and leaves the unwary an abandoned wreck.

That which is uncreate refers to the higher triad, ātma-buddhi-manas, as distinguished from the personality and its bodies. The statement that the hall of learning is needed but for probation applies to the hall of ignorance as well. The set of material planes, physical, astral and lower mental, are but the buildings and equipment of a school for man, in which he is taught by means of toys. There is no experience that does not modify the soul and give it some wisdom; but he who is alive to the educative purpose of it all, and is eager to learn and to extract from the experience of embodied life lessons of eternal value, will not find the toys attractive in themselves. He will be like the bee that takes the honey from the flower and goes away, not intoxicated by its scent and colour.

Māra is a personification of the attractiveness of external things. Madame Blavatsky describes him as follows:

Mara is in exoteric religions a demon, an Asura, but in esoteric *philosophy it is personified temptation through* men's vices, and translated literally means "that which

> kills" the soul. It is represented as a king (of the Maras) with a crown in which shines a jewel of such lustre that, it blinds those who look at it, this lustre referring of course to the fascination exercised by vice upon certain natures.

In *The Light of Asia*[1] Sir Edwin Arnold has given us a vivid picture of this prince of darkness, as he came forth leading the ten chief sins, his angels of evil, against the Lord Buddha, as He sat under the Bodhi Tree, when nearing His Illumination.

> The moth attracted to the dazzling flame of thy night-lamp is doomed to perish in the viscid oil. The unwary Soul that fails to grapple with the mocking demon of illusion, will return to earth the slave of Mara.
>
> Behold the hosts of Souls. Watch how they hover o'er the stormy sea of human life, and how, exhausted, bleeding, broken-winged, they drop one after another on the swelling waves. Tossed by the fierce winds, chased by the gale, they drift into the eddies and disappear within the first great vortex.

The subject of "lost souls" is very complex. Some are like the children in a class at school who are not ready to pass on with the bulk of their fellow-students into the next grade at the end of the year, either because they are too young or because they have been lazy. Then, too, there are cases where the personality has become so immeshed in matter during bodily life that it has nothing to give to the ego, and it may then be cut off. Thirdly, there are the terrible fruits of the practice of black magic. It would take too long to discuss the subject here; I have dealt with it at some length in the article on *Lost Souls* in Volume I of *The Inner Life*.

[1] *Op. cit.*, Book VI.

Some of the expressions in these passages have all the strength of Oriental imagination. We must not think too literally of abandoned wrecks and broken wings. He who falls from the Path on account of material desire certainly does wreck his spiritual prospects for the time being, but even in that case he has learnt something which will be useful to the soul later on. In all cases it is best for a man to learn with wise thought; only when that is neglected will bitter experience be necessary to take its place.

It is by no means requisite that any human being shall go through every kind of experience. The more advanced and the wiser a man becomes, the more he will see in everything, and he will learn much from trifles that others might pass by as insignificant. It is said that a fool cannot learn even from a wise man, but a wise man can always learn, even from a fool. To know that fire is hot it is not necessary to put one's hand into it; a fool may do so, but the wise man has other ways of learning the fact that fire burns. Yet it is a great blessing that those who will not think and thus learn willingly, should be taught in the stern school of experience, without which they would learn nothing at all and make no progress.

The law of karma, that brings to men the experiences that they have given to others, is thus a benefactor and ultimately a liberator, not an instrument of vengeance or punishment. Suppose, for example, that a foot-pad waylaid a gentleman, knocked him down, perhaps killed him, and took his money. Under the law he would have to meet with some such painful experience himself, sooner or later. The robber was capable of such an act because he himself was a coarse being, lacking sensitiveness and imagination; otherwise he would have thought of the feelings of his victim or of the latter's wife and family, and such thought would have stayed his hand. Because he is coarse, crass, unimaginative, the foot-pad needs the violent kind of experience that he gives to others; nothing less will stir him. Later, when through kârmic retribution he has had some suffering, he will remember it when he is about to strike another, and will say to himself: "That is not a very nice thing for that poor man" He will then begin to reform, thanks to the law, which is always educative, never punitive.

CHAPTER XXXVII

THE WORLD'S MOTHER

If through the Hall of Wisdom thou would'st reach the vale of bliss, disciple, close fast thy senses against the great dire heresy of separateness, that weans thee from the rest.

C.W.L.—Herbert Spencer came very near to a revelation of the spiritual truth about evolution, when he described it as a progressive change from a state of incoherent homogeneity to one of coherent heterogeneity of structure and function. To him evolution meant that things which in the beginning were similar and separate, later become different but united. This specialization is seen in the human body, which has different organs which work for the whole; thus the digestive system digests food for the whole body, and the hands grasp, the feet walk, the eyes look, not for the sake of the hands, the feet and the eyes, but for the whole body. Similarly, society becomes more and more highly organized as time goes on. Men become more and more differentiated from one another, as the professions in life advance in knowledge and skill. The doctor cures all, the teacher teaches all, the bridge-builder builds bridges for all. One man works for the benefit of many, and the work of many flows back to benefit him.

When men get the organic sense and feeling for their fellows they cease to be a mob of incoherent homogeneous human beings and become heterogeneous and coherent. A man with that spirit will do his best for his community, or nation, or humanity, leaving it to the law of unity to bring him what he needs from the other organs of the great body. The incoherent homogeneous elements of matter or of society cannot organize themselves; it is the inner principle that draws them together and makes swift progress possible for them through mutual help. The unity is love, the force behind evolution, the *energy* of life; it is buddhi, the greatest wisdom. There is a profound difference between co-operation and brotherhood—the former springs from an intelligent appreciation of the mutual relations of men, the latter from a realization in feeling that the same life is dwelling in all.

In the evolution of an individual it is usually the spirit of co-operation that develops first; the business of the world brings people together, then by contact the divine fire of buddhi is struck. Two men, for example, go prospecting together, and support each other in the work. True friendship supervenes. But if it should chance, as it sometimes does, that brotherhood comes first, it will not develop into perfect and useful co-operation unless the intelligence is also awakened and applied to the business of life. An instance in point was the beautiful love between David Copperfield and his impractical wife Dora, whom the novelist was constrained to kill in order to make room for the more practical Agnes, and so give the story a happier termination.

In the occult life candidates who have developed the higher intelligence so that they have a keen appreciation of the principle of co-operation and of spiritual laws, often still find themselves dull and apparently incapable of rapid progress. They await the awakening in themselves of true love, buddhi. That is the burning energy of the inner man. Still, in this second of the stages of true spiritual unfoldment there will often be much agitation and trouble; the divine energy gushes forth irregularly and not always in the wisest way, causing much sorrow to its possessor—until the third spiritual stage, the place of serenity, has been reached. As that serenity is the goal to which the voice of the silence is directing the candidate, he is told to pass *through* the Hall of Wisdom into the vale of bliss. Even in the buddhic plane there is a certain duality, or separateness. We cannot love ourselves; love needs an object, even though it be not a material object, but the divine life manifested in many spiritual souls. Buddhi is the first veil, the Avalokiteshvara of the Higher Self, not the Parabrahman. The "dire heresy of separateness" has to be disposed of on every plane in turn, the physical, the astral, the mental and even the buddhic.

> Let not thy "heaven-born," merged in the sea of Maya, break from the universal Parent (Soul), but let the fiery power retire into the inmost chamber, the chamber of the heart, and the abode of the world's Mother.
>
> Then from the heart that power shall rise into the sixth, the middle region, the place between thine eyes, when it becomes the breath of the One-Soul, the voice which filleth all, thy Master's voice.

The "*heaven-born*" is *chitta, the lower mind. It is* born from the soul above, when manas becomes dual in incarnation. The planes of ātma-buddhi-manas are typified by heaven, while those of the personality are spoken of as earth. We have already observed the distinction of character which divides the five planes of human manifestation into two. The monadic and divine planes, beyond these five, taken together, form a third division. So the seven worlds can also be grouped as three. The lowest division is in the region of sattwa or law. Here we find everything regulated, but man has some freedom because the "heaven-born" is in him—so much of the energy of the Law-maker works through him. It is because man has this liberty and power to go his own way that his life is usually more disorderly, less regulated, than that of the lower kingdoms of external nature.

The middle set of planes contains those of spiritual energy, the indwelling life, without which the rest would be dead and motionless. They are the planes of the divine, the shining, the Avalokita, or "seen", God—the life seen by wisdom, not the form seen by knowledge.

The highest group of planes is that of the Monad, the Self that is bliss and freedom, where are the realities behind every human ideal and the ecstasy beyond consciousness that is the extracted quintessence of beauty, goodness, truth, harmony, comprehension, union and freedom.

What is here called the fiery power is the force named kundalinī in Sanskrit. This may be described as a latent fire, coiled up like a sleeping serpent at the base of the spine in all men except those few in whom it has been specially awakened, and is actively working in the etheric body. It should not be difficult to realize the existence of such a fire, since it is well known that the breath in our lungs constantly feeds a slow fire, and that digestion also is a kind of fire. Kundalinī is more like electrical fire—a force developing heat where there is resistance—than fire that burns fuel, but it is not of the same order of force as electricity.

I have written on this subject in the articles on the Serpent-Fire and the Force-Centres in *The Inner Life* and that on Vitality in Chapter IV of *The Hidden Side of Things*, and I hope to publish shortly a somewhat fuller study, illustrated with coloured plates.[1] There is also an extensive, if somewhat obscure, literature on the subject in Sanskrit, including the *Shatchakranirūpana*, the *Ananda Lahari*, and many other works. There is an excellent translation of the first of these, with a commentary, by Arthur Avalon, called *The Serpent Power*, published by Ganesh & Co., Madras.

The following is a very brief summary of the subject. Kundalinī is the lower end of a stream of a certain kind of the force of the Logos, and it commonly lies sleeping in the chakra or force-centre at the base of the spine. If it is awakened prematurely, that is, before the man has purified his character of every taint of sensual impurity and selfishness, it may rush downwards and vivify certain lower centres in the body (used only in some objectionable forms of black magic), and irresistibly carry the unfortunate man into a life of indescribable horror; at best, it will intensify all that the man has in him, including such qualities as ambition and pride Kundalinī should be wakened only under the personal direction of a Master, who will instruct the student in the use of the will to arouse it, in the manner in which it should be moved when aroused, and in the spiral course along which it must be carried through the chakras or force-centres, from that near

[1] Book on *Chakras* has been since issued by T.P.H., Adyar.

the base of the spine, to those which lie on the surface of the etheric double at the spleen,[1] the navel, the heart, the throat, between the eyebrows, and at the top of the head. This course differs with different types of people, and it is quite a definite physical thing, for the force has literally to burn a pathway for itself through the impurities of the etheric double.

There are chakras in the astral body also, which are already aroused by kundalinī working in that plane in all the cultured people of the higher races. The process of developing those centres has rendered the astral body sensitive to the plane, awakening its feeling, its power to travel about, its sympathetic response to other entities there, its vision and hearing, and astral faculties generally. But the memory of those experiences or the use of the astral faculties while in the physical body, becomes possible in a definite and well-controlled way only when kundalinī in the etheric double has been carried through the corresponding centres.

The special mention of the place between the eyes in our text has reference to the pineal gland and the pituitary body. The forces from both the sixth and seventh astral centres (which are between the eyebrows and on top of the head) usually converge on the pituitary body, when the etheric centre is aroused, and then vivify it and act through it. But there is a certain type of people (who are being addressed in our text) in whom the seventh astral chakra vivifies the pineal gland instead of the pituitary body, and it in that case forms a line of communication directly with the lower mental plane, without apparently passing through the astral plane in the ordinary way. Through that channel come for them the communications from within, while for the other type of people they come through the pituitary body.

When kundalinī awakens of itself, which it rarely does, or is accidentally aroused, it usually tries to pass up the interior of the spine, instead of following the spiral course in which the occultist is trained to guide it. In this case it will probably rush out through the head, and the man will suffer from nothing worse than a temporary unconsciousness.

[1] Hindu works usually mention the chakra at the root of the genital organs as the second. We recognize the existence of such a centre, but we follow the ancient Egyptians in thinking it eminently undesirable that it should be stirred into activity.

The Hindu books hint at, rather than explain, what happens. They make no references to the chakras on the surface of the etheric double, but speak of their roots, which are in the spine. In the spine, running from its base to the top is what is called Merudanda, the rod of Meru, the central axis of creation. In that rod is the channel called sushumnā, and in that again is the channel called chitrinī, which is "as fine as a spider's thread". Upon that are threaded the chakras, like the knots on a bamboo rod. The lowest of the chakras, called mūlādhāra, lies at the base of the spine, and in it kundalinī sleeps, closing the mouth of the merudanda.

The aim of the aspirant is to raise kundalinī through all the chakras till she reaches that which is between the eyebrows. Then the candidate will find that he, as it were, remains behind, while she leaps forward into the sahasrāra, the great "thousand-petalled" lotus at the top of the head. If he goes with her, it will take him out of the body and put a stop for the time being to his practice of meditation in the body. She rises up chitrinī little by little as the candidate uses his will in meditation. In one practice he may not get very far, but in the next he will go a little further, and so on. When she comes to one of the chakras or lotuses she pierces it and the flower, which was turned downwards, now turns upwards. The candidate meditates upon her in some form, and upon her associates, seated in that lotus. An elaborate dhyāna or meditation, full of rich symbology, is prescribed for each lotus. When the meditation is over, the candidate leads kundalinī back again by the same path into the mūlādhāra; but in some schools she is brought back only as far as the heart chakra, and there she enters what is called her chamber.

Kundalinī can be awakened by various methods, but it should be done only under the direction of a guru or competent teacher, the Master who is responsible to the Brotherhood for the training of the candidate. He is not likely to conduct this awakening until the first three fetters on the Path have been destroyed by the candidate's own power, so that he is no longer in serious danger of being stirred by sensuous or material things. Then his "heaven-born", closely united or harmonized with the higher manas, can remain master of the triple house of personality, and when the energy of kundalinī is set free in the body it will be likely to run in pure channels of service to the higher self. Hence the awakening of kundalinī will take place usually somewhere near the Third Initiation, or, in the present kali yuga, or dark age, it is said, even later. Even then it is awakened in various layers, so that* in the early stages it may give nothing more than a general sensitiveness to the higher planes.

Kundalinī is thought of as a goddess. She is what is called the shabdabrahman in the body. *Shabda* means sound. Sound is the creative force, as before described. Speech is considered to be the most outward form of it. It is an expression of thought, which in its true active form is kriyāshakti. Certain letters of the alphabet, which are the foundation of human speech, are said to reside in each of the chakras, and the power of those letters (their portion of the creative word) is awakened when kundalinī enters them after her union with Ṣhiva in the highest centre, causing them to shine brilliantly with her light. The creative speech of Brahmā, the third Logos, has four forms or stages; hence He is called the four-faced one. When kundalinī represents him in the body she also exhibits those four forms, as she rises through the chakras.

Kundalinī is called the world's mother because the outward action of the powers of consciousness is always regarded as feminine. Thus will, wisdom and activity are feminine, being shaktis or powers, outward turned aspects of the divine. She is the representative of all these, as they were expressed in the creation of the world, in the activity of Brahmā, the Third Logos. It has also been said that she is the world's mother because it is through her that the various planes are brought into conscious existence for the occultist.

* The following foot-note by Madame Blavatsky will also throw light on the foregoing explanations.

> The *inner* chamber of the heart, called in Sanskrit, Brahma-pura. The "fiery power" is Kundalini.
>
> The "power" and the "world-mother" are names given to Kundalini—one of the mystic *Yogi powers. It* is Buddhi considered as an active instead of a passive *principle (which it is generally, when regarded only as*

the vehicle, or casket, of the supreme spirit, Atma). It is an electro-spiritual force, a creative power which when aroused into action can as easily kill as it can create.

It is by no means certain what Madame Blavatsky meant by saying that kundalinī is active buddhi, but several speculations may be offered:

In normal men buddhi is not positively active in the outer life, but when the first three fetters have been cast off, the personality is so purified that the astral body will no longer be active merely on its own account, but will faithfully respond to buddhi, now active. At or near this stage kundalinī is often aroused, as we have seen, and when the faculties of the astral body are then laid open to the candidate while in his physical body it is an astral body reflecting buddhi, which now becomes a veritable fire of love in the man's life. That clairvoyance and other psychic powers need not be awakened in the physical brain even at this advanced stage of human progress, is also indicated by Dr. Besant, in her *Initiation, the Perfecting of Man*. She there says, that before a man can come to the Third Initiation he must learn to bring the spirit of intuition (buddhi) down to his physical consciousness, so that it may abide on him and guide him. Then she adds: "This process is usually called 'the development of psychic faculties,' and it is so, in the true meaning of the word 'psychic'. But it does not mean the development of clairvoyance and clairaudience, which depend on a different process."[1]

The entire higher triad (ātma-buddhi-manas) is but the central member or the buddhi of the still more inclusive triad of Monad, ego and personality. That larger buddhi is triple (will, wisdom and activity), and now its third aspect (activity, kriyāshakti) comes into operation in the body, to awaken its organs and liberate its latent powers.

'Tis only then thou canst become a "walker of the sky," who treads the winds above the waves, whose step touches not the waters.

[1] *Op. cit.*, p. 82.

On this, Madame Blavatsky says:

> Kechara, "sky-walker" or "goer". As explained in the 6th Adhyaya of that king of mystic works, the *Jnaneshvari*—the body of the Yogi becomes as one formed of the wind; as "a cloud from which limbs have sprouted out," after which—"he [the Yogi] beholds the things beyond the seas and stars; he hears the language of the Devas and comprehends it, and perceives what is passing in the mind of the ant."

The term "walker of the sky" has various grades of meaning. In Indian story it is, for example, applied to the great Rishi Nārada, as an emissary of the Logos, who could travel through the pure ākāsha from globe to globe. On the lower planes the astral body or the māyāvi-rupa may be taken as an illustration, as they can be used to travel in what is the air or sky to ordinary people.

In the astral world the ordinary man is a kind of cloud, a being full of kāma, that is, desire and emotion, but not by any means a definite entity such as he is on the physical plane. But when he masters his kāma, and gives it definiteness, the astral body is organized as a vehicle; it is no longer kāma but kāma-rupa. Still further, about the time when the first three fetters are dispensed with, the māyāvi-rupa is formed, and that enables the man to operate with his mental body in the astral as well as the lower mental plane. This may be taken as one interpretation of the statement that his step "touches not the waters", which are a symbol for the astral plane.

CHAPTER XXXVIII

THE SEVEN SOUNDS

Before thou sett'st thy foot upon the ladder's upper rung, the ladder of the mystic sounds, thou hast to hear the voice of thy inner God in seven manners.

C.W.L.—It has already been mentioned that *The Voice of the Silence* is intended to guide the candidate as far as the Fourth Initiation. At that point his consciousness is raised to the seventh principle and begins to function in the ātmic or nirvānic plane. The man is then ready to commence treading what is here called the ladder's upper rung, to go through the course of training which prepares for the Fifth Initiation, that of the Asekha Adept. The Path has two equal divisions, which may be called the ladder's lower and upper rungs.

It is said that the Initiate on the ladder's lower rung must hear the voice of his inner God in seven manners. That inner God at his present stage is the higher self, the buddhi, the second principle. In his meditation the aspirant may or may not hear a series of seven sounds, marking his attainment of the seven sub-planes of the buddhic plane; that depends upon his psychic temperament But what he *must* do, in all cases, is to bring the influence of buddhi down into his life on each of the lower planes, so that the activity of all his principles will be governed by it, and thus his inner God will be ever-present in his life.

The latter stage is called the ladder of the mystic sounds; this is perhaps because they are the sounds of the voice of the silence, hidden in the ātma or Self. One must not push too far the exact interpretation of any English word in our text, as it is only a translation; though every Sanskrit and Pāli word in it is rich with technical significance. Still, the word mystic, coming from a root that means to close the eyes, indicates here certain sounds which do not mingle in the outward life at all, but give direction as from above, in the *ex cathedra* manner of pure conscience. It is implied that the sounds about to be mentioned are more accessible, are not "mystic" at all events to the candidate at the stage under consideration. True conscience does not tell you *what* to do, as is commonly supposed, but it *commands* you to follow that which you already really know to be best, when your mind is trying to invent some excuse to do otherwise. It speaks with the authority of the spiritual will, determining our path in life. It is not the ātmā, but the buddhi, the second principle, that gives intuitive knowledge as to right and wrong. Manas gives inspiration, buddhi intuition as to right and wrong, ātmā the directing conscience.

The first is like the nightingale's sweet voice chanting a song of parting to its mate.

The second comes as the sound of a silver cymbal of the Dhyanis, awakening the twinkling stars.

The next is as the plaint melodious of the ocean-sprite imprisoned in its shell.

And this is followed by the chant of the vina.

The fifth like the sound of bamboo-flute shrills in thine ear.

It changes next into a trumpet-blast.

The last vibrates like the dull rumbling of a thunder-cloud.

The seventh swallows all the other sounds. They die, and then are heard no more.

The series of seven sounds mentioned here has caused much puzzlement among those who meditate upon this little book. We must notice first of all the character of the sounds; then we shall see that there are several interpretations of them. They are increasing in materiality and losing in penetrating quality in the order here given. One may notice, for example, the difference between the vīnā and an Indian trumpet of the old-fashioned kind. It is nearly always a surprise to the European, when he first hears the wonderfully delicate music of the vīnā, perhaps in a large and crowded hall, how, without any exhibition of force, it reaches every corner, and how it gives the impression of sound half-removed from our material planes.

The highest sound in the series is likened to a certain chant of the nightingale. It is said that there are occasions when the voice of this bird rises higher and higher in pitch until it is beyond the range of human hearing, although one may still see the throat of the warbler trembling with song. That such high sounds exist is well known to students of science. The note of a siren, for example, can be raised by increased pressure of air or steam, until one after another of those who are listening declare that they can no longer hear it. There is a certain kind of whistle with which German police dogs can be called. When one blows upon this instrument, which looks like an ordinary whistle, no man can hear the slightest sound, but the dog, in another room or some distance away, will instantly prick up its ears, and come leaping and bounding to the exact spot where what is presumably to it the sound originated.

The interpretations of the sounds fall into two groups. The first mentioned in the list may represent the last heard by the candidate. The sounds are enumerated downwards in the order of their creation, after the Oriental manner, so that the first sound in creation is the seventh when the aspirant is approaching the Lord of that creation. So, first comes the dull rumbling of a thunder-cloud, a sound representing or correlated to the physical principle in man, in the middle is the vīnā, representing the antahkarana (according to Madame Blavatsky's classification), and lastly there is the nightingale's melody, associated with ātmā, the silence. That well typifies the seventh, the soundless sound, into which all the others have to be raised, until they die away and are heard no more. The candidate must learn to hear God in the dull rumbling sound of the physical plane, then in the trumpet-blast of the astral, then in the sound of the lower mental that is likened to the music of a bamboo-flute, and so on right up to the world of his highest principle.

The same sounds may be taken in another way as typical of the *intensity* with which the aspirant hears the voice of the higher self. It is one voice, but is heard in seven *manners*. At first it is delicate and sweet, like the nightingale's song, and it often disappears into silence; next it becomes stronger, like "the silver cymbal of the Dhyānis". Louder and louder it becomes, until at last it is constantly heard, as filling all the air, like the dull rumbling of a thunder-cloud. In the early stages of our progress the voice of the higher Self may seem thin and faint, but later it will have for us all the reality of thunder.

Again, in the text the description of these sounds follows upon the mention of kundalinī, which is carried through the chakras. That force awakens in seven layers, or degrees, and so gives the psychic results already mentioned in increasing power. The voice that is heard when kundalinī rises to the place between the eyes will therefore be heard with seven degrees of intensity, typified by the seven sounds here mentioned.

Once more, it is natural that in the densest plane the candidate should hear the inner voice but faintly, like the nightingale's voice. When he rises to the next plane, where the covering of the inner Self is not so dense, its voice will be more easily heard; until finally, when he reaches the highest principle it will be like the rumbling of a thunder-cloud. It is only the illusion of the lower planes that causes us to ascribe delicacy to the higher things. Ultimately we shall find that they have the full body and reality of thunder.

These interpretations are not mutually exclusive. All the experiences which they suggest are possible for the candidate, at the same time.

I remember that on one occasion a question about these sounds was asked in one of our talks on the roof at Adyar. The President and I respectively answered as follows:

A.B.—In meditation, one of the sounds that you begin to hear (for instance, one thing that I heard quite distinctly) was a sound which was like the beating of a tom-tom in an Indian village. I described that to H.P.B., who said: "That is very good, go on." Next I heard some strains of beautiful music, and then something like silver chimes. Another sound was like the ringing of a temple bell, such as you hear in Benares. I never found out that these sounds meant anything more than that I was becoming able to hear in the astral world.

In India there is a school formed by a man of whom the Master M. spoke highly. The people who belong to that, after a certain amount of practice, hear sounds quite clearly in the brain, but I have never found that any of them got further on that account. Many people come to me in the North, asking what the sounds mean. I reply: "I think it is nothing more than that you are becoming clairaudient."

These seven sounds mentioned by H.P.B. I have never been able to sort out. They may mean that you have to wake your consciousness in plane after plane, and that each is meant to symbolize the note of a particular plane, just as down here *Fa* is the combination of the countless sounds in the physical plane blended together. But that does not really explain matters.

C.W.L.—I cannot make them exactly correspond with the planes; they may possibly be sub-planes They may also be intended to symbolize the sounds which accompany the awakening of the seven centres by the Kundalini, for sound is one of the expressions that take place in that particular case. I have never felt at all certain of what she meant. One would be inclined to say that the silver cymbal in different tones would do for all. The thunder certainly does not seem to fit in very well.

A.B.—Of course there are a certain number of sounds in the head which belong entirely to the vascular system. If a person hears such sounds very strongly it means that he is getting into a dangerous state of anæmia

The sounds are not progressive. H.P.B. put things very often in a circle, she sometimes begins with number four and then works round on the two sides. It may also be that she gives these sounds in no sort of order. You might possibly begin with the thunder, then the trumpet blast, and next the ocean sprite, then you might come to the cymbal for the fourth, the flute for the fifth and the vinâ, which is a more delicate sound, for the sixth, and then the nightingale for the seventh, the top.

C.W.L.—If we are allowed to turn them round like that, they will begin to mean something definite.

A.B.—H.P.B., when consulted astrally said: "What fools you all were to take them in that way: you might have arranged them before: thunder, trumpet, ocean-shell, cymbal, flute, vīnā, nightingale." She said that we were abominably literal.

C.W.L.—Similar lists of sounds are to be found in various Sanskrit works. We have taken the following example from the *Shiva Samhitā*:

> The first sound is like the hum of the honey-intoxicated bee, next that of a flute, then of a harp; after this, by the gradual practice of Yoga, the destroyer of the darkness of the world, he hears the sounds of ringing bells; then sounds like the roar of thunder. When one fixes his full attention on this sound, being free from fear, he gets absorption, O my beloved! When the mind of the Yogī is exceedingly engaged in this sound, he forgets all external things, and is absorbed in this sound.[1]

When the six are slain and at the Master's feet are laid, then is the pupil merged into the One, becomes that One and lives therein.

Madame Blavatsky speaks of the six as:

> The six principles; meaning when the lower personality is destroyed and the inner individuality is merged into and lost in the seventh or Spirit.

And of the One here spoken of she says:

> The disciple is one with Brahman or Atma.

When the six principles are "slain", in other words, when they no longer assert their independence, but have become entirely obedient to the will of the Self, the aspirant lives in

[1] *Op. cit.*, v, 27-8.

that One. The seventh voice of buddhi will carry him up into Ātmā. Madame Blavatsky applies the term Brahman to the human âtmâ by analogy. Brahman (neuter) is the One containing the Three; so does âtmâ contain buddhi and manas within itself, when the man has become an Arhat, and learned to live in the triple spirit.

> Before that path is entered, thou must destroy thy lunar body, cleanse thy mind-body, and make clean thy heart.

To the term "lunar body" Madame Blavatsky adds the note:

> The astral form produced by the kamic principle, the Kama Rupa, or body of desire.

On the term "mind-body" she comments:

> Manasa Rupa. The first refers to the astral or personal self; the second to the individuality, or the reincarnating Ego, whose consciousness on our plane, or the lower Manas, has to be paralysed.

Madame Blavatsky did not think in *planes* so completely as do most of the Theosophists of to-day. She had her eye more on the principles, and saw the matter of different levels taking form under their influence Here she speaks of "our plane", meaning the region of personal existence—physical, astral and lower mental. The "astral form" is by no means necessarily the astral body, but rather the personal form built up in the subjective regions of our personal life (the astral and lower mental planes) on account of our bodily form and the personal feelings and thoughts connected with it. In my little book *The Devachanic Plane* and in Dr. Besant's *Ancient Wisdom* an account is given of the four types of life in the heaven-world: (1) personal friendship, (2) personal devotion, (3) the true missionary spirit, and (4) human achievement. They are all emotive—though unselfish, they are not impersonal, but kâmic. They take their form from the character of the physical plane experience. But the pure lower manas would be the antahkarana—it would be the soul's mind, not the body's mind. It would have its activity stimulated *only* from above. It must now be cleansed from all the kāma, to become a pure channel for the soul.

Think of the condition of the astral body of an advanced person. It gives practically no direct response to impacts from outside. It is, by itself, dead to the world. It has no independent life of its own; it has been "slain". If some one went up to the average man and struck him, probably his astral body would burst instantly into flames of anger; that is its immediate response. Not so that of the advanced man. The impact in his case would go inwards through the astral to the buddhic vehicle. That would respond in its own way. Then *its* impact upon the astral would call forth the beautiful colours of the love emotions which are *its* correspondences in the astral body. Dr. Besant has often explained that the astral aura of an advanced man is colourless, or rather, slightly milky-white, when in repose, but that all the most lovely colours which the plane can exhibit flood through it in response to the great man's buddhic response to the world.

Eternal life's pure waters, clear and crystal, with the monsoon tempest's muddy torrents cannot mingle.

Heaven's dew-drop glittering in the morn's first sunbeam within the bosom of the lotus, when dropped on earth becomes a piece of clay; behold, the pearl is now a speck of mire.

Strive with thy thoughts unclean before they overpower thee. Use them as they will thee, for if thou sparest them and they take root and grow, know well, these thoughts will overpower and kill thee. Beware, disciple, suffer not e'en though it be their shadow to approach. For it will grow, increase in size and power, and then this thing of darkness will absorb thy being before thou hast well realized the black foul monster's presence.

There are some people in the world who imagine that it is possible to carry on the lower things and still make progress on the Path. Sometimes they actually think that by various forms of vicious excitement they can generate a great deal of energy which will help to carry them onward and upward. They are afraid of becoming colourless, should they repress the lower activities entirely. It has been said, of course, that the colourless person, the feeble good man, cannot make progress. "I would thou wert cold or hot," says the Spirit in *Revelation*, and "Because thou art lukewarm, and neither cold nor hot, I will spue thee out of my mouth."[1]

This very well represents the facts. The most promising persons, in order of preference, are (1) the vigorous good man, (2) the vigorous bad man, and (3) the ordinary good man. No man can be an effective criminal unless he has a strong development of some divine quality. His badness is the result of unbalance—such as great will-power and courage, or great intelligence, without love for his fellow-beings. Or great love and will-power, without intelligence, can make an equally dangerous and harmful man, for he may become a fanatical leader of forces of discontent and disruption. The mere good man, weak in all qualities—in will, intelligence and love—makes little progress, though it may be steady. Great men have great faults, but they may get rid of them quickly; little men have little faults, which often seem to last for ever.

There is in all this no recommendation to evil living. It indicates that mere repression of lower tendencies will not make for rapid progress, but that there must be positive and vigorous exertion in the expression of what is high and good While making that effort a person may possibly fall. The very will-power or knowledge or love that he has gained by his exertions will make the man's fall deep and terrible, should he become unbalanced. Thus the magnitude of a man's sin may be a sign of possible rapid future progress for him; but that progress will begin only when the man through kārmic suffering has realized his error and purged away the impurities incidental to

1 Revelation 3, 15-16.

his fall. Nothing much can be done, however, until that purification has taken place. Madame Blavatsky deals vigorously with this point in her *First Steps in Occultism*, as follows:

> There are those whose reasoning powers have been so distorted by foreign influences that they imagine that animal passions can be so sublimated and elevated that their fury, force and fire can, so to speak, be turned inwards; that they can be stored and shut up in one's breast, until their energy is, not expanded, but turned towards higher and more holy purposes: namely, until their collective and unexpanded strength enables their possessor to enter the true Sanctuary of the Soul and stand therein in the presence of the Master—the HIGHER SELF. For this purpose they will not struggle with their passions nor slay them. They will simply, by a strong effort of will, put down the fierce flames and keep them at bay within their natures allowing the fire to smoulder under a thin layer of ashes. They submit joyfully to the torture of the Spartan boy who allowed the fox to devour his entrails rather than part with it. Oh, poor, blind visionaries!

> As well hope that a band of drunken chimney-sweeps, hot and greasy from their work, may be shut up in a Sanctuary hung with pure white linen, and that instead of soiling and turning it by their presence into a heap of dirty shreds, they will become masters in and of the sacred recess, and finally emerge from it as immaculate as that recess. Why not imagine that a dozen skunks imprisoned in the pure atmosphere of a Dgon-pa (a monastery), can issue out of it impregnated with all the perfumes of the incenses used? Strange aberration of the human mind.

This portion of our text concludes with the following uncompromising passages:

> Before the mystic power can make of thee a God, Lanoo, thou must have gained the faculty to slay thy lunar form at will.

> The Self of matter and the Self of Spirit can never meet. One of the twain must disappear; there is no place for both.

> Ere thy Soul's mind can understand, the bud of personality must be crushed out, the worm of sense destroyed past resurrection.

The mystic power is once more kundalinī, the representative in the body of "the great pristine force which underlies all organic and inorganic matter". Madame Blavatsky's note on the subject is as follows:

> Kundalini, the serpent power or mystic fire; it is called the serpentine or the annular power on account of its spiral-like working or progress in the body of the ascetic developing the power in himself. It is an electric fiery occult or fohatic power, the great pristine force which underlies all organic and inorganic matter.

CHAPTER XXXIX

BECOME THE PATH

Thou canst not travel on the Path before thou hast become that Path itself.

C.W.L.—To this the following foot-note is appended:

This Path is mentioned in all the mystic works. As Krishna says in the *Jnaneshvari:* "When this path is beheld . . . whether one sets out to the bloom of the east, or to the chambers of the west, *without moving*, O holder of the bow, *is the travelling in this road.* In this path, to whatever place one would go, that place *one's own self becomes.*" "Thou *art the path,*" is said to the Adept Guru, and by the latter to the disciple, after Initiation. "I am the way and the path," says another Master.

It has already been explained (in the commentary on *At the Feet of the Master*) that the thoughts and feelings which are at first difficult to grasp and maintain become quite easy in the course of time. When the aspirant has so trained and developed himself that the buddhic outlook and response to life become perfectly natural and spontaneous to him, we may say he has become the Path itself. Sometimes such a consequence of continued effort and practice is called "second nature". That expression, however, gives one something of a feeling that the new qualities have been put on, and afterwards become habitual. That is unfortunate. It is our original and best nature, our higher. nature, that shows itself in the higher life; it seems to be something new to us only because it has heretofore been obscured by our material integuments and the pressure of circumstances in the worlds of our personal being.

An interesting metaphysical truth is indicated in the foot-note. Our evolution is not a transit, nor even a growth. It is not a process of going somewhere, nor an increase of size. It is an unfoldment of the powers potential in our lives. As already stated, in the planes of the ego materiality takes second place, the powers of consciousness—will, wisdom and activity, (or will, love and thought)—dominate almost completely the matter of the planes. Therefore space is not the jailor which it is down here, and consciousness need not travel through it in order to appear in another place. The following conversation between a Guru and his pupil has been related to illustrate this point. The Guru told the pupil to walk across the room, and then asked:

"What were you doing? Were you moving?"

After meditating upon the matter, the disciple gave the following answer, which was declared to be correct:

"No, *I* was not moving. I was watching the body move. I was thinking, feeling and willing; the body alone was moving."[1]

This fact is true for all of us; we know of the body's motion merely on account of observing it by means of the senses, just as we do that of any other object. The sensation of rushing along in an open motor-car, for example, resolves itself, when one shuts one's eyes, into an actual feeling of air rushing by, and a sense of power which, acting through the imagination, exhilarates the body. The same experience could be reproduced by suitable apparatus, composed of wind and motion machines, without any transportation of the body. Again, most people who have travelled at night in Pullman berths have had the experience of waking and wondering whether they were going head first or feet first, or even whether

[1] See *The Seven Rays*, p. 13.

the train was moving or not, and they have usually settled the question by slipping up the blind and inferring their direction from an observation of passing lights and shadows.

The fact that, in order to go from one place to another, travelling is not necessary for the ego, is shown also in the way in which it can simultaneously appear in the devachanic images of a number of people in the lower mental plane in different parts of the world.

Though, at the stage of development presupposed in this teaching, the candidate is working at the perfection of his personality, at the same time his inner work is particularly concerned with the development of buddhi, the spiritual soul. To put it in other words, he is climbing through the buddhic plane. Hence his becoming the Path is shown in a great development of sympathy and love for others, as indicated in the following verses:

> Let thy Soul lend its ear to every cry of pain like as the lotus bares its heart to drink the morning sun.
>
> Let not the fierce sun dry one tear of pain before thyself hast wiped it from the sufferer's eye.
>
> But let each burning human tear drop on thy heart and there remain; nor ever brush it off until the pain that caused it is removed.
>
> These tears, O thou of heart most merciful, these are the streams that irrigate the fields of charity immortal. 'Tis on such soil that grows the midnight blossom of Buddha, more difficult to find, more rare to view, than is the flower of the Vogay tree. It is the seed of freedom from rebirth. It isolates the Arhat both from strife and lust, it leads him through the fields of being unto the peace and bliss known only in the land of silence and non-being.

When Christ said, "I am the way, and the truth, and the life: no man cometh unto the Father, but by me,"[1] He declared a mystic truth, for the Christ is one with the buddhic aspect of the world-consciousness. There is only one consciousness; on full recognition of this fact the Initiate can become an Arhat—but unless he goes through that Christ principle he cannot reach the Father, the âtmâ, above. That truth, explained with wonderful inspiration and clarity in Dr. Annie Besant's *Esoteric Christianity*, is, however, only one aspect of the matter, for the Christ incarnate embodied the same principle in His outward life in Palestine, which has moved millions of men—because He did not shrink from pain. Most men try to escape pain as much as possible, but Christ accepted His own and added to it that of all other people as well. Men who follow the buddhic path instinctively say, when trouble comes to them: "Many are suffering; why should I desire to be exempt?" More than that, in the fullness of their sympathy, they feel that other suffering to the breaking point, before they reach the serenity of Arhatship, the illumination that puts death under them, that makes them glow with the joy of liberty, whatever pain may betide. Such liberty would lead to careless rest, could men have it before experiencing the suffering of the Christ, in which the pain of the cross is as nothing beside that of His compassionate response to the cry of a world in pain. Then comes the point at which the man says: "What does it matter whether I suffer or not?" His mind is so busy with service that he can scarcely attend to himself.

Such an expression as "the peace and bliss known only in the land of silence and non-being" can be understood only by those who are willing to think of metaphysical realities. Most of such Oriental expressions as this are based on the fundamental idea that the universal God expresses himself as sat, chit and ânanda, that is, as being, consciousness and bliss.

Being is well understood; people see it all around them; consciousness they also know by experience; but happiness they *seek*. All seek themselves. Happiness is not something that we shall gain, obtain and possess; it is our true state of Self. But beyond both matter and consciousness is the real inner life,

[1] *S. John*, 14, 6.

which is silence and non-being from the standpoint of the external, and yet is the bliss of true being.

> Kill out desire; but if thou killest it, take heed lest from the dead it should again arise.
>
> Kill love of life: but if thou slayest Tanha, let this not be for thirst of life eternal, but to replace the fleeting by the everlasting.
>
> Desire nothing. Chafe not at Karma, nor at nature's changeless laws. But struggle only with the personal, the transitory, the evanescent and the perishable.

Common desire is the love of external things for the sake of astral or sensuous enjoyment. We have already seen that the disciple must not seek the satisfaction of such desires, but must give up all the energy of his personality—physical, emotional, and mental—to the work of spiritual evolution and the service of the inner life in himself and other men.

Tanhâ is the root of these desires, because it is the thirst for sentient life. The ego on its own plane is far from being fully conscious, but what consciousness it has gives it a feeling of great pleasure, and arouses a kind of hunger for a fuller realization of life. It is that which is behind the world's great clamour for a fuller life. As before explained, the forces of the higher mental plane pass through the causal body for the most part without affecting it in the case of ordinary persons, as the ego is not yet developed and trained so as to respond to more than a few of the vibrations of its own level. There are no coarse vibrations on that plane, such as it can respond to in its younger days, so it descends to the lower planes for the sake of feeling more fully alive. For a long time therefore its consciousness is most vivid when things of the physical plane are presented to it, but later, when the astral nature is awakened, the pleasures of that plane prove to be still more intense.

It is not possible in the physical body to realize how keen are the delights of the astral life. So much is that the case that they often turn aside and delay persons who have overcome the same sort of pleasure of the physical plane. Yet that danger is not great for those who in physical life are definitely seeking the things of the Path, if they are persons of advanced type, as they are in a position to realize still higher delights, which have a far greater attraction. The same thing is true of each plane in turn.

Still, the disciple must be on guard not to give up the lower pleasures merely for the sake of relatively higher ones, but always to keep his eye upon his ideal goal, beyond *all* transitory pleasures. He must not thirst to enjoy the age-long pleasures of the heaven-world, but must give up *all* that is transitory and personal. While, on the one hand, he will not seek to obtain the objects of desire, on the other he will not shrink from the lessons that karma places before him; he will not wish that his field of experience should be other than it is. He knows that it is because nature's laws are unchanging that he can use experience for growth. Were it not for the orderly nature of the world, it would be impossible for the intellect to grow or for man to use his powers at all. So he has no resentment against karma, which is the embodiment of the Law.

> Help nature and work on with her; and nature will regard thee as one of her creators and make obeisance.
>
> And she will open wide before thee the portals of her secret chambers, lay bare before thy gaze the treasures hidden in the very depths of her pure virgin bosom. Unsullied by the hand of matter, she shows her treasures only to the eye of Spirit—the eye which never closes, the eye for which there is no veil in all her kingdoms.
>
> Then will she show thee the means and way, the first gate and the second, the third, up to the very seventh. And then, the goal; beyond which lie, bathed

in the sunlight of the Spirit. glories untold. unseen by any save the eye of the Soul.

All students of the material sciences are familiar with the fact that " nature is conquered by obedience ". All the forces that we employ in modern life, such as the pressure of steam or electricity, are examples of our working with nature. It is perhaps rather unsympathetic to use the word conquered, when the fact is that all our power in the world is the result of harmony between man and nature. The man in a boat who sets his sail so that he may go against the wind is not overcoming the wind, but is harmonizing his affairs with its laws. By working with the laws man gains in power, not by fighting against them.

The occultist knows that the same principle is true on every plane, and not only with regard to the matter of each world but also to the forms of life that dwell there, high or low in the scale of evolution. Therefore the knowledge of nature's mechanical laws, which has led to so much power and wealth for mankind, represents only one aspect of the harmony that should subsist between the two. A feeling of friendly sympathy towards the animal, the plants, and even the minerals, and towards the nature spirits and the devas, is equally important, if not more so, for the progress of man. Nature is composed of life as well as matter, and it is through sympathetic feeling that that life becomes known, and harmonized with human life. To look upon the world as a place full of forbidding entities is the unfortunate custom of our age, but the man who faces life with a feeling of kindliness to all living things will not only see and learn more than others, but will have a smoother passage on life's sea. There is a tradition in India of the "lucky hand" of certain persons who have this sympathy, and for whom plants will grow well when for others they fail. It has also been explained many times by authorities in occult science that because of his love for all beings the true yogi or sannyāsi may wander among the mountains and in the jungle quite without danger from wild animals or reptiles.

In ordinary human life this sympathy works in many ways. The modern business man knows that the first requisite for his success is to establish friendliness with those with whom he wants to deal. The same quality is necessary for teaching children, who often regard grown-up people as strange, arbitrary beings, not at all of their own class, but somewhat foreign, as an earth man might regard one of Mr. Wells' fanciful men from Mars. But when sympathy is established, all that strangeness goes, and real education becomes possible.

The nature spirits are in the same position as the children, except that they are not dependent upon us and can easily avoid our vicinity, as the more pleasing kinds of them usually do when modern civilized man arrives, with his noisy, clumsy and cruel ways, and his unclean, repellant aura and cloud of thought-forms. It is a fact that were men sympathetic with the other kingdoms, did they plant forests and not only destroy them, and did they feel kindly towards nature in general, we should enjoy more equable climate and more successful cultivation. It must, of course, be said that the modern movement in favour of gardens round houses, and trees and flowers even in the roads of our cities, all tends in the right direction, and that in special ways of cultivation of the earth and of particular flowers and fruits and grains and trees, and even animals, men have done much to help the work of the nature-spirits. But with more sympathy still better results would have accrued.

This sympathy has occasionally been shown, especially by the poets. Dr. Rabindranath Tagore's essays and poems exhibit it in a very high degree; in fact, the spread of this quality may be regarded almost as his special contribution to modern civilization. Another well-known instance is that of the philosopher Emerson who, on returning from his winter lecture tours to his home at Concord, used to shake hands with the lower branches of his trees. He declared that he could feel that the trees were glad at his return, and no doubt that quality of sympathy was a great aid to his inspiration.

Men who live in their gardens, like Luther Burbank of California, often say that they are distinctly conscious of the feeling that comes to them from certain plants, bushes and trees. Men in Canada, whose duty calls them to live constantly in the forests—to inspect them, mark trees and do other work—have told me that they feel a life in the woods distinct from that elsewhere, that they know that there are some places and trees which like men, and others which do not.

Such sympathy is perfectly natural. If you feel special love and admiration for a certain human being, there is a tendency on his part to become interested in you and to return the affection. A stage lower, if you are affectionate with an animal it becomes strongly attached to you. Still lower, in the vegetable and mineral kingdoms, the same rule obtains, though its effects are less obvious. From this arises the tradition that flowers and plants will grow better for some persons than for others, other things being equal. It is personal magnetism that calls it out; and that is what at a higher level we call affection.

There is no need to say anything here about the seven gates mentioned in this passage, for the whole of the third Fragment of this book is taken up with the seven portals, and there we shall study them in detail.

CHAPTER XL

THE ONE ROAD

There is but one road to the Path; at its very end alone the Voice of the Silence can be heard. The ladder by which the candidate ascends is formed of rungs of suffering and pain; these can be silenced only by the voice of virtue. Woe then to thee, disciple, if there is one single vice thou hast not left behind; for then the ladder will give way and overthrow thee; its foot rests in the deep mire of thy sins and failings, and ere thou canst attempt to cross this wide abyss of matter thou hast to lave thy feet in waters of renunciation. Beware lest thou should'st set a foot still soiled upon the ladder's lowest rung. Woe unto him who dares pollute one rung with miry feet. The foul and viscous mud will dry, become tenacious, then glue his feet unto the spot; and like a bird caught in the wily fowler's lime, he will be stayed from further progress. His vices will take shape and drag him down. His sins will raise their voices, like as the jackal's laugh and sob after the sun goes down; his thoughts become an army, and bear him off a captive slave.

C.W.L.—We have seen, in *The Masters and the Path*, that there are four ways of coming to the beginning of the probationary path: by contact with those who are already on the Path; by deep thought; by hearing and reading the sacred word, and by the practice of virtue.[1] Then, on the probationary path, there are four qualifications to be attained, of which the last is given in *At the Feet of the Master* as Love, and it is said that without this the other qualifications are in vain.[2]

This, then, is the one road to the path proper—the way of *love*, of unselfishness in thought, word and deed.

All the old selfish habits of body and mind must be overcome by positive virtue. The word virtue as used here cannot mean mere passive goodness or absence of wrong-doing; it must be taken in its old meaning of strength. Virtues are forms of strength of the soul. When the soul dominates the personal life it will be seen to be full of such virtue. In the meantime a great battle is necessary. In very many cases the candidate for the Path must bring forth all his determination to stamp out completely any fault of selfishness that he may find in himself in the course of his daily self-examination. This can best be done by picturing a scene in which the fault has been exhibited, and then reconstructing it in the imagination, so that in it the corresponding virtue is shown; then one may dwell on that for a little while, and resolve that henceforth, under such circumstances, the virtue, not the fault, will be expressed.

It is sometimes very hard to overcome habitual faults; hence the frequent mention of suffering and pain. It gives great pain, for example, to the drunkard, to resist "just one more, one last drink". But if he holds firm to his resolves never to take strong drink again, not even once, in time the suffering will disappear, and he will know a higher kind of pleasure than that which he obtained from the stimulus of drink. It is exactly the same with impure or selfish emotions and thoughts; many a man fails because he dwells upon an unworthy thought "just once more". It is just that one that he must give up, and refuse to harbour in his mind. To give up their faults people have sometimes to suffer great wounds to their pride. In all these cases humility is a great help, because it makes men willing to change themselves.

[1] *Op. cit.*, Ch. vi.

[2] *Ante*, p. 288.

Still, there are many whose lives have already been considerably purified, who feel little or nothing of this pain. It has, indeed, been suggested that in this passage Āryasanga has exaggerated the suffering. That is not so, but he has expressed it in extreme terms, so that no one will meet with suffering on the Path, expecting the reverse, and all will be ready to pay toll to the past, to face what suffering there is, and to bring it to an end for ever by the practice of virtue. We may remember here the encouraging words of the *Gītā*: " Even if thou art the most sinful of all sinners, yet shalt thou cross over all sin by the raft of wisdom. As the burning fire reduces fuel to ashes, O Arjuna, so doth the fire of wisdom reduce all karmas to ashes."[1] And again: " Never doth any who worketh righteousness, O beloved, tread the path of woe."[2]

The necessity of getting rid of vices at the very beginning has been emphasized in all yoga systems, as mentioned before.[3] Only when the virtues were firmly established in his character could the student be allowed to pass on to the later steps of the Path, including practices of posture, breathing, control of the senses and meditation. The reason for this demand is that as the pupil advances on the Path the forces of his will and thought become much more powerful than ever before, and there will come times when the ego pours his energy down into the body. If there be still remnants of any vice in the body that energy will give it new strength, so that the fall of the aspirant will be far greater than anything that is possible for one not so far advanced. Powers are powers, for good or ill, so the candidate should purify himself before seeking them, lest he injure others and himself. There is one place on the Path, just after the Second Initiation, where the danger is greatest of all, especially from the vice of pride, as has been explained at length in *The Masters and the Path*.[4]

Kill thy desires, Lanoo, make thy vices impotent, ere the first step is taken on the solemn journey.

[1] *Op. cit.*, IV, 36-37.
[2] *Ibid.*, VI, 40.
[3] *Ante*, p. 391.
[4] *Op. cit.*, Ch. xi.

Strangle thy sins, and make them dumb for ever, before thou dost lift one foot to mount the ladder.

Silence thy thoughts and fix thy whole attention on thy Master, whom yet thou dost not see, but whom thou feelest.

Merge into one sense thy senses, if thou would'st be secure against the foe. 'Tis by that sense alone which lies concealed within the hollow of thy brain, that the steep path which leadeth to thy Master may be disclosed before thy soul's dim eyes.

Āryasanga's repetition of the injunction to get rid of desires and vices shows the importance which he attached to this part of the work. Not only are any such defects enormously intensified as the powers of the candidate develop, but also his responsibility increases, and he becomes capable of making far more karma than before.

The sixth sense, the mind, has its physical organ in the brain. People do not usually employ this when faced by the various objects and experiences of life. They live too much in their astral bodies. They "like" certain things, and "dislike" others, quite without reason, quite without considering what they are, and which are really good and bad, or useful and useless. That will not do, of course, for anyone who wants to tread the occult path. He must consider all things dispassionately, and revalue them according to their usefulness to the soul.

In the brain there are also the organs by means of which direct perception of things beyond the reach of the physical senses may be had. The pituitary body is a link between the physical body and the astral body, and so on. In the same hollow in the brain, but a little further back, lies the pineal gland, which is connected directly with the mental body, and serves to bring impressions down from the mental plane. Some people develop the pituitary body first, some the pineal gland—each must follow the method prescribed by his own guru.

> Long and weary is the way before thee, O disciple. One single thought about the past that thou hast left behind will drag thee down, and thou wilt have to start the climb anew.
>
> Kill in thyself all memory of past experience. Look not behind or thou art lost.

Once more we find Āryasanga emphasizing the worst aspect of the matter, so that none shall find the path harder than he may have thought it to be before entering upon it. Relatively, that path is not long, when one considers that it is only the last fourteen lives, out of a series of many hundreds or even thousands, which are usually spent between the First and Fifth Initiations. Further, in many cases the work of those fourteen lives is done in but a few, taken consecutively, without devachānic interludes—which makes the time short indeed.

It is true that "the road winds uphill all the way", but it need not necessarily be weary. It is when one thinks only of the goal that the journey is weary. A student entering College will find his three or four years there intensely weary if he is thinking only of getting his degree and going out into the world with it, and is not really interested in his studies. But if he has planned out his work, which will bring him naturally to his degree if properly carried out, and if he is really interested in the subjects of his study, he may then forget all about the years that lie ahead, and may have a fascinating time. So also on the Path the work is full of interest for heart and mind, and he who finds it so will make it shorter in fact as well as in appearance than he who cares only for reaching a certain prescribed goal.

It is the same in meditation; some who practise it faithfully feel it to be a tedious thing, but do it all the same, for the sake of its results. Others find it full of interest, and therefore gain much more from it. Let the candidate not think of his own progress on the Path; as so often recommended, let him forget himself and work for the world, and his progress will take care of itself. Self-examination and self-training are necessary, but that is only like preparing and oiling machinery; it should not take much time, the work being the important thing.

It is true that sometimes people find it necessary to force themselves at first along certain lines of work and thought, or meditation, which they feel that they ought to take up. Very well, go on with the dreary task, if such it appears to be, and if the motive is pure, you will soon find that the dreariness departs, a new interest arises, and the work becomes full of delight.

The statement that one single thought about the past can drag the candidate right down to earth again should certainly give pause to anyone who proposes to enter the Path, and yet is unwilling to give up some pet vice, however trifling. It is not the act so much as the thought of it that drags one down. Madame Blavatsky says, in *The Secret Doctrine*:

> Purity of mind is of greater importance than purity of body ... An act may be performed to which little or no attention is paid, and it is of comparatively small importance. But if thought of, dwelt on in the mind, the effect is a thousand times greater. The thoughts must be kept pure.[1]

I recollect a story about Colonel Olcott which illustrates this point. A young man who much wanted to live the higher life came to him one day and asked him if he must give up smoking. The Colonel replied: "Well, if you can't you must, but if you can you needn't." Certainly strength of will and purity of thought are of paramount importance, and there is no progress without them, no matter how clean the body; and the Colonel emphasized the fact very successfully. But it might be added also that smoking is a dirty habit; it befouls the bodies, and often causes much annoyance and discomfort to others. The worst of its dirty selfishness physically is that the smoke is made damp with saliva and then sent off to enter other people's lungs. It is a horrible feature of modern life that we are often compelled to contact and breathe smoke which has been so treated.

As to the effect of a thought of a quality belonging to the past, Madame Blavatsky also says:

> The student must guard his thoughts. Five minutes' thought may undo the work of five years; and though the five years' work will be run through more rapidly the second time, yet time is lost.[2]

[1] *Op. cit.*, Vol. III, 570.
[2] *Ibid.*, p. 579.

A distinction must be made here between a thought which is merely a floating form which has entered the mind, and thought proper, which is a deliberate act. It is the latter that can do so much harm. An unworthy thought may drift into the mind, but if it is not dwelt upon, encouraged and strengthened, little harm is done.

That one who falls thus may quickly rise again is encouraging. That old Greek allegory in which every time that the hero falls to earth, worsted in the conflict, he gains new strength from it, applies to man. Better that he should win the battle once and for all without falling; but in any case he is destined to triumph ultimately. Much may be learned by the intelligent and willing pupil without bitter experience, just as one may learn that fire is hot without putting one's hand into it; but all that is necessary will be learnt sooner or later in one way or another.

> Do not believe that lust can ever be killed out if gratified or satiated, for this is an abomination inspired by Mara. It is by feeding vice that it expands and waxes strong, like to the worm that fattens on the blossom's heart.
>
> The rose must re-become the bud, born of its parent stem, before the parasite has eaten through its heart and drunk its life-sap.
>
> The golden tree puts forth its jewel-buds before its trunk is withered by the storm.
>
> The pupil must regain the child-state he has lost ere the first sound can fall upon his ear.

Sir Edwin Arnold speaks of Māra, as he is understood by the Buddhists, in vigorous and graphic terms, in connection with the temptation of Buddha just before His illumination:

> But he who is the Prince
> Of Darkness, Mâra—knowing this was Buddh
> When he should find the Truth and save the worlds—
> Gave unto all his evil powers command

Wherefore there trooped from every deepest pit
The fiends who war with Wisdom and the Light,
Arati, Trishnã, Rãga, and their crew
Of passions, horrors, ignorances, lusts,
The brood of gloom and dread; all hating Buddh,
Seeking to shake his mind.[1]

Still, Madame Blavatsky says: "But Mâra is also the unconscious quickener of the birth of the Spiritual." The resistance that Mâra opposes to the aspirant enables him to develop his strength. An athlete might move his arms up and down much easier without dumb-bells than with them, yet he would not develop the same strength so quickly, if at all. That even evil is made use of for good was once illustrated by the remark of a very spiritual man who took a high Initiation. For some time before it he had been terribly maligned, and the important work on which he had set his heart had been spoiled. One day someone offered him a word of sympathy, which was quite unnecessary, for he said: "The fact is, I owe a debt of gratitude to those people who tried to injure me, though I did not realize it at the time; for without their aid I should not yet have taken that Initiation." An ordinary man would have been full of anger or of depression, but in such a man as this Mâra calls out an equal strength only of loving sorrow or compassion. Thus may even the greatest enemy become our friend while we are in the way with him.

It is, of course, not the ignorance but the innocence of childhood that is requisite for real spiritual progress. Mere goodness is not progress; it is only preparatory purification. Progress is the development of the ego on *its own* planes, which, when shown in the personality, appears as strength of character—in will and love and thought. In the three stages of the relation of a pupil to his Master, it is the third and highest that contains the idea of childhood, for he is first a probationary pupil, then an accepted one, and thirdly a Son of the Master.

[1] *The Light of Asia*, Book the Sixth

CHAPTER XLI

THE LAST STEPS

The light from the one Master, the one unfading golden light of Spirit, shoots its effulgent beams on the disciple from the very first.

Its rays thread through the thick, dark clouds of matter.

Now here, now there, these rays illumine it, like sun-sparks light the earth through the thick foliage of the jungle growth. But, O disciple, unless the flesh is passive, head cool, the Soul as firm and pure as flaming diamond, the radiance will not reach the chamber, its sunlight will not warm the heart, nor will the mystic sounds of the akashic heights reach the ear, however eager, at the initial stage.

C.W L.—As the sun is always shining behind the clouds, so is the higher self constantly shedding its beams on the aspirant. The flashes of inspiration and intuition that come now and again into the darkness of our minds in what we call our best moments are derived from that high source. It is a wise policy to try to capture those best moments, to hold them in imagination, and to dwell upon them in meditation, and thus to bring the whole life into that diamond-like condition that is mentioned in the text.

With reference to the "mystic sounds of the ākāshic heights" Madame Blavatsky adds the following foot-note:

> The mystic sounds, or the melody, heard by the ascetic at the beginning of his cycle of meditation, called Anahatashabda by the Yogis. The Anahata is the fourth of the Chakras.

The fourth centre or chakra is that at the heart. When the consciousness is centred in the heart during meditation it is most susceptible to the influence of the spiritual soul or higher self. The heart is the centre in the body for the higher triad, ātma-buddhi-manas. The head is the seat of the psycho-intellectual man; it has its various functions in seven cavities, including the pituitary body and the pineal gland. He who in concentration can take his consciousness from the brain to the heart should be able to unite kāma-manas to the higher manas, through the lower manas, which, when pure and free from kāma, is the antahkarana. He will then be in a position to catch some of the promptings of the higher triad. That higher consciousness tries to guide him, through the conscience; he cannot guide it until he is one with buddhi-manas. The foregoing explanation is condensed from notes on some oral teachings of Madame Blavatsky, appended to the third volume of *The Secret Doctrine*.[1]

Indian tradition on the subject says that when kundalinī rises she dissolves the qualities of the various chakras through which she passes and carries their essence upwards. When she reaches the fourth, the heart chakra, the yogī hears the sound from above, called anāhata-shabda. *Shabda* is sound; *an-āhata* means "not beaten"; so it is that sound which is made without beating things together. The term is therefore symbolical of that which is above the planes of personality. The practitioner's touch with the higher triad begins at this point. Those who want to increase the contact between the higher and lower manas should not dwell in meditation on anything below it. The following meditation, translated from the *Gheranda Samhitā*, is one of those prescribed for the heart centre. It illustrates the way in which the

[1] *Op. cit.*, Vol. III, pp. 562-4.

yogi gradually withdraws his attention from his surroundings and concentrates it upon his Ideal.

Let him find in his heart a broad ocean of nectar
  Within it a beautiful island of gems,
Where the sands are bright golden and sprinkled with jewels,
  Fair trees line its shores with a myriad of blooms,
And within it rare bushes, trees, creepers and rushes,
  On all sides shed fragrance most sweet to the sense.

Who would taste of the sweetness of divine completeness
  Should picture therein a most wonderful tree,
On whose far-spreading branches grow fruit of all fancies—
  The four mighty Teachings that hold up the world,
There the fruit and the flowers know no death and no sorrows,
  While to them the bees hum and soft cuckoos sing.

Now, under the shadow of that peaceful arbour
  A temple of rubies most radiant is seen.
And he who shall seek there will find on a seat rare,
  His dearly Beloved, enshrinèd therein,
Let him dwell with his mind, as his Teacher defines,
  On that Divine Form, with His modes and His signs[1]

Unless thou hear'st, thou canst not see. Unless thou seest, thou canst not hear. To hear and see, this is the second stage.

We have already considered the significance of seeing and hearing[2]. Unless the candidate is responsive to the inner voice, that is, unless he understands spiritual laws, he will never see the outer things as they are. He must learn to look at the things of matter with the eyes of the spirit, as a Master once expressed it. When he sees the material or outward things in that way, he will more and more understand the inner voice. This is like the alternation which is necessary between meditation and experience. To go through life in a busy way, without stopping to meditate upon it, is to miss much of the significance of its events; one should spare a little time each day to let the

[1] See *Concentration*, Ch. x.

[2] *Ante*, p. 367.

inner light play upon them. On the other hand, to shut oneself in one's study and give one's whole time to thought would yield little profit; in that way a man would acquire endless misconceptions, for experience is required to correct and enlarge our meditation. It is the balanced interplay of the inner and the outer that the pupil must seek. He must aim to be harmonized—to use the expression repeated again and again in the *Gītā*.

The inner and outer worlds correspond perfectly to one another, point for point in God's system. Says Madame Blavatsky in *The Secret Doctrine*:

> In the realm of hidden Forces, an *audible* sound is but a subjective colour, and a perceptible colour, but an *inaudible* sound.[1]

Colour is spoken of here, not form; it makes the statement more accurate, for we really *see* only colours, not forms.

It is impossible to say with any certainty why this state of hearing and seeing harmonized together is called the second stage. We cannot tell what system of stages Āryasanga was expounding, for a veil is drawn over his instructions at this point. The line of stops marks a missing portion dealing with the third stage. When the teaching emerges again (after this hiatus) we find Āryasanga dealing with later stages exactly as the *Yoga Sūtras* give them, namely (5) pratyāhāra, entire control of the senses, (6) dhāranā, concentration, (7) dhyāna, meditation, and (8) samādhi, contemplation.

> When the disciple sees and hears, and when he smells and tastes, eyes closed, ears shut, with mouth and nostrils stopped; when the four senses blend and ready are to pass into the fifth, that of the inner touch—then into stage the fourth he hath passed on.

There are some yogis who do literally stop the mouth and nose when going into meditation or trance. The fingers are so placed as to keep the eyes, the nostrils and the mouth closed, and these men have also trained the tongue so that they can turn it

[1] *Op. cit.*, Vol. III, p. 508.

upwards and backwards into the cavity above the mouth, and thus prevent the inlet of air. This is called khecharī mudrā, as practised by certain hatha yogīs. It is not done by the rāja yogīs, and is not recommended here. There is a stage at which the pupil can close his eyes and reproduce within himself (or experience in the astro-mental region) the sensations of smell, taste, sight and touch. Now, in order to withdraw himself to a still higher state he must attend to the *inner* touch, which is hearing. By giving his attention to the sound within, and tracing it into its finer and finer recesses, he brings himself to the point where he may practise pratyāhāra, the restraint of *all* sensation, the inner as well as the outer, that of the hall of learning as well as that of the hall of ignorance. This practice is described in the next verse:

> And in the fifth, O slayer of thy thoughts, all these again have to be killed beyond re-animation.

The attention is quite commonly withdrawn to a large extent by most people when, for example, they are especially interested in a book; they do not then respond to the impressions made upon the senses by the various odours, sights and sounds surrounding them. To put oneself into that condition at will is pratyāhāra, and it is a preparation for really successful meditation. The killing beyond re-animation means nothing more than that the senses, like good dogs, will lie down when told to do so, and will not get up again until they are called. There is a foot-note at this point, as follows:

> This means that in the sixth stage of development, which, in the occult system, is Dharana, every sense as an individual faculty has to be "killed" (or paralysed) on this plane, passing into and merging with the seventh sense, the most spiritual.

Dhāranā is the sixth step of yoga, as given in the *Yoga Sutras*. It is that concentration of mind which we have already studied,[1] and it follows upon pratyāhāra. Since mind or chitta

[1] *Ante*, p. 352

is regarded as a sixth sense, when dhāranā is complete and that mind thereby ceases to function in relation to the things of the external world, intuition, here called the seventh sense, arises. Life teaches us in two ways, by tuition that the world gives us, and by intuition, the working of the inner self. As men proceed on their evolutionary pilgrimage, their intuition increases and they do not depend so much as before on the instruction that the world gives. This is only another way of saying that the man who uses his inner powers can learn much more from a little experience than other men can from a great deal. Because of the activity of his innate intelligence the developed man is able to see the great significance of even small things; but the undeveloped mind is full of curiosity. It is constantly eager for novelty, because, not being good at thinking, it soon exhausts the obvious significance of commonplace things. This mind is the one that craves miracles in connection with its religious experience, as it is blind to the countless miracles that surround it all the time.

> Withhold thy mind from all external objects, all external sights Withhold internal images, lest on thy Soul-light a dark shadow they should cast.

> Thou art now in Dharana, the sixth stage.

In the practice of concentration it is always necessary to consider both the external and the internal sources of interruption. One must prevent the mind from taking an interest in any external thing, for if this is not done, the slightest sound will awaken its curiosity and spoil the concentration. Also one must stop the mind from bringing up within itself images relating to the past or the future; during the practice one must be completely uninterested in what happened yesterday or what is likely to happen to-morrow. When this concentration has been successfully achieved, the next and seventh stage of practice begins, which is called dhyāna, that is, meditation.

> When thou hast passed into the seventh, O happy one, thou shalt perceive no more the sacred Three, for thou shalt have become that Three thyself. Thyself and

mind, like twins upon a line, the star which is thy goal burns overhead. The Three that dwell in glory and in bliss ineffable, now in the world of Maya have lost their names. They have become one star, the fire which is the Upadhi of the flame.

And this, O Yogi of success, is what men call Dhyana, the right precursor of Samadhi.

Passing from dhāranā to dhyāna, from concentration to meditation, the aspirant on this Path enters the buddhic consciousness. That is then "thyself". The mind here spoken of is the higher manas, for the lower manas has been silenced. The manasic principle has been raised into that of buddhi, so the two are like "twins upon a line", the two lower corners of a triangle, as is indicated by the following foot-note:

Every stage of development in Raja Yoga is symbolised by a geometrical figure. This one is the sacred triangle and precedes Dharana. The △ is the sign of the high chelas, while another kind of triangle is that of high Initiates. It is the symbol "I" discoursed upon by Buddha and used by him as a symbol of the embodied form of Tathagata when released from the three methods of the Prajna. Once the preliminary and lower stages passed, the disciple sees no more the △ but the—, the abbreviation of the—, the full septenary. Its true form is not given here, as it is almost sure to be pounced upon by some charlatans and desecrated in its use for fraudulent purposes.

The star that burns overhead is the ātmā. But it refers also, as Madame Blavatsky says in another foot-note, to the star of Initiation, which shines over the head of the Initiate. As the object to be attained is the Fourth Initiation, that of the

Arhat, it is the star of that Initiation, which leads to the ātmic or nirvānic plane, that is his goal.

At this stage, instead of looking upwards in thought, and regarding the higher triad (ātma-buddhi-manas) as above oneself, as was the case heretofore, one finds oneself to be in the buddhic state, manas being united with buddhi as manas-taijasī. The "meditation" of the Initiate at this stage will ultimately lead on to a further union of buddhi and ātmā. Upon the attainment of that union the higher triad will have become one star, described in a foot-note as "the basis, *Upādhi, of the ever unreachable flame, so long as the ascetic* is still in this life". The fuel is the personality; the fire is this triple spirit; the flame is the Monad. Even the Adept, while remaining in physical incarnation, does not enter fully into the state of the Monad. Says Madame Blavatsky:

> Dhyana is the *last* stage *before* the *final* on this earth unless one becomes a full Mahatma. As said already, *in this state the Raja Yogi is yet spiritually* conscious of self, and the working of his higher principles. *One step more,* and he will be on the plane beyond the seventh, the fourth according to some schools. These, *after* the practice of Pratyahara—a preliminary training, in order to control one's mind and thoughts—count Dharana, Dhyana and Samadhi, and embrace the three under the generic name of Sannyama. Samadhi is the state in which the ascetic loses the consciousness of every individuality, including his own. He becomes the All.

It is significant that the three should lose their *names*. They are not forms, for their region is that of consciousness. The lower planes of the personality are planes of form; then come the planes of name or "meaning", but the Monad is beyond name, beyond what men call consciousness.

The text goes on to indicate that, having attained to the *practice of* samādhi, the aspirant has now become an Arhat, and has reached the goal of the endeavour discussed in this Fragment.

CHAPTER XLII

THE GOAL

And now thyself is lost in Self, thyself unto Thyself, merged in that Self from which thou first didst radiate.

Where is thy individuality, Lanoo, where the Lanoo himself ? It is the spark lost in the fire, the drop within the ocean, the ever-present ray become the All and the eternal radiance.

And now, Lanoo, thou art the doer and the witness, the radiator and the radiation, light in the sound, and the sound in the light.

C.W.L.—As a man rises in life to a realization that the personality is merely " it ", and thus raises his centre of consciousness to the higher self, so there comes the time when he discovers as a fact of experience that that consciousness is only " you ", not " I ".[1] When that comes about, at or about the Fourth Initiation, the lower self becomes lost in the true Self, and what the man has thought or felt to be his individuality goes. And just as he who has achieved the buddhic state recognizes and accepts the consciousness of others as his own, and feels their joys and sorrows as his own; so now does this man find only one true " I " in all.

The distinction between the realization obtained by the initiate of lower degree, and that of the Arhat, between the consciousness of the buddhic plane and that of the ātmic, has been

[1] See *ante*, pp. 376, 383

given in the *Bhagavad-Gita*. In the former state the man sees *the same Self equally dwelling in all beings; in the latter he* sees that all are in the one Self.

This, according to *Yoga Sutras*, is the state of kaivalya, of "oneness", of freedom, on the full attainment of which the distinction between seer and seen, between subject and object, is destroyed.

> Thou art acquainted with the five impediments, O blessed one. Thou art their conqueror, the master of the sixth, deliverer of the four modes of truth.
>
> The light that falls upon them shines from thyself, O thou who wast disciple, but art Teacher now.
>
> And of these modes of truth:
>
> Hast thou not passed through knowledge of all misery—truth the first?
>
> Hast thou not conquered the Maras' king at Tu, the portal of assembling—truth the second?
>
> Hast thou not sin at the third gate destroyed, and truth the third attained?
>
> Hast thou not entered Tau, the path that leads to knowledge—the fourth truth?
>
> Madame Blavatsky adds:
>
> The four modes of truth are, in Northern Buddhism: Ku, suffering or misery; Tu, the assembling of temptations; Mu, their destructions; and Tau, the Path. The "five impediments" are the knowledge of misery, truth about human frailty, oppressive restraints, and the absolute necessity of separation from all the ties of passion, and

even of desires. The "Path of salvation" is the last one.

There are the Four Noble Truths taught to the world by the Lord Buddha. These were Sorrow, Sorrow's Cause, Sorrow's Ceasing and the Way. These have been put before the Western world with wonderful beauty and accuracy in Sir Edwin Arnold's matchless poem, *The Light of Asia*, from which the following verses are quoted. But all who seek inspiration on the Path should not fail to read the whole work.

Ye that will tread the Middle Road, whose course
 Bright Reason traces and soft Quiet smoothes;
Ye who will take the high Nirvāna-way,
 List the Four Noble Truths.

The First Truth is of *Sorrow*. Be not mocked!
 Life which ye prize is long-drawn agony:
Only its pains abide; its pleasures are
 As birds which light and fly.

Ache of the birth, ache of the helpless days,
 Ache of hot youth and ache of manhood's prime;
Ache of the chill grey years and choking death,
 These fill your piteous time.

Sweet is fond Love, but funeral-flames must kiss
 The breasts which pillow and the lips which cling,
Gallant is warlike Might, but vultures pick
 The joints of chief and King.

Beauteous is Earth, but all its forest-broods
 Plot mutual slaughter, hungering to live;
Of sapphire are the skies, but when men cry
 Famished, no drops they give.

Ask of the sick, the mourners, ask of him
 Who tottereth on his staff, lone and forlorn,
"Liketh thee life?"—these say the babe is wise
 That weepeth, being born.

The Second Truth is *Sorrow's Cause*. What grief
 Springs of itself and springs not of Desire?
Senses and things perceived mingle and light
 Passion's quick spark of fire:

So flameth Trishnā, lust and thirst of things.
Eager ye cleave to shadows, dote on dreams;
A false Self in the midst ye plant, and make
A world around which seems;

Blind to the heights beyond, deaf to the sound
Of sweet airs breathed from far past Indra's sky;
Dumb to the summons of the true life kept
For him who false puts by.

So grow the strifes and lusts which make earth's war,
So grieve poor cheated hearts and flow salt tears;
So wax the passions, envies, angers, hates;
So years chase blood-stained years

With wild red feet. So, where the grain should grow
Spreads the birān-weed with its evil root
And poisonous blossoms; hardly good seeds find
Soil where to fall and shoot;

And, drugged with poisonous drink, the soul departs,
And, fierce with thirst to drink, Karma returns;
Sense-struck again the sodden Self begins,
And new deceits it earns.

The Third is *Sorrow's Ceasing*. This is peace
To conquer love of self and lust of life,
To tear deep-rooted passion from the breast,
To still the inward strife;

For love to clasp Eternal Beauty close;
For glory to be Lord of self; for pleasure
To live beyond the gods; for countless wealth
To lay up lasting treasure

Of perfect service rendered, duties done
In charity, soft speech, and stainless days:
These riches shall not fade away in life,
Nor any death dispraise.

Then Sorrow ends, for Life and Death have ceased;
How should lamps flicker when their oil is spent?
The old sad count is clear, the new is clean;
Thus hath a man content.

The Fourth Truth is *The Way*. It openeth wide
 Plain for all feet to tread, easy and near,
The *Noble Eightfold Path*; it goeth straight
 To peace and refuge. Hear!

Manifold tracks lead to yon sister-peaks
 Around whose snows the gilded clouds are curled;
By steep or gentle slopes the climber comes
 Where breaks that other world.

Strong limbs may dare the rugged road which storms,
 Soaring and perilous, the mountain's breast;
The weak must wind from slower ledge to ledge,
 With many a place of rest.

So is the Eightfold Path which brings to peace;
 By lower or by upper heights it goes.
The firm soul hastes, the feeble tarries. All
 Will reach the sunlit snows[1]

The five impediments in the way of the candidate for Arhatship may be taken in various forms. They are the five mentioned by Madame Blavatsky in the foot-note just quoted, or they are the first five fetters, or they are the five kleshas mentioned in the *Yoga Sutras*, and already discussed.[2]

And now, rest 'neath the Bodhi tree, which is perfection of all knowledge, for, know, thou art the master of Samadhi—the state of faultless vision.

Behold! thou hast become the light, thou hast become the sound, thou art thy Master and thy God. Thou art thyself the object of thy search: the voice unbroken, that resounds throughout eternities, exempt from change, the seven sounds in one, the Voice of the Silence.

Aum Tat Sat.

[1] *Op. cit.*, Book the Eighth.

[2] *Ante*, pp. 359 61.

The termination Aum Tat Sat is one of the Mahāvākyams or "great sayings" of the Hindus. The meaning of Aum we have already considered.[1] Tat refers to the Supreme. Philosophically, the pronouns he and she are unsuitable to refer to the Supreme, so Tat, meaning "That", is employed. Beyond "it" and "you" is That, which is "I". So the expression means that it is *That* which is the *Real*. All good works begin and end with this thought.

PART VII

FRAGMENT II

THE TWO PATHS

CHAPTER XLIII

THE OPEN GATE

C.W.L.—We come now to the second Fragment which Madame Blavatsky translated from *The Book of the Golden Precepts*—entitled *The Two Paths.* This is not necessarily a continuation of the first Fragment, called *The Voice of the Silence*, although it does begin by addressing one who has just reached the goal of Arhatship. There is nothing to show that the three Fragments stand in any special relation to one another. They are to all intents and purposes three separate books dealing in much the same manner with the same subject. It is, however, a great advantage to the aspirant to hear the teaching about the Path again and again in slightly different forms. It renews his enthusiasm, draws attention to points which he may have overlooked, and generally gives him breadth of vision.

The present Fragment begins by addressing one who has just achieved the summit of the Path, and the question arises: will he go onwards into nirvānic bliss, heedless of those who remain behind, or will he turn back at the threshold and help others who are climbing; will he take liberation for himself, or will he stay to help the world?

> And now, O Teacher of compassion, point thou the way to other men. Behold all those who, knocking for admission, await in ignorance and darkness to see the gate of the sweet Law flung open!

The voice of the candidates:

Shalt not thou, Master of thine own mercy, reveal the doctrine of the heart? Shalt thou refuse to lead thy servants unto the Path of liberation?

The opening paragraph of this Fragment may at first seem a little strange to us in these modern days. We are familiar with the thought that the Path is open to anyone anywhere, regardless of race, creed, sex, caste or colour, who lives the life that is prescribed for it. Why, then, should any people be waiting in darkness and ignorance for a gate to be flung open for them?

The fact is that at the time when the Lord Buddha taught in India, the religion of the Brâhmanas had become very rigid. Originally, that faith had been intensely joyous and free, but in course of time the caste system had been extended by the priests and rulers to all kinds of details. The plains of India were thickly populated with Atlanteans and Atlanto-Lemurians when the Aryans descended into the country about ten thousand years B.C. So the Manu found it necessary to forbid intermarriage, and about 8,000 B.C. he ordained the caste system in order that no further admixture might be made, and that those already made might be perpetuated. He founded at first only three castes—Brâhmana, Rajan and Vish. The first were pure Aryans, the second Aryan and Toltec, the third Aryan and Mongolian.

The castes were hence called the Varnas, or colours—the pure Aryans white, the Aryan and Toltec intermixture red, and the Aryan and Mongolian yellow. The castes were allowed to intermarry among themselves, but a feeling quickly grew up that marriages should be restricted within the caste. Later, those who were not Aryan at all were included under the general appellation of Shudras, but even here in many cases a certain small amount of Aryan blood may appear. Many of the hill tribes are partly Aryan—some few are wholly so, like the Siaposh people and the Gipsy tribes.

There are passages in the Hindu scriptures to show that it was *possible for individuals of exceptional character and ability* to be raised in caste rank, but it must have been a very rare occurrence, and certainly for some time before the advent of the Lord Buddha it had been generally held that only a Brâhmana could hope for liberation, and anyone who wished to reach that goal must first contrive to be born as a Brâhmana. This was not a very hopeful doctrine for the majority of the people, since the Brâhmanas were never numerous—even to-day there are only about thirteen millions of them in a population of some three hundred millions—and they did not allow the lower caste people to study the sacred books.

But the Buddha's teaching flung the gates wide open. He taught that equal respect should be shown to one of any caste who lived the life, and conversely that a Brâhmana who does not live the life was not worthy of respect, as in the following verse from the *Vasala Sutta*:

> Not by birth does one become low caste,
> Not by birth does one become a Brâhmana;
> *By actions alone one becomes low caste,*
> By his actions alone one becomes a Brâhmana

Many Brâhmanas have told me that they actually feel the truth of this in practical life; they find themselves more drawn to those of lower castes who live the ideals of the Brâhmana life than to members of their own caste who neglect its ideals and live at a lower standard.

The aim of the Lord Buddha was not to found a new religion, but to reform Hinduism. For a time almost all India called itself Buddhist. There were Buddhist Hindus just as at present in the north-west there are many who call themselves *Sikh Hindus. Buddhism as a religion has long vanished from* India; the twenty million or so of whom we read in statistics as being in India belong to the Province of Burma, which is geographically and ethnographically quite a separate land. But the effect that the Lord Buddha desired to produce still remains to a large extent in the Hindu religion of the present day. As an instance of this one may mention the effect upon animal sacrifices, against which the Buddha spoke very strongly; they were very common before His time, but now they are quite rare. Again, in India to-day every holy man is regarded with reverence by all, whatever may have been his caste before he became a sannyâsî. And people all over the country respect the *Bhagavad-Gita* as of the highest authority, yet it is a book of the most liberal character. In it the Lord says:

> The same am I to all beings; there is none hateful to me nor dear. They verily who worship me with devotion, they are in me, and I also in them. Even if the most sinful worship me, with undivided heart, he too must be accounted righteous, for he hath rightly resolved; speedily he becometh dutiful and goeth to eternal peace, O Kaunteya; know thou for certain that my devotee perisheth never. They who take refuge with me, O Pārtha, though of the womb of sin, women, Vaishyas, even Shudras, they also tread the highest path.[1]

It must not be assumed that Shrī Krishna is here placing women and others on a lower level, but that he is refuting a number of popular superstitions, among them the idea that those who are in female bodies are necessarily inferior and so cannot succeed in high spiritual aims.

Madame Blavatsky explains in a foot-note that there are two schools of the Buddha's doctrine, the esoteric and the exoteric, respectively called the "heart" and the "eye" doctrine, and that the former emanated from the Buddha's heart while the latter was the work of His brain or head. Another interpretation that was given to me relates the terms to the eye and heart of the candidate: the scheme of things may be learnt by the eye, but the higher path can be entered only when the heart is in tune with the inner life.

The whole passage is based upon an alleged hesitation on the part of the Buddha as to whether He should preach. It is said that as He sat under the Bodhi tree on the morning following His Illumination, He doubted whether the world would understand and follow Him, until He heard a voice as of the earth in pain, which cried: "Surely I am lost; I and my creatures!" And then, again: "Oh, Supreme, let thy great Law be uttered!"[2]

Quoth the Teacher:

The paths are two; the great perfections three; six are the virtues that transform the body into the tree of knowledge.

[1] *Op. cit.*, ix, 29-32.
[2] *The Light of Asia*, Book the Seventh.

To this Madame Blavatsky adds the following foot-note:

> The tree of knowledge is a title given by the followers of the Bodhidharma (Wisdom Religion) to those who have attained the height of mystic knowledge—Adepts. Nagarjuna, the founder of the Madhyamika School, was called the dragon-tree, the dragon standing as a symbol of wisdom and knowledge. The tree is honoured because it is under the Bodhi (wisdom) tree that Buddha received His birth and enlightenment, preached His first sermon, and died.

Swāmī T. Subba Rao had a somewhat different interpretation of this symbol of a tree. He said that the body of the candidate had become a channel of knowledge (and we may *add of force as well), so that it was one of the twigs on the* Tree which is the total wisdom of the world. We may add, too, the idea that the Initiate is part of the great tree that is the Hierarchy, the Great White Brotherhood, that has its roots far up in the higher planes, and whose branches ramify into every part of human life, and even down to the lower kingdoms. Those who have read the later chapters of *The Masters and the Path* will appreciate this ancient symbol of a tree, for there it is shown how the Occult Hierarchy branches outward from one great Root.

In this statement about the two paths, the three great perfections, and the six virtues, we have an instance of the methodical character of the Buddha's teaching. He always helped His followers to remember His teaching by giving it to them in a tabular form. There were, for example, the Four Noble Truths, each represented by a single word which would call to recollection a quite definite set of ideas. There were also the Noble Eightfold Path, the Ten Sins, classed as three of the body, four of speech and three of the mind, and the Twelve Nidānas, or successive causes of material life and sorrow for man.

The transcendental virtues, or pāramitâs, are sometimes reckoned as six, sometimes seven, but more commonly as ten.

When in Ceylon, I learned of them as ten from the High Priest Sumangala: the first six, he said, are perfect charity, perfect morality, perfect truth, perfect energy, perfect kindness, and perfect wisdom; the other four that are sometimes added especially for the priests are perfect patience, perfect resignation, perfect resolution, and perfect abnegation. In the *Awakening of Faith* of Ashvagosha, translated into English by Teitaro Suzuki, the Pāramitās are thus enumerated: Charity (dāna), morality (cīla), patience (ksānti), energy (vīrya), meditation (dhyāna), wisdom (prajnā), and the four additional ones: expediency (upaya), prayer or vow (pranidhāna), strength (bala), knowledge (jnāna). In the foot-note to the *Voice of the Silence*, 1924 edition, a list taken from Eitel's *Chinese Buddhism* is given thus: charity, morality, patience, energy, contemplation and wisdom; and in addition for the priests: use of right means, science, pious vows, and force of purpose.

When in Ceylon I compared the statements of Orientalists with the feelings and thoughts of the Buddhists themselves. There is a great difference between the two, for the former are generally very wooden, but the latter are full of life. Yet the learned monks have an accuracy of knowledge at least equal to that of the most erudite Orientalists. Sir Edwin Arnold, in his *Light of Asia*, has given a very remarkably accurate representation of the living side of Buddhism. Some have said that he read Christian ideas and feelings into Buddhism, but that was not so in the least; I can testify that the sentiments described in the poem really exist among the Buddhist people.

> Who shall approach them?
>
> Who shall first enter them?
>
> Who shall first hear the doctrine of two paths in one, the truth unveiled about the Secret Heart? The law which, shunning learning, teaches wisdom, reveals a tale of woe.
>
> Alas, alas, that all men should possess Alaya, be one with the great Soul, and that, possessing it, Alaya should so little avail them!

> Behold how, like the moon reflected in the tranquil waves, Alaya is reflected by the small and by the great, is mirrored in the tiniest atoms, yet fails to reach the heart of all. Alas, that so few men should profit by the gift, the priceless boon of learning truth, the right perception of existing things, the knowledge of the non-existent!

The Secret Heart is the esoteric doctrine. It is a symbol that comes down to us from Atlantean days. In the innermost shrine of the great temple in the City of the Golden Gate there lay upon the altar a massive golden box in the shape of a heart, the secret opening of which was known only to the high priest. This was called "the Heart of the World", and signified to them the innermost mysteries that they knew. In it they kept their most sacred objects, and much of their symbolism centred around it. They knew that every atom beats as a heart, and they considered that the sun had a similar movement, which they connected with the sun-spot period. Sometimes one comes across passages in their books which give the impression that they knew more than we do in matters of science, though they regarded it all from the poetic rather than from the scientific point of view. They thought, for example, that the earth breathes and moves, and it is certainly true that quite recently scientific men have discovered that there is a regular daily displacement of the earth's surface which may be thought of as corresponding in a certain way to breathing.

When Āryasanga uses the term "secret heart" he also means all the inner mysteries Madame Blavatsky's foot-note says:

> The Secret Heart is the esoteric doctrine.

Here the teacher by "shunning learning" certainly means that there are times when we must turn our attention away from the mere gaining of knowledge from the outside through the senses, that we may give time to the development of the inner learning through intuition. We cannot be wise without having sufficient learning or knowledge with regard to the things that we have to deal with in the world, in our particular sphere of duty; but on the other-hand we should be much in error if we thought that the greatest thing in life was to accumulate great stores of knowledge, or were even to imagine that such knowledge had intrinsic value, apart from the use that we can make of it in the service of mankind.

In Europe there is a tendency to approach things and study them from the outside, while the Eastern method is rather to consider them from within. Both methods are necessary at our present state of evolution. When the buddhic vehicle is developed, and intuition comes down into the physical brain from that level, it will give us true wisdom, perfect knowledge, but in very few people is it yet sufficiently developed.

Even if we are able to keep our heads among the clouds, it is necessary that our feet should rest firmly on the earth, and we must treat impressions coming from within with balanced judgment, just as we apply common sense to the experiences of every-day life. This is necessary, because it is quite easy to mistake impulses, coming from the astral body, for intuitions which come from the higher self. Sometimes it happens, for example, that a dead person seeing that we are interested in some particular point, offers a suggestion on the astral plane, and this may come down into the brain and seem like intuition. Yet, as a matter of fact, that dead person may be a very incompetent observer on the astral plane, and may therefore be giving quite wrong information.

This advice to shun learning is useful not only to those who are on the Path, but also to every one who is at all studious, if we take it to mean, as it does, that we should avoid *mere* learning. A great amount of study of the mere outside of things often leads to materialism. Because they see around them great cataclysms, sacrifice, oppression, sorrow and suffering, and a vast amount of praying to which no answer seems to be vouchsafed, many people come to think that conflict and struggle is the law of life, that nature is not compassionate. But to study the world as fully as possible, all the time regarding it as a great school for the life dwelling in its multifarious forms, leads to wisdom, which enables one to see that all things are moving together for good. When one develops astral and higher forms of vision this fact that all is well is no longer a matter to be understood by careful reasoning; it leaps to the eyes. No one with such vision could be a materialist.

The word Ālaya means simply a dwelling or house. Esoterically, Madame Blavatsky says, it has at least a double meaning, as being both the universal soul, and the Self of an advanced Adept. It is the real dwelling or home of man, the universal aspect of that which is buddhi in the spiritual triad in man. It is the male or positive aspect of the universal soul, the Logos. It is the Over-soul of Emerson, the universal Higher Self of all beings. It is what Plato called Nous, a principle free from matter yet acting with design, the jīvātmā of the Hindus, the source of the divine creative thought. In other words it is in the Second Logos, the universal spiritual soul, of which the buddhi in each man is a ray.

That one should have "knowledge of the non-existent" must certainly look strange to those who do not know the exact philosophical meaning of the last word. To exist means to stand outside of, to have external or objective being. The kind of being that is called existence belongs to all the world that is seen as outside ourselves, but the indwelling life or consciousness has its own state of being—call it "istence" if you like, but not "existence". Nothing could be more real than the reality of this conscious life, which we also possess because we are part of the same Logos—and that is the "non-existent" of which the aspirant must gain knowledge. Every man is essentially divine; but to realize it he must stand out of his own light—then there will be no shadow, no illusion.

CHAPTER XLIV

HEAD-LEARNING AND SOUL-WISDOM

Saith the pupil:

O Teacher, what shall I do to reach to wisdom? O wise one, what, to gain perfection?

Search for the paths. But, O Lanoo, be of clean heart before thou startest on thy journey. Before thou takest thy first step, learn to discern the real from the false, the ever-fleeting from the everlasting. Learn above all to separate head-learning from Soul-wisdom, the "eye" from the "heart" doctrine.

C.W.L.—There is nothing that can be said here on the subject of the real and the unreal that has not already been dealt with at length in the comment on "From the unreal lead me to the real" in *At the Feet of the Master*.[1]

Yea, ignorance is like unto a closed and airless vessel; the Soul a bird shut up within. It warbles not, nor can it stir a feather; but the songster mute and torpid sits, and of exhaustion dies.

But even ignorance is better than head-learning with no Soul-wisdom to illuminate and guide it.

[1] *Ante*, Ch. IV.

No occult progress at all is possible for a man while he is extremely ignorant, however much he may be developed in other ways. Without some knowledge of the Truth, and of the Path, he will not move in a definite direction. Most people have very little knowledge of what it means to be really a man, what are the qualities and actions which make for progress and what for retrogression, and they have no conception of the great destiny to which all are slowly moving. Therefore their progress is very, very slow. We have investigated clairvoyantly as many as a hundred successive lives of some second-class pitris, or men of the second grade, and find scarcely any perceptible growth at the end of that series.

There is, however, a steady though slow evolution of the whole mass of life going on all the time, and the man has shared in this general progress. Absolutely he has gone forward, but relatively he has done little. Mr. Sinnett compared this advance to that of a person going round and round a tower by a winding staircase; he comes to the same position and outlook again and again, but every time just a little bit higher than before. It would seem almost as though men were being treated a little better than they deserve, for we see that even the ignorant man, whose thoughts are selfish in nine cases out of ten, is advancing in this way. But the fact is that even a little force directed towards the higher things is far more potent than a great deal of force turned towards the lower things. If one tenth of a man's thoughts are spiritual he is beyond the average; even in such a case the man is taking nine steps backward for one step forward, but fortunately the nine steps backward are very short and the one step forward is very long. It takes a bad life to balance good and evil, and to fall back a man must be exceptionally bad. Then again, the effect of a little good is very far-reaching on account of the close association that obtains among men, and he who sets it going receives much good karma.

But if ignorance is a great obstacle to progress, knowledge that is not applied is little better; it also does not count for very much. Even if a man is interested in occult matters he may stay apparently at the same level life after life; for if it is not applied the knowledge does little good. To put knowledge into practice is an absolutely necessary condition for rapid progress.

'The seeds of wisdom cannot sprout and grow in airless space. To live and reap experience, the mind needs breadth and depth and points to draw it towards the Diamond Soul. Seek not those points in Maya's realm; but soar beyond illusions, search the eternal and the changeless Sat, mistrusting fancy's false suggestions.

In her foot-note, Madame Blavatsky says that the Diamond Soul, Vajrasattva, is a title of the supreme Buddha, the Lord of all mysteries, called Vajradhara and Ādi-Buddha. In *The Secret Doctrine*, however, she points out the distinction between Vajrasattva and Vajradhara. Vajra is a diamond; *sattva* in such a connection as this means "by nature", that is, a character or soul, so Vajrasattva is one whose nature or character is like a diamond. *Dhara* means holding or bearing, so Vajradhara is one who holds a diamond. Avalokiteshvara, "the Lord who is seen", is Vajrasattva, the Diamond-Soul or Diamond-Heart, and is the synthetic reality of all the Dhyāni-Buddhas. The First Logos is Vajradhara or Vajrapāni, the Diamond-Holder, or the Diamond-Handed One, also called Dorjechang in Tibetan. He is the one beyond all conditioning or manifestation, but He sends into the world of *subjective* manifestation the expression of His Heart—Vajrasattva or Dorjesempa, the Second Logos.[1]

That there should be special points required to draw the candidate into full touch with That is analogous to what we have seen in the process of individualization of an animal In this case, the points are the finer qualities that it develops, such as affection and devotion, by means of which it reaches up into the human condition of consciousness. The mind of man must also put out special points in order that it may unite with the Soul, and for the Initiate those points must rise up into buddhi, which is the principle in the reincarnating self corresponding to the Vajrasattva at a still higher level. Swāmi T. Subba Rao said that it referred to the ātmā drawing the ego into the Monad. The same simile can thus be employed at many different levels.

[1] See *Ante*, pp. 377.

For mind is like a mirror; it gathers dust while it reflects.

This, says Madame Blavatsky, is from the doctrine of Shin-Sien, who taught that the human mind is like a mirror which attracts and reflects every atom of dust, and has to be, like that mirror, watched over and dusted every day. Shin-Sien was the sixth patriarch of North China, who taught the esoteric doctrine of Bodhidharma. In *The Secret Doctrine* she explains the position of Bodhidharma, as follows:

> When the misuse of dogmatical orthodox Buddhist Scriptures had reached its climax, and the true spirit of the Buddha's Philosophy was nearly lost, several reformers appeared from India, who established an oral teaching. Such were Bodhidharma and Nagarjuna, the authors of the most important works of the contemplative School in China during the first centuries of our era.[1]

The dust on the mirror typifies the prejudices, illusions and fancies which are in the astral and mental bodies; these are clearly visible to the sight of the respective planes as decided obstacles to better thought or feeling. The effects of these impediments and the means to get rid of them we have already considered carefully in the talks on *At the Feet of the Master*.[2]

It needs the gentle breezes of Soul-wisdom to brush away the dust of our illusions. Seek, O beginner, to blend thy mind and Soul.

Shun ignorance and likewise shun illusion. Avert thy face from world deceptions; mistrust thy senses: they are false. But within thy body—the shrine of thy sensations—seek in the impersonal for the Eternal Man; and having sought him out, look inward: thou art Buddha.

Common experience tells us that the senses must be mistrusted. The impressions of sight, for example, must be corrected by careful study of the facts, and judgment about

[1] *Op. cit.*, Vol III, p. 429

[2] *Ante*, p. 167.

them, as in the matter of the apparent movement of the sun round the earth. Care must be taken, however, not to read into this statement the idea that the senses are not to be used. They must be employed on every plane for the gaining of knowledge, and for doing the work and duty without which there is no progress.

The eternal man is the reincarnating ego, whose life is age-long as compared with that of the personality, persisting as it does through our complete series of human births and deaths.

The word Buddha is used in three distinct senses. Sometimes, as in this case, it means simply enlightened, illuminated, or wise. Sometimes it is used as a name for the Lord Gautama. In other cases it means the high office in the Occult Hierarchy of the Head of the Second Ray, the great department of teaching and religion, which has been described in *The Masters and the Path.* The Buddhists have a list of twenty-four Buddhas, of whom the present holder of the office is the Lord Gautama, who will be succeeded in the far future by the Lord Maitreya.

> Shun praise, O devotee: praise leads to self-delusion. Thy body is not Self, thy Self is in itself without a body, and either praise or blame affects it not.
>
> Self-gratulation, O disciple, is like unto a lofty tower, up which a haughty fool has climbed. Thereon he sits in prideful solitude and unperceived by any but himself.

Very many men have been spoiled by undue praise; it leads to pride in all who do not see clearly what lies ahead of them or above them. Those pupils who are sufficiently clairvoyant to see the Masters frequently are not so prone to this danger as many others are, because they cannot but compare their own littleness with the Master's greatness, their own farthing rushlight with His glorious sunlight. It is the man who is looking downward, and comparing himself with those who are beneath himself, who is most likely to fall through pride.

But the best way of all is not to think of oneself, but to be constantly occupied with the work of the Master. There is for all of us every day far more of that to be done than we can possibly accomplish; and it is only taking energy and time away from that if we spend it in thinking about our little selves. There are no doubt several reasons why the Masters do not show Themselves more than they do to those who are in the earlier stages of Their service. One of these is that the pupil, seeing the Master so far above him, might be overwhelmed with his own insignificance and lose confidence in his own ability to work for the Master. So, while it is necessary to avoid pride on the one hand, one must equally avoid the under-estimation of one's powers on the other. Here, as ever, the middle path is the right one.

The simile of a tower is indeed a good one, for pride does shut a man away from his fellows. If, for example, he is proud of his learning, he will be anxious to keep others more ignorant than himself, so as to enjoy his superior position, and even when he does give out his knowledge it will only be for the sake of displaying it. Such a man is engaged all the time in enlarging the gulf between himself and other people, so that he may look down on them from above.

> False learning is rejected by the wise. and scattered to the winds by the Good Law. Its wheel revolves for all, the humble and the proud. The doctrine of the eye is for the crowd; the doctrine of the heart for the elect. The first repeat in pride. "Behold, I know"; the last, they who in humbleness have garnered, low confess. "Thus have I heard."

Every religion in course of time gathers round itself many speculations and other accretions. For example, in Hinduism, in the Purānas one reads of dozens of things that people are told that they must do or must not do; many of those have been invented by the priests, either for their own convenience and advantage or because of an excessive estimation of the value of many prayers and ceremonies. Also particular interpretations of earlier sayings are developed into dogmas and attached to the original teaching, as, for instance, the horrible eternal hell teaching which still persists among most Christians.

The esoteric teaching at once scatters these to the winds, as it brings the attention back to the essential and vital truths. Still, to act from the heart is the way only of a strong and advanced man. For the masses, wandering slowly along the broad road of evolution which winds gently up the hill-side, the books are still the main guide. Those people are not yet in the position that is described as follows in the *Garuda Purāna*: 'Having practised the Vedas and the Shastras, and having known the Truth, the wise man can abandon all the scriptures, just as one rich in grains abandons the straw."

Every Buddhist scripture begins with, "Thus says——", or, "Thus have I heard." It is a humble beginning. It does not say, "This is absolutely so, and you must believe it," but, "This is what has been said, and it would be well to try to understand it, and so come to a knowledge of the real facts." It is the attitude of enquiry, not of dogmatism. Yet, strange to say, there have been those who have taken it in another, and quite a wrong sense. They say, "It is no use propounding anything different on this subject, for thus it has been said with authority"!

"Great Sifter" is the name of the heart doctrine, O disciple.

The wheel of the Good Law moves swiftly on. It grinds by night and day. The worthless husks it drives from out the golden grain, the refuse from the flour. The hand of Karma guides the wheel; the revolutions mark the beatings of the karmic heart.

True knowledge is the flour, false learning is the husk. If thou would'st eat the bread of wisdom, thy flour thou hast to knead with Amrita's clear waters. But if thou kneadest husks with Maya's dew, thou canst create but food for the black doves of death, the birds of birth, decay and sorrow.

The heart doctrine is called the Great Sifter because as one works in the world in the manner which it directs, the mistakes one makes and the defects one has are gradually sifted out and removed. If one were doing work without the ideals of the inner doctrine, one might go on making the same kind of mistakes again and again, life after life. Madame Blavatsky somewhere wrote that it was one thing to desire to do good, and another to know what is good to do. Yet, with our imperfect knowledge, we must go forth and do the best we can. It is something like learning a language. It is a mistake to try to learn it quite perfectly from books before one makes any attempt to speak it; one must plunge into it, and make mistakes in it, and in the effort one will learn in due course to speak without mistakes. But that will come about, of course, only if one converses in it with others who already know the language correctly.

Similarly the Master, though He may be unseen, will guide the pupil who is sincerely trying to do his best, into the experiences that will sift out his faults and mistakes. Keep in mind the conviction that the final good will inevitably come, and let the heart be full of love; then you may work without fear of mistakes. They will become smaller and smaller, and fewer and fewer, and will eventually die away.

There is a moral to be drawn from the analogy of flour and bread. The true knowledge that you gain does not give you bread, but merely the flour with which the bread of wisdom has to be made. The kneading is the action of the higher self, which works upon experiences and converts them into real wisdom. In ordinary men most of this kneading is done during the devachânic period, but the pupil of the Master has so broadened the channel between the higher and the lower self that he is gaining wisdom all the time.

He who takes only external knowledge, and studies it over with the lower mind, in the light of mere personal necessity and pleasures, is certainly kneading husks with mâyâ's dew. He is not preparing for the triumph of the higher self; he is not treading the Path, but is preparing the karma of future births and deaths, for the future vehicles and personalities that will decay and die.

CHAPTER XLV

THE LIFE OF ACTION

If thou art told that to become Arhan thou hast to cease to love all beings—tell them they lie.

If thou art told that to gain liberation thou hast to hate thy mother and disregard thy son; to disavow thy father and call him householder; for man and beast all pity *to renounce—tell them their tongue* is false.

Thus teach the Tirthikas, the unbelievers.

If thou art taught that sin is born of action and bliss of absolute inaction, then tell them that they err. Non-permanence of human action, deliverance of mind from thraldom by the cessation of sin and faults, are not for Deva Egos. Thus saith the doctrine of the heart.

C.W.L.—To call a man a householder is to say that his interests are still centred in worldly things, but to do this with contempt, as is implied in the text, would certainly indicate the proud and austere qualities of the left-hand path, leading up to the heights of the black magicians, who regard the best of human love as nothing but mere sentimentality. Even though the candidate may have risen above personal desires, he cannot despise those who are still at the earlier stage of evolution, nor can he ignore them. Compassion and eagerness to help are the qualities of his nature.

That the expression householder must be taken in a metaphorical sense is indicated in a foot-note by Madame Blavatsky, as follows:

> Rathapala, the great Arhat, thus addresses his father in the legend called *Rathapala Sutrasanne*. But as all such legends are allegorical (e.g., Rathapala's father had a mansion with seven doors) hence the reproof to those who accept them literally.

Madame Blavatsky describes the Tirthikas as "ascetic Brāhmanas, visiting holy shrines, especially sacred bathing-places." A Tīrtha is literally a "crossing-place". It is thus a landing or bathing place, or any shrine, which is a crossing place to the other worlds or the higher life. A shrine is thus a place where there is a special connection between the inner and the outer worlds. Probably the orthodox Brāhmanas and Hindus in general who visit such Tīrthas as, for example, Benares or Hardwar, were called unbelievers because they did not in most cases follow the Buddha in His assertion that "within oneself deliverance must be sought."

In the talks on *At the Feet of the Master* we have considered at length the necessity for action, and how there may be intense activity of the body, and yet the man within may be calm, steady, serene and strong. The Deva Egos means the reincarnating egos, according to Madame Blavatsky, but Swāmī T. Subba Rao explained the term as meaning those who aspire to work with the devas and for the helping of the world.

The teaching of the *Book of the Golden Precepts* is obviously intended for those who wish to follow that line of work. At present there are not very many egos in incarnation who are ready for special teaching and training—it would be of little use, for example, to seek among the dwellers in the east end of London for people who are ready to become pupils of the Masters. But as time goes on the numbers requiring attention will increase very rapidly, and within a few hundred years there must be many Arhats prepared to teach them Thus a large number of helpers will be needed, and it is to that work that many of us are called.

The Dharma of the eye is the embodiment of the external and the non-existing.

The Dharma of the heart is the embodiment of Bodhi, the permanent and everlasting.

The word *dharma* may here be translated "*form of* religion" or "belief", and bodhi is simply "wisdom".

The lamp burns bright when wick and oil are clean. To make them clean a cleaner is required. The flame feels not the process of the cleaning. "The branches of a tree are shaken by the wind; the trunk remains unmoved."

Both action and inaction may find room in thee; thy body agitated, thy mind tranquil, thy Soul as limpid as a mountain lake.

Whatever suffering there may be on the path of progress is experienced only by the lower self. The Self seated within knows the value even of the painful experience and is therefore quite satisfied. Many people do not understand that suffering is very largely a question of attitude; in *Esoteric Christianity* our President has explained how some of the great martyrs were filled with joy while undergoing what would be terrible pain to others, because they were thinking of the great honour that was theirs to suffer so for the sake of their Lord. So it is true that at last wrong ideas or ignorance are the basis of all suffering.

Physical suffering is the most difficult to deal with. We may be able sometimes to draw away from the physical body when it is in pain, but that does not mean that we have conquered the pain. If it is the result of a particular disease in which a microbe has to run its course, no amount of assertion will enable an ordinary person to drive it away; but in all cases a cheerful attitude makes a big difference. Most people can conquer astral pain, if they set themselves the task; they can refuse to permit their feelings to dwell upon the idea that gives them sorrow. Undesirable emotions, such as jealousy, envy, pride and fear, may be described as astral diseases; they can always be eradicated by persistent effort to feel the opposite emotions Mental suffering, chiefly worry, is even easier to control.

In the causal body a man might have an uneasy sense of incompleteness or insufficiency—but nothing more than that. Though he may feel disappointment at the defects of his lower representative, he knows enough to be patient and to persevere. He is not ignorant; but it is ignorance that makes our suffering so poignant down here. In childhood, when we were still more ignorant, a trouble lasting one day seemed a terrible tragedy; if we failed to pass an examination the idea of waiting a whole year for the next opportunity seemed to us a calamity, though in later life a year does not seem a long period of time. To the personality a life's failure may seem a tragedy, but to the ego, who has known hundreds or thousands of incarnations, it may not appear so vastly important.

The ego has put down a personality much as a fisherman makes a cast. He does not expect that every cast will be successful, and he is not deeply troubled if one proves a failure. To look after a personality is only one of his activities, so he may very well console himself with successes in other lines of activity. In any case, it is the loss of a day, and he may say, "Oh, well, we will hope to do better to-morrow." Often the personality would like more attention from the ego above him, and he may be sure that he will receive it as soon as he deserves it, as soon as the ego finds it worth while. Mr. Sinnett put forward this desire of the personality in a humorous way by saying that what was needed was a school for teaching egos to pay attention to their personalities.

One stage further on, in the buddhic plane, the man begins to touch the intensity of bliss that is the life of the Logos. At the same time he comes closer into touch with other men; on the lower planes he begins to share their suffering, but on the higher side he knows them as sparks of the divine, and that gives indescribable bliss, which makes the suffering seem as naught. Thus sorrow and suffering are for the personality only, and they exist merely while the consciousness is fixed in the lower planes.

Would'st thou become a Yogi of time's circle? Then, O Lanoo:

Believe thou not that sitting in dark forests, in proud seclusion and apart from men; believe thou not that life on roots and plants, that thirst assuaged with snow from the great Range—believe thou not, O devotee, that this will lead thee to the goal of final liberation.

Think not that breaking bone, that rending flesh and muscle, unites thee to thy silent Self. Think not that when the sins of thy gross form are conquered, O victim of thy shadows, thy duty is accomplished by nature and by man.

Āryasanga is here once more preaching against the seeking of liberation as mere escape from the wheel of births and deaths. The yogī of time's circle is the one who is willing to remain within the process of time, for the sake of helping others. When one considers the vast period of time for which the Lord Buddha and the Lord Maitreya had been preparing Themselves for Their great work, which has been explained in *The Masters and the Path*,[1] one cannot but feel oppressed by the thought of such enormous periods of incarnate existence. Undoubtedly, however, time cannot be to Them exactly what it is to us. Even if "a thousand ages in Thy sight are like an evening gone" does not apply to Them, Their sense of time must be vastly different from ours. Certainly They are also intensely happy in Their work, and where there is happiness, as everybody knows by experience, time is of no account—in fact, under those circumstances we always wish that it could be lengthened.

Very wrong ideas have arisen in most of the religions on the subject of asceticism. In the original Greek the word *asketes* meant simply one who exercises himself as an athlete

[1] *Op. cit.*, Ch. xiv.

does. But ecclesiasticism impounded the word and changed its sense, applying it to the practice of self-denial in various ways for the purpose of spiritual progress, on the theory that the bodily nature with its passions and desires has been the stronghold of the evil inherent in man since the fall of Adam, and that it must therefore be suppressed by fasting and penance. In the Oriental religions we sometimes encounter a similar idea, based on the conception of matter as essentially evil, and following from that the deduction that an approach to ideal good or an escape from the miseries of existence can be effected only by subduing or torturing the body.

In both these theories there is dire confusion of thought. The body and its desires are not in themselves evil or good, but it is true that before real progress can be made they must be brought under the control of the higher self within. To govern the body is necessary, but to torture it is foolish.

There appears to be a wide-spread delusion that to be really good one must always be uncomfortable—that discomfort in itself is directly pleasing to the Logos. Nothing can be more grotesque than this idea. In Europe this unfortunately common theory is one of the many horrible legacies left by the ghastly blasphemy of Calvinism. I myself have actually heard a child say: "I feel so happy that I am sure I must be very wicked"—a truly awful result of criminally distorted teaching.

Another reason for the gospel of the uncomfortable is a confusion of cause and effect. It is observed that the really advanced person is simple in his habits and often careless about a large number of minor luxuries that are considered important and really necessary by the ordinary man. But such carelessness about luxury is the effect, not the cause of his advancement. He does not trouble himself about these small matters because he has largely outgrown them and they no longer interest him—not in the least because he considers them as wrong; and one who, while still craving for them, imitates him in abstaining from them does not thereby become advanced.

It is true that our duty to the world is not accomplished when we have purified ourselves. Then indeed does it become really possible for us to do our best work for our fellow-men, and since in the higher life the maxim "From each according to his power, to each according to his need" prevails, our most *serious duty begins at this point, when the shadows, the lower bodies, have been mastered.*

The silent Self in this passage, refers, says Madame Blavatsky, to the seventh principle, which is ātmā. Our studies in the first Fragment have already shown how this idea of silence is attached to that part of the higher Self.

> The blessed ones have scorned to do so. The Lion of the Law, the Lord of Mercy, perceiving the true cause of human woe, immediately forsook the sweet but selfish rest of quiet wilds. From Aranyaka he became the Teacher of mankind. After Julai had entered the Nirvana, he preached on mount and plain, and held discourses in the cities, to Devas, men and Gods.

All the Northern and Southern Buddhist traditions agree in the statement that the Buddha quitted His solitude as soon as He had reached inner enlightenment and had solved the problem of life, and that He at once began teaching publicly.

The term Āranyaka means a forest-dweller. The books relate that Gautama went into the forest in order to meditate, and there he seated Himself under the bodhi tree and resolved to attain illumination. When that was achieved, He considered whether He would give His teaching to the world; He knew that most of the people would not understand it, and that it might therefore do harm. But then, as was remarked at the beginning of our study of this Fragment, the voice of the earth came to Him, and begged Him to teach. I do not know exactly what was meant by the voice of the earth, but it is said that that led Him to decide to teach mankind on the physical plane.

In this passage there are several titles given to the Buddha. He is called Julai. That is the Chinese name for Tathāgata, which is the title given to every Buddha. Tathāgata means literally "he who has gone likewise", he has followed in the steps of his predecessors.

It is a fact that when the Buddha preached others besides men gathered round to listen to His teaching and enjoy His aura.

> Sow kindly acts and thou shalt reap their fruit. Inaction in a deed of mercy is action in a deadly sin.

I have already quoted this in commenting on *At the Feet of the Master.* Each man has the responsibility for exercising the powers of consciousness that he has so far developed. If he fails to exert himself and neglects to use them, he is guilty of sins of omission, which are just as serious as sins of commission. For example, it is our duty to interfere, when we can do so without doing more harm than good, in cases of wrong or cruelty, such as cruelty to animals or children. The wise man, seeing such things, will not let indignation master him. He must feel also for the man who is guilty of the cruelty. His state is in many ways more pitiable than that of his victim, and he will have to suffer in turn, on account of kārmic law. So, if we can induce him to see the error of his ways and stop his cruelty, we have done good to both. When it is our duty to interfere, and we fail to do so, we share the karma of the wrong-doing. The same is true when we allow others to injure ourselves, without resistance. We are making it easy for them to do wrong; we are tempting them, and assisting them, and the karma is partly ours.

> Thus saith the Sage:
>
> Shalt thou abstain from action? Not so shall thy Soul gain her freedom. To reach Nirvana one must reach Self-knowledge, and Self-knowledge is of loving deeds the child.

It is not until we begin to work for others that we can acquire real knowledge of life In the attempt we learn where we stand, and what qualities must be developed There was an old blind man living in the south of India, who said that his blindness had been indirectly a source of great happiness to him. He was also in the deepest poverty, and had spent his life in wandering from village to village, where he used to advise the people in their difficulties and also assist them in some cases with his yoga powers. He used to tell how, by meditation, he had managed to awaken the memory of his past lives; and he remembered that, some hundreds of years before, he had been a very rich and powerful man, and had used his power to injure those who happened to do what he did not like. He recognized that his blindness and poverty were due to his wrong deeds in that former life. He said he was sure that if he had gone on being a rich man he might never have learned to love his fellows, as he had been quite set in a selfish path of life. But now he had had to mingle with others, most of whom knew suffering; they had been very kind to him, and he had learned to love them. The happiness of that love, he said, as compared with his previous condition, was something so great and incomparable that no suffering was in his opinion too great to purchase it. This man claimed to be a pupil of one of our Masters, and he certainly was an illustration of the teaching that self-knowledge is of loving deeds the child.

> Have patience, candidate, as one who fears no failure, courts no success. Fix thy Soul's gaze upon the star whose ray thou art, the flaming star that shines within the lightless depths of ever-being, the boundless fields of the unknown.

The disciple fears no failure because he knows that the plan of the Logos will be carried out; no one's failure can make any difference to that. We may have the opportunity to do a piece of His work. If we should fail to do it, it will be done in some other way through someone else. It makes no difference to the Logos, though it may make a very great difference to ourselves. It happens constantly that people miss their opportunities, but the great plans are made in view of every contingency. Our Masters never appear to notice when we lose an opportunity, but I think that They are quite aware of it. Madame Blavatsky used sometimes to say about some person: "He has earned the right to have his chance." The Masters always assume that we are going to take our opportunities.

The student who has tried to do some good work and has found the opposing forces too great for him, will not be disappointed or lose patience if he understands that all efforts put forth for good must produce a proportionate result in some way, though the results may be unseen, and though there may be for the personality none of the satisfaction which comes from seeing the good that has been done. It is the same in the case of astral work at night. That work is none the less good and effective when done by those who are not able to bring any memory of it back into the physical brain. The laws of nature do not cease to operate because we cannot see the result, or do not remember what we have done.

Usually the people who have done the greatest work in the world do not see the result of it. Take, for instance, the example of the Christ's three years' of preaching. He died as a malefactor, execrated by the populace, and at his death the number of His followers was only a hundred and twenty; now there are many millions. William Wilberforce, who worked steadily for over forty years against the greatest odds for the abolition of slavery in the British Colonies, heard only three days before his death that total abolition of slavery had at last become law. Impatience and depression would have lost his cause. We are all in the same position, in our lesser ways. There is none who cannot take up some good work, and push on with it with tireless and endless patience, regardless of immediate success or failure.

"The star whose ray thou art" is always that which shines above us; for one it is the ego, for another, more advanced, the Monad, and so on to the Planetary Logos, and even the Logos of our system. To know our own star is also to know the ray to which we belong—which of the seven great rays is the one that especially connects us with the Logos. These seven rays are indicated in the chapter dealing with the Chohans of the Rays in *The Masters and the Path*, and also in *The Seven Rays*, by Prof. Ernest Wood. When the higher self is the master of the personality, it becomes possible for the disciple to specialize in the work of the ray to which that higher self belongs, and then he can make very rapid progress in power and usefulness.

Have perseverance as one who doth for evermore endure. Thy shadows live and vanish; that which in thee shall live for ever, that which in thee knows (for it is knowledge) is not of fleeting life: it is the Man that was, that is, and will be, for whom the hour shall never strike.

Besides patience we need perseverance, and nothing can develop this quality in us better than a clear perception of the fact that we endure all through the ages, and that death is only a passing incident, with no power to deflect us from our path. Sometimes people say: "Why should I take up such and such work? I cannot possibly finish it in this life." But the fact is that there is only one real lifetime—that of the ego, which endures *for ever, for all practical purposes. It is wise to begin any* work in which you are interested, or the great task of eliminating faults, even in old age, for all the good that is done is carried forward to the next body, and in it the impulse to continue the work will be felt while it is young. If one postpones the work to a future life, once more old age may arrive before one has the opportunity that will draw attention to it. If you are now ninety, and you have just heard of Theosophy, and you want to hear of it in your youth in your next life, throw yourself into it now with whatever vigour you may have. There is also the great benefit to be derived from the stay in devachan (unless you happen to be one of those who have the privilege of being able to renounce that period) for in that state whatever work you have done is dwelt upon and worked up into faculty which will be a great help in the next incarnation.

Perseverance is necessary also because no great work can be completed in a short time. Think, for example, of the artist who is painting a great picture; he will have very little to show for it in the first few days, perhaps even weeks, and it is also quite possible that he may not be pleased with what he has been able to achieve at the end of a few weeks, so that he has to begin all over again.

A very useful lesson in perseverance may be derived from a study of the history of the Theosophical Society in the early days. The two great founders, Madame Blavatsky and Colonel Olcott, could not have succeeded in establishing the Society permanently, and giving it the material for future growth, had they not had a clear vision of the inner side of things, a realization that their work was part of a plan lasting throughout eternity, and was therefore sure to succeed. They founded the Society in New York in 1875, and worked prodigiously at *Isis Unveiled*, which was duly published. Still, some five years later they were almost alone in the work, and they found it necessary to go to India, to some friends there, to make a new start. Even then there were endlessly varied troubles, year after year, which would have crushed almost anybody else. Madame Blavatsky, with a body seldom free from pain, could still work tirelessly, could produce *The Secret Doctrine* and other great works, because of her knowledge of the Masters and the inner side of things.

CHAPTER XLVI

THE SECRET PATH

If thou would'st reap sweet peace and rest, disciple, sow with the seeds of merit the fields of future harvests.

Accept the woes of birth.

C.W.L.—Āryasanga is all the time endeavouring to persuade the disciple to follow the higher path of renunciation, and not to accept the peace of nirvāna. Life in the ātmic or nirvānic plane has been defined as rest in omniscience, but we must understand that it is rest only in the sense that there is no consciousness of exertion followed by fatigue. There is on that plane the most tremendous activity; that is the very essence of the nature of being on that plane, as I have already tried to explain.[1]

People want rest because they feel fatigue, but when one is out of the body in full consciousness one finds that the fatigue is gone, and then one no longer desires rest. In such conditions we look upon rest rather as we do upon death down here; we do not want less but more of the power and energy that we enjoy. The Solar Logos does not rest, even for a moment. If He did so, even for a second, we should all cease to be.

Many of those who have reached nirvāna have nothing further to do with the world's evolution; yet it does not seem possible for anyone to have reached that level and not to be pouring forth glory and splendour on those below. Even in

[1] *Ante*, p. 394.

the case of one so devoted that he continually turns all his thought upwards, and none downwards, one would think he could not help shedding devotion on those below.

There are seven paths open to the Adept, and most of them take the candidate away from the earth, yet they are all equally ways of serving the Logos. Presumably every Adept is willing to go where he is most needed and can be most serviceable, but at least it seems necessary to be perfectly willing to remain and accept "the woes of birth", if called upon. Any other attitude, and especially the idea of selfish escape from the world, liberation for one's separate self, could not carry the aspirant so high. To us it may seem that to stay with and help our humanity is the kindest thing to do, and that is very natural, for if we cannot thus love those who are already near and known to us, how shall we love others who are not known? Still, we must not forget that if the Lords of the Flame from Venus had not left Their system and come down into ours to help us, we should be at least one round behind the position that we have so far achieved. It may be the duty of some of us in the future to go to the help of some other system less advanced than ours.

At the same time, there is no question that more and more advanced pupils of the Masters will be needed to carry on Their work on earth. It is open to the Arhat to take no more physical births if he so chooses; but it is evident that our Masters wish us to continue taking birth for the sake of the work.

> Step out of sunlight into shade, to make more room for others. The tears that water the parched soil of pain and sorrow bring forth the blossoms and the fruits of karmic retribution. Out of the furnace of man's life and its black smoke, winged flames arise, flames purified, that soaring onward, 'neath the karmic eye, weave in the end the fabric glorified of the three vestures of the Path.

The opening portion of this passage seems to imply that there is not enough sunlight for all; but that is surely not so.

All can be happy. We make our own shadow, as the earth does. Sorrows and trouble are of our own making; they are our own karma, as is everything that comes to us. What Āryasanga means is that one should always be ready to help others, even at the cost of trouble or loss to oneself.

There are few kinds of action that bring great kārmic suffering. Cruelty does, of course, and there are some others. But most of people's actual suffering comes from the way in which they take the inconveniences of life that karma brings to them. *The suffering is then very distinctly "ready-money karma".* Such, for example, is the selfish mourning for those who have passed on to a happier state of existence, which causes suffering to everybody concerned, often including the dead, who feel the depression and sorrow very greatly. What karma brings to a man is never more than he can bear, *and bear easily; but* that is not the case with what he adds to it of foolish thought, and feeling and action.

> These vestures are: Nirmanakaya, Sambhogakaya, and Dharmakaya, robe sublime.

The three vestures will be discussed fully in our study of the third Fragment. They represent three possibilities which lie open to the man who has attained Adeptship. He can at once accept nirvāna, or take it after having gone through other high spiritual experiences, or remain in touch with the earth as a Nirmānakāya in order to fill the spiritual reservoir, or he can take up work in other globes or systems. This last choice is by no means selfish, of course; it is an impossible supposition that any selfishness could be possible at such a level.

There was a reference in the first edition of this book to "selfish Buddhas", but Madame Blavatsky, after her death, asked our President to remove the passage which contained it, because it was causing so much dangerous misunderstanding. It referred to those who are called the Pratyeka Buddhas. These are great Adepts at the level of the Buddha, but on the first ray. *Because "eka" means "one", some Northern Buddhists* have thought that a Pratyeka Buddha is one who works for himself alone, which appears a blasphemous idea to anyone who knows where They stand. The three Lords of the Flame, who are the pupils of the Lord of the World, are Pratyeka Buddhas.

They came to the earth to serve it and hasten its evolution along the line of the first ray, while the Buddha works on the second. It is foolish to criticize Them for not doing work which is not Theirs. It would be as sensible to find fault with a magistrate for not being a schoolmaster, saying, "See how little he cares about the education of children!" Of these great Beings I have tried to give some slight account in *The Masters and the Path*.[1]

> The Shangna robe, 'tis true, can purchase light eternal. The Shangna robe alone gives the Nirvana of destruction; it stops rebirth, but, O Lanoo, it also kills compassion. No longer can the perfect Buddhas, Who don the Dharmakaya glory, help man's salvation. Alas! shall selves be sacrificed to self; mankind, unto the weal of units?
>
> Know, O beginner, this is the open path, the way to selfish bliss, shunned by the Bodhisattvas of the Secret Heart, the Buddhas of compassion.

The Shangna robe is something very far beneath any of the three vestures above mentioned. It means here the balancing of karma, and the destruction of the personality by quenching all desires, including that for life. It implies an evolution of the causal body far higher than most men have attained, but without the development of love and compassion and the desire to help the world. A man who has thus freed himself from the necessity of rebirth may live as an ego on the higher levels of the mental world for an enormously long time.

In this passage, it is almost as though Āryasanga were complaining against those who take the Dharmakāya vesture, and retire to distant planes or systems But it would be really impossible for him to do that. He could not have thought that there were selfish Buddhas. The Prateyka Buddhas certainly are at the same level of attainment as the Lord Buddha; They have the same quality of compassion that He has, but it is not

[1] *Op. cit.*, Ch. xv.

Their duty to fill the office. For thousands of years before Their attainment of such heights these Great Ones must have been utterly incapable of anything like selfishness. We must remember that *The Voice of the Silence* was written down by a disciple of Āryasanga after the death of the latter, so he is not wholly responsible for it, and it appears that here the disciple must have allowed his own misconception to colour the ideas of his teacher.

> To live to benefit mankind is the first step.
>
> To practise the six glorious virtues is the second.
>
> To don Nirmanakaya's humble robe is to forego eternal bliss for self, to help on man's salvation. To reach Nirvana's bliss but to renounce it, is the supreme, the final step—the highest on renunciation's path.
>
> Know, O disciple, this is the secret path, selected by the Buddhas of perfection, who sacrificed the Self to weaker selves.

The six glorious virtues are the pāramitās, already considered in Chapter XLIII. They represent one of the systems of travelling on the path. Another is given in the set of qualifications expounded in *At the Feet of the Master*, followed by the four stages of the Path proper.

It is not quite true that the Nirmânakāya gives up bliss, for Adeptship is itself the attainment of bliss. What is true is that the Adept could remain always on the stupendous levels which He has reached, but instead He comes down to help. By doing that, however, He does not forego the eternal bliss which is inherent in Him; He merely decides to work at lower levels.

> Yet, if the doctrine of the heart is too high-winged for thee, if thou needest help thyself and fearest to offer help to others—then, thou of timid heart, be warned in time: remain content with the eye doctrine of the Law.

Hope still. For if the secret Path is unattainable this day, it is within thy reach to-morrow. Learn that no efforts, not the smallest—whether in right or wrong direction—can vanish from the world of causes. E'en wasted smoke remains not traceless. "A harsh word uttered in past lives is not destroyed, but ever comes again." The pepper plant will not give birth to roses, not the sweet jessamine's silver star to thorn or thistle turn.

Thou canst create this day thy chances for thy morrow. In the great journey, causes sown each hour bear each its harvest of effects, for rigid justice rules the world. With mighty sweep of never-erring action it brings to mortals lives of weal or woe, the karmic progeny of all our former thoughts and deeds.

Take then as much as merit hath in store for thee, O thou of patient heart. Be of good cheer and rest content with fate. Such is thy Karma, the Karma of the cycle of thy births, the destiny of those who, in their pain and sorrow, are born along with thee, rejoice and weep from life to life, chained to thy previous actions.

If one cannot rise immediately to the resolve to be utterly unselfish there is no need to despair One must work on in the right direction until one reaches the position where that ideal will seem perfectly natural and comparatively easy of accomplishment. Sometimes people feel that because they cannot fulfil a great ideal that is put before them there is nothing that they can do which is worth doing. They collapse, and do nothing at all, in consequence. But that is a great mistake. The Lord Buddha was very wise in dealing with all kinds of people, and He took care to avoid this kind of discouragement, by speaking of the highest path to His monks alone. He preached the middle *path to the general public, and told them to live the highest* and noblest life of which they were capable, so that later on they would be in a position to enter His Order. He said that they were to-day creating their opportunities for to-morrow, that is for their next incarnation. There is no need to despair, for the man who takes one opportunity receives tenfold more opportunities, and he who uses what powers he has as fully as possible, without overstraining himself, certainly develops those powers at a surprising rate.

The last paragraph makes reference to those who are born together. It is a fact that people evolve in groups, the same people coming closely together in different relationships again and again. What happens to one in any such group reacts very much upon the others, for both good and ill. It should be an additional incentive to those who are aspiring to realize that whatever they are able to attain will be of great benefit to a number of people whose destinies are thus bound up closely with their own.

CHAPTER XLVII

THE WHEEL OF LIFE

Act thou for them to-day, and they will act for thee to-morrow.

'Tis from the bud of renunciation of the self, that springeth the sweet fruit of final liberation.

To perish doomed is he who out of fear of Mara refrains from helping man, lest he should act for self. The pilgrim who would cool his weary limbs in running waters, yet dares not plunge for terror of the stream, risks to succumb from heat. Inaction based on selfish fear can bear but evil fruit.

The selfish devotee lives to no purpose. The man who does not go through his appointed work in life has lived in vain.

Follow the wheel of life; follow the wheel of duty to race and kin, to friend and foe, and close thy mind to pleasures as to pain. Exhaust the law of karmic retribution. Gain Siddhis for thy future birth.

C.W.L.—There are people who feel that because they cannot do great things or make rapid advance no effort is worth making. That is a great mistake. At least they can live to help those with whom karma has brought them into contact. They will never find themselves in a better position until they make the most of their present environment. If they will do this, when the time comes for them to make the great effort involved in taking the First Initiation, loving friends will be there to help. Real friends are those who are *the friends of the ego. These never bind one down, for the* satisfaction of their own very limited and human, and often really selfish, emotions. They always give one the freedom that is required to follow the higher path.

Some good people refrain from helping others, fearing that they themselves may be prompted by a selfish motive. Very often charity is bestowed upon the unfortunate not really with the desire to help them, but to relieve the giver of the unhappiness that he feels at the sight of suffering. Such a person would never go out of his way to find people in trouble, *in order that they might be helped. Again, there are others* who systematically give a portion of their large incomes to charitable organizations, so that they may enjoy the remainder with no qualms of conscience. *Knowing this, a disciple* sometimes questions himself as to whether his own motive is pure. But to refrain from helping because he doubts his own motive is surely a form of selfishness. Whatever our motive may be, we must help, though only that counts for real progress on the Path which is done purely to help the sufferer, without thought of self.

It is necessary to use discrimination in helping. As the Hindus say, help should be given to the right person, at the right time, and in the right place. Yet the necessity for thought should not cause hesitation. We may not always be certain which is the wiser of two courses of action, but we must nevertheless decide upon one of them, so that the opportunity to do good may not be entirely overlooked. Sometimes it is only by thought that we can help, but that, as I have said before, is very important.[1] The strength of many a man who is doing vigorous work in the world comes largely from others who are *engaged in radiating spiritual force in meditation.*

The wheel of duty to race and kin, to friend and foe does, as a matter of fact, offer the best of opportunities for progress.

[1] *Ante*, pp. 71, 75, 109-10, 184, 191, 320-21.

The Lords of Karma see to it that each person is given the conditions which are suited to his growth. They give a man the particular work that is likely to develop the qualities that he needs. At a low level of development there may be ten thousand places where a man can have the conditions needed for his progress. But when a man is more highly evolved his environment has to be chosen with the greatest care, for every-one must be put absolutely in the position where he can best advance. It is therefore quite inaccurate to say that a man succeeds in spite of his circumstances; difficulties are put in his way in order that he may transcend them, and that his character and powers may grow.

The man who does his daily duties well will soon be trusted with higher ones. Every one who can be trusted to do good and conscientious work is eagerly wanted by Those who guide the destiny of mankind. Be faithful in small things, and you will be made ruler over many things, as the Bible says. To be ruler over many things is a responsible position, and in occultism it is given only to those who have proved themselves faithful in the small things. That is the test that the Master gives. Many people neglect plain everyday duty for some visionary work in the future, perhaps of doubtful utility, and not intended specially for them. Many also regret the ties that they formed before they knew of Theosophy, when they now find them hampering. But they must do their duty. Unsuitable ties will drop away when the time comes when that freedom will be most useful for the aspirant's development, and what is more important, for the world's work. But if they are broken prematurely they will only entangle the man again and much trouble and pain will be caused.

If sun thou canst not be, then be the humble planet. Aye, if thou art debarred from flaming like the noon-day sun upon the snow-capped mount of purity eternal, then choose, O neophyte, a humbler course.

Point out the way—however dimly, and lost among the host—as does the evening star to those who tread their path in darkness.

Behold Migmar, as in his crimson veils his eye sweeps over slumbering Earth. Behold the fiery aura of the hand of Lhagpa extended in protecting love over the heads of his ascetics. Both are now servants to Nyima, left in his absence silent watchers in the night. Yet both in Kalpas past were bright Nyimas, and may in future days again become two suns. Such are the falls and rises of the karmic law in nature.

Be, O Lanoo, like them. Give light and comfort to the toiling pilgrim, and seek out him who knows still less than thou: who in his wretched desolation sits starving for the bread of wisdom and the bread which feeds the shadow, without a Teacher, hope or consolation, and let him hear the Law.

In a foot-note, H.P.B. says:

Nyima, the sun in Tibetan astrology. Migmar or Mars is symbolised by an eye, and Lhagpa, or Mercury, by a hand.

There are here several points of interesting analogy. The two planets mentioned give their light at night, when the sun is out of sight, and all is dark. It is so with us. We have to help those who are in greater darkness than ourselves; there is no one who cannot find someone more ignorant than himself whom he may teach. Even if those around us are not ready to enter the Path, we can lead them in the right direction towards it.

At the time of the transference of life from the moon to the earth, the planets glowed and shone like small suns. But Mars is mainly a desert now, and that is why he reflects the yellow or *reddish light.* From the standpoint of the poetic author of these verses, they are doing their best work in giving light to man now. The idea illustrates the fact that we are not necessarily doing our best work when we shine most. Also, when a building has to be erected, the foundations must be put in first. They do not count for anything in the matter of appearance, being hidden out of sight, but on them the building will be erected. So in the common work of every day the candidate is performing useful service to society, and at the same time developing the higher siddhis which are the spiritual powers of the ego.

The Teacher now tells the candidate what to say to those whom he is trying to bring to the Path.

> Tell him, O candidate, that he who makes of pride and self-regard bond-maidens to devotion; that he, who cleaving to existence, still lays his patience and submission to the Law as a sweet flower at the feet of Shakya-Thub-pa, becomes a Srotapatti in this birth. The Siddhis of perfection may loom far, far away; but the first step is taken, the stream is entered, and he may gain the eye-sight of the mountain eagle, the hearing of the timid doe.

> Tell him, O aspirant, that true devotion may bring him back the knowledge, that knowledge which was his in former births. The deva-sight, and deva-hearing are not obtained in one short birth.

Shâkya-Thub-pa is the Lord Buddha. The Srotāpatti is, as has been explained, "he who enters the stream". An analogy can be drawn between the outward act of laying one's service at the feet of the Teacher, and the inner change when the well-developed manas realizes the presence of buddhi, and bows down before that higher principle, resolving henceforth to use all its powers in obedience to its behests. In the ordinary life of men it is generally the mental nature that is allowed to have the last word. For example, in the matter of vivisection,[1]

[1] See *ante*, pp. 288 90.

many people whose feelings shrink from the practice with loathing, still decide that it must go on, because they think it is the only way to obtain certain knowledge which will help humanity. But the minority, who are in the right, say: "No, it is impossible that vivisection can lead to good. Our higher nature says with a clear voice that it is utterly wrong." If these people were in the majority they would stop it, and then some other way would be found to secure human health; the mind would be set to work in obedience to the higher intuition to find a better way.

Every one who feels enthusiasm on hearing about the Path is sure to have worked for it in a former birth, perhaps in many previous lives. It is encouraging to know this, for then one may expect to recover quickly the attainments of former lives, the deva-sight and deva-hearing which are the faculties of responding to the inner voice and of seeing life and the world with the eyes of the spirit.

> Be humble, if thou would'st attain to wisdom: be humbler still, when wisdom thou hast mastered.
>
> Be like the ocean which receives all streams and rivers. The ocean's mighty calm remains unmoved; it feels them not.
>
> Restrain by thy divine thy lower self. Restrain by the eternal the divine.
>
> Aye, great is he who is the slayer of desire: still greater he in whom the Self divine has slain the very knowledge of desire.
>
> Guard thou the lower lest it soil the higher.

As I have said before, he who stands in the presence of the Masters cannot but be humble, conscious as he is of the great gulf that exists between Them and himself. Not that even the physical presence of the Master, however, causes any uneasiness or depression; on the contrary, in His Presence we feel at our best and we realize that we can achieve because He has achieved. It is so also with the gaining of knowledge. The man who can grasp some big ideas can also see what remains to be learned that he does not yet know, and how much mystery there is in familiar things that others think to be quite simple and well-understood. So he who has much knowledge is likely to be humble, and the aspirant is warned that when pride rises in him it is a sign that he is unconsciously shutting in front of himself the door to further and higher knowledge.

The candidate must also practise moving among the disturbances of the world, which play upon him all the time—physically, astrally and mentally—without permitting them to agitate him. He must so train the lower vehicles that they will respond not to these outer calls, but to the inner commands. The ego is divine; with its aid the lower self must be controlled; and when that is done even the ego will have to be controlled by the Monad, the eternal Self. That all this may be done, the pupil must constantly guard the vehicles, attending to purity of food and drink and magnetism, of words and feelings and thoughts, as has been fully explained in *The Masters and the Path.*

> The way to final freedom is within thy Self. That way begins and ends outside of self.
>
> Unpraised by men and humble is the mother of all rivers in Tirthika's proud sight; empty the human form, though filled with Amrita's sweet waters, in the sight of fools. Withal the birthplace of the sacred rivers is the sacred land, and he who wisdom hath is honoured by all men.

The orthodox Christian usually considers that there are three stages in the growth of a soul First, the man acts rightly for fear of hell. Secondly, he does so with the desire of reaching heaven. Thirdly, he does right for love of Christ, who sacrificed Himself to bring men to that condition of feeling. There is, however, a fourth stage, when the way is found by realizing ourselves as one with the Self. Then the man does right because it is right, not even for the sake of making the

Master happy or of expressing gratitude to Him. Our deliverance is thus from within. No external consideration can determine our steps of progress on the Path. It is not a question of how long we have been at a certain level; we shall take the next step when we have developed the necessary qualities and powers within ourselves. No one need be anxious about this, for as the Tamil proverb says: "Ripe fruit does not remain upon the branch."

The Tīrthika, as we saw before, is the Brâhmana ascetic who visits the sacred shrines, and is evidently regarded here as feeling somewhat proud of having done so. Just so, some of the Hadjis—the Muhammadans who have made a pilgrimage to Mecca—are proud because they have done that. Such men are somewhat like the society people of our own day who are proud to say they have seen the latest play or have read the book of the day—though what they have learned in the process it may be difficult to say. Perhaps Āryasanga's scribe, being a Buddhist, was not above sectarian feeling, for he seems to regard all the Tīrthikas as being of this type!

The great attraction of Benares, Hardwar, Kumbhakonam and other Tīrthas is the bathing in the sacred rivers. At the place last named the pilgrims resort to a huge tank, but they believe that it is fed from underground by the Ganges. But our Buddhist scribe points out, with some apparent pride, that the source of the principal sacred rivers of India is the sacred land, that is, Tibet. It is a remarkable fact that the great rivers, the Ganges, the Indus and the Airāvatī or Irrawadi do rise all very near together in the Himālayas, and, going in different directions, east, south and west, sweep round and enclose the upper part of India in their giant embrace of thousands of miles. Those proud ascetics do not recognize that Tibet, a country which they despise, is the mother of their sacred rivers, says the writer, and he draws an analogy between Tibet and India, making India the body, which contains the sweet waters of immortality only in the incorrect vision of fools, and Tibet the source of wisdom, to be honoured by all men, that is all those who are not fools!

CHAPTER XLVIII

THE WAY OF THE ARHAT

Arhans and Sages of the boundlesss vision are rare as is the blossom of the Udambara tree. Arhans are born at midnight hour, together with the sacred plant of nine and seven stalks, the holy flower that opes and blooms in darkness, out of the pure dew and on the frozen bed of snow-capped heights, heights that are trodden by no sinful foot.

C.W.L.—At the present stage of evolution men who have attained the Arhat level are very rare. That is quite natural, since humanity is expected to attain the Asekha initiation only at the end of the seventh round, and the Arhat stage precedes that usually by only seven lives. Still, Arhatship is quite within our reach; it is principally a matter of our understanding what to aim at, and then using our wills to achieve that goal. Under the influence of the Lord Buddha thousands became Arhats. All that was due to His tremendous magnetism. Soon His successor will be with us, and we shall then also have unusual advantages.

The symbolism of this passage is probably capable of several different interpretations. The midnight hour may very well be taken as that darkest moment before the dawn when the candidate seems to be forsaken by everybody, even by his Master. It is at the fourth Initiation that the seventh principle comes into operation, as the candidate advances to the ātmic plane. The sacred plant of seven stalks may symbolize this, and the number nine also, because that seventh principle is really three in one, which with the other six makes nine. The number nine is considered most sacred by the Hindus.

It is only by going through the greatest trials, by descending into the very depths of darkness, that the qualities required in the candidate for this initiation may be attained. The holy flower opens and blooms in that darkness, yet it comes as a result of development on the buddhic plane.

> No Arhan, O Lanoo, becomes one in that birth when for the first time the Soul begins to long for final liberation. Yet, O thou anxious one, no warrior volunteering fight in the fierce strife between the living and the dead, not one recruit can ever be refused the right to enter on the path that leads toward the field of battle.
>
> For either he shall win or he shall fall.
>
> Yea, if he conquers, Nirvana shall be his. Before he casts his shadow off, his mortal coil, that pregnant cause of anguish and illimitable pain, in him will men a great and holy Buddha honour.
>
> And if he falls, e'en then he does not fall in vain; the enemies he slew in the last battle will not return to life in the next birth that will be his.
>
> But if thou would'st Nirvana reach, or cast the prize away, let not the fruit of action and inaction be thy motive, O thou of dauntless heart.
>
> Know that the Bodhisattva who liberation changes for renunciation to don the miseries of secret life, is called thrice honoured, O thou candidate for woe throughout the cycles.

Swâmî T. Subba Rao interpreted the fight between the living and the dead as the opposition between those who know and those who do not know. It will be remembered that this distinction was also made by the Master Kūthūmi when teaching Alcyone; he said that there were only two classes of people, those who know and those who do not know, those who have seen the way and those who have not yet seen it. He also said that those to be pitied most were not the bigoted and intolerant, but the millions who do not know that there is anything beyond the world worth striving for, and are happy in their ignorance. Madame Blavatsky interpreted the strife to be between the immortal higher ego and the lower personal ego, these being the living and the dead respectively.

The door is never closed against those who really wish to draw nearer to the occult path. He who wants to do so must be given his opportunity to try. And then, even if he fails it will not be in vain, for some of his enemies, his vices and weaknesses, will have been destroyed, and will not trouble him again. It is rare for anyone to blunder so badly as to be put himself back into a distinctly lower grade in life, as for instance, in India into a lower caste; but if a man takes up black magic containing a great deal of powerful evil and exerts himself very much in that line, he may wrench away the personality altogether from the ego, and create such bad karma as to make it necessary for him to go back to primitive conditions. Such cases are very rare A person who has been really unworthy of his class or caste, is usually thrown back into unpleasant surroundings in the same class or just below it. It would, however, be great unwisdom not to try to rise because there may be danger of a fall from a higher and more responsible position.

On the other hand, a man who attains, it is said in the text, will be honoured as a great and holy Buddha. Of course, the Arhat is not technically a Buddha But he is Buddha, that is to say, wise or enlightened.

Madame Blavatsky explained that "the secret life" is that of the Nirmānakaya His greatness is hidden from the sight of man, and yet he continues to live in this world. The term is here used in a general way not only for those who remain on the threshold of liberation in order to fill the reservoir of spiritual force, but *for all who remain behind*, thus including the official Members of the Hierarchy, such as our Masters. We generally reserve the term in these days, however, for those who follow one of the seven great lines after taking the Fifth Initiation—Those *who fill the reservoir*.

We meet here once more the idea of the path of woe. The statement is somewhat misleading, and rather a misuse of the term woe. It is true that a Master who is using the physical body does not obtain the enjoyment of working on the nirvānic plane, but He would smile at the suggestion that he was in woe. When a man gains the nirvānic consciousness, he does not lose it because he keeps a physical body, except when He is actively engaged on the lower planes. At any moment, between writing two letters or any two pieces of work on the physical plane, He can slip away at once into the higher consciousness, and carry on its work, which is infinitely more satisfying, and altogether more glorious and blissful than anyone can imagine down here.

It is true that coming back from the higher planes to physical existence *is like going down from the sunlight into* a very dark dungeon; but you would not think of that if in that place there was someone whom you very much loved and wished to help. Physical life does involve the renunciation of *the higher glory*, but the definite object of helping fills the soul to such an extent that certainly there is no suffering. Indeed, at a much lower stage of evolution, a person who knows that someone else is suffering and needs real help that he can give, and yet neglects that call and goes away to enjoy himself somewhere else, would afterwards be deeply troubled by remorse, so that his suffering would ultimately be greater than if he had renounced his pleasure in the first place. Really, the greatest happiness for all of us comes from doing the best that we know.

There is a large number of candidates who do not actually fall, but are not conscious of making progress. Many of these are subject occasionally to depression, and have the feeling that their efforts have been in vain, since there is nothing to show for them. They should not allow themselves to be depressed, because that spoils the astral atmosphere for other people, and is therefore selfish. But quite apart from that, it is foolish, because they ought to know that all the time they are making real inner progress. Long before they become aware of it in the physical brain, the astral and perhaps the mental body have been organized by their meditation, and they may be doing very definite and useful work in the inner worlds in a variety of ways. The whole life may seem to be a failure, but nevertheless much has been done which will be carried forward into the next life, and will then make possible some conspicuous progress, perhaps even on the physical plane.

In any given life a man develops both good and evil qualities. The latter show themselves in the four lower sub-planes of the astral world. As these reflect their influence in the mental plane only on its four lower sub-planes, they do not affect the ego at all. The only emotions that can appear in the three higher astral sub-planes are those which are good, such as love, sympathy and devotion. These affect the ego in the causal body, since it resides on the corresponding sub-planes of the mental world. Therefore every feeling and thought of a higher kind can be seen, even in this mechanical way, to have a permanent result in the higher self. And since it is the ego that treads the Path, he is making quite definite steps of progress with every right effort. So there is no reason to despair, nor to put off until to-morrow what we can do to-day just because we cannot do everything at once.

The Path is one, disciple, yet in the end, twofold Marked are its stages by four and seven portals. At one end bliss immediate, and at the other bliss deferred. Both are of merit the reward: the choice is thine.

The one becomes the two, the open and the secret. The first one leadeth to the goal, the second to self-immolation.

When to the permanent is sacrificed the mutable, the prize is thine; the drop returneth whence it came. The open Path leads to the changeless change—Nirvana, the glorious state of absoluteness, the bliss past human thought.

Thus, the first Path is liberation.

Yes, there is only one way, and that is by the unfolding of character. There is no limit to the *possibilities of the ego in* that respect; the noblest qualities of the greatest men exist in bud in all our fellow-men and will unfold into flower sooner or later. *And at the end, when one has done all that is possible in* the human kingdom, with the limitations of the human brain and environment, the path becomes twofold, and one must *choose between liberation and renunciation. Here the term* liberation means the acceptance of nirvâna, though sometimes it is used for mere escape from the wheel of births and deaths at *a lower level, as we have already seen in studying At the Feet of the Master.*

Those who do not follow the White Lodge use other methods, which often develop psychic powers to a relatively high point. But as the path of grey magic is not hedged round by restrictions, as is that taught by the Great White Lodge, sooner or later the man misuses his powers—for the temptation is too great. Sometimes, however, the followers of other lines end by coming into touch with the true teaching and pledging themselves to the Lodge. In America especially there is a great amount of more or less public teaching of occultism of the grey variety. But the real path is one—the Path of Holiness, the building of character.

The four portals mentioned here are the four initiations *leading to Arhatship, described at length in The Masters and the Path.* Another arrangement divides it into seven stages, as we shall see in the third Fragment of this book.

At the highest levels of attainment on this path the aspirant will recover the memory of his past lives, though at the same time his consciousness will have widened enormously, so as to take in that of great hosts of beings, and he will realize that his power and love are not his own, but God's. Only separateness will have been lost, and looking back he will see that he has been living under a delusion of separateness. He will see, too, that his past lives were very commonplace; that the turning-point in them were not usually the events that he considered to be the most striking and important while he was experiencing them, but that very often the little things of daily life were the events that really made for the greatest progress.

> But Path the second is renunciation, and therefore called the Path of woe.
>
> The secret path leads the Arhan to mental woe unspeakable; woe for the living dead, and helpless pity for the men of karmic sorrow; the fruit of Karma Sages dare not still.
>
> For it is written: "Teach to eschew all causes; the ripple of effect, as the great tidal wave, thou shalt let run its course."

By the "mental woe unspeakable" of the Arhan, which is another form of the word Arhat, on the secret path is meant the suffering that comes through sympathy. He sees all the pain and sorrow of the world; but at the same time he sees all the joy as well. He feels the greatest compassion for the "living dead", that is, for the great majority of mankind, who do not even know that there is something to strive for. Then, secondly, there is "helpless pity" that is aroused by seeing the kărmic suffering, the results of foolishness, which he cannot—we should say, rather, dare not—still. We can explain to people the principle of karma, so that they will take their painful experiences in the best way, and thus mitigate the suffering to some extent, but we cannot do away with the results of past actions.

Even in exoteric Christianity, the "forgiveness" of sins is not explained as meaning that the results of sins will be abolished. In the Anglican Church, for instance, when a priest is ordained and the power is conferred on him to forgive sins, in accordance with the words which in the Christian scriptures are attributed to the Christ: 'Whosoever sins ye remit, they are remitted unto them, and whosoever sins ye retain, they are retained", it is explained to him that what he has power to do is to set the offender right again with God, when by his n he has put himself in the wrong, or, in other words, he can ırn the man once more into the current of evolution, after he as set himself athwart it and so blocked his own advance. ehind that Christian conception there is a beautiful idea, but ore beautiful still is the Theosophical realization that one can ever get away from the Divine, that even the man who falls to avichi is still part of the Deity.

It has repeatedly happened that good and earnest students ıve refrained from giving help lest they should be interfering ith a person's karma. No one can interfere with the law of ırma, any more than with the law of gravitation. If you hold a book in your hand, it contains the potential energy of avitation, and the moment that the force you are employing to ld it up is withdrawn the book falls. The law of karma operates the same way. Karma not paid off is similar to potential ergy; *it may be suspended for thousands of years or for* ndreds of lives, but when the time comes it will manifest itself.

People sometimes think of karma as merciless. But it is t so. It is just as impersonal as any other law of nature. ı *the physical plane laws work without any regard to good* bad intentions. If a child falls over a precipice the amount injury it sustains depends upon the height of the fall, and ıether the ground is hard or soft, and not at all on such moral nsiderations as whether it was trying to pull a companion out danger, or wanted to pick a flower for its mother, or whether threw itself over in a fit of passion. Similarly, if a man tches hold of a hot bar of iron, he may do it to prevent its ling on someone else, or with intent to strike someone with the injury done to the hand will be the same in either case. at is the way in which karma works on the physical plane. t on the mental plane intentions count for a great deal, for make our own character for the future by our thinking.

So one should never abstain from giving help when pos- le. If when you have done your best you fail, then you may : "His karma did not allow of his being helped," or else: ly karma did not give me the privilege of helping him", but t is all. All that really matters is that we work for others. ork is *expansive* and cumulative; *if* you bring one person Theosophy, he may bring another ten, and each of those, more.

Another sense in which we can take this verse, "the fruit of karma sages dare not still", is that even if a great Adept were to do away with some apparent evil—with all poverty, for instance—He would effect no real good, but only go against the law of the Logos. I do not mean that the Logos wills such evil; it would be blasphemous to say that His scheme includes necessary suffering, that He causes it. Suffering comes only by doing what He has expressly told us not to do. It is true that all have suffered; no one, so far as we know, has always chosen the right thing and never made mistakes; but the suffering has always put us right when we have refused to learn in any other way, and thus the law has made certain for all of us the ultimate attainment of the indescribable bliss of nirvāna.

The open way, no sooner hast thou reached its goal, will lead thee to reject the Bodhisattvic body, and make thee enter the thrice glorious state of Dharmakaya, which is oblivion of the world and men for ever.

The secret way leads also to Paranirvanic bliss—but at the close of Kalpas without number; Nirvanas gained and lost from boundless pity and compassion for the world of deluded mortals.

But it is said: "The last shall be the greatest." Samyak Sambuddha, the Teacher of perfection, gave up his Self for the salvation of the world, by stopping at the threshold of Nirvana, the pure state.

We have already considered the three vestures, and seen that no idea of selfishness can attach to one who takes any of them. The Nirmānakāyas are like the contemplative orders, filling the reservoir of spiritual force for the use of the Adepts who are in touch with our world. There are some fifty or sixty posts which the latter may fill. The Nirmānakāya still retains his permanent atoms, and so could, I suppose, if he wanted, fill one of these posts if it became vacant. The post of Bodhisattva falls vacant once in each root-race, but there are already many appointed to fill the office far into the future, who are now being prepared. Many of those who became Arhats during the incarnation of the Lord Buddha remain as Nirmānakāyas, because of His teaching.

All these offices and positions must be filled, and those who renounce nirvāna are only volunteering to do what we might call the dirty work. The Adept, if one may put it so, feels not so much the loss of pleasure, as the knowledge that working on the nirvânic level would be a million times more effective than down below. And yet someone must do that lower work. In the scheme of the Logos, the smallest bit of work is as necessary as the greatest, just as the oiling of a great locomotive is as necessary as the driving of it.

The Bodhisāttvic body here alluded to is that of all those who remain to help the world—not only that of the very limited number of those who will be Buddhas.

Stopping at the threshold of nirvāna means that one does not enter in and entirely leave the lower planes, as some do, and as the Buddha might have done had He so chosen. He who thus remains has the higher consciousness to the fullest extent, and also retains His consciousness even down to the physical plane, and so can work on any plane required. It is said that the Buddha is, at His level, free of the solar system, that He can move to any of the planets of the system, just as some of us can move to other planets of our chain. Yet even for Him there must be a limit, because He has not yet entered into the consciousness of the Logos. I do not know whether His consciousness includes the sun; Swāmī T. Subba Rao once spoke of the sun as a place of life so intense that even a Dhyān Chohan can hardly enter it.

The buddhic plane appears to take us anywhere through our chain of worlds. Nirvânic consciousness would mean consciousness anywhere in the solar system. At the Fourth Initiation a touch of nirvāna is given, but that does not mean the full consciousness of that plane. It is entry into the lowest part of it, and one has still to rise, sub-plane by sub-plane, until full consciousness of the plane is acquired.

Of the Buddha it is said that He attained Paranirvāna. Thus it is possible to consider different levels of nirvāna—the different sub-planes of the ātmic plane, then the two planes of our system beyond that, and on into the higher cosmic planes.

> Thou hast the knowledge now concerning the two ways. Thy time will come for choice, O thou of eager Soul, when thou hast reached the end and passed the seven portals. Thy mind is clear. No more art thou entangled in delusive thoughts, for thou hast learned all. Unveiled stands Truth and looks thee sternly in the face. She says:
>
> "Sweet are the fruits of rest and liberation for the sake of self; but sweeter still the fruits of long and bitter duty: aye, renunciation for the sake of others, of suffer ing fellow-men."
>
> The Bodhisattva who has won the battle, who holds the prize within his palm, yet says in his divine compassion:
>
> "For others' 'sake this great reward I yield"—accomplishes the greater renunciation.
>
> A Saviour of the world is he.
>
> Behold! The goal of bliss and the long Path of woe are at the furthest end. Thou canst choose either, O aspirant to sorrow, throughout the coming cycles!
>
> Aum vajrapani hum.

The greater renunciation is renouncing the higher work, after seeing it, in order to do the lesser work, which we have seen to be just as necessary. Such a matter as the renunciation of the desires of the personality is an altogether lower renunciation.

We must not import into our thought here any tinge of the popular Christian idea of a Saviour who comes to save us from eternal torment. The idea is, of course, nothing but a horrible *distortion of the earlier and truly Christian teaching*, as for example that of Origen, who believed in the deification of man through Christ. Every one who has risen into true communion with the Master has become identified with Him, and is safe or sure to complete the treading of the Path in the present cycle. The *original meaning of the term* "*saved*" has been explained in *The Masters and the Path*.[1]

When we speak of the *Nirmānakāyas* as the *Guardian* Wall, we do not for a moment imagine that they are protecting us against evil powers who are waiting for an opportunity to pounce upon mankind. They are engaged, as said before, in filling the reservoir with force used by the Great White Brotherhood, *to give help and guidance intelligently* wherever it is possible, and to save mankind from many mistakes which it might otherwise commit, and from the suffering which would then ensue.

This Fragment ends not with "Om mani padme hum", as did the first, but a different formula: "Aum vajrapāni hum," Vajra means a thunder-bolt, as well as a diamond. The term *reminds us of* Jove with his thunderbolts and of the Norse God Thor. This thunderbolt is the dorje, the rod of power, of which I have given a sketch in *The Masters and the Path*.[2]

PART VIII

FRAGMENT III

THE SEVEN PORTALS

CHAPTER XLIX

THE PĀRAMITĀ HEIGHTS

Acharya, the choice is made, I thirst for wisdom. Now hast thou rent the veil before the secret path, and taught the greater Yana. Thy servant here is ready for thy guidance.

C.W.L.—There is a foot-note to the word Āchārya, which means a spiritual preceptor or guru. It explains that among the Northern Buddhists these are chosen from among the saintly men learned in gotrabhū-jnāna. The gotrabhū is the man who is ready for any one of the Initiations, he who has all the qualities and only awaits permission to present himself. Gotrabhū-jnāna is the knowledge of those qualifications. The Masters—Adepts who take pupils or apprentices—are They who have that knowledge.

The term Yāna has already been discussed in Chapter XXX.

'Tis well, Shravaka. Prepare thyself, for thou wilt have to travel on alone. The teacher can but point the way. The Path is one for all, the means to reach the goal must vary with the pilgrims.

The word shrāvaka comes from the root *shru* which means to listen. The "listener" is one who attends to the religious instructions, says a foot-note, and when from theory he passes into the practice or performance of asceticism, he becomes a Shramana, from *shrama*, exertion. The two terms have much the same meaning as the *akoustikoi* and *askitai* among the Greeks.

All who tread the Path must gain the same qualities or virtues, but the modes of training for this are very varied. There are seven great types of men, or seven rays, and along each of these aspirants are drawn to teachers of their own rays. Even within the same type the teaching is adapted to individual needs, so the pupils of one Master often receive quite different treatment. Thus a Master may send one of His pupils into seclusion and another out into the struggle of the world. He may give one the satisfaction of knowing that he is being taught, and leave another without that knowledge for a great length of time. Of this training and the different types some considerable account has been given in *The Masters and the Path.*

> Which will thou choose, O thou of dauntless heart? The Samtan of eye doctrine, fourfold Dhyana, or thread thy way through Paramitas, six in number, noble gates of virtue leading to Bodhi and to Prajna, seventh step of wisdom?
>
> The rugged path of fourfold Dhyana winds uphill. Thrice great is he who climbs the lofty top.
>
> The Paramita heights are crossed by a still steeper path. Thou hast to fight thy way through portals seven, seven strongholds held by cruel, crafty powers—passions incarnate.

Little is said in this Fragment about the fourfold dhyāna, but much about the pāramitās. The steps in meditation or dhyāna are always spoken of as three, as we have seen in studying the first Fragment, and these taken together are called sanyama. These three are dhārana, dhyāna and samādhi, or concentration, meditation and contemplation, and there is the preliminary practice of pratyāhāra, making the fourth. We have also studied the pāramitās in the second

Fragment. Here the path for the attainment of those virtues is spoken of as having seven portals, at each of which the candidate has to struggle with and slay a great fault or sin.

It seems a little misleading to put meditation and the development of these qualities one against the other, for both are necessary. One cannot meditate without having these qualities, and one cannot develop the qualities to perfection without meditation. It may have been that even at his day Āryasanga was contrasting the path of retirement, of the man who avoided the difficulties and distractions of the world in order to go by himself to meditate apart from men, with the path of the spiritual life lived in the midst of the world of men, which requires the practice of ideals in all the affairs of daily life. He would then have been speaking of the former as a lofty path, but of the latter as greater still, or rather steeper still. Instances of men achieving perfection amidst the business of daily life are quite common in the Hindu books The great gurus of the *Mahābhārata* were active in the council-chamber and on the battlefield, and a merchant is also mentioned, in the person of Tulādhāra. In the *Bhagavad-Gītā* the path of duty and action is taught, and Shrī Krishna tells Arjuna, His pupil, that Janaka and others attained to perfection by action, and he should do the same, performing action without personal attachment to the fruit of it, but for the sake of mankind[1]

A glance at the opposites of the pāramitās will show the nature of the cruel, crafty powers which must be fought. The man who is self-centred forgets that he is one unit in a whole, that, as Epictetus said, without mankind around him he would not even be a man. Charity and general ethical development or morality in its full sense do away with this self-centredness, and open the man up so that he thinks more of others than of himself, and becomes a benefactor to those who suffer, a good companion to his peers, and a responsive pupil to his teacher.

People often allow their patience to be ruffled by resentment. They "feel hurt", and are discontented, complaining inwardly, if not outwardly. This means that they forget that just because there is a law of justice, which is all the time engaged in repaying past debts between man and man, there

[1] *Op. cit*, III, 20.

must be some apparent injustice. Sometimes a man wants to see the result of his own work at an early stage, because he is thinking of himself, not of the work, and he wants to boast about it or at least to congratulate himself upon its achievement. At a later stage, he is sorry because his efforts made for a good purpose seem to fail; there is still something of discontent and impatience in that. Later he will see that it was the effort that was the important thing, not the results. When these feelings trouble him no more, he will have acquired patience.

Again, the natural man is lazy. He likes to bask in the sun, and will not exert himself until hunger moves him, or there arises a vainglorious desire to hang more scalps to his belt, which urges him to rise while his fellow-savages are sleeping. Tireless, dauntless energy is not "natural". Observe our President, utilizing every moment of the day, always working, never wasting time. Do you suppose it was natural to her in the past to be always at work? She does it because she has seen the beauty of the goal—to be a helper of mankind.

Meditation also is not "natural". It calls for much trouble, a strong exertion of the mind, and the keeping of the body in subjection. The acquirement of wisdom also involves study and effort, and sometimes the courage to face uncomfortable and even dangerous experiences.

> Be of good cheer, disciple; bear in mind the golden rule. Once thou hast passed the gate Srotapatti, "he who the stream hath entered"; once thy foot hath pressed the bed of the nirvanic stream in this or any future life: thou hast but seven other births before thee, O thou of adamantine will.

Seven lives is the average period between the First Initiation and the Fourth, but if the will is sufficiently strong a man can attain the goal in less. It is analogous to the preparation of a student for an examination; it is considered that a certain period of time spent in study should fit the average candidate to pass, but any given man may take a longer or a shorter time. Two lives have often brought a man from his

First Initiation to Arhatship; some few people have achieved that goal in one life. The same rule then holds good for the attainment of Adeptship, for the Arhat is just half way.

> Look on. What seest thou before thine eye, O aspirant to God-like wisdom?
>
> "The cloak of darkness is upon the deep of matter; within its folds I struggle. Beneath my gaze it deepens, Lord; it is dispelled beneath the waving of thy hand. A shadow moveth, creeping like the stretching serpent coils. . . . It grows, swells out, and disappears in darkness.
>
> It is the shadow of thyself outside the Path, cast on the darkness of thy sins.

Here one would prefer to say faults and failings rather than sins. These become much more dangerous on the Path than ever they were before. Therefore an iron determination to eradicate them utterly and at once is required for treading the way. When one sees a fault in oneself, one should go and do exactly the opposite, unflinchingly and steadily, until it is completely gone. Few people are willing to do this. Sometimes they beg one to be open with them and tell them just what it is that keeps them back. If one does it, one risks losing their friendship. Generally they become indignant and say that they know that they have many faults but not the one to which you have drawn their attention and that they do not think much of your judgment or intuition. There are exceptions, but that is the general rule.

On the Path a man has to live by his own rules, not simply to follow the rules or conventions of the social environment in which he finds himself. This increases his difficulties and dangers He is trying his utmost—of that we may be sure, for if he were not, he would be throwing away the fruits of the efforts of many lives, and that would be madness. Others have no means of judging him. He holds in his hand a key which others do not possess, and for him therefore all things wear a new aspect. He needs the kind thoughts of others—

ot criticism of what they do not understand—for he is not isensitive, and they will aid him to rise rapidly and become a ower to uplift the world.

"Yea, Lord; I see the Path; its foot in mire, its summit lost in glorious light nirvanic: and now I see the ever-narrowing portals on the hard and thorny road to Jnana."

Thou seest well, Lanoo. These portals lead the aspirant across the waters on to the other shore.

"The other shore" is a phrase that is constantly used. here are two distinct forms of symbology which make use of iis metaphor. In one, the whole of life is likened to the :ean, and men are ferried to the other shore, to the state :yond death and rebirth, by the Mahâyâna or the Hînayâna. he second is a more technical meaning. At the first great iitiation, a man steps out from the general evolution, which he is now completed, and begins the special one. As much as is :rmissible of the ceremony that then takes place has been 'inted in *The Masters and the Path*, including the words: You have entered upon the stream. May you soon reach e further shore."[1] That shore is, of course, Adeptship.

Each portal hath a golden key that openeth its gate; and these keys are:

1. Dana, the key of charity and love immortal.

This is not mere charity in the sense of giving alms, nor hat is commonly called a charitable attitude, though that is uch more than the former. It means utter readiness to give ieself and all one has in service. There are not many :ople in the world who have reached that stage, who are ady to employ all their time, energy, money, feelings and oughts to this end. And even for those who have reached at point there is a further stage, for there may still exist the

[1] *Op. cit.*, Ch. VII.

fault of identifying the work with oneself instead of oneself with the work. There are many who are willing to take up great work, but few who will forget themselves to the point of doing any insignificant piece of work of which no notice will be taken and for which no thanks are given. The disciple of the Master has to look round and see what has to be done that he can do that is not being done. He must not look with disfavour upon the humblest task, thinking, " I am too good for this ". In the Master's work no part is more important than any other, though some portions are more difficult than others, and therefore require special training or unusual faculties or ability.

To sacrifice yourself thoroughly you must also sacrifice your feelings. If these are liable to be hurt, you will waste a lot of force in being offended that should have been put into the work. We must always do our best, and not stop to think: "What a fine fellow I am."

Then we must also have "love immortal". Tennyson said of the dead:

> They watch like God the rolling hours
> With larger, other eyes than ours,
> To make allowance for us all.

God knows all, and He does not lose patience. We are apt to lose patience with one another, and quickly get tired of making allowances, but He does not. It has been well said: *Tout comprendre, c'est tout pardonner.*[1]

2. Shila, the key of harmony in word and act, the key that counterbalances the cause and the effect, and leaves no further room for karmic action.

The word shīla is generally translated simply " conduct ", but here the writer emphasizes the idea of harmony. He who practises shīla will be ever attentive to his own dharma, studious of what he can do with the powers that he has in the position in which karma has placed him. This is the quality also which will close up his kārmic account as quickly as

[1] " To understand all is to pardon all."

possible, and enable him to enjoy ever-increasing freedom and opportunity to do good.

3. Kshanti, patience sweet, that nought can ruffle.

While the candidate at this stage of his journey must acquire a great measure of this quality, it still remains to be perfected later on. To be utterly unruffled is a very high condition. The Arhat is spoken of as the perfect—the venerable—yet he has five fetters to cast off before reaching Adeptship, and of these the last but one is the possibility of being ruffled by anything whatever.

4. Vairagya, indifference to pleasure and to pain, illusion conquered, truth alone perceived.

The whole of the third part of our commentary on *At the Feet of the Master* is taken up with the quality of vairāgya, which is there translated desirelessness. As was said before, it is usually translated indifference or dispassion.

This quality is possessed by the man who is keenly alert about his work, but never allows personal considerations to stand in his way. He has got rid of feelings that can be hurt, but has not lost sympathy. He is indifferent to the things which commonly sway men, is not disturbed by passions, but has calm, cool judgment. This so-called indifference does not mean that the man will not put enthusiasm into his work, but that he will do so when it is painful and troublesome just as much as when it is full of pleasure. When the quality is well developed, the man will see that most of our pleasures and pains are illusions, and are caused by a wrong way of taking things. He will see the truth of the saying of the ancient Stoic that it is our opinions about things that trouble us more than the things themselves.

5. Virya, *the dauntless energy that fights its way* to the supernal truth, out of the mire of lies terrestrial.

Each person who approaches the Path has his own special qualities, on account of which he will find some of these portals especially easy to pass and others difficult. The quality of patience, for example, would generally be much easier for the Eastern disciple, and the quality of energy for the Western. When this list was first placed before us, some of us wondered why the more difficult qualities were placed at the beginning. Really it was not so. The Lord Buddha was an Indian and he drew it up for the Indian people, and probably He placed first on the list the steps which they were likely to find the easiest.

It certainly is difficult, when one has first developed a great deal of energy, or vīrya, to acquire the sweet patience, or Kshānti, afterwards. A person who has this energy and hears about the path wants immediately to tread it to the very end—but without patience he will cause such a disturbance all along the way, and create such a quantity of troublesome karma that he will delay himself considerably. On the other hand the man who has the patience and not the energy will perhaps be content to go along very slowly—and his progress will then be slow indeed.

There is a tendency of this kind at present in the East. I remember that in Ceylon I was once told that in ancient times people really attained nirvāna, but that now times were evil—it was what was called a dark age, a kali yuga—and these achievements were no longer possible, though perhaps in some far-distant, golden future they would again become so. But the great teachers are with us still, and though, as the Christian Scripture says, straight is the gate and narrow is the way, yet now as ever that gate can be found and that way can be trodden.

In these matters, no man can tell where he stands. To many Theosophy comes as a recollection; that means that they knew something about it in former lives. If in those lives a man has worked hard to reach the Path, in this life a little more work will bring him to it. But if he is only now beginning that effort he has a long way to go, and it would be an almost superhuman feat for him to enter the stream in this incarnation.

The efforts that many Theosophists are making imply a great strain; that is why there is sometimes so much disturbance in the Theosophical Society, so much irritability and quarrelling. I have heard people say that other Societies have far less trouble of this kind. That is naturally the case. If you join a geographical or geological or other similar society, you are simply joining a set of people who are working together to acquire more knowledge, generally of a particular kind. But in the Theosophical Society many people are putting a great strain upon their astral and mental bodies and that reacts upon their physical bodies. I think, therefore, that as we shall continue to deal with a set of sensitive and not yet perfect people, who are pressing forward more rapidly than nature in its normal course intended, the history of the Society will probably continue to record many disturbances, though the time is bound to come for each one of its members when he will acquire the "patience sweet that nought can ruffle".

6. Dhyana, whose golden gate once opened leads the Narjol towards the realm of Sat eternal and its ceaseless contemplation.

In earlier editions of this book, you will find that the word narjol is mis-spelt naljor. This was a mistake, corrected in the later editions. The mis-spelling was due to the fact that Madame Blavatsky read the word astrally, and reading a book astrally you see at the same time what is written on the front of the page, and also the reverse of the characters as from behind. Of course, you would not focus your attention on the reverse aspect of the print or writing; you would normally notice only the pages spread out before you—those would be quite distinct, and the reverse would then be out of focus. Still, reading in this way it is quite easy to make mistakes and get some things reversed. This is especially true of numbers; you can see at once if you are looking at 7 the wrong way about, but 18 can easily be mistaken for 81.

Madame Blavatsky sometimes got numbers reversed in this way. She used often to look astrally at rare books, of which only one or two copies exist, and some of us would go to the British Museum to verify a quotation which she had stated as being, let us say, on page 139, and would find that it was on page 931. Generally we found her quotations accurate, though sometimes there were small inaccuracies; once, I remember, she left out the word not, which did make quite a difference to the sense! Seeing that Madame Blavatsky did not know Sanskrit, Pāli or Tibetan, and had to depend entirely on her memory when using words in those languages, as she so frequently did, the wonder is not that she made some mistakes, but that she made so few.

The word narjol, which has led us into this little digression, is a Tibetan word which means adept or saint, or, even better, yogi. Its derivation is from a word meaning "peace". The narjol is therefore one who strives after the inner peace.

It is dhyāna or meditation which opens the gates of the higher self. Most of our Theosophical information, and of what is written in the ancient Scriptures, has come to us by way of clairvoyance. There is a mass of investigation waiting to be done by clairvoyance. In occult chemistry, for example, we have examined the elements and some compounds, but there is a vast work to be done in that field by someone who has the faculty of etheric vision and magnification, and the patience to observe and count the atoms over and over again.

The Stanzas of Dzyān must have been written by one who could read the minds of the directing Devas, and thus see what they were aiming at. What we say about rings and rounds may not be exact, but the information given about the astral and mental planes, being the result of thousands of observations, is reasonably sure to be so. There may still arise errors from premature generalization—that happens in every science—from the mistaking of the abnormal for the normal, or from the oversight of some class of phenomena bearing on a general theory. Such, for example, was our former idea about the interval between lives, and the way in which egos incarnated regularly in successive sub-races, which was announced as the normal course of evolution until we discovered another type of egos who kept mostly to one sub-race and reincarnated twice as frequently as the others. There may be half a dozen more types for all we know; all we can say is that we have not yet come across them.

The old Scriptures are especially valuable because they were largely written by people who could see clairvoyantly. Many are repelled from them because of the way in which they present their ideas, sometimes by their archaic flavour. Every age has had its own methods of expression. Our modern way is quite bald; we put things as plainly as we can. In ancient Egypt, to take a different example, everything was told in a very poetic garb. The Gnostic books also wrapped everything up in elaborate symbology. Therefore, if one wants to study the *Book of the Dead*, or *Pistis Sophia*, even supposing one gets an accurate translation, which is not always the case, one has still to try to put oneself back into the attitude of mind of the times when they were written, and that is very difficult. It also takes time—more than the modern man can usually give to it, if he is also engaged in earning his livelihood in some other way.

In the old days in every part of the world life was much more leisurely. It was the custom to make things comfortable and easy for everybody, and generally to put off till to-morrow any business that could possibly be avoided to-day. In looking up a great number of past lives, I found the same thing everywhere. There were no trains to catch or newspapers or magazines to bring out by a certain time of day or on a certain date. The nearest approach that I have found to a regular serial publication was a series of letters, brought out at intervals which were very long and quite irregular—so that sometimes months elapsed between the issues.

In spite of all this, men did attain Adeptship in those old days, but they must have found it hard to acquire vīrya, the dauntless energy required for the path. Still, the unresting activity, the ceaseless hurry of our modern Western world, is not exactly the same thing as vīrya. It is often by outward compulsion that people show their energy. If they are not punctual and assiduous in business, the competition is such that other men will pass ahead of them and they will not be able to make a living. But the student of occultism is moved by his own inner compulsion, and is always working steadily—but without hurry or flurry, for he wants his work to be well done.

Probably the principal danger in this matter is that of doing too little, of letting things go undone which ought to be done. Yet some people spoil their work by undertaking too much. Mrs. Besant is a magnificent example of the middle course; she is always at work, and plans all her time to the best advantage, but she does not attempt more than she can do. She will often say about a thing: "This is not my work, for I have no time for it."

There is truth in the saying that the busiest man always has the most time. It is so because he does not mismanage his time. But there are men who take upon themselves more work than they can really do, sometimes because they have the feeling, which may be well founded, that no one else among the people around them can do the work quite as well. This was once the case many years ago with a certain General Secretary of one of the Sections of the Theosophical Society. He was a splendid worker of great ability, and his opinion that he could do things best was probably justified. But he undertook so much that work left undone for lack of time accumulated until, when his successor came into office, things were in an almost hopeless muddle.

It is better to tread the middle path in this matter, to portion out your work carefully, and to spare some of the time to teach and to train other workers. It is often much more trouble to show someone else how to do a piece of work than to do it oneself, but one hopes that when one has shown him once or twice, or if necessary ten times, he will be able to do it alone a hundred times, so that in the end there will be gain.

> 7. Prajna, the key to which makes of a man a God, creating him a Bodhisattva, son of the Dhyanis.
>
> Such to the portals are the golden keys.

We have now come to the last of these qualities, Prajnā, which means, once more, wisdom—more in the sense of a faculty of consciousness than of knowledge that is wisdom because it penetrates to the life behind the form. Jnâna, also translated wisdom, is not a faculty, but prajnā is.

It is said that this quality makes the Bodhisattva. This latter term is used here in a wide sense. Technically, a Bodhisattva is one who is destined to become a Buddha, who has given to a living Buddha the pledge that in a future life he will take up that office. But all men alike will pass through the level of the Bodhisattva, on their various lines. There are seven great planetary lines, and Masters taking pupils are at work along each of them. Every man, going along his own line, will ultimately be drawn into contact with a Master standing at the head of that line. There is, however, the possibility of a man's changing from one line to another through devotion to a particular Master, but this requires a certain extra amount of study and effort; for a man most readily adapts himself to occult training on his own line.

He who becomes a Buddha must thousands of years beforehand have made his vow to a *living Buddha*, and it is said that from that time onward the influence of the Buddha overshadows him, and that when in due course he attains Buddhahood, the great influence of the spiritual Buddha hovers over the incarnate Buddha. The Lord Gautama is said to have taken his vow to Buddha Dipankara, and the latter is supposed to have been also present in the background during the years when the Buddha Gautama was preaching. One can only repeat what has been said on these high matters, but certainly it is a very beautiful idea. It is also a natural one, for we know that on a much lower level the Master is always overshadowing the disciple, who is part of His consciousness.

CHAPTER L

TUNING THE HEART

Before thou canst approach the last, O weaver of thy freedom, thou hast to master these Paramitas of perfection—the virtues transcendental six and ten in number—along the weary path.

For, O disciple! before thou wert made fit to meet thy Teacher face to face, thy Master light to light, what wert thou told?

Before thou canst approach the foremost gate thou hast to learn to part thy body from thy mind, to dissipate the shadow, and to live in the eternal. For this, thou hast to live and breathe in all, as all that thou perceivest breathes in thee; to feel thyself abiding in all things, all things in Self.

C.W.L.—To meet thy Master light to light expresses a wonderful truth. When the pupil comes into touch with his Master's consciousness, and the latter enfolds him for the first time, his aura shines forth brilliantly with the Master's light, as I have explained in *The Masters and the Path*.[1]

These verses go again over much of the ground traversed at the beginning of the first Fragment To part the body from

[1] *Op. cit.*, Ch. v.

the mind means literally that one must learn to make the māyāvi rupa, and metaphorically that one must discriminate what is reality and understand that one is not the body. The astral body is the shadow of the physical one; this must not be destroyed, but its influence over the pupil must be done away with. One must use it, but not allow it to dominate one. To live in the eternal is not to leave the world, but to judge things all the time from the standpoint of the eternal life. All these things we have considered in studying *At the Feet of the Master.*

He who learns to live from the point of view of the eternal, of the reincarnating ego, soon learns that nothing that happens to one from the outside matters at all. When we read the *Lives of Alcyone*, we see that many of the characters in them went through much suffering. Some of those characters were ourselves, and we know that the suffering was temporary and does not affect us now. Looking back, we sometimes wonder how some of the characters endured such suffering. Well, they did, and came through it safely. It is not always so easy to feel that one will come through present suffering all right, because one is in the midst of it, instead of looking at it in perspective. One cannot expect to see clearly the whole of an experience or an event in which one is actually immersed. A soldier on the battlefield, for example, sees very little of what is going on, and does not usually know the importance of the particular movement or manœuvre in which he is taking part; his share of the work may seem trivial, and yet it may be an important factor in deciding the battle, or it may be spectacular and prominent and yet not be really vital to the success of his side.

Nevertheless, I do not think we can overrate the importance of the Theosophical Society. It is one of the most important movements that the world has ever seen. To the outer world, the rulers and statesmen, it looks like any other Society—a mere handful of people. Yet it was founded by the two Masters who will be the heads of the sixth root-race, and They are choosing from among us the people who are fit to take part in that race in its early development. But we can very easily overrate our own personal share in the work of the Society. No one is indispensable, as we have had occasion to find out in the course of the Society's history. Even our great leaders, Madame Blavatsky and Colonel Olcott, have departed, but the Society has survived their loss, and gone on spreading its ideals and permeating the world with them, because the Masters remain.

Disciples of the Masters have to learn to identify their consciousness with that of their fellow-men and therefore certain exercises are often set for the purpose. The results are often surprising when the pupil begins by trying to enter the consciousness of various animals. They have very limited lines of thought, and actions for which people will often credit them with motives drawn from human experience are often due to something different. On the other hand, they follow their few lines of thought much further than is commonly realized; so that in some ways we credit them with very much more than is in them, but in others with very much less.

Often a pupil is put into the body of someone else, in order that he may understand that other's position, and also that he may realize himself in different forms. A rather drastic experience of the kind was related to me by Mr. Damodar K. Mavalankar many years ago. He was one day taken out of his body, and flung into that of a drunken sailor in some dock in a foreign country. He was a Brâhmana, with all the Brâhmana's hereditary shrinking, if it may be so described, from contact with what is low or unclean—a feeling stronger than almost any Western person can quite understand. Naturally, it was a terrible shock. He found himself immersed in what to him was unspeakable filth. Yet in the midst of this horror which had suddenly fallen upon him he was able to continue to realize himself, and to say to himself: "I am not this; I am Damodar." And he was able to remain calm, and to think: "This too is humanity; I have to sympathize also with this." So he came out of the test with credit.

Many people, if subjected to such a test, would have got into a great flurry, would have thought it a dreadful nightmare, and in struggling madly to get free would have injured themselves. To most, perhaps, the first feeling would have been one of disgust. But an Adept does not feel like that. He does not condone any wrong; He would realize that very much more than we could, but He is not disgusted. He recognizes all the stages of human life. He remembers that He has been through something like this Himself—ages ago, perhaps on some other planet. His buddhic consciousness is also perfectly unfolded, and when that is the case one is able to enfold sinners within oneself. There is no repulsion for the man who is doing wrong; one feels only the desire to give whatever help is possible. Generally, however, only a little can be given to people in those stages, and that must be given cautiously. Not only sympathy is necessary, but also wisdom to understand what he can respond to, and patience and tact to make him realize the excellence of a life a little superior to that which he has been leading.

It is through this experience of identification that one learns wise sympathy, and I think that is the only way in which it can be done perfectly. One sees then why a man does certain things, and how they appear to him. Those who have not that experience must do their best to try to see things from the point of view of others.

> Thou shalt not let thy senses make a playground of thy mind.
>
> Thou shalt not separate thy being from Being, and the rest, but merge the ocean in the drop, the drop within the ocean.
>
> So shalt thou be in full accord with all that lives; bear love to men as though they were thy brother-pupils, disciples of one Teacher, the sons of one sweet mother.

The first of these verses reminds one of the earlier portion of the first Fragment, where it says: "The mind is the great slayer of the real. Let the disciple slay the slayer." It is such a slayer because we have allowed prejudices to grow up in it. It is commonplace knowledge that we never see another person, but only our thought of him. To slay the slayer, however, does not mean that we are to try to get along without the intellect, and trust solely to our impulses, which are a stage lower. We must rise to the intuitional level, which is above the intellect, and allow that to determine to what objects our thoughts shall be directed.

If people could see the effect of prejudice in the mental body, they would be surprised. The matter of that body is, or should be, in a constant rhythmical flow, and different parts of it, or rings, have to do with thought along different lines. If one has a prejudice along some one line of thinking, there is a congestion in the ring which has to do with that line; the matter in that place no longer flows freely. The appearance made on the mental body by this congestion is exactly like that of a great wart. We ought to be able to look out through any portion of the mental body, but the effect of that wart is to interfere with our vision. When we try to look out through this part of the mental body things will appear distorted, as has been explained before.[1]

It is in this way that the mind is the slayer of the real. Even the best people have some prejudices. Someone, for example, who prides himself on being free from them in one direction—let us say about caste or colour—will have them in another, perhaps in regard to manners. He does not mind whether a man's skin be brown, or white, or red, or yellow; but if the man should happen to eat off his knife, or pronounce words in a provincial way, he is not at all indifferent

The worst of these prejudices are generally those of the existence of which we are quite unaware, with which perhaps we have grown up from childhood. They are exceedingly hard to eradicate. The only way to conquer them completely is by love. If the man's manners offend us, he will learn better ones in time—if not in this incarnation, then in the next—but the man is part of the Logos, just as we are. The love of God, like the peace of God, passeth understanding, and not only excuses all, but feels no need to excuse.

We must learn to bear love to all men as though they were our brother-pupils. The tie between pupils of the same Master is the strongest in the world, except that which exists between members of the Brotherhood In time, the pupil will learn to extend the quality of love that he has acquired under these conditions of unity, until he feels it towards all whom he sees.

Of teachers there are many; the Master-Soul is one, Alaya, the universal Soul. Live in that Master

[1] *Ante*, p. 167.

as its ray in thee. Live in thy fellows as they live in it.

This is the same idea of unity, put even more beautifully.

Before thou standest on the threshold of the Path: before thou crossest the foremost gate, thou hast to merge the two into the one and sacrifice the personal to the Self impersonal, and thus destroy the path between the two—Antahkarana.

The general meaning of this verse is quite clear to us, but the use of the word antahkarana is a *little unusual*, especially as Madame Blavatsky has annotated it. She says: "Antahkarana is the lower Manas, the path of communication or communion between the personality and the higher Manas or human Soul. At death it is destroyed as a path or medium of communication, and its remains survive in a form as a Kāmarupa—the shell."

In the latter part of the third volume of *The Secret Doctrine*, Madame Blavatsky sometimes uses the word kāma-manas for what we now call the lower mind, meaning a mind the character of which is built up during the personal life under the influence of kāma. The antahkarana could then be regarded as the lower manas pure and undefiled, the ray of the higher manas. During life, it is possible for a man to get into touch with the higher manas through that channel, and as we have seen in *The Masters and the Path*,[1] the pupil addresses himself to the task of so widening the channel that it is always fully open, and the active higher manas may express himself all the time in the personality. But after death the average man has not the freedom that he had before to initiate new activities or to try new experiments; he is now in the world of the effects of the causes he set going during earth life, and must first work out his collected lower emotions on the astral plane, and then his collected higher emotions on the lower mental plane, in the devachanic condition. So, in a sense, his antahkarana has ceased to function as a downward channel.

[1] *Op. cit.*, Ch. VIII.

This does not apply, however, to the man who is the master of his own feelings and thoughts or to the pupil who ranges the astral and lower mental planes at will.

During life the ego in the causal body has entrusted some of his own energy, as it were, to the search for useful experience to which his personality was adapted, and in so far as the personality failed in its mission, that energy, those rays of the higher manas, have been lost, remaining but as a centre for the shell, or even for the production of a dweller on the threshold if they are strong enough to last over to the next incarnation.

In current Theosophical terms, after death the man remains in the astral plane for a period, longer or shorter, according to the quantity and virility of his selfish desires, be they gross or refined or mixed. Then he meets with his second death, the death of the astral body, and goes on into devachan, a special condition on the lower mental plane, in his lower mental body, in which he works up to perfection all his unselfish ambitions and desires. While he is in this latter state, some part of the discarded astral corpse may still be roaming about in a congenial environment, if that body was coarse All this has been very fully explained in my little works *The Astral Plane* and *The Devachanic Plane.* Anything like a full description of these after-death states here would swell this book to unwieldy proportions

When writing the article on Lost Souls, which has been incorporated in *The Inner Life*, I thought of a simple explanation of the connection between the higher and lower mind. By far the greater part of the ego belongs to the highest sub-plane of the mental; a lesser portion belongs to the second sub-plane, and still less to the third. We may therefore imagine a diagram representing the ego on those three sub-planes, as being shaped something like a conventional heart, tapering to a point at the bottom. In the ordinary person only that little point comes down into the personality—so that a very small portion of the ego is in activity in reference to it.

Probably not more than a hundredth part of it is active in people who are unevolved. With occult students a little of the second sub-plane is generally in activity also. More advanced students have a great deal of that sub-plane in activity, and in the stage below that of the Arhat, about one half the ego is active.

The hold that the ego has over his lower vehicles is only very partial, and the antahkarana may be regarded as the arm stretched out between the little piece of the ego that is awakened, and the part put down, the hand, which frequently forgets about the higher and often even works against it. When the two are perfectly joined this attenuated thread ceases to exist.

In Sanskrit the word antahkarana means the inner organ or inner instrument, and the destruction of that would imply that the ego would no longer need an instrument, but would work directly on the personality.

The ego actually loses a part of himself when the cohesion of the ego as a whole is weaker than the forces of entanglement, but he has also gained something during the life, and generally (always excepting the case of a very wicked life) the gain is more than the loss sustained through the entanglement with the lower manas. A little of himself and a little of the lower manas is left in the kâma rupa at the second death. The antahkarana should therefore be thought of as the link which joins the higher and the lower self, and which disappears when one will operates the two.

> *Thou hast to be prepared to answer Dharma, the stern law, whose voice will ask thee at thy first, at thy initial step:*
>
> "Hast thou complied with all the rules, O thou of lofty hopes?
>
> "Hast thou attuned thy heart and mind to the great mind and heart of all mankind? For as the sacred river's roaring voice whereby all nature-sounds are echoed back, so must the heart of him who in the stream would enter thrill in response to every sigh and thought of all that lives and breathes."

Madame Blavatsky here gives us a long foot-note, explaining that the Northern Buddhists, and indeed all Chinamen, find in the deep roar of some of the great and sacred rivers the key-note of nature. She points out that it is a well-known fact in physical science, as well as in occultism, that the aggregate sound of nature—such as is heard in the roar of great rivers, the noise produced by the waving tops of trees in large forests, or that of a city heard at a distance—is a definite single tone of quite an appreciable pitch. All that is true, and one who has learned to do so can always hear the underlying tone of nature. Every planet also has its own sound; it intones its own note as it moves through space, and by this tone the Logos knows whether all is going well with His worlds, somewhat in the same way that a practised engineer can tell by the sound of his engine whether all is well with his machinery. So must the aspirant listen constantly to the life in all around him.

This brings us back to that quality of sympathy which this book so strongly insists upon. Often we think we understand our nearest friends, but really we do not, as is often quite apparent to an outside observer.[1] But a Master always understands; He cannot possibly misunderstand. He may say that He does not approve of something that He sees; yet He is always in perfect sympathy, and understands without our needing to say a single word. We must try to understand others by endeavouring to see things as they see them, by understanding what their thoughts are, not by doing what they do.

Disciples may be likened to the strings of the soul-echoing vina; mankind, unto its sounding-board; the hand that sweeps it to the tuneful breath of the great World-Soul. The string that fails to answer 'neath the Master's touch in dulcet harmony with all the others, breaks and is cast away. So the collective minds of Lanoo Shravakas. They have to be attuned to the Acharya's mind—one with the Over-Soul—or break away.

[1] *Ante*, pp. 95, 104, 279

The Occult Hierarchy makes use of disciples as the strings of a vînâ, on which it may sound the splendid music of the march of evolution, that all that music may then resound among mankind. What would you do, were you a musician, with a string that did not wish to blend itself with the rest, but tried to force itself into more prominent notice? You would throw it away. Anyone who has an axe of his own to grind, who wants knowledge or liberation, or anything else for himself, is not fit to be a pupil of the Master. With this in view every pupil will be tested. He will be given pieces of work which, if he neglects them, will be left undone. If the work is important, the Master will always have an understudy ready, but when it is just on the fringe of things it may be left, and that string will be cast aside.

The disciple must have not only harmony with the great purpose of the Master, but also with the rest of the workers. A man must do the work of his own department and not interfere with that of others; when their work touches his, he can only either help or hinder them, and it is his duty to help, to make things as easy as possible for a brother. This mutual forbearance and help acts like oil in machinery; when oil is lacking it may still work, but not so smoothly or well, and more energy will be needed to make it go. If one puts all one's energy into the work, and yet wastes much of it in friction, that is almost the same as giving but a part of it. One must have in mind, not his own advancement, nor even the success of his own department, but the good of the whole.

> Thus do the brothers of the shadow—the murderers of their Souls, the dread Dad-Dugpa clan.

All through her writings Madame Blavatsky applies the name Dugpa to the brothers of the shadow—black magicians, as we often call them. Perhaps it is rather an unfortunate name to have chosen, because the dugpas do not quite deserve all the hard things she has said about them.

In Tibet, before Buddhism penetrated that land, there was much worship of elementals and nature-spirits, and offerings of a propitiatory character were regularly made to them. The religion was on a low level, as all religions of a propitiatory nature must be. "The Bhons and Dugpas," says Madame Blavatsky, "and the various sects of the 'Red-caps', are regarded as the most versed in sorcery. They inhabit Western and Little Tibet and Bhutan." The old religion thus still lives.

The same thing has happened in other religions. In Christianity, for example, as I have before pointed out,[1] Jehovah still lingers—a tribal deity, who was jealous of other gods. The Jews knew nothing of one supreme Deity until they were carried away into Assyrian captivity; then they tried to identify the Supreme God whom they then heard of with their own tribal god, and much confusion resulted. Unhappily Christianity became entangled in this, and it still appears in the English Communion Service. In the early part of that service the Jewish Ten Commandments are read, where a jealous god is spoken of, but later on in the same service we find that God is called "God of God, Light of Light, Very God of Very God". The old idea of propitiation also passed on into Christianity, in the curious idea that God was bought off by the death of His own Son.

In Tibet, though Buddhism sent no less than three missions to that country, and the people are mostly Buddhists of a sort, the old religion comes up again and again, for it had a great hold on the hearts of the people. The same phenomenon may be found in the Italian Appenines, where the old Etruscan religion, far older than the Roman, is still to be seen. The Catholic Church has set itself against this in vain. Another instance is evident in Ceylon. The people there are Buddhists, and there are some Christians, descendants of those who were converted by the Portuguese. Still, in moments of real necessity—of serious illness or calamity—Buddhists and Christians alike revert to the old "devil-worship". If you ask them why they do so, they will reply: "Of course we are Buddhists or Christians, and are civilized; but there may, after all, be something more in the old faith, and there is no harm in making things quite safe."

The termination *pa* means simply "people". Thus, the followers of the Master Kūthūmi are called in Tibet Kūt-Hūm-pa. The Bhon-pa are the followers of the aboriginal religion. The descendants of the converts made by the first mission

[1] *Ante*, pp. 306-8.

are called Ninma-pa. That first incursion of Buddhism rapidly became corrupted by the old faith The Kargyu sect represents the converts of the second mission, which was sent to Tibet some centuries later than the first. The Dug-pa, or Red-caps, belong to this sect, and so are two removes from the Bhon-pa. It also became impure, and allowed the old beliefs to creep in.

Then came the third and last reform, by Tsong-ka-pa. The followers of this are the Gelug-pa, or Yellow-caps. To this sect belong the Dalai Lama and the Teshu Lama, and the present government of the country. To it also belong outwardly our two Masters. The people of this sect wear, on great occasions, yellow robes, and curious high-pointed helmet-like caps.

Āryasanga belonged to the Yellow-caps; so, of course, did Alcyone, in his last incarnation, as the former's disciple. Perhaps Alcyone somewhat strengthened his teacher's expressions when speaking of the Red-caps. To call them "murderers of their souls" is hardly in keeping with the spirit of the Buddhist religion.

The Dug-pa clan, then, is not quite so bad as it has been painted. They are Buddhists, with nature-worship superimposed. This old worship, its enemies say, included animal sacrifices, and even human sacrifices at one time.

The Yellow-caps are opposed to them, because they are striving to maintain a purer Buddhism. Their rules are stricter, and admit much less of nature-worship, though even they have not been able to keep entirely free from it, so that some day a fresh reform may well be undertaken. From the Dug-pa clan some have joined the Yellow-caps, and have even attracted the attention of our Masters, so they cannot be altogether bad. The Bhon-pa are not a very advanced or dignified kind of black magicians, so to call them "brothers of the shadow" gives them more credit than they deserve, even on their own line.

Hast thou attuned thy being to humanity's great
pain, O candidate for light?

> Thou hast? Thou mayest enter. Yet, ere thou settest foot upon the dreary path of sorrow, 'tis well thou should'st first learn the pitfalls on thy way.

Once more we have that idea of the path of woe. There is no sorrow on this Path; strenuous effort there is, but with it the greatest joy in the work. Of this joy many teachers have spoken, with the result sometimes that their pupils, encountering the early difficulties, have been disappointed. Āryasanga evidently was anxious not to mislead any pupil of his, so he laid stress on the difficulties.

There is a difficult stage through which all have to pass a stage between two certainties. Many in this position care nothing for the things of the world. They do not care, for example, whether they have money, fine houses and clothes, or not. If wealth should come to them, it would be a responsibility that they would meet like any other, but they would be equally content if they had just sufficient. The lower things have fallen away, and yet the higher ones are still matters of faith, not of knowledge and experience. In this condition the man inevitably has a monotonous and sometimes a miserable time, which may last for a longer or shorter period, and may possibly occur several times.

But when the higher is clearly seen, all is changed, and the Path becomes radiant with happiness Then the lower things have lost all attraction. Take the case of our President. If she devoted her time and talents to worldly ends, she could certainly win great fame and position along one or other of several lines; but if you were to ask her whether it would be a pleasure to give up what she has chosen and follow a line of worldly ambition, she would surely say: "Certainly not; why should I? Nothing could possibly equal the delight of the Master's service."

There is far greater joy in the life of the disciple than in any worldly life, however beautiful the surroundings may be. He renounces personal possessions of every sort, but what does he want with them? In India often a great man, who has been perhaps the Prime Minister of a State, and has had great influence, fame and wealth, one day quietly drops the whole thing, puts on a yellow robe, and goes out owning nothing whatever. He does it knowing quite well both forms of life, and clearly seeing that the life that he has left is poor in real wealth and joy in comparison with that which he will lead as a hermit or a wandering sannyāsī. It is often the case that one in a prominent position, such as the late Czar of Russia, can do very little to help the world. Such a position does not therefore appeal to the occultist. I remember the case of a highly advanced student who was given the choice between remaining an obscure person and rising to a leading position in one of the greatest countries of the world. He chose the latter alternative, and in due course became Prime Minister of Britain. In that position he found himself cramped by powerful and selfish interests, and opposed by the power of the Church. Feeling the weight of his responsibility he was driven into a policy of conciliation. Though his objects were to give greater freedom to the people and to consolidate the Empire, and he did achieve success in the latter aim, he always regretted his choice—perfectly unselfish as it had been—and he died a disappointed man.

CHAPTER LI

THE FIRST THREE GATES

Armed with the key of charity, of love and tender mercy, thou art secure before the gate of Dana, the gate that standeth at the entrance of the Path.

C.W.L.—Aryasanga now runs over once again the seven portals, taking them as stages on the path, and looking at them especially from the standpoint of the pitfalls that endanger the aspirant. The brighter side of the matter, the encouragement and strength that the candidate receives, are for the moment not being thought of; it is desirable to remember this, lest the Path should seem too sad.

Dāna, as already explained, means more than simple almsgiving, more even than the feeling of charity; it implies the complete giving of oneself to the service of humanity, holding nothing back.

Behold, O happy pilgrim! The portal that faceth thee is high and wide, seems easy of access. The road that leads therethrough is straight and smooth and green. 'Tis like a sunny glade in the dark forest depths, a spot on earth mirrored from Amitabha's paradise. There nightingales of hope and birds of radiant plumage sing, perched in green bowers, chanting success to fearless pilgrims. They sing of Bodhisattva's virtues five, the *fivefold source of Bodhi power, and of the seven steps in knowledge.*

Pass on! For thou hast brought the key; thou art secure.

This verse gives us a beautiful and poetic description of the Path as its first part appears to the happy pilgrim. At first he thinks it is full of joy and very pleasant and easy to tread. It is easy, when one has seen the *Holy Grail* to give up all else and follow it. But after a while the vision may fade, the first enthusiasm wears itself out, and the man begins to grow weary. It is the way of human nature to want constant change. See how people rush after a novelty, and how, after a short time their interest slackens, the pursuit becomes monotonous, and they turn their attention to something else.

Studies in the lives of Alcyone showed us that most people make very little progress, even in a series of twenty or thirty lives. One man wrote, after hearing what name he bore in the *Lives*, and learning that he was very much the same fifty thousand years ego as he is now: "If anyone had told me before that twenty-five thousand years ago I was anything but a savage in the woods, I could not have believed it." I answered him: "If twenty-five thousand years ago you had been a savage in the woods, the chances are that you would still be one to-day."

If, however, a person does become enthusiastic for a spiritual object, he at once makes a rapid move forward; if he cannot continue his enthusiasm it is a pity, but probably in the rush he has accomplished as much as was intended for him in the present life. Now we have not only the motive to go forward, but we have also a great deal of knowledge to enable us to do so, and that helps to prevent us from falling back.

We must try to keep our enthusiasm always, and not allow ourselves to be affected by moods so that it is at the mercy of what happens to influence us on the physical plane, or on the psychical planes. We had a great testing of our enthusiasm when Madame Blavatsky died. I remember how it tended to fade when she left us. She had the faculty of keeping us all going, and when she went we felt limp, though some of us had succeeded in getting into direct touch with the Masters.

> And to the second gate the way is verdant too, but it is steep and winds uphill; yea, to its rocky top. Grey mists will overhang its rough and stony height, and all be dark beyond. As on he goes, the song of hope soundeth more feeble in the pilgrim's heart. The thrill of doubt is now upon him; his step less steady grows.
>
> Beware of this, O candidate; beware of fear that spreadeth, like the black and soundless wings of midnight bat, between the moonlight of thy Soul and thy great goal that loometh in the distance far away.
>
> Fear, O disciple, kills the will and stays all action. If lacking in the Shila virtue, the pilgrim trips, and karmic pebbles bruise his feet along the rocky path.

The pupil generally comes in with a splendid outburst, and then slackens down. This is because he expected, though he may not have confessed it even to himself, that his life was going to be all changed; perhaps he imagined that he would have a life full of phenomena or that he would always realize the presence of the Master, and so be able to keep constantly at his highest level. His life *is* changed, but not in the way he thought.

When doubt appears it is for some students doubt of the entire body of Theosophical knowledge; they have not yet come into conscious touch with the Masters, and they begin to doubt Their very existence, and to wonder whether they are following an *ignis fatuus*. I hope no such doubt will come to any of us, but if it does it is best to fall back on first principles. Go back to the beginning; inspect your motives; examine the evidence.

Then there is doubt of oneself, which sometimes assails the beginner; one may not be showing out the divinity that one wishes. But one must go on trying, without doubting, because success is *absolutely* assured for every man, and doubt is a great obstacle to attainment. Let a person who is sure from the outset that he will not be able to do it try to learn swimming. He will never learn. The doubt sends him under the water more than any real difficulty. Another, who has confidence, will learn almost at once.

The trouble with many aspirants to the Path is that they have this doubt as to whether they can achieve. Well, they must go on working for it, and get rid of their prejudice against themselves, for that is what it is, by reasoning it away. They must say to themselves: "I am going to do it, whether I can or not!"

Āryasanga's similes are always beautiful. He speaks here of the moonlight of the soul. It shines with a reflected light from the Logos, the sun, and also from the spiritual soul, buddhi, and the spirit, ātmā. He must let nothing come between, or the soul will be left in darkness.

"The soundless wings of the midnight bat" gives a vivid picture of the way in which fear steals upon a man. Fear is one of the most deadly things, and it is pressing in upon us on every side, for the world is full of it in a multitude of varieties of form. The man in business, for example, is in a constant little turmoil of fear; the employee is afraid of what his superior will think of him, or of losing his place. Religious people are afraid of death, of hell, of the fate of their departed friends, and all sorts of absurd things. Many children live in constant fear of their elders, their fathers and schoolmasters, as I have explained in the earlier commentary.[1]

Āryasanga well says: "Beware of fear". It darkens the soul, and makes it a dimmer reflection of the Logos. The Logos is love, and, said S. John, "Perfect love casteth out fear".[2]

The Shīla virtue is harmony, good conduct. The occultist has a moral code different from that of the world—different in being far more strict. He is not bound by the rules and conventions of society, but by something far stronger—the princi-

[1] *Ante*, p. 291.
[2] I. John, 4, 18.

ples of the spiritual life, which allow not the slightest deviation from truth, love and a life of service, with no room at all for personal self-indulgence.

> Be of sure foot, O candidate. In Kshanti's essence bathe thy soul; for now thou dost approach the portal of that name, the gate of fortitude and patience.

We have come to the third portal. Kshānti is patience and fortitude. Steady enthusiasm is required; not the nervous, anxious, spasmodic kind of enthusiasm that wears out its possessor before it has accomplished anything useful.

> Close not thine eyes, nor lose thy sight of Dorje: Mara's arrows ever smite the man who has not reached Vairagya.

Māra is the king of desire, the personification of desire; so it is said that his arrows ever strike those who have not reached the condition of vairāgya or desirelessness.

Madame Blavatsky gives us a note about Dorje, or Vajra, the thunderbolt, the Rod of Power, which was also mentioned in the second Fragment. She says:

> Dorje is the Sanskrit Vajra, a weapon or instrument in the hands of some Gods (the Tibetan Dragshed, the Devas who protect men), and is regarded as having the same occult power of repelling evil influences by purifying the air as ozone in chemistry. It is also a Mudra, a gesture and posture used in sitting for meditation. It is, in short, a symbol of power over invisible evil influence, whether as a posture or a talisman. The Bhons and Dugpas, however, having appropriated the symbol, misuse it for purposes of black magic. With the yellow-caps, or Gelugpas, it is a symbol of power, as the cross is with

the Christians, while it is in no way more superstitious. With the Bhons, it is, like the double triangle reversed, the sign of sorcery.

The Rod of Power which is kept at Shamballa and used in Initiations and at other times is probably the strongest talisman on this planet. At the same time it is a great symbol of that power which is resistless, which, felt in ourselves, makes fear impossible for us.

Talismans are not mere relics of mediæval superstition, as some people think. If anyone who is in the least degree sensitive will go to the case in the British Museum that contains old Gnostic gems, he may easily convince himself of that fact, for the influence emanating from some of them is very plainly to be felt. A talisman is a small object loaded with magnetism, and its purpose is to repel all influences that do not harmonize with the magnetism with which it is charged. Its action may be compared to that of a gyroscope, which revolves in such a way that it will sometimes break to pieces rather than allow its motion to be changed in direction.

A jewel makes the best talisman, since it preserves magnetism best, being the highest type of mineral. In ordinary circumstances, fear begins faintly, and only gradually gathers strength. In all such cases, a talisman charged with the right kind of magnetism is a help, for it repels those first faint vibrations. The wearer thus has time to gather himself together, to call up his own strength and to set in motion in his astral body vibrations of the opposite kind.

Āryasanga returns to the subject of fear:

> Beware of trembling. 'Neath the breath of fear the key of Kshanti rusty grows; the rusty key refuseth to unlock.
>
> The more thou dost advance, the more thy feet pitfalls will meet. The path that leadeth on is lighted by one fire—the light of daring burning in the heart. The more one dares, the more he shall obtain. The more

he fears, the more that light shall pale—and that alone can guide. For as the lingering sunbeam that on the top of some tall mountain shines is followed by black night when out it fades, so is heart-light. When out it goes, a dark and threatening shade will fall from thine own heart upon the Path, and root thy feet in terror to the spot.

Beware, disciple, of that lethal shade. No light that shines from Spirit can dispel the darkness of the nether Soul unless all selfish thought has fled therefrom, and that the pilgrim saith: "I have renounced this passing frame; I have destroyed the cause: the shadows cast can, as effects, no longer be." For now the last great fight, the final war between the higher and the lower self, hath taken place. Behold, the very battlefield is now engulfed in the great war, and is no more.

But once thou hast passed the gate of Kshanti step the third is taken. Thy body is thy slave.

It is clear from these verses that the candidate must learn to put the lower self aside utterly. Fear belongs to that, for the higher self can have nothing to fear in all the world—the only fear that a real man can have, said an old Roman philosopher, is that he himself should fail to use to the full all his virtues or powers for good.

Selfishness also belongs to it, and in this matter the habit of hundreds of incarnations may have to be reversed; for some time one may find oneself somewhat selfish even when the heart is definitely turned against it; it is comparable to what happens when the engines of a steamboat are suddenly reversed, in order to stop it—the boat still goes forward, against the engines. But presently the forward momentum will be entirely neutralized, and then the boat will obey the engines perfectly.

Until one gets rid of this selfishness the higher self cannot shine fully into the personality. The ego or soul itself may have what looks like selfishness, though it is quite different from that of the personality. It may ignore others, if it remains just manas, and not manas-taijasī, manas strongly connected with buddhi, and so may be selfish in that way; but it could never make the mistake of thinking that it can gain through the loss of another, an error that is common enough down here. Men often do things in trade, for example, which they know to be wrong; they think they have gained, that they have over-reached their neighbours, but they make a great mistake. Quite apart from the law of karma, which is bound to operate, the man has set his mind to plan how to cheat, and he will have to suffer the reaction of all the force of thought and desire that he has set going in that direction. He has set up a habit, and the next time that an opportunity occurs to do some underhand thing it will be a little easier for him to yield to the temptation, and a little harder to check himself and do the right. If he could see the whole of the transaction and not merely one little corner of it, he would realize that he has not gained, but has lost enormously.

An ego could not be as blind as that. The man who cheats, because he sees only the immediate results on the physical plane, is like a general who should neglect all the rest of the battle-field in order to take one small position. He might capture that position, but he would lose the battle.

If you have reached the stage where you have destroyed selfishness, you can say: "I have destroyed the cause;"—the cause of all trouble and sorrow down here.

The battle-field that is now engulfed and is no more is the antahkarana, which disappears when the higher has swallowed up the lower, and no longer exists.

It appears that Āryasanga had in the background of his mind an idea of the correspondence between these seven portals and the seven principles in man. The first three are related in some way to the three lower principles in the personality, while the fourth is concerned with that pure lower mind which is the ray of higher manas, and is the antahkarana. At this point the temptations begin to be those of the higher principles, and thus belong to the inner man.

CHAPTER LII

THE FOURTH GATE

Now for the fourth prepare, the portal of temptations which ensnare the *inner* man.

Ere thou canst near that goal, before thine hand is lifted to upraise the fourth gate's latch, thou must have mastered all the mental changes in thyself, and slain the army of the thought sensations that, subtle and insidious, creep unasked within the Soul's bright shrine.

C.W.L.—It is within the experience of many aspirants to the Path that the common faults which have been met and conquered in ordinary life reappear later on in a different form. You may have killed pride, for example, in its ordinary worldly forms, but it will reappear again as spiritual pride. So also you may have got rid of desire for worldly gain, but it comes up again as desire for personal progress or knowledge for personal satisfaction, for the sake of feeling that one has knowledge. Then, even when sympathy has begun to make itself a power in the life, selfishness tries to capture it and make you desire only to get rid of the cause of your own discomfort and unhappiness, by putting the object of suffering out of sight. It is something like the case of a housewife—if there be one of this kind—who dislikes to see dust in the room, so sweeps it under the carpet, instead of keeping the place properly clean.

Even hatred turns up again, incredible as it may seem that so coarse a vice should appear among those who are striving to live the higher life. Some of our students come perilously near it, if another differs from them on any subject, let us say that of the planetary chains, or the question as to whether Mars and Mercury belong to our earth chain or not! Of course, if one asks point-blank, "Do you hate So-and-so because his opinion on this point is different from yours?" he will deny it; but he will not go to visit the other man, and if they should chance to meet he will feel much disturbed and be disagreeable, or else he will cover that feeling up with an artificial ease, a smooth surface, like oil on water.

This is a singularly persistent fault, and it has been responsible for some of the world's big troubles. Was not the whole Christian world convulsed and rent asunder in the fourth century because of one dot on one letter of a word? It made the difference in the word as to whether the Second Logos was of the *same* substance as the First or of *like* substance. This was the whole dispute which raged round Alexandria between the so-called Arians and the orthodox. And now, are not millions of Christians on the one side and millions of Christians on the other kept apart, all because of the question as to whether the Third Logos came out direct from the First, or from the First through the Second? This is the famous "filioque controversy" on what is called the Procession of the Holy Ghost, which led to the disruption between the two great sections of the Christian Church. The Eastern, or Greek, Church holds that the Holy Ghost, the Third Logos, proceeded from the Father—single procession—but the Western, or Roman, Church holds that He proceeded from the Father and the Son—double procession. The quarrel is all about something of which no one can know anything, and is of no practical importance to anybody. From diagrams shown to us, we Theosophists can infer that both sides are right, but neither will welcome the suggestion.

In Buddhism, to take another example, two large sections of co-religionists are divided by the question as to whether the platform erected on the water for the performance of certain ceremonies should be composed of three planks or of four. They have to perform their ceremonies separately on this account!

What does it matter whether Mars and Mercury belong to our chain or not? We can be just as good men and women, just as good citizens, just as earnest Theosophists, just as good servants of the Masters, and one hopes just as good friends, whatever our opinions may be. Personally, I study and observe as carefully as I can, and then give out what I know, as it seems to me my duty to do, but I have never pretended to infallibility, and am learning more every day. I should never think of finding fault with anybody who disagrees with what I say. I have indeed more than once heard our great President say how deeply she hopes that no one will ever make a dogma of anything she has said, and put her up as an obstacle to future progress in our Society, and as a cause of division. If she has any anxiety at all, it is in regard to this danger.

Theosophists are supposed to have given up the idea of the infallibility of any particular source of knowledge. The question for us when a new idea is promulgated is, "Does it ring true? Does it inspire, elevate, illuminate?"—not, "Who said it? What book did you get that from?" There are, however, some who, having given up blind faith in the Bible, have transferred it to *The Secret Doctrine*, which, though a mine of wonderful wisdom, is not perfect, as its author said. It is, she said, but a selection of fragments of the fundamental tenets of the secret doctrine, paying special attention to some facts which have been seized upon by various writers, and distorted out of all resemblance to the truth. And she quoted the words of Montaigne: "I have here made only a nosegay of culled flowers, and have brought nothing of my own but the string that ties them." *The Secret Doctrine* will be a treasure house for Theosophists for hundreds of years; let us not attach to it the curse of dogmatism. No one can say the last word in occultism. The knowledge that we have acquired up to the present is only like the lifting of a little corner of a great veil; we have no idea of what may be revealed by the raising of another part.

Before one can hope to pass this fourth portal, says Āryasanga, one must have mastered the mental changes in oneself. Moods come and go, and colour one's outlook very effectually. It is difficult for a man to realize that when he is in a cloud of depression the world outside is really no blacker than it was before. When a great, upsetting sorrow has fallen upon him, it is with something of a shock that he goes out and sees that the sun is still shining and people are smiling and even laughing.

A man who is very miserable himself sometimes feels quite angry at seeing others as happy as usual. He thinks the world is very hard, and that it does not care much about *him.* He forgets that yesterday, when he was happy, some others were distressed, and he did not care about them, but went along quite comfortably. *I know that depression is a very real* thing, but it is always self-created or self-permitted. Sometimes it comes from ill-health, over-fatigue or nervous strain. At others it comes from the astral world, where there are many so-called dead people in a state of depression. It is therefore not always one's own fault that the depression should come, but it is one's own fault if one allows it to stay.

Quite a large number of people seem to imagine that their attitude towards things makes a difference. "Oh, no, you will never get me to believe that!" such a person will say, imagining that his disbelief disposes of the matter in question. *But if a thing is a fact, it remains a fact, whether he believes* it or not. This is one of the queer little ways in which human conceit shows itself.

One must also take care that casual thoughts do not interfere with one's being of service, nor be blind to a chance of doing a good service to a man because one does not like something about him—the way he cuts his hair, for example. Such a thing sounds trifling, but it shows the condition of one's mind and character. Often it is a thought about race, class or caste that stands in the way. The Brāhmana in India frequently neglects his duty to the pariah on account of this. No one denies the enormous difference of class, but every one ought to have a fair opportunity to raise himself socially and morally as much as is possible for him. Of course, one cannot change the condition of millions of people very greatly in a short time, one cannot raise the Panchamas to the state of Brāhmanas, but one can always show the greatest kindness and consideration to these people, and help any one of them who can receive the help.

If thou would'st not be slain by them, then must thou harmless make thy own creations, the children of thy thoughts, unseen, impalpable, that swarm round humankind, the progeny and heirs to man and his terrestrial spoils. Thou hast to study the voidness of the seeming full, the fulness of the seeming void.

The fulness of the seeming void is a phrase replete with meaning. It applies to many different conditions. First one thinks of the koilon, the æther of space. Commonly people think of space as something that is empty, but the fact is that it is filled with a density of substance that can scarcely be imagined. It is the apparently solid matter that is "empty". The matter that we see consists of holes in the real matter, of bubbles blown in koilon. As a French scientist recently said: "Il n'y a plus de matière. Il n'y a que des trous dans l'étère."[1] The latest verdict of science with regard to the æther of space is that its density is ten thousand times that of water, and about five hundred times the density of the heaviest metal, the densest thing you can think of.

The Hindus speak of root-matter or mūlaprakriti; of which koilon is a densification, I think. They say that when the Logos realizes Himself, when He differentiates Himself from the Absolute and looks back, as it were, upon that Absolute, He does not see it, but a veil thrown over it—and that veil is mūlaprakriti. In *The Secret Doctrine*, Madame Blavatsky quotes the words of Swāmī T. Subba Rao on this subject, as follows:

> When once it [*i.e.*, the Logos, "... the first manifestation (or aspect) of Parabrahman"] starts into existence as a conscious being, ... from its objective standpoint, Parabrahman appears to it as Mulaprakriti. Please bear this in mind ... for here is the root of the whole difficulty about Purusha and Prakriti felt by the various writers on Vedantic philosophy . . . This Mulaprakriti is material to it (the Logos), as any material object is to us. This Mulaprakriti is no more Parabrahman than the bundle of attributes of a pillar is the pillar itself; Parabrahman is an unconditioned and absolute reality, and Mulaprakriti is a sort of veil thrown over it. Parabrahman by itself cannot be seen as it is It is seen by the Logos with a veil thrown over it, and that veil is the mighty expanse of Cosmic Matter . . . "[2]

[1] "There is no longer any matter. There is nothing but holes in the ether."
[2] *Op. cit.*, Vol. I, p. 462. See also *ante*, p 374.

The Logos here mentioned is the Logos of our Universe, in which are millions of solar systems—not the Logos of one solar system. It was He who blew His breath into the root-matter, who dug holes in space, so that the universe came into being. Fourteen thousand millions of these bubbles make a physical atom, and eighteen of these make an atom of hydrogen, which is the lightest of the chemical elements.

It is therefore a fact that all that we know as matter is nothing else but holes in the real matter. The pressure of that root-matter is several million tons per square inch. When men learn to exclude this pressure, they will be able to use that tremendous force to run their machinery. They will be able to utilize the force of the Logos that is in the atom, which holds itself against that great pressure. But it will first be the force involved in the disintegration of the physical atom that will be tapped.

The fulness of the seeming void and the voidness of the seeming full can be studied in a variety of familiar experiences. The atmosphere is full of the thoughts of other people and other beings. As it says in *The Occult World*:

> Every thought of man upon being evolved passes into the inner world, and becomes an active entity by associating itself, coalescing we might term it, with an elemental—that is to say, with one of the semi-intelligent forces of the kingdoms. It survives as an active intelligence —a creature of the mind's begetting—for a longer or shorter period proportionate with the original intensity of the cerebral action which generated it. Thus good thought is perpetuated as an active, beneficent power, an evil one as a maleficent demon. And so man is continually peopling his current in space with a world of his own, crowded with the offspring of his fancies, desires, impulses and passions; a current which re-acts upon any sensitive or nervous organisation which comes in contact with it, in proportion to its dynamic intensity.[1]

Again, one may be meditating in a room that is empty or full of other people. In the latter case, it may be empty for him, because those other people are not greatly affecting him. In the former case it may yet be full of powerful unseen presences and influences attracted there by the meditation, and engaged in pouring out their force upon him who seems to be alone.

[1] *Op cit*, p. 111.

Something similar is to be seen in the varied circumstances of life. Many seemingly big events pass over us and leave us unaffected, while some tiny occurrence may affect the whole life. The death of a near relation, or the loss of one's fortune, looks so great when it happens that one thinks it will make a permanent landmark in one's life, and yet it may make scarcely any difference in the end. That has been my experience. As a young man I lost all the considerable money which I possessed, in the great financial disaster of 1866. It seemed a great event at the time; yet it has made no difference to me. But my meeting casually with a person who told me about Madame Blavatsky has made all the difference to my life. The meeting seemed to be by chance, but it must have been intended and arranged in that seeming void that is really so full in every possible way.

In the same way, a passing Deva looked in upon me one Sunday morning when I was giving a talk to some Theosophists at Adyar. He showed me some of the ways in which the Devas would influence men through religion in the beginnings of the sixth root-race. I then thought it but the kindly act of a friend passing by, but now I am sure it was much more than that, in view of what has resulted from it. It led to our knowledge of very much about the beginnings of the new race, to the investigation on which the second part of *Man: Whence, How and Whither* was based, and a little later to joint investigation by Dr. Besant and myself, which resulted in the first part of the same book. Looking forward into that community of the future, I saw that she would be remembered by that book when all that she has written before it will have been forgotten; but her greatest book, by which she will be remembered in history, has still to be written.

> O fearless aspirant, look deep within the well of thine own heart, and answer. Knowest thou of Self the powers, O thou perceiver of external shadows?

Purity is a great thing, but it is not enough. The little baby is pure, because it knows nothing of good or evil. Knowledge also is needed in order that we may act, and also the will to put that knowledge into action. The animals are purer than man, the vegetables purer still; they have not the imagination of man, that causes him to seek material pleasure in defiance or disregard of natural laws. Yet it is necessary that man should go through this experience with matter in order that he may have knowledge, and may then return to the Divine from which he descended, regaining his purity. We come out from the Logos a divine cloud, but return to Him a divine being with definite powers.

The man on the Path has recognized the divine self in himself, and is emerging from the influence of the world of shadows. Their reality is only relative, and is now no reality to him beside that of the indwelling life, which offers him a far richer field of conscious experience than the excitement produced by the impacts of external things. He has thought the shadows to be real, absolutely real, more real than anything else, throughout many incarnations, and it was all necessary, for without their attraction he would never have awakened, never have paid attention, never have learned anything at all.

If thou dost not then thou art lost.

For, on path fourth, the lightest breeze of passion or desire will stir the steady light upon the pure white walls of the Soul. The smallest wave of longing or regret for Maya's gifts illusive, along Antahkarana—the path that lies between thy Spirit and thy self, the highway of sensations, the rude arousers of Ahamkara—a thought as fleeting as the lightning flash will make thee thy three prizes forfeit—the prizes thou hast won.

Āryasanga is now talking about *vairâgya*, and he says that when one is striving to perfect that, the least response to the attractiveness of things, or desire for them throws one back again into the ranks of those who are disturbed. This recalls the simile of the soul as limpid as a mountain lake in the second Fragment.[1] Here he takes the simile of a lamp to express the steadiness that must be attained in this stage. Even a casual thought *will throw* one back; that is true, but we must remember the qualification: if it is one's own

[1] *Ante*, p. 474.

thought. As I have before explained, if it is merely a reflection of someone else's thought, merely a drifting thought-form that has attracted the attention, and that is not taken up and made one's own, then there is not the same disturbance to one's purity and tranquillity, to one's vairāgya.

Sometimes very good people are distressed by such passing thoughts, and they feel that they must be very wicked to have such ideas. But if they do not take them up and nourish them and send them out reinforced to do greater work of destruction, they have not really committed a fault. It is quite true that we should not be conscious of an evil or impure thought if it did not touch something akin to itself in us. But that is only saying that we are not yet perfect. If a thought of that nature floated through the mind of an Adept, He would not even notice it; but if there were many of them round Him, He might require to brush them aside, as one brushes away flies and mosquitoes. Do not, therefore, be troubled unnecessarily about the instinctive stirrings of anger, or selfishness, or undesirable stray thoughts; they are a legacy from the past or they belong to your environment. But do not adopt them, for if you do you will not only fail to attain vairāgya, but will forfeit the three prizes already won, and start climbing again from the very beginning of the Path.

Antahkarana is here called the highway of sensations. It is the mysterious means by which material things can affect consciousness, the channel between object and subject, that which causes an impact upon a sense-organ to appear in consciousness as a sensation. Such sensation, direct perception of things, is more vivid than any description in words. To have heard, seen or felt something gives one a greater sense of its reality than merely to have thought about it That is why clairvoyant perception of the other planes is worth so much more than the descriptions that we can give. It is also the reason why the yoga books say that all the testimony of others, and all his judgments about things as yet unseen by him, will at last have to be replaced by the aspirant with his own direct perception, which alone can give a clear vision of the truth.

Sensations are here called the rude arousers of ahamkāra. *Aham* means "I", and *kāra* is "making"; therefore ahamkāra means the "I-maker". The very vividness of that direct experience calls out the vividness of our sense of our own existence by the contrast. And as this process occurs at all levels, it calls out the vividness of the false personality while the man is still in the world; but when he is well on the Path and the illusion of the personal self has been quite destroyed, it calls out the Self that is the Ātmā, the will, in the spiritual man. We have already studied this higher form of ahamkāra, often mentioned in Hindu philosophy, in the first Fragment.[1]

For know that the Eternal knows no change.

Briefly, one must be willing to give up the lower for the sake of the higher; one cannot take worldly goods into the kingdom of heaven. The laws and conditions of the higher world will not change to suit the desire of any aspirant.

"The eight dire miseries forsake for evermore; if not, to wisdom sure thou canst not come, nor yet to liberation," saith the great Lord, the Tathagata of perfection, "he who has followed in the foot-steps of his predecessors."

The eight dire miseries are: malice, sloth, pride, doubt, desire, delusion, ignorance and future lives. The last one seems curious at first sight; but the meaning is quite clear—that life in this world is misery in comparison with what the higher planes have to offer us.

The title Tathāgata is here translated "He who walks in the steps of his predecessors". In Ceylon we were told that it meant "He who has been rightly sent". That means one who has been sent by the Great White Brotherhood as its Messenger to the world; and one so sent would necessarily follow in the steps of those who came before Him. That is why the story of Initiation appears with little variation in the traditions of different nations, especially in the form of what is called the solar myth.

[1] *Ante*, p. 375.

Stern and exacting is the virtue of Vairagya. If thou its path would'st master, thou must keep thy mind and thy perceptions far freer than before from killing action.

Thou hast to saturate thyself with pure Alaya, become as one with nature's Soul-thought. At one with it thou art invincible: in separation, thou becomest the playground of Samvritti, origin of all the world's delusions.

Then there is a long foot-note explaining Samvritti:

Samvritti is that one of the two truths which demonstrates the illusive character or emptiness of all things. It is relative truth in this case. The Mahayana school teaches the difference between these two truths—Paramarthasatya and Samvrittisatya (Satya, truth). This is the bone of contention between the Madhyamikas and the Yogacharyas, the former denying and the latter affirming that every object exists owing to a previous cause or by a concatenation. The Madhyamikas are the great Nihilists and deniers, for whom everything is Parikalpita, an illusion and an error in the world of thought and the subjective, as much as in the objective universe. The Yogacharyas are the great spiritualists. Samvritti, therefore, as only relative truth, is the origin of all illusion.

It is discrimination, the first of the four qualifications, that can enable one always to distinguish between the real and the relatively real which we sometimes call the unreal. Every time that one pierces the unreal and sees the real it becomes easier to do it again, because that by which we recognize the real is the God within us. The more that is awakened the easier will it be to see its purpose in all things, and its life in other people.

The same pure Ālaya, which is in us and also behind the Divine Mind in nature, has been realized by the seers of all religions. A learned Muhammadan once told me that the well-known sentence of Islam: "*Lā ilāha illā,llāh*", means not "There is no God but God," as it is generally translated, but "There is nothing but God." He explained that the Arabic words could be literally taken to have the former meaning, but the latter was the esoteric meaning, imparted secretly among themselves. That is the true proclamation of monotheism; not simply that there are many Gods, but one only is worthy of the name, and of adoration. This esoteric interpretation, if accurate, constitutes a strong link with Hinduism, which speaks of "*One only, without a second*", *the One in whom, they say*, is both being and non-being.

> All is impermanent in man except the pure bright essence of Alaya. Man is its crystal ray; a beam of light immaculate within, a form of clay material upon the lower surface. That beam is thy life-guide and thy true Self, the watcher and the silent thinker, the victim of thy lower self. Thy Soul cannot be hurt but through thy erring body; control and master both, and thou art safe when crossing to the nearing "gate of balance".

Nothing but the One is permanent. The personality of a man lasts a very short time—till the end of his devachanic period; the ego lasts through the whole series of human incarnations, perhaps to the extent of a chain-period; the monad no doubt lasts longer still, but even that is impermanent. *Only the One remains.* Not that we shall lose ourselves. We can truly say, with Emily Bronte:

> Though earth and man were gone,
> And suns and universes ceased to be,
> And Thou wert left alone,
> Every existence would exist in Thee.

The Monad in man is a spark of the one flame. As long as it is in time it will appear to be evolving. Speaking with the deepest reverence, even the Logos appears to be doing the same. He answers to all that is best and greatest in our conception of God, yet it is true that He will not be the same at the end of the solar system as He was at the beginning; for that to Him is an incarnation.

The "form of clay material" is only useful to man in so far as it helps the development of the divine spark in him. The material part cannot affect the divine spark in the sense of actually harming it, but it can advance or retard its unfolding, which for it are the equivalents of help or injury. Therefore it is called the victim of the lower self.

The fourth portal is here called the gate of balance, as it concerns the middle principle in man. It is always a question as to whether the outer or the inner will now gain the ascendancy; the candidate having developed and purified his lower principles, physical, astral and mental, must now put his weight on the side of the higher principles, and make their development his chief business.

> Be of good cheer, O daring pilgrim to the other shore. Heed not the whisperings of Mara's hosts; wave off the tempters, those ill-natured sprites, the jealous Lhamayin in endless space.

There is a note to the word Lhamayin, which says they are elementals and evil spirits adverse to men, and their enemies. There are no creatures that do evil for evil's sake, but there are elementals who are harmful to man; they are living their own life, and we get in their way. The elementals are much like the wild creatures. They are not man's enemies, but they dislike man's intrusion into their domain, and they feel resentment because men have treated them badly

Nature-spirits are joyous creatures; the worst that can be said of them is that they play little mischievous tricks which are tiresome to the people concerned. They object to man because he does so many things which to them are odious and a source of trouble. They live a glad and contented life in the countryside, and love to frolic about with the young of the wild creatures, and they love them and the flowers and trees. They *have no trouble in their innocent life*; and they feel no pressure of necessity, for they need not toil for food and clothing as man has to do.

Into this sylvan happiness comes man; he hunts and kills the animals who are their friends; he cuts down the trees they love, in order to plant crops or build houses; he pollutes the air with the filthy emanations of alcohol and tobacco. All their beautiful country is made to them a horrible wilderness, and they are forced to flee away. Thay may feel somewhat as an artist does when he sees some beautiful landscape spoilt and made hideous with factories, whose chimneys belch forth black smoke, and fumes kill the grass and flowers and trees. We call it progress ; it may be so for us, but the nature-spirit feels it differently, for his home is ruined and his friends are killed.

So it comes about that the nature-spirits shun man, and when a man takes a walk in a wood or along a lane they slip away at his approach. He may be able to overcome this aversion of theirs, just as one can sometimes overcome the timidity of the wild creatures. A Yogi can caress the wild animals that come near him as he sits in meditation. If one goes into the country and forces oneself to lie quiet and still for an hour or two, the little wild things, such as squirrels and birds, will come near. Similarly, if one lives for a long time in one place the nature-spirits gradually find out that one is a harmless specimen of mankind, and in time will be quite willing to make friends, and at last they will sport round one, and be quite proud of having a human friend. In the astral plane these creatures regard men as intruders of a troublesome and dangerous character, much as we should regard an invading army. They therefore make it their business to try to frighten the new-comer. These are not, however, tempters. It is principally the evil thought-forms of man himself that play that rôle.

There are certain men, whom we sometimes call the black magicians, who work to oppose the spiritual progress of humanity, believing quite honestly that our high emotions are not good things, but relics of animal desires and sentiments. Such magicians may see a person in some special situation, one who is making swift progress on the Path, and may at the time be in a condition to be affected by them. It may then seem worth their while to send against him an elemental calculated to upset him, and so cause a disturbance which will block the Masters' work. This is the nearest thing that exists to the tempting demon of popular Christian belief. Still, no aspirant should fear these, for the worst black magician can do nothing to or through a man who is one-pointed, thinking only of the Master's work, not of himself.

Hold firm! Thou nearest now the middle portal, the gate of woe, with its ten thousand snares.

Have mastery o'er thy thoughts, O striver for perfection, if thou would'st cross its threshold.

Have mastery o'er thy Soul, O seeker after truths undying, if thou would'st reach the goal.

Thy Soul-gaze centre on the one pure light, the light that is free from affection, and use thy golden key.

. . . .

Āryasanga may well speak of ten thousand snares, for many times does the candidate imagine that he has achieved vairāgya or desirelessness, only to find that in some subtle way he encounters the same snares over and over again. Even the soul, the higher manas, has to be under the control of the buddhic nature. As we have seen, at the first Initiation the buddhic life begins, if not before, and the candidate treads that plane sub-plane by sub-plane. This work can only be carried to perfection if the soul itself, the higher manas, co-operates, becoming a servant in turn to that higher principle. Then, when that work is done, and the candidate is ready for the next plane, he will take his Fourth Initiation, and step over another threshold.

To be free from affection here means from being affected; as we have already seen, that is the significance of vairāgya.

CHAPTER LIII

THE FIFTH AND SIXTH GATES

The dreary task is done, thy labour well-nigh o'er. The wide abyss that gaped to swallow thee is almost spanned.

. . . .

Thou hast now crossed the moat that circles round the gate of human passions. Thou hast now conquered Mara and his furious host.

Thou hast removed pollution from thine heart and bled it from impure desire.

C.W.L.—We must not misunderstand the statement that the candidate's labour is well-nigh over. The Nirmānakāya, at His far higher level, still labours, and the same may be said of the Logos Himself. But perhaps a distinction should be drawn between the drudgery of the labour of getting rid of the faults of the personality, and the glorious work that continues on the higher planes after the personality is conquered.

The same thought applies to the question of strain. Incessant *work is a great strain on the physical body, but in the* planes of the ego work is pure joy; there is then no difference between work and play, such as exists on the lower planes.[1] Once a man has seen the great sacrifice of the Logos, and the way in which the Masters throw Themselves into His work,

[1] *Ante*, p. 394.

there remains no possibility for him but to plunge into the stream of it, and do all that he can to help.

We are still considering a man who is not quite pure, because he is still capable of a little selfishness. A thought is impure that has the slightest tinge of self in it, however good it may otherwise be. There may be a little thought of pride, such as: "People will think well of me for doing this." That would be called impure, when we are considering this high level of the Path. Not only must we keep impurity away, but we must see that it never occurs to us at all.

> But, O thou glorious combatant, thy task is not yet done. Build high, Lanoo, the wall that shall hedge in the holy isle, the dam that will protect thy mind from pride and satisfaction at thoughts of the great feat achieved.

> A sense of pride would mar the work. Aye, build it strong, lest the fierce rush of battling waves, that mount and beat its shore from out the great World Maya's ocean, swallow up the pilgrim and the isle—yea, even when the victory's achieved.

> Thine 'isle' is the deer, thy thoughts the hounds that weary and pursue his progress to the stream of life. Woe to the deer that is o'ertaken by the barking fiends before he reach the vale of refuge—"Jnan-marga," "path of pure knowledge" named.

To hold the position that he has now gained, against the strong pressure of the thoughts of millions of other people around him, of which we have so often spoken, the aspirant now needs strong concentration and positive power of thought. This strength is necessary before he can successfully carry out that meditation which will raise him to the highest levels of the buddhic plane.

The "isle", Madame Blavatsky tells us, is the higher ego or thinking self. *From it all lower thoughts must be wiped out*, so that the higher may manifest. Yet one must become in no sense a medium. There is a vast difference between making a place empty, and letting someone from the outside enter into it and take possession; that is the difference between the yogi and the medium. Here also lies the difference between the Theosophist and the Spiritualist. Both agree that man is eternal and that his progress has no limit. But the latter considers that it is good for a man to be a medium for good spirits, while the former insists upon the preservation of his own positive consciousness under all circumstances, and maintains that there is nothing which passive mediumship can give which is not obtainable by conscious clairvoyance.

Āryasanga says, "Woe to the deer that is overtaken." That means woe to the ego that falls into prejudice because he has been overcome by the pressure of outside thoughts. He cannot then reach the place of true thought. Madame Blavatsky says of the path of pure knowledge, or Jnāna-mārga, that it "is literally the path of Jnāna, or the path of pure knowledge, of Paramārtha or (Sanskrit) Svásamvedana, the self-evident or self-analysing reflection." Jnāna is, among the Hindus, the higher knowledge, wisdom, not the lower knowledge concerning the world, which is called vijnāna.

> Ere thou canst settle in Jnan-marga and call it thine, thy Soul has to become as the ripe mango fruit; as soft and sweet as its bright golden pulp for others' woes, as hard as that fruit's stone for thine own throes and sorrows, O conqueror of weal and woe.
>
> Make hard thy Soul against the snares of self; deserve for it the name of Diamond-Soul.
>
> For as the diamond buried deep within the throbbing heart of earth can never mirror back the earthly lights, so are thy mind and Soul: plunged in Jnana-marga, these must mirror nought of Maya's realm illusive.

Of our personal sorrow Longfellow has sung:

> But now it has fallen from me,
>   It has sunken into the sea,
> And only the sorrows of others
>   Throw their shadows over me.

We must go a step further than that and not let any sorrows cast shadows over us. When you merely feel the sorrow of another you are not helping him, but adding to his trouble; but when you feel real sympathy you are pouring out vibrations of love, and are giving real help to him. The Master always feels the sympathy, but never the sorrow. He cannot suffer, even though he be truly one with those who are suffering, because He is one with them and knows the joy of their existence on higher planes and the wonderful glory of that state towards which they are evolving with unerring certainty.

The danger for most people is that when they cast out sorrow from their hearts, they tend to lose sympathy as well, and in such a case they may enter the left-hand path, the path of black magic. The brothers of the shadow become perfectly callous to the feelings of others, as well as to their own; they ruthlessly repress all feelings on the ground that they are a waste of force.

> When thou hast reached that state, the portals that thou hast to conquer on the path fling open wide their gates to let thee pass, and nature's strongest mights possess no power to stay thy course. Thou wilt be master of the sevenfold Path: but not till then, O candidate for trials passing speech.

It seems probable that the trials passing speech are not dangers and difficulties so great as to be quite indescribable, but of a kind unknown to ordinary men, and known only to the ego. The path along which Āryasanga is guiding his people is an inner path for the ego. When the personality has been conquered in the outer worlds, the ego has to scale the heights of planes above him, and therefore has to do what cannot be described.

Another possible interpretation is that the candidate finds himself now able to do what at first he was unable to believe that he could. The ordinary man would be inclined to say, for example, that the purity and unselfishness of which we have constantly been speaking are beyond him, and quite impossible of attainment, that they are a counsel of perfection. But some day, if he tries to acquire them, if he keeps on desiring it and trying, he will awake to find that it is perfectly natural and easy for him to have these qualities.

The ordinary man says that a thing is impossible, and so he does not try; but we have learned, like Napoleon, to erase that word from our dictionary. It is not impossible for the reader of this page to attain Adeptship within twenty-four hours; that would be possible if he had sufficient will—a will, however, which no one seems to have. *But leaving time out of* the question, it is possible for him to attain Adeptship; if he fixes his eye on the goal, and goes straight ahead without thinking about the passage of time, he will comparatively soon find himself there.

Till then, a task far harder still awaits thee: thou hast to feel thyself all thought, and yet exile all thoughts from out thy Soul.

Thou hast to reach that fixity of mind in which no breeze, however strong, can waft an earthly thought within. Thus purified, the shrine must of all action, sound, or earthly light be void: e'en as the butterfly, o'ertaken by the frost, falls lifeless at the threshold—so must all earthly thoughts fall dead before the fane.

Behold it written:

"Ere the gold flame can burn with steady light, the lamp must stand well guarded in a spot free from all wind." *Exposed to shifting breeze, the jet will flicker* and the quivering flame cast shades deceptive, dark and everchanging, on the Soul's white shrine.

Here is a poetical description of concentration—such fixity of the higher manas that even on that plane nothing can enter from the outside. This is the same thing as dhāranā, mentioned in the first Fragment,[1] though in this Fragment it is called vīrya, which means strength—not physical strength, of course, but the dauntless and unshaken manhood of the ego.

Dhāranā is called the sixth stage, in the first Fragment, but here vīrya is the fifth portal. There is no confusion of numbers in this, for the fifth portal leads to the sixth stage; in that stage the man is using the quality which he acquired in the fifth stage to admit him to the sixth through the fifth portal.

The same quality is the passport to the buddhic plane; when the man has risen to this level he has silenced the higher mental activity for the time, and now, instead of his own thoughts he feels himself all thought—he is one with others, and their thoughts are his. At this stage he feels the quality of unity of the Solar Logos; to him it is now a definite reality, a matter of direct experience, no longer a beautiful idea or an occasional thrilling inspiration. As to whether all this will come down to any extent into the physical brain—that is another matter; most of it cannot. And the concentration and meditation of these high stages are done for the most part out of the body during sleep.

We often talk of fighting earthly thoughts and feelings. That is a stage in which one is putting oneself on an equality with them; but the stage of which we are now speaking is one in which they fall dead at the threshold of the aura. The rates of vibration of the respective bodies are so tremendous that the lower thought-forms are knocked aside and cannot penetrate. There are many illustrations of this in the physical plane. If a wheel is rotating slowly, one can throw a ball through the spokes, but not if it is turning rapidly. If a jet of water is sufficiently strong, one cannot cut it with a sword; the weapon is thrown back as though the water were solid. One of the well-known children's fairy stories tells of a man *who could stand out in the rain, and whirl his sword so rapidly*

[1] *Ante*, p. 352.

above his head that not one drop could get through the circle and fall upon him!

The quotation about the lamp is taken from the *Bhagavad-Gītā*. It further says: "To such is likened the Yogī of subdued thought, absorbed in the yoga of the Self."[1] and goes on to explain that he then sees the Self by the Self, and in the Self is satisfied, that he thinks there is no greater gain beyond it, and is not shaken any more, even by heavy sorrow.[2]

This experience of the yogī is a true intuition, because it comes from within, from a deeper part of the nature than even the causal levels. How such an intuition will come down into the personality, if it does so, depends upon the type of person who experiences it. There are two main modes for its transmission—one which comes through the higher to the lower mental plane, and the other direct from the buddhi to the astral body.

Which of these lines one will more easily follow depends upon the manner in which one was individualized from the animal kingdom long ago. Some attained that level through deep understanding, others through a rush of high emotion, probably of devotion to a human master. In the former mode it will come into the lower mind as a conviction, requiring no reasoning to establish its truth at present, though it must have been understood in previous lives or out of the body in the lower mental plane. In the case of those who individualized by emotion the intuition is received through the feelings, not the mind.

In neither case can these intuitions come through satisfactorily unless the vehicles are steady. It is like transmitting a musical note. If it has come not only through the air, but through a thick wall, it may be muffled, and the sound may become quite different from what it was. If it has to pass through some disturbance—a hurricane for example—it will be still less clear. The latter simile very well indicates the case when the astral and mental bodies are full of disturbance.

[1] *Op. cit.*, vi, 19.

[2] *Ibid.*, vi. 22.

And then, O thou pursuer of the truth, thy mind-soul will become as a mad elephant, that rages in the jungle. Mistaking forest trees for living foes, he perishes in his attempts to kill the ever-shifting shadows dancing on the wall of sunlit rocks.

I do not know whether such a thing as this really happens in the jungle; but the idea is that when an elephant goes mad, he either mistakes the trees for living foes or, what is even worse, charges against the rocks and perishes. In the same way, some have had the experience that when the mind feels the newly awakened energy of the higher self coming from above, it rebels with a last burst of ferocity against its new master, unwilling in its pride and fear to give up its independence, which it has enjoyed so long. Then it rages, and the last reserves of the army of doubts and suspicions are routed out from every depth and corner, and come forth to do battle against the light, mistaking its every movement for a hostile foe. The mind is a stronghold of pride, and what there is left of that quality rises up in hatred against its superior, just as the persecutors of Jesus rose and killed Him, unable to bear the comparison of His purity and greatness with their own earthly mould.

Beware, lest in the care of Self thy Soul should lose her foot-hold on the soil of Deva-knowledge.

Beware lest in forgetting Self thy Soul lose o'er its trembling mind control, and forfeit thus the due fruition of its conquests.

Deva-knowledge here refers, as before, to the knowledge of the divine underlying all manifestation. There is a danger that the candidate, anxious to see that he is going the right way, should become, not selfish, but self-centred. There is a real distinction between these two. None of us would willingly take anything for ourselves knowing that it would injure another person. That defect would be indicated in the aura by a dull brown-grey. But there is a danger of being self-centred, taking things too much from one's own point of view.

That is indicated in the aura by a hardening of the outer surface, which prevents impressions from coming in.

The other warning relates to the one Self, which must not be forgotten. The aspirant must ever remember that all are one, that the divine unity is in each. This is a practical instruction for every plane. Physically a man must be clean, honest and true, so as not to contaminate society; astrally and mentally his feelings and thoughts must be pure and lofty, not that he may have the pleasure of being so, but for the sake of all around.

> Beware of change, for change is thy great foe. This change will fight thee off, and throw thee back out of the path thou treadest, deep into viscous swamps of doubt.

The warning against change looks a little curious at first, especially when we remember that we are all the time changing and that in treading the Path we have become that Path, and are thus very busily engaged in changing ourselves. What is meant is that one must take care, during the period of change, not to change one's basis, or essential attitude. There is a trying time when one gives up the worldly things that one used to value, and has not yet a permanent hold on the new and higher things. These latter have been visible in special moments when we have been at our best, but we have fallen away from them again and again, into that condition of spiritual dryness mentioned by so many mystics. What is required is that one shall hold to the vision all through those fluctuations, not changing that essential position.

These changes may be caused in several ways. Sometimes it is merely that the physical brain gets a little congested or anæmic; that affects the vehicles, but must not be allowed to affect the real man. When the fluctuations come, we should say: "I knew this would come. I know that I saw clearly before. Now the vision is dim and I begin to doubt; but I know I shall come out of this depression, that it is merely a fluctuation in my astral body."

Sometimes it is a great shock and trial for people to give up the picturesque faith of their childhood, when they realize that it cannot fit the facts of life, and can no longer satisfy the needs of mind and heart. Then there often comes doubt of everything, and a rudderless condition which has in extreme cases been known to last for several lives. In that case one must listen and read and think, and hold on to the hypotheses that best explain the facts, until doubt has been laid to rest by the knowledge that sooner or later will surely come. It is, of course, not necessary to pass through a sceptical stage; it is quite possible to drop the accretions and widen out one's religion little by little, until one arrives at the Theosophical understanding of its message.

Prepare, and be forewarned in time. If thou hast tried and failed, O dauntless fighter, yet lose not courage: fight on, and to the charge return again and yet again.

The fearless warrior, his precious life-blood oozing from his wide and gaping wounds, will still attack the foe, drive him from out his stronghold, vanquish him, ere he himself expires. Act then, all ye who fail and suffer, act like him; and from the stronghold of your Soul chase all your foes away—ambition, anger, hatred, e'en to the shadow of desire—when even you have failed . . .

Remember, thou that fightest for man's liberation, each failure is success, and each sincere attempt wins its reward in time. The holy germs that sprout and grow unseen in the disciple's Soul, their stalks wax strong at each new trial, they bend like reeds but never break, nor can they e'er be lost. But when the hour has struck, they blossom forth.

But if thou cam'st prepared, then have no fear.

In the course of a foot-note to this, H.P.B. refers to the well-known belief that every additional saint *is a new soldier* in the army of those who work for the liberation of mankind, and that in Northern Buddhist countries, where the doctrine of the Nirmānakāyas is taught, every new Bodhisattva is called a liberator of mankind. We must remember, of course, that she refers to all who have become Arhats, not only to the great being who fills the office of Bodhisattva. Every one who makes progress makes it for all.

The candidate cannot have personal ambition on this path. The idea of glory for oneself is selfish, and long before this stage is reached the aspirant has set his will resolutely against such desires. The pupil of the Master thinks not "What do I want?", but "What does the Master want?". When we realize that we are sparks of the divine Fire we can think only of what God wants. We are parts of Him; separately we can have no glory; so the idea of glory for oneself is quite a delusion.

No man who goes on trying can possibly fail. He may not succeed in doing just what he wanted to do at a given time; but if he has put force into his effort it cannot be wasted, and as action and reaction are equal and opposite, every time he tried it reacted upon himself to give him greater strength for the future. Further, every man who tries must succeed, because the whole trend of evolution is on his side. He does not know what may be the thickness of the kārmic wall of obstacles through which he must *break, nor at what moment* he may come through to light on the other side.

Under these circumstances it is simply foolish to despair, or to stop trying, because as yet one has no visible success. In Frederick Myers' grand poem, *St. Paul, we find it said:* "O man, why art thou despairing? God will forgive thee all but thy despair." To despair is the sin against the Holy Ghost; to despair of your own power is to despair of His power that is working through you, so that you shut yourself off from Him.

Āryasanga tells the candidate to be like the warrior who fights, and wins the battle just as he himself expires. He must hold out to the very last, and never give in. The teacher *knew that death is but a trivial thing,* not to be taken into account in our work. It will come to each of us at its proper time; some who are old may still have many years to live, and others who are young will be suddenly taken away. We shall go on with our work just the same after it comes as we did before.

Henceforth thy way is clear right through the Virya gate, the fifth one of the seven portals. Thou art now on the way that leadeth to the Dhyana haven, the sixth, the Bodhi portal.

The Dhyana gate is like an alabaster vase, white and transparent; within there burns a steady golden fire, the flame of Prajna that radiates from Atma.

Thou art that vase.

We have here a wonderfully beautiful illustration—the alabaster vase, with a steady golden fire within. It well typifies the buddhic body or sheath, which is utterly transparent and offers no obstruction to the unity of life at that level. Dhyāna is the higher meditation in that body—in which one takes something and tries to understand its innermost meaning, or in which one fixes one's thought upon a Great One and tries to understand oneself as part of Him. There is no longer any outer knowledge; no standing outside and thinking of the object as apart from oneself; one realizes its nature by becoming one with it, contemplating it from within.

Thou hast estranged thyself from objects of the senses, travelled on the path of seeing, on the path of hearing, and standest in the light of knowledge. Thou hast now reached Titiksha state.

O Narjol, thou art safe.

The same word titikshā has been applied, as we have seen, to one of the qualifications, one of the points of good conduct, meaning endurance. The term is now applied again at a higher stage. In a foot-note Madame Blavatsky says it means "supreme indifference; submission, if necessary, to what is called 'pleasure and pain for all', but deriving neither pleasure nor pain from such submission—in short, the becoming physically, mentally and morally indifferent and insensible to either pleasure or pain."

That is not very clearly put. The candidate does not act from considerations of pleasure and pain; he simply does what he knows to be his duty. He still feels pleasure and pain in his vehicles, as other people do. Yet it may be said that so great is the joy of this level, so intently are the thoughts fixed upon the goal, that pleasure and pain have lost their power. Though the Christ might feel to the full and cry out, "My God, My God, why hast Thou forsaken me?" still there rings in his heart the cry, "My God, My God, how Thou dost glorify me," as I have explained in describing the Fourth Initiation, in *The Masters and the Path*.[1]

CHAPTER LIV

THE SEVENTH GATE

Know, conqueror of sins, once that a Sowani hath crossed the seventh path, all nature thrills with joyous awe and feels subdued. The silver star now twinkles out the news to the night-blossoms, the streamlet to the pebbles ripples out the tale; dark ocean waves will roar it to the rocks surf-bound, scent-laden breezes sing it to the vales, and stately pines mysteriously whisper: "A Master has arisen, a Master of the Day."

C.W.L.—The Master of the Day means one who has become safe for the present cycle; therefore it refers to the candidate who has taken the first Initiation, as well as to him who has reached the further shore. That all nature rejoices at such an event is the simple fact, which is here so beautifully and poetically expressed. Many people at such a time find themselves unaccountably happy, and sometimes are conscious of a decided spiritual thrill. The majority of people of our civilized races are scarcely sufficiently sensitive to be conscious of these events, but sensitive individuals might very well feel: "I am curiously happy to-day. I wonder what has happened." It is felt in nature in that way—as a general sense of well-being.

Most people are busy developing the mind, and they have in consequence lost much sensitiveness, which arises much more with the development of feelings and emotions than with that of the mind. The higher types of savages are far more sensitive in many ways, but usually only in a vague and indefinite manner and without any control over their sensitiveness. They receive impressions, and are often able to foretell events in a general way. All this comes back to us, but in a clear and definite form on a higher turn of the spiral, with the development of the higher emotions. When that unfoldment comes we shall not only feel the sense of well-being and happiness of these great occasions, but will also know why we feel, and from what centre comes the great song of joy. The rest of nature, although below our level, is not yet centred on material things as much as many men are. Unless he is busily occupied with a desire rising from hunger or some other need of the body, an animal will generally be somewhat responsive to the thrill.

The great object of the Theosophical Society is not so much to provide the mental development, as to raise those who are ready into responsiveness to buddhic influences, to re-awaken the *sensitiveness of its people on a higher turn of the* spiral, and prepare them for the new race. It does not deprecate mental development—far from it—but it prepares for the next stage, when intuitional love will produce harmony and *brotherhood, and will employ the developed intellect to build a* new civilization, based on those ideals. Our Society, being in close sympathy with the higher planes, is very sensitive to the forces liberated when another "Son of Man" comes to birth. It receives the first touch of the great outrush, and this gives it new impetus; its work increases and spreads, and there is an advance in numbers and in brotherly feelings.

Sometimes, however, this stimulation of life produces *friction, due to a loss of the sense of proportion. Some* great idea arises in the mind of a member; the inrush of force intensifies it—and that is very good if he is a well-balanced man, and can pursue his own ideas without depreciating those of other people. But where there is unbalance and narrowness, differences of opinion may be made stronger. We have our special lines of work in Theosophy. Some take up one form of activity and some another, but danger arises when a man begins to think that his line is the one which the whole Society ought to take up and emphasize. When other people try to follow out their ideas, he tends to think that they are not doing the best for the Society, because they do not come and help him. It is not unnatural that enthusiasm should sometimes cause friction in such cases, when brotherly love and real tolerance fall a little behind.

Our great President has occasionally explained how she has often worked with others at a "second or third best idea" of theirs. She knew what was best, but would quietly yield for the sake of harmony, and that people might have the experience of carrying out their ideas. If a person comes to her with some plan of which he is very full, though it is often not the best thing, she does not discourage him, but says, "Go ahead, try it, and prosper." The man tries it, and perhaps after a year or two he finds that it was not the best, and he modifies it; but sometimes good results have been brought about in this way.

It is nearly always wise to let people try their ideas, but always sad when they urge them too strongly upon others. Experience tells us ever more and more that the most important thing in the Society is harmony among the workers. Indeed, it may be said that harmony among the workers is more important than success in any piece of work. So, let each man follow the best inspiration that comes to him, but let him have the fullest possible sympathy for others also in their individual ideas. If without peril to the spirit of harmony which makes the Society a perfect channel for higher forces, an open door to the Great Ones, we can engage in vigorous activity, it is well indeed, but not otherwise.

The silver star mentioned in the text may also be thought of as the star of Initiation. It is the sign of the thought and the presence of the King. In the ceremony of Initiation the one who acts for Him, the One Initiator, calls to Him to ratify that which has been done, and the answer is the flashing out of the silver star.

He standeth now like a white pillar to the west, upon whose face the rising sun of thought eternal poureth forth its first most glorious waves. His mind, like a becalmed and boundless ocean, spreadeth out in shoreless space. He holdeth life and death in his strong hand.

Yea, he is mighty. The living power made free in him, that power which is Himself, can raise the tabernacle of illusion high above the Gods, above great Brahm and Indra.

Through the Great White Brotherhood comes to the world all the Light that relieves the darkness of human life, and accelerates enormously the evolution of mankind. Often the symbol of the East has been used to typify the position of the Brotherhood, and the member thereof who has his face turned to help the outer world may therefore be said to be turned to the West.

The illusion referred to here is that of separateness. The aspirant has now won his freedom from that illusion, and on the Path he will raise himself step by step, plane by plane, until he has destroyed the illusion on each of them, and is master of himself on all the planes of human life. There seems to be no limit to the height to which a man can rise, so the reference to Brahma and Indra is no exaggeration, though it is no doubt intended in a general sense. It reminds us also of the line in *The Light of Asia*: "Higher than Indra's ye may lift your lot."[1]

A practical bearing of this illustration is to be found in the change of ray, described in *The Masters and the Path*. It is possible in the Hierarchy of our earth to advance further on the first ray than on the second, and further on the second than on any of the remaining five; so, anyone who has raised himself to the Seventh Initiation on one of the last five rays must change to the second or the first ray, if he wants to go on to the Eighth Initiation, and on to the first ray only if he wishes to go still further. *The Secret Doctrine* compares Indra to the Second Logos, the Sun-God, and Brahmā is the Third Logos, the Creator. In the Hierarchy these two are represented by (1) the Head of the second ray, the Buddha, and (2) the Mahāchohan, who governs the five rays, three to seven. The Lord of the World is on the first ray, and He has raised His lot higher than that of the other two.

[1] *Op. cit.*, Book the Eighth.

Now he shall surely reach his great reward!

Shall he not use the gifts which it confers for his own rest and bliss, his well-earned weal and glory—he, the subduer of the great delusion?

Nay, O thou candidate for nature's hidden lore! If one would follow in the steps of holy Tathagata, those gifts and powers are not for self.

Would'st thou thus dam the waters born on Sumeru? Shalt thou divert the stream for thine own sake, or send it back to its prime source along the crests of cycles?

Once more we come to the question of liberation from the wheel of births and deaths, with its attendant idea of rest. At this stage there can be no feeling of fatigue and labour such as we have down here, but looking from below the lot of an Adept who remains embodied for millions of years does appear appallingly tedious. Still, the candidate to whom Āryasanga is speaking is looking from below, and the teacher desires that he shall have no unwillingness to face that future, though he may at present be able to see only the darker side of the picture. It is perhaps impossible for him to describe the joys of that higher life; they cannot be expressed in terms of any worldly happiness that we know; it is somewhat dangerous therefore to hold out its joys as an attraction to the candidate, as it might cause him to fix his mind on some lower form of happiness, all unwitting, and that would delay his progress.

Mount Meru or Sumeru, is the Mount of the Gods, corresponding in a general way to the Olympus of the Greeks. All good flows from that source; that stream flows into every member of the Brotherhood, and it should flow through him to the world—otherwise he is literally damming up the stream. But in that case, of course, he will become one of the failures.

If thou would'st have that stream of hard-earned knowledge, of wisdom heaven-born, remain sweet running waters, thou shouldst not leave it to become a stagnant pond.

Know, if of Amitabha, the Boundless Age, thou would'st become co-worker, then must thou shed the light acquired, like to the Bodhisattvas twain, upon the span of all three worlds.

On this Madame Blavatsky has the following note:

In the Northern Buddhist symbology, Amitabha or boundless space (Parabrahman) is said to have in his paradise two Bodhisattvas—Kwan-shi-yin and Tashishi—who ever radiate light over the three worlds where they lived, including our own, in order to help with this light (of knowledge) in the instruction of Yogis, who will, in their turn, save men. Their exalted position in Amitabha's realm is due to deeds of mercy performed by the two, as such Yogis, when on earth, says the allegory.

This is a little complicated, and requires some explanation. Madame Blavatsky here makes Amitābha the equivalent of Parabrahman, but it is difficult to see how that could be so, when the former is the Boundless Light, the Boundless Wisdom, the Essence of all the Buddhas. Parabrahman is the first member of the great Trinity, and Avalokiteshvara is the second, which is also Amitābha, described as the "middle principle" of the Buddha. With that second or middle principle it is possible for us to become co-workers, but not with Parabrahman.

However, she often speaks of the two as one, as the Parabrahman is the *concealed wisdom*, and he *manifests* as Avalokiteshvara, the manifested Ishvara, the Logos. Looking upward from below, there is in us, and in all, a God who is seen (the second of the Three) and a God who is concealed (the first of the Three).[1]

[1] *Ante.*, p. 373.

The middle principle is also called the Bodhisattva, and is described as dual, male and female, namely, Kwan-shi-yin, the male aspect, and Kwan-yin the female aspect of Avalokiteshvara. The latter, it is said, "assumes any form at pleasure in order to save mankind."

All the three worlds, says a foot-note, refers to "the three planes of being, the terrestrial. astral and spiritual." Madame Blavatsky is here using the term "astral" in an unusual way, as she has also done in *The Secret Doctrine* when touching on the present topic. She takes the whole of man, from the Monad down to the material bodies, and divides him into three parts, first the spiritual, which is the Monad; secondly, the astral, which comprises our ātma-buddhi-manas, or the rupa beyond sense; and thirdly the material or terrestrial, comprising our lower mental, astral and physical bodies.

We may take the reference to the two Bodhisattvas also in another sense, as referring to the two great Brothers, the Lord Gautama and the Lord Maitreya, who represent the middle principle in the Hierarchy, the former dealing with the higher worlds, and the latter turned downwards, as it were, to deal with the personalities of men in the lower planes. The story of the wonderful effort and sacrifice of these two Brothers has been told in *The Masters and the Path*.[1]

But perhaps the most practical interpretation of the allegory from the human point of view is this. Gautama became one with Amitābha—that is, He became the Buddha. He continues His work on the higher planes, but in the world of men He works through the dual Bodhisattva, whose male form is Kwan-shi-yin, the Lord Maitreya, and whose female form is Kwan-yin, the mysterious companion and shakti of the former in almost all religions.

Know that the stream of superhuman knowledge and the Deva-wisdom thou hast won, must, from thyself, the channel of Alaya, be poured forth into another bed.

Know, O Narjol, thou of the secret path, its pure fresh waters must be used to sweeter make the ocean's

[1] *Op. cit.*, Ch xiv.

bitter waves—that mighty sea of sorrow formed of the tears of men.

The superhuman knowledge refers probably to the key of knowledge which is given to the Initiate when he takes his first step. The man who has passed through several Initiations has certain blocks of knowledge which he is not allowed to communicate to others. He acts under that knowledge, and necessarily it makes certain differences in what he does and the way he lives. Others may observe these things, and follow them by imitation or through devotion. Those who are natural protestants object to this kind of imitation of great people. They draw attention to the fact that a person may be great in some directions but not at all so in many others, that one who follows may easily fall into superstition, as the people did in the story of the cat and the bedpost.[1] They also say that a life of self-reliance develops power. All that is true; but there is benefit to be gained and danger to be faced in both methods; so each should go the way that is natural to him, taking care at the same time to try to understand and respect the man who follows the other path. If we imitate the action of a person who knows a little more than we do, it is not unreasonable. A child imitates grown-up people because he is convinced that they know more than he does, and in most cases he is right. It is just as well that the average child regards his father as the greatest man in the world, and one would not think of telling him that his idea is wrong.

The *Deva-wisdom* is probably the Divine Wisdom, which we call Theosophy. It is knowledge of the worlds as the dwelling-place of God's life, not merely as external regions. Āryasanga always makes a distinction between what one really knows and what one only believes. If he were speaking at one of our Theosophical meetings he might say: "You ought to believe in the existence of the astral and mental planes, because it is a rational necessity. But you do not know it unless you have direct experience." Such knowledge is superhuman only in the sense that it is beyond the reach of normal humanity at the present time, though it will be within the reach of the average person in due course.

[1] *Ante.*, p. 212.

Direct experience makes a great difference to one's realization of these verities. I remember Mr. W. T. Stead once saying that he had made extensive studies and investigations into things psychic, but one day he had a clairvoyant vision which gave new colour and reality to it all. He was falling asleep when he saw before him a little picture of the sea-shore, with the waves dashing against the rocks. It was a small thing, but it taught him much. "Now," he said, "I understand what a clairvoyant means when he says he sees this or that"

It made an enormous difference to Dr. Besant and myself when we began to see the inner planes for ourselves. We were familiar from the outside with facts about the astral and mental worlds, but direct vision gave them life for us. Even with regard to physical plane matters, the man who learns only from books has a cut and dried type of knowledge, but the man who has *lived* his knowledge has it full of colour and light. I remember well this difference among the Buddhist monks whom I used to meet in Ceylon. One would be perfect master of the books, and could quote from them to illustrate every point about his religion; while another, who had had some experience in meditation, would quote less but say far more.

Clairvoyance does not spring suddenly into existence, in a form in which it can be relied upon. Much careful training is required to enable a person to see accurately, to realize the significance of what he sees, and to eliminate the personal equation. One may put a telescope into a man's hands and expect that he will then know all about the stars—but he will know very little until he has been trained to use it properly, and has brought to bear upon what he sees a great deal of knowledge and intelligence. Astronomers have found that they must also make allowance for the personal equation in their considerations.

In clairvoyance this appears in many forms—one may see things a little too large, a little too blue, or too red, and so forth. Personal bias also is evident in the form of prejudice—one lady clairvoyant, for example, who was also an ardent Christian, would persist in associating ideas of baptism with any pouring out of water that she might happen to see, and she was quite offended when others could not agree with her view. With all our efforts we cannot see things fully, as would be necessary for perfect accuracy. It may be that even at Their level of Adeptship, the Masters make allowances for Their "*personal equations*" *when working in the lower planes.*

The Initiate has, however, absolute certainty, from experience, of a number of matters, which enables him to be a channel for the higher forces. It alters the polarity of his mental and causal vehicles, so that he can be used as others cannot, however highly they may be developed along other lines.

> Alas! When once thou hast become like the fixed star in highest heaven, that bright celestial orb must shine from out the spatial depths for all, save for itself; give light to all, but take from none.

It must not be assumed that the star is sorry to have to shine; it does so because it cannot help it. "*Beings follow their own nature; what shall restraint avail?*" *says The Bhagavad-Gītā.*[1] Restraint always produces sorrow; he who loves the world wants to shine upon it for ever; the sorrow would be if he could not do so.

One great example of this is given by the mighty entities who live in the forms of the rice grains or willow leaves of the sun, in order that through them light, heat and vitality may be shed upon the system. This is always spoken of as a sacrifice on their part. But it is spontaneous, their way of expressing their inner nature. *Instead of living a life of splendid activity* on some higher plane of which we have no idea, they keep physical bodies, and live there for the benefit of the worlds which float around our sun. They form a guardian wall in very truth, a channel through which Ālaya may flow into another bed.

> Alas! When once thou hast become like the pure snow in mountain vales, cold and unfeeling to the touch, warm and protective to the seed that sleepeth deep beneath its bosom—'tis now that snow which must receive

[1] *Op. cit.*, III, 33.

the biting frost, the northern blasts, thus shielding from their sharp and cruel tooth the earth that holds the promised harvest, the harvest that will feed the hungry.

The simile of the snow is very beautiful, but must not be pushed too far. The disciple has to become like pure snow—white, stainless, spotless. No doubt when Āryasanga spoke of this to his disciples, he pointed to the snow-covered peaks which were always in sight.

The snow is unfeeling not in the sense of being harmful in any way, but as being not itself affected by the cold. No matter how much colder the temperature of the air may become, the snow remains just the same. Because it is itself unaffected it is able to protect the earth from the more intense cold. That is the position to which the aspirant must rise. He must be unfeeling only in the sense that he does not mind if he himself is troubled or injured by any outward thing, whatever it may be, but he must remain protective to the seed that sleeps below.

The seed is the deity in man. It is beginning to awaken in all those who are turning their attention to higher things and are striving to develop themselves. It is this seed that must be cherished in others. An Upanishad tells us that in the acorn exists the oak tree potentially; it has only to unfold itself, and draw in from the air, the earth and the sunlight that which will enable it to manifest. In the same way the divine spark within us, the Monad, has the whole possibility of the Logos that we shall be one day, but it has still to unfold itself.

We must provide for those divine seeds the conditions under which they can best unfold themselves in the lower worlds. We must therefore receive the biting frost, the northern blast, so as to shield the other people, who might be affected and kept back by it. There are some who are ready for spiritual teaching, and they must be fed with spiritual food. These are the hungry, and we must give them the food they need for growth. They do not quite know what they want, but as soon as it is put before them they grasp it. That has been the experience of some of us with regard to Theosophy. The moment that it came before us we felt: "That is exactly what I have been waiting for", although before we heard of it we did not know what we wanted. There are many other people waiting in the same way to recognize it, and we must be like the snow, whose function is to protect while the cold lasts, and then, when the sun shines, to melt away and efface itself.

That is exactly what we do for children in the home; when times are hard or there is trouble of any kind, we take care that the children do not know of it. If there is a lack of food the children are fed first, and the father and mother go short. Mercifully there is so much of the divine instinct in us that we know that it is our duty to protect the young and helpless.

The same spirit has to be carried into other branches of life. We are a little ahead of the people who know nothing. They are the people to be pitied most, not those who think they are in great mental trouble and difficulty, struggling towards the light, such as the people who are worried because their religion does not express to them all that they need; these are not the people who most need sympathy, because at least they are awake and struggling towards the light. It is the great orphan humanity, those who do not know there is anything to struggle for, who most need sympathy. We cannot do much for them. The only thing one can do for a chick in a shell is to keep it comfortably warm. The warmth is the life that we can pour out. We must be kindly, brotherly and upright. When they need teaching, we can give it to them; but we can *always* give them love and make beautiful thoughts for them, for though they will not receive the exact thought they will feel the warmth, as the chicken does in the egg.

It has been said that it is very well to preach and teach, but the greatest of all sermons is a noble life. One reason for that is that such preaching affects the people who do not yet know what they want. The mass of people are engaged in making a living and looking after their families, and they do not trouble themselves about Theosophy or religion. In England, which is regarded in Europe as a religious country, the accommodation provided in places of worship is insufficient for one-tenth of the population. The churches and chapels of various kinds are generally not even half-full, so we may say that not more than a twentieth of the population habitually attend any sort of religious service. Our beautiful Theosophical lectures make little or no impression on this mass of people; one might just as well whistle a tune or read a piece of poetry. But they are always watching the more educated and developed people, and they form their own opinion of those who are better placed educationally or socially. The man who leads a good, honest, pure, unselfish life is thus actually preaching all the time to all those people who cannot be affected by anything that is said.

An objection to many missionary efforts is that they put preaching before example. A missionary settles, for example, in a bungalow in an Indian country town, close to the European magistrate and tax collector, who is almost a king in his division. Nearly all the Hindus round about are strict vegetarians and teetotallers; but the missionary has meat killed for himself, and generally he keeps a decanter of whiskey or other strong drink at hand, even when he does not share in the shooting of birds and small animals in which his European friends indulge. Then he preaches the purity and love of Christ, and sometimes dares to abuse the objects of worship of the people. Usually he produces no effect, except among some hypocrites who can obtain material benefits through connection with him. In schools, he often manages to undermine the children's religion without implanting his own. He rarely converts a good Hindu into a good Christian, which in any case would be no advantage, but occasionally he changes a good Hindu into an indifferent Christian. It would be better if he would set himself to live a saintly life such as the Hindus can understand, and then speak of Christ as his divine Guru, who has inspired him and made him what he is Even for his own purpose this would be better propaganda, because the Hindus are broad-minded, and are generally willing to allow Those whom others worship a place beside their own Divine Incarnations.

We often hear people say that Eastern lands are being rapidly Christianized when what is meant is that they are taking up modern civilization—such as electric light and sanitation, and are dropping certain social customs, such as the seclusion of the better-class women and early marriage, which were common enough in Christian Europe a century or two ago. Perhaps they forget how the orthodox Christians in Europe fought against science and social reform, and how these improvements had to win their way in the teeth of the kind of "Christianity" which the missionaries are themselves for the most part still preaching. The situation would be comical, were it not both hypocritical and cruel.

Self-doomed to live through future Kalpas, unthanked and unperceived by men; wedged as a stone with countless other stones which form the Guardian Wall, such is thy future if the seventh gate thou passest. Built by the hands of many Masters of compassion, raised by their tortures, by their blood cemented, it shields mankind, since man is man, protecting it from further and far greater misery and sorrow.

Withal man sees it not, will not perceive it, nor will he heed the word of wisdom . . . for he knows it not.

But thou hast heard it, thou knowest all, O thou of eager, guileless Soul . . . and thou must choose. Then hearken yet again.

I cannot help thinking that Āryasanga's pupils must have been rather inferior in certain ways, because again and again he seems to find it necessary to reiterate that they must not expect anything for themselves. That has been said to us too, but I venture to hope that we who are students of occultism have reached a stage where we do not mind being unthanked and unperceived by men.

The idea of wanting these recognitions seems to be significant of rather a lower stage. One is not looking for any thanks or pleasure in connection with the results of one's work, yet one acts carefully and with prevision. It is the duty of the occultist to see beforehand what will be the probable consequence of his action or speech, and not to do anything rash. It is our business to do our best, and to see that failure is not due to our lack of effort, but it is all the same to us whether we see results or not.

'Suppose, for example, that a member of our Society is sent out to start a Lodge in some new district. He gives all the devotion that he has, shows all the tact at his command, and does his best in every way. Then, whether many or few join does not trouble him. It would be foolish for him to say regretfully: "If somebody else had been here they would have succeeded." The man was sent there to do his own best, not that of some other person. It is a mistake for a man to compare himself with others.

The expression "*Guardian Wall*" has caused a great deal of misunderstanding. It is a beautiful symbol, but, like other symbols, it must not be pressed too far. There is no evil of any sort menacing humanity which is not of its own generating. We ourselves are our only possible enemies. No one can hurt a man save himself, and no one can really help him save himself. Others can only put him in the way to learn how to help himself, or put him in a position where if he is not careful he may injure himself. The man in the outer world says that he is injured by another man who defames him; but the fact is that when he is angry the man in his anger injures himself. He need not feel angry. People say that it is natural to do so; that may be so for the undeveloped man, but it is not so for him who has learned a little more.

The expression "since man is man" is capable of two meanings. It may be taken as indicating that the Guardian Wall has existed ever since man became man, or it may mean that it was brought into existence because man is only man, and is therefore liable to injure himself very seriously, unless he receives help and protection and guidance from above. Probably both meanings are true. We know that the Lodge of Adepts is very ancient, that it existed long before our humanity reached the level when it could produce Adepts, and in those days They belonged to other and previous chains.

CHAPTER LV

THE ARYA PATH

On Sowan's Path, O Srotapatti, thou art secure. Aye, on that Marga, where nought but darkness meets the weary pilgrim, where torn by thorns the hands drip blood, the feet are cut by sharp, unyielding flints, and Mara wields his strongest arms—there lies a great reward immediately beyond.

Calm and unmoved the pilgrim glideth up the stream that to Nirvana leads. He knoweth that the more his feet will bleed, the whiter will himself be washed. He knoweth well that after seven short and fleeting births Nirvana will be his . . .

Such is the Dhyana path, the haven of the Yogi, the blessed goal that Srotapattis crave.

C.W.L.—The term Sowan is another Buddhist expression, which has the same meaning as Srotāpatti—the man who has taken the First Initiation. At the end of what is here called the path of dhyāna, the meditation by which he steadily works his way upward through the levels of the buddhic plane, he takes his Fourth Initiation, and immediately enters the nirvānic plane.

He does not rest at that point, however, but then treads the Arhat path to the gate of Prajnā. That term is no doubt connected with the casting off of the last fetter, which is ignorance or avidyā. It has been suggested that the translation ignorance, which is so common, is somewhat unfortunate, and that unwisdom would have been better. The idea is that no matter how much knowledge about things as seen from the outside a man may have he is still ignorant; but when he realizes those things from within, when he has realized the same Self, the One dwelling equally in all, he can see the inner side of all these things, and then he has wisdom. Jnâna is wisdom, and the *jnā* in prajnā has the same meaning, the *pra* being a prefix implying activity or moving forth. Therfore prajnā is sometimes translated consciousness, and sometimes intelligence, discernment or simply wisdom.

It means in practice not that the Adept has all knowledge, but that He is in a position to obtain the result of any knowledge he wishes. For example, the Master Morya, when first I had the privilege of meeting Him, spoke English very imperfectly and with a strong accent. Since then he has acquired far greater fluency in English, though something of the accent still remains. The Master Kūthūmi has always, within our experience, spoken English with the greatest fluency and without any trace of accent, but at the same time with one or two little peculiarities such as any man might have, which enable one to identify His style.

I remember an early experience when one of the Masters wished to send a letter in the Tamil language. As He did not know that tongue, He instructed a pupil of His, who did know it, to think what He wanted to say; then He watched in that man's mind how the thoughts would be expressed, and so precipitated a letter which was correct, though He did not in His body know the meaning of the written symbols used.

I remember that my inner feelings of devotion and reverence received a little shock at the idea that a Master did not know Tamil; but I discovered very soon that it would not be worth while for an Adept to know everything from our point of view. I remembered a remark made by an exceedingly clever man with regard to some matter of astronomy or some other science. A friend of his had expressed surprise when he showed ignorance of the matter, and said: "What, do you mean to say you didn't know that?" He replied:

"No, I did not know it, and even now that you have told me, I shall put the thought aside and probably forget all about it. My brain will hold only a certain amount of information, and I am going to be a specialist on my own line."

Brain capacity is limited, and to acquire a vast amount of information that has scarcely any bearing on our life and work is not wise. I once knew a young man who told me that he had been a very ardent reader of the books of a large reference library in the north of England, until one day he made a calculation as to how long it would take him merely to read all the books that he wanted to study in that particular library alone. His computation showed that it would take him about five hundred life-times if he spent eight hours a day in that occupation! He then decided to select his future reading very carefully.

It is one of the big problems of life to decide just what knowledge one should try to acquire. Karma brings within our reach all that we need to know for our immediate progress. It is possible for us to go beyond that and spend our time and energy on study which is not useful in our lives, though it may be of importance to someone else. The more we learn the more we realize the paralyzing immensity of things; we are like small insects in a great room, looking at it from one corner.

We realized something of this immensity when looking up a long series of lives. For the long time involved we had to use the precession of the equinoxes to mark periods of time; the astronomers make that period about twenty-five thousand years, but higher vision showed it to be thirty-one thousand. The inexactitude of scientific information in these matters is due to the limited period of time over which the investigations could extend—a few hundred years, or a few thousand if the records of the Chaldeans are to be taken into account. The observations have thus been limited to a very small arc of a circle, from which the dimensions of the whole had to be calculated, so the least error in approximation becomes multiplied many times. But that is nothing beside an Age of Brahmā, with its 311,040,000 million years. And the greatest distances we can clearly imagine are naught besides the light-years which separate the stars.

We can imagine two kinds or types of learned men. One might become learned by acquiring an immense amount of knowledge; another, by surrounding himself with a well-chosen set of books and having the knowledge how to turn to those books and get from them the information which he needed. The knowledge of the Adept is somewhat of the second type; He does not necessarily possess books, but He has the power to get at any knowledge that He wants almost in a moment. If the Adept wants knowledge on a particular subject, He can make Himself one with it and get at the core of it instantly, and then observe the surrounding details as He may require them.

The Adept approaches the subject from a higher plane, and therefore it might appear to us on lower levels that there were many things which He did not know. It seems to me possible that if an Adept moved among us now, we might find that we knew more than He along certain lines; but if we came to deal with realities, with the core of the matter, with the real grasp of its essentials, the Master would know more than any of us. Let us try to understand it by considering the study of geology. The student buys a number of manuals, and studies the subject month after month, and perhaps year after year. What would a Master do if He wanted to know geology? Somewhere on the buddhic or nirvânic plane, He would grasp the idea that lies at the back of the science and make Himself one with that; then, from that point of view, He would reach down into any details He might require. Therefore, while undoubtedly some of us may have detailed information of which a given Master is not possessed, He has powers of knowledge different from ours.

An Adept, wishing to occupy His physical energies and time with the very definite purposes that He always has in view, may very well put aside many things and not bother about them. But in addition to that, we must take into account the fact that His consciousness is not only definitely greater than ours, but also different in kind, and no doubt quite indescribable to us who have not yet reached that state

The Arhat has still seven lives before him as a general rule, before he attains Adeptship, but they need not be lived in a physical body. He must descend as far as the astral plane, but the taking of a physical vehicle for those seven lives is quite optional. While in the astral body he may at any moment that he chooses enjoy the nirvânic consciousness, but as in the physical body it is only possible for one to reach a plane below the highest that one can reach while in the astral body, the Arhat incarnated physically can have that nirvânic experience only when he leaves his body during sleep or in trance. The normal home of the Arhat's consciousness is the buddhic plane. If he were speaking to anyone on the physical plane, or doing a piece of work that required attention, his consciousness would be fixed in the physical brain, but when he turns aside and rests for a moment it slips back to its normal home. He has a number of planes open to him, and can focus his consciousness at any particular level, as he chooses, although there will always be a background of the buddhic or the nirvânic consciousness.

One must be careful not to misjudge people who habitually use the higher consciousness. There have been cases where such a person was misunderstood by some people who spoke to him and did not immediately get a comprehensible reply, because of the fact that his attention was abstracted at the time. Sometimes people have got an impression of coldness or aloofness under these circumstances. It is wiser to be on the alert to understand what is happening, and if we receive a preoccupied answer, to go away and try another time. Many a time I have approached the Master in His home, and noticed by the appearance of His aura that He was preoccupied; in such a case one waits until the Master has finished, or one goes away to do some other work and then returns.

All the symbolism, in this and similar passages, about the weary pilgrim being torn by thorns and washed with blood and so forth is rather unpleasant to me. It is, of course, a materialistic way of symbolizing difficulties which all aspirants feel to some extent, but I should prefer to employ more agreeable illustrations. People differ, naturally, and one recognizes that what seems almost repulsive to some is taken very much as a matter of course by others. I have never been able to bring myself to like the Sufi symbolism in which they speak of drinking wisdom as wine, or some parts of the symbolism in the Purânas typifying quite materially the devotion of the Gopis to Shri Krishna. Of course, I know what the Sufi means—that just as the man is entirely filled with his wine and forgets everything else, so must he be filled with the divine wisdom until it is everything to him. I would rather say, with the Psalm, "As the hart panteth after the water brooks, so panteth my soul after thee, O God."[1] Nevertheless, we do not wish to criticise those who use a symbolism different from our own.

> Not so when he hath crossed and won the Arhata Path.
>
> There Klesha is destroyed for ever, Tanha's roots torn out. But stay, disciple . . . yet one word. Canst thou destroy divine compassion? Compassion is no attribute. It is the law of laws—eternal harmony, Alaya's Self; a shoreless universal essence, the light of everlasting right, and fitness of all things, the law of love eternal.
>
> The more thou dost become at one with it, thy being melted in its being, the more thy Soul unites with that which is, the more thou wilt become compassion absolute.
>
> Such is the Arya path, path of the Buddhas of perfection.

In foot-notes to this passage Madame Blavatsky writes: "Klesha is the love of pleasure or of worldly enjoyment, evil or good," and "Tanhā, the will to live, that which causes rebirth" The kleshas are technically considered among the Hindus as five forms of attachment to the world which are the great troubles and obstacles of the path. They have been dealt with in our comments on the first Fragment.[2] Tanhā, as explained before, is the thirst of the ego for the strong vibrations of material existence, which, in the early

[1] *Psalm*, 42, 1.

[2] *Ante.*, pp. 359-61.

stages of his evolution, help to awaken him to a more vivid realization of his own existence.

There is also a foot-note on the subject of compassion, as follows:

> This compassion must not be regarded in the same light as "God, the divine Love" of the Theists. Compassion stands here as an abstract, impersonal law, whose nature, being absolute harmony, is thrown into confusion by discord, suffering and sin.

I have always felt that perhaps our great Founder did a little less than justice to the Theists there. She says that one must not think of the Absolute Compassion as God, the Divine Love. I believe myself that one should so think of it, only that one should make one's idea of God, the Divine Love, a higher, a greater and nobler thing than many have made it.

In many devotional books it has been made very personal indeed. In some of the Roman Catholic books of devotion, and in books of the Quietists we find expressions such as "Christ, the Lover of his Church" which are more suited to love between people on the physical plane. In India also those who follow Chaitanya, and some others, employ similar material expressions; they speak of a love like human love, though glorified.

Probably Madame Blavatsky was thinking of these things, and warning us not to identify absolute compassion with that idea of divine love. Divine love is stronger than that, yet too abstract to be put into words; it is not a quality of God, but it is *He*; He is all love and there is nothing that is not love. So I think this compassion absolute is simply what we mean by God, not a personal God, but the utter Reality which lies behind all. And because that is absolute love we, being one with all others in that, must feel the need to help others.

> Withal, what mean the sacred scrolls which make thee say:

"Aum! I believe it is not all the Arhats that get of the nirvanic path the sweet fruition."

"Aum! I believe that the Nirvana-dharma is entered not by all the Buddhas."

Yea, on the Arya path thou art no more Srotapatti, thou art a Bodhisattva. The stream is crossed.

When it is said that the nirvāna-dharma is not entered by all the Buddhas, the term buddha is used in a general way, meaning those who are illuminated or enlightened or wise. Madame Blavatsky said: "In the Northern Buddhist phraseology all the great arhats, Adepts and saints are called Buddhas." And when it says "Thou art a Bodhisattva" it means one who is preparing to become a buddha in that general sense, and may be taken as equivalent to the term Arhat. Here the text speaks of the ārya path, where before it said "the ārhata path." The word ārya means noble, and it may be that the term arhat applied to the path has a tinge of its general meaning of worthy or venerable, so that it would be not simply the path of the Arhat, but the venerable or noble path, as distinguished from the other path, that of accepting nirvāna, which, as we have seen before, Āryasanga or his reporter is inclined to slight.

It has already been explained that the word bodhisattva has at least three meanings, of which one is that it names the office in the Hierarchy of the future Buddha who is the Teacher of Devas and men for a particular root-race. In a foot-note here Madame Blavatsky says that popular feeling rightly places this great being even higher in its reverence than a perfect Buddha. The Buddha is, of course, a higher official, but inasmuch as the Bodhisattva who for our root-race is the Lord Maitreya, is the great Teacher in the lower worlds, He may be said to be more directly and closely in touch with them, and therefore may take a more vital and living place in their devotion, in much the same way as affection and loyalty for some Prince who is in charge of a province may be greater than that felt for the great Emperor far away, who is seldom or never seen.

It has often been asked "Do the Buddhists worship Buddha?" Colonel Olcott, when writing his *Buddhist Catechism* had to deal with the question: "Was the Buddha God?" To his answer, "No", the Burmese Buddhists raised objection, though the Sinhalese Buddhists were quite satisfied. The Lord Buddha is regarded in Ceylon as the Perfect Man, a Teacher towards whom the deepest gratitude is felt. But in Burma the religion is more coloured with devotion, and the Lord Buddha is practically worshipped. In a sense, both views are correct. All men are divine in essence; in imperfect men the divinity is veiled, but in the Lord Buddha God was shining forth.

These local differences of philosophical and devotional outlook are due to the temperament of the people of the two countries; Buddhism contains both aspects. Every great religion has begun by providing for all types of men; but in each case as the centuries rolled on certain portions or aspects of the teaching were allowed to fade while others were brought into prominence. Christianity nowadays provides almost exclusively for the devotional type of people; of the knowledge and philosophy that it had in the form of the Gnostic teaching but little is left. The Muhammadan religion also appeals principally to the devotional element, though there is philosophy among the Sufis. The Jewish religion is in the same plight; in it, however, the Talmud offers a philosophical system. Of all religions, it is perhaps only Hinduism that at present shows out both the philosophical and devotional sides with equal brilliance and fervour.

CHAPTER LVI

THE THREE VESTURES

'Tis true thou hast a right to Dharmakaya vesture; but Sambhogakaya is greater than a Nirvani, and greater still is a Nirmanakaya—the Buddha of Compassion.

C.W.L.—We come now to the three vestures, on which Madame Blavatsky has a very long note, which I will comment upon piecemeal. The vestures refer to the lines of activity open to him who has taken the Fifth Initiation. Very little has ever been said about the seven paths that lie beyond Adeptship, but we have summarised what information is available in the following passage:[1]

> When the Human Kingdom is traversed, and man stands on the threshold of His superhuman life, a liberated Spirit, seven paths open before Him for His choosing. He may enter into the blissful omniscience and omnipotence of Nirvāna, with activities far beyond our knowing, to become, perchance, in some future world an Avatāra, or divine Incarnation this is sometimes called, 'taking the Dharmakāya vesture'. He may enter on 'the Spiritual Period'—a phrase covering unknown meanings, among them probably that of 'taking the Sambhogakāya vesture' He may become part of that treasure-house of spiritual forces on which the Agents of the Logos draw for Their work, 'taking the Nirmānakāya vesture'. He may remain a member of the Occult Hierarchy which rules and guards the world in which He has reached perfection. He may pass on to the next Chain, to aid in building up its forms. He may enter the splendid Angel—Deva—Evolution. He may give himself to the immediate service of the Logos, to be used by Him in any part of the Solar System, His Servant

[1] From *Man Whence, How and Whither*, pp 12-13.

and Messenger, who lives but to carry out His will and do His work over the whole of the system which He rules. As a General has his Staff, the members of which carry his messages to any part of the field, so are These the Staff of Him who commands all, "Ministers of His that do His pleasure."

In earlier days, in the moon chain, these paths probably opened before the Arhat, because that was the level of attainment set for humanity in that chain. The line of those who remain in the Hierarchy on our earth leads to the Sixth Initiation, that of the Chohan, and still further to a seventh, that of the Mahāchohan. That is the last Initiation that is possible on rays three to seven, but on the second ray a further step may be taken, that of the Buddha, and on the first ray yet one more, that of the Lord of the World.

In the division of the seven ways into three sections as given here, no doubt the path of work in the Hierarchy would be included among those described as Nirmānakāyas, along with the other path of the Nirmānakāya proper. Our Masters, who keep Their physical bodies for certain purposes connected with Their work, still give most of Their help to men on higher levels They work habitually on the causal bodies of men, and sometimes on the buddhic and ātmic sheaths.

The Nirmānakāya usually retains his causal body, that is the Augoeides, the glorified form which he has been building up in the course of his evolution. With that he usually also retains the permanent atoms of the lower mental and the astral and physical bodies, so that he can whenever he chooses (which is a very rare thing) make for himself a vehicle on any of those planes, and show himself in it. Ordinarily, he lives in his causal body, and spends his time in the generation of spiritual force, which is poured into the reservoir, and is then distributed by the members of the Hierarchy and Their pupils. Both these classes, Madame Blavatsky said, "Prefer to remain invisibly (in spirit, so to speak) in the world, and contribute towards men's salvation by influencing them to follow the good Law."

Further on she speaks of the Nirmānakāya as "that ethereal *form* which one would assume when leaving his physical he would appear in his astral dody—having in addition all the *knowledge of an Adept*. The *Bodhisattva* develops it in Himself as he proceeds on the path. Having reached the goal and refused its fruition, he remains on earth, as an Adept; and when he dies, instead of going into Nirvāna, he remains in that glorious body he has woven for himself, invisible to uninitiated mankind, to watch over and protect it."

Madame Blavatsky is here using the term astral body in quite a different sense from that in which she commonly employed it and in which it is now used, but she used it in this way also in her article on The Mystery of Buddha in the third volume of *The Secret Doctrine*. She there explains that Shrī Shankarāchārya, who appeared in India shortly after the death of the Lord Buddha, was *in a sense* a reincarnation of the Buddha, inasmuch as He used the "astral" remains of Gautama, and she says, such "astral bodies" must be regarded in the light of separate or independent Powers or Gods rather than material objects. She concludes: "Hence the right way of representing the truth would be to say that the various principles, the Bodhisattva, of Gautama Buddha, which did not go to Nirvāna, re-united to form the middle principle of Shankarāchārya, the earthly Entity."[1]

In order to understand this mystery of Buddha we must first realize the constitution of the physical atoms and then how these evolve by being used in the human body both in a general way to build up its particles and in a special way as permanent atoms. When you look at a physical ultimate atom with etheric sight you first of all see that it resembles a wire cage: then, looking more closely, you find that each wire is made up of a finer coil, and that in all there are seven sets of such spirillæ. One of these spirillæ is developed into activity in each round of evolution, so as we are now in the fourth round of our earth chain incarnation there are only four spirillæ in activity at present in the majority of atoms. In each round a new set will be developed, so that in the seventh round the entire seven spirillæ will be active; the atoms will therefore be better atoms in the seventh round than they are now, and the people who will live in that round will therefore find it far easier than people do to-day to respond to inner things and to live the higher life.

This awakening or evolution of the atoms is due to their being used in the bodies of living creatures, from the mineral

[1] *The Secret Doctine*, Vol. III, p. 381.

to man. Everything is built of atoms, which are floating around us in unthinkable numbers. There must be some of them which have never been used at all, but others have frequently been taken into and thrown off from the bodies of living beings. Some few have experienced constant association with man, having been adopted as permanent atoms, to be carried from life to life through the man's cycle of reincarnations. The atoms thus live with us and form our bodies. It is said that once in seven years every particle in the physical body is changed; some scientists have stated the period as three years. It is probable that the bony structure changes much more slowly, but it seems to me reasonable to imagine that the fleshy material is renewed entirely in about three years. The particles of the blood change more rapidly still; one would not be surprised to learn that they are entirely replaced every few days.

All atoms absorbed into living things are changed considerably. Those which form part of the earth are very little evolved by that, but those which compose precious stones are considerably developed. Vegetables and animals offer a still better opportunity, but the best possible evolution for atoms is to be drawn into the bodies of human beings. Among men, those who are living the occult life offer better conditions than men less advanced, since they have purer bodies because of what they eat and drink (or rather because of what they do not eat nor drink). As we evolve we also attract better atoms and our bodies more and more tend to reject those less evolved.

When a man reaches Adeptship he cannot express himself through the ordinary atoms that we find about us. They must be specially advanced and refined atoms, because his various vehicles are required to be so very much purer than ours, and capable of vibrating at rates which ours cannot maintain When a person reaches the level of a Buddha, it is quite impossible for him to find atoms useful to him, except such as have been used as permanent atoms, and have therefore been in the human body all the time, except during the intervals between incarnations. Permanent atoms are very much more evolved than others. They are at the fullest development of seventh round atoms in men who are about to become Adepts. They are as highly developed as atoms can possibly be, and are charged with all the qualities which they have brought over from previous births.

All the permanent atoms of all who, in connection with this world or probably even this chain of worlds, have attained Adeptship and have cast them off, have been collected together by the Lord Gautama, or for Him. He was the first Buddha of our human race. All those who had been Buddhas before Him had come from some other evolution, and had no doubt brought whatever they needed in the way of bodies with them. But the Lord Gautama, who was the first really human Buddha, had to find His bodies from the material of this chain. Therefore He, or some greater Ones for Him, made these bodies. His causal body was built up of the "remains", or permanent atoms of all the causal bodies which had been used by such great Ones; His mental body was built of the mental units gathered from such people, and His astral body was made of Their permanent astral atoms. There were not quite enough of these to make the entire vehicle, so some ordinary atoms, the best available, had also to be employed; but these were galvanized into activity, by the others, and they are replaced by permanent atoms obtained from every new Adept who takes the Sambhogakāya or the Dharmakāya vesture. Thus has been built up a set of bodies which is absolutely unique There are no other such bodies in the world, and there is no material to make another such set. They were used by Gautama Buddha, and afterwards preserved.

We are now in a position to understand Madame Blavatsky's statement that the principles of the Buddha were employed as the middle principles of Shrī Shankarāchārya, but the physical Shankarāchārya was quite a different man, and the Ātmā of Shankarāchārya was absolutely distinct from that of the Buddha. These three intermediary bodies were used by Shankarāchārya, and are now being used by the Lord Maitreya. Madame Blavatsky employed a curious nomenclature in her article. S. Paul divided man into three parts—spirit, soul and body. By the spirit he meant what we call the Monad; by the soul the ego, and by the body the personality, no doubt. Madame Blavatsky is alluding to the same triple division; but she says that the Buddha is a person so exalted that you cannot think of His component principles in the same way as those of a man. So instead of speaking of the Monad of the Buddha, she speaks of it as the *Dhyāni Buddha*. Then she calls the intermediate principles His Bodhisattva. Thirdly, she calls the physical body of the Buddha the Manushya Buddha. And so we have these three things as the principles of the Buddha: the Monad of the Buddha, which, because He is one with it in a way which is not the case with us now, is called the Dhyāni Buddha; the Bodhisattva; and then the Manushya Buddha, which is His manifestation on the physical plane. The astral and mental bodies, which have not been dissipated, are also included in the Bodhisattva.

At first many of us were much confused by Madame Blavatsky's terminology, but as the facts became more fully known to us we began to see what she means when she says that the Manushya Buddha dies and passes away, the Dhyāni Buddha enters Nirvāna, and the Bodhisattva remains on the earth to carry on the work of the Buddha. The Bodhisattva means the principles of the Buddha, which the present Bodhisattva uses. As the Lord Maitreya is using these, it is not these which we see on the Wesak day, for that is called the Shadow of the Buddha.[1] It is but a reflection of Him in the same way as the living image is a reflection of the astral and mental bodies of the pupil,[2] but He functions through it and uses it.

I have explained in *The Masters and the Path* that the work of the Lord Buddha was, in some way incomprehensible to us, not entirely successful. He and the Lord Maitreya were both far in advance of the rest of humanity, but at the time when the first human Buddha was needed, neither of Them was quite sufficiently advanced to take that high position. When the time came, the Lord Gautama, in his great love for humanity, said that He would at any cost fit Himself to fill this position, that He would make the great sacrifice necessary to push Himself on very much more quickly.[1]

He did this, and the whole of the Buddhist world venerates Him for it to an extent which no one can understand unless he has lived there. He lived the life of the Buddha and did the work, and it would seem to us looking at it a wonderful life. It is impossible to find any defect in it, to discover anything short of perfection in His life and teaching

[1] See *The Masters and the Path*, Ch. xiv.
[2] *Ibid.*, Ch. v.

and work, and yet it is said that some parts of it were not fully completed. In order to compensate for whatever was lacking, two arrangements were made. The first was that the Lord Buddha Himself undertook to appear once a year and give His blessing—He appears, on Wesak day, and gives an outpouring of spiritual force which helps the world very much. Then there was to be an incarnation almost immediately after His death, and that requirement was fulfilled by the birth of Shrī Shankarāchārya.

The first we ever heard about the occult relation between the Lord Buddha and Shrī Shankarāchārya was from the teaching given in *Esoteric Buddhism*, by Mr. Sinnett. In that he said that the Buddha reincarnated as Shrī Shankarāchārya, that Shankarāchārya was simply Gautama in a new body. Now very early we knew that that was not so, for the reason—besides many others—that Shankarāchārya was a first ray man, and the Lord Buddha was the head of the second ray. Madame Blavatsky quotes that remark of Mr. Sinnett's, and says that it is true in a certain occult way, but that it was very misleading as it was put. She was asked if Shankarāchārya was the Lord Gautama under a new form. Her answer was that there was the astral Gautama inside the outward Shankarāchārya, whose Ātmā was nevertheless His own divine prototype, the heavenly mind-born son of Light.

When Madame Blavatsky says that Shrī Shankarāchārya was a Buddha, but not an incarnation of the Buddha, she means that He is a Pratyeka Buddha, that is a Buddha on the first ray. He still lives at Shamballa in the body which He brought from Venus The bodies of the Lords of the Flame are not like ours at all. They do not change their particles, but have been compared to bodies of glass; they look like ours, but very much more glorified, and I suppose that They brought them entire from Venus, and that they are built of the physical matter of that evolution. Madame Blavatsky says that Shankarāchārya was an avatāra in the full sense of the word, the abode of a flame of the highest of manifested spiritual beings. As an avatāra is literally one who "crosses over" or "descends", not one of our humanity, the term is strictly applied in this case, as He is one of the three Lords of the Flame from Venus who remain on our earth as assistants and pupils of the Lord of the World.

To return to the general subject of the Nirmânakâyas, Madame Blavatsky's foot-note further says: "It is part of the exoteric Northern Buddhism to honour all such great characters as saints, and even to offer prayers to them, as the Greeks and Catholics do to their saints and patrons; on the other hand, the esoteric teachings countenance no such thing." By Greeks she means members of the Greek Church—the ancient Greek did not usually make it a custom to offer prayers, and certainly not to saints. When she says that the esoteric teachings do not countenance prayer to the Nirmānakāyas, she means that no esoteric student would pray to a Nirmānakâya to give him help, because he knows that They are not connected with individuals at all, but are fully engaged in pouring out Their splendid energies in Their own line of work.

Still, it is said that these Great Beings, the Buddhas of Compassion, are reverenced popularly more than those who have taken the other paths. Madame Blavatsky also says "This same popular reverence calls 'Buddhas of Compassion' those Bodhisattvas who, having reached the rank of an Arhat (*i.e.*, having completed the fourth or seventh Path), refuse to pass into the nirvānic state or 'don the Dharmakāya robe and cross to the other shore', as it would then become beyond their power to assist men even so little as Karma permits."

The main ideas here are perfectly clear, but the terminology is a little confusing. Every Adept has crossed to the other shore; that is the termination of the path which he began to tread when he entered upon the stream. As is said in the text, "the stream is crossed" before the choice of these three vestures is made; and it is the Adept, not the Arhat in the ordinary sense, who makes the choice. He who dons the Dharmakâya vesture crosses to the other shore, but in a fuller sense.

The Sambhogakâya, Madame Blavatsky continues, "is the same but with the additional lustre of three perfections, one of which is entire obliteration of all earthly concerns." He enters a spiritual line of evolution, and takes nirvāna at a later stage. He retains the nirvānic atom, the nirvānic body, but I think none of the lower atoms. He usually shows himself at that level as the triple spirit. Included in this class is probably that order of perfected men who have joined the Staff Corps of the

Logos. They are no longer especially attached to our earth, but are in the service of the Logos, to be sent by Him anywhere within His system.

Then comes the Dharmakāya robe, which is "That of a complete Buddha, *i.e.*, no body at all, but an ideal breath; consciousness merged in the universal consciousness, or soul devoid of every attribute." This means that the man who takes the Dharmakāya vesture retires into the Monad. He drops his permanent atoms altogether, and works only on high planes, the lowest for him being the nirvānic. He burns his boats behind him, as it were, and starts out on cosmic life, but I believe that if he chooses he may yet show himself as the triple spirit, but he does not retain, I think, even the nirvānic atom.

All through our evolution we keep the same causal body until we are able to raise our consciousness to the buddhic plane, and then the mere act of focusing oneself in the buddhic body causes the causal vehicle to vanish As soon, however, as one brings one's consciousness down again on to the higher mental plane the causal body reappears; it is not the same as it was before, because the particles have been dissipated, but it seems in every way exactly the same body. A similar process takes place in the case of the Dharmakāya vesture. The man has dropped his nirvānic atom, his manifestation on the nirvānic plane, but I believe if he puts himself down to that level for a moment he instantly draws to himself an atom exactly similar, a nirvānic vesture through which he may manifest as the triple spirit.

Comparing the three, it may be said that the Dharmakāya keeps nothing below the Monad, though what the vesture of the Monad may be on its own plane we do not know. The Sambhogakāya retains his manifestation as a triple spirit, and I think he can reach down and show himself in a temporary Augoeides. The Nirmānakāya appears to preserve his Augoeides and keeps all his permanent atoms, and therefore has the power to show himself at whichever level he chooses. Yet the three are all equal in development; the difference is only that he who casts aside the permanent atoms is therefore unable to make himself visible on the lower levels, and he throws them away because he no longer needs them for his kind of work. The man who retains them has the power to come down to those levels and work upon them, but it cannot rightly be said that those who choose to do the other work are in any way less important, lower in value or honour. We might think of him who is dealing at a higher level with great solar forces as the more important, but that would be a mistake, for the whole solar system is a manifestation of the Logos.

Madame Blavatsky speaks of all these kâyas as buddhic bodies. In so doing, she is using the term buddhic as an adjective of buddha, and is using buddha as the equivalent of our term Asekha Adept, one who has passed the Fifth Initiation. We have restricted the term to those who have taken the Buddha Initiation; our Masters stand two steps lower than that, but They are spoken of as "living Buddhas" in Tibet.

The closing passage in the note says: "The esoteric school teaches that Gautama Buddha, with several of his arhats, is such a Nirmānakāya higher than whom, on account of his great renunciation and sacrifice for mankind, there is none known." We must not take this to mean that Gautama Buddha and several of His arhats make one Nirmānakâya, but that He is such a Being, and several of His followers have also taken the same line. Then it is said that none higher is known to mankind. This statement is perfectly accurate if it means that of our humanity no other has yet reached so high a level as the Lord Gautama.

Even the Bodhisattva, the Lord Maitreya Himself, who long ago was equal with Him, as I have explained in *The Masters and the Path*, has not yet taken the step which would make Him a Buddha. Had He done so, He could not occupy His present position as Head of the teaching department of the world. He is often called Maitreya Buddha by the Buddhists, but that is an honorific title.

There is one level in the Hierarchy, higher even than that of the Buddha—the level of the great King who is the One Initiator, but as he is one of the Lords of the Flame who came from Venus, it remains true that Gautama Buddha is the highest of our humanity.

Now bend thy head and listen well. O Bodhisattva —compassion speaks and saith: "Can there be bliss when all that lives must suffer? Shalt thou be saved and hear the whole world cry?"

Now thou hast heard that which was said:

Now thou shalt attain the seventh step and cross the gate of final knowledge, but only to wed woe—if thou would'st be Tathagata, follow upon thy predecessor's steps, remain unselfish to the endless end.

Thou art enlightened—choose thy way.

Once more Āryasanga brings forward his prevailing idea, and urges his followers to take the path of compassion. He says one cannot desert one's brothers when they are suffering. We have already considered the question of suffering quite fully, and realized that though the Arhat may still work in the world that is full of suffering, his consciousness on the higher planes knows the glory that is behind it all, knows the heights of happiness which all men will infallibly reach, so that it is impossible for him to suffer as ordinary men do who see so little of the glory of life. The Arhat, who is here addressed as a Bodhisattva, is in a position to share the triumphant song of the Lord Buddha, so well expressed in *The Light of Asia*:

> Ye are not bound! The Soul of things is sweet,
>   The Heart of Being is celestial rest;
> Stronger than woe is will that which was Good
>   Doth pass to Better—Best.
> I, Buddh, who wept with all my brothers' tears,
>   Whose heart was broken by a whole world's woe,
> Laugh and am glad, for there is Liberty![1]

When Āryasanga urges his followers to remain unselfish to the endless end, he uses an expression curiously similar to a phrase which in Christianity is translated "World without end"; the Latin form is *in secula seculorum*, in the ages of the ages. It means until the end of our set of worlds, or perhaps

[1] *Op. cit.*, Book the Eighth.

ntil the end of our present chain. The suggestion is that we hould remain in touch with humanity until the work of the resent human *cycle is complete, ,and humanity has reached* s goal.

Our own method of offering ourselves is a little different om that; we have put ourselves completely at the disposal of ie Masters, not asking that They should send us to this work r that, but leaving it absolutely to Them, saying: "Here am ; send me." Aryasanga's desire was that his pupils should llow the line that he himself had chosen. Perhaps he felt iat many more workers were urgently needed in that particular eld. He was speaking at a certain period of Indian history, i the reign of King Harsha, when there seems to have been a ecay of religion, when people were thinking more of outward rms *than of the real life behind, when everything had become* uch specialized and somewhat artificial; under these circumances perhaps he felt the necessity for more teachers, for the vival *of the religious life and the ideal of service.*

Finally he urges the pupils to be Tathāgata, to follow in e steps of the Lord Buddha. He tells them that they are w enlightened and should choose their way. Next comes a ie of dots—while the person is choosing, apparently, and then : breaks out into a magnificent peroration:

Behold, the mellow light that floods the eastern sky. In signs of praise both heaven and earth unite. And from the four-fold manifested powers a chant of love ariseth, both from the flaming fire and flowing water, and from sweet-smelling earth and rushing wind.

Hark! . . . from the deep unfathomable vortex of that golden light in which the Victor bathes, all nature's wordless voice in thousand tones ariseth to proclaim:

Joy unto you, O men of Myalba. A pilgrim hath returned back from the other shore. A new Arhan is born.

I have already spoken of the way in which all nature rejoices when a new Initiate is born. In this, it is now said, both heaven and earth unite. The spirit of the earth gains an added sense of well-being. That spirit is a great entity, not on our human line at all, for whom the whole earth acts as a physical body. It is difficult to grasp the nature of such a being. When we think of the earth as merely a huge globe, whirling through space, without specialized organs, we might wonder how it can serve any being as a body. But if all the creatures that live upon it contribute to the consciousness of the spirit of the earth it needs no other eyes than theirs. It lives in their life and so gains experience. Again, the earth moves on its way as one of a mighty choir of planets, each one sounding its own note in the music of the spheres, possessing within itself all the things which we have to reach out to get.

This entity lives on a scale very different from ours. Our bodies happen to have a certain size and to live for a certain time; that seems to us the correct standard, so a tiny creature with a small span of life seems despicable, and a large creature with a long life-period is respected. But size and length of life are no criteria of development or advancement. Some antediluvian animals were enormously bigger than the elephant, but they were much less intelligent, just as to-day the rhinoceros and hippopotamus have less mind than the dog. We need not assume, therefore, that because the spirit of the earth has a globe eight thousand miles in diameter for a body, and because for him one incarnation is an entire world period, he is more intelligent than we are. Consciousness is a point in each of us. That of the spirit of the earth seems to be curiously multiplex, and, notwithstanding his great size, to be less advanced in some ways than that of many of the great Devas who move about his body.

If we stand upon a hill and look over the surrounding country we find it permeated with something of the life of the spirit of the earth. That life seems to divide itself into parts, temporarily or permanently. A beautiful view, which has been admired by many people, is ensouled by a vague individuality which is part of that spirit. Such admiration, whether from human beings or great Devas, seems to excite the life in that portion, so that it answers to the feeling of delight When we admire a fine view it is acting upon us, but we also are acting upon it. This response is in addition to what is felt by the life in the mineral, vegetable and animal kingdoms.

When a man is initiated the influence to which he has tuned himself on higher planes rushes through every part of his being. Though there is little effect in the solids, liquids and gases of the physical plane, there is a great deal of radiation from the etheric double, and from his astral and mental bodies, and this is felt, as we have already seen by the kingdoms of nature, and by such men as are in a condition to respond.

The fourfold manifested powers are those of earth, water, fire and air—the four Devarājas or Mahārājas, who are the administrators of karma for us down here, the under-servants, as it were, of the Lipika, the Great Lords of Karma. Their names among the Hindus are, it is said, Dhritarāshtra, Virudhaka, Virupaksha and Vaishravana, and each of them is at the head of one line of development. Dhritarāshtra is said to be the head of the Gandharvas, the spirits of the air, the great Devas who express themselves by music; to them is always assigned the east, and they are always symbolized by the colour white, as horsemen arrayed in white, riding white horses, and carrying targets of pearl. Under Virudhaka come the Kumbhandas. They are the Angels of the south, the spirits of water, so connected because the southern part of the world has far more water than earth. They are represented as blue, the colour of water, and are said to carry sapphire shields. Under Virupaksha are the Nāgas, Angels of the west, spirits of the fire, whose colour is red and who carry coral shields. These Ezekiel described as *fiery creatures full of eyes within*, and also as winged wheels. Then come the Yakshas, ruled by Vaishravana. To them the north is consecrated; they are the earth Devas or Angels, and their colour is always gold—that of the gold hidden in the earth.[1]

Madame Blavatsky explains Myalba as "our earth—pertinently called hell, and the greatest of all hells, by the esoteric school The esoteric doctrine knows of no hell or place of punishment other than a man-bearing planet or earth. Avichi is a state, not a locality." Although some people suffer after death in the astral plane, it cannot quite be regarded as punishment. They are suffering from their own disordered

[1] See *The Light of Asia*, Book the First

imaginations or low desires, and although things may sometimes be bad on that plane, the worst of it is not so mean and sordid as some of the things which happen down here; all who have had experience on higher planes will agree with Madame Blavatsky that there is nothing quite so bad as physical life anywhere else.

"A pilgrim hath returned back from the other shore" evidently means that someone has gained the higher level, but still chooses to remain and work among men in this world. Generally we think of the other shore as the Fifth Initiation, not as the Fourth, but here it is used in the more restricted sense.

Aryasanga closes with the salutation:

PEACE TO ALL BEINGS

Similar blessings are to be found at the end of every Buddhist or Hindu religious book. Aryasanga closes his book with very great rejoicing He has sometimes spoken of the path of woe, but he ends with a pæan of wonderful joy and beautiful peace.